DATE DUE

AP 9 MY 3 0 07			
DE 2 '99			
MY 6 '99			
NO 2 9 '99 FE 1 6 00			
NO 2 1 '00			
DE 1 2 '00			
AP 2 9 '01			
DE 2 9 '0 JE 9 04			
NO 1 6 JE 7 05			
NO 2 8 05			
DE 1 1 06			

DEMCO 38-296

REASON TO
H●PE

REASON TO HOPE

A PSYCHOSOCIAL PERSPECTIVE ON VIOLENCE & YOUTH

Edited by Leonard D. Eron,

Jacquelyn H. Gentry, & Peggy Schlegel

American Psychological Association

Washington, DC

Copies may be ordered from
APA Order Department
P.O. Box 2710
Hyattsville, MD 20784

In the UK and Europe, copies may be ordered from
American Psychological Association
3 Henrietta Street
Covent Garden, London
WC2E 8LU England

Typeset in Century Schoolbook by PRO-Image Corporation, Techna-Type Div.,
York, PA

Printer: Data Reproductions Corp., Rochester Hills, MI
Cover Designer: Anne Masters, Washington, DC
Technical/Production Editors: Paula R. Whyman and Susan Bedford

Library of Congress Cataloging-in-Publication Data
Reason to hope : a psychosocial perspective on violence and youth /
  edited by Leonard D. Eron, Jacquelyn H. Gentry, and Peggy Schlegel.
     p.   cm.
  Includes bibliographical references and index.
  ISBN 1-55798-272-4 (acid-free paper)
  1. Socially handicapped youth—United States.   2. Violence—United
States—Psychological aspects.   3. Juvenile delinquency—United
States—Prevention.   I. Eron, Leonard D.   II. Gentry, Jacquelyn H.
III. Schlegel, Peggy.   IV. American Psychological Association.
HV1431.R42   1994
364.3′6′0973—dc20   94-30938
                                                                      CIP

British Cataloguing-in-Publication Data
A CIP record is available from the British Library

Printed in the United States of America
First Edition

The work of the APA Commission on Violence and Youth was supported in part by a grant from the Sol Goldman Charitable Trust of New York City.

Contents

Contributors

Joyce Barham, Mental Health Consultant, Rockville, Maryland

Judith V. Becker, PhD, College of Medicine, University of Arizona

Leonard Berkowitz, PhD, Department of Psychology, University of Wisconsin—Madison

Patricia Bowie, MPH, School of Public Health, University of California, Los Angeles

S. Andrew Chen, PhD, Department of Counseling and Educational Psychology, Slippery Rock University of Pennsylvania

Lawrence J. Dark, JD, Urban League of Portland, Portland, Oregon

Anthony R. D'Augelli, PhD, Department of Psychology, Pennsylvania State University

Edward Donnerstein, PhD, Department of Communication, University of California, Santa Barbara

Leonard D. Eron, PhD, Institute for Social Research, University of Michigan

Eva L. Feindler, PhD, Clinical Psychology Doctoral Program, Long Island University

Arnold P. Goldstein, PhD, Center for Research on Aggression, Syracuse University

Nancy G. Guerra, EdD, Department of Psychology, University of Illinois at Chicago

W. Rodney Hammond, PhD, School of Professional Psychology, Wright State University

Hope M. Hill, PhD, Department of Psychology, Howard University

Alan E. Kazdin, PhD, Department of Psychology, Yale University

Teresa D. LaFromboise, PhD, Department of Education, Stanford University

Vasilios K. Lagos, PsyD, Westchester School for Special Children, Yonkers, New York

Judith C. Levey, PhD, Westchester School for Special Children, Yonkers, New York

Debra J. Pepler, PhD, Department of Psychology, York University, Canada

Lori H. Rosenthal, Department of Psychology, University of Massachusetts at Amherst

Ronald G. Slaby, PhD, Education Development Center, Newton, Massachusetts

Susan B. Sorenson, PhD, School of Public Health, University of California, Los Angeles

Fernando I. Soriano, PhD, Department of Behavioral Science, University of Missouri—Kansas City

Ervin Staub, PhD, Department of Psychology, University of Massachusetts at Amherst

Patrick H. Tolan, PhD, Department of Psychiatry, University of Illinois at Chicago

Reiko Homma True, PhD, Division of Mental Health and Substance Abuse Services, San Francisco, California

Betty R. Yung, PhD, School of Professional Psychology, Wright State University

Brian L. Wilcox, PhD, Center on Children, Families, and the Law, University of Nebraska, Lincoln

Preface

This volume is testimony to psychology's conviction that the unique perspective the discipline has to offer must become part of the public dialogue on the prevention and control of violent behavior. Regarding youth involvement in violence—as victims, perpetrators, or bystanders—psychology offers a scientific basis for optimism, because a close study of violent behavior shows that for the most part such behavior is learned and, having been learned, can be unlearned. Even more to the point, psychologists have found that it is possible to set up conditions in which people do not learn to act in violent ways in the first place. So, as psychologists and editors, our message in this book is one of hope.

But it is not only psychologists who are optimistic. Others, who are, perhaps, more frequently on the front line of violence, concur. For example, in a recent conversation we had with Isaac Fulwood, Jr.—retired career police officer, former Chief of Police in Washington, DC, and member of the American Psychological Association (APA) Commission on Violence and Youth—he reflected on the hope that he now feels:

> Already I see communities mobilizing to reclaim our children: I see it when parents get involved with schools, when family members are kind to each other and to their neighbors, when churches are serving their youngsters, and when police know when to call in services instead of making arrests. We don't have to wait for breakthroughs and miracles . . . . we are building hope when we celebrate each of these steps!

The APA Focus on Violence

Like many citizens, psychologists have been troubled by violence in this nation's communities, work places, and families, and have been especially concerned about the influence of violence on the lives of young people. As the largest and most influential association of psychologists in the world, the American Psychological Association (APA) has redoubled its efforts toward making the contributions of psychology to the understanding, prevention, and treatment of violence accessible to other psychologists as well as to a broader audience of other social scientists, practitioners, and the public.

Psychologists, like many other professionals working in the field of violence, realize that although the problem of violence is not as hopeless as many believe, it is more complicated than many want to believe. Building more prisons or hiring more police in the community may help to contain some individuals who are violent. These actions do not prevent violence from occurring in the first place. Even programs aimed at preventing violence, such as those that target high risk groups, are confronted with the fact that many of the characteristics of American society may inadvertently hinder such efforts and may actually operate to encourage and sustain violence. For example, the media sometimes legitimize and even glamorize violence. Clearly, a complex mix of factors must be considered when attempting to reduce violence.

It is a specific mix of these factors—psychological, sociocultural, economic, and societal—that this book has been developed to address. This volume is a result of the work of the APA Commission on Violence and Youth, one of several APA expert groups that have studied aspects of violence in recent years.[1]

The APA Commission on Violence and Youth

Responding to concerns about the influence of violence on our nation's young people, in May 1991 the APA Public Interest Directorate established the Commission on Violence and Youth. It was organized to bring psychological expertise to bear on the problems that have been emerging as increasing numbers of young people become victims, witnesses, or perpetrators of interpersonal violence, and as even more live under the constant threat of violence.

APA charged the Commission with five tasks:

1. to articulate the state of psychological knowledge related to violence and youth;
2. to define existing practical problems and how psychological knowledge can be applied to resolve or constructively intervene in these problems;
3. to describe effective intervention models;
4. to recommend promising directions for public policy, research, and program development; and
5. to recommend APA policies, projects, or programs that will constructively influence psychological research, practice, and education on these issues.

---

[1] Over the past 4 years, the APA has initiated a number of special studies to collect, analyze, and disseminate research findings about many factors pertaining to interpersonal violence. In 1990, the APA Council of Representatives approved a policy statement on child abuse that resulted in the establishment of three working groups, one each on treatment, prevention, and legal issues in child abuse and neglect. Concomitantly, the Public Interest Directorate and the Board for the Advancement of Psychology in the Public Interest adopted violence as a high priority theme for programming.

Within a short time, the Public Interest Directorate established the Commission on Violence and Youth, and the Committee on Women and Psychology established the Task Force on Male Violence Against Women. In 1992, the APA Task Force on Television and Society issued its report that underscored the importance of television viewing as it contributes to violent behavior. In 1994, the newly elected APA President Ronald Fox, PhD, established the Presidential Task Force on Violence and the Family, and APA began collaborative work with other organizations to develop a behavioral and social science research advocacy agenda on violence.

With a wide range of expertise in behavioral science, legal issues, and law enforcement, Commission members included the following individuals:

Judith V. Becker, PhD, Tuscon, AZ
S. Andrew Chen, PhD, Slippery Rock, PA
Lawrence J. Dark, JD, Columbia, SC
Edward Donnerstein, PhD, Santa Barbara, CA
Leonard D. Eron, PhD (Chair), Ann Arbor, MI
Eva L. Feindler, PhD, Brookville, NY
Isaac Fulwood, Jr., Washington, DC
Arnold P. Goldstein, PhD, Syracuse, NY
W. Rodney Hammond, PhD, Dayton, OH
Hope M. Hill, PhD, Washington, DC
Ronald G. Slaby, PhD, Newton, MA
Fernando I. Soriano, PhD, Stanford, CA

Meeting for the first time in July 1991, Commission members decided to focus their work on preventive and rehabilitative interventions initially. Individual Commissioners took responsibility for reviewing research and writing reports on specific topics related to youth violence. Other experts were called on to conduct research reviews on specialized topics that were considered essential, such as those pertaining to the complex mix of factors influencing violence, alluded to above.

The fall 1991 meeting included hearings with testimony from both professional and grassroots groups. They included researchers and program staff in the areas of sexual assault, law enforcement, health care, and community services, as well as representatives of the religious community and state and federal government agencies. Children from Howard University's Violence Prevention Project in Washington, DC, along with teenagers and young adults from several inner-city groups, described their experiences and fears in the face of violence that pervades everyday life in their neighborhoods. As one immigrant adolescent poignantly told the Commission, "My parents sent me here from El Salvador so I would be safe; sometimes I think I would be safer if I go back!"

In each of the Commission meetings, colleagues from many disciplines and professions offered new information, led discussions, and participated in the deliberations. Their views and experiences markedly enriched the Commission's work. These collaborators included:

Ruby Takanishi, PhD, Executive Director, Carnegie Council on Adolescent Development, Washington, DC
Tom Blagburn, District of Columbia Police Department
Eli Anderson, PhD, Dept. of Sociology, University of Pennsylvania, Philadelphia, PA
Joyce Barham, mental health consultant, Rockville, MD
Doris Clanton, aide to Senator John Glenn, Washington, DC
Doreen S. Koretz, PhD, National Institute of Mental Health, Rockville, MD
Kenneth Powell, MD, Centers for Disease Control, Atlanta, GA
Ellen Scrivner, PhD, National Institute of Justice, Washington, DC
Susan Solomon, PhD, National Institute of Mental Health, Rockville, MD

> Joel Wallman, PhD, The Harry Frank Guggenheim Foundation, New York, NY
>
> Amy Goldman, PhD, Sol Goldman Charitable Trust, New York, NY
>
> Stacy Daniels, PhD, Ewing Marion Kauffman Foundation, Kansas City, MO
>
> Eileen Kelly, MSW, National Association of Social Workers, Washington, DC
>
> Milton Grady, ACSW, MSW, National Association of Social Workers, Washington, DC
>
> Jack Wiggins, PhD, President, American Psychological Association, Cleveland, OH
>
> Evvie Becker-Lausen, PhD, U.S. Senate Subcommittee on Children, Families, Drugs, and Alcoholism

The Commission also maintained collegial work with a large number of psychologists by holding open forums at the APA Annual Conventions. Additionally, the Commission maintained systematic contact with its Cadre of Experts, an international group of about 150 professionals working on issues of violence and youth.

The research reviews, discussions of their implications, and recommendations presented here were summarized before this current volume was edited for publication, and the 96–page summary document was issued by APA at a Washington, DC, press conference in August 1993. The summary report, *Violence and Youth: Psychology's Response*, has been enthusiastically received and used by policymakers, educators, service providers, and others involved in efforts to curb the violence that terrorizes our nation.

Financial support of the Commission on Violence and Youth was made possible by a combination of APA budget and personnel resources, member donations, and grant funds. The Sol Goldman Charitable Trust awarded grants to APA to provide general support for the Commission's work and to print and distribute the preliminary summary report that was issued in August 1993.

We trust that this book will help to amplify the principles and recommendations that were outlined in the summary by presenting much of the material on psychological theory, research, policy, and practice that informed the earlier report. It should be a valuable reference for those who are or will become engaged in research, policy development, advocacy, community service, professional practice, and, in general, the responsible care of our nation's children and youth.

We are particularly hopeful that prevention of violence among youth will become an abiding interest of our readers and an increasing focus of behavioral and social scientists, even though prevention research and its applications have sometimes been considered "soft" science in the past. Remembering our most recent conversation with former police chief Isaac Fulwood, we would concur with his belief that

> Prevention is not a "mushy-headed" concept—it involves discipline, respect, thoughtfulness, and responsible decision making. It is the kind of experience that makes youngsters know they are important and helps them create a vision of a productive future.

Everyone is responsible for helping the children of this country create a vision that will inspire them to use their talents constructively and develop their potential fully. Everyone can help to curb the violence that disrupts their development and too often ends their lives. The editors, authors, and publisher of this book believe that psychology has an important and unique contribution to make to creating visions of a future in which violence is noticeably absent for all.

Acknowledgments

A volume such as this is a product of many kinds of expertise and talents, and we are grateful to the many people who made it possible for the APA Commission on Violence and Youth to develop and refine the scientific information that is presented here. It would be impossible to list all of the advisers and supporters by name, but a few warrant special mention.

In the American Psychological Association, Henry Tomes, PhD, and James M. Jones, PhD, were instrumental in establishing violence as a priority in the Public Interest Directorate and in organizing the Commission on Violence and Youth; they gave steadfast policy support and guidance to the Commission. Claudia Menashe was tireless, cheerful, and reliable in handling the daily administrative tasks that facilitated the Commission's work and follow-up activities. Anne Woodworth's meticulous library research and reference checks buttressed the scholarly documentation for the chapters.

We value the substantive guidance, editorial advice, and production assistance given by Gary VandenBos, PhD, Executive Director, and a number of staff in the APA Publications and Communications Office. In particular, we are grateful for the publishing expertise of APA Books staff, for the operational wisdom of Mary Lynn Skutley, manager of editorial development, and for the careful and wise editing of Paula R. Whyman, technical/production editor.

As consultants to the Commission on Violence and Youth, Ellen Scrivner, PhD, and Joyce Barham provided important background information to the group and gave invaluable advice on the process and products of the Commission's work.

A number of professionals inside and outside APA contributed their ideas by reviewing the work of authors whose work appears in this volume. Their insightful comments, challenging questions, and substantive suggestions strengthened the book. The reviewers include: Clinton Anderson; Jean M. Baker, PhD; Kevin Berrill; Kenyon S. Chan, PhD; William Davidson, PhD; Lemyra DeBruyn, PhD; Paul Gendreau, PhD; L. Philip Guzman, PhD; Darnell Hawkins, PhD; James M. Jones, PhD; Iseli K. Krauss, EdD; Donald Lollar, EdD; John P. Murray, PhD; Jerald L. Newberry; Edgar O'Neal, PhD; Gerald Patterson, PhD; Melissa Ring, PhD; David Rowe, PhD; Stanley Sue, PhD; Carolyn Swift, PhD; James Tedeschi, PhD; Harry C. Triandis, PhD; Penelope Trickett, PhD; and the APA Committee on Women in Psychology.

Finally, we thank the many APA members and others interested in violence and youth who corresponded with the Commission, sent materials for our use, and offered suggestions at the Annual Convention Open Forums with Commission members. This volume reflects a large collective effort to understand problems of violence and youth. We trust that it will have some influence in ameliorating those problems.

Leonard D. Eron, PhD
Jacquelyn H. Gentry, PhD
Peggy Schlegel, MSW

1

Introduction

Leonard D. Eron and Ronald G. Slaby

Youth and violence; the words seem inextricably linked. That is certainly the impression one gets when reading the headlines, listening to the news, or watching prime time television in America today. And the pictures that bear witness to the words are indeed frightening and dramatic, regardless of whether the youth that are captured on film are the victims or the perpetrators of violence. The pictures and words almost convince us that it is inevitable, this marriage of violence and youth.

But psychology's message with regard to violence is one of hope. We know that violence is not random, uncontrollable, or inevitable. Violence is learned, and it can be unlearned. In addition, individual characteristics, family experiences, peer relations, access to firearms, involvement with alcohol and other drugs, exposure to media violence, and larger cultural and societal forces all play a role in violence among youth, and many of these factors are also amenable to change. Moreover, there is considerable evidence that psychologists and others can intervene effectively in the lives of young people in many ways to reduce or prevent their involvement in violence.

Contemporary books on violence in America often begin by presenting statistics to support the conclusion that there is indeed an epidemic of violence in this country. And, although we will present such statistics in this book, most of our readers will need little convincing that the problem of violence, particularly with regard to youth, has reached epidemic proportions in the 1990s.

Although statistics on youth involvement in violence are alarming, more humanized accounts of violence are perhaps more pertinent and powerful. They remove the abstraction from aggregated statistics on various forms of violent crimes, comparative homicide rates "per 100,000" among different age, ethnic, and gender groups, and tables showing percentages of young children who are beaten, molested, or murdered by their "caregivers." Consider, for example, the following accounts of youth involvement with violence:

> In upstate New York a 19-year-old male student approached a female acquaintance in a video shop and asked her to go out with him. She refused; he left and 10 minutes later returned with a gun and shot her in the heart.

1

*

A 17–year-old African American girl from Boston reported to the State Task Force on Adolescent Violence that she had attended the funerals of 16 friends and classmates who had died by violence. One fatality was the result of an argument about who was next in line at the barber shop.

*

Arriving at a domestic violence shelter after having been beaten by her husband, a teenage Pueblo Indian woman was told that if she did not return to her home, she would be under perpetual house arrest and would never be allowed custody of her children. When she returned home, her teenaged husband shot her to death and then killed himself.

*

With anticipated assistance from a 12–year-old accomplice, a 13–year-old female honor student in Loraine, Ohio, brought a fish fillet knife to school with the intention of stabbing a teacher who had reprimanded her the day before. About a dozen of her classmates bet a total of $200 on the outcome of the murder plan.

*

In Dallas, Texas, a Hispanic boy received 17 facial stitches at the emergency room after being beaten up because he stepped on someone's shoe without saying excuse me.

*

In August, 1992, a 19–year-old Vietnamese refugee living in Florida was beaten to death when he responded to the racial taunts of five white youths.

*

A teenage boy in Brooklyn reported asking his mother for $150 to buy gym shoes. He used the money instead to buy a bullet-proof vest and, with apparent nonchalance, described to reporters an elaborate set of "when and where" rules he had devised for using the vest.

*

A 10–year-old resident of Cabrini-Green housing project in Chicago who lacked such protection simply concluded, "You can't go outside. You got to duck and dive from the bullets. They be shootin' most every day."[1]

Such testimony may create reactions of outrage, discomfort, anxiety, anger, or sadness in the reader. However, the recital may also serve as an impetus to action, compelling a strong commitment to violence prevention research and intervention that focuses on the population that is most vulnerable to violence in this country: America's youth.

The purpose of this book is to stimulate such a commitment. Its intended audience includes all psychologists as well as other social and biological sci-

---

[1]The preceding incidents were drawn from our research and from testimony given at public hearings on violence and youth. Identifying details have been altered to protect the anonymity of the individuals involved.

entists who we hope will be inspired by this volume to continue doing solid research on the causes and prevention of violence. We also hope that practitioners of psychology and members of other helping professions will be encouraged by the findings and conclusions presented here and that these findings will help to inform their practice. Policy makers who read the recommendations and rationales behind them will be better informed to make the important decisions about public programs that are needed to stem and reverse the increasing tide of violence engulfing the youth of this country. Finally, we hope the volume will be helpful to individual citizens who also have it in their power to make the individual, familial, and societal changes that are necessary to achieve this end.

Why Youth Are of Primary Importance

Perhaps the strongest single predictor of an individual's risk of perpetrating violence is a history of having engaged in aggressive behavior as a child. In fact, by the time a youngster has reached the age of 8, it is possible to predict reasonably well from the extent of his or her aggressive behavior in school how aggressive the youth is likely to become in adolescence and adulthood, including whether he or she will exhibit criminal and antisocial behavior (Eron, Huesmann, Dubow, Romanoff, & Yarmel, 1987; Farrington, 1994; McCord, 1994).

Late adolescence is an age level at which many feel intervention efforts should be focused. However, the learning of aggressive behavior begins early in life, and aggression is often learned well by an early age. Despite occasional or even frequent attempts to discourage or control aggression, the individual rewards, social approval, and media portrayals that support this behavior are often so abundant that it persists. That is why prevention and treatment programs for older adolescent and adult offenders have had limited success. Although it is never too late to make changes in one's violent behavior patterns, by the time a developing individual has reached late adolescence change is often extremely difficult; distinctive ways of behaving and of justifying this behavior have often become so firmly established that they are resistant to change. Primary and secondary preventive interventions will therefore have the best opportunity for success when they start in early childhood and continue throughout adolescence. To understand the causes of violence it is necessary to focus on the early childhood experiences and the developmental pathways that lead to involvement with violence in later life (see chapter 2 in this volume).

Myths About Violence

One widespread belief is that violence is often the direct and inevitable result of extreme anger or inadequate impulse control. However, inadequate impulse or emotional control serves only to put individuals at risk for making errors of disinhibition or inappropriateness in their choice of behaviors in a given situation, similar in some ways to the disinhibiting effects of alcohol. Inadequate impulse control puts an individual at risk for violence only if violent acts are that person's preferred response choice because of previous learning experiences.

Another limiting belief is that, when it comes to violence, "biology is destiny." As we discuss later in this chapter, biopsychological approaches can be useful, but biology alone does not allow us to understand human violence in a way that offers practical strategies for a reduction in the incidence and extent of violence. For biological processes to exert an influence on aggressive behavior, they must work through life history events, especially learning experiences.

A third misconception is that violence is caused by a single factor. As the chapters in this volume indicate, no one factor by itself can account for the occurrence of violent behavior. Whether or not a given individual will perform a violent act at a given time is determined by many factors, biological, physiological, chemical, political, economic, and sociological. However, as many authors in this volume stress, violence is ultimately a learned behavior, even though its learning is affected by all of the previously noted factors. The way these factors interact with and impinge on the learning process determines the likelihood of the occurrence of violent behavior.

The Incidence of Violence in America

Death by violence occurs within virtually every segment of American society. At current rates in the United States, over 25,000 individuals die each year because someone has killed them (Federal Bureau of Investigation [FBI], 1992). In the United States, the homicide rate for young males[2] is not only the highest among 21 developed countries investigated, it is also more than 4 times higher than the country (Scotland) with the next highest rate, and more than 40 times higher than the country (Japan) with the lowest rate (Fingerhut & Kleinman, 1990).

Although it is widespread among all groups of people, death by violence in the United States is more highly prevalent among youth, minority groups, and males. For example, violence is the leading cause of death for young African American males. Although the overall death rate is lower for females than for males, violence is also the leading cause of death for young African American females (see chapters 3–8 in this volume for information on the experience of violence for ethnic minority groups and for girls and young women).

Death by violence represents only the tip of the iceberg. Injury caused by violence is even more pervasive and widespread. In the United States, over 1.4 million noninstitutionalized individuals over 12 years of age suffer injuries each year because someone has assaulted them (Bureau of Justice Statistics, 1990). Children are at particularly high risk for certain forms of injury that are caused by violence (National Committee for Injury Prevention and Control

---

[2]The APA Commission on Violence and Youth defined *youth* as the period during which an individual is likely to be in school, ages 3 to 22.

[NCIPC], 1989). With the possible exception of homicide, children and youth suffer more victimizations than do adults in virtually every category, including physical abuse, sibling assaults, bullying, sexual abuse, and rape (Finkelhor & Dziuba-Leatherman, 1994). An estimated 1.6 million children suffer serious injury or impairment each year because someone abused or neglected them (National Center on Child Abuse and Neglect, 1988). Common injuries to children that are caused by abuse or neglect include broken bones, head injuries, lacerations, intestinal perforations, obstructions from trauma to the abdomen, and burns (Newberger, 1982). Female children and adolescents are at particularly high risk of nonfatal injuries from sexual abuse, rape, and assault, usually perpetrated by males.

Psychology's Response

In the past, psychology has made valuable contributions to the understanding of violence by bringing the study of human aggression into the realm of science, by making a comparative study of nonhuman and human aggression, and by developing an important body of research that serves as a guide in understanding and controlling human aggression. More than one-half century of psychological research on the development and control of aggression has created a valuable repository of scientific findings, formulations, methods, and intervention strategies. Chief among these findings is the overwhelming evidence that human aggression is largely learned and therefore can be reduced or prevented through learning (Eron, 1987; Slaby & Roedell, 1982).

Especially in the last decade, psychology as a discipline has been involved in trying to understand and prevent overt violence. In the recent past, the American Psychological Association has formed commissions and task forces to investigate and evaluate the status of knowledge in this area and to make recommendations for further actions in such areas as violence toward women, victims of crime, television and violence, family violence, and child abuse.

In addition to psychology's organized response as a discipline, over the last 50 years many individual psychologists have been doing research on the causes and prevention of violence, and many psychologist practitioners have been conducting programs to mitigate or prevent violence.

The Approach of the Book

As mentioned earlier, the factors contributing to aggression are varied and many. No one factor by itself is a sole cause of aggression. Violence occurs only when there is a convergence of a number of factors, and even then violence is not inevitable. For an individual to respond to these various and interacting forces with aggression, the individual must have learned, somehow, sometime in the past, that this is an acceptable way to respond. In his or her history the individual must have experienced or observed this behavior, seen it rewarded, and might have practiced it in actuality or in fantasy. Having adopted violence as an acceptable response in particular situations, the individual is prepared to respond in a violent way when those situations arise.

In this book, the ways in which violent behavior develops and is learned are explored; particular emphasis is placed on the social and cultural factors that impinge on the process and help to mold it. Those populations who are especially susceptible to becoming perpetrators or victims because of the impinging social factors, including members of ethnic minority groups, girls and young women, youth with disabilities, and gay and lesbian youth, are discussed. Recommendations are made for research, services, and policy formation that we believe are necessary in order to reduce youth violence in this country.

Most important, solutions are examined as well as problems. We believe that just as the need to address the problem of youth violence systematically and effectively has never been greater, the field of psychology has never been in a better position to play a central role in developing solutions.

In coordinating chapters for this book, we chose to emphasize psychosocial influences on violence and violence prevention and intervention. Other influences, such as the ones described earlier, have not been given much emphasis primarily because doing justice to those approaches would require additional volumes. Nonetheless, we recognize the importance of these approaches. For example, we do not underestimate the importance of biological influences on behavior and the role of psychology in investigating them. Biological psychology has had a long tradition as a distinct field within psychology[3]. In this "decade of the brain," new methods of brain imaging have accelerated research on the biological bases of behavior, and this research area has grown in depth and in communication across disciplinary lines.

Biological approaches include the study of genetic influences on behavioral variation. An active field tied to psychology is behavior genetics, which concerns the relative contributions of nature and nurture to behavioral variation (i.e., individual differences). This subfield has ties with molecular genetics, and searches are underway for specific genes that may affect behavioral traits (Plomin, 1990).

Although biological aspects of youth and violence are only briefly touched on in this book, we believe that the biological perspective can make several contributions to the understanding of violence and violence prevention. These contributions include investigating (a) the relative role of nature and nurture in the intergenerational transmission of violence, (b) the physiological differences between violent and nonviolent individuals, (c) the physiological and psychological effects of alcohol and other drugs on individuals' involvement with violence, (d) the drug interventions that are effective for particular subpopulations (with important consideration given to both medical side effects and the ethical use of medication), and (e) the evolutionary context of violent behavior.

Behavior–genetic methods have been used to investigate the heritability of crime and delinquency, both of which may involve violence. Childhood disorders that are hypothesized to predict later violence, such as hyperactivity and conduct disorder, may be partially heritable. Evidence has been found for

---

[3]We thank David Rowe, PhD, for graciously contributing the material that follows on biological issues pertaining to violence and youth.

gene x environment interactions in crime and delinquency (e.g., Cadoret, Cain, & Crowe, 1983; Mednick, Gabrielli, & Hutchings, 1984).

These studies should not be misinterpreted as indicating that any single "violence" gene exists. Rather, violence appears to be related in part to a set of traits, such as a fearless, uninhibited temperament, impulsiveness, cognitive impairments, and low IQ, that can interact with other factors to produce violent behavior. Not only do psychosocial and environmental factors influence violence, but genetic variation may also contribute to violent behaviors through pathways that help cause variation in these factors. These temperament differences among individuals may help explain why, even in poor, urban communities where violence rates are quite high, only a minority of youths are violent.[4] Indeed, the behavior–genetic perspective may also be helpful for understanding the different outcomes of siblings, who, although they share similar family and neighborhood environments as well as similar genetic contributions from their common parents, may nevertheless differ in their specific genetic and behavioral patterns.

The presence of genetic variation in possible violence-related temperament factors suggests that, in the future, physiological differences may be found between individuals who are more or less prone to violence. Promising biological correlates include two levels of cerebral spinal fluid serotonin (a chemical signal in the brain) metabolites, low heart rates and reduced skin conductance response, and low levels of the brain enzyme monoamine oxidase (Ellis, 1991; Raine, Venables, & Williams, 1990). This list of potential physiological correlates of violence is still short, but may grow with further research.

A third direction in the biological approach is the use of medicines as interventions. Most directly related to violence is the current treatment of childhood hyperactivity by stimulant drugs such as Ritalin (Henker & Whalen, 1989). Although the drug treatment of children remains controversial, behavioral improvements are sometimes observed. On the other hand, the medical treatment of hyperactive children has not been a panacea. Even treated hyperactive children and adolescents continue to have problems when it comes to violence. Although we share concerns with others that drug interventions can be socially misused, we appreciate that this area will remain an active one for biologically oriented psychologists and psychiatrists.

In summary, biological perspectives on violence may complement the psychological and psychosocial approaches that are elaborated on more fully in this volume. Most psychologists recognize that behavior involves the interaction of biological, psychological, and social determinants, and that analyses of these different levels support rather than contradict one another.

We also do not underestimate the influence of alcohol and other drug use on violent behavior. Most studies have found that, in 60% of homicides, the perpetrator, the victim, or both had used alcohol, and violence frequently occurs in places where alcohol is consumed (NCIPC, 1989; Wilson & Hernstein,

---

[4]Previously in this chapter, the possibility was raised that the failure of social conditions alone to explain this anomaly was due to the differential learning histories of children growing up in similar environments.

1985). The connection between alcohol consumption and interpersonal violence has been attributed to alcohol's power to disinhibit. Whereas the involvement of alcohol in violence is well-documented because of the common
use of blood alcohol tests on homicide victims, far less is known about the role
of narcotics, marijuana, and other controlled substances. Some drugs may
have a similar disinhibitory effect on violence, and other drugs (e.g., PCP or
"angel dust") have sometimes been blamed for causing violent behavior (Goldstein, Hunt, Des Jarlais, & Deren, 1987).

Beyond the potential for drugs to contribute directly to violent behavior,
drugs also play two important and well-documented indirect roles in interpersonal violence (NCIPC, 1989). Because some drugs are both addictive and
expensive (e.g., heroin and cocaine), many users of these drugs commit crimes
involving violence to support their addictions. Because many drugs are both
illegal and valuable, drug dealers frequently become involved in violence related to the marketing of drugs. The National Institute on Drug Abuse estimated, conservatively, that at least 10% of homicides occur during drug sales
(Harwood, Napolitano, Kristiansen, & Collins, 1984).

Several recent findings suggest that habitually violent and impulsive
criminals who commit crimes under the influence of alcohol show unusual
biochemical findings, characterized by a particularly low cerebrospinal fluid
5–hydroxyindoleacetic acid (i.e., serotonin) level and a low blood glucose nadir
in the glucose tolerance test (Virkkunen & Linnoila, 1990). However, these
biochemical conditions do not differentiate impulsive violent individuals from
impulsive nonviolent individuals. Thus, it appears that biochemical conditions
may interact with learned response choices, leading only those impulsive individuals for whom violence is a dominant response pattern to show a high
propensity for violent behavior.

Many drug prevention and intervention programs have been developed,
and some have proven to be effective (Tobler, 1992), thereby presumably having an indirect effect on preventing interpersonal violence. Few of these programs, however, make systematic connections to violence prevention. Coordinated and integrative efforts are needed in the development and evaluation
of drug prevention and violence prevention programs. Drug treatment programs have been effective in reducing addiction.

Organization of the Book

The influences on violence are as numerous as they are on any complex behavior, and one book cannot hope to touch, much less cover, all of them. Like-
wise, the approaches to preventing and reducing violence and rehabilitating
violent individuals are many and varied. In this book, we decided to focus on
six major areas, primarily from a psychosocial perspective:

1. etiology of violence,
2. experience of violence among ethnic groups,
3. experience of violence among selected vulnerable populations of
   youth,

4. societal influences on youth violence,
5. prevention and intervention, and
6. research and public policy needs.

The first five areas were chosen for examination and exploration because the members of the APA Commission on Violence and Youth believe that psychology has had the greatest impact in these areas in the past and that future developments in psychology's understanding and prevention of violence must focus on these areas. The last section of the book, research and public policy needs, presents, in general, what the Commission members believe that psychology must do to reach these goals.

In the remaining portion of this chapter, we briefly introduce each of these six sections by discussing some topics pertinent to these areas. Individual chapters will be described in more detail in introductions to each section throughout the book.

Etiology of violence. The two chapters in this section of the book focus on etiological factors that contribute to the development and the prevention of youth violence from the points of view of developmental socialization (e.g, influences of temperament, family, school, peer, and gender roles) and sociocultural socialization (e.g., influences of ethnicity and cultural contexts).

A number of social experiences have been found to increase the risk that an individual will become involved in violence. These include inadequately achieved developmental milestones, unhealthy family and peer relationships, and unfavorable sociocultural conditions. Following are several comments pertaining to the continuity of aggression over time, the role of cognitions, and the influence of socioeconomic inequality and discrimination on violence.

Although the form and the absolute level of an individual's aggression commonly vary considerably throughout the life span, an individual's relative level of aggression among age-mates shows remarkable continuity and predictability over time. Meta-analyses of longitudinal research evidence regarding an individual's patterns of aggression over time have revealed that, for both males and females, about 20%–25% of the variation among same-sex age mates in the perpetration of violence can often be predicted from knowledge of an individual's aggressive behavior several decades earlier (Olweus, 1979, 1982). Furthermore, an individual's aggressive behavior typically becomes more highly predictable as he or she grows older (Olweus, 1979). For example, a 22-year longitudinal follow-up study revealed that aggressive behavior of boys in early childhood is predictive of serious antisocial behavior in adulthood, including criminal offenses, spouse abuse, and a tendency toward severe punishment of one's children (Huesmann, Eron, Lefkowitz, & Walder, 1984). Patterns of victimization have been found to show levels of continuity and predictability similar to those of aggression, although these findings appear to be limited to the school years, when individuals usually have little opportunity to control their social environment. Childhood victimization was found to predict depression in adulthood, but it did not predict an individual's harassment at age 23, presumably because adults generally have greater freedom to avoid victimization by controlling their own social and physical environments (Olweus, 1993).

Although interpersonal violence has been investigated primarily within the various social domains of family, peer relations, media, school, and particular social settings, investigation of violent behavior across these social domains has begun to reveal striking individual consistencies (Parke & Slaby, 1983; Slaby & Roedell, 1982). Children and youth typically navigate among these social domains on a daily basis, and they show substantial consistency in their relative level of violence across social domains, even though their absolute level typically differs considerably from setting to setting.

Similarities between youthful victims and perpetrators have also been found. For example, school children who are identified by their peers as commonly behaving as aggressors or victims, share a number of social experiences and patterns of thought that put them at risk for involvement with violence. For one, aggressors and victims share a common social experience of being strongly rejected by their peers as friends and playmates (Perry, Kusel, & Perry, 1988; Slaby, Wilson-Brewer, & DeVos, 1994).

However, despite this and other similarities and despite their interactive influences, youthful aggressors and victims differ from one another in a variety of ways (Fagan, Piper, & Cheng, 1987). For example, peer-nominated aggressors are likely to show behavioral intent to use physical and verbal aggression to solve social problems, whereas peer-nominated victims may show behavioral intent to avoid dealing with the social problem (Slaby, Wilson-Brewer, & DeVos, 1994). In the most comprehensive investigation to date of young bullies and victims (ages 13–16), it was found that bullies were generally characterized by their impulsive tendencies, positive attitudes toward violence, strong need to dominate others, little empathy for others, and physical strength. Victims, on the other hand, were generally anxious, lacking in self-esteem, socially isolated, physically weak, and afraid to defend themselves (Olweus, 1991).

Violence is not triggered merely by these individual characteristics and environmental events but also by the way in which an individual perceives these events, makes meaning of them, anticipates others' reactions, and chooses to act on these events. From as early as the preschool years and throughout adulthood, highly aggressive or violent individuals have been found to show habits of thought that reflect lower levels of social problem-solving skills and higher endorsement of beliefs that support the use of violence (Dodge, 1986; Parke & Slaby, 1983; Slaby & Guerra, 1988; Slaby & Stringham, in press; Shure & Spivack, 1988).

Highly aggressive children and violent adolescent offenders typically define social problems in hostile ways, adopt hostile goals, seek few additional facts, generate few alternative solutions, anticipate few consequences for aggression, and give higher priority to their aggressive solutions. Combined with their deficits in social problem-solving skills, aggressive children and violent adolescent offenders commonly hold general beliefs that support the use of aggression, such as the beliefs that the use of aggression is legitimate, increases self-esteem, and helps to avoid a negative image (e.g., Guerra & Slaby, 1989; Huesmann & Guerra, 1994; Slaby & Guerra, 1988; Shure & Spivack,

1988). Because the cognitive patterns that underlie violent behavior appear to be learned early in childhood, are habitual in nature, and, yet, are potentially modifiable through direct intervention, treatment programs that change these cognitive patterns should lead to relatively enduring changes in violent behavior (Guerra & Slaby, 1990; Kazdin, 1987).

Finally, although a high rate of interpersonal violence among the poor is a social fact in the United States, there has been little investigation of the different patterns of violent behavior found within low socioeconomic status groups. Interwoven with the effects of poverty on violence are the racial differences that will be described here and elsewhere in this book.

Here we would like to stress that it has been very difficult to disentangle poverty from race or ethnicity as independent predictors of violence. It appears that economic inequality, rather than absolute level of material deprivation, is most strongly predictive of group differences in the rate of violence, because homicide rates are highest for countries and areas in which the difference in levels of material wealth between the rich and poor is the greatest (Hawkins, 1993; Messner, 1990). Furthermore, economic discrimination against the poor appears to increase the societal rate of homicide (Hawkins, 1993). It has been suggested that "the close association of violent crime with urban lower-class life is a direct result of the opportunities that are *not* available" (Silberman, 1980, p. 117–118).

Although programs designed to foster equal economic opportunity have been developed in attempts to overcome the profound economic inequalities that exist in the United States, such programs have rarely been perceived as related to violence prevention. Investigation is needed into the potential connections between economic opportunity programs and violence prevention programs and the effects they have on one another.

Experience of violence: Ethnic minorities. There are some groups, primarily ethnic minority groups, that appear to dominate the statistics as victims of violence.[5] Much of the research to date on these vulnerable groups has been epidemiological in nature. There has been little or no research to demonstrate unique psychological or behavioral characteristics among the groups that might explain the differential occurrence of violence. Because of this, the chapters in this section largely focus on the epidemiology of violence among four ethnic groups: African Americans, U.S. Latinos, Native Americans, and Asian and Pacific Island Americans. However, the authors also discuss some of the psychological aspects of ethnicity that influence reactions and responses to victimization.

Here and in the next section, we briefly discuss hate violence as a particular form of violence often perpetrated against members of ethnic minority

---

[5]For example, with regard to African American and White victims of violence, the lifetime odds of dying by interpersonal violence in the United States have recently been estimated (Federal Bureau of Investigation, 1989). Excluding violent deaths by suicide, by war, or by acts of law enforcement, it has been estimated that 1 in 27 African American males in America will die by violence (compared with 1 in 205 White males); 1 in 117 African American females in America will die by violence (compared with 1 in 496 White females).

groups. Hate violence appears to have its roots in individuals' learned prejudices against particular social groups.

The attitudinal bases for prejudice were described over 40 years ago (Allport, 1954). At about the same time an instrument to assess the "authoritarian personality" known as the "Fascist Scale" (i.e., F-Scale) was developed and has been used to predict a wide variety of anti-Semitic and other discriminatory social behaviors (Adorno, Frenkel-Brunswik, Levinson, & Sanford, 1950). Although the body of research that was generated from these formulations has advanced the understanding of the development of prejudice, little is known about the connection between the development of prejudice and violence (Aboud, 1988). It has been observed that

> from a practical point of view, it is important to identify the genesis of hate crime so that it can be curtailed, recognizing that there are many persons who do not see it as a problem requiring any special attention. (Weiss, 1990, p. 78)

Although many school-based educational programs have been designed to reduce stereotyping, prejudice, and discriminatory behavior, no available programs specifically designed for the prevention of hate violence have been identified (Schwartz & Elcik, 1994). One such program is currently in development (McLaughlin & Brilliant, 1994). Recommendations for the prevention of hate crime fall into five categories: (a) human relations education programs, (b) self-defense organization and training for victim groups, (c) community dispute mediation efforts, (d) increased penalties, and (e) prosecution (Weiss, 1990). The potential effectiveness of these strategies is unknown because to date no adequate outcome research has been done.

Specific recommendations offered by Weiss (1990) include (a) encouraging all jurisdictions in the U.S. to enact, or continue to enact, and enforce laws against hate violence; (b) enhancing law enforcement capabilities; (c) encouraging community leaders to heighten awareness and to denounce hate violence; (d) rendering adequate assistance to victims of hate violence; (e) coordinating intra-agency efforts among government, law enforcement, and community organizations; (f) reorienting emergent antihate crime vigilante groups toward nonviolent enforcement strategies; (g) enhancing efforts to protect children from child abuse and neglect; (h) developing, through applied research, strategies for engendering tolerant values among American children; and (i) developing a means for social rehabilitation of hate violence criminals. To date, none of these seemingly sensible recommendations have developed into programs that have been the subject of adequate scientific evaluation.

Experience of violence: Vulnerable populations. Historically, African Americans have been the most frequent targets of hate violence in the United States (Weiss, 1990). However, hate violence can also target other groups, such as women, gays and lesbians, and individuals with disabilities (Ehrlich, 1992; Herek & Berrill, 1992; Levin & McDevitt, 1993), groups that are discussed in chapters 8–10 in this section.

Data exist primarily on anti-African American and anti-Semitic violence, and many instances of hate violence are not documented as such. Nonetheless, there is some consensus that groups not classified by ethnicity are increasingly becoming the targets of hate crimes. For example, in a recent report to the National Institute of Justice, it was observed that "homosexuals are probably the most frequent victims" of hate violence (Finn & McNeil, 1987, p. 2). In 1984, the National Gay and Lesbian Task Force (NGLTF) conducted a survey of lesbians and gay men in eight U.S. cities (Berrill, 1986). More than one fifth of the men and nearly one tenth of the women reported having been physically assaulted because of their sexual orientation.

The Hate Crimes Statistics Act signed into law in July 1990 calls for the gathering of data on hate crimes against people based on their sexual orientation. Anti-gay assaults may have increased in frequency during the last few years, with many incidents now including spoken references to AIDS by the assailants. Attitude research suggests, however, that AIDS may be less a cause of anti-gay sentiment than a focal issue that crystallizes heterosexuals' preexisting hostility toward gay people (Herek, 1989). A statewide survey of junior and senior high school students in New York revealed greater hostility toward gay people than toward racial or ethnic minorities, and students' responses often included threats of anti-gay violence (Governor's Task Force on Bias-Related Violence, 1988). The bulk of reported anti-gay attacks are perpetrated by male assailants, usually juveniles or young adults in groups who are not known by their victim (NGLTF, 1987).

Whether girls and young women are also targets of hate violence is less clear. Some believe that the victimization of members of the female gender has to do with an underlying hatred toward women fostered by societal influences such as pornography and the underresponse to domestic violence and sexual crimes (e.g., date rape) in this country. Others focus more on gender-related socialization or the different physical stature of women as making them more vulnerable to violence.

Societal influences on youth violence. By societal influences we refer to those aspects of everyday life in the United States that are not formal ecological and sociological variables such as ethnicity and social class but that impinge on and affect the individual's behavior. In chapters 11–14, we cover four major societal influences (i.e., gangs, guns, media, and mobs), while realizing that many other forces play a similarly important role in instigating violence. For example, alcohol and other drugs often influence the occurrence of violence, as discussed previously.

Media as a societal force can be particularly detrimental when it comes to youth and violence. Because we believe that this force has been greatly underestimated, we also address it here. Unlike many other forms of so-called unintentional injury, interpersonal violence can be socially transmitted through observational experiences, as well as through direct interactive experiences. The potential for violence to be socially learned and transmitted has been documented through research on the viewing of television or film violence (e.g., Bandura, 1973; Condry, 1989; Eron & Huesmann, 1984; Huston et al., 1992; Liebert & Sprafkin, 1988; Parke & Slaby, 1983; Pearl, Bouthilet,

& Lazar, 1982), the witnessing of domestic violence (e.g., Rosenberg & Rossman, 1990), and the potential for interpersonal violence to spread and escalate rapidly in communities (e.g., Loftin, 1985). Unlike the social transmission of communicable diseases, violence spreads through processes of learning based on the observation, interpretation, and imitation of the behavior of others.

Since the first congressional investigations were undertaken in 1953 to address the question of the impact of television violence on children's aggressive behavior and juvenile delinquency, research evidence over nearly 4 decades has documented the potential risk of learning violence from television. In a report designed to follow-up on the Surgeon General's Commission report of 1972, the National Institute of Mental Health (NIMH) report (1982) concluded that "violence on television does lead to aggressive behavior by children and teenagers who watch the program" (p. 6).

More important than the potential for immediate effects on the viewer of a single exposure, there appear to be long-term cumulative effects as well, which help shape the developing youngster's character and personality, including the willingness and readiness to engage in violence (Huesmann, Eron, Lefkowitz, & Walder, 1984).

In addition to increasing the viewers' potential for perpetrating violence, television violence viewing has been found to lead to a behavioral and physiological indifference toward violence that is perpetrated against others (e.g., Cline Croft, & Courrier, 1973; Thomas, Horton, Lippincott, & Drabman, 1977). In addition, an increased "mean world" syndrome based on a growing mistrust of others and an exaggerated view of both the prevalence and the appropriateness of violence in the real world is encouraged (e.g., Gerbner, Gross, Jackson-Beeck, Jeffries-Fox, & Signorielli, 1978). The major research has moved from asking whether there are effects of viewing television violence to seeking explanations and ways to reduce or prevent the effects (Huesmann, Eron, Kline, Brice, & Fischer, 1983; Huston et al., 1992; Liebert & Sprafkin, 1988; Parke & Slaby, 1983; Slaby & Quarfoth, 1980).

A large number of professional organizations that are concerned with the well-being of children and families (e.g., American Academy of Pediatrics, American Medical Association, American Psychological Association, National Parent Teachers Association) have recommended that professionals take a more active role in reducing the impact of violent media. Research and intervention programs have indicated that some of the impact of media violence can be reduced by "empowering" parents in their roles as monitors of children's television viewing (e.g., Collins, Sobol, & Westby, 1981; Singer & Singer, 1981). In addition to home-based interventions, a number of programs have been designed to build "critical viewing skills" that may ameliorate the impact of televised violence on parents and children (Eron, 1986; Singer & Singer, 1991), although the effectiveness of these programs is still under evaluation. Recommendations regarding regulatory and policy issues in relation to children's television have also been made (e.g., Huston, Watkins, & Kunkel, 1989; Kunkel & Watkins, 1987; Palmer, 1988). The potential for the medium of television not only to reduce its role as a source of risk, but also to play a major beneficial role as the most powerful public teacher in reducing violence deserves thorough consideration in light of television's previous successes in health campaigns (Pearl, Bouthilet, & Lazar, 1982; Palmer, 1988; Slaby, 1994). The Corporation for Public Broadcasting has recently launched a national campaign to reduce youth violence. Beginning in 1995, television programming will be coordinated with community outreach activities to create the largest educational campaign in the history of public television.

Along with the media, the ready availability of guns has broadened the scope and severity of violence among youth. Although injury and death that result from interpersonal violence can be inflicted through a wide variety of means, firearms are involved in a majority of homicides, and the proportion of firearm homicide is particularly high among youth. Firearms accounted for 60% of all U.S. homicides in 1987 (Earls et al., 1992). For those 15–19 years of age, firearms accounted for 71% of all homicides (Fingerhut & Kleinman, 1990). For African American male teenagers, the firearm homicide rate increased 66% from 1984 to 1987, while the nonfirearm homicide rate increased only 13% (Fingerhut & Kleinman, 1990).

In addition to fatal firearm injuries, nonfatal firearm injuries are widespread in America. In 1985, for every firearm death there were an estimated 7.5 nonfatal injuries (236,000 altogether) of which 28% required hospitalization (Rice, MacKenzie, & Associates, 1989).

Two types of interventions are generally considered in attempts to reduce injury caused by firearms. Educational interventions have been designed primarily to reduce unintentional firearm injuries. Laws and enforcement policies have been designed primarily to limit the number, type, and distribution of firearms. Research is needed to evaluate the effectiveness of both educational and regulatory interventions in reducing violent injury and death involving firearms. In one study, comparisons were made between two cities that differed primarily in their gun control policies — Seattle, Washington, in the United States, where guns can be easily obtained, and Vancouver, British Columbia, in Canada, where stringent restrictions exist on the purchase of guns (Sloan et al., 1988). Although the overall assault rate was similar in both cities, fatal assaults were much higher in Seattle primarily because of shooting fatalities. Within the United States, geographical differences in gun ownership have also been found to be correlated with that fraction of homicides, suicides, and assaults that are committed with guns (Alexander, Massey, Gibbs, & Alterkruse, 1985; Cook, 1991). Societal consensus and regulatory policy needs to be developed regarding "legitimate" and "nonlegitimate" access to, distribution of, and use of various types of firearms (Moore, 1982).

Preventive and rehabilitative interventions. The three chapters in this section (chapters 15–17) emphasize preventive and interventional strategies and programs for children and adolescents as both victims and perpetrators of violence. Interventions have been designed to address the problem of violence at the community level, the family level, and the individual level.

Community-based interventions offer the possibility of crossing many environmental contexts in which violence is learned, the community, school, peer groups, and family. In contrast to treatment programs in which individuals who are deemed to be at risk are identified for intervention by a single therapist, community-based interventions typically emphasize the need to integrate community support systems and organizations in order to develop a coordinated and systematic approach to preventing violence among youth.

For example, the New York City Department of Health has designed, and is currently in the process of implementing, a community-based program that targets reducing interpersonal violence among minority males, ages 15–24, the group that is at highest risk (New York City Department of Health, 1990). The "Safe Havens Project" seeks to make an impact on children, families, and their support systems through a wide variety of sources (e.g., school, police, job training programs, substance abuse programs, health care centers, media) and a coordinated set of city-wide activities (e.g., public awareness campaign, skills development, conflict resolution training).

Youth who are not successfully reached by community-based prevention and treatment programs may often be those for whom violence has been repeatedly learned and reinforced within the context of the family. The family usually provides the first, and potentially most intense learning experiences that have broad and enduring consequences for an individual's use of violence. In addition, children and youth are frequently in direct danger of injury or even death at the hands of family members or they may become perpetrators of violence against family members. A number of factors have been suggested to account for high rates of violent interaction within many families (Gelles & Straus, 1979). These include (a) the large amount of time spent interacting with one another, (b) the wide range of activities (and thus possible sources of dispute) in which families engage, (c) the high intensity of involvement with one another, (d) the assumed right or responsibility to influence other family members, (e) the right to privacy that insulates family behavior from external monitoring and assistance, (f) the involuntary membership (particularly for young children) and the expectation of stability in the relationships that prevent conflicts from being resolved or terminated by leaving the situations, and (g) the cultural norms and legal protections that legitimize violence among family members to a greater extent than violence outside of the family.

Family experiences that are found to contribute to an individual's risk of involvement with violence include (a) physical abuse or neglect (Egeland, Sroufe, & Erickson, 1983; Engfer & Schneewind, 1982; George & Main, 1979; Hoffman-Plotkin & Twentyman, 1984; Widom, 1989), (b) heavy use of physical punitiveness (Eron, Walder, & Lefkowitz, 1971; Martin, 1975; Slaby & Roedell, 1982), (c) parental permissiveness for aggression (Olweus, 1979), (d) active encouragement of the use of aggression outside of the home (Bandura & Walters, 1959), (e) the witnessing of marital violence (Jaffe, Wolfe, Wilson, & Zak, 1986; Rosenberg & Rossman, 1990), and (f) high levels of coercive family interaction (Patterson, 1982).

At the family level, parent training is often seen as the key component in preventing or reducing violence. Programs in parent management training have been systematically developed and thoroughly investigated over the past two decades by Patterson and his colleagues (e.g., Patterson, 1982, 1986; Patterson, Capaldi, & Bank, 1991). Based on the view that coercive interaction patterns in the family inadvertently contribute to the development, maintenance, and escalation of violence both within and outside of the family, this program focuses on training parents of young children (3 to 12 years) to define and respond to coercive behavior in the home in new, effective, and noncoercive ways. A related program of functional family treatment has been designed to alter those interaction and communication patterns among family members that may foster coercive behavior (e.g., replace defensiveness with mutual support) (Alexander & Parsons, 1982).

A number of interventions have been developed to target individuals through programs that are delivered through schools or other educational, correctional, or health institutions (Wilson-Brewer, Cohen, O'Donnell, & Goodman, 1991). Some of these programs are designed for early intervention in the preschool years (e.g., Shure, 1992; Slaby, Roedell, Arezzo, & Hendrix, 1994). These programs are generally designed to teach social–cognitive skills, including alternative solution generation, social perspective taking, and peer negotiation skills. These programs are becoming more and more popular as one school district after another seeks to solve its school violence problems by use of such apparently simple techniques with good face validity. They are seldom developed or evaluated with acceptable scientific procedures, and when they are successful it is difficult to ascertain which treatment components and combinations of components are effective. Nevertheless, several intervention programs have been built on sound theoretical foundations and have demonstrated some effectiveness in changing individuals' social–cognitive skills and their violence-related behaviors (e.g., Guerra & Slaby, 1990; Slaby, Wilson-Brewer, & Dash, 1994; see also chapters 15 and 16 in this volume).

Recommendations. The final section of the volume is devoted to recommendations for future research and policy directions, which are covered separately in chapters 18 and 19. The authors of the chapter on research surveyed the state of current knowledge in specific areas. It was apparent from each of these evaluative surveys that there were still many gaps in knowledge, and new methodologies were available to help shed light on these areas. These gaps and newer methodologies are summarized in the section on recommendations for research. Changes and innovations in public policy that are necessary in order to deal appropriately with the problems of youth violence in society are summarized in the chapter on policy recommendations.[6]

Conclusion

Interpersonal violence is indeed one of the most prevalent, stable, socially transmittable, societally destructive, and problematic health risks Americans face. Nevertheless, violence is by no means an inevitable, random, or unchangeable problem. What is needed is the will to treat violence as an unacceptable and preventable problem, combined with a coordinated set of scien-

---

[6]Specific recommendations in both of these chapters were published in the predecessor to this volume, *Violence and Youth: Psychology's Response.*

tifically derived, practical, and effective interventions that are carried out systematically and consistently in the homes, schools, communities, media, and health centers of this country.

The need and the opportunity for the field of psychology to play a key role in helping to solve the problem of violence has never been greater. It is our hope that this book will serve as a strong impetus toward that end.

References

Aboud, F. (1988). *Children and prejudice.* Cambridge, MA: Basil Blackwell.

Adorno, T., Frenkel-Brunswik, E., Levinson, D., & Sanford, R. N. (1950). *The authoritarian personality.* New York: Harper.

Alexander, G. R., Massey, R. M., Gibbs, T., & Alterkruse, J. (1985). Firearm-related fatalities: An epidemiologic assessment of violent death. *American Journal of Public Health, 75,* 165–166.

Alexander, J. F., & Parsons, B. V. (1982). *Functional family therapy.* Monterey, CA: Brooks/Cole.

Allport, G. W. (1954). *The nature of prejudice.* Reading, MA: Addison-Wesley.

Bandura, A. (1973). *Aggression: A social learning analysis.* Englewood Cliffs, NJ: Prentice Hall.

Bandura, A., & Walters, R. H. (1959). *Adolescent aggression.* New York: Ronald Press.

Berrill, K. (1986). *Anti-gay violence: Causes, consequences, responses.* Washington, DC: National Gay and Lesbian Task Force. (Available from the National Gay and Lesbian Task Force, 1517 U St., NW, Washington, DC 20009.)

Bureau of Justice Statistics. (1990). *Criminal victimization in the United States, 1988. A national crime survey report.* Washington, DC: U. S. Department of Justice.

Cadoret, R. J., Cain, C. A., & Crowe, R. R. (1983). Evidence for gene–environment interaction in the development of adolescent antisocial behavior. *Behavior Genetics, 13,* 301–310.

Centers for Disease Control. (1987). Premature mortality due to homicide and suicide—United States, 1984: Perspectives in disease prevention and health promotion. *Morbidity and Mortality Weekly Report, 36*(32), 531–534.

Cline, V. B., Croft, R. G., & Courrier, S. (1973). Desensitization of children to television violence. *Journal of Personality and Social Psychology, 27,* 360–365.

Collins, W. A., Sobol, B. L., & Westby, S. (1981). Effect of adult commentary on children's comprehension and inferences about televised aggressive portrayal. *Child Development, 52,* 158–163.

Condry, J. (1989). *The psychology of television.* Hillsdale, NJ: Erlbaum.

Cook, P. J. (1991). The technology of personal violence. In M. Tonry (Ed.), *Crime and justice: A review of research* (pp. 1–74). Chicago: University of Chicago Press.

Dodge, K. A. (1986). A social information-processing model of social competence in children. In M. Perlmutter (Ed.), *Minnesota symposium on child psychology* (Vol. 18, pp. 77–125). Hillsdale, NJ: Erlbaum.

Earls, F. J., Slaby, R. G., Spirito, A., Saltzman, L. E., Thornton, T. N., Berman, A., Davidson, L., Fagan, J., Goodman, A., Hawkins, D., Kraus, J. F., Loftin, C., Moscicki, E., Muehrer, P., O'Carroll, P., Sudak, H., Visher, C., Widom, C. S., Wintemute, G. & Baer, K. (1992). Prevention of violence and injuries due to violence. In *Injury control: Position papers from the third national injury control conference: Setting the national agenda for injury control in the 1990s* (pp. 159–254). Atlanta, GA: Centers for Disease Control.

Egeland, B., Sroufe, L. A., & Erickson, M. (1983). The developmental consequence of different patterns of maltreatment. *Child Abuse and Neglect, 7,* 459–469.

Ehrlich, H. J. (1992). *Campus ethnoviolence: A research review* (Institute Rep. No. 5). Baltimore, MD: National Institute Against Prejudice and Violence.

Ellis, D. (1991). Monoamine oxidase and criminality: Identifying an apparent biological marker for antisocial behavior. *Journal of Research in Crime and Delinquency, 28,* 227–251.

Engfer, A., & Schneewind, K. A. (1982). Causes and consequences of harsh parental punishment. *Child Abuse and Neglect, 6,* 129–139.

Eron, L. D. (1986). Interventions to mitigate the psychological effects of media violence on aggressive behavior. *Journal of Social Issues, 42,* 155–169.

Eron, L. (1987). The development of aggressive behavior from the perspective of a developing behaviorist. *American Psychologist, 42,* 435–442.

Eron, L. D., & Huesmann, L. R. (1984). Television violence and aggressive behavior. In B. B. Lahey & A. Kazdin (Eds.), *Advances in Clinical Child Psychology,* (Vol. 7, pp. 35–55). New York: Plenum.

Eron, L. D., Huesmann, L. R., Dubow, E., Romanoff, R., & Yarmel, P. W. (1987). Aggression and its correlates over 22 years. In D. Crowell, E. Evans & C. O'Donnell (Eds.), *Aggression and violence: Sources of influence, prevention and control* (pp. 249–262). New York: Plenum.

Eron, L. D., Walder, L. O., & Lefkowitz, M. M. (1971). *The learning of aggression in children.* Boston: Little, Brown.

Fagan, J., Piper, E. E., & Cheng, Y. (1987). Contributions of victimization to delinquency in inner cities. *The Journal of Criminal Law and Criminology, 78*(3), 586–613.

Farrington, D. P. (1994). Childhood, adolescent and adult features of violent males. In L. R. Huesmann (Ed.), *Aggressive behavior: Current perspectives* (pp. 215–240). New York: Plenum.

Federal Bureau of Investigation. (1989). *Uniform Crime Reports.* Washington, DC: U.S. Department of Justice.

Federal Bureau of Investigation. (1992). Crime in the United States: Uniform Crime Reports, 1991. Washington, DC: U.S. Department of Justice.

Fingerhut, L. A., & Kleinman, J. C. (1990). International and interstate comparisons of homicide among young males. *Journal of the American Medical Association, 263*(24), 3292–3295.

Finkelhor, D., & Dziuba-Leatherman, J. (1994). Victimization of children. *American Psychologist, 49,* 173–183.

Finn, P., & McNeil, T. (1987). *The response of the criminal justice system to bias crime: An exploratory review.* Contract report submitted to the National Institute of Justice, U.S. Department of Justice. (Available from Abt Associates, Inc., 55 Wheeler St., Cambridge, MA 02138.)

Gelles, R. J., & Straus, M. A. (1979). Determinants of violence in the family: Toward a theoretical integration. In W. Burr, R. Hill, F. I. Nye., & I. Reiss (Eds.), *Contemporary theories about the family* (pp. 549–581). New York: Free Press.

George, C., & Main, M. (1979). Social interactions of young abused children: Approach, avoidance, and aggression. *Child Development, 50,* 306–318.

Gerbner, G., Gross, L., Jackson-Beeck, M., Jeffries-Fox, S., & Signorielli, N. (1978). TV violence profile no. 9: Cultural indicators. *Journal of Communication, 28,* 176–207.

Goldstein, P., Hunt, D., Des Jarlais, D. C., & Deren, S. (1987). Drug dependence and abuse. In R. W. Amler & H. B. Dull (Eds.), *Closing the gap: The burden of unnecessary illness* (pp. 89–101). New York: Oxford University Press.

Governor's Task Force on Bias-Related Violence. (1988). *Final Report.* (Available from Division of Human Rights, 55 West 125th Street, New York, NY 10027.)

Guerra, N. G., & Slaby, R. G. (1989). Evaluative factors in social problem solving by aggressive boys. *Journal of Abnormal Psychology, 17,* 277–289.

Guerra, N. G., & Slaby, R. G. (1990). Cognitive mediators of aggression in adolescent offenders: 2. Intervention. *Developmental Psychology, 26,* 269–277.

Harwoood, H., Napolitano, D., Kristiansen, P. & Collins, J. (1984). Economic cost to society of alcohol and drug abuse and mental illness, Final report. (Unpublished) Rockville, MD: ADAMHA.

Hawkins, D. F. (1993). Inequality, culture and interpersonal violence. *Health Affairs, 12,* 80–95.

Henker, B., & Whalen, C. K. (1989). Hyperactivity and attention deficits. *American Psychologist, 44,* 216–223.

Herek, G. M. (1989). Hate crimes against lesbians and gay men: Issues for research and policy. *American Psychologist, 44,* 948–955.

Herek, G. M., & Berrill, K. T., (Eds.). (1992). *Hate crimes: Confronting violence against lesbians and gay men.* Newbury Park, CA: Sage.

Hoffman-Plotkin, D., & Twentyman, C. T. (1984). A multimodal assessment of behavioral and cognitive deficits in abused and neglected preschoolers. *Child Development, 55,* 794–802.

Huesmann, L. R., Eron, L. D., Klein, R., Brice, P., & Fischer, P. (1983). Mitigating the imitation of aggressive behavior by changing children's attitudes about media violence. *Journal of Personality and Social Psychology, 44,* 899–910.

Huesmann, L. R., Eron, L. D., Lefkowitz, M. M., & Walder, L. O. (1984). The stability of aggression over time and generations. *Developmental Psychology, 20,* 1120–1134.

Huesmann, L. R., & Guerra, N. G. (1994). Normative beliefs about aggression and aggressive behavior. Manuscript submitted for publication.

Huston, A. C., Donnerstein, E., Fairchild, H., Feshbach, N. D., Katz, P. A., Murray, J. P., Rubinstein, E. A., Wilcox, B. L., & Zuckerman, D. (1992). *Big world, small screen: The role of television in American society.* Lincoln: University of Nebraska Press.

Huston, A. C., Watkins, B. A., & Kunkel, D. (1989). Public policy and children's television. *American Psychologist, 44,* 424–433.

Jaffe, P., Wolfe, D., Wilson, S., & Zak, L. (1986). Similarities in behavior and social maladjustment among child victims and witnesses to family violence. *American Journal of Orthopsychiatry, 56,* 142–146.

Kazdin, A. E. (1987). Treatment of antisocial behavior in children: Current status and future directions. *Psychological Bulletin, 102,* 187–203.

Kunkel, D. & Watkins, B. (1987). Evaluation of children's television regulatory policy. *Journal of Broadcasting and Electronic Media, 31,* 367–389.

Levin, J., & McDevitt, J. (1993). *Hate crimes: The rising tide of bigotry and bloodshed.* New York: Plenum.

Liebert, R. M., & Sprafkin, J. (1988). *The early window: Effects of television on children and youth.* Elmsford, NY: Pergamon Press.

Loftin, C. (1985). Assaultive violence as a contagious social process. *Bulletin of the New York Academy of Medicine, 62,* 5.

Martin, B. (1975). Parent–child relations. In F. D. Horowitz (Ed.), *Review of child development research* (Vol. 4, pp. 463–540). Chicago: University of Chicago Press.

McCord, J. (1994). Aggression in two generations. In L. R. Huesmann (Ed.) *Aggressive behavior: Current perspectives* (pp. 241–254). New York: Plenum.

McLaughlin, K., & Brilliant, K. (1994). *Juvenile bias crime prevention program.* Unpublished curriculum. (Available from Education Development Center, 55 Chapel Street, Newton, MA 02160.)

Mednick, S. A., Gabrielli, W. F., & Hutchings, B. (1984). Genetic influence in criminal convictions: Evidence from an adoption cohort. *Science, 224,* 891–894.

Messner, S. F. (1990). Income inequality and murder rates: Some cross-national findings. *Comparative Social Research, 3,* 185–198.

National Center on Child Abuse and Neglect. (1988). *Study of national incidence and prevalence of child abuse and neglect.* Washington, DC: U.S. Department of Health and Human Services.

National Committee for Injury Prevention and Control. (1989). *Injury prevention: Meeting the challenge.* New York: Oxford University Press.

National Gay and Lesbian Task Force. (1987). *Anti-gay violence, victimization, and defamation in 1986.* Washington, DC: Author.

National Institute of Mental Health. (1982). *Television and behavior: Ten years of scientific progress and implications for the eighties (Vol. 1). Summary Report.* Washington, DC: U.S. Government Printing Office.

New York City Department of Health. (1990, May). *New York City Violence Prevention Initiative.* New York: Author.

Newberger, E. H. (1982). *Child abuse.* Boston: Little, Brown.

Olweus, D. (1979). Stability and aggressive patterns in males: A review. *Psychological Bulletin, 86,* 852–875.

Olweus, D. (1982). Continuity in aggressive and inhibited withdrawn behavior patterns. *Psychiatry and Social Science, 1,* 141–159.

Olweus, D. (1991). Bully/victim problems among schoolchildren: Basic facts and effects of a school based intervention program. In D. J. Pepler & K. H. Rubin (Eds.), *The development and treatment of childhood aggression* (pp. 411–448). Hillsdale, NJ: Erlbaum.

Olweus, D. (1993). Victimization by peers: Antecedents and long-term outcomes. In K. H. Rubin & J. B. Asendorf (Eds.), *Social withdrawal, inhibition, and shyness in childhood*. Hillsdale, NJ: Erlbaum.

Palmer, E. L. (1988). *Television and America's children*. New York: Oxford University Press.

Parke, R. D., & Slaby, R. G. (1983). The development of aggression. In P. H. Mussen (Ed.), *Handbook of child psychology*, (Vol. 4, 4th ed., pp. 547–641). New York: Wiley.

Patterson, G. R. (1982). *Coercive family processes*. Eugene, OR: Castilia Press.

Patterson, G. R. (1986). Performance models for antisocial boys. *American Psychologist, 41,* 432–444.

Patterson, G. R., Capaldi, D., & Bank, L. (1991). An early starter model for prediction delinquency. In D. J. Pepler, & K. H. Rubin (Eds.), *The development and treatment of childhood aggression* (pp. 139–159). Hillsdale, NJ: Erlbaum.

Pearl, D., Bouthilet, L., & Lazar, J. (1982). *Television and behavior: Ten years of programs and implications for the 80's*. Washington, DC: U.S. Government Printing Office.

Perry, D. G., Kusel, S. L., & Perry, L. C. (1988). Victims of peer aggression. *Developmental Psychology, 24,* 807–814.

Plomin, R. (1990). The role of inheritance in behavior. *Science, 248,* 183–188.

Raine, A., Venables, P. H., & Williams, M. (1990). Relationship between CNS and ANS measures of arousal at age 15 and criminality at age 24. *Archives of General Psychiatry, 27,* 1003–1007.

Rice, D. P., MacKenzie, E. J., & Associates. (1989). *Cost of injury in the United States. A report to Congress*. San Francisco: Institute for Health & Aging, University of California and Injury Prevention Center, The Johns Hopkins University.

Rosenberg, M. S., & Rossman, B. B. R. (1990). The child witness to marital violence. In R. T. Ammerman & M. Herson (Eds.), *Treatment of family violence: A sourcebook* (pp. 183–210). New York: Wiley.

Schwartz, W., & Elcik, L. (1994). *A directory of anti-bias education resources and services*. (Available from ERIC Clearinghouse on Urban Education, Box 40, Teachers College, Columbia University, New York, NY 10027.)

Shure, M. (1992). *I can problem solve: An interpersonal cognitive problem-solving program for children*. Champaign, IL: Research Press.

Shure, M., & Spivack, G. (1988). Interpersonal cognitive problem solving. In R. G. Price, E. L. Cowen, R. P. Lorion, & J. Ramos-McKay (Eds.), *14 ounces of prevention: A casebook for practitioners* (pp. 69–82). Washington, DC: American Psychological Association.

Silberman, C. E. (1980). *Criminal violence, criminal justice*. New York: Vintage Books.

Singer, D. G., & Singer, J. L. (1991). *Creating critical viewers*. New York: National Academy of Television Arts & Sciences.

Slaby, R. G. (1994). Combating television violence. *The Chronicle of Higher Education*, Vol. XL (No. 18), pp. B1–B2.

Slaby, R. G., & Guerra, N. G. (1988). Cognitive mediators of aggression in adolescent offenders: 1. Assessment. *Developmental Psychology, 24,* 580–588.

Slaby, R. G., & Quarforth, G. R. (1980). Effects of television on the developing child. In B. W. Camp (Ed.), *Advances in behavioral pediatrics* (Vol 1., pp 225–266). Greenwich, CT: JAI Press.

Slaby, R. G., & Roedell, W. C. (1982). Development and regulation of aggression in young children. In J. Worell (Ed.), *Psychological development in the elementary years* (pp. 97–149). San Diego, CA: Academic Press.

Slaby, R. G., Roedell, W. C., Arezzo, D., & Hendrix, K. (1994). *Early violence prevention: Tools for teachers of young children*. Washington, DC: National Association for the Advancement of Young Children.

Slaby, R. G., & Stringham, P. (in press). Prevention of peer and community violence: The pediatrician's role. *Pediatrics, 94* (supplement).

Slaby, R. G., Wilson-Brewer, R., & Dash, K. (1994). *Aggressors, victims, and bystanders: Thinking and acting to prevent violence*. Newton, MA: Education Development Center.

Slaby, R. G., Wilson-Brewer, R., & DeVos, E. (1994). Aggressors, victims, and bystanders: An assessment-based middle school violence prevention curriculum. Final report of grant #R49/CCR103559. Atlanta, GA: Centers for Disease Control and Prevention. (Available from the National Technical Information Service, 5285 Port Royal Road, Springfield, VA 22161.)

Sloan, J. H., Kellerman, A. L., Reay, D. T., Ferris, J. A., Koepsell, T., Rivara, F. P., Rice, C., Gray, L., & Logerfo, J. (1988). Handgun regulations, crime, assaults, and homicide: A tale of two cities. *New England Journal of Medicine, 319,* 1256–1262.

Thomas, M. H., Horton, R. W., Lippincott, E. C., & Drabman, R. S. (1977). Desensitization to portrayals of real-life aggression as a function of exposure to television violence. *Journal of Personality and Social Psychology, 35,* 450–458.

Tobler, N. S. (1992). Drug prevention programs that can work: Research findings. *Journal of Addictive Diseases, 11,*(3), 1–28.

Virkkunen, M. & Linnoila, M. (1990). Serotonin in early onset, male alcoholics with violent behavior. *Annals of Medicine, 22,* 327–331.

Weiss, J. C. (1990). Violence motivated by bigotry: Ethnoviolence. *Encyclopedia of Social Work* (18th ed., supplement, pp. 307–319). Washington, DC: National Association of Social Work Press.

Widom, C. S. (1989). The cycle of violence. *Science, 244,* 160–166.

Wilson, J. O., & Hernstein, R. J. (1985). *Crime and human nature.* New York: Simon & Schuster.

Wilson-Brewer, R., Cohen, S., O'Donnell, L., & Goodman, I. F. (1991). *Violence prevention for young adolescents: A survey of the state of the art.* Washington, DC: Carnegie Corporation of New York.

Part I

Etiology of Violence

Introduction

As the individual child develops and matures, he or she learns how to interpret the surrounding world as hostile or benevolent, how to solve interpersonal problems in prosocial or in antisocial and violent ways, how to manage or mismanage frustration, and how to meet emotional, social, and physical needs through either legal or illegal means. This learning takes place in multiple contexts: in the family, school, peer group, neighborhood, and larger community, each of which are affected by social and cultural forces in the society at large.

In chapter 2, "Theoretical and Developmental Perspectives on Youth and Violence," Debra Pepler and Ronald Slaby examine individual and contextual factors in a developmental context to explain how aggression may be acquired, how it may develop, and what accounts for continuous and consistent individual differences in patterns of aggressive behavior. Many of the theoretical formulations that have implications for preventing and reducing violence are reviewed. Because the independent contributions of nature, nurture, and the larger societal context are difficult to tease out, interactional models may provide the best framework from which to understand how violence develops.

Pepler and Slaby note that temperament, hyperactivity, impulsivity, intelligence, cognitive styles, and social skills (influenced by both nature and nurture to varying degrees) are among the many individual factors considered that appear germane to violence among youth. Contextual factors, such as family, school, and peer contexts, also interact with each other and with the individual factors to influence violence. Family demographics, such as socioeconomic status; parental characteristics, such as antisocial personality; parenting techniques, such as harsh or inconsistent discipline; and parent–child relations, such as the absence of bonding, each appear to make a contribution to the propensity for violence.

Many of these factors act synergistically when a child enters the school system, interfering with peer relations and affecting the child's ability to learn and function in the classroom. These effects in turn can portend increased aggressive behavior and participation in coercive cliques with other youth who have similar characteristics and problems. The institutional context of the school, including limited space, poor design features, and the imposition of rigid behavior routines may also increase propensity for violence.

As Pepler and Slaby conclude, developmental psychology should provide an increasingly sharp focus on individual and contextual factors affecting the developmental trajectory toward violence and develop interactional models to account for them. Research data in the context of interactional models can then guide and fine tune prevention and intervention efforts.

In chapter 3 "Sociocultural Factors in the Etiology and Prevention of Ethnic Minority Youth Violence," authors Hope Hill, Fernando Soriano, S. Andrew Chen, and Teresa LaFromboise hypothesize critical relations among cultural characteristics of ethnic groups, structural inequities in the larger society, and developmental needs of adolescents on the one hand, and the appearance and development, or prevention, of youth violence on the other.

The authors note that the close association between minority groups and social status makes it difficult to separate the independent roles of culture and social status in youth violence. For example, many social factors (e.g., unemployment, poverty, high population density, and drug abuse) are associated with being both victims and perpetrators of violence. As these same social factors are disproportionately prevalent among members of ethnic minority groups, there is a risk that characteristics of the ethnic culture rather than the social factors impinging on that culture will be seen as precursors to violence when in fact ethnic cultural factors may be protective against violence.

As Hill et al. note, there has been little research on the protective functions that ethnic cultures might perform in preventing youth violence. To stimulate research in that regard, the authors focus on the cultural values of four ethnic minority groups: African American, Hispanic, Native American, and Asian/Pacific Island American youth. As several other chapters in this book stress, it is important to remember that these major ethnic groups are composed of subgroups that may differ widely. In fact, so much heterogeneity exists that readers are cautioned about generalizing results of research and practice from one subgroup to another.

In this chapter, the authors describe a process of proactive socialization that may promote the ethnic culture as a source of strength and protection against violence. Although the authors acknowledge that larger societal factors (e.g., chronic poverty) may impede the ability of ethnic cultures to protect against violence, they hold great hope that by incorporating ethnic cultural variables (e.g., values, strengths) in interactive models of violence and then testing those variables appropriately, prevention and treatment of violence among ethnic minority youth will be greatly enhanced.

Together these chapters help to identify the numerous individual and contextual factors that should be considered in building an interactive psychosocial model of the development of violence among youth. They also provide a broad etiological context in which to consider the epidemiology of violence among ethnic groups, the experience of violence with regard to other vulnerable populations, societal forces that impinge on violence, preventive and treatment interventions, and research and policy recommendations, all of which are discussed in the remaining chapters of this book.

2

Theoretical and Developmental Perspectives on Youth and Violence

Debra J. Pepler and Ronald G. Slaby

A developmental perspective on how youth may become aggressive and violent is central to the understanding of these behaviors because it helps to explain the processes underlying the appearance, continuity, and changes in aggression and violence in youth over time. Knowledge of both individual and contextual factors that place children at risk for becoming violent, as well as for becoming involved with violence as victims or bystanders, provides a basis for early identification of those children who are at risk and for articulation of strategies to prevent or reduce violence.

In this chapter, we provide a selective overview of theoretical formulations regarding the etiology and development of aggression and violence, and we describe data about individual (e.g., temperament, learned problem-solving skills) and contextual (e.g., school, family, and peers) factors that elucidate how patterns of violence develop and how they can be changed. We also examine gender differences in the development of aggression and violence, looking at biological factors, type of aggression, socialization experiences, and developmental outcomes of aggression and violence. Finally, using the theory and data we have presented, we suggest guidelines for prevention, intervention, and social policy development. (We believe that our chapter is applicable to all youth. However, in chapter 3, a discussion of larger contextual factors, such as culture, provides increased understanding of the development of violent behaviors and the victim experience for particular groups of individuals.)

Theories of Aggression and Violence

From the time psychology first became a discipline, psychologists have grappled with the problem of human aggression and violence. Many psychological theories have been articulated and investigated in an attempt to understand the acquisition, maintenance, and control of aggression. Whereas early theories were limited in both their explanatory power and their implications for controlling aggression, recent theories have presented a more complete account of the underlying processes within a developmental framework that provides a broad perspective on aggressive behavior and how to control it. Psychological theories of human aggression are reviewed in a more comprehensive fashion elsewhere (e.g., Geen & Donnerstein, 1983; National Research Council, 1993; Parke & Slaby, 1983). Here, we highlight those aspects of the theoretical formulations that provide key points of leverage for preventing and reducing aggression and violence.

Instinct Theories

Early psychological theories provided little insight into the control of aggression because they regarded human aggression as the direct product of instinct or biological factors. According to *psychoanalytic theory* (Freud, 1950), human beings were assumed to be universally endowed with the opposing internal forces of Eros (positive energy) and Thanatos (destructive energy). These forces were assumed to be biologically based and to require expression. According to *ethological theory* (Lorenz, 1966), human beings were assumed to share with nonhuman animals an instinctual aggressive energy that could be released by specific stimuli without any prior learning.

These instinct theories brought attention to the fact that human beings are endowed with neurophysiological mechanisms that enable them to behave aggressively. However, they failed to reflect the influence of learned social and cognitive factors that determine whether and how aggressive behavior will occur, as well as how it can be prevented. Furthermore, the assumption that individuals who are deprived of aggression-releasing stimuli will increase their tendency to behave aggressively until they attack someone or dissipate their "aggressive energy" in some other way has led to widespread and misleading recommendations for aggression control. Contrary to the recommendations derived from the instinct theories, research has indicated that the discharge of "pent-up" aggressive energy directed toward "safe" targets will typically increase rather than decrease aggressive behavior (Parke & Slaby, 1983).

Drive Theories

The notion that human beings are motivated to behave aggressively not by instinct but by internal drives instigated by external stimuli, such as frustrating experiences, promised to provide a basis for controlling aggressive behavior. According to the most influential version of this position, the *frustration-aggression theory* (Dollard, Doob, Miller, Mowrer, & Sears, 1939, p. 1), "the occurrence of aggressive behavior always presupposes the existence of frustration and contrariwise, the existence of frustration always leads to some form of aggression." Subsequent evidence has indicated that the relation between frustration and aggression is far from inevitable. Frustration is not an inevitable precursor to aggression nor is aggression an inevitable consequence of frustration. Nevertheless, this theoretical formulation succeeded in shifting attention from explanatory factors that were internal and currently unchangeable to factors that were external and potentially controllable.

Although the drive formulation implied that aggressive behavior could be prevented by eliminating "frustrating experiences," this potential solution was unattainable because the experience of frustration was so broad and subjective (e.g., attack, insult, failure, delay, loss of valued objects, and thwarting of goal directed behavior). It was also assumed that following frustration, the motivation to act aggressively was inevitable and undiminished even if the aggressive behavior itself had been inhibited (e.g., by the threat of punishment). This unexpressed motivation to act aggressively might impel one to reduce the drive through either *displacement* (aggression against a target associated with weaker punishment) or *catharsis* (direct or vicarious acts of aggression that may be unrelated to the original instigator). Recommended interventions to reduce aggressive behavior through displacement or catharsis have been largely ineffective or counterproductive. It now appears that frustration is simply one of many potential instigators of aggressive behavior, and an individual's response to frustration is largely determined by learned social and cognitive factors.

Cognitive–Neoassociation Theory

In his recent discussions of the connection between frustration and aggression, Berkowitz (e.g., 1989, 1993) recommended several important modifications to the 1939 frustration–aggression formulation. His theory provides a bridge between traditional drive theories and the social learning and social cognitive theories we discuss in the next section. Agreeing with other contemporary researchers that all aggressive actions do not arise in the same way, Berkowitz (1989, 1993) noted that many assaults actually are instrumental behaviors carried out chiefly to achieve some goal (e.g., money, social approval, self-esteem restoration) other than the target's injury. He contends that the proclivity to use aggression instrumentally can be learned much as other instrumental behaviors are learned. He maintained, following Feshbach's (1964) terminology, that frustration-engendered assaults should be regarded as one type of hostile aggression, behavior whose primary aim is the target's injury or destruction. Going further, Berkowitz also argued that a failure to attain an anticipated goal (his definition of a frustration) produces an instigation to aggression only to the degree that this failure is decidedly unpleasant to the thwarted person. Berkowitz thus contended that the linkage between frustration and aggression is only a special case of the tendency for strong negative affect to generate aggressive inclinations.

According to his formulation, strong negative affect automatically activates an anger/aggression syndrome (a network of feelings, thoughts, memories, and motor reactions) that is associated with the instigation to attack some target, principally, but not only, the perceived source of the unpleasant affect. Particular situational stimuli that are associated in the person's mind, either with previously encountered aversive events or with rewarded aggression, can also activate the anger/aggression syndrome.

The cognitive-neoassociationistic model recognizes the important roles played by learning and cognitive processes. For example, it points out that learning can strengthen or weaken the initial, fairly automatic reactions. In addition, this model suggests that after the first automatic reactions, as the person thinks about the aversive incident (e.g., as to whether the incident was intended by an external agent as a personal attack), cognitive processes can intervene to intensify or modify or lessen the extent to which there is consciously experienced anger and an open attack on some available target.

All in all, then, this formulation is a drive theory in that, along with other modern emotion theories (e.g., Frijda, 1988), it holds that a relevant emotion-arousing event (in this case, a decidedly unpleasant occurrence) tends to activate a particular motor program (in this case, motor responses linked to aggression).

Theories of the Development of Violence and Aggression

Although the early instinct and drive theories of aggression have challenged and clarified the concepts of aggressive behavior, they have provided a limited basis for explaining how aggression is acquired and develops, what accounts for continuous and consistent individual differences in patterns of aggressive behavior, and how to reduce or prevent aggression. Advances in answering these questions have been made through social learning and social–cognitive theories and other models of long-term change and development. These theories have provided important strategies for reducing or preventing the development and expression of aggression and interpersonal violence. We now highlight some of the ways in which these theories have contributed to the understanding of the development and treatment of violence.

Social Learning Theory

Regarded as a single theory, *social learning theory* (Bandura & Walters, 1959, 1963; Bandura, 1973, 1983, 1986) has actually evolved considerably since it was first proposed to account for aggression. This formulation is based on the premise that "people are not born with preformed repertoires of aggressive behavior. They must learn them" (Bandura, 1983, p. 4). Although biological factors are assumed to constrain the type of aggressive response and the rate of learning, as well as to predispose organisms to learn critical features of their immediate environment, human beings are viewed as less constrained and less specifically predisposed by biological factors than are other species. Unlike instinct and drive theories that focus on the inner factors that impel an individual to act aggressively, social learning theory focuses primarily on controllable environmental influences, as well as learned cognitive and self-regulative influences.

According to social learning theory (e.g., Bandura & Walters, 1959, 1963), aggressive behavior is acquired and maintained primarily through (a) observational learning (e.g., viewing aggressive behavior modeled in real life and in the media), (b) direct experience (e.g., receiving rewarding or punishing consequences for aggression), and (c) self-regulative influences (e.g., applying self-reward or punishment and engaging or disengaging one's aggressive behavior from evaluative self-reactions). Investigations of observational learning have led to recommendations about ways of altering the effects of viewing violence in real life or in the media to reduce subsequent violence, as well as ways of encouraging effective and prosocial alternatives to violence to help prevent violence. Investigations of direct experiences related to aggression have led to recommendations by which parents, teachers, peers, and other socialization agents can apply direct rewards and penalties for children's behavior to reduce and prevent violence and to foster effective alternatives to violence. Investigations of the self-regulative influences on aggression have led to recommendations about how children's own social interpretations, beliefs, expectations, and justifications might be fostered or changed in ways that can reduce or prevent violence.

Application of social learning theory to intervention and treatment programs has stimulated the development of a wide variety of treatment methods that combine and extend these three primary sources of social learning (observational learning, direct experience, and self-regulation) to include modeling, role-playing, social skills training, coaching, performance feedback, and self-monitoring. Whereas applications of social learning theory have typically focused on the aggressive behavior of children and youth, little attempt has been made to investigate how children of different ages and levels of development can use and respond to these strategies for controlling aggression. Although social learning theory focused initially and primarily on the observational learning and direct experiences that may lead to aggression (Bandura & Walters, 1959, 1963), recent investigations of self-regulative control have provided a connection and partial integration with theories of social–cognitive development (Bandura, 1983, 1986; see also Parke & Slaby, 1983).

Social–Cognitive Models

Several social–cognitive models have brought additional focus to various ways that cognitive factors may help to account for the acquisition, maintenance, developmental changes, and control or prevention of aggression and violence. These models have focused on various ways in which cognitive factors relate to aggression. Cognitive factors are hypothesized to (a) be acquired through learning and development; (b) contribute to an individual's own proactive exposure to and interpretation of social experiences that foster aggression; (c) mediate an individual's aggressive response to particular social experiences; (d) account for individual continuities and consistencies in patterns of aggression, victimization, and bystander support for violence; and (e) be amenable to change in ways that prevent or reduce aggression.

Although they share a common set of principles, overlapping social–cognitive models have not yet been integrated into a single theory. Social–cognitive models have drawn on a variety of earlier formulations, including mechanisms of self-regulation (Bandura, 1973), principles of cognitive development (Piaget, 1970; Werner, 1948), models of problem solving (d'Zurilla & Goldfried, 1971), notions of information processing (Miller, Galanter, & Pribram, 1960;

Newell & Simon, 1972), formulations of social skills (McFall, 1982), processes of attribution (Kelley, 1972), concepts of social scripts (Schank & Abelson, 1977), and perspectives on social judgments (Walters & Parke, 1964). Although social–cognitive models have commonly placed primary emphasis on the role of cognitive factors, several formulations have included related emotional factors such as anger, hostility, and emotional arousal. Recent intervention efforts have also focused on anger control training (e.g., Lochman, Lampron, Gemmer, & Harris, 1987).

Social information-processing model. The social information-processing model of competent social responding (Dodge, 1980, 1986, 1993) posits that cognitive deficiencies and hostile biases are shown by aggressive children at each step in a five-step sequence of information-processing skills involved in solving social problems: encoding, mental representation, response access, response evaluation and selection, and enactment. For example, at the encoding stage aggressive children have been found to attend to fewer cues than do nonaggressive children and to show a hostile bias in their interpretation of social cues. At the stage of mental representation, aggressive children may have difficulty with affective and social perspective taking. Similar differences have been explored at each of the remaining steps.

Dodge (1991) has drawn a distinction between "reactive" and "proactive" aggression in children, similar to distinctions proposed earlier between "emotional" and "instrumental" aggression (Berkowitz, 1983) or between "hostile" and "instrumental" aggression (Hartup, 1974), to differentiate those aggressive children who react to others in an angry and volatile manner from those who use aggression proactively against others to achieve their goals. There is currently some debate as to whether these represent state or trait characteristics (e.g., Coie, Dodge & Kupersmidt, 1990). Interventions issuing from this model have been aimed at reducing or preventing aggression by increasing aggressive children's social information-processing skills and challenging their hostile biases (e.g., Pepler, Byrd, & King, 1991).

Cognitive-script model. The cognitive-script model (Huesmann, 1988; Huesmann & Eron, 1984, 1989) has addressed aggressive behavior as the product of learned cognitive schemas. According to this model, children learn programs or "scripts" regarding aggression that remain stable because of repeated rehearsal through fantasizing, observation, or actual behavior. These scripts are retrieved from memory and activated in response to related environmental cues. The retrieved scripts affect children's emotional reactions to social situations and control their behavior. Children's behaviors are also influenced by their beliefs about what is normative. These beliefs act as self-regulating internal standards that filter out inappropriate behaviors. Interventions are aimed at changing children's "scripts" and normative beliefs regarding aggression.

Other social–cognitive formulations. Through interactions within the family and peer contexts, children develop internalized cognitive mediators for social interactions. These mediators include strategies for solving social problems, beliefs that support aggression, hostile attributional biases, and social scripts (e.g., Dodge, 1986; Huesmann, 1988; Huesmann & Eron, 1984, 1989; Slaby & Guerra, 1988). If aggressive children view the social world as hostile, they are likely to react with anger and aggression. Others in their social worlds will respond in kind, establishing increasingly coercive interaction patterns that persist across contexts and over time. In addition to the models described above, several other social–cognitive formulations have been informative in describing the cognitions that support aggression and in developing effective interventions to reduce aggressive behavior problems.

The *social problem-solving* paradigm (Rubin & Krasnor, 1986; Spivack & Shure, 1974) provides a framework for assessing specific cognitive skill deficits predictive of young children's aggressive behavior and for intervening to build the cognitive skills that lead to reductions in aggressive behavior (e.g., generating alternative solutions to interpersonal problems and anticipating their consequences). A wide variety of procedures have been used to help young children build both the cognitive and social skills involved in solving social problems in effective and nonaggressive ways, including solving hypothetical dilemmas, "thinking aloud," role playing, transferring training from hypothetical to real life situations, and providing performance feedback. (See Shure, 1992, for a recent edition of these procedures.)

The *cognitive mediators* paradigm (Guerra & Slaby, 1989, 1990; Slaby & Guerra, 1988; Slaby & Stringham, in press) also referred to as the "habits of thought model," has presented a strategy for assessing and changing individuals' content of thought (in the form of generalized beliefs that support the use of violence), as well as their process of thought (in the form of skills in solving social problems) and their style of thought (impulsive or reflective processing of content). An intervention that changed the habits of thought of adolescent offenders who were incarcerated for crimes of violence led to reductions in their subsequent aggressive, impulsive, and inflexible behaviors (Guerra & Slaby, 1990). This assessment and intervention strategy has also been applied to assess and alter those violence-supporting patterns of thought that put individuals at risk for involvement with violence, not only as aggressors, but also as victims or bystanders (Slaby, Wilson-Brewer, & DeVos, 1994).

The *cognitive–social learning mediators* paradigm (Perry, Perry, & Rasmussen, 1986) has extended earlier social learning theory to include assessment of children's expectancies and confidence that their own aggressive behavior will elicit successful outcomes.

Some cognitive mediators lead aggressive children to view the social world as hostile and to react with angry, aggressive thoughts. Such hostile social cognitions guide children's behavior and become increasingly resistant to change (Slaby & Roedell, 1982). Children with hostile and aggressive social–cognitive orientations may actively elicit interactions from their social environment that become increasingly coercive, both at home and at school (Patterson, DeBaryshe, & Ramsey, 1989). This focus on children's learned cognitive content regarding aggression has also been applied to both aggressive children and those victimized by aggression (Perry, Kusel, & Perry, 1988).

The *attribution* paradigm (Ferguson & Rule, 1983) has focused on the ways in which an individual's own perceptions and judgments regarding the harmdoer's causal responsibility (e.g., accidental, foreseeable, nonmalevolently intentional, malevolently intentional) and moral culpability (blame) may mediate the individual's anger and aggressive behavior. Varying the information about the mitigating circumstances of another's aggression has been found to affect the instigation but not the inhibition of retaliatory aggression (Rule, Dyck, & Nesdale, 1978).

The *development of interpersonal understanding* paradigm (Selman, 1980; Selman et al., 1992) provides a developmental framework to account for the ways in which knowledge, personal meaning, and social management skills in any given area of risk can influence risk-taking behaviors, including those behaviors that lead to friendship or fighting. These psychosocial factors are shown to evolve through developmental levels from an egocentric and undifferentiated perspective to a highly differentiated and well-integrated coordination of social perspectives, similar to that previously proposed by Piaget (1970) and by Werner (1948). For example, the personal meaning that an individual applies to aggressive behavior has been described as evolving through several developmental levels of interpersonal understanding: dismissive, impersonal rule-based, personal rule-based, personal need-based (isolated), personal need-based (integrated), and insightful. A variety of intervention techniques have been explored in an attempt to reduce aggressive behavior while strengthening effective negotiation behaviors by stimulating change in children's developmental level of social cognition and behavior. These techniques include teaching skills in problem solving, decision making, and interpersonal negotiation, as well as counseling pairs of children in their responses to both hypothetical and real-life situations.

Developmental Theories of Violence and Aggression: Continuity and Change

Several attempts have been made to account for the processes of learning and development related to long-term continuity and change in aggressive and violent behavior. These formulations provide a broader developmental view of when, where, and how intervention might be applied most effectively to reduce or prevent violence.

Social-interactional model. The social-interactional model (Patterson, 1982; Patterson et al., 1989; Patterson, Reid, & Dishion, 1992; Reid & Patterson, 1989) has focused on the primary contexts of social learning during successive phases of development. Patterson and his colleagues acknowledge the relation of factors such as parent criminality, socioeconomic disadvantage, child temperament, and marital conflict to the development of antisocial child behavior, but argue that their influence is mediated by the degree to which they compromise day-to-day parenting practices.

In the first phase of the social interactional model, maladaptive parent–child interaction patterns and ineffective parent practices are viewed as key determinants of young children's coercive and antisocial behavior patterns, including aggressive behavior. These behavior patterns transfer in the second phase to other contexts, such as the school, where children's aggressive patterns may interfere with learning and academic achievement and the development of positive relationships with peers. In the third phase of development, during late childhood or early adolescence, academic failure and peer rejection lead aggressive children to show increased risk for depressed mood and involvement in a deviant peer group. In short, this model suggests that as the child develops, the primary focus for effective intervention may shift from parents, to schools, and to peer groups.

Developmental–organizational. A developmental–organizational framework (Greenberg & Speltz, 1988) focusing on attachment has been proposed to integrate social learning and developmental theories. Attachment processes have been implicated as one of several risk factors in the development of externalizing behaviors such as violence (e.g., Easterbrooks, Davidson, & Chazan, 1993). Three complementary attachment processes have been hypothesized to lead to behavior problems (Greenberg, Speltz, & DeKlyen, 1993). First, young children may develop disruptive behavior at home in an attempt to regulate the proximity and attention of caregivers who have been unresponsive or unpredictable. Second, insecurely attached children may develop working models of relationships characterized by anger, mistrust, chaos, and insecurity. Finally, attachment may promote the motivation to respond positively or with resistance to social interactions. Resistant children are, in turn, more difficult to socialize. This resistance in combination with impoverished caregiving under stressful environmental conditions may severely jeopardize the quality of care. Accordingly, home-based interventions during infancy that are designed to increase the caregiver's capacity to provide optimal care and to strengthen the formation of early attachment between infant and caregiver are regarded as potentially important in preventing later cycles of disruptive behavior and maladaptive responses that may stimulate and maintain aggression.

Developmental pathways. The developmental sequences in disruptive-antisocial behaviors shown by boys from childhood to adolescence have been described as involving different pathways (Loeber et al., 1993). Boys on the Overt Pathway to Violence typically follow a developmental sequence of escalating behaviors from aggression (annoying or bullying others at ages 8–13 years) to fighting (fighting with individuals or gangs at ages 12–14 years), and eventually to violence (e.g., attacking, strongarming, or forcing sex on someone at ages 12–14 years). Although boys rarely enter this pathway toward violence from other disruptive behavior pathways, they often broaden the range of their disruptive behaviors into other pathways, such as the Early Authority Conflict Pathway (a sequence of stubborn behavior, defiance, and authority avoidance) or the Covert Pathway (a sequence of minor covert behavior, property damage, moderate forms of delinquency, and serious forms of delinquency). This analysis supports the hypothesis that intervention designed to reduce or prevent early forms of aggression may be beneficial in preventing an escalation into later forms of fighting and violence, as well as a broadening into multiple forms of disruptive antisocial behavior.

In summary, psychological theories of aggression have generated a wealth of theoretical, conceptual, and empirical knowledge that helps to clarify the processes by which connections are developed and maintained between various social, biological, cognitive, and social experiences and aggressive or violent behaviors. When the empirical body of knowledge about individual and contextual factors influencing youth violence is examined with an eye for strategies that can help to solve the problems of aggression and violence, however, one can see that much more needs to be done to apply and extend what is known.

Individual and Contextual Factors in the Development of Aggressive and Violent Behavior

Both nature and nurture have been implicated in the development of aggressive and violent behavior. Biological factors, such as temperament and the tendency toward impulsivity, are presumed to influence children's interactions with their environments and others' reactions to them during childhood and adolescence. Individual characteristics that develop as a result of the interaction between the biological factors and the environment, such as intelligence and social–cognitive factors, also determine children's susceptibility to developing aggressive behavior patterns. These latter factors include emotional responsivity, social–cognitive styles, social skills, scripts, and beliefs. They shape children's interpretations of and responses to their environments and are, therefore, critical to an understanding of which children are likely to succumb to negative social influences.

With regard to these factors, longitudinal studies have demonstrated considerable individual continuity in patterns of aggression from childhood to adulthood (e.g., Farrington, 1992; Huesmann, Eron, Lefkowitz, & Walder, 1984). In a review of longitudinal research, Olweus (1979) concluded that measures of aggressive behavior over periods of 5 to 10 years had average correlations from .60 to .69. Based on his longitudinal research, Farrington (1991) postulated a general continuity in antisocial and deviant behavior that persists from childhood to adulthood. The continuity of aggressive behavior is likely a function of continuity in both the child's constitution and environmental factors (Eron & Huesmann, 1990). Individual differences in children's temperaments or behavior styles may differentially predispose them to adopting consistently aggressive patterns of behavior (Slaby & Roedell, 1982). Although long-term studies indicate continuity in the underlying individual characteristics, the manifestation of the antisocial tendencies may vary with age, changing from temper tantrums and aggressive outbursts, and cruelty to animals (Ascione, 1993) in early childhood to delinquency and violent crime in adolescence and adulthood. Recent research indicates that the best predictor of chronic delinquent offending and violence in adolescence is antisocial behavior in childhood (Capaldi & Patterson, 1993). In the effort to prevent violence, resources should be directed toward reducing early signs of antisocial behavior.

It is difficult to determine the extent to which the association between individual factors and aggressive behavior patterns are genetically or environmentally based. On one hand, children's biological characteristics may shape their environments (Lytton, 1990). On the other hand, the associations between individual factors and aggression may be a function of acquired biological deficits, such as prenatal and perinatal complications (Brennan, Mednick, & Kandel, 1991), exposure to neurotoxins, or deficits in children's social environments (Loeber, 1990).

Selected Individual Factors

Temperament. An early risk factor for developing a predisposition for aggressive and violent behavior may be a fearless, uninhibited temperament. The National Research Council (NRC; 1993) report cites physiological data to support the hypothesized association between temperament and aggression. A fearless, uninhibited temperament is associated with low heart rates; low heart rates have been found in children and adolescents with aggressive conduct disorder (Raine & Jones, 1987). This biological trait shows developmental continuity: There is also evidence of lower heart rates among criminals at later stages of development (Farrington, 1987b). The association between a fearless, uninhibited temperament and later conduct problems and violent behavior most likely derives from an interaction between children and their environments. For example, it may be that young children with this temperamental style are difficult to socialize as they do not respond as readily to parenting techniques such as reinforcement and punishment. In middle childhood, these children may be thrill-seekers and drawn to peer interactions that provide excitement, daring, and adventure. Given additional risk factors, such as poor parental monitoring, low socioeconomic status, and a delinquent peer group within the community, a fearless, uninhibited temperament may predispose a child to a developmental trajectory of aggression and violence.

Another risk factor for developing an aggressive behavioral style is a difficult temperament, which may overlap somewhat with the fearless, uninhibited temperament, described above. A difficult temperament in early childhood has been associated with aggressiveness and delinquency in later childhood and adolescence (Bates, Bayles, Bennett, Ridge & Brown, 1991; Farrington, 1987a; Olweus, 1980). This association may also be a product of the nature–nurture interaction. For example, Olweus (1980) reported that mothers of boys with a difficult temperament became increasingly more permissive with their children's aggressive behaviors which, in turn, continued to flourish. In a life-course analysis of ill-tempered children, Caspi, Elder, and Bem (1987) found that children with a pattern of temper tantrums in late childhood became ill-tempered adults. They proposed that early personality styles are sustained through the progressive accumulation of their own consequences (cumulative continuity) and by eliciting maintaining responses from others during social interaction (interactional continuity).

Attention deficit disorder with hyperactivity. An interactional framework has also been used to describe the association between attention deficit disorder with hyperactivity (ADD-H) and antisocial behavior patterns. Loeber (1990) suggested that hyperactivity and its associated behaviors, such as impulsivity and attentional difficulties, act as catalysts for the continuity in behavior problems. A high proportion of children with a diagnosis of ADD-H have been found to report delinquent behaviors in early adolescence (Moffitt & Silva, 1988; Moffitt, 1993). A combination of ADD-H and conduct problems in the early years places children at a very high risk of later delinquency (e.g., Farrington, Loeber, & Van Kammen, 1990). Furthermore, the childhood profiles of violent offenders have been shown to comprise hyperactivity, impulsivity, and attention problems (Farrington, 1991). Recent research suggests that cognitive deficits may be a significant mechanism underlying the association between ADD-H and subsequent delinquency and violent crime. Among children with ADD-H, Moffitt and Silva (1988) found that the children most likely to develop delinquent behavior patterns were those who exhibited cognitive impairment on measures of verbal and visual integration and performed poorly on a measure of verbal memory. The cognitive handicaps experienced by some children, and ADD-H children in particular, may inhibit not only their academic functioning, but also the learning of prosocial skills and moral concepts (Loeber, 1990). In a recent review paper on the neuropsychology of conduct disorder, Moffitt (1993) highlights the need for more research to explain the links between such neuropsychological deficits and conduct problems.

Intelligence. In longitudinal studies, IQ has been identified as a predictor and correlate of childhood aggression and adult violence (e.g., Farrington, 1991; Huesmann et al., 1984). There is some question, however, about the independent contribution of IQ to the prediction of aggression. For example, Huesmann and Eron (1984) found that IQ was no longer a significant predictor of aggression at age 30 once the effects of aggression at age 8 had been extracted. They postulated that low IQ may contribute to the early development of aggressive behavior patterns, but once these are established, low IQ plays a minimal role in the further trajectory toward adult antisocial behavior. This is consistent with current findings about the relation between early disruptive behavior, poor school achievement, and delinquent behavior. Therefore, although it is often suggested that aggressive behavior is a result of academic failure, a stronger case may be made that aggressive behavior contributes to failure at school which, in turn, contributes to delinquent tendencies in later childhood and adolescence (Patterson et al., 1989; Huesmann, Eron, & Yarmel, 1987). The role of early disruptive behavior in school in contributing to later delinquency was confirmed in a recent analysis by Tremblay et al. (1992). The most predictive model for delinquent boys was a direct causal link between disruptive behavior in grade 1 and subsequent delinquent behavior; poor school achievement was not a necessary causal factor.

Contextual Factors in the Development of Aggressive and Violent Behavior

Whatever the balance between the contributions of nature and nurture, it is likely that an interactional model will most accurately describe the development and continuity in aggressive and violent behavior patterns. The developmental perspective suggests that individual factors interact with a complex mix of familial, school, peer, and other ecological factors to produce aggressive and violent behavior patterns in childhood that extend into adolescence and adulthood.

Among the models of long-term change and development discussed earlier, we selected the social interactional model developed by Patterson and his colleagues to elucidate these interactions. The social interaction model, in our opinion, currently provides the most comprehensive and flexible developmental framework with which to consider the changing influences of the family, school, peer group, and broader community (Patterson et al., 1989, 1992).

Family context. Parental and family influences can be classified into four domains: family demographics (e.g., socioeconomic status), parental characteristics (e.g., antisocial personality), parenting techniques (e.g., lack of monitoring, inconsistent discipline) and parent–child relationships (e.g., parental rejection) (Loeber & Stouthamer-Loeber, 1986). These influences have been studied singly and in combination.

For example, Patterson and his colleagues have described how certain parenting practices provide the breeding grounds for aggressive behavior problems in youth (Patterson, 1982, 1986; Patterson et al., 1989, 1992). Their research indicates that families of aggressive children support the use of aversive and aggressive behaviors in their children by inadvertently reinforcing such behaviors and by failing to adequately reinforce prosocial ones (Patterson, 1982). Through these practices, parents of aggressive children appear to fail to teach compliance and appropriate social problem solving, which in turn leads to coercive family interactions and the development of aggressive behavior patterns in the children. Indeed, the reciprocally aversive exchanges between parents and aggressive children suggest that these children may be both the architects and the victims of aggressive interactions (Cairns, Cairns, Neckerman, Gest, & Gariepy, 1988; Patterson, 1982).

Other researchers have also implicated parenting practices in the development of aggression. In a meta-analysis of family influences, Loeber and Stouthamer-Loeber (1986) concluded that lack of parental supervision was one of the strongest predictors of the development of conduct disorder and delinquency in youth, problems that frequently involve violence. A number of studies have also cited a lack of parent–child involvement and parental rejection of the child as predictors of later aggressive behavior problems and delinquency (e.g., Eron, Walder, & Lefkowitz, 1971; Farrington, 1991; Loeber & Stouthamer-Loeber, 1986; Olweus, 1980).

The parenting practice of harsh physical punishment has been specifically implicated in the development of aggressive behavior patterns in youth (e.g., Eron, Walder, Toigo, & Lefkowitz, 1963; Farrington, 1991; Straus, 1991).

Dodge, Bates, and Pettit (1990) found that physical harm in early childhood was associated with children's aggression toward peers, above and beyond any co-occurring family ecological factor or child health problem or temperament. Dodge and his colleagues found that harshly punished children were likely to develop biased and deficient patterns of processing social information, patterns that were found to predict the development of aggressive behavior. These include a failure to attend to relevant cues, a bias to attribute hostile intentions to others, and a lack of competent behavioral strategies. They concluded that abuse at the hands of parents leads children to think and solve problems in deviant ways that later lead to the development of aggressive behavior patterns and a continuation of the cycle of violence (Dodge et al., 1990). In a recent review paper, Straus (1991) argued that although physical punishment may produce conformity in children in the short term, over time it tends to increase the probability of delinquency and eventual adult violent crime inside and outside the family. Longitudinal studies of aggressive behavior problems have shown consistency of aggression over three generations and consistency of punishment patterns over two generations (Huesmann et al., 1984).

On the other hand, although there is a widespread belief in the intergenerational transmission of violence, Widom (1989, 1990) concluded that there is limited empirical evidence that abuse leads to abuse. Widom notes that extant studies are plagued with methodological problems. Moreover, although the data indicate that parents are more likely to abuse their children if they, themselves, were abused as children, fewer than 20% of adults abused as children perpetuate the abuse with their own children (Widom, 1990). Also, it is difficult to specify when parents cross the line of community standards from caring discipline to child abuse (Slaby & Roedell, 1982). Given that survey statistics in the United States indicate that over 90% of the parents of 3- and 4-year-old children use physical punishment as a discipline strategy (Straus, 1991), this is clearly an area for future research.

The interacting effects of the four domains of family influence may be particularly hard to disentangle. According to Patterson (1982), the effects of family demographic variables on the development of children's aggressive behavior may be mediated by parenting practices, which may, in turn, break down under stressful family circumstances. Patterson and Dishion (1988) tested the relations among stress, parental characteristics, and parenting practices using a stress amplification model. Briefly, stress within the family exacerbated parents' antisocial tendencies, which in turn related to irritable discipline practices and children's aggressive behavior patterns. This illustrates how parental characteristics and stressful family influences may operate together to place a child at risk for developing conduct problems (Loeber, 1990). Other research, however, indicates that antisocial personality disorder in parents may be associated with conduct disorder in children, independent of parenting practices (Frick et al., 1992).

In summary, several factors are involved in the development of aggression within the family context including family demographics, parental characteristics, poor parent–child relationships, and parenting practices, particularly harsh physical punishment. The breakdown of family processes in each of the four domains separately and together appears to lay the foundation for the development of aggressive and violent behaviors in youth. Once established at home, these aggressive behavior patterns readily transfer to the school and peer contexts. The process is not inevitable, however. Many of the family influences seem to be controllable and, once identified, have implications for intervention and prevention efforts.

School context. The school context, in general, may create a milieu that is conducive to aggression. The National Research Council Report on Violence (1993) cited four characteristics of school milieus that may contribute to violence: (a) a relatively high number of students occupy a limited amount of space; (b) the capacity to avoid confrontations is somewhat reduced; (c) the imposition of behavioral routines and conformity contribute to feelings of anger, resentment, and rejection; and (d) poor building design features facilitate the commission of violent acts.

Empirical studies of the relation between aggression and violence and the size of the class or school have shown mixed results. For example, in England, the incidence of bullying, one form of aggression, was found to be related not only to the level of economic disadvantage in the neighborhood but also to the size of the class and school (Stephenson & Smith, 1989). In Norway, however, the number of students per class and per school were not found to be relevant variables in the reported incidence of bullying (Olweus, 1991). In addition, there were no significant differences between urban and rural areas in the frequency of bullying.

With regard to the imposition of behavioral routines, the incidence of aggression has been related to the heavy and inflexible use of school rules in the classroom (Pratt, 1973). The relationships among teachers, teacher hostility, and lack of rapport between staff members were also found to affect the school environment adversely with regard to aggression (Pratt, 1973). Inconsistent responses to disruptive classroom behavior also create an environment conducive to aggression. Frude and Gault (1984) found that a lack of consensus regarding classroom management can lead to major inconsistencies in the limits of toleration of students' behavior. When incidents of disruption occur (e.g., student refusal to cooperate, lying, stealing, and temper tantrums), an increase in the amount of bullying has been reported (Laslett, 1977).

The school milieu appears to be affected by individual characteristics of students, peer context, and family context factors. For example, observations of aggressive children in class indicate that they spend significantly more time out of their seats and disrupting others than nonaggressive children (e.g., Cobb & Hops, 1973). They interact more frequently with teachers and also tend to spend more time in task-inappropriate solitary activity, such as clowning, daydreaming, and wandering around the room (Dodge, Coie, & Brakke, 1982). Their behavior appears to affect both academic achievement and peer relations. Indeed, given the disruptive nature of their classroom behavior, it is not surprising that aggressive children experience academic difficulties. Their off-task behavior is likely to interfere with attending to lessons and completing assignments. Having fallen behind in earlier grades, they may also not engage in learning tasks because they lack the academic skills to approach the assigned work (Dodge et al., 1982).

The disruptive behavior of aggressive children is also likely to be bothersome to both teachers and peers, setting up negative social perceptions and interactions at school. The exacerbation of learning and peer problems, in turn, may portend further academic failure and continued deviance. This developmental path has been identified in longitudinal research showing that preadolescent aggression toward peers predicted school suspensions, early school withdrawal, and police and court contacts (Kupersmidt & Coie, 1990).

Children's experiences at home also impinge on the school context. Patterson and his colleagues have shown how antisocial behavior patterns learned at home interfere with learning in the school context and with positive relationships with peers (Patterson, 1982; Patterson et al., 1989, 1992). This developmental sequence was tested by Dishion (1990), who found that poor parenting practices were associated with aggressive behavior, which was, in turn, a disruptor of academic achievement. Furthermore, parenting practices were indirectly related to boys' peer relations in the school setting. Boys' aggressive behavior and academic achievement were found to mediate the association between parenting practices and peer relations (Dishion, 1990).

Several other studies, not discussed here, have also noted significant school effects in the incidence of aggressive behavior (e.g., Craig & Pepler, 1992; Kellam & Rebok, 1992). Considerably more research is required to identify the school characteristics and the interpersonal processes within the school that contribute to or reduce aggression. In the meantime, school interventions may profitably be patterned on models of family interventions. For example, focusing on coercive processes within the family, Patterson (1982) has developed parent training interventions that appear most promising for reducing dysfunctional interactions and aggressive behavior problems in the home (Kazdin, 1987; see also chapter 15 of this book). Such interventions could be tailored to and tested in the schools. In addition, Deutsch (1993), has outlined four key components of an educational program to encourage the values, attitudes, knowledge, and behavior that foster constructive rather than destructive relations in schools. These components include cooperative learning, conflict resolution training, the constructive use of controversy in teaching particular subjects, and the creation of dispute resolution centers in schools.

Peer context. A child who enters school with a well-developed repertoire of aggressive behaviors and few social skills will encounter problems with peer interactions. Observations of aggressive children in peer interaction reflect the aversive behavior patterns established at home. Aggressive children exhibit significantly more inappropriate play, insults, threats, hitting and exclusion of peers than average children (Dodge, 1983). They are less likely to engage in social conversation or to continue in group activities than other children (Coie & Kupersmidt, 1983; Dodge, 1983). The consequence of these negative peer interactions is peer rejection.

Aggression is highly correlated with rejection by peers (Coie, Dodge & Kupersmidt, 1990). In the early school years, overt aggression toward peers is associated with rejection; with age, indirect aggression becomes more closely linked to rejection by peers (Coie et al., 1990). Rejection by peers is also associated with victimization (Perry, Kusel, & Perry, 1988). In fact many of the behaviors that are considered rejecting, such as exclusion from the peer group, are described as indirect forms of bullying and victimization (Olweus, 1991).

The importance of peer relations in subsequent adjustment was highlighted in a review by Parker and Asher (1987). They postulated a causal model suggesting that deviant behavior, such as aggression, leads to low acceptance by peers, which in turn leads to further development of deviant behaviors and association with deviant peers. Therefore, for aggressive children, rejection by peers is presumed to set the course toward maladjustment in adulthood. At this point, however, there is some lack of clarity with respect to the role of peer relations and rejection in maladjustment. Kupersmidt, Coie, & Dodge (1990) suggest several hypotheses regarding this dynamic. First, peer rejection may be a marker variable, a manifestation of a more basic risk factor that accounts for maladjustment in adulthood. Second, peer rejection may be a source of stress and isolation for a child, which inhibits adaptive development. Finally, rejection by peers may be a direct cause of maladjustment by either restricting positive contacts or encouraging negative ones.

The end of this sequence ushers in the third stage in the social-interactional model proposed by Patterson and his colleagues (Patterson et al., 1989, 1992). After factors in the family and school contexts have influenced young children and, in turn, have been influenced by them, aggressive children are at increased risk for depressed mood and involvement in a deviant peer group during later childhood and early adolescence.

Although aggressive children may be disliked by some classmates, they appear to establish relationships with peers like themselves in "coercive cliques" (Cairns et al., 1988). There is a trend for rejected aggressive children to associate less and less with popular and skilled members of the social group and more with other rejected children (Cairns & Cairns, 1991; Snyder, Dishion, & Patterson, 1986). Aggressive children seek out and associate with children who will accept them and who are like themselves, in terms of behavior, values, and goals (Hymel, Wagner, Butler, 1990). As such, they become members of the "outgroup" rather than the "ingroup" and their socialization experiences are further imbalanced in the direction of negative behaviors. Within these newly formed social groups, aggressive children have little opportunity for positive peer interactions that are presumed to play an important role in the development of cognitive and social skills. This limited opportunity for positive peer interaction places rejected children at risk for continuing to learn and use aggressive behaviors (Parker & Asher, 1987).

The deviant peer group is presumed to provide a training ground for delinquent behaviors and drug and alcohol use (Patterson et al., 1989, 1992). Many studies support the link between involvement with antisocial peers and delinquency. In longitudinal analyses comparing violent and nonviolent adults to others, Farrington (1991) reported that adolescent involvement in group violence and vandalism was associated with the maintenance of antisocial behaviors into adulthood.

Again, the conditions that set the stage for the detrimental processes within the peer group are likely established within the family context early in a child's life and reinforced within the school context. In the Dishion (1990) study cited earlier, poor parenting discipline practices were found to be associated with peer rejection through two mediating variables: antisocial behavior and academic failure. Dishion found that boys who were rejected by their peers had been exposed to more coercive and hostile family experiences compared with average children. On the other hand, parents can support the prosocial development of their children by coaching on how to initiate and maintain friendships, modeling of positive peer relations, arranging contact with peers, and selecting neighborhoods (Dishion, 1990). In support of the relationship between parenting practices and peer relations, one study, for example, showed that during adolescence, parent supervision and involvement relate to prosocial friendships (Snyder, Dishion, & Patterson, 1986).

This link between children's experiences within the family and at school points to the important relations among systems within the child's life. Patterns of social interaction are multiply determined and, therefore, assessments of effects should encompass the full range of factors including individual factors, interindividual interactions, social networks, internetwork relations, and cultural, ecological, and economic conditions (Cairns & Cairns, 1991). Although this makes the task of understanding the development of aggressive behavior patterns appear impossibly complex, Cairns and Cairns suggest that "an explicit recognition of the complexity of the task and the simultaneous operation of different levels of influence must precede a thoughtful appraisal of simplifying assumptions" (1991, p. 250). One such model has been proposed by Dishion, Patterson, & Griesler (1994). To date, some mechanisms that propel children on an aggressive and violent trajectory have been identified; however, there is still much research to be done in order to elucidate the multiple processes and pathways that lead to violent behavior.

Gender Differences in the Development of Aggressive and Violent Behavior

In a developmental analysis of aggression and violence, it is essential to consider the role of gender in determining children's manifestations of and responses to violence. Two decades ago, Maccoby and Jacklin (1974) concluded that gender differences in aggression were well-substantiated. Since then, the strength of gender differences and their biological bases have been called into question (e.g., Hyde, 1984; Tieger, 1980). Research on gender differences in the development of aggression has been limited by the assumption that aggression is primarily a male domain. The majority of studies of children's aggression have been conducted exclusively with boys; therefore, there is scant data on the development and long-term consequences of girls' aggression. There is a growing recognition that biology is not the primary determinant of gender differences in aggression (Adams, 1992). The extent to which biological factors contribute to sex differences in aggressive behaviors has been a point of controversy leading, in some cases, to different interpretations of similar data sets (Maccoby & Jacklin, 1980; Tieger, 1980). Although biological differences may account for some of the gender disparities in aggression, many psychosocial factors influence the nature of aggression that is exhibited by males and females. Therefore, to understand gender differences in aggression, the type of aggression; contextual variables in the family, school, peer group, and larger societal context; and differences and similarities between genders in terms of developmental outcomes of aggression must also be considered. For a more comprehensive consideration of gender differences in aggression, see Bjorkqvist and Niemela (1992) and Campbell (1993).

Biological Contributions to Gender Differences in Aggression

Several biological factors have been identified as potential causal mechanisms in gender differences in aggression, particularly in accounting for the robust differences in physical violence perpetrated by men and women (Harries, 1990). In an examination of the role of hormones in human aggression, Benton (1992) concluded that testosterone has an organizing effect on brain structures and a role in the expression of human aggression. According to Benton, however, the role of testosterone is small and relatively unimportant compared to psychosocial factors that are experienced during development. Neurophysiological explanations have also been advanced to account for the expression of aggression (e.g., Potegal, 1992). Although substantial evidence for the role of biological factors in differences in male and female aggression has been accumulated from animal research, the task of understanding the unique contribution of biology to gender differences in human aggression is more complex. Hood and her colleagues caution that in research on human gender differences, biological sex is completely confounded with social and psychological factors, hence it is premature to speculate about biological causes of gender differences until the interactions among biological, social, and psychological factors are understood (Hood, Draper, Crockett, & Petersen, 1987).

Type of Aggression

Gender differences are more pronounced in physical aggression than in other types of aggression (Eagly & Steffen, 1986; Hyde, 1984). This difference in physical aggression is apparent in early childhood (Fagot, Hagan, Leinbach, & Kronsberg, 1985) through to adulthood, when homicides and other serious violent crimes are much more likely to be committed by men than by women (Harries, 1990). Observations of physical aggression on the school playground indicate that boys attack at twice the rate of girls (Serbin, Marchessault, McAffer, Peters, & Schwartzman, 1993). In this study, much of boys' physical aggression on the playground was mild and expressed within the context of rough-and-tumble play. When other forms of aggression are examined, such as indirect or verbal aggression, gender differences are less pronounced (Bjorkqvist, Osterman, & Kaukiainen, 1992). Indirect aggression, which is delivered circuitously and not face-to-face, is reported to be more typical of girls than boys (Cairns, Cairns, Neckerman, Ferguson & Gariepy, 1989; Lagerspetz, Bjorkqvist, & Peltonen, 1988). This type of aggression is characterized by alienation, ostracism, and character defamation (Cairns et al., 1989).

Although the type of aggression expressed by males and females may stem in part from biological differences (e.g., after puberty males are on average physically stronger and larger than females), it may also relate to differences in social contexts. For example, boys' peer interactions are characterized by higher levels of physical activity and more rough-and-tumble play than those of girls. Physical aggression between boys often develops out of rough-and-tumble episodes (Smith & Boulton, 1990). Indirect aggression may be more effective within girls' peer contexts of small intimate groups, than in boys' more extensive and less well-defined peer groups (Lagerspetz et al., 1988). Although it is important to recognize situational influences on aggression, we must be cautious in generalizing about gender differences because the variability within gender is often greater than that between genders (Favreau, 1993; Hyde, 1984), and as little as 5% of the variance in aggression is explained by gender differences (Pulkkinen, 1992).

As both boys and girls move from predominantly physical forms of aggression to more sophisticated strategies, gender differences may be less pronounced. Bjorkqvist et al. (1992) proposed a developmental progression in aggressive strategies from physical to verbal to indirect, which unfolds as a function of cognitive, verbal, and social maturation. The apparent decreases in gender differences with age (Hyde, 1984) may reflect a convergence in styles of male and female aggression. With development, the context for the expression of aggression may differ for males and females, with males continuing to offend within the community and females moving their aggression to intimate relationships behind closed doors. Attitudes may also effect gender differences in aggression. Physical aggression in females is viewed much more negatively by peers in childhood compared with that of males (Serbin et al., 1993). In adulthood, men's aggression may be viewed as a means of assuming power and control, whereas women's aggression may be viewed less positively, as a failure of self-control (Campbell, 1993).

Gender-Related Socialization Within the Family

To clarify gender similarities and differences in the nature of aggressive behavior, a number of contextual factors, including specific socialization experiences within the family, must be considered. From an early age, these are likely to differ for boys and girls. Consider the link discussed earlier between parenting practices, such as harsh physical punishment, and the development of aggression and violence in youth. Eron (1992) postulated that boys would be more aggressive than girls because parents use more harsh punishment in response to boys' than to girls' aggression. In a recent review, however, Lytton and Romney (1991) concluded that gender differences in aggression were not likely to be caused by differential parenting practices. Their meta-analysis indicated that parents discourage aggressive or antisocial behavior only slightly and nonsignificantly more in girls than in boys.

Recent research suggests differential familial processes in boys' and girls' antisocial trajectories. Kavanagh (1993) found that different family interaction behaviors and management practices were predictive of girls' compared with boys' reported antisocial behaviors. In particular, girls who were not positively engaged in family interactions and had fathers who were negatively engaged were most likely to be rated as antisocial. Family perceptions of boys' and girls' aggression also differ. Adolescent girls who were aggressive and uncooperative were judged as problematic by their parents and by themselves (Kavanagh & Hops, 1994). In contrast, adolescent males who were aggressive were not seen as such by themselves or by their parents. A similar bias to rate girls' aggression as more deviant was found in a study with younger children by Condry and Ross (1985).

Interactional patterns in families also appear to differ with regard to gender. In observations of family problem solving interactions, Kavanagh and Hops (in press) found girls to be more aggressive with their parents than boys, even though parents' ratings of boys' and girls' aggressive behavior problems did not differ. Mothers interacting with daughters displayed less facilitative and problem solving behavior and tended to be more aggressive than mothers interacting with sons.

Although these gender differences and the development of aggression and violence in the context of the family require considerably more research attention, two additional points bear special consideration. Given girls' greater propensity to play at home (Maccoby, 1986), their development may be more contingent on family circumstances than that of boys. Also, the intimacy of relations within the family may present opportunities for girls to express their aggression that are not present in the larger social contexts of school and community (Pepler & Moore, 1993). Compared with girls, boys' aggressive behaviors may be more visible and more troublesome within the broader contexts of school and community (Maccoby, 1986).

Gender-Related Socialization Among Peers

Acceptance of aggression within the peer group may play a major role in the development and expression of aggression by boys and girls. Boys' aggression appears to be more accepted by peers than girls' aggression. In one survey, Huesmann, Guerra, Zelli, and Miller (1992) found that boys were more likely to approve aggression than girls. Serbin et al. (1993) found that boys rated as aggressive by peers were aggressive on the playground, but contrary to expectations were highly involved with peers. Girls identified by peers as aggressive were disliked by their classmates and did not carry out their aggression within a social context of peers. They concluded that boys' peer groups likely perceive aggression as normative and an extension of rough-and-tumble play. Girls' peer groups, on the other hand, likely perceive girls' aggression as atypical and indicative of a wide range of internalizing and externalizing problems.

Interestingly, girls perceived as aggressive spent more time in mixed-sex groups than in same-sex groups (Serbin et al., 1993). The aggressive girls may have sought out male peers because they were ostracized by the other girls. Conversely, girls in mixed-sex groups may exhibit more aggression than girls in same-sex groups as a function of the social context. Both boys and girls are more likely to have physical conflicts with boys than with girls (Cairns et al., 1989; Serbin et al., 1993). This highlights the difficulty of distinguishing actual gender differences in aggression and its expression from the contexts in which they are measured.

Societal Context

The traditional roles of men and women in society have often been assumed to be based on biological determinants: Men have been seen as combatants responsible for protecting and providing for their families, whereas women have been seen as caregivers responsible for the well-being of the children and the home. The stereotypic man is "strong, stoic (sometimes to the point of being unfeeling), competitive, aggressive, independent, active, agentic, and exploitive" (Zahn-Waxler, 1993, p. 83). The stereotypic woman is "delicate, emotional, dependent, passive, nurturing, relationship oriented, valuing connection and commitment, and seeking self-validation from others" (Zahn-Waxler, 1993, p. 83). Although feminism has challenged these traditional roles, they are still pervasive in the television and films viewed by the youth of society. Through identification with and imitation of same-sex models in the media and in real life, and through differential family, peer, and educational socialization experiences, boys' and girls' developmental pathways are likely to differ according to sex-role expectations. These sex-specific socialization experiences may contribute to gender differences in aggression.

Researchers have noted a decline in the magnitude of gender differences with regard to aggression over the past decade (e.g., Hyde, 1984; Viemero, 1992). Several factors may underlie this change. It may be due to changing societal norms and roles for the genders, particularly for females. Aggression may be more acceptable and normative for girls and women than it used to be (Eron, 1992). Socialization practices with respect to girls' aggression may have changed, given the increasing pressure on girls toward competitiveness, achievement, and social success (Hyde, 1984; Viemero, 1992). There may have been an accompanying change in normative standards, so that adults and peers are less likely to identify girls' aggression as atypical. Cairns and Cairns (1984) noted that in late childhood social norms for boys and girls reflect the role and physical differences that will emerge in adolescence and early adulthood. As traditional roles for females are ignored or rejected, gender equivalences in aggressive behavior may emerge. The changing patterns of gender differences over the past two decades may also be related to methodological changes in the studies of aggression (Rabbie, Goldenbeld, & Lodewijkx, 1992).

Developmental Outcomes

The models describing the development and consequences of aggressive behavior are generally based on boys' developmental trajectories, given the limited longitudinal data on girls with regard to aggression. The longitudinal studies described below are somewhat contradictory with respect to developmental trajectories. Some evidence indicates that aggressive girls and boys follow similar developmental courses and other evidence suggests that they do not follow identical courses. The differing trajectories of males and females may be related to different socialization experiences or different social orientations.

Developmental outcomes of aggression show both similarities and differences between boys and girls. In their longitudinal study, Huesmann et al. (1984) found that early aggressiveness of both boys and girls predicted later aggressive personality scores, harsh punishment of children, and criminal acts. Robins (1986) reported that although girls had significantly fewer conduct problems than boys, the rank orders of the frequency of conduct problems for boys and girls were similar. The outcomes for boys and girls with conduct disorder differed, however, in adulthood. In her follow-up of children referred to clinics for antisocial behavior problems, Robins (1966, 1986) noted that girls were somewhat less likely than boys to be diagnosed with antisocial personality disorders as adults. On the other hand, both boys and girls referred for conduct problems were at increased risk for drug and alcohol abuse in adolescence and adulthood. Girls were more likely than boys to experience internalizing disorders such as anxiety and depression in adulthood.

Given the differences in boys' and girls' developmental trajectories, it seems logical to search for the long-term sequelae of aggressive behavior problems in somewhat different domains for males and females. Whereas a proportion of aggressive boys may develop into adults who engage in violent crimes within the community, this is less likely for girls (Magnusson, 1988). Girls, on the other hand, may express their aggressive tendencies within the confines of the family and close relationships. A review of violent offenders indicated that most of the violent women were convicted of attacks on their own families or neighbors (McClintock, 1963).

In examining the long-term consequences of girls' aggression, researchers should expand their list of outcome variables to include the risk of serious aggression within close relationships. In a follow-up study of female delinquents, Lewis and her colleagues found that these women were less likely than a matched sample of men to be arrested for violent offenses (Lewis et al., 1991). Other aspects of these women's lives, however, reveal significant dysfunction and violence. More than half of the women had been involved in "extraordinarily violent relationships with men" (Lewis et al., 1991, p. 200). Over two thirds of the women had children, and their child-rearing was described with a litany of problems, leading Lewis et al. to conclude that they had "negligible abilities to provide even minimal support for the next generation" (1991, p. 201). In short, the relationships of these women reflected the violence of their youth.

There is much to be learned about the potentially different mechanisms and outcomes in the developmental trajectories of aggressive boys and girls. To date the research has been dominated by investigations of the outcomes for males, whose aggression is usually physical and direct as compared with the indirect, verbal, and interpersonal nature of female aggression. At present, there is some evidence to suggest somewhat different factors in the development of aggression in boys and girls. As knowledge of these increases, we will be able to articulate different components for intervention, depending on not only the age, but also the gender of the children at risk. Although male aggression and violence may have a more visible and measurable impact in crime statistics, the developmental outcomes for girls may present an equal or greater burden for society. Although a smaller number of girls than boys accelerate to severe public displays of aggression and violence in adulthood, aggressive girls often become mothers of the next generation and, as such, have considerable potential in sustaining or augmenting the problems of aggression and violence in society.

Guidelines for Prevention, Interventions, and Social Policy

The developmental perspective provides key insights for understanding and intervening in the problem of violence within society. A recognition of the different manifestations of disruptive and aggressive behaviors throughout childhood and adolescence will guide the assessment and treatment of children who are at risk at various stages of development. The following guidelines summarize the results of developmental research with implications for prevention, intervention, and social policy.

Developmental Continuity

- The strongest developmental predictor of a child's involvement in violence is a history of previous violence.
- Early aggression will commonly escalate into later violence and broaden into other antisocial behavior.
- In the absence of systematic intervention, individuals show extensive continuity and consistency in their patterns of aggression.

Contributions of Nature and Nurture

- Violence is not prewired, inevitable, or unchangeable.
- It is difficult to separate the respective roles of inherited factors, acquired biological factors (such as birth trauma or head injury), and learned psychosocial factors in the development of violence.
- Children who show a fearless, impulsive temperament very early in life may have a predisposition for aggressive and violent behavior.
- Some evidence suggests that the developmental trajectory for females who become violent is different from that of violent males.

Family Factors and Child Rearing

- Family characteristics and a breakdown of family processes and relationships contribute to the development of antisocial behaviors, including violence.

- Harsh and continual physical punishment by parents has been implicated in the development of aggressive behavior patterns.
- Positive interactions with parents and other adults may act as protective factors for children who are at risk for violence.

School Factors and Academic Achievement

In early childhood, aggressive and disruptive classroom behavior contributes to poor school achievement and poor peer relations. Particular features of the school context may also help create a milieu that is conducive to aggression.

Emotional and Cognitive Development

- Although many believe that violence is the direct, inevitable result of extreme anger or inadequate impulse control, research suggests that inadequate impulse or emotional control puts an individual at risk for violence only if violent acts are that person's preferred response learned through past experiences.
- The cognitive deficits that sometimes accompany Attention Deficit Disorder with Hyperactivity (ADD-H) may contribute to the development of violent behavior.

Influence of Social and Cultural Factors on Cognitive Development

- Because aggressive habits learned early in life are the foundation for later behavior, social and cultural influences in early childhood may have a life-long impact on a child's attitudes toward violence and likelihood of involvement with violence.
- Particular social experiences commonly contribute to violence, but no specific social experiences inevitably lead to violence.
- Individuals learn and develop enduring patterns of connection between their social experiences and their involvement with violence as aggressors, victims, and bystanders who support violence.
- Individuals can learn new patterns of connection by which to control their involvement with, and response to, social experiences that commonly contribute to violence.

Role of Developmental Perspectives in Antiviolence Interventions

- Youth at greatest risk of becoming extremely aggressive and violent tend to share common experiences that appear to place them on a trajectory toward violence.
- Intervening to counteract, buffer, deflect, or otherwise mitigate developmental factors that are conducive to violence can reduce the risk that children or youth will become involved in violence as aggressors, victims, or bystanders who condone violence.

- Early intervention is likely to be more effective than later intervention; however, later intervention can also be effective.
- Interventions can be effective by changing children's and youths' involvement with and response to social experiences, their social perceptions, and their individual patterns of connection.
- Interventions will be most effective when adapted to the key points of leverage that characterize an individual's developmental level.
- Interventions can benefit all individuals, and they are likely to be most effective for those at highest risk for involvement with violence.

Conclusion

The developmental perspective highlights several challenges in addressing the problem of violence within society. First, aggressive children do not constitute a homogeneous group. Therefore, a risk and protective factor approach to understanding the development and sequelae of aggressive behavior problems should include multiple child indicators that are biological and ecological and that incorporate variables from the family, school, and peer contexts. Second, during childhood and adolescence, the problems of violence and victimization have multiple causes, manifestations, and pathways. Third, uniform, time-limited assessments and interventions will not address the diversity and longevity of the problems. Finally, prevention and intervention efforts must be tailored to children's developmental levels and must address the critical influences of children's social milieus at various stages of development. At present, the developmental perspective is providing more clarity about the problem of violence within society and how to reduce and prevent it. With an increasingly sharp focus on the problem, prevention and intervention efforts can be fine-tuned to identify children at risk and ameliorate their life prospects.

References

Adams, D. (1992). Biology does not make men more aggressive than women. In K. Bjorkqvist & P. Niemela (Eds.), *Of mice and women: Aspects of female aggression* (pp. 17–26). San Diego, CA: Academic Press.

Ascione, F. R. (1993). Children who are cruel to animals: A review of research and implications for developmental psychopathology. *Anthrozoos, 6,* 226–247.

Bandura, A. (1973). *Aggression: A social learning analysis.* Englewood Cliffs, NJ: Prentice Hall.

Bandura, A. (1983). Psychological mechanisms of aggression. In R. G. Geen & E. I. Donnerstein (Eds.), *Aggression: Theoretical and empirical reviews* (Vol. 1, pp. 1–40). San Diego, CA: Academic Press.

Bandura, A. (1986). *Social foundations of thought and action.* Englewood Cliffs, NJ: Prentice Hall.

Bandura, A., & Walters, R. H. (1959). *Adolescent aggression.* New York: Ronald.

Bandura, A., & Walters, R. H. (1963). *Social learning and personality development.* New York: Holt, Rinehart & Winston.

Bates, J. E., Bayles, K., Bennett, D. S., Ridge, B., & Brown, M. M. (1991). Origins of externalizing behavior: Problems at eight years of age. In D. J. Pepler & K. H. Rubin (Eds.), *The development and treatment of childhood aggression* (pp. 93–120). Hillsdale, NJ: Erlbaum.

Benton, D. (1992). Hormones and human aggression. In K. Bjorkqvist & P. Niemela (Eds.), *Of mice and women: Aspects of female aggression* (pp. 37–48). San Diego, CA: Academic Press.

Berkowitz, L. (1983). Aversively stimulated aggression: Some parallels and differences in research with animals and humans. *American Psychologist, 38,* 1135–1144.

Berkowitz, L. (1989). Frustration-aggression hypothesis: Examination and reformulation. *Psychological Bulletin, 106,* 59–73.

Berkowitz, L. (1993). *Aggression: Its causes, consequences, and control.* New York: McGraw-Hill.

Bjorkqvist, K., & Niemela, P. (Eds.). (1992). *Of mice and women: Aspects of female aggression.* San Diego, CA: Academic Press.

Bjorkqvist, K., Osterman, K., & Kaukiainen, A. (1992). The development of direct and indirect aggressive strategies in males and females. In K. Bjorkqvist & P. Niemela (Eds.), *Of mice and women: Aspects of female aggression* (pp. 51–64). San Diego, CA: Academic Press.

Brennan, P., Mednick, S., & Kandel, E. (1991). Congenital determinants of violent and property offending. In D. J. Pepler, & K. H. Rubin (Eds.), *The development and treatment of childhood aggression* (pp. 81–92). Hillsdale, NJ: Erlbaum.

Cairns, R. B., and Cairns, B. D. (1984). Predicting aggressive patterns in girls and boys: A developmental study. *Aggressive Behavior, 10,* 227–242.

Cairns, R. B., & Cairns, B. D. (1991). Social cognition and social networks: A developmental perspective. In D. J. Pepler, & K. H. Rubin (Eds.), *The development and treatment of childhood aggression* (pp. 249–278). Hillsdale, NJ: Erlbaum.

Cairns, R. B., Cairns, B. D., Neckerman, H. J., Ferguson, L. L., & Gariepy, J.-L. (1989). Growth and aggression: I. Childhood to early adolescence. *Developmental Psychology, 25,* 320–330.

Cairns, R. B., Cairns, B. D., Neckerman, H. J., Gest, S. D., & Gariepy, J. L. (1988) Social networks and aggressive behavior: Peer support or peer rejection. *Developmental Psychology, 24,* 815–826.

Campbell, A. (1993) *Men, women, and aggression.* New York: Basic Books.

Capaldi, D. M., & Patterson, G. R. (1993, March). *The violent adolescent male: Specialist or generalist?* Paper presented at the biennial meeting of the Society for Research in Child Development, New Orleans, LA.

Caspi, A., Elder, G. H., & Bem, D. J. (1987). Moving against the world: Life course patterns of explosive children. *Developmental Psychology, 23,* 308–313.

Cobb, J. A., & Hops, H. (1973). Effects of academic survival skill training on low-achieving first graders. *Journal of Educational Research, 67,* 108–113.

Coie, J. D., Dodge, K. A., & Kupersmidt, J. B. (1990). Peer group behavior and social status. In S. R. Asher & J. D. Coie (Eds.) *Peer rejection in childhood* (pp. 17–59). Cambridge, England: Cambridge University Press.

Coie, J. D., & Kupersmidt, J. B. (1983). A behavioral analysis of emerging social status in boys' groups. *Child Development, 54,* 1400–1416.

Condry, J. C., & Ross, D. F. (1985). Sex and aggression: The influence of gender label on the perception of aggression in children. *Child Development, 56,* 225–233.

Craig, W. M., & Pepler, D. J. (1992, June). *Contextual factors in bullying and victimization.* Paper presented at the Canadian Psychology Association conference, Quebec, Canada.

Deutsch, M. (1993). Educating for a peaceful world. *American Psychologist, 48(5),* 510–517.

Dishion, T. J. (1990). The family ecology of boys' peer relations in middle childhood. *Child Development, 61,* 874–892.

Dishion, T. J., Patterson, G. R., & Griesler, P. C. (1994). Peer adaptations in the development of antisocial behavior: A confluence model. In L.R. Huesmann (Ed.), *Current perspectives on aggressive behavior* (pp. 61–95). New York: Plenum.

Dodge, K. A. (1980). Social cognition and children's aggressive behavior. *Child Development, 51,* 162–170.

Dodge, K. A. (1983). Behavioral antecedents of peer social status. *Child Development, 54,* 1386–1399.

Dodge, K. A. (1986). A social information-processing model of social competence in children. In M. Perlmutter (Ed.), *Minnesota symposium on child psychology* (Vol. 18, pp. 77–125). Hillsdale, NJ: Erlbaum.

Dodge, K. A. (1991). The structure and function of reactive and proactive aggression. In D. J. Pepler, & K. H. Rubin (Eds.), *The development and treatment of childhood aggression* (pp. 201–218). Hillsdale, NJ: Erlbaum.

Dodge, K. A. (1993). Social–cognitive mechanisms in the development of conduct disorder and depression. *Annual Review of Psychology, 44,* 559–584.

Dodge, K. A., Bates, J. E., & Pettit, G. S. (1990). Mechanisms in the cycle of violence. *Science, 250,* 1678–1683.

Dodge, K. A., Coie, J. D., & Brakke, N. P. (1982). Behavior patterns of socially rejected and neglected preadolescents: The roles of social approach and aggression. *Journal of Abnormal Child Psychology, 10,* 389–410.

Dollard, J., Doob, L. W., Miller, N. E., Mowrer, O. H., & Sears, R. R. (1939). *Frustration and aggression,* New Haven, CT: Yale University Press.

d'Zurilla, T. J., & Goldfried, M. R. (1971). Problem solving and behavior modification. *Journal of Abnormal Psychology, 78,* 107–126.

Eagly, A. H., & Steffen, V. J. (1986). Gender and aggressive behavior: A meta-analytic review of the social psychological literature. *Psychological Bulletin, 100,* 309–330.

Easterbrooks, M. A., Davidson, C. E., & Chazan, R. (1993) Psychosocial risk, attachment, and behavior problems among school-aged children. *Development and Psychopathology, 5,* 389–402.

Eron, L. D. (1992). Gender differences in violence: Biology and/or socialization? In K. Bjorkqvist & P. Niemela (Eds.), *Of mice and women: Aspects of female aggression* (pp. 89–98). San Diego, CA: Academic Press.

Eron, L. D., & Huesmann, L. R. (1990). The stability of aggressive behavior—Even unto the third generation. In M. Lewis & S. M. Miller (Eds.), *Handbook of developmental psychopathology* (pp. 147–156). New York: Plenum.

Eron, L. D., Walder, L. O., & Lefkowitz, M. M. (1971). *The learning of aggression in children.* Boston: Little, Brown.

Eron, L. D., Walder, L. O., Toigo, R., & Lefkowitz, M. M. (1963). Social class, parental punishment for aggression, and child aggression. *Child Development, 34,* 849–867.

Fagot, B. I., Hagan, R., Leinbach, M. D., & Kronsberg, S. (1985). Differential reactions to assertive and communicative acts of toddler boys and girls. *Child Development, 56,* 1499–1505.

Farrington, D. P. (1987a). Early precursors of frequent offending. In J. Q. Wilson & G. C. Loury (Eds.), *Families, schools, and delinquency prevention* (pp. 27–50). New York: Springer-Verlag.

Farrington, D. P. (1987b). Implications of biological findings for criminological research. In S. A. Mednick, T. E. Moffitt, & S. A. Stack (Eds.), *The causes of crime* (pp. 42–64). Cambridge, England: Cambridge University Press.

Farrington, D. P. (1991). Childhood aggression and adult violence: Early precursors and later life outcomes. In D. J. Pepler & K. H. Rubin (Eds.), *The development and treatment of childhood aggression.* Hillsdale, NJ: Erlbaum.

Farrington, D. P. (1992). The need for longitudinal experimental research in offending and anti-social behavior. In J. McCord & R. E. Tremblay (Eds.), *Preventing antisocial behavior.* New York: Guilford Press.

Farrington, D. P., Loeber, R., & Van Kammen, W. B. (1990). Long-term criminal outcomes of hyperactivity-impulsivity-attention deficit and conduct problems in childhood. In L. N. Robins & M. Rutter (Eds.), *Straight and devious pathways to adulthood* (pp. 62–81). New York: Cambridge University Press.

Favreau, O. E. (1993). Do the n's justify the means? Null hypothesis testing applied to sex and other differences. *Canadian Psychology, 34,* 64–78.

Ferguson, T. J., & Rule, B. G. (1983). An attributional perspective on anger and aggression. In R. G. Geen & E. I. Donnerstein (Eds.), *Aggression: Theoretical and empirical reviews* (Vol. 1, pp. 41–74). San Diego, CA: Academic Press.

Feshbach, S. (1964). The function of aggression in the regulation of aggressive drive. *Psychological Review, 71,* 257–272.

Freud, S. (1950). *Beyond the pleasure principle* (J. Strachey, Trans.). New York: Liveright.

Frick, P. J., Lahey, B. B., Loeber, R., Stouthamer-Loeber, M., Christ, M. A.G., & Hanson, K. (1992). Familial risk factors to oppositional defiant disorder and conduct disorder: Parental psycho-pathology and maternal parenting. *Journal of Consulting and Clinical Psychology, 60,* 49–55.

Frijda, N. (1988). The laws of emotion. *American Psychologist, 43,* 349–358.

Frude, N. & Gault, H. (1984). *Disruptive behavior in the schools*. Chichester: Wiley.

Geen, R. G., & Donnerstein, E. I. (Eds.). (1983). *Aggression: Theoretical and empirical reviews, Vol. 1*. San Diego, CA: Academic Press.

Greenberg, M., & Speltz, M. (1988). Attachment and the ontogeny of conduct problems. In J. Belsky & T. Nezworski (Eds.), *Clinical Implications of attachment* (pp. 177–218). Hillsdale, NJ: Erlbaum.

Greenberg, M., Speltz, M., & DeKlyen, M. (1993). The role of attachment in the early development of disruptive behavior problems. *Development and Psychopathology, 5,* 191–213.

Guerra, N., & Slaby, R. (1989). Evaluative factors in social problem solving skills by aggressive boys. *Journal of Abnormal Child Psychology, 17,* 277–289.

Guerra, N. G., & Slaby, R. (1990). Cognitive mediators of aggression in adolescent offenders: Intervention. *Developmental Psychology, 26,* 269–277.

Harries, K. D. (1990). *Serious violence: Patterns of homicide and assault in america*. Springfield, IL: Charles C Thomas.

Hartup, W. W. (1974). Aggression in childhood: Developmental perspectives. *American Psychologist, 29,* 336–341.

Hood, K. E., Draper, P., Crockett, L. J., & Petersen, A. C. (1987). The ontogeny and phylogeny of sex differences in development: A biopsychosocial synthesis. In D. B. Carter (Ed.), *Current conceptions of sex roles and sex typing: Theory and research* (pp. 49–78). New York: Praeger.

Huesmann, L. R. (1988). An information-processing model for the development of aggression, *Aggressive Behavior, 14,* 13–24.

Huesmann, L. R., & Eron, L. D. (1984). Cognitive processes and the persistence of aggressive behavior. *Aggressive Behavior, 10,* 243–251.

Huesmann, L. R., & Eron, L. D. (1989). Individual differences and the trait of aggression. *European Journal of Personality, 3,* 95–106.

Huesmann, L. R., Eron, L. D., Lefkowitz, M. M., & Walder, L. O. (1984). Stability of aggression over time and generations. *Developmental Psychology, 20,* 1120–1134.

Huesmann, L. R., Guerra, N. G., Zelli, A., & Miller, L. (1992). Differing normative beliefs about aggression for boys and girls. In K. Bjorkqvist & P. Niemela (Eds.), *Of mice and women: Aspects of female aggression* (pp. 77–87). San Diego, CA: Academic Press.

Hyde, J. S. (1984). How large are gender differences in aggression? A developmental meta-analysis. *Developmental Psychology, 20,* 722–736.

Hymel, S., Wagner, E., & Butler, L. J. (1990). Reputational bias: View from the peer group. In S. R. Asher & J. D. Coie (Eds.), *Peer rejection in childhood* (pp. 156–188). Cambridge, England: Cambridge University Press.

Kavanagh, K. (1993, March). *Relationship of gender to family interactions and reports of early adolescent antisocial behaviors*. Paper presented at the meetings of the Society for Research in Child Development, New Orleans, LA.

Kavanagh, K., & Hops, H. (1994). Good girls? Bad boys?: Gender and development as contexts for diagnosis and treatment. In T. H. Ollendick & R. J. Prinz (Eds.), *Advances in Clinical Child Psychology* (Vol. 16, pp. 45–79). New York: Plenum.

Kazdin, A. E. (1987). Treatment of antisocial behavior in children: Current status and future directions. *Psychological Bulletin, 102,* 187–203.

Kellam, S. G., & Rebok, G. W. (1992). Building developmental and etiological theory through epidemiologically based preventive intervention trials. In J. McCord & R. E. Tremblay (Eds.), *Preventing antisocial behavior: Interventions from birth through adolescence* (pp. 162–195). New York: Guilford Press.

Kelley, H. H. (1972). *Causal schemata and the attribution process*. Morristown, NJ: General Learning Press.

Kupersmidt, J. B., & Coie, J. D. (1990). Preadolescent peer status, aggression, and school adjustment as predictors of externalizing problems in adolescence. *Child Development, 61,* 1350–1362.

Kupersmidt, J. B., Coie, J. D., & Dodge, K. A. (1990). The role of poor peer relationships in the development of disorder. In S. R. Asher & J. D. Coie (Eds.), *Peer rejection in childhood* (pp. 247–308). Cambridge, England: Cambridge University Press.

Lagerspetz, K., Bjorkqvist, K., & Peltonen, T. (1988). Is indirect aggression typical of females? Gender differences in aggressiveness in 11- to 12-year old children. *Aggressive Behavior, 14,* 403–404.

Laslett, R. (1977). Disruptive and violent pupils: The facts and the fallacies. *Educational Review, 29,* 152–162.

Lewis, D. O., Yeager, C. A., Cobham-Portorreal, C. S., Klein, N., Showater, C., & Anthony, A. (1991). A follow-up of female delinquents: Maternal contributions to the perpetuation of deviance. *Journal of the American Academy of Child and Adolescent Psychiatry, 30,* 197–201.

Lochman, J. E., Lampron, L. B., Gemmer, T. C., & Harris, S. R. (1987). Anger coping intervention with aggressive children: A guide to implementation in school settings. In P. A. Keller & S. R. Heyman (Eds.), *Innovations in clinical practice: A source book* (Vol. 6, pp. 339–356). Sarasota, FL: Professional Resource Exchange.

Loeber, R. (1990). Development and risk factors of juvenile antisocial behavior and delinquency. *Clinical Psychology Review, 10,* 1–41.

Loeber, R., & Stouthamer-Loeber, M. (1986). Family factors as correlates and predictors of juvenile conduct problems and delinquency. In N. Morris & M. Tonry (Eds.), *Crime and justice: An annual review of research,* (Vol. 7, pp. 29–149). Chicago: University of Chicago Press.

Loeber, R., Wung, P., Keenan, K., Giroux, B., Stouthamer-Loeber, M., Van Kammen, W. B., & Maughan, B. (1993). Developmental pathways in disruptive child behavior. *Development and Psychopathology, 5,* 103–133.

Lorenz, K. (1966). *On aggression.* New York: Harcourt, Brace & World.

Lytton, H. (1990). Child and parent effects in boys' conduct disorder: A reinterpretation. *Developmental Psychology, 26,* 683–697.

Lytton, H., & Romney, D. M. (1991). Parents' differential socialization of boys and girls: A meta-analysis. *Psychological Bulletin, 109,* 267–296.

Maccoby, E. E. (1986). Social groupings in childhood: Their relationship to prosocial and antisocial behavior in boys and girls. In D. Olweus, J. Block, & M. Radke-Yarrow (Eds.), *Development of antisocial and prosocial behavior: Research, theories, and issues* (pp. 263–284). San Diego, CA: Academic Press.

Maccoby, E. E., & Jacklin, C. N. (1974). *The psychology of sex differences.* Stanford, CA: Stanford University Press.

Maccoby, E. E., & Jacklin, C. N. (1980). Sex differences in aggression: A rejoinder and reprise. *Child Development, 51,* 964–980.

Magnusson, D. (1988). *Individual development from an interactional perspective.* Hillsdale, NJ: Erlbaum.

McClintock, F. (1963). *Crimes of violence.* London: Macmillan.

McFall, R. M. (1982). A review and reformation of the concept of social skills. *Behavioral Assessment, 4,* 1–33.

Miller, G. A., Galanter, E., & Pribram, K. H. (1960). *Plans and the structure of behavior.* New York: Holt, Rinehart & Winston.

Moffitt, T. E. (1993). The neuropsychology of conduct disorder. *Development and Psychopathology, 5,* 135–151.

Moffitt, T. E., & Silva, P. A. (1988). Self-reported delinquency, neuropsychological deficit, and history of attention deficit disorder. *Journal of Abnormal Child Psychology, 16,* 553–569.

National Research Council. (1993). *Understanding and preventing violence.* Washington, DC: National Academy Press.

Newell, A., & Simon, H.A. (1972). *Human problem solving.* Englewood Cliffs, NJ: Prentice Hall.

Olweus, D. (1979). Stability of aggressive reaction patterns in males: A review. *Psychological Bulletin, 86,* 852–872.

Olweus, D. (1980). Familial and temperamental determinants of aggressive behavior in adolescent boys: A causal analysis. *Developmental Psychology, 16,* 644–660.

Olweus, D. (1991). Bully/victim problems among school children: Some basic facts and effects of a school based intervention program. In D. J. Pepler & K. H. Rubin (Eds.), *The development and treatment of childhood aggression* (pp. 411–448). Hillsdale, NJ: Erlbaum.

Parke, R. D., & Slaby, R. G. (1983). The development of aggression. In P. H. Mussen (Series Ed.), & E. M. Hetherington (Vol. Ed.), *Handbook of child psychology* (Vol. 4, pp. 547–641). New York: Wiley.

Parker, J. G., & Asher, S. R. (1987). Peer relations and later personal adjustment: Are low-accepted children at risk? *Psychological Bulletin, 102*, 357–389.

Patterson, G. R. (1982). *Coercive family process.* Eugene, OR: Castalia.

Patterson, G. R. (1986). Performance models for antisocial boys. *American Psychologist, 41*, 432–444.

Patterson, G. R., DeBaryshe, B. D., & Ramsey, E. (1989). A developmental perspective on antisocial behavior. *American Psychologist, 44*, 329–335.

Patterson, G. R., Dishion, T. J. (1988). Multilevel family process models: Traits, interactions, and relationships. In R. Hinde & J. Stevenson-Hinde (Eds.), *Relationships within families: Mutual influences* (pp. 283–310). Oxford, England: Clarendon Press.

Patterson, G. R., Reid, J. B., & Dishion, T. J. (1992). *Antisocial boys.* Eugene, OR: Castalia.

Pepler, D. J., Byrd, W., & King, G. (1991). A social–cognitively based social skills training program for aggressive children. In D. J. Pepler & K. H. Rubin (Eds.), *The development and treatment of childhood aggression* (pp. 361–379). Hillsdale, NJ: Erlbaum.

Pepler, D. J., & Moore, T. E. (1993, August). *Daughters of abused women: At risk?* Paper presented at the 101st Annual Convention of the American Psychological Association, Toronto, Canada.

Perry, D. G., Kusel, S. J., & Perry, L. C. (1988). Victims of peer aggression. *Developmental Psychology, 24*, 807–814.

Perry, D. G., Perry, L. C., & Rasmussen, P. (1986). Cognitive social learning mediators of aggression. *Child Development, 57*, 700–711.

Piaget, J. (1970). Piaget's theory. In P. Mussen (Ed.), *Carmichael's manual of child psychology* (Vol. 1, pp. 703–732). New York: Wiley.

Potegal, M. (1992). Aggression and aggressiveness in female golden hamsters: The attack priming effect as tour guide to the central mechanisms of aggression. In K. Bjorkqvist & P. Niemela (Eds.), *Of mice and women: Aspects of female aggression* (pp. 330–350). San Diego, CA: Academic Press.

Pratt, T. M. (1973). Positive approaches to disruptive behavior. *Today's Education, 62*, 18–19.

Pulkkinen, L. (1992). The path to adulthood for aggressively inclined girls. In K. Bjorkqvist & P. Niemela (Eds.), *Of mice and women: Aspects of female aggression* (pp. 113–121). San Diego, CA: Academic Press.

Rabbie, J. M., Goldenbeld, C., & Lodewijkx, H. F. M. (1992). Sex differences in conflict and aggression in individual and groups settings. In K. Bjorkqvist & P. Niemela (Eds.), *Of mice and women: Aspects of female aggression* (pp. 217–228). San Diego, CA: Academic Press.

Raine, A., & Jones, F. (1987). Attention, autonomic arousal, and personality in behaviorally disordered children. *Journal of Abnormal Child Psychology, 15*, 583–599.

Reid, J. B., & Patterson, G. R. (1989) The development of antisocial behavior patterns in childhood and adolescence. *European Journal of Personality, 3*, 107–120.

Robins, L. N. (1966). *Deviant children grow up.* Baltimore: Williams & Wilkins.

Robins, L. N. (1986). The consequences of conduct disorder in girls. In D. Olweus, J. Block, & M. Radke-Yarrow (Eds.), *Development of antisocial and prosocial behavior: Research, theories, and issues* (pp. 385–414). San Diego, CA: Academic Press.

Rubin, K. H., & Krasnor, L. R. (1986). Social–cognitive and social–behavioral perspectives on problem solving. In M. Perlmutter (Ed.), *Cognitive perspectives on children's social and behavioral development. The Minnesota Symposia on Child Psychology* (Vol. 18, pp. 1–68). Hillsdale, NJ: Erlbaum.

Rule, B. G., Dyck, R., & Nesdale, A. R. (1978). Arbitrariness of frustration: Inhibition or instigation effects on aggression. *European Journal of Social Psychology, 8*, 237–244.

Schank, R. C., & Abelson, R. P. (1977). *Scripts, plans, goals and understanding.* Hillsdale, NJ: Erlbaum.

Selman, R. L. (1980). *The growth of interpersonal understanding.* San Diego, CA: Academic Press.

Selman, R. L., Schultz, L. H., Nakkula, M., Barr, D., Watts, C., & Richmond, J. B. (1992). Friendship and fighting: A developmental approach to the study of risk and prevention of violence. *Development and Psychopathology, 4*, 529–558.

Serbin, L. A., Marchessault, K., McAffer, V., Peters, P., & Schwartzman, A. E. (1993). Patterns of social behavior on the playground in 9–11-year-old girls and boys: Relation to teacher perceptions and to peer ratings of aggression, withdrawal and likability. In C.Hart (Ed.), *Children on the playground* (pp. 162–183). NY: SUNY Press.

Shure, M. B. (1992). *I can problem solve: An interpersonal cognitive problem-solving program.* Champaign, IL: Research Press.

Slaby, R. G. (1989). *Aggressors, victims, and bystanders: An assessment-based middle school violence prevention curriculum.* Unpublished grant proposal, Education Development Center, Newton, MA.

Slaby, R. G., & Guerra, N. G. (1988). Cognitive mediators of aggression in adolescent offenders: 1. Assessment. *Developmental Psychology, 24,* 580–588.

Slaby, R. B., & Roedell, W. C. (1982). The development and regulation of aggression in young children. In J. Worrell (Ed.), *Psychological development in the elementary years* (pp. 97–149). San Diego, CA: Academic Press.

Slaby, R. G., & Stringham, P. (in press). Prevention of peer and community violence: The pediatrician's role. *Pediatrics.*

Slaby, R. G., Wilson-Brewer, R., & DeVos, E. (1994). *Aggressors, victims, & bystanders: An assessment-based middle school violence prevention curriculum.* Final report of research grant #R49/CCR-103559 to the Centers for Disease Control & Prevention, Atlanta, GA. (Available from the National Technology Information Center, 5285 Port Royal Road, Springfield, VA 22161.)

Smith, P. K., & Boulton, M. (1990). Rough and tumble play, aggression and dominance: Perception and behaviors in children's encounters. *Human Development, 33,* 271–282.

Snyder, J. J., Dishion, T. J., & Patterson, G. R. (1986). Determinants and consequences of associating with deviant peers during preadolescence and adolescence. *Journal of Early Adolescence, 6,* 29–43.

Spivack, G., & Shure, M. B. (1974). *Social adjustment of young children: A cognitive approach to solving real-life problems.* San Francisco: Jossey-Bass.

Stephenson, P., & Smith, D. (1989). Bullying in the junior school. In D. Tattum & D. Lane (Eds.), *Bullying in schools* (pp. 45–59). Stoke on Trent, England: Trentham.

Straus, M. (1991). Discipline and deviance: Physical punishment of children and violence and other crime in adulthood. *Social Problems, 38,* 133–154.

Tieger, T. (1980). On the biological basis of sex differences in aggression. *Child Development, 51,* 943–963.

Tremblay, R. E., Masse, B., Perron, D., Leblanc, M., Schwartzman, A. E., & Ledingham, J. E. (1992). Early disruptive behavior, poor school achievement, delinquent behavior, and delinquent personality: Longitudinal analyses. *Journal of Consulting and Clinical Psychology, 60,* 64–72.

Viemero, V. (1992). Changes in patterns of aggressiveness among Finnish girls over a decade. In K. Bjorkqvist & P. Niemela (Eds.), *Of mice and women: Aspects of female aggression* (pp. 99–106). San Diego, CA: Academic Press.

Walters, R. H., & Parke, R. D. (1964). Social motivation, dependency, and susceptibility to social influence. In L. Berkowitz (Ed.), *Advances in experimental social psychology* (Vol. 1, pp. 231–276). San Diego, CA: Academic Press.

Werner, H. (1948). *The comparative psychology of mental development.* Madison, CT: International Universities Press.

Widom, C. S. (1989). Does violence beget violence? A critical examination of the literature. *Psychological Bulletin, 106,* 3–28.

Widom, C. S. (1990). The intergenerational transmission of violence. In N. A. Weiner & M. E. Wolfgang (Eds.), *Pathways to criminal violence* (pp. 137–201). Newbury Park, CA: Sage.

Zahn-Waxler, C. (1993). Warriors and worriers: Gender and psychopathology. *Development and Psychopathology, 5,* 79–89.

3

Sociocultural Factors in the Etiology and Prevention of Violence Among Ethnic Minority Youth

Hope M. Hill, Fernando I. Soriano, S. Andrew Chen, and Teresa D. LaFromboise

The recent data on violence among youth have drawn the attention of both the public and the scientific community. In 1989, for example, homicide was the second leading cause of death among persons between 15 and 24 years of age. In that same year, close to 5%, or an estimated 4.6 million households nationwide, had a member who had experienced one or more violent crimes (U.S. Department of Justice, 1991b).

Data suggest that the incidence and prevalence of violence differ across social and cultural groups in the United States. In particular, violent crime victimization and perpetration rates have consistently revealed differing patterns of violence associated with each of the dominant ethnic minority groups in the United States (Roper, 1991; see also chapters 4–7 of this book).

This is perhaps most clear when considering statistics on violence among youth in these groups. Rather than being the second leading cause of death among 15- to 24-year-olds, for example, homicide is the number one cause of death among African American youth (Fingerhut, Ingram, & Feldman, 1992). And, for U.S. Latino and Native American youth, data show that victimization rates for crimes of violence are higher than those for White non-Latinos (U.S. Department of Justice, 1991a). (For additional demographic and epidemiological data on violence involving members of ethnic minority groups, see chapters 4–7 in this book.)

Researchers have questioned just what it is about racial and ethnic differences in the United States that seems to be associated with varying rates of violence (D. Hawkins, 1990). One important answer has been found by looking at risk factors for violence and at population demographics. The data indicate that social risk factors such as unemployment, high population density, poverty, and drug abuse, among others, are associated with being both victims and perpetrators of violent crimes (Sampson, 1993). At the same time, population demographics indicate that these risk factors are overrepresented among members of ethnic minority groups and may, in part, account for the difference in rates of violence among ethnic minority groups and Whites (Sampson, 1993). This close association between ethnicity and risk factors makes it difficult to separate the independent role of each in violence among these groups.

It is important to note that research suggests that rather than being the result of one or two risk factors, violence may be the result of a number of historical, economic, social, and psychological forces that are associated with the lives of ethnic minority members (D. Hawkins, 1990). Indeed, several studies support the hypothesis that it is the combination of poverty and other variables reflecting structural inequity, racism, and discrimination that place some groups at higher risk for violence than others (D. Hawkins, 1990; McLoyd, 1990; Sampson, 1985; Sampson & Lauritsen, 1990).

Further research is certainly needed both to delineate these other variables and to describe any mediational effects they may have on violence. In addition, more work is needed to understand how smaller systems and larger systems interact. For example, do family process variables in some ethnic cultures mediate the effects of poverty and inequality on violence? How does poverty influence psychological distress, parenting, and socioemotional development that in turn play roles in violence? (See, e.g., McLoyd, 1990.)

In chapter 2, risk and resiliency factors pertaining to several smaller systems levels (i.e., individual, family, school, and peer) were implicated in how violence develops or can be prevented among youth, and these same factors are, of course, often applicable to ethnic minority youth. But psychologists and other social scientists also need to look at potential risk and resiliency factors that are specific to ethnic minority groups. For example, what risk factors make ethnic minority youth more likely to join juvenile gangs that are involved in violence? What protective mechanisms within the culture may come into play to prevent or reduce violence among some ethnic minority youth who are at high risk for violence because of social and economic factors? In other words, how do larger social and cultural factors put some youth within a particular ethnic minority group at high risk for experiencing violence, and how might ethnic culture make others resilient enough to avoid becoming either victims or perpetrators of violence?

Overview

In this chapter, we take a closer look at sociocultural factors as they apply to ethnic minority youth and suggest critical relations between culture, structural inequities, and developmental mandates, on the one hand, and violence among ethnic minority youth on the other. We look at these relations both as they pertain to risk factors and also as they interact with hypothesized ethnic cultural protective mechanisms that may serve as buffers against violence.

Because of their disproportionate experience with violence, we focus on four major ethnic minority groups in the United States: African Americans, U.S. Latinos, Native Americans, and Asian and Pacific Island Americans. We are aware that each group's experience with violence among youth (and within their subgroups[1]) is different in that there are variations in socioeconomic factors and variations in each group's interaction with the mainstream culture. But we are also aware of their common plight: All four groups have a disproportionately higher experience of violence than Whites, and all four groups share a common experience of exploitation and oppression in this country. Moreover, although we have chosen to focus on four ethnic groups, we have done so with the understanding that violence is embedded within the American culture itself, which, in combination with social and psychological forces, influences the propensity toward violent behavior among all youth.

Because research on the influence of larger social and cultural systems on violence among ethnic minority youth is currently sparse, much of what we present in this chapter is meant to be heuristic. What we hope to do is to encourage theorists, researchers, and program developers to include sociocultural variables related to ethnicity in their work and to suggest some important areas on which to focus.

The chapter is divided into six sections. In the first section, we consider violence and culture, particularly the way in which psychology has examined their relationship to ethnic minority groups in the past. We also briefly look at the way in which violence is a part of the larger American culture. In the second section, we examine the influence of social forces by focusing on structural inequities as risk factors for violence. These involve racism and discrimination, poverty and inequality, and the status mobility system. In the third section, we explore developmental mandates of youth and how risk factors for violence may interact with such mandates. We focus specifically on proactive socialization and bicultural competency as one way of reducing violence. This discussion is followed by the fourth section, in which we describe traditional values of the four ethnic groups that can potentially serve as protective mechanisms against youth violence. In the fifth and sixth sections, respectively, we present specific recommendations for future research in the area and for prevention and treatment intervention with regard to ethnic minority youth.

Again, we acknowledge that the ethnic minority groups we discuss are extremely heterogeneous and are influenced greatly by norms involving social class. Therefore, in this chapter we focus on the economically disadvantaged among ethnic minority groups. We also acknowledge that some of the factors we discuss (e.g., access to quality schooling and jobs) may also be germane to economically disadvantaged youth among the White population.

---

[1]There is vast heterogeneity among each of these subgroups, but space limitations preclude being specific about many of them in this chapter. Triandis (personal communication, February 23, 1993; see also Triandis, 1987), for example, has noted many cultural differences within subgroups of an ethnic minority group, including those regarded as deviations from norms. Those cultures that are "tight" are quite concerned about deviations from the norm, and those that are "loose" are able to tolerate more deviation. Using the Asian-American group as an example, he has found that Thais are "loose," the Japanese are quite "tight," and the Chinese somewhere in between. Subgroups' values may also influence the development of violence. We refer the reader to McGoldrick, Pearce, and Giordano (1982) for excellent general discussions regarding values among some subgroups (e.g., Mexican, Cuban, Puerto Rican subgroups of the U.S. Latino population).

How Psychology Has Studied Violence and Culture

Historical Overview

As a field, psychology has been studying aggressive and violent behavior for over 50 years; an earnest engagement in research started in the early 1940s. (For a more comprehensive review of theory and research, see chapter 2.) Before that time, psychologists theorized about aggression and violence, but they mainly focused on genetic, instinctual, or biological bases of aggression and criminal activity (Krebs & Miller, 1985), some of which were biased against members of ethnic minority groups and were used by racists to reinforce negative stereotypes.

It was not until Dollard et al. published their book, *Frustration and Aggression*, in 1939 (Dollard, Doob, Miller, Mowrer, & Sears, 1939) that psychology's narrow focus on genetics, instinct, and biology was generally expanded. Their theory, referred to as the "frustration–aggression hypothesis," suggested that all aggression was inextricably tied to levels of frustration (Miller, 1941). However, even with this new challenge to earlier biological and genetic models of aggression, theories continued to emerge that blamed ethnic and racial groups for what were then perceived as their deficiencies in culture or values (Montiel, 1970).

For example, early theorists (e.g., Rose, 1978; Wolfgang & Ferracutti, 1967) advanced the concept of a "subculture of violence" among the lower classes. This subculture was seen as having deviant beliefs and values in comparison with the perceived normative values of the middle class, deviance that led to violence.

With regard to African Americans, according to Harries (1990), the assumptions in these early models were that deficient child rearing conditions and a stressful environment had led to "new modal personality types" and the possibility of regionally distinct African American subcultures, both of which promote violence. It has been argued that this conceptualization of a culture of violence is flawed (Hill et al., 1989), in that "culture" denotes an elaborated, time-tested, and enduring system that serves as a guide for conceptualizing the world, and early work in this field did not examine culture in this light. Nevertheless, the biased view of an African American subculture led some to consider this "subculture" to be the main causal factor in violence.

The psychological and social science literature has also been biased against other ethnic minority groups. For example, Mirande (1977) has shown that the earliest literature on U.S. Latinos and violence was largely pejorative. This literature, dating primarily before 1965, was largely critical of Latino culture and its focus on the family. One of the most persistent beliefs perpetuated by social scientists was that U.S. Latinos were "controlled" by their traditional culture. That is, they were considered passive receptors of their culture. Many of the problems encountered by U.S. Latinos, such as violence and delinquency were said to result from bondage to their traditional culture, which made assimilation into the mainstream difficult, if not impossible (Soriano, 1994).

Heller (1966) represented the pejorative view of Latinos when she observed that

> The kind of socialization that Mexican-American children generally receive at home is not conducive to the development of the capacities needed for advancement . . . by stressing values that hinder mobility—family ties, honor, masculinity, and living in the present—and by neglecting the values that are conducive to it—achievement, independence, and deferred gratification. (pp. 34–35)

In the early 1970s, coinciding with the advent of minority researchers, a more sympathetic view of U.S. Latinos emerged.[2] Latino values, such as familism, began to be seen as positive characteristics. These social scientists argued that the U.S. Latino culture is not unstable and pathological but one that provides its members with a sense of security and love, often thought to be lacking in mainstream U.S. culture (Romano, 1973). In the early 1980s, U.S. Latino and non-Latino social scientists began to critically assess both of these views. They called for more objective and empirically based studies of U.S. Latinos and their families (Chandler, 1979; Ramirez & Arce, 1981). This emphasis on empirical research has yielded findings that have helped to better understand U.S. Latino culture.

Historically, psychology has ignored Native American and Asian/Pacific Island American cultures in research in general and with regard to violence in particular. The historical failure of psychology to adequately understand Native Americans is discussed in Trimble (1977). Similar information about the Asian/Pacific Island minorities in the United States can be found in Sue and Wagner (1973), and more particular information on the "subculture" of the Japanese subgroup is found in Kitano (1969). Chen (1988) has found that Asian Americans are unique in experiencing a "double" minority status in that, in addition to being a racial minority, they possess an Eastern cultural heritage that is perceived as different and inferior by most Americans.

Current Status

Like those in many other social science fields, psychologists are still struggling in their efforts to understand the role that culture plays in influencing behavior such as violence and aggression. In a recent article in the *American Psychologist*, Betancourt and Lopez (1993) summarized the current status of the study of culture, ethnicity, and race in American psychology. They concluded that research on culture and ethnicity is still the exception rather than

---

[2]Representative of these new minority social scientists was Miguel Montiel. In a cogent and incisive critique of past research on U.S. Latinos, Montiel (1970) argued that much of the past literature perpetuated many erroneous stereotypes because of its unquestioned reliance on the psychoanalytic model and view that sees machismo as the root of all problems encountered by U.S. Latinos. Of those who hold this view, he said they are, "inherently incapable of defining normal behavior and this automatically labels all Mexican and Mexican American people as sick—only in degree of sickness do they vary" (p. 62).

the rule when it comes to mainstream psychology in the United States. (See also responses to this article by Lee, 1994, and Reid, 1994.)

We believe that much of the current psychological research on ethnic culture and violence fails to account for important variability that is found within populations (e.g., culture becomes a source of error variance). Another problem in studying culture and violence in the United States is that some psychologists have used the term "culture" indiscriminately to denote subpopulations (Price-Williams, 1985) and internalized cognitions (e.g., beliefs, values, and norms; see discussion that follows). When used to refer only to subpopulations, as in some cross-cultural studies of violence, group differences are left to post hoc explanations, many of which falsely assume ethnic group homogeneity. And even when linked to internalized cognitions, cultural traits influencing those cognitions are assumed to be equally salient to all members of a particular racial or ethnic group, which is rarely the case. In all of these situations, the understanding of ethnic minority cultures and their effect on various behaviors, including violence, has been obscured.[3]

The Many Definitions of Culture

Culture has been defined in many ways. It has been characterized as the sum total of the ways of living developed by a group to meet basic biological and psychosocial needs (Pinderhughes, 1989). Leighton described culture as "elements such as values, norms, beliefs, attitudes, folkways, behavior styles, and traditions that are linked together to form an integrated whole that functions to preserve the society" (cited in Pinderhughes, 1989, p. 6).

Kroeber and Kluckhohn stated that "culture refers to distinct preferred or actual patterns of behavior, communication and cognition that are held in common and accepted by members of a distinct group of people" (cited in Soriano, in press). Much more recently, Triandis offered a complementary definition of culture that makes more specific reference to psychological constructs of attitudes, beliefs, and norms:

> Culture consists of shared patterns of categorizations, beliefs, attitudes, norms, roles, values and behaviors (e.g., communication), that were adaptive during the history of a distinct group, and were transmitted to those who could interact with that group, because of a common language and contiguity in time-space. (H. C. Triandis, personal communication, February 23, 1993)

---

[3]To avoid these common errors in studying violence among ethnic minority youth, culture must be strategically and purposefully incorporated into research and program designs. Researchers need to decide how culture will be conceptualized and operationalized a priori. They need to decide from the start whether they will treat culture simply as a nominal independent variable used to stratify a sample and then used to compare groups or whether they will make a more serious effort to incorporate specific cultural concepts that would lead to a better understanding of culture and its role in behavior. Finally, researchers must take care to distinguish cultural concepts from other interacting, mediating, or associated social variables, such as poverty or geographical location. See Betancourt and Lopez (1993) for other issues involving research on ethnic minority populations.

This last definition of culture may be the most useful, as it accommodates the reality that members of ethnic minority groups may be bicultural (La-Fromboise, Coleman, & Gerton, 1993; Ramirez & Castaneda, 1974) and that they may choose differing and distinct forms of behavior because of their histories in both cultures. These include customs passed on through communication (verbal and nonverbal language) and internalized attitudes, beliefs, values, norms, and roles from both the majority and ethnic minority cultures to which they belong. The unique cultural patterns that develop from this intermingling of cultures are then passed on from generation to generation, to be shaped by the contemporary bicultural reality in which group members live.

According to Pedersen (1991), such unique cultural patterns of thought and action help to guide ideas, influence decisions, and take control of life choices, including those that lead to violence. Cultural patterns have also been associated with specific cultural identities, self-schemas, and typologies (Markus, 1977).

With regard to self schemas and culture, for example, in an insightful review article on culture and the self, Markus and Kitayama (1991) suggested that cultures and peoples are generally linked to one of two construals of self: independent or interdependent. Western cultures largely adopt an independent or monocultural notion of self, which emphasizes an autonomous self-identity independent of context and an emphasis on one's difference from others. Other cultures, such as African, Latino, Asian, and Native American cultures, adopt an interdependent view, which emphasizes a social contextual view of self and an appreciation of fitting in with others. Markus and Kitayama (1991) showed that an individual's view of self as independent or interdependent influences cognition (attribution), emotion (self- vs. other-focused), and motivation (e.g., whether internal or external approval of actions is primary). As seen in chapter 2, cognition, emotion, and motivation are crucial in understanding violence in a developmental context. The fact that many ethnic minority groups' cultures of origin emphasize an interdependent construal of self should have implications not only for the development of violent patterns but also for the prevention and reduction of violence among these groups. So, how independent and interdependent orientations influence violence among members of the majority and minority cultures remains one of the most important questions for research to examine.

Psychologists, Culture, and Norms

Many contemporary psychologists readily acknowledge the indirect role of culture in behavior by saying that it provides the "prescriptive standards," including norms, values, laws, customs, and moral traditions, that serve as a guide to "proper" conduct (Krebs & Miller, 1985). However, as we have described above, psychologists often ignore important cultural differences that influence norms and thus fail to account for important variables and attendant behaviors, such as violence.

For example, in studying aggression and violence, psychologists have mainly focused on the influence of the majority's cultural norms underlying aggressive and prosocial behavior, erroneously implying the existence of a single standard of behavior. Perhaps it is this assumption regarding such "normative behavior" that led to early criticisms of the cultural values and beliefs of ethnic and racial groups (Bayton, 1941; Katz & Braly, 1933; Rudoff, 1971; Trujillo, 1974).

Although the study of norms of the mainstream cultures continues to be important to learning about violence, in heterogeneous American society such research should always include an examination of intercultural or cross-cultural differences, which would include group-specific norms among ethnic and racial minority groups.

The American Culture and Violence

As mentioned previously, any analysis of social and cultural factors in ethnic minority violence would be incomplete without a specific focus on the often conflicting role of violence in the larger American culture. First, it should be noted that American society, as a whole, seems to foster a high level of violence. For example, in a recent study of violence in industrialized countries, Fingerhut and her colleagues (1992) reported that the United States leads the world in homicides and interpersonal violence (see also Holinger, Offer, Barter, & Bell, 1994, for a summary of cross-cultural data with regard to homicide and youth). These data support the often heard colloquial expression that "violence is as American as apple pie."

Violence in this country, as in many others, is often glorified or eschewed depending on the context in which it is displayed, the extent to which it is socially sanctioned, the target, and the goal. From the contemporary popularity of Arnold Schwarzenegger as "The Terminator" to Monday night football, Americans' taste for violence in entertainment often seems voracious (see chapter 11 for a discussion of media's role in influencing and promoting violence). Even though the media is criticized by many in the majority culture for promoting violence, it seems to be criticized even more harshly when members of ethnic minority groups are involved. For example, some gangster rappers (and those who profit from their work) have capitalized on the American appetite for the depiction of violent sex in slick music videos targeted toward youth. Understanding the role of social and economic rewards for depictions of violence and sex in the larger American culture, and the influence of social conditions fostering violence rather than simply the characteristics of gangs or of particular groups of ethnic minority youth, is central in understanding the emergence of rap music that is violent (however, these factors may also explain the emergence of most depictions of violence and sex in the media).

In other ways, America is conflicted about violence. Although most Americans abhor the violence in the streets of this country, interpersonal violence in law enforcement and in the disciplining of children is seen by many as a prerogative or even a necessity. And spousal or partner violence continues to be implicitly condoned by the inactivity of the police and judicial systems in the United States (A. Jones, 1994).

Structural Inequity and Youth Violence

Major factors affecting ethnic groups and violence are the structural inequities woven into the very fabric of American society. These include racism and discrimination, poverty and inequality, and the status mobility system. We consider these structural inequities to be important risk factors for violence among ethnic minority youth.

Racism and discrimination. Despite the advances in civil rights in the past 25 years, Hacker (1992) contends that racism continues largely unabated in this country, and its effects are still as negative and insidious. In his searing analysis of race relations in the United States, he contends that a primary effect of racism is that it consigns some groups to the margins of society, in which they lead painful lives and often face premature death (e.g., consider the homicide rates among ethnic minority youth). Others have also written eloquently on the impact of racism (e.g., J. M. Jones, 1972; R. Jones, 1991), providing a basis for understanding how racism and discrimination have compromised the functioning of both Whites and people of color.

Racism has been used to justify discrimination against ethnic minorities. For example, racist stereotypes of African Americans as primitive and inferior have been used as a justification for exclusion of African Americans from mainstream opportunities (Hacker, 1992). Racist stereotypes of Native Americans as lazy and savage have led to attempts to denigrate and eradicate their cultures, and therefore many sources of strength. The fact that their unemployment rate is much higher than the national average (LaFromboise, 1988) is seen by many as an affirmation rather than a refutation of racist stereotypes, leading to further discrimination against them. Even more "positive" stereotypes, such as Asian Americans being the alleged "model minority" who experience few social problems may result in discrimination toward those Asian Americans who do experience poverty and unemployment and are in need of attention from social policies and services. Many of the Asian youth who join gangs, for example, are influenced by the cultural exclusion, poverty, poor health, language deficiencies, adjustment problems in schools, poor housing conditions, and lack of services that exist in Asian-American communities across the United States today.

Furthermore, discrimination may also influence an individual's ability to ward off racism. For example, a study by Soriano and Ramirez (1991) recently showed that Mexican Americans who are discriminated against in their jobs because of their ethnicity are more likely to score higher on depression and anxiety, and lower on self-esteem, psychological factors that may make it more likely that they will internalize racist messages.

Racism and discrimination have varied in intensity over the years. For example, there is currently a national hysteria over the presence of immigrants in the United States. This concern has focused historically on two groups: Latinos and Asians (Grossman, 1993), but most recently Black immigrants have also been targeted (e.g., at the time of this writing Haitians could not pursue claims for political asylum in the United States). Latino immigrants are accused of depleting the U.S. economy through educational and other public service costs. Historically, however, Asian Americans are one of the groups to have been legally prohibited from entering the United States (Chen, 1988). Only 3% of Americans are Asian in origin. This low percentage (reported by the 1990 Census) reflects more than 100 years of discriminatory exclusion of Asian immigrants from entering the United States. In 1882, Congress responded to an outbreak of anti-Asian violence by suspending the immigration of Chinese laborers. J. C. Ting, a law professor at Temple University in Pennsylvania and an assistant commissioner of U.S. Immigration and Naturalization Services from 1990 to 1993, stated: "It's no exaggeration to say that U.S. immigration law was created for, and still is based upon, the exclusion of Chinese immigrants" (Ting, 1993, p. C7).

During World War II, Japanese Americans were seen as war criminals and sent to concentration camps. Today, racism is expressed both toward Asian immigrants from poor countries who are thought to deplete economic and social resources in the United States and toward Asians as "model minorities" who are often seen as monopolizing business opportunities in communities where other ethnic minorities live. These anti-immigrant attitudes are promoting an increase and a solidification in anti-Latino, anti-Black, and anti-Asian sentiments, which affect all these ethnic minority group members, not just new immigrants.

Racism and its relation to violence is perhaps most evident in the history of Native Americans. Before Whites arrived in this country, the Native American population was estimated to be 5 million. It is estimated that the population of Native Americans and Alaskan Natives has shrunk to approximately 2 million (U.S. Bureau of the Census, 1991), in large part because of violence and oppression. And racism affected relationships in the families that did survive. Attneave (1982) described how, in working with families the 1950s, it was quite common to encounter parents who had never experienced family living during their school years because they had been shipped off to boarding schools in order to save them from the influence of their "pagan and savage" homes. It is also important to note that boarding schools were the first place that most Native Americans came in contact with corporal punishment of children, punishment that was often akin to physical abuse (Cross, 1987; May, 1987).

Institutionalized racism. It has been cogently argued that racism and discrimination are operationalized through social policies and structural opportunities in society and that these have set the stage for violence among oppressed people, both during colonization (Bulhan, 1985; Fanon, 1963, 1967; Memmi, 1967) and today (Bulhan, 1985; D. Hawkins, 1990; A. N. Wilson, 1990). As one form of racism, institutional racism has been a particularly pernicious element in the lives of ethnic minorities, limiting opportunities for youth to fulfill developmental tasks.

Although Hacker describes institutional racism directed against African Americans in the following passage, it is applicable to other people of color:

> American institutions begin with an initial bias against African American applicants, since the presumption is that most Blacks cannot or will not

meet the standards the organization has set. Historically , virtually all of the people associated with [institutions such as universities, airlines, and law enforcement] have been White, which has in turn created both the image of these institutions and the way they operate. In this sense they are White organizations, from which it follows that their members are expected to think and act in White ways. This is not as difficult for White people, although some have to make an extra effort if they wish to master class-based aspects of the manner and style. However, for Blacks the situation is qualitatively different since they see themselves as being judged by more coercive criteria, which call on them to deny large parts of themselves. (Hacker, 1992, p. 23)

For many ethnic minority youth, institutional racism is seen in their educational experiences, from day care to high school, and in the sparse and low-paying employment settings for youth without a college education. In these institutional settings, youth may have to deny large parts of themselves in order to survive, may internalize negative images of their group from the dominant society, and may fail to adopt an ethnic cultural identity. Each of these factors has been thought to make youth highly vulnerable for socialization toward violence (A. N. Wilson, 1990). This may be particularly true when ethnic minority members are not present among those who hold leadership positions. For example, racism may affect U.S. Latino youth significantly in school, where U.S. Latino teachers are few and therefore may be unavailable to mitigate racism's effect. De La Rosa and Maw (1990) report that U.S. Latino teachers represent only 2.9% of public and 2.8% of private-school teachers in this country.

Poverty and inequality. Poverty, not race or ethnicity, has been found to be the greatest predictor of violence (Centerwall, 1984; Sampson, 1993). As D. Hawkins (1990) emphasized, this fact must be considered in studying violence:

> Despite some findings to the contrary, a significant correlation has been shown to exist among societal inequality, discrimination, and homicide. . . . Deprivation, whether relative or absolute is linked to high rates of homicide. Among all groups in the United States regardless of race, homicide is found disproportionately among the lowest socioeconomic groups. (p. 160)

However, several researchers (D. Hawkins, 1990; Sampson, 1987, 1993) have suggested that the relationships between poverty, violence, and race are more complicated than they may seem. Poverty, meaning simply the lack of sufficient income, is not primarily implicated in violence (D. Hawkins, 1990). Rather, it is the absence of sufficient income to meet basic necessities in a given geographical context, compounded by inequity and lack of or limited access to needed resources because of discrimination and institutional racism, that may account for the increased violence among ethnic minority groups. Among African Americans, for example, Sampson (1993) concluded that the relationship between race and violence can be largely accounted for by the over-representation of variables such as segregation, family disruption and joblessness, social isolation, and sparse social networks, in addition to limited financial resources. (See chapters 4–7 for a detailed description of how each of the ethnic minority groups described here fares in relation to these social variables.)

McLoyd (1990) has presented an analytic model of how poverty affects African American children, which has implications for violence among these youth. According to her model, poverty influences children through its impact on the parents' behavior toward their children. Specifically, the psychological distress caused by poverty in urban settings is believed to diminish parents' capacity for supportive and consistent parenting and to increase their use of coercive methods. Coercive parenting behaviors, in turn, have been demonstrated to increase aggressive behavior in children (Eron, Walder, & Lefkowitz, 1971; Patterson, 1982).

Thus, the effect of poverty on violence is likely to be conditional on several other variables, from family systems to larger community settings. In these latter settings, a most notable effect is the rate of mobility and change within the context of neighborhoods. Sampson (1993) found that mobility was positively associated with violent crime rates in poor neighborhoods but not in more affluent areas. The conclusion of this study is that "communities characterized by rapid population turnover and high levels of poverty have significantly higher violent crime rates than mobile areas that are more affluent or poor areas that are stable" (Sampson, 1990, p. 6). Smith and Jarjoura (1988) also discovered a significant interaction between mobility and low income in explaining violence across 57 neighborhoods in three American cities.

The major factor implicated in mobility is the downward spiral that W. J. Wilson (1987) has described as causing a community to become increasingly "underclass." Wilson's examination of significant economic and social factors in the 1960s through the 1980s can help explain how such a downward spiral has played a role in the increase of youth violence in inner cities and metropolitan areas (Fingerhut et al., 1992).

According to W. J. Wilson (1987), the economy of this country during this time period dramatically shifted from manufacturing industries to service industries. Many manufacturing jobs were shipped out of the Northeast and Midwest cities to Asia where wages are lower. Factories all over the United States closed. This resulted in the substantial decline of traditional jobs in cities for individuals who had a high school education and for those who had not attained that educational level, which included members of many ethnic minority groups. As hundreds of thousands of factory jobs were demolished, many people of color were left without a viable way to earn a living, because the replacement jobs in the service industries generally required a higher level of skill and training than they had achieved (Prothrow-Stith, 1991).

At the same time that this was occurring, many in the middle class were moving out of the inner cities, leaving only the poorest of the poor in these areas, those too disenfranchised to be anywhere else (W. J. Wilson, 1987). As a result, communities were destabilized, social networks were fractured, critical institutions were closed, and organizing for political action abated. Moreover, the ethnic minority youth who remained were thus denied models of those who had successfully traversed the pathways to upward mobility. Together these occurrences left the inner cities, and many ethnic minority youth, vulnerable to the epidemic of violence and drug trafficking that would soon follow (W. J. Wilson, 1987).

This account of the downward spiral in inner cities and other metropolitan areas seems to offer an explanation, at least in part, of how ethnic minority youth from these communities have become increasingly vulnerable to violence because of larger societal changes. This kind of community change disrupts the economic pathways that lead these youth into the mainstream economy, instead leading to continued poverty, one of the most significant predictors of youth involvement in violence. One particular pathway to the mainstream economy is through the education and job structure, or status mobility system (Ogbu, 1983, 1988).

The status mobility system. The status mobility system in the United States is the way that youth develop pathways to America's social and economic resources. To say it more colloquially, it is the socially approved strategy for getting ahead.

Access to social and economic resources in this country are critical to defining one's worth and value and one's sense of "personhood." As Inkeles has insisted,

> full adult status in the U.S. and especially one's manhood is defined in terms of the ability to compete for and obtain a desirable job, to earn a reasonably good income, to manage one's affairs . . . and maintain a good and stable home and family. (cited in Ogbu, 1983, p. 173)

Furthermore, acquiring an education and a job are to some degree the basis for attaining a measure of personal power and control of one's life. Without such an education, job, and sufficient income, we believe that it is very difficult for any American to manage his or her own private affairs, participate effectively in politics, and establish and maintain a stable family life.

Ogbu (1983, 1988) has cogently argued that there are four major forces that account for the differential rates of success and failure of ethnic minority groups in navigating the status mobility system. First are the impact of structural inequities on shaping educational resources and the unequal power relationship that allows the dominant group to control minority access to jobs and schooling. Second is the introduction of a job ceiling for minorities that limits their occupational choice. Third is the response of parents to the effects of these systemic constraints and the means by which they socialize their children to negotiate the social mobility system. Finally, fourth is the extent to which some minorities respond to social inequity by developing what has been labeled an "oppositional social identity and an oppositional cultural frame of reference" (Fordham & Ogbu, 1986).

Bulhan (1985), drawing on the work of Fanon (1963), has argued that the expressions of violence among many disadvantaged youth are directly tied to their inability to navigate the status mobility system. A. N. Wilson (1990) has argued that violence among African American youth (and we would argue, other minority youth) is tied to vain attempts to achieve basic, positive human ends in an environment that does not support these efforts, which results in attempts to achieve them by negative means:

> It represents an often misguided furious struggle for self-affirmation by many African Americans while entangled in a White American-spun spider's web specifically designed and constructed to accomplish their disaffirmation. . . . For too many African American youth, being cut off from the paths to legitimate and self-determined personal accomplishment as a result of the underdeveloped power of the African American community, the violent subduing of others may often be their only significant achievement and 'claim to fame.' Their capacity to perpetrate violence is the great equalizer in a world characterized by great inequalities. (p. xvii)

The way in which a specific ethnic minority group enters this country may also influence the ability of youth to negotiate the status mobility system. Ogbu (1983) describes three categories of minorities in the United States: autonomous, immigrant, and involuntary. The autonomous minorities are minorities in number, but perhaps not in power (e.g., those coming to the United States with significant means and status). Immigrant minorities are those who come to the United States voluntarily with the intention of improving their social, economic, and possibly political status (e.g., some Latinos and Asians). Involuntary or caste-like minorities are those who have been incorporated into the United States through conquest or slavery. African Americans are an example of caste-like minorities, given their history of slavery and thereafter their relegation to menial occupational status (Fordham & Ogbu, 1986; Myrdal, 1944). Thus, the higher rate of homicide among African American youth, for example, cannot be explained without paying considerable attention to their ethnic group's historical legacy: their embeddedness and longevity in a system of structural inequities, their legislated inferiority, the inequity in major social institutions, and the discriminatory and ethnic bias that are associated with their African origins. Native Americans, characterized as "aliens in their own land" (LaFromboise, 1988) can also be considered caste-like minorities whose land, culture, and strengths have been systematically decimated throughout the history of their relations with those in the dominant culture. According to Fordham and Ogbu (1986), Native Americans were conquered and sent to live on reservations (Spicer, 1962) against their will. Mexican Americans in the Southwest were also conquered and displaced from power, and Mexicans who later immigrated to the United States were given the status of the conquered group and treated in the same manner (Acuna, 1972; Ogbu, 1978). Although Asian/Pacific Island Americans came to this country of their own volition, they still faced blatant discrimination. Such treatment was epitomized by the 1882 Chinese Exclusion Act and the internment of Japanese Americans during World War II (Chen, 1988).

The initial point of access to the status mobility system is schooling. Ogbu (1983) contends that conflicts between the mainstream culture and the cultures of certain minority groups, in combination with the results of structural inequity, negatively influence minority youth's attitudes toward education as well as their level of educational attainment. Without higher education or

skill-specific training, access to the other major component of the status mobility system—the job market—is seriously undermined.

Finally, skin color should be mentioned as it pertains to the status mobility system, particularly for African Americans and U.S. Latinos. Historically, the darker the complexion and the more ethnically distinct the facial
features, the more bias an individual may experience in their education and
the more limited their access to job opportunities may be in mainstream
America.

Developmental Mandates and Youth Violence

Another major consideration of youth involvement in violence is the degree to
which the psychological demands of normal developmental stages can be successfully addressed in prosocial ways.[4] For example, developmental theorists
(Erikson, 1968; Kagan & Coles, 1973) have included in the basic developmental tasks of adolescence the need to establish a sense of identity (including a
sexual identity) and to experiment and take risks in social situations. The
quest for a sense of personal self-efficacy, the push for individuation and separation from families of origin, and the need to be able to project a life for
themselves into the future are parts of this process. As formidable as these
tasks are for all youth, difficulties may be magnified for youth in inner cities.
For example, when parents of ethnic minority youth are oppressed by social
and economic circumstances (see McLoyd, 1990), they may be less able to
provide the structure that a teenager needs when he or she separates from
the family. Perhaps this is part of the reason that inner-city ethnic minority
youth are drawn to gangs. Gangs offer a sense of belonging and provide structure (e.g., rules and norms) as well as a sense of group and individual identity
(e.g., colors and rank). (See chapter 14 in this volume.)

Prothrow-Stith (1991) highlighted the importance of a sense of future for
adolescents and a sense of possibility in that future, noting that cognitive
development at this age allows youth to understand the relationship between
the present and the future. As she stated, "Having a future gives a teenager
reasons for trying and reasons for valuing his life" (p. 57). Unfortunately, cognitive development during adolescence does not always preclude youth from
having a child-like idea of death, of which finality is not always a part (Holinger et al., 1994). Activities that some youth in some inner-city gangs engage
in result in a decreased likelihood that they and those around them will project a life for themselves in the future, and these youth will tell you so in their
own words (Children's Express, 1993).

In terms of self-efficacy, experiences such as educational success, extra-
curricular activities, sports, and community projects become critical in build-

---

[4]Chapter 2 discussed family, school, and peer influences on developing youth and the propensity for violence. In this section, we focus more on how social risk factors may influence normal
adolescent development and lead to violence among ethnic minority youth.

ing a sense of competence that allows the youth to meet developmental challenges in the present and to have a sense of future mastery that is based on present accomplishments. These activities provide opportunities for young people to experience goal achievement and competence in social relationships (e.g., same- and other-sex peer groups) and in instrumental tasks that test their physical, emotional, sexual, and intellectual prowess. If such tasks are successfully accomplished in adolescence, the individual may be well on his or her way to young adulthood with the integrity and competence necessary to handle adult tasks in a productive and healthy manner.

Adolescence is also the time that disadvantaged ethnic minority youth are able to fully appreciate that, for many of them, developing a sense of self-efficacy is restricted by racism and discrimination, by poverty, and by the lack of relative power of their groups in American society. (Although anecdotal evidence suggests that this realization may occur at much younger ages for many inner-city youth.) Concurrently, these disadvantaged ethnic minority youth see other youth succeeding, attaining recognition, and obtaining material possessions. (Indeed, the mass media has helped to socialize all youth to think that they need certain material possessions to be successful in their own eyes and in the eyes of others, particularly their peers.)

To the extent that they are blocked from the social and economic pathways through which they could attain recognition and achieve success by the mainstream culture's standards, ethnic minority youth may also experience more frustration and anger than any adolescent would normally tolerate. These youth may then adopt a value system characterized by a sense of "instant being" and the acquisition of material symbols of success by any means necessary, rather than suffering the "agony" of a future in which social and economic resources seem unlikely to be open to them in the mainstream culture (Hill, 1994). The media further reinforces the view of violent crime as a means toward these ends by characterizing violence as a normative response when desires are thwarted or frustrated (see chapter 11).

For economically disadvantaged ethnic minority youth, the ability to use opportunities in their environment to achieve developmental goals is not only limited by lack of access, but also may be affected by unresolved conflicts of cultures. Boykin and his colleagues (Boykin, 1979; Boykin & Ellison, in press; Boykin & Toms, 1985) maintain that members of many ethnic minority groups have to negotiate three cultural realms: (a) the indigenous ethnic culture that embodies the cultural values from the original homeland, (b) the minority realm that embodies the elements of minority racial status, and (c) the mainstream culture. There may be conflicts between any of these three realms that affect the development of ethnic minority youth.

For example, failing to recognize and understand the conflicting demands of multiple cultural realms can result in continual conflicts between youth and social institutions (e.g., school and the workplace). In many groups, values such as communalism that are rewarded at home may be rejected or even punished by teachers in school (Boykin & Ellison, in press). As will be discussed later in this chapter, proactive socialization and bicultural competence may mitigate these effects.

Resiliency, Risk Factors, and Ethnic Culture

So far in this chapter we have focused mainly on risk factors that are likely to influence the relatively higher rate of violence among ethnic minority youth. However, it is equally, if not more, important to focus on resilience and related protective mechanisms that have the potential for ameliorating violence. In this section, we examine the values of ethnic group cultures as possible protective mechanisms against other risk factors for violence, including the ones described in this and other chapters of this book. One of our hypotheses is that proactive socialization in an intact ethnic culture and the achievement of bicultural competence are major protective mechanisms against violence among ethnic minority youth.

Resilience and Protective Mechanisms

According to Rutter (1990), "resilience is concerned with individual variations in response to risk factors" (1990, p. 183). Protective mechanisms, in his view, are "more specific and narrowly defined than that of resilience" (p. 184) and may serve to modify the individual's response to a particular risk factor.

Psychologists have now established protective mechanisms in the field of psychiatric risk research. These have included such buffers as secure and supportive personal relationships, task accomplishment, and opportunities that are available at critical turning points in people's lives (Rutter, 1990).

Werner and Smith (1977, 1982, 1992) have conducted some of the most notable studies on resilience, examining protective mechanisms in relation to biological and psychosocial risk factors in the development of the individuals. Their seminal studies found that about one third of "at-risk" individuals did not develop psychological or developmental problems despite facing such challenges as experiencing moderate to severe perinatal stress, living in chronic poverty, being reared by parents with little formal education, growing up in a disorganized family environment, and experiencing desertion or divorce and the effects of parental alcoholism or mental illness.

Although there have been several retrospective and prospective studies involving resilience (O'Connell, 1985; Tress, 1986; Viederman, 1979; Werner, 1988; Werner & Smith, 1982, 1992), none have specifically examined the role of ethnic culture in promoting resilience against risk factors for ethnic minority youth involvement in violence. Furthermore, we are aware of only a few studies that examine the values of specific ethnic cultures as serving as protective mechanisms against violence. Despite this current lack of substantial data, we believe that the values of ethnic cultures can indeed do just that. We hope that by sharing our speculations in this regard, we will promote research, theory development, and services that incorporate ethnic minority cultural values.

How Ethnic Culture Protects Against Violence

Ethnic culture serves as a potential protective mechanism in the face of risk factors for violence in several ways. First, ethnic cultures may bind groups together in the service of survival and protection from forces that would destabilize or destroy them (Nobles, 1991b; A. N. Wilson, 1990). For example, ethnic cultures may provide a set of norms and values that influence behavior and social interactions in the face of stress, provide a way of interpreting reality, and guide how adults socialize youth to overcome social and economic obstacles (Ogbu, 1985, 1991). These cultures may further provide a foundation from which parents can then socialize offspring to understand, interpret, and know how to achieve in the mainstream culture as well as in their own ethnic culture, to understand and work through racism, and to deal with the inherent conflicts between cultures, when such conflicts arise.

For example, it has been argued that ethnic culture shapes a positive sense of identity for both the group and the individual member (Helms, 1990; Spencer, 1989; A. N. Wilson, 1990). This positive self- and reference-group identity may help to counteract racist and other negative messages from the mainstream culture. Moreover, such a personal sense of ethnic identity may well be a critical component in mediating involvement in violence in the face of risk experiences (Bell & Jenkins, 1991) and reducing risk for other self-destructive behaviors (Holinger et al., 1994).

Several experts (J. D. Hawkins, Lishner, & Catalano, 1985; J. D. Hawkins & Weis, 1985) have suggested that a potentially protective force in socializing adolescents against delinquency, drugs, and violence is the development of bonds to traditional agents of socialization within the minority culture (both adults and institutions, e.g., church or other spiritual settings, school, and community agencies). Youth who have formed these bonds are more likely to be able to withstand the pull of juvenile delinquency, drug involvement, and violence (J. D. Hawkins et al., 1985; J. D. Hawkins & Weis, 1985).

These agents can guide adolescents' development and incorporate them as stakeholders in the community and the society. An example of research on violence that supports this argument is the longitudinal study of boys in New York state by Eron & Huesmann (1984), who found that church attendance in their communities was one of the primary variables that seemed to protect these youth against serious involvement in violence as older adolescents and young adults.

The absence of bonding with community agents as youth separate from their parents can result in the development of a sense of anomie and estrangement in which the adolescent essentially disconnects from all positive socializing elements. Calhoun (1991) warns that adolescents who do not see themselves as bonded to the social contract to which adult society subscribes will see no sense in adhering to it. In an effort to reconnect to some structure in which to achieve developmental tasks, the adolescent will be drawn to those forces in the community that fill this need, and these forces can either impede or promote aggression and violence.

How Proactive Socialization and Bicultural Competence Help Protect Ethnic Minority Youth Against Violence

Proactive socialization. Proactive socialization (Boykin & Ellison, in press; Spencer, 1985) is a process by which ethnic minority youth are consciously socialized to understand and become aware of the multiple demands and expectations of the several cultural realms in which they must operate. It is generally seen as a deliberate and active effort by the family and other systemic entities to strengthen pride in cultural identity and to facilitate biculturality. Its purpose is to integrate selected values of the ethnic culture and the mainstream culture, to fortify the youth, and to enhance his or her sense of personal and group identity.

Proactive socialization has the potential to protect ethnic minority children by providing a strengthened sense of identity that reflects the strengths of the ethnic culture (Bowman & Howard, 1985; Spencer, 1985, 1989) and helps to buffer their experience with racism. Some (Nobles, 1988, 1991b; Oliver, 1989) have argued that the goal of proactive socialization is to socialize the youth to a cultural ethos and value system that will be protective in the face of institutional and individual racism. This includes the active interpretation of subtle messages about the culture that young people receive both in the ethnic culture and from the mainstream. Although many U.S. Latino youth are aware of being stereotyped as gang members, many are unaware that their culture's contributions to the U.S. economy and to national security are substantial. For example, few youth know that U.S. Latinos earned more congressional medals of honor as servicemen during World War II and the Vietnam war than any other cultural group (Velez-Ibanez, in press). Few Americans know that the Choctaw Code Talkers in World War I and the Comanche and Navajo Code Talkers in World War II played a crucial role in winning these wars by developing a code that the enemies could not break (Hirschfelder & Kreipe de Montano, 1993; Weatherford, 1988).

Central to proactive socialization is the push to actively monitor, interpret, and above all to counter the powerful socialization effects of violence from television and other media. For example, helping youth identify with nonviolent leaders in their ethnic minority communities may help counteract the media influence of powerful models who glorify violence and become rich while doing so.

Proactive socialization can also enhance prosocial bonding to agents of socialization who can help youth to counter potential interpersonal violence in their peer groups (Oliver, 1989; A. N. Wilson, 1990). We also believe that proactive socialization may enable minority youth to develop pathways to achievement in the social and economic system of mainstream America through such activities as mentoring.

Bowman and Howard's (1985) study of the socialization practices among three generations of African American families supports the value of proactive socialization in the home. Their study revealed that those parents who practiced a more proactive style of socialization, in which children were made aware of the consequences of their ethnicity and the racial barriers present in society, produced more competent children and adults. According to Bowman and Howard, the parents of successful young people emphasized ethnic pride, self-development, awareness of racial barriers, and egalitarianism in their socialization practice. Although this study did not directly study violence and socialization practices, proactive socialization was found to be a significant factor in children's motivation, achievement, and prospects for upward mobility, factors which in themselves may have an effect on violence. Similarly, a study by Devarics (Holinger et al., 1994) showed that an Afrocentric curriculum resulted in an increase in grades and improved self-esteem among African American students.

Finally, we believe that the absence of proactive socialization may in itself be a risk factor for violence. The absence of such socialization can influence an over-identification with or a personalization of racist behavior and stereotypes, leading to increased violence toward members of one's own ethnic group as well as toward others (Bulhan, 1985; Fanon, 1963; A. N. Wilson, 1990).

For example, at their stage of cognitive and social development, adolescents may find it difficult to separate stereotypic racist responses from personal affronts (Spencer, 1985). Pierce (1970) described the onslaught of subtle insults faced by people of color on a daily basis in his theory of micro-insults. He held that the adolescent who is unable to filter out these stressors, internalizes and personalizes the messages and is vulnerable for acting out rage and anger rather than analyzing the broader picture. For example, consider the store merchant who follows an African American youth from the time he or she enters the store. The youth may not consider that this is stereotypical behavior and may instead take the behavior personally. As noted in chapter 2, such attributions play a large role in determining whether responses to such behavior become aggressive and violent.

Bicultural competence. LaFromboise, Coleman, and Gerton (1993) believe that contrary to models that posit negative effects as a result of an individual being bicultural, the ability of an ethnic minority individual to alternate between their ethnic culture and the mainstream culture in different social situations has positive effects. They cite research showing that individuals who can alternate between cultures may exhibit better cognitive functioning and mental health status than individuals who are monocultural, assimilated, or acculturated. Contemporary Native Americans living in cities seem to gravitate toward this method of alternation. Attneave (1982) described this bicultural view. The individual Native Americans she studied showed an openness to learning and using the tools of the White culture while also making a commitment to keep alive elements of their tribal identities (e.g., language, values, folkways).

LaFromboise, Coleman, and Gerton (1988) posit that the bicultural competence that is part of successful alternation is a result of "(a) knowledge of cultural beliefs and values, (b) positive attitudes toward both majority and minority groups, (c) bicultural efficacy, (d) communication ability, (e) role repertoire, and (f) a sense of being grounded" (p. 403). Proactive socialization, as we show later in this chapter, can certainly lead to these accomplishments.

Although no research has directly examined the relationship between violence and the ability to alternate between cultures, we believe that the connection has potential. For example, knowledge of ethnic cultural beliefs and values that eschew violence can reinforce those same values that may be present in systems that are part of the ethnic minority community (e.g., norms of reciprocity held by parents), thus counteracting other systems (e.g., gangs) that may pervert these values during a period of developmental vulnerability (i.e., adolescence). In this sense, proactive socialization and bicultural efficacy can be seen as empowering minority groups (LaFromboise, Trimble, & Mohatt, 1990) in situations in which they have been rendered relatively powerless by oppression and structural inequity.

Bicultural efficacy can enable an individual to take advantage of mainstream opportunities without compromising his or her sense of cultural identity, and this could lead individuals to overcome social conditions that are traditionally linked with violence (e.g., poverty in inner cities). This may help to mitigate the negative stereotype of the African American who, for example, is seen as achieving economic success in the mainstream only by "selling out." Such stereotypes leave African American youth in a double-bind when considering the value of achieving success in White-dominated institutions. If to be successful is to be economically successful, and the only way to be so without selling out appears to be to flaunt the law (e.g., drug trafficking), then the intergroup violence associated with such activities will be perhaps more "acceptable" and hence more likely to occur. A similar double-bind for Native American youth has been described by Attneave (1982) as the "bucket of crabs" phenomenon that occurs when other Native Americans attempt to "pull down" a peer who tries to climb out of poverty by gaining education and experience in the "White man's" world.

Moreover, by having a sense of "grounding" in their own ethnic culture, without having to eschew economic success in the mainstream culture, youth may be better able to envision a future for themselves that makes a violent end seem less inevitable.

All of this is not to say that by themselves, proactive socialization and bicultural competency will reduce violence among ethnic minority youth. Concurrently, minority and majority members of mainstream society's institutions must be able to value ethnic cultures and, more important, to change the structural inequities (e.g., poverty and unemployment) that are linked to violence among these groups. In fact, the next section of this chapter is devoted to outlining the values of ethnic cultures that have the potential to prevent and reduce violence among all youth.

Culture as a Protective Mechanism: Selected Values of Four Ethnic Cultures

In this section, we look at some of the primary values of four ethnic cultures: U.S. Latino, African American, Asian and Pacific Island American, and Native American.

Latino culture. G. Marin, B. V. Marin, and their colleagues in San Francisco have conducted a series of studies focusing on cultural characteristics of Latinos (cf., G. Marin & B. V. Marin, 1991). Their research has pointed to the existence of a core set of cultural values or scripts characterizing U.S. Latinos, regardless of subcultural membership, acculturation, or income level. These cultural values include the following: familism, allocentrism or collectivism, *respeto, simpatia*, and *personalismo*.

Familism places central importance on the family. For those who hold this value, the family comes before the individual. According to G. Marin and B. V. Marin (1991) familism refers to the sense of obligation to provide emotional and material support to the members of the nuclear and extended family, as well as a perception that relatives are both reliable providers of help and attitudinal and behavioral referents (Sabogal, G. Marin, Otero-Sabogal, B. V. Marin, & Perez-Stable, 1987).

Allocentrism or collectivism is a value whose adherents prefer to belong and work within groups. This value or orientation is the opposite of individualism (G. Marin & Triandis, 1985). As mentioned earlier, Markus and Kitayama (1991) suggested the importance of similar values that they called independent or interdependent construals of self to motivation, emotions, and cognitions.

Respeto—translated, respect—is a value placing great social value and conferring decision-making roles on authority figures, such as parents, elders, teachers, law enforcement personnel, and other government officials. It confers to such individuals ultimate decision-making roles. *Simpatia* is a cultural value that is antithetical to interpersonal conflict. It discourages individuals from engaging in interpersonal conflict. It places great value in keeping the peace at all cost. Assertiveness is antithetical to simpatia. *Personalismo* places great value in interpersonal relationships. Interpersonal relationships are more important than reputation or material gain. Those holding this value will not think twice about arriving late to an appointment if it means helping a friend or acquaintance in need.

Although these cultural values have not been directly studied as to their influence on violence,[5] several relationships suggest themselves both as protective and as risk factors. For example, familism is a cultural value that under normal circumstances would keep U.S. Latino youth from being unduly influenced by delinquent or violent youth groups, such as gangs. However, given family instability or dysfunctions, this same value can serve as a risk factor that draws them to youth groups, such as gangs, because gangs can serve as surrogate families (Soriano, et al., in press). Similarly, given the nature of youth groups, allocentrism or collectivism can serve either to help youths avoid the negative influences of delinquent or violent youth groups or to draw youths to them if they do not belong to a positive reference group.

Simpatia is expected to serve as a protective factor because it is antithetical to conflict and violence. Similarly, *respeto* is expected to be a resiliency factor because it places great importance on authority figures. However, given a lack of appropriate authority figures, *respeto* can conceivably confer authority status on delinquent or violent leaders. *Personalismo* can be seen as either a risk factor or a protective mechanism because it places great importance on interpersonal relationships, whether they are good or negative influences.

---

[5]However, some research is underway in other areas of risk to Latinos. B. Marin's (1991) research suggests that for U.S. Latinos, familism is a protective factor that helps them reduce their risk for such health hazards as HIV infection, AIDS, and cancer caused by tobacco use.

African American culture. Similarly, social scientists (Boykin, 1986; Boykin & Toms, 1985; Dixon, 1976; Hill, 1971, 1986; Nichols, 1991b; Nobles, 1974, 1976, 1985, 1991a; Sudarkasa, 1980) have pointed to several essential cultural values that, according to Hollins (cited in King, 1994) appear to transcend training and occupation. Several scholars (e.g., Dixon, 1976; Johnson, 1992; Nobles, 1991b), but most notably Nichols (1991a) have stressed that the basic cultural orientation of African Americans is more person-centered than object-centered. This suggests that the culture traditionally elevates individuals' relationships with each other over individuals' relationships with objects such as money and material possessions. However, youth who are able to depersonalize relationships and objectify other individuals may well be more vulnerable to involvement in violence (Garbarino, Kostelny, & Dubrow, 1991; Pynoos & Nader, 1990). Therefore, the proactive socialization of African American youth to the traditional person-to-person worldview (Nichols, 1991a) would seem to mitigate against such depersonalization and objectification and would strengthen relationship bonds.

The following are some of the core values of the African American culture (Boykin, 1986; Boykin & Ellison, in press; Boykin & Toms, 1985) that may protect against youth violence.

Harmony and interrelatedness are values that describe the connectedness of the individual to events in nature and elements of the universe. Those who hold these values believe in the "oneness of being" of all humanity (King, 1994) and underscore a respect for the sanctity of life.

Communalism relates to the interdependence of people. In communalism, one's identity is viewed as both personal and collective. It is the perception of self as part of a social order in which sharing resources and giving assistance to others is mutually beneficial to the well-being of the group. This value is best characterized by the African proverb that is popular among African Americans: "I am because we are, because we are, therefore I am" (Mbiti, 1970). Socialization to this value system would be the antithesis of violent actions designed to destroy the group or its members.

Mutuality and reciprocity describe a sense that the consequences of an individual's actions, whether positive or negative, will eventually be visited on that individual. This is reflected in the popular saying, "what goes around, comes around." Youth socialized to this value system learn that violence toward others does not end with them, but that the consequences are likely to be felt by the youth or his or her family.

Spirituality involves the acknowledgement of a higher power, a nonmaterial force that permeates all forms of life (Boykin & Ellison, in press). Youth whose lives are guided by such spirituality or belief in a higher power may hold human lives in high esteem and reject the taking of another's life.

Other cultural values of African Americans that may serve as protective mechanisms against youth involvement in violence include strong religious orientation (Boykin & Toms, 1985; Harvey, 1985; Herskovitz, 1941; Hill et al., 1989; Ladner, 1971; Lewis, 1975; Stack, 1974) and belief in a supreme power; church attendance (Eron & Huesmann, 1984); child-centeredness (i.e., emphasizing the importance of child–caretaker attachment and the safety and continuity of human life; Hill et al., 1989; Kenyatta, 1983; Nobles, 1974);

strong family orientation (Billingsley, 1968; Nobles, 1976); flexibility of roles among men and women (Hill, 1971; McAdoo, 1981); and strong work and achievement orientation (Hill, 1971).

Calhoun (1991) has suggested that engagement in interpersonal violence is supported by the ability of youth to disengage from traditional bonds to society, school, family, and peers, thus leading to anomie, the objectification and depersonalization of individuals. As youth are socialized toward traditional cultural values, a more cohesive relationship with others and a greater connectedness to the well-being of the group should result, thereby reducing interpersonal violence.

Asian and Pacific Island American culture. One of the strongest cultural factors among the Asian and the Pacific Island American cultures is the emphasis on pacificism, harmony in interpersonal relations, and humanism. An individual is connected in a sociocultural order through family, ancestors, clans, the universe, and/or the cosmic order. Within these cultures, discipline and impulse control are the cultural strategies for maintaining harmonious human relations. Asian and Pacific Island cultures place an emphasis on the ethical and rational behavior of the individual. A person's conduct is judged not by whether it is successful in achieving a particular end but by whether it is morally right or wrong.

The Asian cultural code, rooted in Confucianism, emphasizes interpersonal relationships based on the "social order" and its hierarchy of superior–inferior relationships (Fairbank, 1992). Parents are superior to children, men to women, ruler to subject. Individual behavior is guided by prescribed roles to play; therefore, one acts according to one's social responsibilities not according to the "rights" of an individual. In this code, shame and guilt are often used to restrain unruly behavior. Respect and "face saving" are more valued than material gains or physical pleasures.

The predominant cultural response of Asian and Pacific Island Americans in conflict situations is to maintain peace and restore social order. One of the duties for those in positions of power is to anticipate and defuse potential confrontation. Strategies used by the groups to resolve or short-circuit any open conflict include the use of indirect language, a middle person, face saving ploys, a long-range view, and mediation (Ho, 1990). Kurokawa (1969), Su (1969), and Niem and Collard (1972) have also noted that features of Asian cultures related to the inhibitions of exploratory, risk-taking, and aggressive behavior are rooted in the traditional practice of filial piety.

Native American culture. Of all the groups discussed in this chapter, the values of the Native American culture are perhaps the most complex and diverse, because they vary from group to group among over 505 federally recognized tribal entities and an additional 365 state-recognized tribes and bands (Thomason, 1991). This is further complicated by language differences, because over 200 tribal languages are still spoken today (LaFromboise, 1988). This diversity may have important implications for participation in violence. For example, tribes may differ in their historical emphasis on peace or war (H. C. Triandis, personal communication, February 23, 1993) and in the nature of their early contact with Europeans (Axtell, 1981). Both of these factors may influence attitudes toward violence among Native Americans today.

However, even considering this diversity, there are common world views that influence values that are found among most tribes (Trimble, 1981). These include harmony (Northwest Indian Child Welfare Institute [NICWI], 1986), respect (Lewis, 1984), noninterference (Goodtracks, 1973), generosity and reciprocity (NICWI, 1986), and noncompetition (Yates, 1987).

Primeaux (1977) described the world view of the Native American as one in which the "forces of good and evil are interwoven" (p. 55) and interact, and this interaction cannot be separated into physical, mental, or social problems. Instead, according to traditional Native American culture, each problem must be considered holistically. For example, an individual's problem is seen as rooted in the community (LaFromboise, 1988). Solutions to that problem must be collective involving both social and symbolic bonds to the community as well as the community's relation to the natural environment.

Lifestyle values that emanate from this world view can be seen as important in reducing violence. Traditionally, Native Americans have lived in relational networks that support and nurture bonds of mutual assistance and affection and emphasize the importance of interpersonal respect. They place a high value on the well-being of children. The early introduction of spiritual life to Native American children fosters a sense of respect for nature, interdependence and self-discipline. Autonomy within the context of community is highly valued among Native Americans, and for this reason children are expected to make their own decisions and operate semi-independently at an early age (LaFromboise & Low, 1989).

The high value that is traditionally placed on their community's culture, rather than on consumption of goods, is a source of strength, and this continues to the present day. For example, middle-class Native Americans often use their discretionary funds not for the purchase of material possessions, but instead for the opportunity to be involved in traditional ceremonial practices (Fixico, 1986).

Interdependence. Interdependence is a commonality among the four ethnic cultures. Of all the similarities among these groups and between these groups and the mainstream culture, the value of interdependence is most striking. As Markus and Kitayama (1991) have noted, the interdependent construal of self has many consequences. Some of these are quite pertinent to understanding violence among ethnic minority youth as well as its prevention and reduction. For example, they describe cultures with interdependent views as fostering an awareness of one's role vis-a-vis a group and attentiveness to the reactions of others in a particular context. This is as opposed to cultures with independent views that foster attention to one's internal attributes that are considered global rather than situation-specific. Behavior such as violence may involve dynamics that are misunderstood by those with an independent construal of themselves and the world. For example, the importance of "ingroups" and "out-groups" to those with interdependent or "collectivist" cultures (Triandis, 1989) may be underestimated by those of independent or "individualist" cultures. For example, conflicts between youth gangs of the same ethnicity may not be examined for the interdependent functioning of members within each gang, the strength of in-group loyalties, and how these affect cognition, emotion, and motivation that may lead to violence. Proposed descriptions of and solutions to the problem of youth gang violence by those with an independent construal of self may thus be missing important elements that could affect the success of their interventions (see chapter 14 on culturally sensitive gang programming).

This is, of course, only one example of how understanding the way that the self is construed in ethnic minority cultures is important to understanding violence among these youth. The reader is referred to Markus and Kitayama (1991) and Triandis (1989) to judge from general examples how these construals may affect cognition, emotion, and behavior to more specific examples in the field of violence and youth.

When Ethnic Culture Fails to Protect Against Risk Factors

We believe that the strengths of an ethnic culture can and have failed to protect against the social risk factors for youth violence in several ways. First, the social risk factors in the mainstream are often so overwhelming that they diminish or destroy cultural norms and values so that they become ineffective in the socialization process. Second, the ethnic culture may be in such conflict with the mainstream culture that youth get mixed messages as to their worth and value from both cultures. They may be unable to interpret such messages adequately and thus begin to personalize negative reactions and to develop what Fordham and Ogbu (1986) refer to as an "oppositional collectives or social identity and an oppositional cultural frame of reference" (p. 181). Third, culture fails to protect when there is substantial conflict between the mainstream and the ethnic cultures, and children are not proactively socialized or biculturally competent enough to deal with this conflict. In the absence of sufficient cultural socialization, youth may become vulnerable to the code of conduct of the streets or the value system of their adolescent peer group. Fourth, in an effort to adapt to structural inequality in the mainstream and to still achieve mandates for personal power and efficacy, cultures may adopt maladaptive behavioral patterns that are destructive to the individual and to the group (Oliver, 1989).

The following examples from the ethnic groups may illustrate these potential negative effects.

Acculturation. The process of acculturation (as opposed to alternation; LaFromboise, Coleman, & Gerton, 1993) by its very nature can produce substantial conflict between ethnic culture and that of the mainstream. This can be illustrated in the experience of both Native Americans and U.S. Latinos. As Native Americans have sought to assimilate further into the mainstream, they have experienced denigration of culture and, for some, the loss of traditional cultural supports (Baldwin, 1987). The research of Moore (1991) and Vigil (1988) on U.S. Latino gangs shows how acculturation may lead some youth to become more likely to engage in violence. Vigil (1979) has reported that within the barrio in the inner city, low-acculturated (Latino-oriented) youth are better adjusted compared with medium-acculturated youth because of strong family support. This suggests that as some U.S. Latino youth have become more acculturated, there is a potential conflict between the norms and values of the ethnic culture and that of the mainstream, in addition to blocked pathways to economic opportunities and fulfillment of developmental mandates.

Cultural conflict. The impact of cultural conflict and youth violence directed toward the self is dramatically revealed in the experience of many Native American youth who are adopted by White families. The rate of suicide among Native American youth is already three times that of the general population (Dizmang, Watson, May, & Bopp, 1974; however, the reader is cautioned that the rates of suicide among particular tribes differs dramatically). However, Native American youth who are adopted by White families are twice as likely to commit suicide during their teen years as Native American teens who are raised in their own families (La Fromboise & Low, 1989). Also, those youth from tribes considered traditional in maintaining the old ways are less likely to commit suicide than youth from transitional or acculturated tribes cultures (May, 1987).

Adaptation. Oliver (1989) has described the attempts African American males have made to adapt to the maladaptive conditions of racism and inequity in the mainstream culture. He has argued that in this process some African Americans have negated the ethnic culture's integrity in two ways. First, they have failed to adopt an Afrocentric cultural orientation. Second, they have tended, particularly those in lower-income groups, to tolerate the "tough guy" and the "player-of-women" images as acceptable alternatives to traditional definitions of manhood. Although this image was formed in lieu of being able to achieve the traditional markers of manhood in this country, namely a good job, social status, and the ability to provide for one's family, this style of behavior can place the individual at risk for interpersonal violence.

Disengagement. Ironically, many who participate in violent behavior have been exposed to cultural values that are opposed to violence and aggression. Bandura (1986, 1991) has held that violating internal self-regulatory principles (such as those based on cultural values) are possible through one of the following disengaging principles or methods: (a) moral justification or reconstruing conduct ("It's okay to hit him, because it will keep my friends from getting in trouble"), (b) euphemistic labeling or obscuring causal agency ("Teaching him a lesson was no big thing"), (c) advantageous comparison or disregarding or misrepresenting injurious consequences ("I only beat him up, I didn't kill him"), and (d) displacement of responsibility or blaming and devaluating victims ("It's his fault for provoking me").

Understanding such perplexing behavior requires a better understanding of the strength of social and internal regulatory mechanisms opposing violence compared with the environmental and external conditions facilitating it. It is contended that the accurate understanding of these mechanisms requires an understanding of ethnic minority cultures. Research is needed that allows for a better understanding of regulatory mechanisms and of the role that cultural values play in strengthening or weakening behavioral controls related to violence among youth.

Summary

In this chapter, we have focused on socioeconomic and ethnic cultural factors as they relate to violence among ethnic minority youth. We have cited the extant data, however sparse, that suggest a relationship between social and cultural risk factors and protective mechanisms influencing violence among youth in these groups.

The major thesis of this chapter is that the interplay of structural inequity, unfulfilled developmental needs, and the compromising of ethnic cultural protective mechanisms may best explain the disproportionate occurrence of violence among ethnic minority youth. The developmental mandates of all youth during adolescence are similar. But the resources for achieving developmental milestones are significantly fewer for economically disadvantaged ethnic minority youth, particularly in inner cities and particularly if they have not had the opportunity to internalize the values of their own ethnic culture that can protect against violence.

Maslow (1970) described a hierarchy of needs through which humans become self-actualized that is still relevant today. He suggested that all humans must satisfy, in sequence, each of a set of five needs in order to become fulfilled or to live up to their potential. These needs are physiological fulfillment, safety, love, esteem, and self-actualization. Maslow's hierarchy of needs serves to remind us that for any intervention or prevention effort to be successful, consideration needs to be given to such basic human needs as health, nutrition, shelter, sleep, love and esteem, elements that far too many ethnic minority youth and their families lack. In other words, it makes no sense to place all hope in such appealing programs as conflict resolution, literacy skill development, and social skill development, and so on, to reduce youth violence, if basic needs such as nutrition, health, and safety are not being met at the same time.

We have acknowledged the importance of smaller systems (e.g., individual, family, peer) in youth violence and look forward to a time when all systems, including culture, will be present in an overarching theory allowing the data from each to be integrated. Indeed, this chapter is an attempt to point out the sociocultural factors that must be considered when psychology and related disciplines attempt to understand, explain, and prevent youth violence.

Theorists, such as Bandura (1991), are beginning to appreciate the magnitude of the influence of these factors on the social learning process, as seen in the following prescription for theory:

> A comprehensive theory of social transmission must also explain what produces and sustains the values, standards and behavioral norms promulgated by the cultural institutions. . . . An interactional theory that treats

human development as a product of both familial and social system influences holds greater promise of furthering our understanding of the process than does a dichotomized view that pits one system against the other. This broader transmission model provides the vehicle for cultural evaluation and the transmission of cultural patterns both within generations and from one generation to the next. (Bandura, 1991, pp. 57–58)

Although the relationships we describe in this chapter need further empirical support, we and others (e.g., Prothrow-Smith, 1991) maintain that enough consensus exists to begin to act in useful ways. For example, there is enough knowledge to show that for them to be successful, intervention and prevention efforts must take into account the unique cultural characteristics of ethnic minority youths and of their developmental needs within the context of their particular socioeconomic environment. This clearly argues against some overarching intervention to influence all "ethnic minority problems" related to youth violence. One should not look for that "magic" or model program—even for a particular ethnic group. Instead, examining the unique needs and cultural characteristics of youth in particular targeted areas and taking each factor into account in program development seems to be the most promising way to reduce violence (Soriano, in press).

Recommendations for Future Research

1. Studies should be designed to investigate the interaction of social and cultural factors among U.S. Latinos, Native Americans, African Americans, and Asian/Pacific Island Americans.

There is a paucity of research on social and cultural factors and their relationship to youth violence among the ethnic groups discussed in this chapter (see also the lacuna on epidemiological research on these populations in the next section). In general, there was more information available to us about African Americans, but even that was sparse. Furthermore, with few exceptions, much of the research that does exist focuses on isolated social and cultural variables. In the future, there must be studies that integrate social and cultural factors and that help distinguish the impact of culture from the impact of socioeconomic forces.

Because of the impact of the social context on the understanding of violence among ethnic minority youth (Sampson, 1993), research must carefully examine contextual variables such as neighborhood organization, exposure to injuries, housing, health care, role of the school, and so on, in the lives of youth, and determine their interaction with other risk factors. For example, it is clear that ethnic minority youth are at greater risk for experiencing community violence because many of them live in low income urban areas. However, social scientists are beginning to understand how exposure to violence in these communities during childhood has an impact on later involvement with violence, either as victims, perpetrators, or witnesses.

We strongly suggest that future research efforts examine more closely the role of cultural values (Soriano, in press) and construals of self (Markus &

Kitayama, 1991) in social problem behaviors, such as violence. Some questions to be answered are: What are the specific values and lifestyles of the individual cultures that seem have the greatest impact on participation in violence? What are the collective and individual impacts of social systems, family networks, the school environment, and community organizations, and how do they serve as both risk and protective factors in the lives of these youth?

We acknowledge the difficulty in conceptualizing ethnic minority youth violence from a larger social and cultural perspective while attempting to understand individual, family, and peer influences on the four ethnic groups discussed in this chapter. We agree that expanded efforts are also needed in this area.

2. Theoretical models should be generated that integrate the multiple realms that have an impact on youth violence, which will then guide the development of the knowledge base.

It is critical that appropriate models are generated that integrate variables within the social context (e.g., family, school, peer) with individual psychological variables (e.g., temperament) and with the cultural and socioeconomic variables described in this chapter. Bandura's (1991) model has been offered as one example of such an integration.[6]

3. Multidisciplinary research endeavors should be developed among such disciplines as public health, sociology, anthropology, urban geography, and education. It is clear that the complexity of youth violence demands the integration of expertise in psychology with a range of other disciplines in order to address the interaction of social, contextual, and psychological variables. Interdisciplinary models that build on the expertise of psychology and these other relevant fields should guide research and program development.

4. Research should specifically examine the protective mechanisms against risk factors for violence among ethnic minority youth. Perhaps one of the most promising of future research directions is the application of conceptual and methodological designs, which have been developed in the investigation of protective mechanisms, to the study of youth violence. Rutter's (1990) ideas about research on individual and family protective factors that are involved in the development of emotional and behavioral disturbances in children could be helpful in designing research.

5. Studies should examine the impact of strengthening cultural identity as a preventive strategy and should operationalize the theoretical concepts of conflicting cultural demands. We have observed that proactive socialization to cultural norms and values and bicultural competence may strengthen the

---

[6]Bandura's (1986, 1991) model suggests the involvement of three constituent sources of influences on behavior all operating as interacting determinants of each other. These are behavior, cognition (and other individual factors), and environmental influences. Behavior is said to be regulated by a reciprocity of influence between cognition and self-sanctions, conduct, and a network of social influences. Dominant cultural values are an integral part of social and internal regulatory mechanisms. After standards and self-reactive functions are developed, behavior usually produces two sets of consequences: Self-evaluative reactions (guided by an internalized self-sanctions) and social effects assessment, including social pressure (e.g., social/peer pressure). These two consequences may operate as complementary or opposing influences or controls on behavior.

identity of youth in such a way as to be protective against involvement in violence. However, there is a critical need for empirical research both in evaluation of preventive programs and in more investigative studies to ascertain the efficacy of these concepts for violence prevention efforts.

Recommendations for Prevention and Treatment Interventions

Below we summarize our recommendations that address these multiple areas and are derived from the research and theory described in this chapter.

1. The systemic inequities that create the context for youth violence must be modified. At the program level, for example, psychologists must include interventions such as job training opportunities, academic support, and employment opportunities for pre-adolescents and adolescents in order to open up viable pathways toward mainstream social and economic opportunities. Prevention and treatment programs based on social learning and other viable models are not likely to succeed with disadvantaged ethnic minority youth unless inequities in education, employment, housing, and health care are concurrently addressed.

2. Proactive cultural socialization for ethnic minority children must be supported. We have chosen to conceptualize the role of ethnic culture in youth violence as primarily protective and have concluded that the consideration of cultural differences is critical in the control and reduction of violence. Proactive socialization to these cultures by parents, schools, and other community agencies should be supported. However, many parents will themselves need to be socialized to their ethnic culture in order to transmit it to their children. Programs in schools, churches, and community centers that support adult development should include cultural components to introduce parents to their history and culture and assist their efforts in proactive cultural socialization of their children.

In socializing ethnic minority children to their cultures, some cultural schools for Asian and Jewish children, which meet after the full day of school, should be strongly considered as models. In addition, the continued efforts in many school districts around the country (e.g., Washington, D.C. Public Schools) to develop culturally based educational programs should be supported. Native American educational models, such as those of the Navajos and Okawasannee-Mohawks should be considered as well.

3. Contextually focused intervention models that target the multiple environments in which youth operate must be developed. The complexity of the problem of youth involvement in violence necessitates that credible interventions in the future be comprehensive in terms of addressing multiple aspects of the child's functioning as well as the multiple levels of his or her social and cultural environment. In the past, one predominant focus of interventions has been cognitively based and directed at interpersonal problem-solving skills or the development of cognitive and interpersonal skills for conflict resolution. To date, most of these programs have been delivered to children in school (see chapters 15 and 16 in this volume).

In the future, however, it is crucial to expand the focus to the social, cultural, and related factors that have an impact on youth violence. It is necessary to carefully evaluate the existing program models, such as the rites of passage programs (Harvey, 1990; Warfield-Coppock, 1990) that are being used increasingly in the areas of drug prevention and juvenile delinquency. These programs are designed to provide a proactive cultural socialization, increase bonding to social networks, provide positive mentoring role models and relationships, and instill a specific value system for children who are in high-risk situations.

We recommend that all violence prevention programs have as their foundation the support of the family's ability to transmit culture and values. This includes strengthening the support system of families by involving extended family in prevention when these supports are available or helping families to develop supportive surrogate extended families when none exist.

4. Culturally appropriate comprehensive interventions for youth in the context of their norms and values should be developed. In the future, intervention will need to build on the cultural values and strengths of ethnic minority groups. Some examples of these values and strengths have been described for each minority group discussed in this chapter. Deciding how to design programs that are congruent with these and other values and strengths is crucial to successful violence prevention and intervention.

5. Prevention and other interventions must be developed along a continuum of care model within a developmental context. In this chapter, we focus on adolescents and some of their developmental needs, and the developmental needs of younger members of ethnic minority groups are no less important. For example, services on a comprehensive continuum of care would include services for youngsters at risk for involvement in violence because of being physically or sexually abused, witnessing violence in the home or in the community, or exhibiting aggressive behavioral problems in school. These services would differ, however, according to whether the youth were exposed to these risk factors during early childhood, latency, or the adolescent years.

The continuum of care in children's mental health is perhaps a promising model (Friedman & Stroul, 1986) to consider in undertaking the development of culturally appropriate violence prevention interventions for ethnic minority youth at various stages of development. This model directs the development of a range of services offered from early childhood through adolescence, centered on the youth in the context of the family, with interventions in settings ranging from home to community-based institutions to the school.

To provide a continuum of care, links between youth and their families and essential services (e.g., in mental health, social services, education) must be created and maintained. To carry out such interventions clearly requires cross-disciplinary collaboration, multiple areas of intervention, and a significant commitment of time and resources. In short, the very nature of violence among ethnic minority youth is not amenable to one-shot, single-target interventions conducted in one location and over a short period of time. If social science wishes to mitigate violence among youth, a long-term commitment to research and intervention is required.

References

Acuna, R. (1972). *Occupied America: The Chicano's struggle toward liberation*. New York: Harper & Row.

Attneave, C. (1982). American Indians and Alaska Native families: Emigrants in their own homeland. In M. McGoldrick, J. K. Pearce, & J. Giordano (Eds.), *Ethnicity and family therapy* (pp. 55–83). New York: Guilford Press.

Axtell, J. (1981). *The European and the Indian: Essays in the ethnohistory of colonial North America*. New York: Oxford University Press.

Baldwin, O. (1987, August). *Conflicts in values in intercultural and intergenerational relationships: How are they affecting our youth today*. Presentation given at Positive American Indian Development Center Conference, Madison, WI.

Bandura, A. (1986). *Social foundations of thought and action*. Englewood Cliffs, NJ: Prentice Hall.

Bandura, A. (1991). Social–cognitive theory of moral thought and action. In W. M. Kurtines & J. L. Gewirtz (Eds.), *Handbook of moral behavior and development. Volume 1: Theory* (pp. 45–103). Hillsdale, NJ: Erlbaum.

Bayton, J. A. (1941). The racial stereotypes of Negro college students. *Journal of Abnormal and Social Psychology*, January, 97–102.

Bell, C. C., & Jenkins, E. J. (1991). Traumatic stress in children. *Journal of Health Care for the Poor and Underserved, 1*(2), 175–189.

Betancourt, H., & Lopez, S. R. (1993). The study of culture, ethnicity, and race in American psychology. *American Psychologist, 48*, 629–637.

Billingsley, A. (1968). *Black families in White America*. Englewood Cliffs, NJ: Prentice Hall.

Bowman, P. J., & Howard, C. (1985). Race-related socialization, motivation, and academic achievement: A study of Black youths in three-generation families. *Journal of the American Academy of Child Psychiatry, 24*(2), 134–141.

Boykin, A. W. (1979). Psychological/behavioral verve: Some theoretical explorations and empirical manifestations. In A. W. Boykin, A. J. Franklin, & J. F. Yates (Eds.), *Research directions of Black psychologists*, 351–367), New York: Russell Sage Foundation.

Boykin, A. W. (1986). The triple quandary and the schooling of Afro American children. In U. Neisser (Ed.), *The school achievement of minority children* (pp. 57–92). Hillsdale, NJ: Erlbaum.

Boykin, A. W., & Toms, F. (1985). Black child socialization: A conceptual framework. In H. McAdoo and J. McAdoo (Eds.), *Black children* (pp. 33–51). Beverly Hills, CA: Sage.

Boykin, A. W., & Ellison, C. (in press). The multiple ecologies of Black youth socialization: An afrographic analysis. In R. Taylor (Ed.), *Black youth*. Newbury Park, CA: Sage.

Bulhan, Hussein A. (1985). *Frantz Fanon and the psychology of oppression*. New York: Plenum.

Calhoun, C. (1991). Indirect relationships and imagined communities: Large-scale social integration and the transformation of everyday life. In P. Bourdieu & J. S. Coleman (Eds.), *Social theory for a changing society* (pp. 95–130). Boulder: Westview Press.

Centerwall, B. S. (1984). Race, socioeconomic status, and domestic homicide, Atlanta, 1971–2. *American Journal of Public Health, 74*, 813–815.

Chandler, C. R. (1979). Traditionalism in a modern setting: A comparison of Anglo and Mexican American value orientations. *Human Organization, 38*(2), 153–159.

Chen, S. A. (1988). Chinese Americans: Their plights and challenges. *Community Psychologists, 21*(3), 36–37.

Children's Express. (1993). *Voices from the future: Our children tell us about violence in America*. New York: Crown.

Cross, T. (1987). Positive Indian parenting: Honoring our children by honoring our traditions. In *Conference Proceedings of the 5th Annual National American Indian Conference on Child Abuse and Neglect* (pp. 5–18). Norman, OK: American Indian Institute, University of Oklahoma.

De La Rosa, D., & Maw, C. E. (1990). *Hispanic education: A statistical portrait 1990*. Washington, DC: National Council of La Raza.

Dixon, V. (1976). World views and research methodology. In L. S. King et al. (Eds.), *African philosophy: Assumptions and paradigms for research on Black persons*. Los Angeles: Fanon Research and Development Center.

Dizmang, L. D., Watson, J., May, P. A., & Bopp, I. (1974). Adolescent suicide at an Indian reservation. *American Journal of Orthopsychiatry, 44*, 43–49.

Dollard, J., Doob, L. W., Miller, M. E., Mowrer, O. H., & Sears, R. R. (1939). *Frustration and aggression*. New Haven: Yale University Press.

Erikson, E. (1968). *Identity: Youth and crisis*. New York: Norton.

Eron, L. D., & Huesmann, L. R. (1984). The relation of prosocial behavior to the development of aggression and psychopathology. *Aggressive Behavior, 10*, 243–253.

Eron, L. D., Walder, L. O., & Lefkowitz, M. M. (1971). *Learning of aggression in children*. Boston: Little, Brown.

Fairbank, J. (1992). *China: A new history*. Cambridge, MA: Harvard University Press.

Fanon, F. (1963). *The wretched of the earth*. New York: Grove Press.

Fanon, F. (1967). *Black skin, white mask*. New York: Grove Press.

Fingerhut, L., Ingram, D., & Feldman, J. (1992). Firearm and nonfirearm homicide among persons 15 through 19 years of age. *Journal of the American Medical Association, 267*, 3048–3053.

Fixico, M. (1986). The road to middle class Indian America. In C. E. Trafzer (Ed.), *American Indian identity: Today's changing perspectives* (pp. 29–37). Sacramento, CA: Sierra Oaks.

Fordham, S., & Ogbu, J. (1986). Black students' school success: Coping with the "burden of acting White." *Urban Review, 18*(3) 176–206.

Friedman, R. M., & Stroul, B. A. (1986). *A system of care for severely emotionally disturbed children and youth*. Rockville, MD: National Institute of Mental Health, Child and Adolescent Service System Program.

Garbarino, J., Kostelny, K., & Dubrow, N. (1991). What children can tell us about living in danger. *American Psychologist, 46*, 376–383.

Goodtracks, J. C. (1973). Native American non-interference. *Social Work, 18*, 30–34.

Grossman, D. (1993). Defining populations and terms. In D. R. Atkinson, G. Morten, & D. W. Sue (Eds.), *Counseling American minorities: A cross-cultural perspective* (pp. 3–17). Dubuque, IA: William C. Brown.

Hacker, A. (1992). *Two nations: Black, white, separate and unequal*. New York: Scribner.

Harries, K. D. (1990). *Serious violence: Patterns of homicide and assault in America*. Springfield, IL: Charles C Thomas.

Harvey, A. R. (Ed.). (1985). *The Black family: An Afrocentric perspective*. New York: Commission for Racial Justice, United Church of Christ.

Harvey, A. R. (1990). *The rites of passage*. Washington, DC: Maat Institute.

Hawkins, D. (1990). Explaining the black homicide rate. *Journal of Interpersonal Violence, 5*(2), 151–163.

Hawkins, J. D., Lishner, D., & Catalano, R. R., Jr. (1985). Childhood predictors and the prevention of adolescent substance abuse. In C. L. R. Jones, & R. J. Battjes (Eds.), *Etiology of drug abuse*. (NIDA Drug Research Monograph, No. 56). Rockville, MD: National Institute of Drug Abuse.

Hawkins, J. D., & Weis, J. F. (1985). The social development model: An integrated approach to delinquency prevention. *Journal of Primary Prevention, 6*(2), 73–97.

Heller, C. S. (1966). *Mexican American youth: Forgotten youth at the crossroads*. New York: Random House.

Helms, J. E. (1990). *Black and white racial identity: Theory research and practice*. New York: Greenwood Press.

Herskovitz, M. J. (1941). *The myth of the Negro past*. Boston: Beacon Press.

Hill, H. M. (1994, April). *The role of developmental mandates of adolescents in understanding youth violence: Instant being versus the agony of becoming*. Paper presented at the Leadership Washington Conference on Violence, Washington, DC.

Hill, R. (1971). *The strengths of Black families*. New York: Emerson Hall.

Hill, R. (1986). *The Black middle class: Past, present, and future in the state of Black America*. New York: National Urban League.

Hill, R., Billingsley, A., Ingraham, E., Malson. M., Ruben, Stack, C., Stewart, J. B., & Teele, J. (1989). *Research on the African-American family: A holistic assessment of the status of African-Americans* (Vol. 2). Boston: William Monroe Trotter Institute of the University of Massachusetts at Boston.

Hirschfelder, A., & Kreipe de Montano, M. (1993). *The Native American almanac: A portrait of Native America today.* New York: Prentice Hall.

Ho, C. (1990). An analysis of domestic violence in Asian American communities. *Women and Therapy, 9*(1– 2), 129–150.

Holinger, P. C., Offer, D., Barter, J. T., & Bell, C. C. (1994). *Suicide and homicide among adolescents.* New York: Guilford Press.

Johnson, S. T. (1992). Extra-school factors in achievement, attainment, and aspiration among junior and senior high-school-age African American youth. *Journal of Negro Education, 61,* 99–119.

Jones, A. (1994). *Next time she'll be dead: Battering and how to stop it.* Boston: Beacon Press.

Jones, J. M. (1972). *Prejudice and racism.* Reading, MA: Addison Wesley.

Jones, R. (1991). *Black psychology* (3rd ed.). Berkeley, CA: Cobb & Henry.

Kagan, J., & Coles, R. (1973). *Twelve to sixteen: Early adolescence.* Boston: Houghton Mifflin.

Katz, D., & Braly, K. (1933, Oct./Dec.). Racial stereotypes of one hundred college students. *Journal of Abnormal and Social Psychology,* 280–290.

Kenyatta, M. (1983, March). In defense of the Black family: The impact of racism on the family as a support system. *Monthly Review,* pp. 12–21.

King, J. E. (1994). The purpose of schooling for African American children: Including cultural knowledge. In R. Rossi (Ed.), *Schools and students at risk: Context and framework for positive change.* New York: Teachers College Press.

Kitano, H. H. L. (1969). *Japanese Americans: The evolution of a subculture.* Englewood Cliffs, NJ: Prentice Hall.

Krebs, D. L., & Miller, D. T. (1985). Altruism and aggression. In G. Lindzey & E. Aronson (Eds.), *Handbook of social psychology* (Vol. 2, pp. 1–72). New York: Random House.

Kurokawa, M. (1969). Acculturation and childhood accidents among Chinese and Japanese Americans. *Genetic Psychology Monographs, 79,* 89–159.

Ladner, J. (1971). *Tomorrow's tomorrow: The Black woman.* New York: Doubleday.

LaFromboise, T. D. (1988). American Indian mental health policy. *American Psychologist, 43,* 388–397.

LaFromboise, T. D., Coleman, H. L. K, & Gerton, J. (1993). Psychological impact of biculturalism: Evidence and theory. *Psychological Bulletin, 114,* 395–412.

LaFromboise, T. D., & Low, K. G. (1989). American Indian children and adolescents. In J. T. Gibbs & L. N. Huang (Eds.), *Children of color: Psychological interventions with minority youth* (pp. 114–147). San Francisco: Jossey-Bass.

LaFromboise, T. D., Trimble, J. E., & Mohatt, G. V. (1990). Counseling intervention and American Indian tradition: An integrative approach. *Counseling Psychologist, 18*(4), 628–654.

Lee, Y-T. (1994). Why does American psychology have cultural limitations. *American Psychologist, 49,* 524.

Lewis, D. K. (1975). The Black family: Socialization and sex roles. *Phylon, 38,* 221–237.

Lewis, R. (1984). The strengths of Indian families. *Protecting our children: Conference proceedings of the 2nd Annual National American Indian Conference on Child Abuse and Neglect* (pp. 9–17). Tulsa, Oklahoma: American Indian Institute, University of Oklahoma.

Marin, B. V. (1991). *Hagalo hoy por su lalud y su familia* [Do it for yourself and for your family]. Smoking cessation guide. National Cancer Institute. Washington, DC: U.S. Government Printing Office.

Marin, G., & Marin, B. V. (1991). *Research with Hispanic populations.* Newbury Park, CA: Sage.

Marin, G., & Triandis, H. C. (1985). Allocentrism as an important characteristic of the behavior of Latin Americans and Hispanics. In R. Diaz-Guerrero (Ed.), *Cross-cultural and national studies in social psychology* (pp. 85–1040). Amsterdam: Elsevier.

Markus, H. (1977). Self-schemes and processing information about the self. *Journal of Personality and Social Psychology, 35,* 63–78.

Markus, H. R., & Kitayama, S. (1991). Culture and the self: Implications for cognition, emotion, and motivation. *Psychological Review, 98*(2), 224–253.

Maslow, A. H. (1970). *Motivation and personality* (2nd ed.). New York: Harper & Row.

May, P. (1987). Suicide and self-destruction among American Indian youths. *American Indian and Alaska Native Mental Health Research, 1,* 52–69.

Mbiti, J. S. (1970). *African religions and philosophies.* Garden City, NY: Anchor Books.

McAdoo, H. P. (1981). *Black families*. Beverly Hills, CA: Sage.

McGoldrick, M., Pearce, J., & Giordano, J. (Eds.). (1982). *Ethnicity and family therapy*. New York: Guilford Press.

McLoyd, V. C. (1990). The impact of economic hardship on Black families and children: Psychological distress, parenting, and socioemotional development. *Child Development, 61,* 311–346.

Memmi, A. (1967). *The colonizer and the colonized*. Boston, MA: Beacon Press.

Miller, N. E. (1941). The frustration-aggression hypothesis. *Psychological Review, 48,* 337–342.

Mirande, A. (1977). The Chicano family: A reanalysis of conflicting views. *Journal of Marriage and the Family, 39,* 747–756.

Moore, J. W. (1991). *Going down to the barrio*. Philadelphia, PA: Temple University Press.

Montiel, M. (1970). The social science myth of the Mexican American family. *El Grito: A Journal of Contemporary Mexican American Thought, 3,* 56–63.

Myrdal, G. (1944). *An American dilemma: The negro problem and modern democracy* (Vol. 1). New York: Harper.

Nichols, E. J. (1991a). *Cross-cultural man in multi-ethnic society*. Unpublished manuscript.

Nichols, E. J. (1991b). Cultural foundations for teaching African American children. In J. Ratteray (Ed.), *Teaching mathematics*. Washington, DC: Institute for Independent Education.

Niem, T. I., & Collard, R. R. (1972). Parental discipline of aggressive behavior and four-year-old Chinese and American children. *Proceedings of the 80th Annual Convention of the American Psychological Association, 7,* 95–96.

Nobles, W. (1974). W. African roots and American fruit: The Black family. *The Journal of Social and Behavioral Sciences, 20,* 66–77.

Nobles, W. (1976). *A formulative and empirical study of Black families. Final report*. Washington, DC: U.S. Office of Child Development.

Nobles, W. (1985). Black family life: A theoretical and policy implications literature review. In A. R. Harvey (Ed.), *The Black family: An afrocentric perspective* (pp. 23–89). New York: Congress for Racial Justice, United Church of Christ.

Nobles, W. (1988). *African philosophy and psychology*. San Francisco: Black Family Institute.

Nobles, W. (1991a). Extended self: Rethinking the so-called Negro self-concept. In R. J. Jones (Ed.), *Black psychology*. (3rd ed., pp. 295–304). Berkeley, CA: Cobb & Henry.

Nobles, W. (1991b). W. African philosophy: Foundations for Black psychology. In R. Jones (Ed.), *Black psychology* (3rd ed., pp. 47–63). Berkeley, CA: Cobb & Henry.

Northwest Indian Child Welfare Institute. (1986). *Positive Indian parenting: Honoring our children by honoring our traditions*. Portland, OR: Author.

O'Connell Higgins, R. (1985). *Psychological resilience and the capacity for intimacy: How the wounded might "love well."* Unpublished doctoral dissertation, Harvard University, Cambridge, MA.

Ogbu, J. U. (1978). *Minority education and caste: The American system in cross cultural perspective*. San Diego, CA: Academic Press.

Ogbu, J. U. (1983). Minority status and schooling in plural societies. *Comparative Education Review, 27*(2), 168–190.

Ogbu, J. U. (1985). A cultural ecology of competence among inner-city Blacks. In M. Spencer, G. K. Brookins, & W. R. Allen (Eds.), *Beginnings: The social and affective development of black children* (pp. 45–66). Hillsdale, NJ: Erlbaum.

Ogbu, J. U. (1988). Cultural diversity and human development. *New Directions for Child Development, 42,* 11–28.

Ogbu, J. U. (1991). Minority coping responses and school experience. *Journal of Psychohistory, 18*(4), 433–456.

Oliver, W. (1989). Sexual conquest and patterns of Black-on-Black violence: A structural–cultural perspective. *Violence and Victims, 4,* 257–271.

Patterson, G. R. (1982). *Coercive family processes*. Eugene, OR: Castilia Press.

Pedersen, P. (1991). Multiculturalism as a generic approach to counseling. *Journal of Counseling and Development, 70,* 6–12.

Pierce, C. M. (1970). Offense mechanisms. In F. Barbour (Ed.), *The Black 70s*. Boston: Porter Sargent.

Pinderhughes, E. (1989). *Understanding race, ethnicity, and power, the key to efficacy in clinical practice*. New York: Free Press.

Price-Williams, D. R. (1985). Cultural psychology. In G. Lindzey & E. Aronson (Eds.), *Handbook of social psychology,* 993–1042.

Primeaux, M. H. (1977). American Indian health care practices: A cross-cultural perspective. *Nursing Clinics of North America, 12,* 55–65.

Prothrow-Stith, D. (1991). *Deadly consequences.* New York: HarperCollins.

Pynoos, R. S., & Nader, K. (1990). Children's exposure to violence and traumatic death. *Psychiatric Annals, 20,* 334–344.

Ramirez, M., & Arce, C. H. (1981). The contemporary Chicano family: An empirically based review. In A. Baron, Jr. (Ed.), *Explorations in Chicano psychology* (pp. 3–28). New York: Praeger.

Ramirez, M., & Castaneda, A. (1974). *Cultural democracy, bicognitive development and education.* San Diego, CA: Academic Press.

Reid, P. T. (1994). The real problem in the study of culture. *American Psychologist, 49,* 524–525.

Romano, O. I. (1973). The anthropology and sociology of Mexican American history. *Voices: A Journal of Contemporary Mexican American Thought,* 43–56.

Roper, W. L. (1991). The prevention of minority youth violence must begin despite risks and imperfect understanding. *Journal of the U.S. Public Health Service, 106,* 229–231.

Rose, H. M. (1978). The geography of despair. *Annals of the Association of American Geographers, 68,* 453–464.

Rudoff, A. (1971). Criminology: The incarcerated Mexican-American delinquent. *The Journal of Criminal Law, Criminology and Police Science, 62*(2), 224–238.

Rutter, M. (1990). Psychosocial resilience and protective mechanisms. In J. E. Rolf, A. S. Masten, D. Cicchetti, K. H. Nuechterlein, & S. Weintraub (Eds.), *Risk and protective factors in the development of psychopathology* (pp. 181–214). Cambridge, England: Cambridge University Press.

Sabogal, F., Marin, G., Otero-Sabogal, R., Marin, B. V., & Perez-Stable, E. (1987). Hispanic familism and acculturation: What changes and what doesn't? *Hispanic Journal of Behavioral Sciences, 9,* 397–412.

Sampson, R. J. (1985). Neighborhood and crime: The structural determinants of personal victimization. *Journal of Research in Crime and Delinquency, 22,* 7–40.

Sampson, R. J. (1987). Urban black violence: The effect of male joblessness and family disruption. *American Journal of Sociology, 93,* 348–382.

Sampson, R. J. (1990). *The community context of violent victimization and offending.* Paper prepared for the 1990 annual meeting of the American Sociological Association, Washington, DC.

Sampson, R. J. (1993). *The community context of violent crime.* In W. J. Wilson (Ed.), Sociology and the public agency (pp. 259–286). Newbury Park, CA: Sage.

Sampson, R. J., & Lauritsen (1994). Violent victimization and offending: Individual situational, and community-level risk factors. In A. T. Reiss, Jr., & J. Roth (Eds.), *Understanding and preventing violence: Social influences* (Vol. 3, pp. 1–114). Washington, DC: National Academy Press.

Smith, D. R., & Jarjoura, G. R. (1988). Social structure and criminal victimization. *Journal of Research in Crime and Work in the Inner City.* Ithaca, NY: Cornell University Press.

Soriano, F. I. (1994). The Latino perspective: A sociocultural portrait. In J. U. Gordon (Ed.), *Managing multiculturalism in substance abuse services* (pp. 117–147). Newbury Park, CA: Sage.

Soriano, F. I. (in press). *Conducting needs assessments: A multidisciplinary approach.* Newbury Park, CA: Sage.

Soriano, F. I., LaVoie, L. L. M., Perez, V., Rowland, D., Silva, E., & Navarro, M. (in press). Psychosocial, familial, and cultural factors in gang membership and violence. In M. Sotomayor (Ed.), *Latino families: Intergenerational issues.* Milwaukee, WI: Family Service America.

Soriano, F. I., & Ramirez, A. (1991). Unequal employment status and ethnicity: Further analysis of the USPI-ESPI Model. *Hispanic Journal for the Behavioral Sciences, 13*(4), 391–400.

Spencer, M. B. (1985). Black children's race awareness, racial attitudes, and self-concept: A reinterpretation. *Annual Progress in Child Psychiatry and Child Development,* 616–630.

Spencer, M. B. (1989). Cultural cognition and social cognition as identity correlates of Black children's person–social development. In M. B. Spencer, G. K. Brookins, & W. R. Allen (Eds.), *The social and affective development of Black children.* Hillsdale, NJ: Erlbaum.

Spicer, Edward H. (1962). *Cycles of conquest: The impact of Spain, Mexico & the United States on Indians of the Southwest, 1533–1960.* Tucson: University of Arizona Press.

Stack, C. (1974). *All our kind: Strategies for survival in a Black community*. New York: Harper & Row.

Su, C. W. (1969). A study of aggressive behavior in preschool children, *Psychology and Education, 3*, 11–28. (Available from Taiwan Normal University in Chinese only.)

Sudarkasa, N. (1980, November/December). African and Afro-American family structure: A comparison. *The Black Scholar, 11*(8), 37–60.

Sue, S., & Wagner, N. (Eds.) (1973). *Asian Americans: Psychological perspectives*. Palo Alto, CA: Science and Behavior Books.

Ting, J. C. (1993, July 12). Other than a Chinaman. *Washington Post*, p. C7.

Tress, W. (1986). *Das Raetsel der seelischen Gesundheit: Traumatische Kindheit und fruehe Schutz gegen psychogene Stoerungen* [The puzzle of spiritual health: Traumatic childhood and early protection against psychological disturbance]. Verlag fuer medizinische Psychologie im Verlag Vandenhoeck und Ruprecht.

Thomason, T. C. (1991). Counseling Native Americans: An introduction for non-native American counselors. *Journal of Counseling and Development, 69*, 321–327.

Triandis, H. C. (1971). *Attitudes and attitude change*. New York: Wiley.

Triandis, H. C. (1987). Some major dimensions of cultural variation in client populations. In P. Pedersen (Ed.), *Handbook of cross-cultural counseling and therapy* (pp. 21-28). New York: Praeger.

Triandis, H. C. (1989). The self and social behavior in differing cultural contexts. *Psychological Review, 96*, 506–520.

Trimble, J. E. (1977). The sojourner in the American Indian community: Methodological issues and concerns. *Journal of Social Issues, 33*, 159–174.

Trimble, J. E. (1981). Value differentials and their importance in counseling American Indians. In P. Pedersen, J. Draguns, W. Lonner, & J. Trimble (Eds.), *Counseling across cultures* (pp. 203–226). Honolulu: University Press of Hawaii.

Trujillo, L. D. (1974). La evolucion del "bandido" al "pachuco": A critical examination and evaluation of criminological literature on Chicanos. *Issues in Criminology, 9*, 43–67.

U.S. Department of Justice. (1991a). *Criminal victimization 1990: A national crime victimization survey report*. Washington, DC: Bureau of Justice Statistics.

U.S. Department of Justice. (1991b). *Violent crime in the United States*. Washington, DC: Bureau of Justice Statistics.

Velez-Ibanez, C. (in press). *Many visions of one world: An anthropology of U.S. Mexicans of the Southwest*. Tucson: University of Arizona Press.

Viederman, M. (1979). Monica: A 25–year longitudinal study of the consequences of trauma in infancy. *Journal of the American Psychoanalytic Association, 27*, 107–126.

Vigil, D. (1979). Adaptation strategies and cultural life styles of Mexican-American adolescents. *Hispanic Journal of Behavioral Science, 1*, 375–392.

Vigil, J. D. (1988). *Barrio gangs: Street life and identity in Southern California*. Austin: University of Texas Press.

Warfield-Coppock, N. (1990). *Afrocentric theory and applications. Volume I: Adolescent rites of passage*. Washington, DC: Baobab Associates.

Weatherford, J. (1988). *Indian givers: How the Indians of the Americas transformed the world*. New York: Fawcett Columbine.

Werner, E. E. (1988). Vulnerability and resiliency: A longitudinal study of Asian Americans from birth to age 30. In *Proceedings of the 9th Biennial Meeting of the International Society for the Study of Behavioral Development, Tokyo* (pp. 143–152). Tokyo: International Society for the Study of Behavioral Development.

Werner, E. E., & Smith, R. S. (1977). *Kauai's children come of age*. Honolulu: University of Hawaii Press.

Werner, E. E., & Smith, R. S. (1982). *Vulnerable but invincible: A longitudinal study of resilient children and youth*. New York: McGraw-Hill.

Werner, E. E., & Smith, R. S. (1992). *Overcoming the odds: High risk children from birth to adulthood*. Ithaca, NY: Cornell University Press.

Wilson, A. N. (1990). *Black-on-black violence*. Afrikan World: Info Systems.

Wilson, W. J. (1987). *The truly disadvantaged*. Chicago: University of Chicago Press.

Wolfgang, M., & Ferracutti, F. (1967). *The subculture of violence*. London: Tavistock.

U.S. Bureau of the Census. (1991). *Population profile of the United States: 1991*. (Current Population Reports, Series P-23, No. 173). Washington, DC: U.S. Government Printing Office.

Yates, A. (1987). Current status and future directions of research on the American Indian child. *American Journal of Psychiatry, 144*, 1135–1142.

Part II

Experience of Violence:
Ethnic Groups

Introduction

Epidemiological information is critical in designing the most useful prevention and intervention programs to reduce violence among youth. Together with clinical and experimental data, epidemiological information is also crucial in enhancing research and policy development. For example, epidemiological data have confirmed that ethnic minority youth, particularly males, are the group at highest risk for homicide, the ultimate expression of violence. The 1990 homicide rate for non-White males aged 15–24 was more than seven times the rate for White males of the same age (Holinger, Offer, Barter, & Bell, 1994). Such data invite researchers, policymakers, and practitioners to focus their attention in areas in which the potential payoffs in terms of human lives are the greatest.

The factors contributing to the high risk for violence among young ethnic minority group members operate in a complex and imperfectly understood interplay between social, economic, cultural, institutional, and interpersonal influences, and ethnic minority status. For example, poverty may combine with community disorganization, joblessness, and interpersonal problems in families of many ethnic minority groups. Thus, ethnicity in and of itself should not be considered a causal or risk factor for violence (see chapter 3 in this book). Epidemiological data about these influences are also crucial in efforts to reduce violence among ethnic minority youth.[1]

Included in this section of the book are separate chapters on the experience of violence among African Americans, U.S. Latinos, Native Americans, and Asian/Pacific Islander Americans. Each of the chapters describes the population and its subgroups; outlines what is known about the extent, nature, and characteristics of risk for violence among the group's members; describes some psychological and help-seeking responses to victimization; and generates recommendations for future research, service, and policymaking.

Although the chapters in this section do not address the experience of the youth members of the majority population who are also at risk for violence (e.g., White youth living in poverty and or in inner cities), the needs of these

---

[1]For example, in line with epidemiological factors such as these, Hammond and Yung (1993) suggested that violence prevention programing needs to take into account geographic, financial, and attitudinal barriers that other health-related programs have already identified in planning the location of interventive efforts.

youth must not be ignored in policy or intervention strategies to reduce violence. It should also be noted that the chapters in this section do not focus primarily on female youth (see chapters 9 and 16 in this book), because male youth far outnumber female youth with regard to being victims of nonsexual violence, such as homicide (Holinger et al., 1994). Again, female ethnic minority group members should not be disregarded when strategizing research, policy, and practice with regard to violence (see Koss et al., 1994).

There are, however, many similarities between the experience of violence among ethnic minority youth and among youth in general, as has been pointed out by Hammond and Yung (1993). Ethnic minority infants and young children, like their White peers, are most likely to be violently harmed by parents and caretakers. Ethnic minority adolescents, like all youth, are most at risk of assaults and murders by peers who are close to their age and at least acquainted with them (Christoffel, 1990, as cited in Hammond & Yung, 1993). Also, violent victimization is more prevalent among ethnic minority youth who are poor and who live in the inner city, which is true for nonminority youth as well (Fingerhut, Ingram, & Feldman, 1992, as cited in Hammond & Yung, 1993). Finally, ethnic minority youth experience the same developmental needs and pressures as all adolescents (e.g., the need to conform and belong to peer groups). However, ethnic minority youth are likely to be influenced in this regard by ethnic group norms as well as norms in the majority culture (Hammond & Yung, 1993).

As is noted in several chapters, data on the prevalence of violence among ethnic minority group members are not comprehensive, in large part because of the nature of traditional data collection procedures (e.g., official records have often listed race as only Black, White, or "other"). Moreover, some of the data reported in these chapters are not specific to youth, because information collected on violence often does not specify the age of the victims, another data collection problem that needs resolution. Finally, the heterogeneity of groups that are the result of subgroup differences (e.g., among the Asian group, differences for those of Chinese, Thai, Vietnamese, and Filipino origin) are rarely reflected in official statistical reports, research programs, or interventions.

Points of common concern can be seen in each of the chapters. For example, all chapters call for increased funding for research on violence that better distinguishes among ethnic minority groups. All recommend increased recruitment of psychological and other social science researchers and practitioners (e.g., ethnic minority psychologists are still underrepresented in the field; Office of Demographic, Employment, and Educational Research, 1993). Finally, all appeal for conceptual and operational attention to cultural sensitivity in psychological service delivery and the training of professionals.

References

Hammond, W. R., & Yung, B. (1993). Psychology's role in the public health response to assaultive violence among young African-American men. *American Psychologist, 48,* 142–154.

Holinger, P. C., Offer, D., Barter, J. T., and Bell, C. C. (1994). *Suicide and homicide among adolescents.* New York: Guilford Press.

Koss, M., Goodman, L., Fitzgerald, L., Russo, N. F., Keita, G. P., & Brown, A. (1994). *No safe haven: Male violence against women at home, at work, and in the community.* Washington, DC: American Psychological Association.

Office of Demographic, Employment, and Educational Research. (1993). *Profile of APA members.* Washington, DC: American Psychological Association.

4

African Americans

W. Rodney Hammond and Betty R. Yung

Description of the Population

African Americans make up approximately 12% of the total population of the United States (Children's Defense Fund, 1991). The majority of African Americans in the United States are individuals whose ancestors were brought into the nation from different African countries as slaves. However, this ethnic designation also encompasses newer waves of emigrants from Africa and from the West Indies (Ho, 1992). Thus, although sharing identifiable physical and racial characteristics such as darker skin color and in most cases a common heritage of ancestral slavery, the national African American population is a culturally diverse group. In addition to any lasting effects of indigenous traditions and values extended from the multiple countries of origin, African Americans are subject to the varying influences of modern American ethnic communities that may have distinct customs according to geographic region, rural versus urban location, and socioeconomic factors.

In general, African Americans have not achieved a status of parity relative to the White majority in the United States in terms of income, employment, educational attainment, and health. Rates of African American children living in poverty have increased in the past two decades largely because of rising birth rates among unmarried African American adolescents, who account for 45.9% of all teenage births. Child poverty rates for the total national population of African American children are estimated at 45.1%, compared with 15% for White children. Both male and female African American teenagers are more likely to drop out of school than White youth and to suffer the related difficulties in obtaining jobs as the national demand for unskilled workers continues to decline. The unemployment rates even for African Americans completing high school may be as much as 25% higher than the rates for White high school dropouts (Children's Defense Fund, 1991). African Americans are also disproportionately represented in the population suffering early deaths from preventable diseases or conditions such as infant mortality, AIDS, cancer, cardiovascular disease, and violence (Secretary's Task Force on Black and Minority Health, 1986).

Extent of the Risk of Violence

There is virtually no debate in the epidemiological literature that African Americans are the ethnic group at highest risk both for homicide and for nonlethal assaultive violence. National data on homicide incidence and characteristics is tracked primarily by two sources:

1. The Federal Bureau of Investigation's (FBI's) Uniform Crime Reports, Supplementary Homicide Report, collects data on demographic characteristics of victim and offender (age, race, and gender), victim–offender relationship, and crime circumstances (e.g., argument, legal intervention by police, etc.).
2. The National Center for Health Statistics Mortality Data takes records from death certificates. This database includes demographic data on victims but not on perpetrators and not on victim–perpetrator relationship. It captures some information on crime circumstances but does not distinguish between homicides of criminal origin versus "crimes of passion" or episodes of self-defense.

Although there are limitations to each surveillance system, the data sources on homicide are generally considered to be fairly reliable (Rosenberg & Mercy, 1991).

Statistics on homicide collected at the national level consistently have shown significantly higher victimization rates for African Americans than for Whites or other ethnic minorities, regardless of age or gender (National Center for Health Statistics, 1990; National Committee for Injury Prevention and Control, 1989). For both male and female African Americans between the ages of 15 and 34, homicide has been the leading cause of death since 1978 (Centers for Disease Control, 1990). The lifetime risk of death by interpersonal violence has been estimated to be 1 in 27 for African American males and 1 in 117 for African American females, compared with 1 in 205 for White males and 1 in 496 for White females (cited in Prothrow-Stith, 1991). Smaller studies on defined metropolitan regions such as New York, Los Angeles, and Detroit have shown generally elevated levels of risk for the total urban population but a persistent risk disparity for African Americans, particularly males (Mercy et al., 1986; Ropp, Visintainer, Ulman, & Treloar, 1992; Tardiff & Gross, 1986). In Detroit, for example, a study of pediatric deaths conducted between 1980 and 1988 indicated that urban African American males, aged 15–18, had homicide rates more than 16 times greater than White males of the same age (Ropp et al., 1992).

Murder rates for African American females of all ages have been generally found to be 3 to 5 times higher than those of White females (e.g., Harlow, 1991). However, within the general African American population, males between 15 and 24 are the subpopulation known to be most at risk for homicide. Comparisons of the 1988 mortality rates of males between these ages show that African Americans are homicide victims at an annual rate of 101.8 per 100,000, compared with a rate of 11.5 for White males of the same age (Centers for Disease Control, 1990). In recent years there have been alarming increases in homicide victimization for African American males in their late teens; percentage increases noted in regional or national studies have ranged from 55% to 70% (Centers for Disease Control, 1990; Fingerhut, Kleinman, Godfrey, & Rosenberg, 1991; Ropp et al., 1992).

For African Americans as well as the general population, it is much more difficult to estimate the extent of assaultive violence that does not result in death. Gaps in the availability of reliable data on nonfatal violence have to do with both a lack of accurate record-keeping systems at both local and national levels and the presumed underreporting of violent incidents (National Committee for Injury Prevention and Control, 1989; Rosenberg & Mercy, 1991). Existing data provide some evidence of higher incidence of child physical abuse (Hampton, 1987) and of spouse or partner abuse (Harlow, 1991; Stark & Flitcraft, 1991) in African American families than that found within other ethnic minority and White families. However, child physical abuse may be overreported among low-income African American families, and some studies have reported no ethnic differences in family violence patterns, particularly when controls for social class were introduced (Asbury, 1993; Hampton, 1987).

African American adolescents living in inner cities have self-reported levels of personal victimization and weapons-carrying that far exceed those reported in national surveys (Centers for Disease Control, 1991a; Menacker, Weldon, & Hurwitz, 1990; Sheley, McGee, & Wright, 1992). African American male adolescents report higher rates of carrying weapons than do African American female adolescents. One study conducted in a small North Carolina city indicated that 22% of the male respondents and 16% of the female respondents (in a sample that was 97% African American) reported occasional or frequent carrying knives or guns (Cotten et al., 1994). National data on ethnically mixed samples of high school students indicate a substantially lower weapons-carrying rate of 15.5% (U.S. Department of Health and Human Services, 1994).

Chronic exposure to violence is a particular problem for African American children living in certain communities. In a study of African American eighth graders living in an extremely violent neighborhood in Chicago, Shakoor and Chalmers (1991) found that 73% of the survey population had seen someone shot, stabbed, robbed, or killed. High percentages of first and second graders surveyed in Washington, DC, reported witnessing muggings (45%) or shootings (31%), and 39% said they had seen dead bodies (Richters & Martinez, 1994). These findings are highly comparable to results from similar surveys in Chicago (Bell & Jenkins, 1994) and New Orleans (Osofsky, Wewers, Hann, & Fick, 1994).

Similarly, inner-city African American adolescents report witnessing violent crime at rates that exceed comparison groups of suburban or rural youth. Gladstein, Slater-Rusonis, and Heald (1992) found that 42% of their metropolitan African American sample reported having seen someone shot, 25% had seen someone stabbed, and 23% had seen someone murdered. By contrast, suburban White adolescents reported percentages of 4%, 9%, and 1%, respectively. The reported percentages of violence exposure for African American adolescents are similar to those found by Schubiner, Scott, and Tzelepis (1993).

It is difficult to determine the extent of risk for sexual victimization such as familial sexual abuse or stranger or date rape among African American children and adolescents because samples and methodologies in the literature on such violence tend to be nonequivalent (Asbury, 1993). U.S. Department of Justice (1991) crime reports suggest that African American women tend to have higher incidence of rape than other ethnic minority girls and women. Scott, Lefley, and Hicks (1993) found a higher frequency of previous rape or incest for African American women than for Hispanic and non-Hispanic White women in a population of female rape victims. However, other studies of rape and child sexual abuse have shown no ethnic differences in incidence (Asbury, 1993).

Little information is available on sexual victimization or sexual assault perpetration patterns of African American male children and adolescents. Gladstein et al. (1992) reported a 6% incidence of self-reported rape victimization among a sample of 403 inner-city African American male adolescents. In another self-report survey, African American male adolescents reported higher rates than Native American and White male teenagers of forcing sex on a partner of unspecified gender (Gruber, DiClemente, & Anderson, 1994).

Nature and Characteristics of Risk

The nature and circumstances under which violent episodes occur among African Americans vary significantly according to age and gender. However, for all African Americans, the risk of violence by intimates or acquaintances is far greater than the danger from random violence committed by strangers or in connection with another crime such as robbery; for women and children, much of the violence risk is within family (Goetting, 1988; Harlow, 1991; Humphrey & Palmer, 1986; Stark, 1990). Perpetrator and victim are generally of the same race. Analyses of racial and ethnic homicide patterns over a several-year period have indicated that more than 90% of African American murder victims of all age groups were slain by other African Americans (FBI, 1987, 1989).

Up to age 5, African American children are more likely to be killed or injured by parents than by strangers, and these incidents are most often a result of an attempt to administer discipline (Christoffel, 1990; Crittenden & Craig, 1990). Risk is somewhat higher for males and the perpetrator is most often the mother (Christoffel, 1990; Crittenden & Craig, 1990; Hampton, 1987). Factors contributing to vulnerability for physical abuse and battering death of young children have been identified to include poverty; metropolitan residence; low birth weight; handicapping condition; young unmarried mothers, especially teenagers; mothers with less formal education; and history of abuse in the parent's family (Christoffel, 1990; Crittenden & Craig, 1990; Hampton, 1987; Winpisinger, Hopkins, Indian, Hostelter, 1991).

Risk for children of all ethnic groups generally declines up to adolescence, at which point the patterns related to violence change considerably. Adolescents of all ethnicities are more likely to be killed by a near-age peer. Violence-related mortality and injury for African American male adolescents involves firearms in most cases (Centers for Disease Control, 1990) and is most often due to arguments among friends or acquaintances (Humphrey & Palmer, 1986; Ropp et al., 1992; Sheley et al., 1992). Several investigators have underscored that, in many cases, the arguments between peers that erupt into violence tend to begin as trivial episodes (Lauritsen, Laub, & Sampson, 1992; Prothrow-Stith, 1991; Roberts, 1990). Newspaper accounts lend anecdotal evidence of this pattern and provide details of incidents in which African American teenagers died over minor incidents of name calling, gossip, an accidental bump, arguments over possessions, or a "wrong" look at someone who happened to be carrying a knife or a gun.

Although the exact nature of the relationship is not well understood, it appears that poverty is one of the strongest correlates of adolescent homicide risk for both males and females (Christoffel, 1990; Prothrow-Stith, 1991). Urban residence is an equally prevalent fatality predictor. The Detroit pediatric death study showed that in 1988 urban African American males were murder victims at the rate of 185.85 per 100,000, compared with around 90 per 100,000 for their suburban African American counterparts (Ropp et al., 1992). In a study of gun-related violence in and around inner-city schools, Sheley et al. (1992) concluded that, apart from the general risk factors of poverty and urban residence, the specific predictive factors most closely associated with victimization were (a) whether family members carried guns; (b) the extent to which students themselves carried guns in and out of school; (c) whether students used and sold drugs; and (d) whether they affiliated with others who carried guns to school. Other research has examined the factors associated with perpetration of violence among urban African American adolescents, finding that self-reported violent behavior was most significantly correlated with three indicators: exposure to violence and victimization in the community, degree of witnessing family conflict, and severity of corporal punishment used at home (DuRant, Cadenhead, Pendergrast, Slavens, & Linder, 1994). A total of 84% of the adolescents in this sample reported engaging in at least one form of violent behavior. Young women in this group engaged in violence less frequently than did young men, but in some categories they were relatively close to the rates for males in their violent behavior (e.g., for physical fighting within the past year, 65% of the males and 55% of the females reported participating in one or more incidents).

Violence against late adolescent and early adult African American females is most likely to be perpetuated by boyfriends or spouses, although if they are residents of central cities, these women also have higher levels of risk for stranger-to-stranger attacks than do White women or women of other races (Harlow, 1991). Risk factors for spouse abuse identified by Harlow include age below 35, marital status of separation or divorce, low income, unemployment, inner-city residence, and renting rather than owning one's own home. Other studies have identified additional correlates of vulnerability to be pregnancy, alcohol abuse, previous physical victimization by either the batterer or the victim, or all of these (Asbury, 1987; Stark & Flitcraft, 1991).

Battering is a frequent antecedent to fatal spouse abuse (Stark, 1990), which has been found to occur among African Americans more frequently than among other ethnic groups. Mercy and Saltzman (1989) studied fatal violence patterns among spouses in the United States for a 10-year period using data from the FBI Supplemental Homicide Reports. In their examination of racial and ethnic differences among spousal homicide victims, they found that African Americans accounted for 45.4% of all spouse homicide victims and that their rates were 8.4 times greater than that for Whites. Battering may result in a homicide of either the victim or a revenge slaying of the abuser (Goetting, 1988; Mercy & Saltzman, 1989; Stark, 1990). Mercy and Saltzman (1989) in fact found that African American males were at greater risk of spouse homicide victimization than African American wives or White spouses of either sex.

Although it appears to be a popularly accepted theory that much of the increase in violence among young African American males has to do with drug trafficking and gang membership, at the national level the percentage of homicides attributable to these factors is small compared with the total deaths (Prothrow-Stith, 1991). For example, Rogers (1993) examined gang-related homicides (i.e., those in which either the victim or the assailant was a gang member and the homicide occurred in the context of gang activity) and non-gang-related murders in Los Angeles, a city with one of the worst gang problems in the country. He found that, over a 10-year period, non-gang-related homicides were roughly four times more common than gang-related murders and that, although both types of homicide were increasing, the rates of increase were highly similar so that the differential between them remained fairly constant. Clearly, either gang involvement or narcotics trafficking are inherently risky activities; in large metropolitan areas they are believed to partially account for substantially higher and rising homicide rates (Meehan & O'Carroll, 1992; Mercy et al, 1986; Spergel et al, 1990; Tardiff & Gross, 1986). Although some researchers have not found a significant proportion of homicides related to gang involvement in narcotics trafficking (e.g., Meehan & O'Carroll, 1992), violence-related dangers to African American youth resulting from gang membership or selling drugs should not be minimized (Sheley et al., 1992; Spergel et al., 1990). Sheley et al. reported that the sale of drugs was strongly associated with violence around inner-city schools. Spergel et al. estimated that there are more than 1,400 gangs (with membership exceeding 120,000) in the United States and that 55% of all gang members are African American.

Because of the high percentages of firearm-associated deaths among African American youth, there has been increased research attention given to the relationship between weapons-carrying and involvement in violence. African American adolescents who carry guns or knives are more likely than non-weapons-carriers to be male, to have been witnesses of violent crime, to have been threatened or injured by a weapon, to fight with peers or strangers or to assault family members more frequently, to have arrest records, and to hold beliefs that carrying a gun is not associated with increased personal risk. Patterns were similar for both male and female weapons-carriers; however, the correlations were much stronger for African American male adolescents

(DuRant, 1994; Kulig, Valentine, & Steriti, 1994; Webster, Gainer, & Champion, 1993).

The greater risk to African Americans from violence among intimates should not downplay their risk from other sources. U.S. Department of Justice (n.d.) figures collected on hate crimes committed in 1991, including intimidation, vandalism, assault, robbery, and murder, indicated that African Americans were the group most frequently victimized by racially motivated hate crime, accounting for 35.5% of all such crimes reported.

Ethnicity: Interpreting and Responding to Victimization

Because of the alarming rise in violence affecting African American children and adolescents, there is a growing body of literature examining the effects of experiencing or witnessing the many forms of violence to which this vulnerable population is exposed. Unfortunately, many of these studies do not always make distinctions that would be helpful such as differentiating between the effects of witnessing versus experiencing violence, the levels and severity of violence exposure, and comparisons of impact among different ethnic groups and within-family victimization or witnessing versus exposure to community violence. In spite of these limitations, existing studies provide a compelling portrait of disturbing emotional and behavioral consequences to victimized African American children, adolescents, and adults.

African American children and adolescents—both victims and witnesses—show evidence of posttraumatic stress disorder (Fitzpatrick & Boldizar, 1993), depression (Fitzpatrick, 1993; Lorion & Saltzman, 1994; Martinez & Richters, 1994), and anxiety (Osofsky et al., 1994; Martinez & Richters, 1994; Schubiner et al., 1993). There are age and gender variations in the manifestations of these symptoms. Younger children are more likely to show more symptoms in each of these categories (Fitzpatrick, 1993; Fitzpatrick & Boldizar, 1993; Martinez & Richters, 1994). Some studies, but not all (e.g., Martinez & Richters, 1994), have shown effects more evident in girls and young women (Fitzpatrick, 1993; Fitzpatrick & Boldizar, 1993; Lorion & Saltzman, 1994).

Reported behavioral consequences for both victims and witnesses of violence are severe. These experiences have been associated with increased fighting; weapons-carrying; gang involvement; and other health risk behavior such as school failure, school suspensions, and substance abuse (Cotten et al., 1994; DuRant et al., 1994; Kulig et al., 1994; Webster et al., 1993). It also appears that African American children and adolescents who have experienced or witnessed (or both) violence are more likely than other victims to exhibit emotional distress and behavior problems (DuRant et al., 1994; Fitzpatrick, 1993; Miller, Handal, Gilner, & Cross, 1991).

It is also apparent that victimized African American adolescents rarely seek psychological help and may not even go to a doctor for medical assistance except in cases in which the injuries are grave. Gladstein et al. (1992) reported on the percentages of inner-city African American adolescents who saw a physician or a counselor following a violent incident. Respondents usually sought medical services if they had been shot (87%) and less frequently if they had been raped and a weapon was used (50%) or they were stabbed (45%). Only 25% of the shooting victims and 9% of the stabbing victims sought psychological services.

Other research suggests a lack of inclination to seek professional or other sources of help in cases of rape. Wyatt's (1992) study of rape victims reported that African American women were less likely than White women (64% vs. 36%) to disclose the sexual assault to anyone until years later. Only 23% of African Americans reported incidents of rape to the police or to a women's center, whereas 31% of the White women made such reports.

This is especially problematic because the short- and long-term effects of rape can be devastating. Wyatt (1992) did not find ethnic differences in the responses of African American and White women to the trauma of rape. The most commonly reported effects were psychological (e.g., fear, anger, anxiety, depression, and preoccupations with the abuse incident), followed by physical effects (e.g., sleep or appetite disturbances, sexually transmitted diseases, and pregnancy) and problems in their sex lives (e.g., avoidance of sex, diminished enjoyment). A majority of both African American and White women reported long-term negative psychological effects, including mistrust of men, chronic depression, and fears of being alone or being out at night. Similarly, Rhodes, Ebert, and Meyers (1993) also reported negative effects on the psychological and social adjustment of young pregnant and parenting African American women who had been raped, concluding that these women had lower self-esteem and more external locus of control than nonvictimized women in the sample.

There is little research shedding light on the reluctance of African American adolescents and young adult women to seek professional assistance after a victimization experience. In the Wyatt (1992) study, there were ethnic differences in women's beliefs about why they were victimized. African American women who had been raped were more likely than White women to offer explanations about their victimization that involved the riskiness of their living circumstances and to hold a general belief that African American women are at greatest risk for rape, suggesting that some may simply accept their vulnerability or victimization as inevitable. Responses of African American adolescents in Minnesota to a health-related survey indicated that a majority did not feel that adults such as school personnel care about their welfare (Rode & Bellfield, 1992). Such feelings would certainly contribute to a reluctance to go to such sources for assistance with problems of any type.

Knowledge Gaps and Research Needs

There is considerable need for continued empirical research and building of conceptual understanding of violence among African Americans. Theoretical formulations attempting to explain the phenomena have been developed by multiple disciplines, including psychology, sociology, criminology, and public health. These conceptualizations have implicated a variety of causative factors or correlates, such as poverty, structural conditions within the community, racism, self-hatred, cultural acceptance of violence, family disorganization and dysfunction and its cyclical consequences, biological phenomena, and interpersonal variables such as faulty cognitive patterns (reviewed in Hammond & Yung, 1991). Much of the research on the origins of African American violence has been criticized as offering inadequate guidance for policymaking and the development of programs of prevention and intervention (Hawkins, 1990; Oliver, 1989a, 1989b).

The call for additional empirical research suggests a general need for study of the ethnic, cultural, and subcultural variations in the prevalence, distribution, correlates, and consequences of violence and specific need for investigations that focus on subgroup analysis by narrow age and gender groupings (Christoffel, 1990; Hampton, 1987). Among other objectives, such research should provide detailed descriptions of the narrow situational circumstances of violent episodes, distinguishing among child, adolescent, and adult episodes (Christoffel, 1990). Research on physical and sexual abuse of young African American women should include data on partner violence, both within and outside of marriage relationships. Multivariate analytical approaches should be used that would take into account the multiple relevant factors contributing to the occurrence and outcomes of violent encounters, with a view toward identifying the most salient factors as targets for intervention (Rosenberg & Mercy, 1991). The effects of chronic exposure to violence as witness needs continued study, with particular focus on identification of familial and interpersonal factors that might mitigate harmful sequelae (Richters & Martinez, 1994). Examinations of regional or metropolitan trends should be undertaken to identify particularly high-risk locations for intervention efforts (Ropp et al., 1992). Finally, there are crucial needs for studies of the effectiveness of different prevention approaches, especially those that focus on behavioral outcomes and that provide for longitudinal followup as well as assessment of intermediate effects (Cohen & Wilson-Brewer, 1991; Wilson-Brewer & Jacklin, 1990).

Although research on the genesis and circumstances of violent crime is still needed, simultaneous attention is needed on the design of programs of prevention and intervention. Psychologists need to understand that knowledge and control of violence crosses disciplinary lines and they therefore should be committed to working in collaboration with professionals in other fields such as criminal justice, education, and public health to supply their unique contributions to the effort. In particular, the cognitive and behavioral interventions that can be provided by psychologists can help aggressive individuals learn to control anger and manage impulses as well as assisting potential victims to formulate constructive responses to situations in which violence is threatened. Service needs recognized to be particularly crucial include improved programming for victims of all types of violence, especially abused women and children and young victims with firearms injuries. Screening, early identification, and intervention with high-risk children and youth (e.g., those living in extremely violent neighborhoods) has also been strongly recommended (Bell, Hildreth, Jenkins, Levi, & Carter, 1988; Shakoor & Chalmers, 1991). Major task forces and conferences addressing violence have stressed the need for psychosocial and educational programming that would develop violence reduction skills, particularly for adolescents (Christoffel,

1990; National Committee for Injury Prevention and Control, 1989; Wilson-Brewer & Jacklin, 1990). Furthermore, it has been encouraged that youth programs should be developed that focus specifically on the unique needs and social environment of central city African American youth (Centers for Disease Control, 1991b; Isaacs, 1992; Mizanin, in press).

In addition, there is a scarcity of psychologist practitioners who are knowledgeable about the complexities of the multiple factors related to violent behavior, who have good awareness of multicultural issues, and who have had significant education and clinical exposure supporting culturally sensitive service provision toward violence reduction (Centers for Disease Control, 1991b; Wilson-Brewer & Jacklin, 1990).

Public Policy Recommendations

1. Public education is needed to dispel myths that perpetuate a "blame the victim" viewpoint, particularly to dispute theories that suggest that violence is prevalent among African Americans as a result of widespread community acceptance of violence as a legitimate solution to conflict.

2. Support should be made available for preprofessional training initiatives designed to prepare practitioners and researchers for career focus on this priority area. Particular needs have been noted for appropriately trained African American professionals.

3. Federal and state agencies should identify and recruit African American and other culturally competent professionals to serve on grant review panels to ensure that attention is given to research and program development in the area of violence in the African American community.

4. Funding is vitally needed to support culturally sensitive violence prevention programming for African American children, youth, and families either to reach individuals before violent patterns develop or to minimize consequences of victimization. Initiatives should be designed to address the many forms of violence that threaten the health and lives of African Americans, including expressive violence among family members and other intimates, hate crime, and risks associated with drug use and sales and gang membership. Priority should be placed on providing violence prevention and intervention services in normative settings such as schools, health clinics, churches, community-based agencies, and doctors' offices. This is particularly crucial in light of research suggesting that African American adolescents and young adults may be reluctant to seek help for victimization.

5. Public policy should support initiatives to introduce programming at the family level that raises awareness of violence risk. Funders should stimulate research and program development that highlights the protective role parents and other caretakers may take in violence prevention.

6. The potential contributions of media as either a positive or negative influence on the understanding and perpetuation of violence among African Americans should be recognized. Popular media may glorify violence or overfocus on predatory crime episodes that give false impressions about the sources of greatest risk and feed racially based fears and stereotypes. Ways should be sought to sensitize producers of popular media to the impact of images conveyed and to make use of both popular and educational media to facilitate violence reduction risk. Government agencies should provide incentives for the creation of culturally sensitive health education media directed to reducing violence.

7. Gun control legislation should be supported because guns are the weapons used most often in assaults and homicides among African Americans.

8. Increased funding is needed to advance the state of knowledge about the problem of violence in the African American community and to identify and test solutions.

References

Asbury, J. (1987). African-American women in violent relationships: An exploration of cultural differences. In R. Hampton (Ed.), *Violence in the Black family: Correlates and consequences* (pp. 89–106). Lexington, MA: Lexington Books.

Asbury, J. (1993). Violence in families of color in the United States. In R. Hampton, T. Gullotta, G. Adams, E. Potter, & R. Weissburg (Eds.), *Family violence: Prevention and treatment* (pp. 159–178). Newbury Park, CA: Sage.

Bell, C., Hildreth, C., Jenkins, E., Levi, D., & Carter, C. (1988). The need for victimization screening in a poor outpatient medical population. *Journal of the National Medical Association, 80,* 853–860.

Bell, C., & Jenkins, E. (1994). Community violence and children on Chicago's Southside. *Psychiatry, 56,* 46–54.

Centers for Disease Control. (1990). Homicide among young black males—United States, 1978–1987. *Morbidity and Mortality Weekly Report, 39,* 869–873.

Centers for Disease Control. (1991a). Weapon-carrying among high school students. *Journal of the American Medical Association, 266,* 2342.

Centers for Disease Control. (1991b). Forum on youth violence in minority communities: Setting the agenda for prevention. *Public Health Reports, 106,* 225–253.

Children's Defense Fund. (1991). *The state of America's children: 1991.* Washington, DC: Author.

Christoffel, K. K. (1990). Violent death and injury in US children and adolescents. *American Journal of Diseases of Childhood, 144,* 697–706.

Cohen, S., & Wilson-Brewer, R. (1991). *Violence prevention for young adolescents: The state of the art of program evaluation.* Washington, DC: Carnegie Council on Adolescent Development.

Cotten, N., Resnick, J., Browne, D., Martin, S., McCarraher, D. & Woods, J. (1994). Aggression and fighting behavior among African-American adolescents: Individual and family factors. *American Journal of Public Health, 84,* 618–622.

Crittenden, P., & Craig, S. (1990). Developmental trends in the nature of child homicide. *Journal of Interpersonal Violence, 5,* 202–216.

DuRant, R. (1994). The relationship between weapon carrying and engaging in violent behavior among black adolescents [Abstract]. *Journal of Adolescent Health, 15,* 91.

DuRant, R., Cadenhead, C., Pendergrast, R., Slavens, G., & Linder, C. (1994). Factors associated with the use of violence among urban black adolescents. *American Journal of Public Health, 84,* 612–617.

Federal Bureau of Investigation. (1987). *Crime in the United States: 1986*. Washington, DC: U.S. Department of Justice.

Federal Bureau of Investigation. (1989). *Uniform crime reports for the United States: 1988*. Washington, DC: U.S. Department of Justice.

Fingerhut, L., Kleinman, J., Godfrey, E., Rosenberg, M. (1991). Firearm mortality among children, youth, and young adults 1–34 years of age, trends, and current status: United States, 1979–1988. *Monthly Vital Statistics Reports, 39*, 1–15.

Fitzpatrick, K. (1993). Exposure to violence and presence of depression among low-income, African-American youth. *Journal of Consulting and Clinical Psychology, 61*, 528–531.

Fitzpatrick, K., & Boldizar, J. (1993). The prevalence and consequences of exposure to violence among African-American youth. *Journal of the American Academy of Child and Adolescent Psychiatry, 32*, 424–430.

Gladstein, J., Slater-Rusonis, E., & Heald, F. (1992). A comparison of inner-city and upper-middle class youths' exposure to violence. *Journal of Adolescent Health, 13*, 275–280.

Goetting, A. (1988). Patterns of homicide among women. *Journal of Interpersonal Violence, 3*, 3–20.

Gruber, E., DiClemente, R., & Anderson, M. (1994). Differences in risk-taking behavior among Native American, Black and White adolescents in a midwestern state [Abstract]. *Journal of Adolescent Health, 15*, 59.

Hammond, R., & Yung, B. (1991). Preventing violence in at-risk African-American youth. *Journal of Health Care for the Poor and Underserved, 2*, 359–373.

Hampton, R. (1987). Family violence and homicides in the Black community: Are they linked? In R. Hampton (Ed.), *Violence in the Black family: Correlates and consequences* (pp. 135–156). Lexington, MA: Lexington Books.

Harlow, C. (1991). *Female victims of violent crime* (Rep. No. NCJ-126826). Washington, DC: U.S. Department of Justice, Office of Justice Programs, Bureau of Justice Statistics.

Hawkins, D. F. (1990). Explaining the Black homicide rate. *Journal of Interpersonal Violence, 5*, 151–163.

Ho, M. (1992). *Minority children and adolescents in therapy*. Newbury Park, CA: Sage.

Humphrey, J. A., & Palmer, S. (1986). Race, sex, and criminal homicide: Offender-victim relationships. In D. Hawkins (Ed.), *Homicide among Black Americans* (pp. 57–68). Lanham, MD: University Press of America.

Isaacs, M. (Ed.). (1992). *Violence: The impact of community violence on African American children and families*. Arlington, VA: National Center for Education in Maternal and Child Health.

Kulig, J., Valentine, J., & Steriti, L. (1994). A correlational analysis of weapon-carrying among urban high school students: Findings from a cross-sectional survey. *Journal of Adolescent Health, 15*, 90.

Lauritsen, J., Laub, J., & Sampson, R. (1992). Convention and delinquent activities: Implications for the prevention of violent victimization among adolescents. *Violence and Victims, 7*, 91–108.

Lorion, R., & Saltzman, W. (1994). Children's exposure to community violence: Following a path from concern to research to action. *Psychiatry, 56*, 55–65.

Martinez, P., & Richters, J. (1994). The NIMH community violence project: II. Children's distress symptoms associated with violence exposure. *Psychiatry, 56*, 22–35.

Meehan, P., & O'Carroll, P. (1992). Gangs, drugs, and homicide in Los Angeles. *AJDC, 146*, 683–687.

Menacker, J., Weldon, W., & Hurwitz, E. (1990). Community influences on school crime and violence. *Urban Education, 25*, 68–80.

Mercy, J., & Saltzman, L. (1989). Fatal violence among spouses in the United States, 1976–85. *American Journal of Public Health, 79*, 595–599.

Mercy, J., Goodman, R., Rosenberg, M., Allen, N., Loya, F., Smith, J., & Vargas, L. (1986). Patterns of homicide victimization in the city of Los Angeles, 1970–79. *Bulletin of the New York Academy of Medicine, 62*, 427–445.

Miller, T., Handal, P., Gilner, F., & Cross, J. (1991). The relationship of abuse and witnessing violence on the Child Abuse Potential Inventory with black adolescents. *Journal of Family Violence, 6*, 351–363.

Mizanin, J. (Ed.). (in press). *Forum on youth violence: Prevention in Ohio*. Cleveland, OH: Mizanin.

National Center for Health Statistics. (1990). *Prevention profile. Health, United States, 1989* (DHHS Publication No. PHS 90-1232). Hyattsville, MD: U.S. Government Printing Office.

National Committee for Injury Prevention and Control. (1989). *Injury prevention: Meeting the challenge.* New York: Oxford University Press.

Oliver, W. (1989a). Black males and social problems: Prevention through Afrocentric socialization. *Journal of Black Studies, 20,* 15–39.

Oliver, W. (1989b). Sexual conquest and patterns of black-on-black violence: A structural-cultural perspective. *Violence and Victims, 4,* 257–271.

Osofsky, J., Wewers, S., Hann, D., & Fick, A. (1994). Chronic community violence: What is happening to our children. *Psychiatry, 56,* 36–45.

Prothrow-Stith, D. (1991). *Deadly consequences: How violence is destroying our teenage population and a plan to begin solving the problem.* New York: HarperCollins.

Rhodes, J., Ebert, L., & Meyers, A. (1993). Sexual victimization in young, pregnant and parenting, African-American women: Psychological and social outcomes. *Violence and Victims, 8,* 153–163.

Richters, J., & Martinez, P. (1994). The NIMH Community Violence Project: I. Children as victims and witnesses to violence. *Psychiatry, 56,* 7–21.

Roberts, S. (1990). Murder, mayhem, and other joys of youth. *Journal of NIH Research, 2,* 67–72.

Rode, P., & Bellfield, K. (1992). *The next generation: The health and well being of young people of color in the Twin Cities. A report based on the Minnesota Adolescent Health Survey.* Minneapolis, MN: Urban Coalition of Minneapolis.

Rogers, C. (1993). Gang-related homicides in Los Angeles County. *Journal of Forensic Sciences, 38,* 831–834.

Ropp, L., Visintainer, P., Uman, J., & Treloar, D. (1992). Death in the city: An American childhood tragedy. *Journal of the American Medical Association, 267,* 2905–2910.

Rosenberg, M., & Mercy, J. (1991). Assaultive violence. In M. Rosenberg & J. Mercy (Eds.), *Violence in America: A public health approach* (pp. 14–50). New York: Oxford University Press.

Schubiner, H., Scott, R., & Tzelepis, A. (1993). Exposure to violence among inner-city youth. *Journal of Adolescent Health, 14,* 214–219.

Scott, C., Lefley, H., & Hicks, D. (1993). Potential risk factors for rape in three ethnic groups. *Community Mental Health Journal, 29,* 133–141.

Secretary's Task Force on Black and Minority Health. (1986). *Report of the Secretary's Task Force on Black and Minority Health: V.* Washington, DC: U.S. Department of Health and Human Services.

Shakoor, B., & Chalmers, D. (1991). Co-victimization of African American children who witness violence: Effects on cognitive, emotional, and behavioral development. *Journal of the National Medical Association, 83,* 233–237.

Sheley, J., McGee, Z., & Wright, J. (1992). Gun-related violence in and around inner-city schools. *AJDC, 146,* 677–682.

Spergel, I., Currey, G., Chance, R., Kane, C., Ross, R., Lexander, A., Simmons, E., & Oh, S. (1990). *Youth gang problems and response. Stage 1. Assessment.* Washington, DC: U.S. Department of Justice, Office of Juvenile Justice and Delinquency Prevention.

Stark, E. (1990). Rethinking homicide: Violence, race, and the politics of gender. *International Journal of Health Services, 20,* 3–26.

Stark, E., & Flitcraft, A. (1991). Spouse abuse. In M. Rosenberg & J. Mercy (Eds.), *Violence in America: A public health approach* (pp. 123–157). New York: Oxford University Press.

Tardiff, K., & Gross, E. (1986). Homicide in New York City. *Bulletin of New York Academy of Medicine, 62,* 413–426.

U.S. Department of Health and Human Services. (1994). Health risk behaviors among adolescents who do and do not attend school—United States, 1992. *Morbidity and Mortality Weekly Report, 43,* 129–132.

U. S. Department of Justice. (n.d.) Press release reporting summary results on 1991 data collected by the FBI in response to the Hate Crime Statistics Act.

U. S. Department of Justice. (1991). *Violent crime in the United States* (Rep. No. NCJ-127855). Rockville, MD: Author.

Webster, D., Gainer, P., & Champion, H. (1993). Weapon carrying among inner-city junior high school students: Defensive behavior vs. aggressive delinquency. *American Journal of Public Health, 83,* 1604–1608.

Wilson-Brewer, R., & Jacklin, B. (1990). *Violence prevention strategies targeted at the general population of minority youth.* Background paper prepared for the Forum on Youth Violence in Minority Communities: Setting the Agenda for Prevention. Newton, MA: Education Development Center.

Winpisinger, K., Hopkins, R., Indian, R., & Hostelter, J. (1991). Risk factors for childhood homicides in Ohio: A birth certificate-based case-control study. *American Journal of Public Health, 81,* 1052–1054.

Wyatt, G. (1992). The sociocultural context of African American and White American women's rape. *Journal of Social Issues, 48,* 77–91.

5 _____

U.S. Latinos

Fernando I. Soriano

Description of the Population

U.S. Latinos have been called the "invisible minority" because, compared with their size, not much is said or known about this significant population (National Education Association, 1968). Latinos represent approximately 22.4 million people, or about 9% of the total U.S. population, and are presently one of the largest and fastest growing minorities in the United States (A. Garcia, 1991).

In terms of country of origin, the Mexican-origin subgroup, which represents 63% of Latinos in the United States, is the largest, followed by the Puerto Rican subgroup, which represents 11% of the U.S. Latino population. The third largest is the Cuban subgroup, representing 5% of the U.S. Latino population. More recently, there has been a steady increase in the number of Latinos entering the United States from Central and South American countries, such as from El Salvador, Nicaragua, and other Central and South American countries. Together, these "other" subgroups make up a sizable 22% of the Latino population in the United States (U.S. Bureau of the Census, 1991).

On the basis of available information, U.S. Latinos are projected to surpass the African American population in absolute numbers by the year 2010 (National Council of La Raza, 1992). Moreover, future estimates of the Latino population range from 18.1 to 26.5% of the total U.S. population by the year 2080. That is, it is expected that by the year 2080, about 1 out of 5 persons in the United States will be Latino (Spencer, 1986). Much of this expected growth among U.S. Latinos is simply due to more accurate counting of Latinos. Other significant reasons are high fertility rates, a higher percentage of child-bearing women compared with non-Latinos, as well as a continued entry of new immigrants into this country.

The largest increase in U.S. Latinos between census counts in the United States occurred between the 1970 and 1980. This represented an increase of 60%—from 9.1 to 14.6 million (U.S. Bureau of the Census, 1985b). From 1980 to 1990, the U.S. Latino population increased 53%, from 14.6 to 20.4 million. According to the U.S. Bureau of the Census (1991), the Latino population, totaling about 22.4 million, has been growing eight times as fast as the non-Latino population (Del Pinal & De Navas, 1990).

U.S. Latinos are concentrated primarily in the Southwest. Texas and California have more than 55% of the total Latino population, and most are of Mexican descent. New York has about 10% of the Latino population, and Puerto Ricans make up the largest Latino population there. Florida is home to much of the U.S. Cuban population and currently has about 8% of the Latino population (Del Pinal & De Navas, 1990).

The U.S. Latino population is young. The median age of Latinos is 25.9 years, which is lower than the non-Latino age of 33.2 years. About 21% of the total U.S. Latino population are under the age of 9, compared with 15% of non-Latinos. However, the youngest Latino subgroup is the Mexican American group, which has a median age of 23.6 years. The median age for Puerto Ricans is 26.8, whereas that of Cubans is 41.4 years (Del Pinal & De Navas, 1990). Nearly one third (30%) of Latinos are under 15 years of age, compared with 21% of non-Latinos. Conversely, about twice as many non-Latinos (22%) were 55 years or older, compared with Latinos (11%; J. M. Garcia & Montgomery, 1991).

U.S. Latino families tend to be larger than non-Latino families. In 1989, the average number of persons in Latino households was 3.39 compared with 2.57 for non-Latinos. This larger household size for Latinos is a reflection of the higher fertility rates among Latinos. In 1986, U.S. Latino women of childbearing age (18–44 years) had 105.6 births per 1,000 women compared with only 68.2 for Whites (McKay, 1988). In 1982, U.S. Latino women had an average of 1.6 children compared with 1.3 of non-Latino women (U.S. Bureau of the Census, 1985a).

Extent of the Risk of Violence

As with comprehensive demographics on Latinos in the United States, data on social problems facing Latinos (e.g., violence victimization rates) are not as yet systematically collected. National health, juvenile justice, and crime data typically provide aggregate national statistics and at times provide a breakdown by race, primarily an African American and White comparisons. Only rarely are data provided on ethnic groups and subgroups, such as U.S. Latinos.

It is clear from available data, for example, what the national homicide rates are for African Americans, but conspicuously absent are reliable national data on Latinos, particularly for U.S. Latino youth.[1] Instead, U.S. Latino

---

[1]Adding to this complexity is the sketchy, incomplete, or lacking data on U.S. Latinos compared with those available on non-Latinos. There are various reasons for this lack of data. First, there is lack of agreement on what a Latino or Hispanic is (i.e., Latinos defy racial categorizations, because they are neither a racial group nor exclusively a part of one). Second, U.S. Latinos are a heterogeneous population comprised of various subpopulations having different histories and origins, even if they share a common influence and confrontation with the Spanish conquistadores. Third, it is fiscally and politically convenient to ignore a population that is significantly underserved and is confronting social and health challenges. Consequently, the sparse data on this large population make it difficult to develop a clear and comprehensive overview of violence among U.S. Latinos, and in particular, Latino youth.

data have to be pieced together from available regional data for some individual cities, individual states or at times for several states. Furthermore, the scant information available focuses on either one Latino subgroup, such as on the Mexican-origin subgroup, or does not specify the subgroups comprising aggregate data. Also largely absent are data allowing for age by gender by ethnic group comparisons. This relative lack of data must be taken into account when considering the statistics on violence among this population.

Homicide

The most extreme measure of violence is homicide. While systematic data on this outcome among U.S. Latinos is lacking, anecdotal and regional data suggest that such cities such as Los Angeles, Chicago, New York, and Miami experience relatively high rates of homicide among their Latino populations. For example, Block (1988) showed that compared with African American or White non-Latino youth of the same age, Latinos aged 15–19 have the highest homicide victimization rates (104 per 100,000 for Latinos, 62 per 100,000 for African Americans, and 12 per 100,000 for White non-Latino youths). Unfortunately, until better data are gathered for U.S. Latinos nationally, the most that can be done in terms of the overall homicide rate is to guess, as Prothrow-Stith (1991) did: "Asked to make an educated guess I would say that in many Latino communities the assault and homicide rates are probably just as catastrophic as in inner city black communities" (p. 66).

As mentioned earlier, the limited available data on comparing U.S. Latino homicide rates with that of non-Latino Whites comes from regional studies from individual cities. For example, an early study by Porkorny (1965) showed Latino rates to be 2.3 times those of Anglos in Houston, Texas, from 1958 to 1961. Smith, Mercy, and Rosenberg (1988) cited an unpublished study by Loya et al. (1980) that reported data suggesting that Latinos in Los Angeles had a homicide rate that was 2.2 times that of Anglos between 1970 and 1980. Smith et al. (1988) reported data from a study on homicide rates for the five Southwestern states where more than 60% of all U.S. Latinos reside (Arizona, California, Colorado, New Mexico, and Texas). They found that the Latino homicide rate (20.5 per 100,000 people) was more than 2.5 times that of Anglos (7.9 per 100,000 people).

Unlike many other studies not reporting gender differences, Smith et al. (1988) found that Latina and Anglo females had similar homicide rates: 4.8 per 1,000 and 4.2 per 1,000, respectively, which are markedly lower than those for Latina and Anglo males. For example, Latino males had a rate of 39.3 per 100,000 homicides and 11.7 per 100,000 for Anglo males. Latinos aged 20–24 years had the highest homicide rates for males and females: 83.3 and 8.7, respectively.

Prothrow-Stith (1991) reported on data from Los Angeles indicating that the homicide rate of U.S. Latino males increased nearly 300%, from 9.1 per 100,000 to 32.6 per 100,000 between 1970 and 1979. Some researchers have found that Latinos have even higher homicide rates than African Americans (e.g., a study in Chicago by Block, 1988).

Sewell et al. (1989) provided mortality data for New Mexico for the year ending in 1982 and found that among males, homicide was the second cause of mortal external injury for Latinos, the third for Native Americans, and the fourth for non-Latino Whites. Homicide accounted for 12.5% of injury deaths for Latino males, 8.1% for Native Americans, and 6.1 for non-Latino Whites. For females, homicide was the third leading cause of mortal external injury for Latinas, the second for Native Americans, and the fourth for White non-Latinas. Sewell et al. also found that for all cultural groups including White non-Latinos, the 20–24 age cohort had the highest rate of external injuries (including both genders). For each age cohort, Native Americans showed the greatest incidence of mortal external injury, followed by Latinos and White non-Latinos.

Zahn (1988) presented aggregate homicide data for Philadelphia, Newark, Chicago, St. Louis, Memphis, Dallas, Oakland, San Jose, and Ashton. Her data suggested that African American males had the highest homicide rates, followed by U.S. Latino and White non-Latino males (84.4, 46.8, and 16.2, respectively, per 100,000 people). This same pattern of homicide among cultures held true for females, but their rates per 100,000 people were significantly lower: 14.4, 5.3, and 3.9, respectively. The average age of victims was the youngest for Latinos (29.4), followed by African Americans (32.2) and White non-Latino males (38.2). There are other researchers who reported similar trends for Latinos in other parts of the United States (Batten, Hicks, & Penn, 1991; Mauer, Rosenberg, & Keemer, 1990; Shai & Rosenwaike, 1988; Smith, Mercy, Rosenberg, 1986).

Shai and Rosenwaike (1988) compared homicide rates among different U.S. Latino immigrant groups (non-U.S. born). As with previous studies, African American males had the highest rate of homicide (73.7 per 100,000), followed by Mexican-born males (60.4 per 100,000) and White non-Latino males (10.9 per 100,000). A similar but attenuated trend was evident for female African Americans, Latinas, and White non-Latinas: 13.8, 5.0, and 3.1 per 100,000, respectively. The surprising finding had to do with Puerto Rican-born males, who had higher rates of homicide (75.6 per 100,000) compared with African American males (73.7 per 100,000). Cuban-born males also showed elevated rates compared with Mexican-born males (63.1 and 60.4 per 100,000, respectively).

U.S. Latina females showed a similar trend with Puerto Rican-born females (8.4 per 100,000) showing the highest rates among Latino groups. The Cuban-born female rate (7.9 per 100,000) was also higher than the Mexican-born female rate (5.0 per 100,000) but higher than the White non-Latina rate (3.1 per 100,000; Shai & Rosenwaike, 1988).

A study by Desenclos and Hahn (1992) introduced a measure of "years of potential life lost" to estimate the number of years of life lost to intentional and unintentional injuries and illnesses. They found that the rate per 1,000 of years lost was highest for African Americans, 140.0; followed by Native Americans/Alaskan Natives, 100.9; Latinos, 74.3; and non-Latino Whites, 68.3. However, violence—either self- or externally inflicted (e.g., suicide and homicide)—accounted for the greatest proportion of years lost for Latino males (18.4%), followed by African American (17.3%) and White non-Latino

(10.5%) males. Among females, African Americans lost the most number of years to violence (7.5%), followed by both Latinas and White non-Latinas (6.7% for both).

Gangs and Violence

It is estimated that U.S. Latino gangs are responsible for more than one third of all homicides (Genelin & Copelin, 1989). Nationally, Spergel et al. (1990) indicated that more than one third of gang members are Latino and that most of these are Mexican American or Puerto Rican. Research suggests that for Latino and non-Latino juveniles, gang membership increases the likelihood of juveniles engaging in delinquency or antisocial behavior (Spergel, 1990). Matched comparison studies by Busch and his colleagues (Busch, Zagar, Hughes, Arbit, & Bussell, 1990; Zagar, Arbit, Sylvies, Busch, & Hughes, 1990) involving Latinos showed that violent juveniles convicted of a homicide were characterized as likely to come from families with criminally violent members, be gang members, have severe educational difficulties, and have problems with alcohol abuse. A recent government report indicated that Los Angeles County experienced approximately 771 gang-related homicides in 1991 (California Department of Justice, 1993).

Researchers warn that although there is a correlation between gang membership and violence or delinquency among Latinos and non-Latinos, this link is not necessarily causal (Fagan, 1990; Soriano et al., in press). Latino youths and their families are more likely to live under conditions that increase their risk of not only gang membership but a host of other antisocial behaviors (e.g., delinquency, illegal substance use, etc.). See chapter 14 in this book for a more detailed discussion on youth gangs and violence.

Violence Among all Latino Youth

Of the scant data available nationally on U.S. Latinos and violent crimes, the following statistics are offered for various years. Generally, from 1979 to 1986, Latinos experienced higher rates of violent crimes than did non-Latinos (U.S. Department of Justice, 1991d). Among Latino teenagers, the rate of victimization for crimes of violence from 1985 to 1988 was generally lower than for non-Latinos aged 12–15, 47.2 per 1,000 and 63 per 1,000, respectively. However, the differences were less for 16–19-year-olds: 60.2 per 1,000 for Latinos and 73.5 per 1,000 for non-Latinos (U.S. Department of Justice, 1991c). About 44% of perpetrators of 12–15-year-olds were strangers compared with 52% of 16–19-year-olds (ethnic group comparisons were not available). Conversely, among 12–15-year-olds, perpetrators tended to be nonstrangers, such as well-known or casual acquaintances (50%); it was 38% for 16–19-year-olds.

Other statistics show that the victimization rates for U.S. Latinos 12 years or older for personal crimes of violence are higher (37.3 per 1,000) than for Whites (28.8 per 1,000) and only slightly less than for African Americans (39.7 per 1,000; U.S. Department of Justice, 1991b, p. 6). The rates for Latino male victimization for violent crimes were substantially higher (49.5 per 1,000) than for non-Latinos (36.3 per 1,000). Latino females also showed higher rates of victimization by violence (25.0 per 1,000) compared with non-Latino females (21.9 per 1,000). Unfortunately, the data do not allow an examination of youth groups.

Broken down by type of violent crime, the incidence rate of U.S. Latino victimization during the progress of a robbery in 1990 was 13.9 in 1,000, or slightly less than 3 times the rate for non-Latinos (5 per 1,000), for persons 12 years and older. The rate of robbery for African Americans was 13 per 1,000, or slightly lower than that of Latinos (U.S. Department of Justice, 1991b). Unfortunately, the data do not allow an examination of youth groups.

For aggravated assaults, the rate for U.S. Latinos who were 12 years and older was 10.1 per 1,000, which is about 25% higher than the rate for Whites (7.6 per 1,000) and 15% lower compared with African Americans (26 per 1,000; U.S. Department of Justice, 1991b, p. 6). Regarding female sexual victimization, the limited data suggest that Latinas and non-Latinas have similar rates of experiencing completed and attempted rapes, 1.5 and 1.6 per 1,000, respectively (U.S. Department of Justice, 1991e). However, Latinas and Latinos had higher rates of victimization for violent crimes than did non-Latino males and females (30.3 and 49.9 per 1,000 compared with 25.5 and 44.7 per 1,000, respectively; U.S. Department of Justice, 1991e). Unfortunately, the data do not allow an examination of youth groups.

Physical and Sexual Abuse and Rape

Few studies of physical and sexual abuse among U.S. Latinos have been done, but some studies do suggest that sexual abuse in particular may be relevant to violence among these youths. Moore (1991) found, for example, that approximately one third (29%) of Latina gang members reported incestuous encounters. Moore also found a positive correlation between incestuous experiences (a close relative such as an uncle, brother, grandfather) and poverty, education, and Mexican-born fathers. In a study by Chavez, Edwards, and Oetting (1989), Latina school dropouts were twice as likely as controls to have been raped or sexually assaulted (10% vs. 20%). Latina dropouts were also found to be more likely to develop serious illnesses, alcohol and drug abuse, and be beaten by parents (10% vs. 22.5%).

Although there are no national epidemiological studies (to my knowledge) on physical and sexual abuse of U.S. Latino youth, one can surmise that being a poor population (more than one third of Latino youths are under the poverty line—36% compared with 17.5% for non-Latinos) and one that is among the least educated (J. M. Garcia & Montgomery, 1991) puts this population at risk, because each of these items has been found to be a risk factor for abuse (U.S. Department of Health and Human Services, 1992).

Nationally, rapes reported to the police are highest for poor, inner-city minority females with one exception: Latinas (Sorenson & Siegel, 1992). Confirming this is a study of both males and females by Sorenson and Siegel (1992), who found that the lifetime prevalence of sexual assault among non-Latino Whites was 2.5 times that of Latinos. However, as I discuss later, some at-risk groups of youth (e.g., youth involved in gangs) may have signficantly higher rates of rape than those reported by Sorenson and Siegel.

Nature and Characteristics of Risk

The limited data on the prevalence and incidence of youth violence among U.S. Latino populations suggests the need to examine available data on risk factors associated with violence. The research on violence risk factors suggests that age, marital status, education, income, occupation or employment status, home ownership, and place of residence are all associated with adult and youth violence (U.S. Department of Justice, 1985). In addition, the ownership of guns has been found to be important in understanding violence among all youths (Holinger, Offer, Barter, & Bell, 1994; see chapter 12 in this book).

Age

Violent crime is more likely to affect young rather than older individuals; 12–24-year-olds have the highest victimization rates for violent crimes (U.S. Department of Justice, 1991d). Homicide was the second leading cause of death among 15–34-year-olds in 1988. Seventy-one percent of arrestees for violent crimes are under 30 years of age (U.S. Department of Justice, 1988). This age range accounts for almost half of the total U.S. Latino population (48%) compared with 35% of non-Latinos. The median age is 23.6% for Mexican Americans, who make up about two thirds of the Latino population (62.6%); the median age for non-Latinos is 33.2 (J. M. Garcia & Montgomery, 1991).

Marital Status

Violence victimization rates are highest for those who have never married. For the never-married population (age 12 and older), the victimization rate was 72 per 1,000, which was more than 3 times the rate for those married: 19 per 1,000 (U.S. Department of Justice, 1988). Because it is a young population, about one third (32.6%) of Latinos have never married, compared with 26% of non-Latinos (J. M. Garcia & Montgomery, 1991).

Education

Those with an education of 9–11 years have the highest violence victimization rates at 39 per 1,000 (U.S. Department of Justice, 1988, p. 26). Educational attainment is one of the most troublesome challenges for U.S. Latinos. About 1 out of every 2 Latinos (49%) have less than 4 years of high school, compared with 1 out of 5 non-Latinos (20%; J. M Garcia & Montgomery, 1991).

U.S. Latinos have the highest dropout rates of any major group in the United States. Currently, by ages 16–17, about 1 in 5 Latinos (19.5%) leaves school without a diploma, compared with 6% of African Americans and 7.1%

of non-Latino Whites (De La Rosa & Maw, 1990). Research by Chavez et al. (1989) suggests that U.S. Latino and non-Latino dropouts are more likely to be exposed to violence. They found that nearly half had experienced being badly beaten. At least 20% of the female dropouts had experienced being sexually assaulted or raped. One in 5 male dropouts had held a gun on someone in a confrontation. One in 5 Mexican American dropouts had cut someone with a knife.

Income

One of the most consistent correlates of violence is poverty (U.S. Department of Justice, 1988, 1991a). Those with low household incomes are more likely to be victims of violent crimes. Specifically, the data suggest that those with household incomes under $7,500 are 2.5 times more likely to be victimized than those with incomes $50,000 and above (U.S. Department of Justice, 1991d).

More than 1 in 5 U.S. Latino households (21.1%) earn less than $10,000 compared with 14.5% of non-Latino families. The median household income for Latinos is $22,330 compared with $38,069 for non-Latinos. It is estimated that more than one third (38.4%) of Latinos under 18 years of age live in poverty compared with 18.3% of non-Latinos. Hence, Latino youth are more than two times as likely to live in poverty compared with non-Latinos (J. M. Garcia & Montgomery, 1991), and they are more likely to be victims of crime.

Employment Status and Occupation

The data have consistently suggested that victimization is related to the victim's employment status and occupation (U.S. Department of Justice, 1990). Specifically, the data suggest that unemployed people are more than twice as likely to be victims of violent crimes (76 per 1,000) than the employed people (32 per 1,000). U.S. Latinos have an unemployment rate of 10% compared with 6.9% for non-Latinos. Having a professional or managerial occupation reduces the probability of violent crime victimization (U.S. Department of Justice, 1990). Almost 1 in 3 non-Latino males hold managerial or professional occupations (28%) compared with only 11% of Latino males. Alternatively, almost one third of Latino males (29%) hold operator, fabricator, or laborer positions compared with 19% of non-Latino males (J. M. Garcia & Montgomery, 1991).

Home Ownership

Home ownership also has been linked to victimization rates for violent crimes and other offenses (U.S. Department of Justice, 1990). For example, the rate is 134.1 per 1,000 for homeowners for general household victimization compared with 208.9 per 1000 for renters (U.S. Department of Justice, 1991b). The data indicate that 39% of Latinos either own or are purchasing a home compared with 66% of non-Latinos. Conversely, 61% of Latinos rent their dwellings, as compared with 34.2% of non-Latinos (J. M. Garcia & Montgomery, 1991).

Residence

Victimization data suggest that city or inner-city dwellers experience higher victimization rates of violence compared with suburbanites or non-inner-city residents. For example, the rates of violent victimization for people age 12 and older living in a central city area is 41.3 per 1,000 compared with 25.2 per 1,000 for those living in suburban or nonmetropolitan areas (U.S. Department of Justice, 1991b). Census data suggest that more than 9 out of 10 U.S. Latinos (91.8%) live in urban areas compared with 72.8% of non-Latinos (J. M. Garcia & Montgomery, 1991).

Access to Weapons

Because guns are involved in a high percentage of serious violent incidents, it is important to note how U.S. Latino youth fare in this regard. A recent survey of youths conducted by the Centers for Disease Control (CDC) and reported in a newsletter published in October 1991 by the CDC indicated U.S. Latino male students in Grades 9–12 are more likely than their African American or White peers to admit to carrying weapons. When asked how many times during the past 30 days they had carried a weapon, 41% reported carrying a club, knife, or gun at least once, compared with 39% of African American and 29% of White non-Latinos (U.S. Department of Health and Human Services, 1991). Among females, 12% of Latinas carried a weapon compared with 17% of African American and 5% of White non-Latina females.

Together, data about U.S. Latinos with regard to these risk factors suggest that Latinos, and Latino youth in particular, may experience the devastating effects of violence to a greater extent than non-Latinos. Indeed, any of the demographic characteristics taken individually can predispose Latinos to violence, but it is the combination of characteristics that is most troubling to violence experts. In particular, it is the combination of poverty, poor education, high unemployment, and greater exposure to urban areas fraught with violence that impede short-term solutions to problems of violence among Latinos.

Ethnicity: Interpreting and Responding to Victimization

U.S. Latinos and non-Latinos are comparable in their rates of reporting crimes of violence to police, 49.5% and 48.8%, respectively. However, Latinos are less likely to report violent crimes if they involve strangers (42.2%) but are more likely to report these crimes with nonstranger perpetrators (68.5%) compared with non-Latinos, 48.8% and 46.8%, respectively (U.S. Department of Justice, 1990).

As with other cultural groups, there is a need to better understand the meaning and perceptions of violence by U.S. Latinos, which are culturally anchored (Shai & Rosenwaike, 1988). This information is important to understand in developing effective and culturally relevant violence prevention and intervention efforts, and it is also important in helping Latino victims of violence.

Given the rate of violence among U.S. Latino youth, and thus among families and bystanders, the issue of posttraumatic stress disorder (PTSD) needs to be considered. Pynoos and Nader (1988) examined PTSD and community violence. Here, too, an understanding of the Latino culture is necessary in order to intervene effectively with this population.

Knowledge Gaps and Research Needs

Clearly, there is a need for more data on the prevalence and incidence rates of violence among U.S. Latinos and Latinas. In planning additional research, studies need to consider and plan for the fact that Latinos are a heterogeneous group. There are some cultural similarities, but there are also significant differences as well (Sabogal, Marin, Otero-Sabogal, Marin, & Perez-Stable, 1987). The education, age, and income levels of Cubans, for example, are markedly higher than those of Mexican Americans and Puerto Ricans.

Research suggests that U.S. Latinos differ in their levels of acculturation, which has been shown to be a significant independent predictor in the study of many Latino social problems (see O'Keefe & Padilla, 1987). Studies on Latinos should include a specific examination of acculturation effects or at least should control for such effects in studies. Latino subgroup and acculturation issues suggest that future studies should include sufficient numbers of Latinos to allow for subgroup analyses.

Moreover, national and regional studies and surveys need to ensure adequate numbers of U.S. Latinos and other minority members in their samples. Furthermore, the researchers need to report their findings as the findings pertain to each major minority group. When possible, the reporting of the findings should include breakdowns within ethnic subgroups (e.g., Mexican American, Puerto Rican, Hmong, Cambodian, Navajo, Cherokee, southern and northern Black, etc.).

Research is also needed on the independent role of social and economic and cultural factors in violence among youth in the different Latino subgroups (see also chapter 3 in this book). The close correlation between many social and economic indicators with minority status makes it difficult to separate these from variables that are cultural in nature.

As is the case with each major ethnic minority group, there is a shortage of research psychologists and other social scientists who are themselves members of minority groups. This suggests the need to fund focused training programs and to encourage minorities to develop expertise on youth violence issues. Psychology training programs at universities need to increase their commitment to representation of culturally diverse faculty within their departments. Psychology departments should encourage minority faculty who have applied research and service interests with regard to violence and aggression issues, because these topics are likely to increase in importance in the coming years. Psychological journals should encourage and promote the publication of articles that focus on minority populations, particularly from minority perspectives. Conferences should be convened on youth violence among minority populations.

Public Policy Recommendations

1. The available data on U.S. Latinos dispel many of standing myths regarding Latinos as criminally prone (Rudoff, 1971). It is important that public education dispel such lingering myths regarding Latinos and violence.

2. Federal agencies should take cultural differences into account in developing and funding violence prevention and intervention programs.

3. More funding is needed for research targeted to understand the role of culture in violence in U.S. Latino communities. Preliminary results from a qualitative study on Latino violent youth offenders suggests that cultural values, such as family orientation (familism) and simpatia—avoidance of conflict—serve as protective or resilience factors for Latino youth (Soriano et al., in press).

4. Federal agencies that routinely collect national data bearing on violence need to ensure adequate numbers of U.S. Latinos, Native Americans, and Asians in their surveys and epidemiological studies (including sufficient cohorts for adults, adolescents, and children) to provide necessary information on adult and youth violence among Latinos and other large minority groups. Among others, these surveys include the National Youth Survey, National Youth Risk Behavior Survey, National Crime Survey, Children in Custody Survey, and the National Health Interview Survey.

5. The federal government and private foundations interested in this topic (e.g., Kellogg Foundation, Guggenheim Foundation, Kauffman Foundations, etc.) should be encouraged to require that all future studies they fund should include adequate numbers of Latinos and other minority groups (be they national or regional studies). Furthermore, researchers conducting these studies should be required to report on their findings across cultural groups.

6. There is a need for studies to examine intraethnic group heterogeneity. These intraethnic studies need to address the role of gender, acculturation, age, family structure, and process in violence.

7. Studies need to examine the role of discrimination, prejudice, hate crimes, and social isolation on violence victimization and perpetration.

8. There is a serious need for more U.S. Latino researchers. More public funding is needed for scholarships and beginning Latino investigators to increase the number of Latino violence researchers. Professional psychological organizations, such as the American Psychological Association, need to vigorously encourage psychological training pro-

grams to increase the number of Latinos and other minorities who become psychologists.

References

Batten, P. J., Hicks, L. J., & Penn, D. W. (1991). A 28-year (1963–90) study of homicide in Marion County, Oregon. *American Journal of Forensic Medicine and Pathology, 12*, 227–234.

Block, C. R. (1988). Lethal violence in the Chicago community, 1965 to 1981. In research conference proceedings, *Violence and homicide in Hispanic communities* (pp. 31–66). Los Angeles: University of California Press.

Busch, K. G., Zagar, R., Hughes, J. R., Arbit, J., & Bussell, R. E. (1990). Adolescents who kill. *Journal of Clinical Psychology, 46*, 472–484.

California Department of Justice. (1993). *Gangs 2000: A call to action (March 1993)*. Sacramento: California Department of Justice.

Chavez, E. L., Edwards, R., & Oetting, E. R. (1989). Mexican American and White American school dropouts' drug use, health status, and involvement in violence. *Public Health Reports, 104*, 594–604.

De La Rosa, D., & Maw, C. E. (1990). *Hispanic education: A statistical portrait 1990*. Washington, DC: National Council of La Raza.

Del Pinal, J. H., & De Navas, C. (1990). *The Hispanic population in the United States: March 1989* (Series P-20, No. 444). Washington, DC: U.S. Government Printing Office.

Desenclos, J. A., & Hahn, R. A. (1992). Years of potential life lost before age 65, by race, Hispanic origin, and sex: United States, 1986–1988. *Morbidity and Mortality Weekly Report (MMWR), 41*(SS-6), 13–23.

Fagan, J. (1990). Social processes of delinquency and drug use among urban gangs. In C. R. Huff (Ed.), *Gangs in America* (pp. 183–222). Newbury Park, CA: Sage.

Garcia, A. (1991). The changing demographic face of Hispanics in the United States. In M. Sotomayor (Ed.), *Empowering Hispanic families: A critical issue for the '90s* (pp. 21–38). Milwaukee, WI: Family Service America.

Garcia, J. M., & Montgomery, P. A. (1991). *The Hispanic population in the United States: March 1991* (Series P-20, No. 455). Washington, DC: U.S. Government Printing Office.

Genelin, M., & Coplen, B. (1989). *Los Angeles street gangs: Report and recommendations of the County-Wide Criminal Justice Coordination Committee Interagency Gang Task Force, March 1989*. Los Angeles: Interagency Gang Task Force.

Holinger, P. C., Offer, D., Barter, J. T., & Bell, C. C. (1994). *Suicide and homicide among adolescents*. New York: Guilford Press.

Mauer, J. D., Rosenberg, H. M., & Keemer, J. B. (1990). *Deaths of Hispanic origin: 15 reporting states, 1979–81* (DHHS Publication No. PHS 90-1855). Washington, DC: U.S. Government Printing Office.

McKay, E. G. (1988). *Changing Hispanic demographics*. Washington, DC: National Council of La Raza.

Moore, J. W. (1991). *Going down to the barrio: Homeboys and homegirls in change*. Philadelphia: Temple University Press.

National Council of La Raza. (1992). *State of Hispanic America 1991: An overview*. Washington, DC: Author.

National Education Association. (1968). *The invisible minority*. Washington, DC: Author.

O'Keefe, S. E., & Padilla, A. M. (1987). *Chicano ethnicity*. Albuquerque: University of New Mexico Press.

Pokorny, A. D. (1965). A comparison of homicide in two cities. *Journal of Criminal Law, Criminology and Political Science, 56*, 279–287.

Prothrow-Stith, D. (1991). *Deadly consequences: How violence is destroying our teenage population and a plan to begin solving the problem*. New York: HarperCollins.

Pynoos, R. S., & Nader, K. (1988). Psychological first aid and treatment approach to children exposed to community violence: Research implications. *Journal of Traumatic Stress, 1,* 445–473.

Rudoff, A. (1971). Criminology: The incarcerated Mexican-American delinquent. *Journal of Criminal Law, Criminology and Police Science, 62,* 224–238.

Sabogal, F., Marin, G., Otero-Sabogal, R., Marin, B. V., and Perez-Stable, E. J. (1987). Hispanic familism and acculturation: What changes and what doesn't. *Hispanic Journal of Behavioral Sciences, 9,* 397–412.

Sewell, C. M, Becker, T. M., Wiggins, C. L., Key, C. R., Hull, H. F., & Samet, J. M. (1989). Injury mortality in New Mexico's American Indians, Hispanics, and non-Hispanic Whites, 1958–1982. *Western Journal of Medicine, 150,* 708–713.

Shai, D., & Rosenwaike, I. (1988). Violent deaths among Mexican-, Puerto Rican- and Cuban-Born migrants in the United States. *Social Science and Medicine, 26,* 269–276.

Smith, J. C., Mercy, J. A., & Rosenberg, M. A. (1986). Suicide and homicide among Hispanics in the Southwest. *Public Health Reports, 101,* 265–270.

Smith, J. C., Mercy, J. A., & Rosenberg, M. L. (1988). Comparison of homicides among Anglos and hispanics in five southwestern states. *Border Health, 4*(1), 2–15.

Sorenson, S. B., & Siegel, J. M. (1992). Gender, ethnicity, and sexual assault: Findings from a Los Angeles study. *Journal of Social Issues, 48,* 93–104.

Soriano, F. I., LaVoie, L. L. M., Perez, V., Rowland, D., Silva, E., & Navarro, M. (in press). Psychosocial, familial and cultural factors in gang membership and violence. In M. Sotomayor (Ed.), *Latino families: Intergenerational issues.* Milwaukee, WI: Family Service America.

Spencer, G. (1986). Projections of the Hispanic population: 1983 to 2080. In *U.S. Bureau of the Census: Current population reports* (Series P-25, No. 995). Washington, DC: U.S. Government Printing Office.

Spergel, I. A. (1990). Youth gangs: Continuity and change. *Crime and Justice: A Review of Research, 12,* 171–275.

Spergel, I. A., Curry, D., Chance, R., Kane, C., Ross, R., Lexander, A., Simmons, E., & Oh, S. (1990). *Youth gangs: Problem and response. Stage 1: Assessment.* Washington, DC: Office of Juvenile Justice and Delinquency Prevention.

U.S. Bureau of the Census. (1985a). *Persons of Spanish origin in the United States: March 1982* (Series P-20, No. 396). Washington, DC: U.S. Government Printing Office.

U.S. Bureau of the Census. (1985b). *Current population survey.* Washington, DC: U.S. Government Printing Office.

U.S. Bureau of the Census. (1991). *Race and Hispanic origin: 1990 Census Profile Number 2, June 1991.* Washington, DC: U.S. Government Printing Office.

U.S. Department of Health and Human Services. (1991, October 11). Weapon-carrying among high school students—United States, 1990. *Morbidity and Mortality Weekly Report (MMWR).*

U.S. Department of Health and Human Services (1992). *Child abuse and neglect: A shared community concern, March 1992* (DHHS Publication No. ACF 92-30531, Rev.). Washington, DC: U.S. Government Printing Office.

U.S. Department of Justice. (1985). *The risk of violent crime.* Washington, DC: Bureau of Justice Statistics.

U.S. Department of Justice. (1988). *Report to the nation on crime and justice* (2nd ed.). Washington, DC: Bureau of Justice Statistics.

U.S. Department of Justice. (1990). *Hispanic victims.* Washington, DC: Bureau of Justice Statistics.

U.S. Department of Justice. (1991a). *Criminal victimization in the United States: 1990.* Washington, DC: Bureau of Justice Statistics.

U.S. Department of Justice. (1991b). *Criminal victimization 1990: A national crime victimization survey report.* Washington, DC: Bureau of Justice Statistics.

U.S. Department of Justice. (1991c). *Teenage victims.* Washington, DC: Bureau of Justice Statistics.

U.S. Department of Justice. (1991d). *Violent crime in the United States.* Washington, DC: Bureau of Justice Statistics.

U.S. Department of Justice. (1991e). *Female victims of violent crime* (Rep. No. NCJ-126826). Washington, DC: Bureau of Justice Statistics.

Zagar, R., Arbit, J., Sylvies, R., Busch, K. G., & Hughes, J. R. (1990). Homicidal adolescents: A replication. *Psychological Reports, 67*, 1235–1242.

Zahn, M. A. (1988). Homicide in nine American cities: The Hispanic case. In *Violence and homicide in Hispanic communities* (pp. 13–30). Los Angeles: University of California Publication Services.

6

Native Americans

Betty R. Yung and W. Rodney Hammond

Description of the Population

Native American, American Indian, and *Alaskan Native* are terms used to describe the indigenous native people of North America. Composed of many tribes and subpopulations of diverse cultural orientations and characterized by different lifestyles, states of acculturation, and residency (e.g., reservations, rural communities, or cities), Native Americans have been described as the "smallest and perhaps most diverse of all American minority groups" (Nickens, 1991, p. 29). In the United States, there are at least 124 major federally recognized tribes and bands (Klein, 1986), with larger but undetermined numbers of subgroupings (estimated to exceed 450) such as pueblo units or villages with distinct traditions, customs, and mores (LaFromboise & Low, 1991; Trimble, 1990). Evidence of the exceptional diversity of the Native Americans is the large number of present-day languages. Waldman (1988) identified 40 language families with more than 140 dialect variations among North American Indians. L. DeBruyn (personal communication, February 18, 1993) called attention to the other "numerous languages that were lost due to disease, decimation, and warfare from European conquest and colonization" as further testimony to the extraordinary linguistic and cultural heterogeneity of this population.

It is difficult to establish the size of the Native American population because of methods of defining ethnicity and collecting data. The legal definition formulated by the Bureau of Indian Affairs describes a Native American as one who (a) is an enrolled or registered member of a federally recognized tribe or village or (b) has at least one fourth or more in blood quantum and able to demonstrate that fact legally. The most recent U.S. Bureau of the Census (1990) figures estimate the size of the Native American, Eskimo, and Aleut population to be slightly more than 1.9 million, or 0.8% of the total population of the United States. However, some tribes have their own criteria for ethnic identification. In addition, the U.S. Bureau of the Census uses self-identification methods to determine ethnicity. Their methods obviously exclude citizens of Native American background who do not participate in the census or do not want to be so identified for personal reasons but counting other individuals who state an ethnic affiliation but perhaps do not meet legal or tribal definitions (Trimble, 1990).

Among identified Native Americans, the largest concentrations are found within the Western and Pacific regions of the lower 48 states of the continental United States (U.S. Bureau of the Census, 1990), with approximately 47% residing in four states: California, Oklahoma, Arizona, and New Mexico (Ho, 1992). In Alaska, the indigenous people include Eskimos, Aleuts, and the Athabascans of the eastern sector of the state; these groups make up about 16% of the state's population (Ho, 1992; Trimble, 1990). An increasing trend toward moves from reservations to urban locations has been notable since 1970, with only about an estimated one fourth of the Native American population currently living on 278 federal and state reservations (Ho, 1992).

Extent of the Risk of Violence

The extent of risk for fatal violence for Native Americans is not fully known. Reliable epidemiological data at the national level on homicide victimization rates for all ethnic groups other than African Americans cannot be obtained (Prothrow-Stith, 1991; U.S. Department of Health and Human Services, 1990). Federal Bureau of Investigation crime statistics typically classify victims as Black, White, and "other," so there is no national database on murder rates for specific non-African American minority populations (U.S. Department of Health and Human Services, 1990). The same is true of National Center for Health Statistics mortality data (Rosenberg & Mercy, 1991).

Thus, estimates on risk of homicide for Native Americans are based on data gathered in regional or tribal studies. Many studies have suggested that the relative risk for Native Americans is 1.5–3 times that for all Americans (Indian Health Service, 1990; Kahn, 1986; Kettl, 1993; Leyba, 1988; U.S. Department of Health and Human Services, 1990; Wallace, Kirk, Houston, Annest, & Emrich, 1993). Although homicide rates for Native Americans generally have been found to be lower than those for African Americans and about equal to those for Latinos, two exceptions are notable. Sloan et al. (1988) determined that Native Americans in Seattle, Washington, and Vancouver, British Columbia, Canada, had higher rates of death by homicide than did Whites or individuals of all other ethnic minority groups. Becker, Samet, Wiggins, and Key (1990), who studied homicide rates in New Mexico over a 30-year period, found substantially higher rates for both male and female Native Americans than for U.S. Latino and non-Latino men and women.

Gender-related patterns of fatal assaultive violence among Native Americans show similarities to national trends. Native American males have a 4- to 10-fold greater risk for involvement in lethal violent episodes than their female counterparts (Becker et al., 1990; Leyba, 1988). In Leyba's study, 90% of the Native American homicide victims and 88.9% of the perpetrators were male. Age-specific data from homicide studies suggest that risk increases sharply at age 15 for both male and female Native Americans and persists up to age 44 (Becker et al., 1990; Leyba, 1988; Wallace et al., 1993). Becker et al. also found that (a) risk disparity for Native American men between 35 and 44 remains higher than for same-aged men of other ethnic groups, (b) the violent death risk for 15–24-year-old Native American men exceeds that of U.S. Latino and non-Latino White men of the same ages, and (c) homicide incidents for adolescent and young adult Native American men increased more than 82% between 1958 and 1987. A study of homicide among Alaska Natives for a 3-year period showed an additional pattern of high victimization rates extending to older individuals, with murder rates for 45–74-year-old men and women about double that of the total Alaskan population and approximately six times higher than the total U.S. population (Kettl, 1993). Although the Alaska study may not be representative because of the relatively small number of deaths examined ($N = 48$), other research also suggests persistently high rates for middle-aged and older Native Americans and Alaska Natives (Wallace et al., 1993).

The extent of nonlethal forms of interpersonal violence among Native Americans is also difficult to determine. National normative data are not available on many of the dimensions of violence, such as physical child abuse, spouse abuse, and other assaults not resulting in death. In addition, these problems are widely considered to be underreported among all groups (De-Bruyn, Hymbaugh, & Valdez, 1988; National Committee for Injury Prevention and Control, 1989; Rosenberg & Mercy, 1991). Another complication in estimating interpersonal violence rates for Native Americans is misclassification of race in vital records and morbidity registries. Sugarman, Soderberg, Gordon, and Rivara (1993) studied the extent to which injury rates among Native Americans in Oregon are underestimated because the registry system for collecting data on injuries depends either on patient self-report or observation by hospital staff. When matched with patient files of Native American Oregon residents registered with the Indian Health Services, which determine race by documentation of tribal membership or Native American heritage, the annual injury rate for Native Americans was 68% higher than that reported in the hospital surveillance system.

Intertribal variations in reported cases of child physical abuse, a reluctance common to many battered women to seek help for what is considered to be a "family concern," and lack of data on off-reservation incidence contribute to the difficulties in estimating prevalence of family violence among Native Americans (DeBruyn et al., 1988; DeBruyn, Lujan, & May, 1992; DeBruyn, Wilkins, & Artichoker, 1990; Durst, 1991; Lujan, DeBruyn, May, & Bird, 1989). A study of physical violence affecting women in the 12 months preceding childbirth reported rates of battering among Native American women that were twice as high as those of White women and about 1.5 times higher than those of African American women (U.S. Department of Health and Human Services, 1994). Studies of physical abuse and neglect among Native American and Alaska Native children that were reviewed by the Office of Technology Assessment (OTA; 1990) suggested rates ranging from 5.7 to 26 per 1,000—higher than similar estimates (4.9–23.5 per 1,000) for the total child population (cited by Finklehor & Dziuba-Leatherman, 1994).

Apart from the limited research on child abuse among Native Americans, to our knowledge there are no studies focusing specifically on violence affecting Native American children and youth. The University of Minnesota has conducted survey research on health concerns and risk-taking behavior among Native American adolescents that included some data on violence (Blum, Harmon, Harris, Bergeisen, & Resnick, 1992; Blum, Harmon, Harris, Resnick, et al., 1992). Although this research provides some information on patterns of violence, it has not yielded a comprehensive profile. For example, in the reported episodes of fighting and victimization by physical and sexual assault, no questions were included to determine victim–perpetrator relationship; ethnicity of perpetrators; or levels of within-family violence versus victimization by strangers, friends, or acquaintances. There are also many typologies of victimization and risk behavior that have not been investigated in any source, including stranger rape, date rape or other violence, witnessing of violence, and weapons-carrying. A recent study provides some comparative data on the incidence of Native American male adolescents forcing sex on a partner (of unspecified gender), finding that their rates of such behavior (10.6%) were higher than those of White male adolescents (4.6%) but somewhat lower than the 11.7% reported by African American male adolescents (Gruber, DiClemente, & Anderson, 1994).

The Minnesota self-report survey data on involvement in violence by Native American adolescents suggest serious and substantial problems for individuals within this age group. Among the 13,000 Native American youth surveyed, almost one fifth reported being knocked unconscious by another person once or twice during the past year (Blum, Harmon, Harris, Bergeisen, et al., 1992; Blum, Harmon, Harris, Resnick, et al., 1992). Nearly 4 out of 10 of these adolescents said they had hit or beaten up someone at least once in the past year, with 4% admitting to 6 or more such incidents within this time frame and rates for male adolescents nearly double that reported for young women. Higher levels of involvement in violence were reported by respondents who also indicated regular use of marijuana or alcohol (Blum, Harmon, Harris, Resnick, et al., 1992). In comparison to a group of rural White youth in Minnesota, physical abuse episodes (in which the perpetrator was not identified) were twice as prevalent for both male and female Native American youth. Particularly high percentages of both physical and sexual abuse were reported by older adolescent female students in the 11th and 12th grades, with nearly 25% reporting physical abuse and more than 20% reporting sexual victimization (Blum, Harmon, Harris, Bergeisen, et al., 1992; Blum, Harmon, Harris, Resnick, et al., 1992). Native American adolescents also reported significant involvement with gangs; about 15% of the respondents indicated such an affiliation, with no differences noted by gender but with higher percentages reported by younger adolescents. Students who were gang members also were more likely to report multiple incidents of violent behavior; about 18% of those in gangs indicated that they had hit or beaten someone up three or more times during the past year compared with 6% of the larger sample reporting this behavior (Blum, Harmon, Harris, Resnick, et al., 1992).

Nature and Characteristics of Risk

Although assaultive violence crosses all socioeconomic lines, poverty has been identified persistently as the environmental risk correlate most strongly associated with violent victimization among all Americans (Christoffel, 1990; Fingerhut, Ingram, & Feldman, 1992; Loftin & Parker, 1985; Rosenberg & Mercy, 1991; Stark & Flitcraft, 1991). Although explanations for this relationship are not fully developed, it is generally accepted that it is not economic status in itself but its frequently associated conditions such as unemployment and disorganized, unsafe communities that contribute to high potential for violent behavior (see the discussion in Hammond & Yung, 1993). Among Native Americans and other ethnic groups, racism and discrimination contribute to continued oppression and community upheaval and perpetuate the adverse social and environmental conditions that appear to be linked to a higher prevalence of violence (Berlin, 1987). A particular contributor to family and community disruption among many Native American tribes has been forced attendance at boarding schools, in many cases situated great distances from the home reservation (Berlin, 1986, 1987).

A majority of Native American families are known to be living in poverty. According to data from the U.S. Congress (Ho, 1992), the median income in 1986 for Native American families was $13,768, compared with $17,786 for African American families and $29,152 for White families. On reservations, the average income was still lower at $9,942. Among some tribes, unemployment rates as high as 90% were reported (Berlin, 1987). There has been little empirical research specifically investigating the relationship between the incidence of poverty and violent episodes among Native Americans. DeBruyn et al. (1988) found higher rates of abuse and neglect among children living in households headed by single women, a situation frequently associated with lower incomes. Young (1990, 1991) found generally high correlations between the incidence of poverty and the homicide and suicide rates for individuals living in U.S. Indian Service areas. However, this did not hold true across all tribes, with the most noteworthy exception being the Navajo service area. Although the Navajos had the highest poverty rates of all areas studied, they had one of the lowest suicide and homicide rates. In addition, Young (1991) did not find a significant relationship between poverty level and homicide incidence among Native American women.

As for other ethnic groups, Native Americans are most vulnerable to violence perpetrated by an intimate, such as a spouse, parent, other family member, friend, or acquaintance (Kahn, 1986). Leyba (1988) found that the most frequent victim–perpetrator relationship in Native American homicides was that of friend or acquaintance (55.5% combined) and that in 80% of the cases studied, the incident leading to the eruption of the fatal violence was an altercation rather than a random act of predatory violence or violence associated with the commission of another crime.

Other research has identified additional associated variables or predictors of violence among Native Americans. Studies in a Southwest Indian Health Service hospital and four outpatient clinics showed close correlations between child physical abuse and multiple family problems, especially alcohol abuse, intergenerational histories of family violence, and lifestyle disruptions and instability as indicated by frequent moves (DeBruyn et al., 1988; Lujan et al., 1989). These studies further determined that children with disabilities were more likely to experience physical abuse. Approximately 30% of the abused children within the sample had disabilities, although the investigators noted that a number of the disabilities represented involved learning or emotional disorders, which might have been a result rather than the cause of the abuse (Lujan et al., 1989). Another study that examined Native American children who were in mental health treatment indicated that those who had histories of both abuse and neglect were more likely to come from families in which there was parental alcoholism, divorce, single parenting, and generally chaotic family situations (Piesecki, Manson, & Biernoff, 1989; cited in OTA, 1990).

Alcohol abuse within the family, the strongest correlate found in these studies, has also been implicated as a factor in higher incidence of spouse abuse (Durst, 1991) and in fatal violence among friends and acquaintances (Leyba, 1988). A 5-year study of injury-related mortalities in Oklahoma showed that 73% of the Native American homicide victims had a positive blood alcohol count, compared with 48% of the total sample (Oklahoma State Department of Health, 1993). Data are not available on intoxication levels in cases of nonfatal violence and rape, although some research suggests that both male and female Native American adolescents have higher general levels of injury following alcohol use (Gruber, Anderson, & DiClemente, 1994). The same study also showed a relationship between substance use and self-reported postuse perpetration of violence among Native American male adolescents (68%) and females (44%). These rates were higher than those of African American males (51.6%), White males (44%), African American females (34.5%), and White females (28.5%).

Ethnicity: Interpreting and Responding to Victimization

Just as the epidemiological data on violence among Native Americans is incomplete, so is the literature on the sequelae related to the experience of violence for this population. The effects of witnessing violence have not been examined, and the research on the effects of direct victimization has had only limited attention. Existing data suggest that the response patterns of Native American children and adolescents to a victimization experience combine with other risk factors to create particularly adverse and potentially lethal consequences for this group.

Piasecki, Manson, and Biernoff (1989) found that children in mental health treatment who had suffered both abuse and neglect were more likely than their nonabused peers to exhibit cognitive, developmental, and behavioral problems including running away from home and being expelled from school. Blum, Harmon, Harris, Bergeisen, et al. (1992) also found that abused respondents were significantly more likely to have run away from home.

A secondary analysis of Minnesota survey data by the OTA (1990) examined the covariance of physical and sexual abuse among Native American adolescents with diverse behavioral risk factors. In general, those youth who had experienced both physical and sexual abuse were more likely than the rest of the sample to pursue self-destructive paths, with the strongest effects for both male and female adolescents in the areas of suicide attempts and alcohol and drug use. Among adolescents who had experienced both forms of abuse, 72% of both males and females reported some use of beer or wine, and 19% of the young men and 13% of the young women reported very frequent use. Significant numbers of these adolescents also reported marijuana use, with males indicating somewhat higher levels than females (57% vs. 48%, respectively). Nonabused comparison youth reported lower rates of occasional use of alcohol (56% for males and 49% for females), of frequent use of alcohol (12% for males and 8% for females), and of experimentation with marijuana (37% for males and 29% for females). Comparable numbers of both boys and girls with histories of double abuse reported suicide attempts, approximately 42%, compared with 11% of the nonabused adolescents. Physically and sexually abused adolescents also reported more fear of being forced to do something sexual, more sexual activity, and more pronounced feelings of being only in fair or poor health (OTA, 1990).

The greater propensity for maltreated Native American adolescents to misuse alcohol or other drugs is not consistent with findings among the general population of physically and sexually abused adolescents, which report mixed results according to nature of the abuse and gender of the victim (see reviews in Ireland & Spatz-Widom, 1994). In their own research Ireland and Spatz-Widom did not find that childhood abuse was a significant predictor of adolescent arrest for alcohol- or drug-related offenses, although they did find a correlation with arrests for such offenses for young adults. They hypothesized that their findings may simply indicate that the full impact or extent of adolescent chemical involvement may not be realized until adulthood. For Native American adolescents, there is a generally higher incidence of alcohol abuse and other drugs than for other ethnic minority or White adolescent groups. Investigators have suggested diverse etiological explanations for this phenomenon, including that substance abuse represents a coping strategy to reduce feelings of isolation or alienation, a temporary emotional escape from the stresses associated with minority group status, a means of connecting with substance-abusing peers, or a self-destructive behavior related to low self-esteem and poor expectations for the future (Berlin, 1987; OTA, 1990). It is difficult to disentangle the specific effects of physical and sexual violence from these broader social and cultural factors.

The traumatic effects of victimization could be mitigated by personal support systems such as strong bonds with friends, parents, or other adults or interventions by a helping professional. However, Native American adolescents appear to have less feeling of family connectedness than White and other ethnic minority youth. They also report more negative feelings about school and less confidence that church and school leaders care about them. When asked to whom they would turn first if they felt depressed or angry or were having relationship problems with family or friends, 20% of the male and 7% of the female Native American adolescents said they would not seek help at all in most of these situations (Rode & Bellefield, 1992).

Knowledge Gaps and Research Needs

Knowledge about violence among Native Americans suffers from the same lack of understanding about contributing etiological factors that characterizes general conceptualizations around violence among all ethnic groups. The interrelationships of social, cultural, structural, situational, and interpersonal variables with violent acts and minority group status are not perfectly discernible (Prothrow-Stith, 1991; Sampson, 1987). Violence among adults in Native American families has been linked to factors that may also be characteristic of the broader American culture, such as power differentials in male–female relationships, community or tribal sanctions against divorce or separation and against outside interference in domestic disputes, and police attitudes and practices that are not helpful to women in situations of domestic battering (DeBruyn et al., 1990; Durst, 1991).

Much of the conceptual development of Native American violence discusses the ethnic group as a homogeneous entity with little distinction between subgroup variations. Such distinctions are extremely important. Young's (1990, 1991) findings of differential homicide rates among tribes and among men and women support the need for focused study on variations among tribal and gender groups. The growing and substantial levels of violence among Native American adolescents and young adults, highlighted in the research of Becker et al. (1990), Blum, Harmon, Harris, Bergeisen, et al. (1992), and Blum, Harmon, Harris, Resnick, et al. (1992), indicate a need for investigations that target age-specific variables. In addition, much of the related literature is based on studies done with Native Americans living on reservations, with virtually no research on those in off-reservation housing who now constitute a majority of the population.

Psychologists can make an especially valuable contribution to the extensive need for research on the experience of violent victimization for Native Americans. Studies that gauge both short- and long-range consequences of violence victimization and exposure are vitally needed in an effort to build knowledge and capacity of service providers to respond to these phenomena. Specific attention should be paid to identifying links between violence and other risk behaviors, such as suicide attempts and substance abuse; relationships between cultural norms and help-seeking behavior; the effects of repeated exposure to traumatic events; and the factors that might prevent destructive consequences. Psychologists can also assist in the development of new psychometric measures to assess the effects of violent victimization and in determining whether existing measures are culturally appropriate.

Program or Service Needs

For Native Americans, particular needs have been noted for clinical and support services geared toward victims, batterers, and children involved in violent situations. Debruyn et al. (1990) underscored the scarcity of existing service programs on reservations, estimating that there are probably less than 10 shelters in the nation specifically established to serve battered Native American women. As a result, these women must most often seek services in shelters that are geographically remote from the reservations and that have been designed to meet the needs of the mainstream population.

Needs have also been identified for appropriately trained service providers, particularly ones of Native American descent who would have a personal understanding of the needs and culture of the population. Trimble (1990) cited the fact that there are only 30 entries found in the Native American section of the 1988 *Directory of Ethnic Minority Professionals in Psychology*. La-Fromboise (1988) identified the few available role models in academic and service positions in the field of psychology as a significant barrier experienced by Native Americans who might want to pursue graduate education. The OTA (1990) reported that within the 12 Indian Health Service areas (covering 32 states), there were only 17 child- and adolescent-trained mental health care providers to serve a population of young people exceeding 199,000.

Echoing recommendations related to other ethnic groups, the literature on Native American violence emphasizes the need for culturally sensitive violence prevention programming that takes into account the values, beliefs, and customs of the group for which the intervention is designed. Many authors emphasize the need for involvement of tribal leaders in program development in recognition of the fact that the authority figures and opinion leaders of the community must sanction the effort if it is to be successful (Berlin, 1986; DeBruyn et al., 1988).

The general recommendations developed by task forces and interdisciplinary forums on violence and injury prevention are certainly applicable to efforts to reduce violence among Native Americans. Such proposals are designed to change the social, environmental, and structural contexts most likely to generate violent behavior. Of special interest are the recommendations generated in recent conferences on minority violence sponsored by the Centers for Disease Control and those highlighted in the work of the National Committee for Injury Prevention and Control (Centers for Disease Control, 1991; Mizanin, in press; National Committee for Injury Prevention and Control, 1989). Among other priorities, they emphasize the need to design culturally appropriate prevention and intervention programs that build on the traditions and strengths of ethnic minority communities as efforts are directed toward (a) mobilizing communities to take responsibility for addressing the problem of violence; (b) developing data collection and evaluation methods for better documentation of incidence of violent behavior and the effectiveness of preventive interventions; (c) educating citizens, tribal and community leaders, and service providers on violence issues; and (d) addressing broader issues such as poverty, unemployment, and racism.

Public Policy Recommendations

1. Funding is needed for service demonstration programs. Although much basic research is needed on the causes and nature of violence within this population, waiting until perfect knowledge has been attained is an unaffordable luxury. Potentially life-saving interventions

need to be tested and implemented and results shared between communities. Special needs include counseling and shelter for victims of battering, increased legal programs and options, programs of primary prevention, and community educational programs. Because of its strong correlations with all types of violence, alcohol and other drug abuse should be a strongly emphasized component of such programming.

2. Native American-specific research initiatives related to violence should be developed and funded, especially ones that would support longitudinal study; examine within-group variations among ethnic, gender, and age subgroupings; and focus on off-reservation populations.

3. There should be expansion or, at minimum, continuation of funding programs such as National Institute of Mental Health clinical training grants for support of ethnic minorities to pursue doctoral training in psychology. Indigenous researchers and service providers with an understanding of the culture will be in a more credible position to identify problems related to violence, to develop culturally sensitive programs of prevention and intervention, and to advocate for change. Emphasis needs to be maintained on public–academic linkages in training programs that will produce practitioners and applied researchers committed to serve at-risk Native Americans in public settings.

4. Professional literature points out dilemmas related to differences between tribal policies or informal customs that do not adequately protect women and children (e.g., tribal sanctions against a woman leaving her husband even if he is being extremely physically abusive). Public policy should elucidate such conflicts with a view toward determining what changes are possible.

5. Data collection methods at the national level should be improved to assist in gaining a more complete understanding of the extent of the problem. The present system used by the National Center for Health Statistics and the Federal Bureau of Investigation of aggregating all non-African American ethnic minority individuals into an "other" category does not permit the construction of a reliable account of the extent of homicide (generally the easiest form of violence to track) among Native Americans. National studies on the prevalence of child and spouse or partner abuse and rape should be encouraged to include Native Americans in their samples and to provide analyses that distinguish ethnic-specific patterns. Research of this type should use standardized methods of determining ethnicity because differing definitions and means of establishing race present problems in making comparisons between existing studies.

6. The American Psychological Association should place a continued and increased emphasis on rural psychology and public service psychology. It is important to promote these special interests because large concentrations of Native Americans, both on and off reservations, live in rural areas that present unique problems for psychological service delivery because of geographic spread, isolation, lack of other support

services, and lack of transportation for some individuals or families. Also because of high levels of poverty, most Native Americans are more likely to receive services from publicly funded mental health agencies.

References

Becker, T., Samet, J., Wiggins, C., & Key, C. (1990). Violent death in the West: Suicide and homicide in New Mexico, 1958–1987. *Suicide and Life-Threatening Behavior, 20*, 324–334.

Berlin, I. (1986). Psychopathology and its antecedents among American Indian adolescents. *Advances in Clinical Psychology, 9*, 125–151.

Berlin, I. (1987). Suicide among American Indian adolescents: An overview. *Suicide and Life-Threatening Behavior, 17* , 218–232.

Blum, R., Harmon, B., Harris, L., Bergeisen, L., & Resnick, M. (1992). American Indian-Alaska Native youth health. *Journal of the American Medical Association, 267*, 1637–1644.

Blum, R., Harmon, B., Harris, L., Resnick, M., Stutelberg, K., & Robles, A. (1992). *The state of Native American youth health*. Minneapolis: University of Minnesota, Division of General Pediatrics and Adolescent Health.

Centers for Disease Control. (1991). Forum on youth violence in minority communities: Setting the agenda for prevention. *Public Health Reports, 106* , 225–253.

Christoffel, K. K. (1990). Violent death and injury in US children and adolescents. *American Journal of Diseases of Childhood, 144*, 697–706.

DeBruyn, L., Hymbaugh, K., & Valdez, N. (1988). Helping communities address suicide and violence: The Special Initiatives Team of the Indian Health Service. *American Indian and Alaska Native Mental Health Research, 1*, 56–65.

DeBruyn, L., Lujan, C., & May, P. (1992). A comparative study of abused and neglected American Indian children in the Southwest. *Social Science and Medicine, 35*, 305–315.

DeBruyn, L., Wilkins, B., & Artichoker, K. (1990, November). *"It's not cultural": Violence against Native American women*. Paper presented at the 89th Meeting of the American Anthropological Association, New Orleans, LA.

Durst, D. (1991). Conjugal violence: Changing attitudes in two northern native communities. *Community Mental Health Journal, 27*, 359–373.

Fingerhut, L., Ingram, D., & Feldman, J. (1992). Firearm and nonfirearm homicide among persons 15 through 19 years of age. *Journal of the American Medical Association, 267*, 3048–3053.

Finklehor, D., & Dziuba-Leatherman, J. (1994). Victimization of children. *American Psychologist, 49*, 173–183.

Gruber, E., Anderson, M., & DiClemente, R. (1994). Alcohol-specific problem behavior among Native American, Black & White adolescents in a midwestern state [Abstract]. *Journal of Adolescent Health, 15*, 59.

Gruber, E., DiClemente, R., & Anderson, M. (1994). Differences in risk-taking behavior among Native American, Black and White adolescents in a midwestern state [Abstract]. *Journal of Adolescent Health, 15*, 59.

Hammond, R., & Yung, B. (1993). Psychology's role in the public health response to assaultive violence among young African-American men. *American Psychologist, 48*, 142–154.

Ho, M. (1992). *Minority children and adolescents in therapy*. Newbury Park, CA: Sage.

Indian Health Service. (1990). *Injuries among American Indians and Alaskan Natives: 1990*. Rockville, MD: U.S. Public Health Service.

Ireland, T., & Spatz-Widom (1994). Childhood victimization and risk for alcohol and drug arrests. *International Journal of the Addictions, 29*, 235–274.

Kahn, M. (1986). Psychosocial disorders of aboriginal people of the United States and Australia. *Journal of Rural Community Psychology, 7*, 45–59.

Kettl, P. (1993). Homicide in Alaska Natives. *Alaska Medicine, 35*, 168–172.

Klein, B. (1986). *Reference encyclopedia of the American Indian*. New York: Todd.

LaFromboise, T. (1988). American Indian mental health policy. *American Psychologist, 43*, 388–397.

LaFromboise, T., & Low, K. (1991). American Indian children and adolescents. In J. T. Gibbs & L. N. Huang (Eds.), *Children of color: Psychological interventions with minority youth* (pp. 114–147). San Francisco: Jossey-Bass.

Leyba, C. (1988). Homicides in Bernalillo County: 1978–1982. In J. Kraus, S. Sorenson, & P. Juarez (Eds.), *Research conference on violence and homicide in Hispanic communities* (pp. 101–118). Los Angeles: University of California Press.

Loftin, C., & Parker, R. N. (1985). The effect of poverty on urban homicide rates: An errors-in-variable model. *Criminology, 23,* 269–287.

Lujan, C., DeBruyn, L., May, P., & Bird, M. (1989). Profile of abused and neglected American Indian children in the Southwest. *Child Abuse and Neglect, 13,* 449–461.

Mizanin, J. (Ed.). (in press). *Forum on youth violence: Prevention in Ohio.* Cleveland, OH: Mizanin.

National Committee for Injury Prevention and Control. (1989). *Injury prevention: Meeting the challenge.* New York: Oxford University Press.

Nickens, H. (1991). The health status of minority populations in the United States. *Western Journal of Medicine, 155,* 27–32.

Office of Technology Assessment. (1990). *Indian adolescent mental health* (Rep. No. OTA-H-446). Washington, DC: U.S. Government Printing Office.

Oklahoma State Department of Health. (1993). *Oklahoma injury facts.* Oklahoma City: Injury Prevention Service, Oklahoma State Department of Health.

Piasecki, J., Manson, S., & Biernoff, M. (1989). Abuse and neglect of American Indian children: Findings from a survey of federal providers. *American Indian and Alaska Native Mental Health Research, 3,* 43–62.

Prothrow-Stith, D. (1991). *Deadly consequences: How violence is destroying our teenage population and a plan to begin solving the problem.* New York: HarperCollins.

Rode, P., & Bellefield, K. (1992). *The next generation: The health and well being of young people of color in the Twin Cities. A report based on the Minnesota Adolescent Health Survey.* Minneapolis: Urban Coalition of Minneapolis.

Rosenberg, M., & Mercy, J. (1991). Assaultive violence. In M. Rosenberg & J. Mercy (Eds.), *Violence in America: A public health approach* (pp. 14–50). New York: Oxford University Press.

Sampson, R. (1987). Urban black violence: The effect of male joblessness and family disruption. *American Journal of Sociology, 93,* 348–405.

Sloan, J., Kellermann, A., Reay, D., Ferris, J., Koepsell, T., Rivara, F., Rice, C., Gray, L., & LoGerfo, J. (1988). Handgun regulation, crime, assaults, and homicides. *New England Journal of Medicine, 319,* 1256–1262.

Stark, E., & Flitcraft, A. (1991). Spouse abuse. In M. Rosenberg & J. Mercy (Eds.), *Violence in America: A public health approach* (pp. 123–157). New York: Oxford University Press.

Sugarman, J., Soderberg, R., Gordon, J., & Rivara, F. (1993). Racial misclassification of American Indians: Its effect on injury rates in Oregon, 1989 through 1990. *American Journal of Public Health, 83,* 681–684.

Trimble, J. (1990). Application of psychological knowledge for American Indians and Alaska Natives. *Journal of Training and Practice in Professional Psychology, 4,* 45–63.

U.S. Bureau of the Census. (1990). Population and Housing Summary Tape File 1C.

U.S. Department of Health and Human Services, Public Health Service. (1990). *Healthy people 2000: National health promotion and disease prevention objectives* (DHS Publication No. PHS 91-50212).Washington, DC: U.S. Government Printing Office.

U.S. Department of Health and Human Services. (1994). Physical violence during the 12 months preceding childbirth—Alaska, Maine, Oklahoma, and West Virginia, 1990–91. *Morbidity and Mortality Weekly Report, 43,* 133–137.

Waldman, C. (1988). *Encyclopedia of Native American tribes.* New York: Facts on File Publications.

Wallace, D., Kirk, M., Houston, B., Annest, J., & Emrich, S. (1993). *Injury mortality atlas of Indian Health Service areas, 1979–87.* Atlanta, GA: National Center for Injury Prevention and Control, Centers for Disease Control and Prevention.

Young, T. (1990). Poverty, suicide, and homicide among Native Americans. *Psychological Reports, 67,* 1153–1154.

Young, T. (1991). Suicide and homicide among Native Americans: Anomie or social learning? *Psychological Reports, 68,* 1137–1138.

7

Asian/Pacific Island Americans

S. Andrew Chen and Reiko Homma True

Description of the Population

Although Asian/Pacific Island Americans (A/PIs) represent only 2.9% (7.27 million) of the total U.S. population, the number of A/PIs in the U.S. increased by 95% between 1980 and 1990. This rapid growth is expected to continue well into the next century and is projected to reach 18–20 million by 2020 (Ong & Hee, 1992). The increase was stimulated primarily by the 1965 immigration law change and the admission of refugees from Southeastern Asian countries beginning in 1975. Among them, the percentages of children under 19 and between 10 and 19 are 32.2% and 15.9%, respectively (Asian and Pacific Islander Center for Census Information and Services, 1992).

The term *Asian/Pacific Island Americans* is often used by policymakers and the general public, who tend to think of them as a homogeneous group. However, they are a diverse group of people with vastly different backgrounds, including their history, language, culture, socioeconomic status, needs, and problems (Takaki, 1989). Among them, Asian Americans make up 95% of the population, representing 28 ethnic groups, including persons of Chinese, Japanese, Filipino, Asian Indian, Korean, and Vietnamese ancestry (Chen, 1991). Although their number is small, Pacific Islanders consist of approximately 30 different ethnic groups from the Pacific Island region, including Hawaiians, Samoans, Tongans, and Guamanians.

Some of the Asian American groups such as Chinese, Japanese, and Filipinos began immigrating to the United States more than 100 years ago and have fifth- and sixth-generation offspring. However, a majority (65.6%) are foreign born, with wide variations among ethnic groups (e.g., 32.4% of Japanese vs. 79.9% of Vietnamese or 79.4% of Laotians; U.S. Bureau of the Census, 1993). In 1990, 58% of A/PIs lived in the western United States, with the highest concentration living in California. New York, Hawaii, Texas, and Illinois also have significant Asian American populations.

Extent of the Risk of Violence

Because most violence-related national data are not systematically collected on ethnic groups other than African Americans, little is known about the extent of risk or incidence of violence against A/PIs. The official justification by federal and state agencies for not focusing on or identifying A/PIs as a separate group has been that their numbers are too small, too diverse, and too dispersed throughout the country to make meaningful, cost-effective data collection possible.

Homicide

National statistics on A/PI homicides are difficult to interpret, in that rates for suicide and homicide are combined. Among 15–24-year-old A/PIs, the combined suicide and homicide rates, per 100,000 people, were 15.5 in 1987, 13.2 in 1988, and 17.5 in 1989 (U.S. Department of Education, 1992).

More specific data on violent deaths for this population can be found in some studies of smaller geographical areas. The investigation conducted in Los Angeles by Loya et al. (1986) is one of the few studies that identifies Asian Americans (as well as U.S. Latinos) as a separate racial category. Reviewing all criminal homicides among Anglo, U.S. Latino, African American, and Asian victims between 1970 and 1979, they noted that among the homicide victims, the percentage of Asian cases was relatively small at 1.9%. However, they constituted 4.6% and 6.1% of the city's population total in 1970 and 1980, respectively. By contrast, the homicide figures for other races were 47.4% for African Americans, 27.2% for Anglos, and 22.9% for Latinos; they constituted 17.0%, 48.3%, and 27.5%, respectively, of the total population in 1980.

Relative to the victim's relationship to his or her perpetrator, the highest category for Asians was by strangers, 60.2%, whereas the figures for other races for the same category were considerably lower (i.e., 40.0%, 18.0%, and 29.1% for Anglos, African Americans, and Latinos, respectively). The percentage committed by spouses or partners was 7.2% for Asians, whereas the figures for Anglos, African Americans, and U.S. Latinos were 14.0%, 17.2%, and 5.4%, respectively. Similarly, the figures for the nonspouse family category was also significantly lower for Asians at 1.2%, whereas the respective figures were 7.6%, 8.9%, and 6.7% for Anglos, African Americans, and U.S. Latinos. Although specific figures were not provided, the investigators also noted that there was an apparent absence of primary homicides for Asians (i.e., homicides perpetrated by individuals from the same ethnic or racial group as the victim's). The percentage of gang-related homicides for Asians was 4.8% of the total, and the figures for Anglos, African Americans, and U.S. Latinos were 1.0%, 2.0%, and 16.0%, respectively.

Family Violence

An area that has received limited attention is the area of child and spouse abuse within A/PI communities. The rate of offenses against family and children of Asian origin in the United States was reported as 2.7% in the Federal Bureau of Investigation's (FBI's; 1991) "Uniform Crime Report." However, community-based A/PI human service workers often express concern about the presence of hidden family violence in the community and the community's failure to recognize and deal with it as a problem (C. Ho, 1990; Lum, 1988; Masaki, 1992; Nakagawa, 1992; Rimonte, 1989).

Some regional data that can provide more specific information about the nature of A/PI child abuse include the report on a review of A/PI cases seen at a large San Diego Asian Pacific social service agency by Ima and Hohn (1991). Among the 158 cases seen over an 18-month period between 1987 and 1988, the investigators noted that Cambodians and Vietnamese were disproportionately represented compared with their overall population in the community (see Table 1). The investigators speculated that the devastating experience of war trauma in their home countries was contributing to the delayed psychic distress among adults, who take out their frustrations on their children.

By contrast, the incidence of abuse among Hmong families was negligible, which the investigators believed was primarily because of their ability to transpose their close-knit social organization from Laos to the United States and maintain a supportive network among its members. Apparently, Hmongs in other communities have also been successful in maintaining a cohesive social network and are helpful in intervening when potential abuse may occur among their members (McInnis, 1991).

Although there were no Japanese or Chinese cases found, the investigators believed that the absence was not necessarily an indication that they were problem free but that most were English speaking and did not require the bilingual services offered at the agency.

Relative to the types of abuse reported, the investigators noted that the majority of A/PI abuse cases involved physical abuse, with neglect being the next most frequently reported (Table 2). This contrasts with the general U.S. population, for which a significant incidence of child sexual and emotional abuse is reported. Among the Asian subgroups, even though there are similarities in child-rearing patterns, there are important differences in type of maltreatment, which investigators postulated are due to cultural variations in family structure, child-rearing patterns, and different life experiences. The

TABLE 1. Ethnicity of Child Maltreatment Victims (in Percentages)

	UPAC sample (N = 158)	Indo-Chinese/Pacific Islander population[a] (N = 93,622)
Cambodian	23.6	6.0
Hmong	1.3	5.0
Korean	1.3	3.0
Laotian	9.6	9.0
Filipino	24.2	52.0
Samoan	3.8	3.0
Vietnamese	36.3	23.0

Note. From "Child maltreatment among Asian and Pacific Islander refugees and immigrants," by K. Ima & C. F. Hohm, 1991, *Journal of Interpersonal Violence, 6,* p. 272. Copyright 1991 by Sage Publications. Reprinted with permission. UPAC = Union of Pan Asian Communities.
[a]Estimates for Vietnamese, Hmong, Cambodian (Khmer), and Laotian are from Rumbault and Weeks (1986); estimates for Korean, Filipino, and Samoan are based on 1983 U.S. Census data.

TABLE 2.   Type of Child Maltreatment by Ethnicity (in Percentages)

	Vietnamese	Filipino	Laotian	Cambodian	Samoan	Korean	Hmong
Physical abuse[a]	71.9	47.4	53.3	62.2	83.3	100.0	—
Sexual abuse[b]	3.5	13.2	—	—	—	—	—
Emotional abuse[c]	5.3	15.8	13.3	—	—	—	—
Neglect[d]	35.1	42.1	66.7	45.9	16.7	—	100.0
n	57	38	15	37	6	2	2

Note. Percentages do not add up to 100% because the types of child maltreatment are not exclusive. Some children were involved in two or more types of child maltreatment. Each row constitutes a separate cross-tabulation.
[a]Chi-square significant at .06; Cramer's V = .28.
[b]Chi-square not significant; Cramer's V = .21.
[c]Chi-square not significant; Cramer's V = .24.
[d]Chi-square significant at .09; Cramer's V = .26.
From "Chinese maltreatment among Asian and Pacific Islander refugees and immigrants" by K. Ima and C. F. Hohm, 1991, *Journal of Interpersonal Violence, 6,* p. 273. Copyright 1991 by Sage Publications. Reprinted by permission.

groups with a high proportion of physical abuse cases were Samoan (83%) and Vietnamese (72%). Except for Filipinos, child sexual abuse was relatively rare among all other A/PI American groups.

Although in the U.S. population males are slightly more likely to be neglected than females (49.3% vs. 40.6%, respectively), the percentage for A/PI males in the San Diego group was much greater than for females (44.6% vs. 27.5%). Although the breakdown of emotional abuse among the U.S. population was nearly equal between male and female victims, the proportion of A/PI females was more than 4 times that of males (9.9% vs. 2.2%). For sexual abuse, females were more likely to be victims for both groups, but it was proportionately higher (8.8% vs. 1.1%) in the A/PI group than in the U.S. group (17.2% vs. 6.1%). In terms of the relationship between the perpetrator and the sexual abuse victim, 50% of the A/PI cases involved fathers and 50% were people other than parents, whereas the figures for the U.S. population were 36% fathers and 33% others.

Similar to the experience in San Diego, the child abuse information in San Francisco, where there is a large concentration A/PIs under 21 years of age (38%), indicates that the reported incidence of child abuse among A/PIs is low. Among the number of cases reported to the San Francisco Police Department during 1993, the rates per 1,000 population for Asians were 3, 1, and 0.5 for physical abuse, sexual abuse, and neglect, respectively, whereas the respective rates for other ethnic groups were considerably higher: Whites, 9, 10, and 3; Latinos, 12, 7, and 2; and African Americans, 24, 15, and 9 (San Francisco Police Department, 1993).

Like the San Diego cases, the majority of the Asian cases in San Francisco involved physical abuse (64%). However, the percentage of sexual abuse was 25% versus 4.9% in San Diego and the neglect category was 11.2% versus 36.1%. Although there were no reports of Chinese or Japanese cases in San Diego, the majority of cases in San Francisco involved Chinese (53%) and other Asians (46%), who were mostly southeastern Asians. Whereas 78% of the physical abuse cases were committed by a family member, 58% of the sexual abuse cases were committed by a nonrelative or other than a close relative. Because many of the refugee families are living in the high-crime Tenderloin district of San Francisco, many of the nonrelative perpetrators are non-Asian pedophiles living in the area (Lim, 1994).

Although there are few national data on the extent of child sexual abuse among A/PIs, the review of the cases treated at a citywide child abuse crisis and treatment agency in San Francisco by Rao, DiClemente, and Ponton (1992) offers a glimpse into the often ignored area. The researchers conducted a retrospective review of closed A/PI cases seen between January 1986 and December 1988 and compared them with random samples of African American, White, and U.S. Latino victims seen during the same period. During the 3-year period, the ethnic breakdown of children served by the agency was 37.6% African American, 25.9% White, 21.9% Latino, 6.6% Asian, and 7.2% "other." The total number of A/PI cases seen during that period was 98, of which 69 were substantiated as sexual abuse. Of these 69 cases, 30.4% were Filipino, 15.9% were Vietnamese, 15.9% were Pacific Islander, 11.6% were Chinese, 5.8% were Fiji Indian, 5.8% were Cambodian, and 14.6% were other. The significant proportion of A/PI as well as Latino victims were immigrants. Although gender breakdown was not provided in the report, the overall gender breakdown of the cases served at the same agency during 1993 was 70% female and 30% male. The majority of the A/PI cases were also females (Smith, personal communication, February 11, 1994).

The investigators found that when compared with other ethnic groups, there were considerable differences among A/PI victims: the median age was 11.5 versus 8.7, 9.0, and 10.5 for African Americans, Whites, and Latinos, respectively. They were most likely to be living with both parents, 35% versus 10%, 26%, and 23% for African Americans, Whites, and Latinos, respectively, but also proportionately more (18%) were living in a shelter at the time of evaluation compared with other groups. The majority (71%) were immigrants. The percentage of victims experiencing vaginal or anal intercourse was 36%, the same as Whites, whereas the figures for African Americans and Latinos were 58% and 50%, respectively. They were also the most likely to be abused by a male relative, including the father (62%), compared with 36% for Whites and 45% each for African Americans and Latinos.

On the basis of the preliminary review of the data currently available in the United States, the overall incidence of child abuse and sexual abuse among the A/PI group appears to be considerably lower than in the general U.S. population. However, it is generally believed that there is a significant underreporting of the extent of child abuse in A/PI communities because they believe that considerable physical punishment is necessary to bring up obedient children and that punishment is an expression of love, not abuse (Hong & Hong, 1991; Ima & Hohm, 1991). Once in the United States, many A/PI parents are dismayed to find that their rights to punish their children physically are significantly limited.

Although many A/PI parents' actions bordering on child abuse are not reported, certain groups, such as refugees on welfare, are under closer scrutiny by public authorities and are more easily identified for abuse. Although some refugees and recent immigrants do tend to become abusive to their children because of acculturation difficulties, there are certain culturally acceptable child-rearing and healing practices that are judged by U.S. professionals to be abuse or neglect and are therefore mishandled. The case of coin rolling (a traditional Asian treatment used to relieve fever, headache, and chills, which leaves an ugly skin abrasion) among the southeastern Asian refugees (Rosenblatt & Hong, 1989) or use of folk-healing remedies among Central and Latin American immigrants (Krajewski-Jaime, 1991) are some of the examples of situations that can be mislabeled and inappropriately handled by the U.S. authorities and can lead to unnecessary tragedies.

Adolescent Rape, Dating Violence, and Prostitution

Although quantitative data are not available on the extent of violence suffered by A/PI adolescent females, there are anecdotal reports (Yoshihama, Parekh, & Boyington, 1991) suggesting that many A/PI females are victims of stranger rape, date rape, and dating violence. As more A/PI females are beginning to move out of their own communities and socialize in integrated academic or work environments, they are becoming rapidly involved in interracial dating and marriage (Kitano, Yeung, Chai, & Hatanaka, 1986; Weiss, 1973). Because of the long-standing stereotyping and exploitation of A/PI women as easily available sex objects both in the United States and in various Asian countries where American businessmen and soldiers were stationed, they are expected to be available sexually here and are victimized when they resist (Chan, 1987). However, they are reluctant to report or seek help because of feeling of shame, cultural prohibitions, and fears or distrust of authority.

Although little information is available on the extent of child and adolescent prostitution in this population, the group most vulnerable to such exploitation are the adolescent girls who run away from home. Contrary to the idealized image of Asian families as close-knit units, there are a considerable number of adolescents who run away from home, becoming more vulnerable for violent victimization. Reporting on their work with San Francisco's Chinese American runaway adolescents, Louie, Joe, Luu, and Tong (1991) noted that 50 of 447 reported runaways in San Francisco in 1990 were Asians, 56% of whom were females aged 11–16 years. Most identified family problems (e.g., parental marital problems, disagreement with parents, sibling issues, neglect and abuse) as the primary impetus for running away. However, they rarely went to traditional shelters but were often taken in by gang-related groups into a "gang house," fed, clothed and given spending money. In return, they are asked to participate in underground prostitution rings.

Another area, which is mostly hidden in the A/PI community but affects children, is the incidence of spousal abuse, primarily involving wives as victims. However, as some of the communities begin to address the problems by providing A/PI shelters and social services with bilingual staff, they are finding out that many of the women have children who are traumatized by the battery of their mothers and are themselves in danger of being abused. For example, the statistics at the New York Asian Women's Center (1992), which provides bilingual counseling, hotline, and shelter services to abused women, indicates that the majority of women who are served have children (i.e., 45% in the shelter, 64% in overall services). In the Los Angeles shelter, two thirds of the population are children, one fourth of whom have been abused (Rimonte, 1989). Although these children exhibit symptoms of distress similar to other children of abused mothers (e.g., feeling terrified, responsible, and guilty for the violence and for their mother's having to leave the home; being passive and withdrawn; having impaired peer relations), they have the added burden, as the offspring of immigrant mothers, of playing mediator between the home and the outside world and taking on the parental role because of their facility with English (Rimonte, 1989).

Youth Gangs

Although the involvement of A/PI youths in delinquent and criminal activities previously has been thought to be relatively low (Abbott & Abbott, 1968; Kitano, 1976), the emergence of Asian youth gangs in communities with significant Asian concentrations has attracted the attention of the media and law enforcement professionals (Dao, 1992; Vigil & Yun, 1990; Wong, 1992). Although this is not a new phenomenon, the increase in number of crimes and degree of criminality perpetrated by them seems to be increasing, particularly among immigrant youth (Chin, 1990). However, despite media publicity and some disturbing trends, the overall criminal involvement of A/PI youth appears to remain relatively low if one judges from the local data (e.g., San Francisco's juvenile probation records).

Nature and Characteristics of Risk

The literature on violence-related research suggests that age, educational achievement, home ownership, and place of residence are all associated with adult and youth violence (U.S. Department of Justice, 1985). In spite of the absence of specific violence-related data, it appears that A/PIs are at considerable risk for experiencing violence when age, education, poverty, and prior exposure to violence are considered.

Age

Violent crime is likely to have more of an impact on youth than on adults or elderly individuals (e.g., 12–24-year-olds have the highest victimization rates for violent crimes; U.S. Department of Justice, 1991). The percentage of A/PIs below the age of 19 and between the ages 10 and 24 in 1990 was 32.2% and 24.6%, respectively, compared with 26.7% and 20.4%, respectively, for Whites (Asian and Pacific Islander Center for Census Information and Services, 1992). The figures for more recent immigrants and refugees are even higher, particularly among the Southeast Asians (Gardner, Robey, & Smith,

1985). Chen (1992) reviewed data on the ages of victims of anti-Asian violence and found the largest number to be young adolescents.

Education

Although the general level of education is high among A/PIs, leading the media to stereotype them as a model minority, it masks the great variability among subgroups (e.g., 82% of Japanese completing high school vs. 61% of Samoans; Sue & Okazaki, 1990). Even more disturbing are the significant school dropout rates among the subgroups (e.g., 46.1% of Filipino students in California; more than 50% of the Laotian students in Lowell, Massachusetts, during the 1986–1987 school year; U.S. Commission on Civil Rights, 1992).

Poverty

Poverty is reported consistently to be a risk factor for violent crime (U.S. Department of Justice, 1991). Asian Americans are generally perceived to be affluent because of the relatively high median family income (e.g., 3% higher than non-Hispanic White families in 1989). However, because this statistic is based on family income, the figure for A/PIs reflects the fact that they tend to have large families, with most family members working to add to the collective family income. Although Japanese and Chinese have relatively high incomes overall, there is a high poverty rate among subgroups. The overall poverty rate in 1989 for A/PIs was 14%, almost twice the rate for non-Hispanic Whites (U.S. Bureau of the Census, 1993). New refugees and immigrants from Southeast Asia have the highest poverty rates among the group (e.g., Hmong = 63.6%, Cambodians = 42.6%), and many began their lives in the United States receiving welfare. The figures for some of the local communities are even more startling. For example, 34% of children living in poverty and 22% of families receiving Aid to Families With Dependent Children in San Francisco were A/PIs (Coleman Youth Advocates, 1993).

Prior Exposure to Violence

Many of the refugee children and youth have witnessed countless war atrocities, including assaults, rape, and the murder of their parents and other family members. However, although there are considerable data on the extent of trauma suffered by adult refugees, data specific to the experience of children and youth are limited. Interview data on Cambodian high school students obtained by Kinzie, Sack, Angell, Manson, and Rath (1986) provides information on their traumatic experiences prior to coming to the United States and the extent of posttraumatic psychiatric difficulties they continued to experience. Among Southeast Asian refugee groups, Gong-Guy (1987) found that Cambodians suffered the greatest degree of losses and atrocities at the hands of Pol Pot regime during and after the Vietnam War.

Of the 46 Cambodian students interviewed by Kinzie et al. (1986) in an Oregon high school, 40 of them lived for 4 years under the Pol Pot regime from 1975 to 1979, then escaped to Thailand. The researchers interviewed the student group, which included 25 males and 15 females (aged 14–20 years, $M = 17$ years), who had been in the United States an average of 2 years. Overall, 26 were living with some family members, and 14 were living in either American or Cambodian foster homes or alone. Their experiences prior to coming to the United States included the following: Eighty-three percent were separated from their families for a period; almost 98% endured forced labor; 43% saw people being killed; 18% saw their own family members being killed; 68% saw members of their group who were escaping to Thailand get killed; and all saw corpses. The number of lost, killed, or missing family members of this group was high: Eighty percent lost at least one family member, and the average number lost, either dead or missing, was three members of the nuclear family. Although the 6 students who escaped the Pol Pot regime were adjusting well to life in the United States, many of the 40 students reported a variety of symptoms related to posttraumatic stress (e.g., having nightmares and recurring dreams, being easily startled, feeling ashamed of being alive, and experiencing various depressive symptoms).

Yoshihama, Parekh, and Boyington (1991) reported that the United Nations had conducted a study of Vietnamese refugees in 1980, finding that approximately 40% of female refugees had been raped by pirates at sea. Of these, 11% were aged 11–20 years.

Other investigators (Felsman, Leong, Johnson, & Felsman, 1990; Nicassio, LaBarberra, Coburn, & Finley, 1986; Williams & Westermeyer, 1983) also noted significant levels of psychiatric problems among other refugee adolescents, although they did not document the extent of traumas the refugees experienced prior to their entry into the United States. When they are reexposed to violence in the United States and many of them are resettled in low-income neighborhoods, with high incidence of crime and violence, refugees often become targets of the neighborhood's hostility. When they become victimized, the new traumas reawaken and compound their past psychic traumas, which are often manifested as severe anxiety reactions, depressive symptoms, psychosomatic symptoms, and behavior problems.

Gangs, Weapons, and Drugs

On the basis of their work with Chinese American youth gangs, Lyman (1977) and Sung (1979) noted some of the background factors that are thought to attract Chinese American youths to gang affiliation, including financial rewards; feelings of power and camaraderie with other members; status; inability to succeed in school because of English-language problems and culture conflicts; lack of supervision at home (both parents work long hours); and frustration over racism in the larger community. Vigil and Yun (1990) also noted similar factors affecting Vietnamese youth who join gangs; these factors are also likely to be responsible for leading other Asian youths into gang activities (see also chapter 14 in this book).

Concerns have been voiced in recent years by media and law enforcement offices that Chinese gangs are working closely with the Tongs (associations that provide social clubs and other legal activities, as well as illegal activities such as gambling among some groups). According to a 3-year survey conducted in San Francisco of known gangs of all ethnicities (21 were A/PI groups) and their involvement with drug sales and other activities (Waldorf, Hunt, Joe, & Murphy, 1993), it appears involvement of gangs with Tongs in San Francisco is not significant. Afraid that it will affect tourism and business in Chinatown, the Tongs are believed to discourage the development of relationship with gangs except with the long-standing gangs, which serve to provide protection for illegal activities and to collect for debts owed to the Tongs.

However, there may be regional differences in large cities such as New York, which has significant infiltration by the more organized criminal elements such as Triads (Mafia-like organizations from Hong Kong and China). Observing the activities of the emerging gangs in New York, Kwong (1987) sounded an alarm about the dangers of the young Chinese gang members who are linked with the Triads and are involved in the heroin and opium trade. More recently, Dao (1992) reported on the emergence of more ethnically diverse Asian street gangs in New York, who are now competing with the older, more established Chinese Tongs and are involved in extortion, murder, and smuggling of heroin and illegal immigrants through their connection with Asian Triads. Similarly, the *San Francisco Chronicle* reported recently that a key Asian Triad was using "underlings" aged 14–25 to carry out some of their crimes ("U.S. Says," 1993).

When Waldorf et al (1993) interviewed the various ethnic gang group members in San Francisco, they found that most gangs, including A/PI gangs, did not have a well-organized network of drug sales but that most were involved in the sales of some drugs (Asians = 50.0%, Samoans = 81.1%) and other criminal activities to raise money for themselves. Although Asian gang members reported drug sales less often than did the other groups, they reported theft, burglary, and extortion more than did the other groups. Among the drugs used by the gang members, Asians tended use a wide variety of drugs, but they had greater use of rock cocaine than any of the other groups. All of them smoked marijuana and most were using crack cocaine.

With regard to A/PI youth in general, nationwide statistics suggest a low level of alcohol and drug use, which may decrease their risk for violence to some degree. For example, a national survey conducted from 1986 to 1989 by the U.S. Department of Education (1992) of 982 A/PI American males and 917 females showed that of male and female high school seniors, respectively, 43.7% and 34.2 reported having used alcohol occasionally; 9.7% and 8.1% reported having used marijuana, and 1.8% and 2.6% reported having used cocaine.

An indicator often associated with gangs and violence is the availability and possession of weapons. Callahan and Rivara (1992) investigated the prevalence of handgun ownership and easy access to it among high school youth in the Seattle, Washington, area. Twenty-five percent of the A/PI respondents indicated that they had easy access to handguns and 4.1% indicated ownership (see also chapter 12 in this book).

Home Ownership

Another risk factor relevant to A/PIs include status as renters and residence in inner-city areas (U.S. Department of Justice, 1991). The percentage of A/PIs who were renters was 48% compared with 31% of White householders. The percentage of A/PIs living in metropolitan areas was 94%. Because of their limited economic resources, many immigrants and refugees are living in low-income, inner-city areas, where they are forced to compete for scarce resources and are likely targets for victimization by other residents. According to the national review of data during 1993 on anti-Asian acts of violence by the National Asian Pacific American Legal Consortium (1994), A/PIs were the most vulnerable where they resided (28% of the total incidence), followed by commercial business sites (10%).

Anti-Asian Violent Hate Crimes

In spite of the fact that comprehensive data are not available, there are many official reports indicating that A/PIs are frequently victimized, often resulting in fatalities, throughout the United States. In 1986, the U.S. Commission on Civil Rights warned that "anti-Asian activity in the form of violence, vandalism, harassment, and intimidation continues to occur across the nation" (p. 57). Six years later, the U.S. Commission on Civil Rights (1992) reexamined the situation and concluded that it had not improved, identifying areas where A/PIs are particularly vulnerable. For example, in Philadelphia, where A/PIs made up less than 4% of population 1988, they represented 20% of the city's total hate crime victims, the highest among all ethnic groups. In a recently published report by the FBI (1992), 6% of all hate crimes were targeted against A/PIs. Most agree that the actual figure is higher because many A/PIs, especially recent immigrants, are reluctant to report crimes to authorities for a variety of reasons.

In response to the concerns of A/PIs and other minority groups, the U.S. Congress enacted the Hate Crimes Statistics Act in 1990 to begin to collect hate crimes statistics with appropriate ethnic breakdowns. This action was followed by 13 state legislatures, which enacted similar hate crime legislations (Chen, 1992). It is hoped that because of increased responsiveness by government agencies for ethnic-sensitive data collection, future investigations will yield adequate information about the nature of problems so that proactive planning and preventive efforts will be possible.

According to the 1992 Hate Crime Statistics (FBI, 1992), of those who victimized A/PI Americans of all ages in identified hate crimes, 46.5% where White, 11.9% were African American, almost 40% were of unknown ethnicity, and 1% were identified as A/PI Americans.

Although the data are too limited to describe fully the nature and circumstances under which A/PIs *youths* are victimized, a significant number appear to be the result of anti-Asian sentiment among White and other ethnic groups in the community. Among the examples cited in the Civil Rights Commission

Report (1992), the incident involving the Stockton, California, schoolyard massacre in 1988 is the most disturbing. It involved a deranged ex-Vietnam veteran entering the Cleveland Elementary school yard and repeatedly firing an AK-47 assault rifle at the children, killing 5 Indo-Chinese children and wounding 30 others. Although the authorities initially dismissed the possibility that the killings were racially motivated, a more in-depth investigation confirmed that that was the case.

Another case cited involves the beating death of a 15-year-old Vietnamese boy, Hung Troung, in Houston, Texas, by two 18-year-old skinheads in 1990. During the trial, the two assailants, who were known to have racist views and had skinhead ties, admitted that the only reason they had attacked Troung was because he was Vietnamese. Although it is not known at this time if A/PI youth are more vulnerable to racially motivated attacks, they are frequently harassed and attacked in public schools at all grade levels.

Some of the contributing factors toward anti-Asian violence of all age groups cited by the U.S. Commission on Civil Rights (1992) include the following:

- a long history of prejudice and discrimination against them, aggravated by their increased visibility due to a large influx of immigrants and refugees;
- high rates of immigration magnifying the linguistic, cultural, and religious differences of the new arrivals from others in the community, leading to serious misunderstandings;
- the resentment toward the economic success of Japan misplaced to Asian and Pacific Islanders in the United States regardless of their national origin, residence, or citizenship; and
- the common stereotype of Asian Americans as a successful model minority and the misperception that Asian immigrants receive unfair subsidies.

More recently, the National Asian Pacific American Legal Consortium mounted a special initiative to deal with anti-Asian hate crimes and identified additional factors contributing to the distressing national trend. These include the following:

- a decrease in social services attributable to the recessionary economy but blamed on recent immigrants;
- abrupt racial integration of neighborhoods and schools, leading to "move-in" violence;
- insensitive media coverage of minority groups and issues, leading to the perpetuation of stereotypes; and
- poor police response to hate crimes.

Ethnicity: Interpreting and Responding to Victimization

Despite significant cultural diversity that exists among A/PI groups, there are certain cultural traditions, values, and expectations that are shared by a number of them and have an impact on the way A/PI children and youths respond to the experience of victimization. For example, in terms of family structure, most families, particularly immigrant families, are governed by a strong patriarchal system, in which the authority of a father is to be obeyed without question and men are given many preferential privileges.

Although many immigrant parents try to sacrifice their own personal needs to provide educational opportunities and other advantages in life so that their children will succeed in the United States, conflicts occur frequently within families because of diverse pressures that affect each family member differently. Although parents often struggle to deal with daily survival issues and often fail to learn the new language and customs, their children learn the language more quickly and become exposed to greater freedom their non-Asian peers have. Watching their parents struggle ineffectively with the outside world, some children begin to question and challenge their parents' authority, demanding greater freedom. The situation becomes even more conflictual when children are recruited, because of their English-speaking ability, to act as mediators with outside authorities, thus assuming a pseudoadult authority over their own parents and further eroding the parental authority. When faced with seemingly insurmountable frustrations and fearful that they are losing control of their children, some parents become more autocratic than before, even resorting to physical punishment, in order to restore their authority. Many of them believe their actions are justified in order to protect the children from "bad influences" outside, such as drugs, delinquency, promiscuous sex, and so on (M. K. Ho, 1992). Because of the strong emphasis placed on maintaining family loyalty and respect for their parents, many children feel conflicted about seeking outside help even when they are abused. Bringing outside attention on the family problem is discouraged and seen as bringing shame and causing a "loss of face." If the abuse becomes known to outsiders, many children feel somehow responsible and feel guilty.

Endurance and perseverance, in the face of adversity, are other virtues strongly inculcated into the A/PI children. Whatever happens, they are taught to accept it as fate and to endure the pain and tribulations stoically. Expressions of feelings and emotions are discouraged because it is perceived as weakness. Therefore, seeking emotional support to deal with victimization may be more difficult for many of these youth.

While growing up, many Asian girls experience low self-esteem and are not confident about asserting their own needs. They are often restricted from dating, taught about the importance of maintaining their virginity, yet they have trouble protecting themselves against the demands of their dates because they are taught to be submissive to males. The topic of sex is often taboo in their families.

When they are victimized in situations such as stranger rape, date rape, and acquaintance rape, they often blame themselves for what happened, feeling intense shame for being violated, and yet they are afraid to seek help because of the fear of bringing disgrace to their families. They are also taught by their families not to trust American authorities, who are perceived as not being sympathetic to the needs of their community, and that they will only be further subjected to more problems and humiliation. For these reasons, they are often even more reluctant than males to report the incident or to seek professional help; they would rather endure their pain by themselves (Yoshi-hama et al., 1991).

When abuse is perpetrated by fathers or other male relatives, the internal conflict for the victimized girl is even greater, resulting in the loss of faith in her parent or adult relative; she feels intensely shamed and guilty. These feelings could lead to depression, self-hate, and suicidal ideations or attempts. Such tendencies of Asian females was noted in the San Francisco sexual abuse case reviews cited earlier. When compared with other ethnic groups relative to the presence of sexual acting out, anger, and suicidal ideation or attempts, Rao et al. (1992) noted that Asians, most of whom were females, were least likely to display anger (8.7%) or inappropriate sexual behaviors (1.4%) compared with other ethnic groups but that they were most likely to express suicidal ideation or to have made actual attempts (21.7%).

Rao et al. (1992) also found that Asian victims were the least likely to first disclose the sexual abuse to their mothers (27.4%) compared with other groups, perhaps because they realized that they would not be believed or receive their protection. Among the cases, the Asian primary caretakers, mostly mothers, were much less supportive than other groups to the sexually abused child in that they were more likely to disbelieve them, less likely to spontaneously report the abuse to authorities, and were less likely to complete the recommended evaluation and treatment with the victim. The researchers postulated that in addition to their lack of English-speaking ability, which is a deterrent to reporting crimes, other reasons for the Asian parents' reluctance may include lack of trust of government authority, unfamiliarity with the use of health and mental health services, and a cultural tradition of not discussing family problems with outsiders. Other considerations may include a fear that their immigration status may be jeopardized, resulting in their deportation. Also a mother may be caught between competing pressures to protect her daughter and to be loyal and subservient to her husband.

More recently, frustrated by this oppressive treatment of women at home and in the A/PI community, a new trend is emerging among A/PI women to challenge the subservient status expected of them, to fight the victimizations, and to forge a new identity, free of exploitation (Fujitomi & Wong, 1973; True, 1990).

Knowledge Gaps and Research Needs

As described previously, there is only fragmented information about violence among A/PI youth. There is a serious need for more data on the prevalence and incidence of violence among these youth, the nature and characteristic of risks involved, and the contributing factors. When addressing the problem of data collection, it will be critical to get federal and state agencies involved in collecting violence-related information to adopt policies to identify A/PI groups as discrete racial categories. Furthermore, in order to gain a better understanding of the diverse ethnic group differences within A/PI groups, it will be important to obtain information about key ethnic groups including Chinese, Japanese, Koreans, Filipinos, Cambodians, Pacific Islanders, Vietnamese and other Southeast Asians by differentially focusing on regions where they represent a significant portion of the population.

In addition to the investigation of ethnic diversity, other issues that warrant investigation about subgroup differences include analysis of prevalence, correlates, and consequences of violence that takes into account generational, gender, age, and socioeconomic status differences. Given the fact that so many A/PIs are victims or witnesses to violence, the impact of exposure to these violent acts, identification of individual coping strategies, and the effectiveness of various intervention strategies are other areas for investigation.

In the area of available services to meet the violence-related needs, resources have been scarce for A/PIs. Many of the most in need are immigrants with limited English-speaking ability who require linguistically appropriate and culturally sensitive services. However, requests to develop these services are often denied on the basis that the supporting data concerning the extent of problems and need for services are not available (Sue & Morishima, 1982). Several communities, such as Los Angeles, Boston, San Francisco, Seattle, and New York, have developed culturally responsive programs targeted at children, youth, and families. These community programs have demonstrated effectiveness in reducing individual problems, defusing family tension, and preventing and redirecting youth away from gang involvement (Chinatown Youth Council, 1991). Local initiatives such as these are far too few and inadequately funded. In order to deal more effectively with the problems faced by A/PI youth in the United States, more systematic support for prevention and service programs is urgently needed.

Public Policy Recommendations

1. Federal and state agencies should adopt policies that support the development of mechanisms that identify A/PIs as separate minority groups for data collection and research purposes in areas involving them as victims or perpetrators of violence.
2. Federal, state, and private funding agencies should be lobbied to recognize A/PIs as priority populations for increased funding and technical support as related to youth and violence issues.
3. When making funding decisions, funding agencies should ensure a culturally sensitive review and decision-making process through recruitment and inclusion of culturally competent A/PI professionals on their review panels.
4. Immediate funding is urgently needed at local levels to respond to the current crisis involving youth and violence in order to provide culturally sensitive prevention and intervention programs targeted to A/PI children, youth, and families.
5. Prevention and intervention strategies need to begin early with a multifaceted approach long before youth reach adolescence and become easy targets for gang recruitment.
6. Public policies should be developed that support initiatives that intervene at the family level, encouraging research and program devel-

opment that highlights the protective role parents and other caretakers may assume in violence prevention.

7. Attention should focus on interethnic tension among disadvantaged minority groups in inner-city areas and support provided to develop conflict resolution and violence prevention strategies.

8. The media must be educated so that they will assist in dispelling negative racial stereotypes about A/PIs, thus reducing anti-Asian sentiment among the general public.

References

Abbott, K. A., & Abbott, E. L. (1968). Juvenile delinquency in San Francisco's Chinese-American community: 1961–1966. *Journal of Sociology, 4,* 45–56.

Asian and Pacific Islander Center for Census Information and Services. (1992). *Asian and Pacific Islander American profile series.* San Francisco: Author.

Callahan, C. M., & Rivara, F. P. (1992). Urban high school youth and handguns: A school-based survey. *Journal of the American Medical Association, 267,* 3038–3042.

Chan, C. S. (1987). Asian-American women: Psychological responses to sexual exploitation and cultural stereotypes. *Asian American Psychological Association Journal, 12,* 11–15.

Chen, S. A. (Ed.). (1991). *Asians in Pennsylvania.* Harrisburg: Pennsylvania Heritage Affairs.

Chen, S. A. (Ed.). (1992). *In pursuit of justice: National Anti-Asian Violence Task Force report and guidelines for citizen actions.* Washington, DC: Organization of Chinese Americans.

Chin, K. (1990). *Chinese subculture and criminality: Non-traditional crime groups in America.* Westport, CT: Greenwood.

Chinatown Youth Council. (1991). *History of Chinatown Youth Council.* San Francisco: Author.

Coleman Youth Advocates. (1993). *A profile of San Francisco's children.* San Francisco: Author.

Dao, J. (1992, April 1). Asian street gangs emerging as new underworld. *New York Times,* pp. A1.

Federal Bureau of Investigation, U.S. Department of Justice. (1992, December 22). Press release. Washington, DC: Author.

Federal Bureau of Investigation. (1991). *Uniform crime reports for the United States, 1991.* Washington, DC: U.S. Department of Justice.

Felsman, J. K., Leong, F. T. L., Johnson, M. C., & Felsman, I. C. (1990). Estimates of psychological distress among Vietnamese refugees: Adolescents, unaccompanied minors and young adults. *Social Science Medicine, 31,* 1251–1256.

Fujitomi, D., & Wong, D. (1973). The new Asian-American woman. In S. Sue & N. N. Wagner (Eds.), *Asian-Americans: Psychological perspectives* (pp. 252-263). Palo Alto, CA: Science and Behavior Books.

Gardner, R. W., Robey, B., & Smith, P. C. (1985). Asian Americans: Growth, change, and diversity. *Population Bulletin, 40,* 4.

Gong-Guy, E. (1987). *The California Southeast Asian Mental Health Needs Assessment.* Oakland, CA: Asian Community Mental Health Services.

Ho, C. (1990). An analysis of domestic violence in Asian American communities. *Women and Therapy, 9*(1–2), 129–150.

Ho, M. K. (1992). *Minority children and adolescents in therapy.* Newbury Park, CA: Sage.

Ima, K., & Hohm, C. F. (1991). Child maltreatment among Asian and Pacific Islander refugees and immigrants: The San Diego case. *Journal of Interpersonal Violence, 6,* 267–285.

Kinzie, J. D., Sack, W. H., Angell, R. H., Manson, S., & Rath, B. (1986). The psychiatric effects of massive trauma on Cambodian children: I. The children. *Journal of the American Academy of Child Psychiatry, 25,* 370–376.

Kitano, H. H. L. (1976). *The Japanese Americans: The evolution of a sub-culture.* Englewood Cliffs, NJ: Prentice Hall.

Kitano, H. H., Yeung, W., Chai, L., & Hatanaka, H. (1986). Asian American interracial marriage. *Asian American Psychological Association Journal, 11,* 30–32.

Krajewski-Jaime, E. (1991). Folk-healing among Mexican-American families as a consideration in the delivery of child welfare and child health care services. *Child Welfare, 70,* 158–167.

Kwong, P. (1987). *Tongs, gangs, and the godfather in the New Chinatown.* New York: Hill & Wang.

Louie, L., Joe, K., Luu, M., & Tong, B. (1991, August). *Chinese American adolescent runaways.* Paper presented at the annual convention of the Asian American Psychological Association, San Francisco.

Lim, G. (1994, February 11). San Francisco group urges child sexual abuse victims to "break the silence." *Asian Week,* pp. 1, 21.

Loya, F., Garcia, P., Sullivan, J. D., Vargas, L. A., Mercy, J., & Allen, N. (1986). Conditional risks among Anglo, Hispanic, Black, and Asian victims in Los Angeles, 1970–1979: Vol. V. Homicide, suicide, and unintentional injuries. *Report of the Secretary's Task Force on Black and Minority Health* (pp. 117–136). Washington, DC: U.S. Department of Health and Human Services.

Lum, J. (1988, March). Battered Asian women. *Rice,* pp. 50–52.

Lyman, S. F. (1977). Chinese secret societies in the Occident: Notes and suggestions for research in the sociology of secrecy. In S. F. Lyman (Ed.), *The Asian in North America.* Santa Barbara, CA: ABC-Clio.

Masaki, B. (1992). Shattered myths: Battered women in the A/PI Community. *Focus, 3,* 3.

McInnis, K. (1991). Ethnic sensitive work with Hmong refugee children. *Child Welfare, 70,* 571–579.

Nakagawa, M. (1992, August 14). Domestic violence not a foreign concept in Asian households. *Asian Week,* pp. 1–13.

National Asian Pacific American Legal Consortium. (1994). *Audit of violence against Asian Pacific Americans, 1993: Anti-Asian violence, a national problem.* Washington, DC: Author.

New York Asian Women's Center. (1992). *Tenth anniversary report: 1982–1992.* New York: Author.

Nicassio, P. M., LaBarberra, J. D., Coburn, P., & Finley, R. (1986). The psychosocial adjustment of the Amerasian refugees: Findings from the personality inventory for children. *Journal of Nervous and Mental Disease, 174,* 541–544.

Ong, P., & Hee, S. J. (1992). The growth of the Asian Pacific American population: Twenty million in 2020. In *The state of Asian Pacific America: Policy issues to the year 2020* (pp. 11–24). Los Angeles: LEAP Asian American Public Policy Institute and UCLA Asian American Studies Center.

Rao, K., DiClemente, R. J., & Ponton, L. E. (1992). Child sexual abuse of Asians compared with other populations. *Journal of the American Academy of Child and Adolescent Psychiatry, 31,* 880–886.

Rimonte, N. (1989). Domestic violence among Pacific Asians. In Asian Women United of California (Eds.), *Making waves: An anthology of writings by and about Asian American women* (pp. 327–336). Boston: Beacon Press.

Rosenblatt, H., & Hong, P. (1989). Coin rolling misdiagnosed as child abuse. *Canadian Medical Association Journal, 140,* 417.

Rumbaut, R., & Weeks, J. (1986). Fertility and adaptation: Indochinese refugees in the United States. *International Migration Review, 20,* 428–466.

San Francisco Police Department. (1993). *Reported cases of child abuse.* San Francisco: Author.

Sue, S., & Morishima, J. K. (1982). *The mental health of Asian Americans.* San Francisco: Jossey-Bass.

Sue, S., & Okazaki, S. (1990). Asian American educational achievements: A phenomenon in search of an explanation. *American Psychologist, 45,* 913–920.

Sung, B. L. (1979). *Transplanted Chinese children: Report to the administration for children, youth and families.* Washington, DC: Department of Health, Education and Welfare.

Takaki, R. (1989). *Strangers from a different shore: History of Asian Americans.* Boston: Little, Brown.

True, R. H. (1990). Psychotherapeutic issues with Asian American women. *Sex Roles, 22,* 477–486.

U.S. Bureau of the Census. (1993). *We, the American . . . Asians.* Washington, DC: U.S. Department of Commerce.

U. S. Civil Rights Commission. (1986). *Recent activities against citizens and residents of Asian descent* (Publication No. 88). Washington, DC: U.S. Commission on Civil Rights.

U. S. Commission on Civil Rights. (1992). *Civil rights issues facing Asian Americans in the 1990's.* Washington, DC: Author.

U.S. Department of Education, National Center of Educational Statistics. (1992). *The condition of education.* Washington, DC: U.S. Government Printing Office.

U.S. Department of Justice. (1985). *The risk of violent crime.* Washington, DC: Bureau of Justice Statistics.

U.S. Department of Justice. (1991). *Criminal victimization in the United States, 1990.* Washington, DC: Bureau of Justice Statistics.

U.S. says it's broken key Asian mafia gang. (1993, October 13). *San Francisco Chronicle.*

Vigil, J. D., & Yun, S. C. (1990). Vietnamese youth gangs in Southern California. In R. Huff (Ed.), *Gangs in America* (pp.146–162). Newbury Park, CA: Sage.

Waldorf, D., Hunt, G., Joe, K., & Murphy, S. (1993). *Final report of the crack sales, gangs and violence study.* Alameda, CA: Institute for Scientific Analysis.

Weiss, M. S. (1973). Selective acculturation and the dating process: The pattern of Chinese-Caucasian inter-racial dating. In N. N. Wagner & S. Sue (Eds.), *Asian-Americans: Psychological perspectives* (pp. 86–94). Palo Alto, CA: Science and Behavioral Books.

Williams, C. L., & Westermeyer, J. (1983). Psychiatric problems among adolescent Southeast Asian refugees: A descriptive study. *Journal of Nervous and Mental Disease, 171,* 79–85.

Wong, W. (1992, April 10). Asian gang life as "power, fun." *Oakland Tribune,* p. 2.

Yoshihama, M., Parekh, A. L., & Boyington, D. (1991). Dating violence in Asian/Pacific communities. In B. Levy. (Ed.), *Dating violence: Young women in danger* (pp. 184–195). Seattle, WA: Seal Press.

Part III ⎯⎯⎯⎯⎯⎯⎯⎯⎯⎯⎯⎯⎯⎯⎯⎯

Experience of Violence: Vulnerable Populations

Introduction

Violent victimization is a significant problem for all American children and youth (Finkelhor & Dziuba-Leatherman, 1994). Prevailing cultural attitudes greatly enhance the risk for victimization, within this general population, among certain groups based on their gender, sexual orientation, or physical and mental characteristics. This section contains chapters that call attention to the special vulnerability of girls and young women, gay and lesbian youth, and children and adolescents with disabilities.

Among these groups, there is high potential for diverse kinds of victimization including sexual, physical, emotional, or verbal abuse. Victims may suffer long-term negative psychological consequences that go beyond any physical harm sustained. However, the circumstances, sources and nature of risk, dynamics of violent acts, and reactions to victimization vary to some degree among these groups.

In chapter 8 on girls and young women, Susan Sorenson and Patricia Bowie focus primarily on violence involving victims and perpetrators who are known to one another, because this accounts for the largest proportion of violence among this population. Physical violence, including child physical abuse and dating violence, and sexual violence, including child sexual abuse and date and acquaintance rape, are among the most prevalent forms of violence toward this group. In terms of prevention and intervention, although services to girls and young women are urgently needed, the authors stress keeping the spotlight on perpetrators as well.

Victimization of gay, lesbian, and bisexual youth, and children and adolescents with disabilities may result from intolerance, fear, and hate directed toward groups who have identifiable or imagined "differences" from the majority. In chapter 9 on gay, lesbian, and bisexual youth, Anthony D'Augelli and Lawrence Dark reveal the high rate of violent victimization among these populations and how it appears to be increasing as youth become more open about their sexual orientation, and hence are more visible, and as AIDS-related fears increase. They describe the developmental challenges of and distinct stresses on these youth, which may render them more vulnerable to the effects of violence and less likely to receive help if they are victimized. D'Augelli and Dark argue that interventions to reduce violence toward members of these groups must be targeted to two populations: the heterosexual population and the gay male, lesbian, and bisexual youth population. The public must be educated regarding issues involving sexual orientation, including violence, and the authors advocate incorporating pertinent information into school curricula. For gay, lesbian, and bisexual youth, they recommend better monitoring of victimization patterns, providing help for victims by creating safe settings (e.g., in schools), and creating public policy initiatives to reduce bias-related violence and discrimination.

In chapter 10 on children with disabilities, Judith Levey and Vasilios Lagos examine the incidence and prevalence of maltreatment of this population, which appears to be 1.7 times greater than maltreatment of children without disabilities. They note that in the majority of cases, children with disabilities are abused by someone known and trusted, such as a family member, caretaker, or close friend. They also describe risk factors related to the child, the parents or caretakers, and their interaction. The authors conclude that, considering the limited communicative and cognitive skills of some of these children as well as the increased stress on caretakers resulting from the child's greater care requirements and sometimes more hard-to-manage behavior, it is not too difficult to understand why these children are at greater risk for abuse.

Each chapter notes concerns about a lack of reliable data for documentation of the problem of violence. Underreporting of violence is a special concern among these groups. Contributors to an inability or reluctance to report include shame or embarrassment; guilt; fear of reprisal; or circumstances related to age, presence of a disability, or lack of access to resources. Such factors suggest that the actual prevalence of violence may far exceed the present indicators that already substantiate above-average risk for certain kinds of victimization among these groups. Data evaluating prevention and treatment programs are also noted to be sparse. Public policy issues and recommendations vary but universally call for increased education to reduce bias and discrimination and increased support around the specific needs of these vulnerable populations.

Reference

Finkelhor, D., & Dziuba-Leatherman, J. (1994). Victimization of children. *American Psychologist, 49*, 173–183.

8

Girls and Young Women

Susan B. Sorenson and Patricia Bowie

Homicide and child physical and sexual abuse are problems shared by both boys and girls.[1] However, girls and young women are at higher risk than boys and young men of childhood sexual abuse and dating violence, including date and acquaintance rape. Many factors may contribute to the increased risk to girls and young women for these types of violence, including societal attitudes that may implicitly sanction some of the violence (e.g., Dobash & Dobash, 1980; Donat & D'Emilio, 1992; Horsfall, 1991) and inadequate health, police, and judicial responses to violence against women by their male intimates. These and associated influences also may be related to the underreporting of violence against women and young girls (e.g., Ageton, 1983; Koss, 1988; Koss, 1992).

There are few data on the experience of and sequelae of interpersonal violence at various points in the life span for either males or females. Some research (e.g., Burnam et al., 1988) indicates that sexual abuse during childhood, (as opposed to adulthood) regardless of gender, is associated with a greater likelihood of developing certain mental disorders. From a developmental perspective, one can assume that if a young woman is victimized in her first dating relationship, she may be less likely to perceive alternatives and options than if she had a history of more positive, healthy, and violence-free relationships. The development of self-esteem, coping and problem-solving skills, attitudes toward violence, and so on, is likely to be shaped by exposure to violence. Violence across the life span and the factors that shape and mediate its impact require further investigation.

The sociocultural and life course context of violence against women has received relatively little systematic study. For example, differential exposure to street crime may affect girls' and young women's perceptions of intimate violence (their highest risk of violent victimization) as well as the perceptions of the surrounding community. Specifically, a woman who lives in neighborhoods in which the sound of gunfire is not uncommon may perceive a beating by her boyfriend as less significant than what is occurring on the street. This

Writing of this chapter was supported, in part, by the Centers for Disease Control by a grant to the Southern California Injury Prevention Research Center (CCR903622).
[1]Individuals from birth to approximately college age.

relativistic perspective may be reinforced by the responses of friends and relatives who, with some frequency, attend funerals for homicide victims, and by the police and judiciary who are actively engaged in dealing with cases of violent street crime. Thus, community context may shape how a victimized young woman labels her experiences as well as how and if others offer support and intervention. Research, for the most part, has ignored the potential interface between violence within and outside the home. The study of social and life contexts of violent experiences will help illuminate girls' and young women's experiences of and efforts at coping with violence.

While acknowledging the importance of investigating such factors as they pertain to violence against girls and young women, our primary purpose in this chapter is to describe the extent of the risk to girls and young women in certain categories of violence, which at times entails a comparison of the extent of such risk to boys and young men. This review of patterns of violence toward girls and young women is organized by the nature and context of the violence: homicide and physical fighting; child physical abuse; child sexual abuse; and dating violence, including adolescent date and acquaintance rape. General risk patterns are presented; additional chapters (e.g., chapters 4–7, 9, and 10) address specific subpopulations. Important areas regarding violence against girls and young women that we do not cover include sibling abuse, psychological abuse, gang rape, and sexual harassment (e.g., Hart & Brassard, 1987; Laviola, 1992; Rozee-Koker & Polk, 1986; Russell, 1984). Moreover, although they make up a relatively small but not insignificant proportion of assailants, the role of girls and young women as perpetrators of violence is not a primary focus of this chapter.

Homicide and Physical Fighting

Homicide is the fourth leading cause of death among 0– to 14–year-olds in the United States (National Center for Health Statistics, 1990). For both girls and boys, risk of homicide is highest during infancy and the toddler years, drops during the childhood and preteen years, and increases again during adolescence (Jason & Andereck, 1983). Homicides of girls and boys during early childhood most likely are committed by a parent or other caretaker, are due to beatings, and have unclear precipitating circumstances (Christoffel, 1984).

The pattern of homicide changes during adolescence, so that a majority of the homicides are precipitated by an argument, most victims are killed with a firearm, and a majority of the victims know but are not related to their assailant and are male (Fingerhut, Ingram, & Feldman, 1992; O'Carroll & Mercy, 1986). Although it was believed that mothers (i.e., women) were the most common perpetrators of fatal and nonfatal physical violence toward young (i.e., preschool) children and that men were the most common perpetrators of the homicide of older children, a shift has occurred to more male perpetrators of violence toward younger children (see, e.g., Bergman, Larsen, & Mueller, 1986). To illustrate, the father of the child and the mother's male intimate are 1.5 times more likely than the mother to be a suspect in the homicide of a child (Sorenson, Richardson, & Peterson, 1993).

Girls and boys share a roughly similar risk of homicide at young ages; women have lower rates of homicide than men during adolescence and adulthood. Race or ethnicity and age define the predominant risk groups, not sex of the victim. African American and U.S. Latino boys and girls are at higher risk of homicide than their non-U.S. Latino White peers, and 0– to 4–year-olds, regardless of sex, are at higher risk than 5– to 14–year-olds (Paulson & Rushforth, 1986; Sorenson et al., 1993). To illustrate, African American girls are at greater risk than both White boys and White girls (O'Carroll & Mercy, 1986). This race-based discrepancy continues through older ages (Fingerhut et al., 1992).

For every homicide, there are approximately 100 incidents of nonfatal assault (Rosenberg & Mercy, 1986). Physical fighting is a common form of violence among adolescents and a prominent cause of injuries and homicide (see, e.g., Centers for Disease Control, 1985). In a recent survey of physical fighting among high school students over a 30–day period, nearly 8% of the students reported being in a physical fight that required treatment by a physician or a nurse (*Morbidity Mortality Weekly Report* [MMWR], 1992). Students were most likely to fight with family, friends, or a date. Girls were one fourth as likely as boys to have engaged in fighting during the month.

Currently popular adolescent violence prevention programs with an educational approach focus on the development of negotiation, communication, anger management, problem solving, and coping skills (e.g., Hammond, 1991; Hammond & Yung, 1993; Prothrow-Stith, 1987). Such programs reinforce the idea that violence is not an acceptable form of resolving conflict and assume that individual skill development will help reduce violence and violent interactions. Adequate evaluations of such efforts are difficult yet necessary in order to assess the efficacy of these educational programs.

Child Physical Abuse

Community-based epidemiologic studies of child physical abuse have concentrated on abusive behavior by parents; additional research is needed on sibling abuse. In a 1985 survey, 62% of parents reported using physical violence against their children in the previous year (Straus & Gelles, 1986). Acts of physical violence ranged from pushing and slapping to the use of knives and guns. Severe violence was reported by 11% of the parents and was defined as hitting, kicking, beating, threatening, or using knives or guns against a child.

Children typically spend more time with their mothers, which may explain why mothers report slightly higher rates of nonsexual violence toward their children than do fathers (Straus, Gelles, & Steinmetz, 1980). In contrast to community-based surveys, reported child abuse cases associate men with more major and minor physical injury to children (Wolfe, 1987). If exposure to the caretaker is taken into account, the gender difference may more closely approximate that observed for fatal violence in which men are the more likely perpetrators.

The risk of abuse for girls is lower than for boys at younger years and increases with age (Straus et al., 1980). The physical growth and maturation of boys increases their ability both to sustain and to inflict injury, thus, risk of physical abuse by parents drops for boys as they grow. Girls are at higher risk than boys for physical abuse during the pre-adolescent and adolescent years. (See chapter 17 for additional information on child and adolescent abuse.)

Child Sexual Assault

Child sexual abuse often is defined as sexual contact with a child that occurs as a result of force, that occurs in a relationship that is exploitative because of a difference in age, or that is perpetrated by a caretaker. Community-based surveys that elicit childhood experiences of adults indicate that 6.8% to 62% of women and 6% to 15% of men have experienced child sexual assault (Finkelhor, 1979; Russell, 1982; Siegel, Sorenson, Golding, Burnam, & Stein, 1987; Wyatt, 1985). The most common form of abuse involves fondling, groping, or touching the body underneath or on top of clothing. Intercourse or attempted intercourse was reported in 16%–29% of the cases, and activities including anal or oral intercourse constituted 3%–11% of the cases (Finkelhor, 1979; Wyatt, 1985). Potential differential disclosure by gender notwithstanding, girls are two to three times more likely to be sexually abused than boys. For boys, family members, mostly uncles and brothers, account for 16%–42% of all sex abuse cases; fathers and stepfathers account for 7%–8%. For girls, family members, mostly caretakers, account for about one fourth of all sex abuse cases (Siegel et al., 1987; Wyatt, 1985). Although the finding is not always consistent (e.g., Wyatt, 1985), girls appear to be at higher risk of sexual abuse from their stepfathers than their biological fathers (Finkelhor, 1979; Russell, 1982).

Most child sexual assault offenders are male. Women are reported to be offenders in fewer than 5% of sexual abuse cases that involve girls and fewer than 20% of the cases that involve boys (Finkelhor & Russell, 1984; Wyatt, 1985). In contrast to widely held societal beliefs, strangers account for a relatively small proportion of child sexual abuse offenders. However, in contrast to girls, abused boys are more likely to be victims of extrafamilial sexual abuse.

It is generally accepted that the psychological impact of sexual abuse endures longer than any physical harm. Identified mental health problems include fear, depression, guilt, suicide ideation, changes in sleeping and eating patterns, sexual acting out, mistrust, hostility, compulsive masturbation, and school problems (Finkelhor, 1991). For both women and men, sexual abuse before the age of 16 presents a higher risk of subsequent mental disorder than if the assault occurred after 15 years of age for both sexes (Burnam et al., 1988). Gender differences in long-term responses to sexual assault, regardless of age of occurrence, follow other documented differences in stress responses: Men are more likely than women to abuse alcohol (Burnam et al., 1988).

Dating Violence

Nearly 1 out of every 10 high school students experiences physical violence in a dating relationship (Roscoe & Callahan, 1985); the proportion increases to 22% among college students (White & Koss, 1991), a rate of battering similar to that in adult populations. Although women and men are similar in their reports of perpetrating violence in an intimate relationship (Makepeace, 1983; Straus & Gelles, 1986), physical size and strength differences between men and women may result in different outcomes when males are the assailants. The same violent behaviors (e.g., slapping) by young women and young men may be interpreted differently, represent a different level of threat, and have different psychological and physical consequences. Thus, not surprisingly, women are more likely than men to report being the victim of severe physical violence in the context of dating (Gamache, 1991).

Most studies of dating violence have excluded sexual assault and define dating violence as physical or verbal abuse. The definition of violence in research on dating relationships ranges from serious injury to behaviors that do not result in injury to threats of physical violence to verbal abuse; the diverse definitions in the literature sometimes complicate data interpretation.

Most violent incidents occur during the steady or serious phase of the dating relationship (Burke, Stets, & Pirog-Good, 1989). Jealousy and uncontrollable anger are given by both women and men as the primary reasons for dating violence (Makepeace, 1986; Roscoe & Callahan, 1985).

Young women are three times more likely than young men to report severe emotional trauma as a result of a violent episode in a dating context (Makepeace, 1986). Victims of relationship violence, regardless of the level of trauma, rarely seek professional help; if help is sought, it is most likely from friends. Between 25% and 35% of both victims and perpetrators report that violence represents love on the part of the aggressor (Roscoe & Kelsey, 1986), which may reflect the dynamics of battering (Graham & Rawlings, 1991). Young women perceive the man's violence as a response to sexual denial; young men report that their own violence serves to intimidate, frighten, or force the woman to give them something (Makepeace, 1986).

Beliefs in the legitimacy of violence in intimate relationships (e.g., Levy, 1991; Walker, 1979) are likely to affect the perceptions regarding and the prevalence of dating violence. The study of dating violence is in its initial stages; more research is needed before firm conclusions can be drawn about physical and verbal aggression in dating relationships.

Adolescent Date and Acquaintance Rape

Estimates of the prevalence of sexual assault or attempted sexual assault range from 10% to 25% for 15- to 24-year-old women (Ageton, 1983; Koss, 1988; Koss, Gidycz, & Wisniewski, 1987). Adolescent girls (ages 16–19) are at very high risk of sexual assault, and the patterns of assault are similar to those for women of all ages; for example, the assailant is most likely to be someone with whom they are acquainted. For adolescents, over half of sexual assaults occur in a dating situation (Ageton, 1983; Koss, 1988). Adolescent rape is most likely to occur in a vehicle or in the home of the victim or the perpetrator (Ageton, 1983).

The majority of young women whose experience fits the legal definition of rape do not identify themselves as rape victims and, like their adult counterparts, do not report the incident to police (Ageton, 1983; Koss, 1988). If an adolescent girl does tell someone about the incident, she most likely tells a friend.

The impact of sexual assault on adolescents is similar to the impact on adults and varies in length and intensity. Common reactions include fear, anxiety, depression, sexual dysfunction, and suicide ideation (Burnam et al., 1988; Koss, 1988; Siegel, Golding, Stein, Burnam, & Sorenson, 1990). The proportion of rape victims who develop posttraumatic stress disorder (PTSD), an anticipated mental health consequence of a sexual assault, is substantial (Resnick, Kilpatrick, Dansky, Saunders, & Best, 1993); the proportion of adolescent sexual assault victims who develop PTSD is not known.

Prevention and treatment programs for both potential perpetrators and victims of dating violence among youth, including date rape, have been described by a number of authors (e.g., Funk, 1993; Jones, 1991; Levy, 1991; NiCarthy, 1991; Powell, 1991; Roden, 1991; Sousa, 1991). (A description of empirically tested programs is provided in chapter 17).

Perpetrator-focused programs are particularly important. Men Against Rape and other efforts to reduce sexual aggression by men on college campuses are examples of perpetration prevention programs that hold promise. (The Men's Anti-Rape Resource Center [Madison, WI] and RAVEN [Rape and Violence End Now, St. Louis, MO] are good resources for additional information about such programs.) Model programs that examine sex roles and other social constructions and contribute to adolescent empowerment (e.g., Creighton & Kivel, 1992) may be particularly helpful in addressing the range of youth violence.

Knowledge Gaps and Service Needs

Diverse definitions of violence, data collection techniques, and research methodologies have been used in youth violence research; not surprisingly, the findings vary greatly and are likely to frustrate those looking for a definitive answer. Nonetheless, the data do provide a framework in which to view types and patterns of violence: Violence perpetrated against girls and young women is most often committed by someone they know (typically a family member or intimate partner); the incident or incidents are most likely to occur in the victim's own home or neighborhood and not to be reported to police. Although girls and young women may be victims of any form of violence, they are at particularly high risk for sexual victimization (i.e., child sexual abuse and rape).

More community-based studies are needed to investigate the phenomenon of violence, both its precursors and sequelae as it relates to gender, particularly among youth. Little is understood about young women as perpetrators of dating violence and sexual assault, perhaps because the issue has been considered almost exclusively a problem of young males. The intergenerational effect of violence is a popular albeit poorly documented theory intended to explain ongoing violent behavior between intimates (Widom, 1989). Further research is needed to study, for example, the inconclusive findings about the association between experiencing or witnessing violence in the family of origin and the occurrence of subsequent violence in dating relationships (Kalmuss, 1984; Sugarman & Hotaling, 1989).

Investigations of youth violence and its effects also would benefit from drawing on established theories of human development and stress and coping.

Future research investigations can increase their contributions by expanding beyond the current practice of focusing on one form of abuse (e.g., sexual abuse) and instead concentrating on the co-occurrence of different forms of abuse and violence (e.g., physical and emotional abuse, physical and sexual abuse).

Service programs need to be directed toward boys and men as potential victimizers as well as girls and women as potential victims. Perpetration prevention programs for boys and men underscore the need to address the problem of aggressive behaviors and keep the spotlight on the actor rather than on girls and women as victims and reactors. The traditional focus on girls and women (especially in sexual assault programs) centers on victimization prevention which, while important, tends to reinforce (albeit inadvertently) the idea that girls and women are responsible for their victimization.

Public Policy Recommendations

1. Increase funding for research examining gender differences in the types, patterns, and the short- and long-term impact of various forms of youth violence.
2. Fund programs that help children, adolescents, and adults develop negotiation, communication, anger management, problem-solving, and coping skills that exclude violence as an acceptable form of resolving conflict.
3. Expand existing youth violence prevention programs to address issues of male-to-female violence. A number of the existing programs are ethnically sensitive, ethnically specific, or incorporate issues of race- or ethnicity-based conflict. Youth violence prevention efforts would be more effective in reducing violence against girls and young women if they addressed gender-based violence openly and directly.
4. Develop and support antiviolence programs that emphasize perpetration prevention as well as victimization prevention. Programs concentrating on boys and men and their actions and attitudes will help reduce violence against girls and women.

References

Ageton, S. (1983). *Sexual assault among adolescents.* Lexington, MA: DC Heath.

Bergman, A. B., Larsen, R. M., & Mueller, B. A. (1986). Changing spectrum of serious child abuse. *Pediatrics, 77,* 113–116.

Burke, P. J., Stets, J. E., & Pirog-Good, M. A. (1989). Gender identity, self-esteem and physical and sexual abuse in dating relationships. In M. A. Pirog-Good & J. E. Stets (Eds.), *Violence in dating relationships: Emerging social issues* (pp. 72–93). New York: Praeger.

Burnam, M. A., Stein, J. A., Golding, J. M., Siegel, J. M., Sorenson, S. B., Forsythe, A. B., & Telles, C. A. (1988). Sexual assault and mental disorders in a community population. *Journal of Consulting and Clinical Psychology, 56,* 843–850.

Centers for Disease Control, University of California at Los Angeles. (1985). *The epidemiology of homicide in the city of Los Angeles, 1970–79.* Atlanta, GA: U.S. Department of Health and Human Services, Public Health Service.

Christoffel, K. K. (1984). Homicide in childhood: A public health problem in need of attention. *American Journal of Public Health, 74,* 68–70.

Creighton, A., & Kivel, P. (1992). *Helping teens stop violence* (2nd ed.). Alameda, CA: Hunter House.

Dobash, R.E., & Dobash, R. (1980). *Violence against wives: The case against patriarchy.* London: Open Books.

Donat, P. L. N., & D'Emilio, J. (1992). A feminist redefinition of rape and sexual assault: Historical foundations and change. *Journal of Social Issues, 48,* 9–22.

Fingerhut, L., Ingram, D., & Feldman, J. (1992). Firearm and nonfirearm homicide among persons 15–19 years of age. *Journal of the American Medical Association, 267,* 3048–3053.

Finkelhor, D. (1979). *Sexually victimized children.* New York: Free Press.

Finkelhor, D. (1991). Child sexual abuse. In M. Rosenberg & M. A. Fenley (Eds.), *Violence in America: A public health approach* (pp. 79–94). New York: Oxford University Press.

Finkelhor, D., & Russell, D. E. (1984). Women as perpetrators: Review of the evidence. In D. Finkelhor (Ed.), *Child sexual abuse: New research and theory* (pp. 171–87). New York: Free Press.

Funk, R. E. (1993). *Stopping rape: A challenge for men.* Philadelphia: New Society.

Gamache, D. (1991). Domination and control: The social context of dating violence. In B. Levy (Ed.), *Dating violence: Young women in danger* (pp. 69–83). Seattle: Seal Press.

Graham, D., & Rawlings, E. I. (1991). Bonding with abusive dating partners: Dynamics of Stockholm syndrome. In B. Levy (Ed.), *Dating violence: Young women in danger* (pp. 119–135). Seattle, WA: Seal Press.

Hammond, W. R. (1991). *Dealing with anger: Givin' it, takin' it, workin' it out.* Champaign, IL: Research Press.

Hammond, W. R. (1993). Psychology's role in the public health response to assaultive violence among young African American men. *American Psychologist, 48,* 142–154.

Hart, S. B., & Brassard, M. R. (1987). A major threat to children's mental health: Psychological maltreatment. *American Psychologist, 42,* 160–165.

Horsfall, J. (1991). *The presence of the past: Male violence in the family.* Winchester, MA: Allen & Unwin.

Jason, J., & Andereck, N. D. (1983). Fatal child abuse in Georgia: The epidemiology of severe physical child abuse. *Child Abuse and Neglect, 7,* 1–9.

Jones, L. E. (1991). The Minnesota School Curriculum Project: A statewide domestic violence prevention project in secondary schools. In B. Levy (Ed.), *Dating violence: Young women in danger* (pp. 258–266). Seattle, WA: Seal Press.

Kalmuss, D. (1984). The intergenerational transmission of marital aggression. *Journal of Marriage and the Family, 46,* 11–19.

Koss, M. P. (1988). Hidden rape: Sexual aggression and victimization in a national sample in higher education. In A. W. Burgess (Ed.), *Sexual assault, Vol. II* (pp. 3–25). New York: Garland.

Koss, M. P. (1992). The underdetection of rape: Methodological choices influence incidence estimates. *Journal of Social Issues, 48,* 61–75.

Koss, M. P., Gidycz, C. A., & Wisniewski, N. (1987). The scope of rape: Incidence and prevalence of sexual aggression and victimization in a national sample of higher education students. *Journal of Consulting and Clinical Psychology, 55*, 162–170.

Laviola, M. (1992). Effects of older brother, younger sister incest—A case study of the dynamics of 17 cases. *Child Abuse and Neglect, 16*, 409–421.

Levy, B. (1991). Support groups: Empowerment for young women abused in dating relationships. In B. Levy (Ed.), *Dating violence: Young women in danger* (pp. 232–239). Seattle, WA: Seal Press.

Makepeace, J. M. (1983). Life events, stress and courtship violence. *Family Relations, 32*, 101–109.

Makepeace, J. M. (1986). Gender differences in courtship violence victimization. *Family Relations, 35*, 383–388.

Morbidity Mortality Weekly Report (MMWR). (1992). *Physical fighting among high school students—United States, 1990. 41*, 91–94.

National Center for Health Statistics. (1990). Annual summary of births, marriages, divorces, and deaths: United States, 1989. *Monthly Vital Statistics Report, 38*, 20–21.

NiCarthy, G. (1991). Addictive love and abuse: A course for teenage women. In B. Levy (Ed.), *Dating violence: Young women in danger* (pp. 240–257). Seattle, WA: Seal Press.

O'Carroll, P. W., & Mercy, J. (1986). Patterns and trends in Black homicide. In D. Hawkins (Ed.), *Homicide among black Americans* (pp. 29–42). Lanham, MD: University Press of America.

Paulson, J. A., & Rushforth, N. B. (1986). Violent death in children in a metropolitan county: Changing patterns of homicide, 1958–1982. *Pediatrics, 78*, 1013–1020.

Powell, C. (1991). Dealing with dating violence in schools. In B. Levy (Ed.), *Dating violence: Young women in danger* (pp. 279–284). Seattle, WA: Seal Press.

Prothrow-Stith, D. (1987). *Violence prevention: Curriculum for adolescents*. Newton, MA: Education Development Center.

Resnick, H. S., Kilpatrick, D. G., Dansky, B. S., Saunders, B. E., & Best, C. L. (1993). Prevalence of civilian trauma and posttraumatic stress disorder in a representative national sample of women. *Journal of Clinical and Consulting Psychology, 61*, 984–991.

Roden, M. (1991). A model secondary school date rape prevention program. In B. Levy (Ed.), *Dating violence: Young women in danger* (pp. 267–278). Seattle, WA: Seal Press.

Roscoe, B., & Callahan, J. E. (1985). Adolescents' self report of violence in families and dating relations. *Adolescence, 20*, 545–553.

Roscoe, B., & Kelsey, T. (1986). Dating violence among high school students. *Psychology, 23*, 53–59.

Rosenberg, M., & Mercy, J. (1986). Homicide: Epidemiologic analysis at the national level. *Bulletin of the New York Academy of Medicine, 62*, 376–394.

Rozee-Koker, P., & Polk, G. (1986). The social psychology of group rape. *Sexual Coercion and Assault: Issues and Perspectives, 1*, 57–65.

Russell, D. E. H. (1982). The prevalence and incidence of forcible rape and attempted rape of females. *Victimology, 7*, 81–93.

Russell, D. E. H. (1984). *Sexual exploitation*. Beverly Hills, CA: Sage.

Siegel, J. M., Golding, J. M., Stein, J. A., Burnam, M. A., & Sorenson, S. B. (1990). Reactions to sexual assault: A community study. *Journal of Interpersonal Violence, 5*, 229–246.

Siegel, J. M., Sorenson, S. B., Golding, J. M., Burnam, M. A., & Stein, J. A. (1987). The prevalence of childhood sexual assault: The Los Angeles epidemiologic catchment area project. *American Journal of Epidemiology, 126*, 1141–1153.

Sorenson, S. B., Richardson, B. A., & Peterson, J. G. (1993). Youthful homicide victims: Race/ethnicity patterns in the city of Los Angeles, 1980–1989, *American Journal of Public Health, 83*, 725–727.

Sousa, C. (1991). The dating violence intervention project. In B. Levy (Ed.), *Dating violence: Young women in danger* (pp. 223–231). Seattle, WA: Seal Press.

Straus, M., & Gelles, R. (1986). Societal change and change in family violence from 1975 to 1985 as revealed by two national surveys. *Journal of Marriage and the Family, 48*, 465–479.

Straus, M., Gelles, R., & Steinmetz, S. K. (1980). *Behind closed doors: Violence in the American family*. New York: Doubleday.

Sugarman, D. B., & Hotaling, G. T. (1991). Dating violence: A review of contextual and risk factors. In B. Levy (Ed.), *Dating violence: Young women in danger* (pp. 100–118). Seattle, WA: Seal Press.

Walker, L. E. A. (1979). *The battered woman*. New York: Harper & Row.

White, J. G., & Koss, M. P. (1991). Courtship violence: Incidence in a national sample of higher education students. *Violence and Victims, 6*, 247–256.

Widom, C. S. (1989). Does violence beget violence? A critical examination of the literature. *Psychological Bulletin, 106*, 3–28.

Wolfe, D. A. (1987). *Child abuse: Implications for child development and psychopathology*. Newbury Park, CA: Sage.

Wyatt, G. E. (1985). The sexual abuse of African-American women and white-American women in childhood. *Child Abuse and Neglect, 9*, 507–519.

9

Lesbian, Gay, and Bisexual Youths

Anthony R. D'Augelli and Lawrence J. Dark

Studies of bias-related violence demonstrate that the most frequent kind of victimization occurs when the victim is perceived to be lesbian or gay (Berrill, 1990; Comstock, 1991; Finn & McNeil, 1987; Herek, 1989). Summarizing the available surveys of antilesbian and antigay victimization, Comstock (1991, p. 39) found that 23% of adult lesbians and gay men reported that they had objects thrown at them; 17% had been punched, hit, kicked, or beaten; 17% reported vandalism or arson; 7% had been spit at; and 7% reported assault with a weapon. These frequencies reflect victimization at the time of the study, and surveys requesting information on lifetime incidents show that more than 50% have experienced some kind of violence. Comstock's analysis also revealed that 32% of those surveyed had been chased or followed, suggesting that victimization might have been more frequent or more severe if attackers had been more successful. A recent longitudinal study in New York City corroborates the results of these community surveys (Dean, Wu, & Martin, 1992). Dean et al. found that more than one third of their large sample of gay men reported violence during 1 of the 6 years of the study and that 15% reported violence in 2 or more years of the study. In addition to physical violence and threats of violence, lesbians and gay men reported routine verbal harassment. Berrill's (1990) review of 10 victimization surveys of lesbians and gay men showed verbal abuse rates ranging from 58% of a sample of Alaskans to 87% of a sample of Pennsylvanians.

The available information shows not only that violence is common among this population but that it has been increasing. Reported violence that is based on sexual orientation has risen 127% in the past 6 years, despite a modest decline in 1993 (National Gay and Lesbian Task Force Policy Institute, 1994). Victim assistance agencies serving the lesbian and gay population in Boston, Chicago, Minneapolis/St. Paul, New York, and San Francisco documented 1,822 antigay episodes in 1991, an increase of 31% over 1990 (National Gay and Lesbian Task Force Policy Institute, 1992). These episodes included harassment, threats, physical assault, vandalism, arson, police abuse, and murder. As Berrill (1992) noted, given that these geographically diverse cities recorded such trends, it is likely that many other communities in the United States have experienced similar increases in violence. Herek (1995) noted that many of these surveys are based on nonprobability samples of lesbians and gay men, but they are consistent with a national telephone survey using a probability sample that showed that nearly half of the sample (47%) had been discriminated against because of their sexual orientation and that 5% of the men and 10% of the women reported physical assault in the year prior to the survey. The National Gay and Lesbian Task Force (NGLTF) and local groups attribute the rise in such incidents to greater reporting by victims as well as changes in the incidence of actual victimization, some of which may be related to AIDS. For example, since the early 1980s, prevalence studies have shown AIDS-related attacks against lesbians and gay men to be widespread (Herek & Berrill, 1992; Herek & Glunt, 1988). The Philadelphia Lesbian and Gay Task Force (Gross & Aurand, 1992) found that 18% of the men and 4% of the women reported that victimization was accompanied by HIV- and AIDS-related abuse. Also, some groups, such as the Southern Poverty Law Center (1987) and Anti-Defamation League of B'nai Brith (1991), maintain that the rise in violence toward lesbians and gay men may be part of the general rise in hate crimes that are the result of a deterioration in relations among racial, ethnic, religious, and other social groups nationally (see also Levin & McDevitt, 1993). Finally, the increased visibility of lesbians, gay men, and bisexuals in society not only provides more targets for victimization, but it also may produce a backlash that encourages various forms of victimization.

Table 1 contains summary data from the most recent report from the Philadelphia Lesbian and Gay Task Force's survey of discrimination and violence directed against adult lesbian and gay Pennsylvanians on the basis of their sexual orientation (Gross & Aurand, 1992). Comparable data on the victimization of lesbian, gay, and bisexual youth are unavailable; the few published reports related to such violence are reviewed later in this chapter.

At Special Risk for Violence: Lesbian, Gay, and Bisexual Youth

Lesbian, gay, and bisexual youth are especially vulnerable to victimization of various kinds; it is also likely that the psychological consequences of victimization will be more severe than they might be for older lesbians, gay men, and bisexuals. There are several reasons why youth are more likely to be victimized. First, simply by virtue of being adolescents they are at greater risk of violence than adults (Hammond & Yung, 1993). Compared with adults, adolescents are disproportionately the victims of violent crime (Select Committee on Children, Youth, and Families, 1989). A recent U.S. Department of Justice report confirms that teenagers are more vulnerable than adults to both violent and property crime (Whitaker & Bastian, 1991). Second, lesbian, gay, and bisexual youth are uniquely subject to violence resulting from societal heterosexism and homophobia, although heterosexual youth perceived as lesbian or gay may also be targeted. Third, lesbian, gay, and bisexual youth will be subject to violence because of their association with the HIV epidemic. Finally, lesbian, gay, and bisexual youth are victimized as a result of backlash resulting from their greater visibility in society (Berrill & Herek, 1990; Hun-

TABLE 1.   Discrimination and Violence Against Lesbians and Gay Men in Philadelphia

- Twenty-five percent of the men and 31% of the women reported discrimination in employment, housing, or public accommodations.
- Fifty percent of the men and 53% of the women reported discrimination at one point in their lifetimes.
- Seventy-eight percent of the men and 87% of the women expect future discrimination.
- Sixty-five percent of the men and 50% of the women experienced verbal abuse within the past year; lifetime rates were 89% and 74%, respectively.
- Twenty-four percent of the men and 16% of the women were the victims of criminal violence; lifetime rates were 57% of the men and 35% of the women.
- Eighteen percent of the men and 4% of the women reporting verbal abuse within the past year said attacks were accompanied by AIDS-related abuse.
- Twenty-four percent of the men and 13% of the women experienced harassment or violence from police over their lifetimes.
- Fifty-seven percent of the men and 30% of the women reported harassment or violence in junior high school, senior high school, or college.
- Thirty-one percent of the men and 31% of the women reported harassment or physical violence from family members over their lifetimes.

Note: The data in this table pertain only to the city of Philadelphia and were compiled by L. Gross and S. Aurand. Results are based on a 1991–1992 sample of 553 women and 860 men. The complete report, which contains these and other data, can be found in L. Gross and S. Aurand. (1992, September). *Discrimination and violence against lesbian women and gay men in Philadelphia and the Commonwealth of Pennsylvania.* Philadelphia: Philadelphia Lesbian and Gay Task Force.

ter, 1990). With increased social acceptance of homosexuality over the past two decades, more lesbian, gay, and bisexual youth are aware of their sexual orientation at earlier ages, have the language to articulate their identities, disclose their identities to others ("come out") earlier, and find greater support from other similar youth (Herdt, 1989; Savin-Williams, 1990, 1995). In addition, contemporary lesbian, gay, and bisexual youth, if they are open about their sexual orientation, may be more assertive about their identities and more confrontive than prior generations of youth (Leck, 1994; Signorile, 1993). Their increased openness and assertiveness puts them in direct conflict with family and peers, as well as with all of the traditional institutions and support systems of society, most importantly the schools (Rofes, 1989, 1994). This amplified social vulnerability to victimization of lesbian, gay, and bisexual youth is especially problematic because of the distinctive character of their adolescent years (Savin-Williams, 1995).

Developmental Issues

Adolescence is a time of tremendous cognitive, social, and biological change. Exploration of sexual behavior, expression, and identity is a core normative aspect of adolescent development. Early adolescence is generally seen as a period of sexual awakening and discovery (D'Augelli & Bingham, 1993; Koch, 1993). The physiological, psychological, and social changes related to pubertal development are difficult for many adolescents to manage, but lesbian, gay, and bisexual youth face even more difficult challenges in developing a positive sexual identity in proximal (i.e., parents, family, peers, teachers, schools) and distal (i.e., neighborhood, community, the media, etc.) social environments that are strongly conditioned by heterosexist assumptions that devalue lesbian, gay, or bisexual orientations. Contemporary research suggests that lesbian, gay, and bisexual youth are first aware of their same-sex attraction at about 10–12 years of age; they ordinarily label themselves as lesbian, gay, or bisexual at about age 15; and they disclose their identities to someone else for the first time at about age 16 (there is considerable variability in such ages; see D'Augelli & Hershberger, 1993; Herdt & Boxer, 1993). They deal with these complex personal matters with far fewer resources and with far greater risks than their heterosexual counterparts. Thus, even without victimization, lesbian, gay, and bisexual youth are at risk for mental health problems. These developmental challenges of lesbian and gay male youth have only recently gained the attention of researchers and professionals (Anderson, 1994; Boxer & Cohler, 1989; Cates, 1987; Cwayna, Remafedi, & Treadway, 1991; Gonsiorek, 1988; Kourany, 1987; Mallon, 1992; Remafedi, 1987a, 1987b, 1987c; M. Schneider, 1988, 1989, 1991; M. Schneider & Tremble, 1986; Slater, 1988). Often, however, lesbian, gay, and bisexual youth are neglected in discussions of adolescence. A current example of such neglect can be seen by the near total absence of discussions of lesbian, gay, or bisexual youth in a recent *American Psychologist* issue on adolescence (Takanishi, 1993).

Youth who become aware of their sexual orientation during adolescence and who choose to disclose their orientation to others (or those whose orientations is disclosed to others without their consent) usually experience psychological conflict in a number of contexts, at home, at school, and in peer relationships. These conflicts can negatively affect their development, particularly their sense of a positive identity and their self-esteem. Anticipating such conflicts, many lesbian, gay, and bisexual youth hide their sexual identity, leading a double life, rather than confronting personal, family, and social situations that are highly threatening (Martin, 1982; Martin & Hetrick, 1988). Many live in constant fear of being discovered. Others deny their sexual orientation, even to themselves, threatening their identity development (Malyon, 1981–1982). This alienation places these youth at risk for various behaviors that are injurious to themselves and others, and also renders them vulnerable to exploitation, harassment, discrimination, and violence. For example, up to 40% of street youth and runaways in some studies are lesbian, gay, or bisexual (Savin-Williams & Cohen, in press). Gay male youth are at particular risk for HIV infection as well (Rotheram-Borus & Koopman, 1991).

Distinctive Life Stresses

Developmental research suggests that many who identify as lesbian or gay first recognize their orientation in early adolescence and that most knew they were lesbian or gay by early adulthood (Herdt, 1989). As increasing numbers of young lesbians and gay men disclose their identities to others, researchers have been better able to study the psychological and psychosocial stressors in their lives (Gonsiorek, 1988; Hetrick & Martin, 1987; Hunter & Schaecher, 1987; Martin & Hetrick, 1988). Recent studies reveal considerable stress in the lives of these youth. Remafedi (1987c) found that 43% of a sample of gay male adolescents reported strong negative reactions from parents about their sexual orientation; 41% reported negative reactions from friends. Most of these youth (72%) had received mental health services for emotional problems (Remafedi, 1987a). A Canadian study also showed evidence of serious mental health problems in a sample of 60 lesbian and gay youth, with more than half reporting periods of extreme anxiety or depression (M. Schneider, 1991). A national survey of lesbian mental health showed that 62% of the 17–24-year-olds in the sample had received counseling (National Lesbian and Gay Health Foundation, 1987). The most frequently occurring problems taken to counselors were family problems (46%), depression (40%), problems in relationships (29%), and anxiety (26%). A study of young gay men revealed a similar constellation of personal and emotional problems (D'Augelli, 1991a). The most frequent concerns were dealing with parents about one's sexual orientation (93% reported it to be a concern), relationship problems (93%), worry about AIDS (92%), anxiety (77%), and depression (63%). A recent study of lesbian, gay, and bisexual youth indicated that more than half experienced problems with depression, anxiety, close relationship conflicts, dissatisfaction with their sex lives, and stresses related to disclosure of their sexual orientation to families and others (D'Augelli & Hershberger, 1993).

The disclosure of sexual orientation to parents and family members is a core issue related to the psychological adjustment of lesbian, gay, and bisexual youth. Research on parental reactions to disclosure of sexual orientation finds considerable upset among parents, many of whom initially respond strongly negatively to the disclosure and recover slowly (Muller, 1987; Strommen, 1989). Cramer and Roach (1988), using an adult gay male sample, found that 55% of the men's mothers and 42% of their fathers had an initial negative response. Robinson, Walters, and Skeen (1989) sampled parents of lesbian and gay adults through a national support group for parents and found that most at first reported sadness (74%), regret (58%), depression (49%), and fear for their child's well-being (74%). Neither study focused specifically on parents of lesbian, gay, or bisexual *youth*. By contrast, Boxer, Cook, and Herdt (1991) studied both youth 21 and younger as well as a sample of these youths' parents. More youth had disclosed to their mothers than to their fathers. Of the lesbian youth, 63% had disclosed to mothers and 37% to fathers; of the males, 54% had disclosed to mothers and 28% to fathers. Parents reported a period of considerable family disruption following the disclosure.

Suicide

In addition to these distinctive stresses, the accumulated evidence suggests a disproportionately high incidence of suicide attempts among lesbian, gay, and bisexual youth. The earliest study of gay male youth showed that 31% of a sample of gay males aged 16–22 had made a suicide attempt (Roesler & Deisher, 1972). Martin and Hetrick (1988) found that 21% of their clients as a social service agency for troubled lesbian and gay youth had made a suicide attempt. Basing his conclusions on earlier studies as well as on reports from community agencies, Gibson (1989) speculated that most suicide attempts by lesbians and gay men occurred in their youth, that lesbian and gay youth are two to three times more likely to commit suicide than their heterosexual peers, and that lesbian and gay male suicide may constitute up to 30% of all completed youth suicides. Gibson estimated that 20%–35% of lesbian and gay youth have made suicide attempts. Gibson's (1989) conclusions were echoed by a similar analysis by Harry (1989b), who concluded that, overall, lesbians and gay men were more likely to make suicide attempts than heterosexuals and that such attempts were more probable at times of conflicts about sexual orientation, especially in adolescence. Unfortunately, Gibson's and Harry's conclusions were based on limited empirical data and rely heavily on reports from organizations that may attract individuals with mental health problems. Nonetheless, these figures are considerably higher than current estimates of high school suicide attempts, which range from 6% to 13% (Friedman, Asnis, Boeck, & DiFiore, 1987; Garland & Zigler, 1993; S. G. Schneider, Farberow, & Kruks, 1989; Smith & Crawford, 1986).

Recent empirical studies have shown similar conclusions about a high risk for suicide among lesbian, gay, and bisexual youth. Remafedi (1987a) found that 34% of his gay male adolescent sample had attempted suicide. In a later study with a somewhat larger sample, Remafedi, Farrow, and Deisher (1991) found that 30% had made a suicide attempt. Those who had attempted suicide were younger, had more feminine gender role concepts, and were more likely to report drug and alcohol abuse. Another study of gay male youth indicated that 23% had attempted suicide at least once and that 59% evidenced serious suicidal thinking (S. G. Schneider et al., 1989). In the Canadian study noted earlier, more than one third reported suicidal thoughts or having made suicide attempts (M. Schneider, 1991). Many young lesbians in the national study mentioned earlier had considered suicide. Of those aged 17–24 years, about one quarter had made an attempt. Only 41% said they had never contemplated suicide (National Lesbian and Gay Health Foundation, 1987). In a study of nearly 200 lesbian, gay, and bisexual youth (D'Augelli & Hershberger, 1993), 42% stated that they had made a suicide attempt. Those who had made suicide attempts reported more psychiatric symptoms, were aware of their sexual orientation at an earlier age, had lower self-esteem, and had lost more friends because of their sexual orientation than those who did not make attempts. Finally, a study of 202 Chicago youth attending a lesbian and gay social service agency's youth support group indicated that about one third of the group had made at least one suicide attempt (Herdt & Boxer, 1993).

Unfortunately, the linkages between personal, familial, and social stresses and suicide attempts, suicidal ideation, or other serious mental health problems have not been systematically studied in this population. Remefedi et al. (1991) found that 44% of the gay male youth studied reported that their suicide attempts were precipitated by "family problems." S. G. Schneider et al.

(1989) found that suicide attempters had not yet established a positive gay identity; attempts occurred most often while youth were "closeted" (i.e., before they acknowledged or disclosed their sexual identities to others). They also found that a family background of paternal alcoholism and abuse, reliance on social support from people who rejected them because of their sexual orientation, and awareness of their sexual orientation at an earlier age were all associated with youths' suicide attempts. M. Schneider (1991) reported decreases in youths' mental health problems when coming-out issues were resolved. Interestingly, there are even fewer reports attempting to delineate the relation between the victimization of lesbian, gay, and bisexual youth and their psychological adjustment, despite evidence that victimization of different kinds is common in their lives and a fair assumption that victimization would add further burden to lives already under unusual stress.

Patterns of Victimization of Lesbian, Gay, and Bisexual Youth

Research on violence directed at lesbians, gay males, and bisexuals seldom takes into account the age of the victims. A rare exception is the longitudinal study by Dean et al. (1992), which showed that younger gay men in New York were more frequently attacked than older men. The "young" males in this study, however, ranged from 18 to 24 years of age. Similarly, the youngest women in the large-scale survey conducted by the National Lesbian and Gay Health Foundation (1987) were 17–24 years of age. Of these women, 29% reported physical abuse, 50% reported rape and sexual assault, and 18% reported incest; again, victimization was highest in this age group. Thus, the little information available that compares age groups suggests that lesbian, gay, and bisexual youth are more likely to be the victims of violence than older lesbians or gay men. Some of this victimization takes place at home; much takes place in schools and in other community settings. Most of the victimization occurs to youth who are open about their orientation, are suspected of being lesbian or gay, or behave in ways stereotypically associated with lesbians and gay men even if they are heterosexually identified. How much of the sexual victimization of young lesbians can be specifically attributed to their sexual orientation is uncertain. There is little doubt that much victimization goes unreported, especially if it occurs in domestic settings or is perpetrated by peers.

Victimization Within the Family

The home is often not a safe haven for many lesbian, gay, and bisexual youth. Many parents believe that they are responsible for their offspring's sexual orientation, a belief that puts the family and the youth in conflict that may lead to violence (Hunter & Schaecher, 1987). Hunter (1990) documented that 61% of sexual-orientation-related violence directed toward youth occurred in the family. In other studies of antilesbian and gay abuse by relatives, 19%–41% of respondents had experienced verbal insults or threats, and 4%–7%

had encountered physical violence (Herek & Berrill, 1992). There is evidence of parental physical abuse of gay males in adolescence (Harry, 1989a). Although some of this abuse may have occurred in adulthood, it is likely that much occurred while the respondents were at home—for most, until the end of their high school years. In a study of lesbian and gay youth at a social service agency in New York dedicated to their needs, Hunter (1990) found that 61% of the violence youth reported as related to sexual orientation had occurred in the family. Pilkington and D'Augelli (in press) found that more than one third of their sample of lesbian, gay, and bisexual youth reported verbal abuse by family members and that nearly one quarter said that fear of victimization at home affected their openness about their orientation. The particular family members (e.g., mothers, fathers, siblings, extended family members) who attack lesbian, gay, and bisexual youth have not been carefully studied. The National Lesbian and Gay Health Foundation survey (1987) indicated that 70% of all women beaten or abused as children were attacked by unspecified male relatives and 45% by female relatives; of those women raped or sexually attacked as children, 31% were male relatives and 45% were other known males; and of those who ever experienced incest (19% of the total sample), 34% were brothers, 28% were fathers, 27% were uncles, and 18% were cousins.

Victimization in Community Settings

In addition to familial conflicts and victimization, lesbian, gay, and bisexual youth who are open about their sexual orientation face verbal harassment and physical attacks at school and in their local communities. Because so much time is spent in school settings, these settings take on particular importance. Between 33% and 49% of lesbians and gay male adults responding to community surveys reported being victimized "in school," presumably in junior and high school (Berrill, 1990). In 1991, 37% of lesbians and gay men surveyed by the NGLTF Policy Institute (1992) reported experiencing harassment, threats, or actual violence in junior and senior high school. A survey of New York State junior and senior high school students showed that nearly one third (31%) witnessed acts of violence directed at students or teachers thought to be lesbian or gay (White, 1988). Gross and Aurand (1992) found that 57% of the sample of adult gay men and 30% of lesbians in Philadelphia reported that they had experienced violence or harassment in junior high school, high school, or college. In the Pilkington and D'Augelli (in press) report, 22% of the males and 29% of the females reported being hurt at school by another student. Most (79%) reported discomfort about disclosure of their orientation at school. Many school problems experienced by lesbian, gay, or bisexual students are often the result of verbal and physical abuse from peers in school. Indeed, alternative programs such as the Harvey Milk High School in New York City have been established partly because of the harassment that youth received in public school, which contributes to poor academic performance, excessive absences, truancy, and dropping out.

Reports from gay males in Remafedi's (1987c) study were similar, with more than half (55%) reporting peer verbal abuse and nearly one third (30%) physical assault. Nearly 40% of the male youths in the Remafedi et al. (1991) study said they had experienced physical violence. Physical attacks by families, peers, or strangers were reported by 41% of the lesbian and gay youth surveyed by Hunter (1990), with nearly half of the attacks attributable to sexual orientation. In a study of gay male youth drawn from the same social service agency as in Hunter's (1990) study, Rotheram-Borus, Rosario, and Koopman (1991) found that 27% reported physical assault, 14% reported rape or sexual assault, and 55% said they had been ridiculed by someone because of their sexual orientation. In the National Lesbian and Gay Health Foundation (1987) study, 52% of the total sample of women said they had been verbally attacked and 6% said they had been physically attacked. Pilkington and D'Augelli (in press) found that 80% of their sample of 15–21-year-olds had experienced verbal abuse, nearly half (44%) had been physically threatened, nearly one third (31%) had been chased or followed, 11% had been spat on, and nearly one fifth had been physically assaulted. Ten percent of the youth had been assaulted with a weapon. Many reported mental health problems, and more than 40% reported a suicide attempt (D'Augelli & Hershberger, 1993). Although victimization patterns were not related to reported suicide attempts, attacks did compromise their mental health (Hershberger & D'Augelli, in press). Nearly half (44%) of another sample of lesbian and gay youth said that they were either physically or emotionally abused, with sexual orientation being the primary reason for the abuse (Hammelman, 1993). Of those abused, 38% had made suicide attempts and 52% stated that they had seriously considered suicide.

Victimization on College and University Campuses

Although college and university campuses are ideally ones in which tolerance and pluralism are cherished values, lesbian, gay, and bisexual students are faced with risky circumstances even in such settings (Evans & D'Augelli, in press; Evans & Wall, 1991). Widespread harassment of undergraduate students who are lesbian, gay, or bisexual has been well documented. In a careful synthesis of survey data from three universities, Comstock (1991) summarized the percentages of respondents who experienced victimization because of their sexual orientation. His analysis indicated that 22% had been chased or followed; 15% had objects thrown at them; 4% had been punched, hit, kicked, or beaten; 11% were the targets of vandalism or arson; 3% were spit at; and 1% was assaulted with a weapon. Comstock concluded that lesbian, gay, and bisexual students are victimized at a rate four times higher than the rate reported by the general student population. A more recent study of 121 undergraduates (D'Augelli, 1992) corroborated earlier findings. Most youth (77%) had been verbally insulted; 27% had been threatened with physical violence, 7% more than once. In terms of actual violence, 13% reported property damage; 22% reported being chased. Six of the youth reported cases of actual physical assault. Incidents were rarely reported to the authorities. Other students were the most frequent perpetrators.

In terms of estimates of violence against lesbian, gay, and bisexual college students, however, it must be noted that findings from such studies are likely underestimates of the incidence of victimization. Many incidents are not reported because victims do not want their sexual orientation known, because they fear additional harassment from authorities, or because they expect no action following their reporting. All evidence suggests that lesbian, gay, and bisexual college students expect verbal harassment and fear physical attack; these high estimates of the probability of victimization are shared by heterosexual students as well (D'Augelli, 1993). Thus, college students still show the hypervigilence common among younger lesbian, gay, and bisexual youth as well; they too endeavor to avoid situations or persons that they perceive may lead to violence. Whether lesbian, gay, or bisexual college students are more successful in avoiding attacks, are attacked less vociferously, or rebound more readily than younger counterparts is unknown.

Research Dilemmas

Most lesbian, gay, and bisexual youth—whether in school of one sort or another or not—often face the challenges of victimization alone, or with the help of a small network of others in whom they have confided and whose trust is predictable. Some, especially those who are seriously hurt, may have no choice but to turn to others, such as parents or teachers, who are unaccepting of their sexual orientation. For some youth, one consequence of their attack is an unexpected disclosure of their sexual orientation. For others, a fragile equilibrium in which neither they nor their family address the youths' sexual orientation may be shattered by victimization (Boxer et al., 1991). Thus, youth may experience additional, or secondary, victimization in the process of help-seeking events that exacerbate the primary victimization (Berrill & Herek, 1992). Currently, to our knowledge there is no research on lesbian, gay, and bisexual youth that directly assesses their responses to victimization, despite the conclusion of most mental health and social service professionals that the range of harmful events to which they are exposed has a profound impact on their development and their mental health. For lesbian, gay, and bisexual adults, for instance, an increased vulnerability, intensified internalized homophobia, depression, guilt, and self-blame are common psychological reactions (Garnets, Herek, & Levy, 1990). Garnets et al. (1990) argued that verbal abuse may be even more problematic, because it does not have the physical reality of assault and thus stymies recovery. It would seem likely that such reactions would be amplified among lesbian, gay, and bisexual youth.

Many critical questions about reactions to victimization remain to be studied. For instance, researchers do not know whether youth who make suicide attempts do so because they have not disclosed their orientations to family or close friends, and they therefore ultimately succumb to the intense stresses associated with hiding. Indeed, undisclosed youth are not involved in research because they do not visit the usual settings in which such research is conducted. Another pattern concerns disclosed youth who are subjected to victimization of different kinds from different sources. It is reasonable to hypothesize that such youth, especially if they are young (and therefore will experience more victimization over a longer period of time) and have little or no support in coping with attacks, will suffer more deleterious consequences, but this has yet to be tested. Furthermore, little is known about how variability in crucial factors such as prior mental health status, personal characteristics (especially self-esteem and coping competence), support from family and friends, and involvement with helping resources of different kinds (especially those affirming the youth's sexual orientation) might mitigate the impact of verbal and physical abuse. It is particularly important to understand such issues among lesbian, gay, and bisexual youth so as to facilitate the development of preventive interventions. Having an empirically tested model that would delineate which youth cope well with the routine verbal harassment that openly lesbian and gay people commonly encounter could lead to identification of strategies to enhance their coping strategies. Knowing which youth respond poorly to assaults will similarly allow for the development of crisis intervention services that might forestall later academic failure, loss of self-esteem, and self-destructive behavior.

Interventions to Prevent Violence Against Lesbian, Gay, and Bisexual Youth

To address increasing victimization against lesbian, gay, and bisexual youth, several strategies are needed. They are (a) the development of more effective ways to monitor the incidence and prevalence of victimization, (b) the provision of services to youth who are the targets of different forms of victimization, (c) the creation of safe settings in schools, (d) the incorporation of issues of sexual orientation into school curricula, and (e) the enactment of public policies that protect lesbian, gay, and bisexual youth and discourage victimization.

Monitoring Victimization Patterns

Despite the greater visibility of the lesbian, gay, and bisexual population over the past two decades, lesbian, gay, and bisexual youth remain an invisible subset of this population. Because of their reluctance to share their orientation with others, documenting the incidence and prevalence of different forms of victimization directed at them is difficult. Much of the victimization occurs in the form of verbal harassment and threats, and these are even less often reported to others than are assaults. In addition, although more violent attacks may come to the attention of parents, school officials, and law enforcement authorities, the role of bias motivation in the attacks may not be clear. The most general solution to this problem involves an appreciation of the scope of victimization directed against this group of youth, so that antilesbian and antigay prejudice can be considered as a motive for victimization.

There are three primary sources of data for documenting victimization: information collected by law enforcement authorities, surveys of victims, and surveys of perpetrators (Herek & Berrill, 1992). The passage of the 1990 U.S. Hate Statistics Act directs the tabulation of bias crimes on the basis of sexual orientation directed against victims of different ages. Unfortunately, it will take many years for this system to become fully operative, and underreporting of crimes motivated by homophobia will remain a problem. Many states have added sexual orientation to statutes that amplify penalties for bias crimes; this too will ultimately increase information about such victimization, despite its limitations. It would also be helpful if school authorities began tracking incidents of harassment and violence in which homophobic attitudes were involved. Providing confidential mechanisms for students to report these incidents will help monitoring and also facilitate appropriate help for victimizers.

Continuing surveying of victims will likely be a more productive source of useful information than data gathered by authorities on the basis of reported incidents. Historically, the most important accounting of discrimination and violence against lesbians, gay men, and bisexuals has been conducted by lesbian, gay, and bisexual community-based organizations such as the Philadelphia Lesbian and Gay Task Force, the Community United Against Violence in San Francisco, and the New York City Gay and Lesbian Anti-Violence Project (Wertheimer, 1992). These and other groups have developed simple survey instruments that can be used in any setting (Gross & Aurand, 1992). Other instruments are also available (Herek, 1993; Herek & Berrill, 1992). Unfortunately, surveying lesbian, gay, and bisexual youth is especially complex. However, one promising strategy, despite its drawbacks, is to sample youth who are involved in the increasing number of support and discussion groups and advocacy and political groups in lesbian–gay community centers. This approach has already yielded important information about victimization patterns (Pilkington & D'Augelli, in press).

Information about perpetrators is difficult to gather even for crimes committed against lesbian, gay, and bisexual adults. However, Comstock's (1991) review indicated some trends among perpetrators (e.g., 94% were males; nearly half were 21 or younger; more were White than people of color; many did not know their victims personally). Comparable data about assailants of lesbian, gay, or bisexual youth have not been gathered. Relevant information about the social climate for victimization of lesbian, gay, and bisexual youth can be found in surveys of students. A survey conducted at a Massachusetts high school showed that 98% of the students had heard homophobic remarks at the school and that 49% had heard such comments often (Governor's Commission on Gay and Lesbian Youth, 1993). A survey on bias-related violence conducted on junior and senior high school students in New York State noted that "one of the most alarming findings in the youth survey is the openness with which respondents expressed their aversion and hostility toward gays and lesbians. . . . Gays and lesbians, it seems, are perceived as legitimate targets which can be openly attacked (White, 1988, p. 97). Little support for gay males was found in a national survey of 15–19-year-old males (Marsiglio, 1993). In that report, 89% found the thought of sex between men "disgusting," and only 12% felt they could befriend a gay person. Those with more negative views held more traditional sex role views, had religious fundamentalist attitudes, and came from less well educated families, characteristics found in other research on prejudice against lesbians and gay men (Herek, 1991). Widespread antilesbian and antigay attitudes on college campuses have also been found (D'Augelli, 1993), and survey methods for gathering such information are available (Herek, 1994).

Provision of Help for Victims

Although there is much variability in response to antilesbian and antigay victimization, there is little doubt that it has immediate, lingering, and delayed impact (Garnets et al., 1990). Among lesbian, gay, and bisexual youth, outcomes associated with harassment and violence have included patterns ranging from school problems and running away from home to substance abuse, prostitution, and suicide (Savin-Williams & Cohen, in press). For severe assaults, intensive crisis intervention may be necessary. For repeated verbal abuse and threats, ongoing supportive counseling should be complemented by efforts to stop the victimization as quickly as possible. These efforts should also include helping youth become involved with support networks of other youth (Herdt & Boxer, 1993). To develop the array of services needed by such youth, junior high school and high school personnel need to become trained in issues related to lesbian, gay, and bisexual development (e.g., Reynolds & Koski, 1994; Ross-Reynolds & Hardy, 1985; Slater, 1988; Sobocinski, 1990). Access to confidential help for those who are dealing with their evolving sexual identity is crucial, because many of these youth may disclose their orientation to others and provoke direct or indirect victimization. School personnel who recommend that youth discuss their sexual orientation with others without carefully investigating probable responses might be inadvertently setting them up for victimization. In addition, help must be provided so that reporting attacks to authorities—whether to police or school officials—does not lead to further harassment by homophobic or heterosexist attitudes or comments.

The Creation of Safe Settings in Schools

The accumulating evidence on victimization of lesbian, gay, and bisexual youth provides an imperative for the need to assure "safe spaces" for them, especially in the schools. Increasing numbers of youth will be "coming out" during their school years, and many will be doing this at earlier ages. Those students who do make their sexual orientation known, or those whose sexual orientation becomes known, need special attention. One of the more promising interventions in this regard is Project 10, a drop-in program for lesbian, gay, and bisexual students in a Los Angeles high school that has been duplicated in other parts of the country (Harbeck, 1994; Uribe & Harbeck, 1991). In addition to such professionally run program offices, schools can enable the creation of support groups for lesbian, gay, and bisexual youth; these are most usefully organized in collaboration with trusted adults who can provide assurances of safety and who can be available if problems emerge. Another setting is a "gay–straight" alliance that includes supportive heterosexual students who are committed to helping schools eradicate bigotry on the basis of sexual orientation (Blumenfeld, 1994).

Incorporating Sexual Orientation Into Curricula

A recent national survey has shown that infrequent personal contact with gay men was associated with more negative attitudes (Herek & Glunt, 1993). Lesbian, gay, and bisexual youth are not only hidden from others in schools and in their communities—thus making personal contact difficult—but they are also hidden in school curricula. The invisibility of lesbian, gay, and bisexual lives in curricula occurs not only in high school (Lipkin, 1994), but also in colleges and universities (D'Augelli, 1991b). This situation allows stereotypes to go unchallenged, increasing a climate in which antilesbian and antigay attitudes can remain normative. The inclusion of material on lesbians, gay men, and bisexuals in classes allows for discussion and demystification. Adding fiction written by lesbian and gay writers for youth audiences can help youth feel less alienated and vulnerable. Discussion of advances in civil rights on the basis of sexual orientation is a reasonable component of history courses. Analyses of prejudice in social science courses can readily include homophobia and heterosexism.

Public Policy Recommendations

Public policy initiatives can play a crucial role in the prevention of victimization of lesbian, gay, and bisexual youth. Even public statements acknowledging the existence of these youth remove the invisibility from their lives and place the responsibility for their protection with authorities such as school professionals. There are two critical types of public statements relevant to the lives of lesbian, gay, and bisexual youth. The most pressing are statements clearly condemning violence on the basis of sexual orientation; such a statement might be best issued as part of a sexual harassment policy initiative. The second relates to discrimination. It is of the utmost importance that institutions serving youth, especially schools, make their programs and services accessible to all youth and explicitly prohibit discrimination that is based on sexual orientation. Such statements of intentions provide a framework from which to assure that lesbian, gay, and bisexual youth receive the same education, services, and support as heterosexual youth. Without such policy statements, the de facto discrimination against lesbian, gay, and bisexual youth will continue, a situation that destines them to enduring several years of neglect or persecution.

The Commonwealth of Massachusetts became the first state to address the challenges of lesbian, gay, and bisexual youth when Governor William Weld signed into law in December 1993 H.3353, An Act to Prohibit Discrimination Against Students in Public Schools on the Basis of Sexual Orientation. The law requires the following:

> No person shall be excluded from or discriminated against in admission to a public school of any town or in obtaining the advantages, privileges, and courses of study of such public school on account of race, color, religion, national origin, or sexual orientation.

The Governor's Commission on Gay and Lesbian Youth's (1993) report, which eventuated in the law, made several other sets of public policy recommendations. Five recommendations for schools were that each school system have (a) policies protecting lesbian and gay students from harassment, violence, and discrimination; (b) training for teachers, counselors, and other staff in crisis intervention and violence prevention; (c) school-based support groups for lesbian and gay students and their heterosexual allies; (d) information in school libraries for lesbian, gay, and bisexual adolescents; and (e) the integration of lesbian and gay issues into all subject areas. The commission also made policy recommendations for families of lesbian, gay, and bisexual youth. The commission recommended that various state agencies provide school-based counseling for families and peer support groups, education for families through public libraries, and parent speakers bureaus to advocate for lesbian and gay youth in the schools. The commission encouraged the Massachusetts Department of Education to sponsor training for teachers, families, and students to learn about the problems of lesbian and gay youth; make presentations to local school groups about the problems facing lesbian and gay youth; and develop and disseminate a "yellow pages" resource book on lesbian and gay youth. These recommendations form the basis for a statewide effort to ensure that lesbian, gay, and bisexual youth receive the same treatment from the schools; the recommendations wisely also help heterosexual students learn tolerance and respect for diversity.

Another set of policy activities is recommended by the Child Welfare League of America (1991) in their publication *Serving Gay and Lesbian Youths*. Some of these are as follows:

1. Provide opportunities for building professional competencies at all levels within agencies on the issues facing gay and lesbian youths through materials, workshops, seminars, conferences, and interagency sharing.
2. Build staff competencies by integrating issues of concern to gay and lesbian youth into training curricula, practice and policy discussions, and other initiatives.
3. Integrate the needs of gay and lesbian youths into service planning and implementation.
4. Create an agency environment that is safe and nurturing for all youth, regardless of their sexual orientation.
5. Using models of successful programs, encourage the development of a positive self-identity for youth who identify themselves as gay or lesbian.
6. Recognize the universal negative effects of bias not only on the treatment of gay and lesbian youth, but on all children and youth.
7. Examine existing indicators that can be used for obtaining basic data about gay and lesbian youths served, including incidence of runaways,

assaults, and name calling; sexual activity; diseases; pregnancy rates; suicide attempts; degree of psychological disturbances; signs of isolation; levels of self-esteem; poor school performance; degree of substance abuse; and degree of individual and family dysfunctions.

8. Encourage and support networking with other service providers to help assure that all of the needs of gay and lesbian youths are properly met.

Conclusion

There are two interlocking challenges facing professionals working to eradicate violence directed against youth who happen to be lesbian, gay, or bisexual. One set of interventions needs to be directed to these youth. All professional views and the increasing empirical research point to these youth as particular likely targets of intolerance and violence. In addition, the unusual stresses associated with developing as a lesbian, gay, or bisexual person in American society make such youth especially vulnerable to negative reactions following victimization. The other set of interventions must be focused on helping their heterosexual peers. This other set of youth must learn more about the diversities of sexual orientations and the nature of the development of human sexualities. They must also appreciate the pervasiveness of mistreatment of people on the basis of their sexual orientation. Finally, heterosexual youth need to come to appreciate that some of their friends are lesbian, gay, bisexual, or uncertain about their sexual orientation. With effective intervention, lesbian, gay, and bisexual youth may feel more comfortable disclosing their sexual orientation to others, knowing that supportive peers, teachers, and families are available for them. Until this time, however, interventions must be directed at protecting lesbian, gay, and bisexual youth from victimization and at restraining victimizers. We suggest that both sets of issues be approached on multiple levels, with efforts focused on individual youth as well as efforts designed to create social settings and social policy.

References

Anderson, D. A. (1994). Lesbian and gay adolescents: Social and developmental considerations. *High School Journal, 77*, 13–19.

Anti-Defamation League of B'nai Brith. (1991). *Audit of anti-Semitic incidents.* New York: Author.

Berrill, K. T. (1990). Anti-gay violence and victimization in the United States: An overview. *Journal of Interpersonal Violence, 5*, 274–294.

Berrill, K. T. (1992). Anti-gay violence and victimization in the United States: An overview. In K. T. Berrill & G. M. Herek (Eds.), *Hate crimes: Confronting violence against lesbians and gay men* (pp. 19–45). Newbury Park, CA: Sage.

Berrill, K. T., & Herek, G. M. (1990). Violence against lesbian and gay men: An introduction. *Journal of Interpersonal Violence, 5*, 269–273.

Berrill, K. T., & Herek, G. M. (1992). Primary and secondary victimization in anti-gay hate crimes: Official response and public policy. In G. M. Herek & K. T. Berrill (Eds.), *Hate crimes: Confronting violence against lesbians and gay men* (pp. 289–305). Newbury Park, CA: Sage.

Blumenfeld, W. J. (1994). "Gay/straight" alliances: Transforming pain to pride. *High School Journal, 77*, 113–121.

Boxer, A. M., & Cohler, B. J. (1989). The life course of gay and lesbian youth: An immodest proposal for the study of lives. *Journal of Homosexuality, 17*(1–2), 315–355.

Boxer, A. M., Cook, J. A., & Herdt, G. (1991). Double jeopardy: Identity transitions and parent-child relations among gay and lesbian youth. In K. Pillemer & K. McCartney (Eds.), *Parent-child relations throughout life* (pp. 59–92). Hillsdale, NJ: Erlbaum.

Cates, J. A. (1987). Adolescent sexuality: Gay and lesbian issues. *Child Welfare, 67*, 353–364.

Child Welfare League of America. (1991). *Serving gay and lesbian youths: The role of child welfare agencies.* Washington, DC: Author.

Comstock, G. D. (1991). *Violence against lesbians and gay men.* New York: Columbia University Press.

Cramer, D. W., & Roach, A. J. (1988). Coming out to Mom and Dad: A study of gay males and their relationships with their parents. *Journal of Homosexuality, 15*(3–4), 79–92.

Cwayna, K., Remafedi, G., & Treadway, L. (1991). Caring for gay and lesbian youth. *Medical Aspects of Human Sexuality, 25*, 50–57.

D'Augelli, A. R. (1991a). Gay men in college: Identity processes and adaptations. *Journal of College Student Development, 32*, 140–146.

D'Augelli, A. R. (1991b). Teaching lesbian/gay development: From oppression to exceptionality. *Journal of Homosexuality, 22*, 213–227.

D'Augelli, A. R. (1992). Lesbian and gay male undergraduates' experiences of harassment and fear on campus. *Journal of Interpersonal Violence, 7*, 383–395.

D'Augelli, A. R. (1993). Preventing mental health problems among lesbian and gay college students. *Journal of Primary Prevention, 13*(4), 1–17.

D'Augelli, A. R. , & Bingham, R. (1993). Interventions to prevent HIV infections in young adolescents. In R. M. Lerner (Ed.), *Early adolescence: Perspectives on research, policy, and intervention* (pp. 353–368). Hillsdale, NJ: Erlbaum.

D'Augelli, A. R., & Hershberger, S. L. (1993). Lesbian, gay, and bisexual youth in community settings: Personal challenges and mental health problems. *American Journal of Community Psychology, 21*, 421–448.

Dean, L., Wu, S., & Martin, J. L. (1992). Trends in violence and discrimination against gay men in New York City: 1984 to 1990. In G. M. Herek & K. T. Berrill (Eds.), *Hate crimes: Confronting violence against lesbians and gay men* (pp. 46–64). Newbury Park, CA: Sage.

Evans, N. J., & D'Augelli, A. R. (in press). Lesbians, gay men, and bisexual people in college. In R. C. Savin-Williams & K. M. Cohen (Eds.), *Developmental and clinical issues among lesbians, gay men, and bisexuals.* New York: Harcourt Brace Jovanovich.

Evans, N. J., & Wall, V. A. (Eds.). (1991). *Beyond tolerance: Gays, lesbians, and bisexuals on campus.* Alexandria, VA: American College Personnel Association.

Finn, P., & McNeil, T. (1987). *The response of the criminal justice system to bias crime: An exploratory review.* Cambridge, MA: ABT Associates.

Friedman, J. M., Asnis, G. M., Boeck, M., & DiFiore, J. (1987). Prevalence of specific suicidal behaviors in a high school sample. *American Journal of Psychiatry, 144*, 1203–1206.

Garland, A. F., & Zigler, E. (1993). Adolescent suicide prevention: Current research and social policy implications. *American Psychologist, 48*, 169–182.

Garnets, L., Herek, G. M., & Levy, B. (1990). Violence and victimization of lesbians and gay men: Mental health consequences. *Journal of Interpersonal Violence, 5*, 366–383.

Gibson, P. (1989). Gay male and lesbian youth suicide. In *Report of the Secretary's Task Force on Youth Suicide* (DHHS Publication No. ADM 89-1623, Vol. 3, pp. 110–142). Washington, DC: U.S. Government Printing Office.

Gonsiorek, J. C. (1988). Mental health issues of gay and lesbian adolescents. *Journal of Adolescent Health Care, 9*, 114–122.

Governor's Commission on Gay and Lesbian Youth. (1993). *Making schools safe for gay and lesbian youth: Breaking the silence in schools and in families.* Boston: Author.

Gross, L., & Aurand, S. K. (1992). *Discrimination and violence against lesbian women and gay men in Philadelphia and the Commonwealth of Pennsylvania.* Philadelphia: Philadelphia Lesbian and Gay Task Force.

Hammelman, T. L. (1993). Gay and lesbian youth: Contributing factors to serious attempts or considerations of suicide. *Journal of Gay and Lesbian Psychotherapy, 2,* 77–89.

Hammond, W. R., & Yung, B. (1993). Psychology's role in the public health response to assaultive violence among African American men. *American Psychologist, 48,* 142–154.

Harbeck, K. M. (1994). Invisible no more: Addressing the needs of gay, lesbian, and bisexual youth and their advocates. *High School Journal, 77,* 169–176.

Harry, J. (1989a). Parental physical abuse and sexual orientation. *Archives of Sexual Behavior, 18,* 251–261.

Harry, J. (1989b). Sexual identity issues. In *Report of the Secretary's Task Force on Youth Suicide* (DHHS Publication No. ADM 89-1622, Vol. 2, pp. 131–142). Washington, DC: U.S. Government Printing Office.

Herdt, G. (1989). Gay and lesbian youth: Emergent identities and cultural scenes at home and abroad. *Journal of Homosexuality, 17*(1–2), 1–42.

Herdt, G. H., & Boxer, A. M. (1993). *Children of Horizons: How gay and lesbian teens are leading a new way out of the closet.* Boston: Beacon Press.

Herek, G. M. (1989). Hate crimes against lesbians and gay men: Issues for research and social policy. *American Psychologist, 44,* 948–955.

Herek, G. M. (1991). Stigma, prejudice, and violence against lesbians and gay men. In J. C. Gonsiorek & J. D. Weinrich (Eds.), *Homosexuality: Research implications for public policy* (pp. 60–80). Newbury Park, CA: Sage.

Herek, G. M. (1993). Documenting prejudice against lesbians and gay men on campus: The Yale Sexual Orientation Survey. *Journal of Homosexuality, 25*(4), 15–30.

Herek, G. M. (1994). Assessing heterosexuals' attitudes toward lesbians and gay men: A review of empirical research with the ATLG Scale. In B. Greene & G. M. Herek (Eds.), *Lesbian and gay psychology: Theory, research, and clinical applications* (pp. 206–228). Newbury Park, CA: Sage.

Herek, G. M. (1995). Psychological heterosexism in the United States. In A. R. D'Augelli & C. J. Patterson (Eds.), *Lesbian, gay, and bisexual identities over the lifespan* (pp. 321–346). New York: Oxford University Press.

Herek, G. M., & Berrill, K. T. (1992). Documenting the victimization of lesbians and gay men: Methodological issues. In G. M. Herek & K. T. Berrill (Eds.), *Hate crimes: Confronting violence against lesbians and gay men* (pp. 270–286). Newbury Park, CA: Sage.

Herek, G. M., & Glunt, E. K. (1988). An epidemic of stigma: Public reactions to AIDS. *American Psychologist, 43,* 886–891.

Herek, G. M., & Glunt, E. K. (1993). Interpersonal contact and heterosexuals' attitudes toward gay men: Results from a national survey. *Journal of Sex Research, 30,* 239–244.

Hershberger, S. L., & D'Augelli, A. R. (in press). The consequences of victimization on the mental health and suicidality of lesbian, gay, and bisexual youth. *Developmental Psychology.*

Hetrick, E. S., & Martin, A. D. (1987). Developmental issues and their resolution for gay and lesbian adolescents. *Journal of Homosexuality, 14*(1–2), 25–43.

Hunter, J. (1990). Violence against lesbian and gay male youths. *Journal of Interpersonal Violence, 5,* 295–300.

Hunter, J., & Schaecher, R. (1987). Stresses on lesbian and gay adolescents in schools. *Social Work in Education, 9,* 180–190.

Koch, P. B. (1993). Promoting healthy sexual development during early adolescence. In R. M. Lerner (Ed.), *Early adolescence: Perspectives on research, policy, and intervention* (pp. 293–307). Hillsdale, NJ: Erlbaum.

Kourany, R. F. C. (1987). Suicide among homosexual adolescents. *Journal of Homosexuality, 13*(4), 111–117.

Leck, G. (1994). Politics of adolescent sexual identity and queer responses. *High School Journal, 77,* 186–192.

Levin, J., & McDevitt, J. (1993). *Hate crimes: The rising tide of bigotry and bloodshed.* New York: Plenum.

Lipkin, A. (1994). The case for a gay and lesbian curriculum. *High School Journal, 77,* 95–107.

Mallon, G. (1992). Gay and no place to go: Assessing the needs of gay and lesbian adolescents in out-of-home care settings. *Child Welfare, 71,* 547–556.

Malyon, A. K. (1981–1982). The homosexual adolescent: Development issues and social bias. *Child Welfare, 60*, 321–330.

Marsiglio, W. (1993). Attitudes towards homosexual activity and gays as friends: A national survey of heterosexual 15- to 19-year-old males. *Journal of Sex Research, 30*, 12–17.

Martin, A. D. (1982). Learning to hide: Socialization of the gay adolescent. *Adolescent Psychiatry, 10*, 52–65.

Martin, A. D., & Hetrick, E. S. (1988). The stigmatization of the gay and lesbian adolescent. *Journal of Homosexuality, 15*(1–2), 163–184.

Muller, A. (1987). *Parents matter: Parents' relationships with lesbian daughters and gay sons.* Tallahassee, FL: Naiad Press.

National Gay and Lesbian Task Force Policy Institute. (1992). *Anti-gay / lesbian violence, victimization and defamation in 1991.* Washington, DC: Author.

National Gay and Lesbian Task Force Policy Institute. (1994). *Anti-gay / lesbian / bisexual violence fact sheet: April 1994 update.* Washington, DC: Author.

National Lesbian and Gay Health Foundation. (1987). *National lesbian health care survey: Mental health implications.* Unpublished manuscript.

Pilkington, N., & D'Augelli, A. R. (in press). Victimization of lesbian, gay, and bisexual youth in community settings. *Journal of Community Psychology*.

Remafedi, G. (1987a). Adolescent homosexuality: Psychosocial and medical implications. *Pediatrics, 79*, 331–337.

Remafedi, G. (1987b). Homosexual youth: A challenge to contemporary society. *Journal of the American Medical Association, 258*, 222–225.

Remafedi, G. (1987c). Male homosexuality: The adolescent's perspective. *Pediatrics, 79*, 326–330.

Remafedi, G., Farrow, J. A., & Deisher, R. W. (1991). Risk factors for attempted suicide in gay and bisexual youth. *Pediatrics, 87*, 869–875.

Reynolds, A. L., & Koski, M. J. (1994). Lesbian, gay, and bisexual teens and the school counselor: Building alliances. *High School Journal, 77*, 88–94.

Robinson, B. E., Walters, L. H., & Skeen, P. (1989). Response of parents to learning that their child is homosexual and concern over AIDS: A national survey. *Journal of Homosexuality, 18*(1–2), 59–80.

Roesler, T., & Deisher, R. (1972). Youthful male homosexuality. *Journal of the American Medical Association, 219*, 1018–1023.

Rofes, E. E. (1989). Opening up the classroom closet: Responding to the educational needs of gay and lesbian youth. *Harvard Educational Review, 59*, 444–453.

Rofes, E. E. (1994). Making our schools safe for sissies. *High School Journal, 77*, 37–40.

Ross-Reynolds, G., & Hardy, B. S. (1985). Crisis counseling for disparate adolescent sexual dilemmas: Pregnancy and homosexuality. *School Psychology Review, 14*, 300–312.

Rotheram-Borus, M. J., & Koopman, C. (1991). Sexual risk behavior, AIDS knowledge, and beliefs about AIDS among predominantly minority gay and bisexual male adolescents. *AIDS Education and Prevention 3*, 305–312.

Rotheram-Borus, M. J., Rosario, M., & Koopman, C. (1991). Minority youth at high risk: Gay males and runaways. In M. E. Colten & S. Gore (Eds.), *Adolescent stress: Causes and consequences* (pp. 181–200). New York: Aldine deGruyter.

Savin-Williams, R. C. (1990). *Gay and lesbian youth: Expressions of identity.* Washington, DC: Hemisphere.

Savin-Williams, R. C. (1995). Lesbian, gay male, and bisexual adolescents. In A. R. D'Augelli & C. J. Patterson (Eds.), *Lesbian, gay, and bisexual identities over the lifespan* (pp. 165–189). New York: Oxford University Press.

Savin-Williams, R. C., & Cohen, K. M. (in press). Coping with verbal and physical abuse among sexual minority youths: Associations with school problems, running away, substance abuse, prostitution, and suicide. In R. C. Savin-Williams & K. M. Cohen (Eds.), *Clinical, developmental, and policy issues facing lesbians, gay males, and bisexuals.* New York: Harcourt Brace Jovanovich.

Schneider, M. S. (1988). *Often invisible: Counselling gay and lesbian youth.* Toronto: Central Toronto Youth Services.

Schneider, M. (1989). Sappho was a right-on adolescent: Growing up lesbian. *Journal of Homosexuality, 17*(1–2), 111–130.

Schneider, M. (1991). Developing services for lesbian and gay adolescents. *Canadian Journal of Community Mental Health, 10,* 133–151.

Schneider, M. S., & Tremble, B. (1986). Training service providers to work with gay or lesbian adolescents: A workshop. *Journal of Counseling and Development, 65,* 98–99.

Schneider, S. G., Farberow, N. L., & Kruks, G. N. (1989). Suicidal behavior in adolescent and young adult gay men. *Suicidal and Life-Threatening Behavior, 19,* 381–394.

Select Committee on Children, Youth, and Families, U.S. House of Representatives. (1989). *Down these mean streets: Violence by and against America's children.* Washington, DC: U.S. Government Printing Office.

Signorile, M. (1993). *Queer in America: Sex, the media, and the closets of power.* New York: Random House.

Slater, B. R. (1988). Essential issues in working with lesbian and gay male youths. *Professional Psychology: Research and Practice, 19,* 226–235.

Smith, K., & Crawford, S. (1986). Suicidal behavior among "normal" high school students. *Suicide and Life-Threatening Behavior, 16,* 313–325.

Sobocinski, M. R. (1990). Ethical principles in the counseling of gay and lesbian adolescents: Issues of autonomy, competence, and confidentiality. *Professional Psychology: Research and Practice, 21,* 240–247.

Southern Poverty Law Center. (1987). Gay-bashing prevalent among hate crimes. *Klanwatch Intelligence Report.* (Available from Southern Poverty Law Center, 200 Washington Avenue, Montgomery, AL 36104)

Strommen, E. F. (1989). Hidden branches and growing pains: Homosexuality and the family tree. *Journal of Marriage and Family Review, 14,* 9–34.

Takanishi, R. (Ed.). (1993). Special issue: Adolescence. *American Psychologist, 48,* 85–201.

Uribe, V., & Harbeck, K. M. (1991). Addressing the needs of lesbian, gay, and bisexual youth: The origins of Project 10 and school-based intervention. *Journal of Homosexuality, 22*(3–4), 9–28.

Wertheimer, D. M. (1992). Treatment and service intervention for lesbian and gay male crime victims. In G. M. Herek & K. T. Berrill (Eds.), *Hate crimes: Confronting violence against lesbians and gay men* (pp. 227–240). Newbury Park, CA: Sage.

Whitaker, C. J., & Bastian, L. D. (1991, May). *Teenage victims* (Tech. Rep. No. NLJ-128129). U.S. Department of Justice, Office of Justice Programs, Bureau of Justice Statistics National Crime Survey.

White, D. H. (1988). *Governor's Task Force on Bias-Related Violence: Final report.* Albany, NY: Governor's Office.

10

Children With Disabilities

Judith C. Levey and Vasilios K. Lagos

In this chapter we review the recent research and literature related to the vulnerability of children with disabilities to maltreatment. Although we do not by any means minimize the impact of neglect, emotional or psychological abuse, or "institutional" abuse on children with disabilities, because the focus of this commission is on *violence* on youth, we emphasize the research that pertains to physical abuse, sexual abuse, or both.

Description of the Population

The Digest of Data on Persons With Disabilities (Ficke, 1992) reports that during the 1988–1989 school year, more than 4 million children (aged 6–21) were provided with special education. Forty-eight percent of these were classified as learning disabled, 23% had speech impairments, 14% were mentally retarded, and 9% were emotionally disturbed; hard of hearing/deaf, multi-handicapped, orthopedically impaired, other health impaired, visually handicapped, and deaf/blind each accounted for 2% or less of this special education population. It should be noted that, although subsequent legislation extended coverage to all children, data on preschool children were not available at the time and were not included in the report. The actual number of children with disabilities in the United States is unknown, as estimates of prevalence may vary as a function of the definitions used by the investigatory agency. For example, the U.S. Department of Education in Public Law 101-476, the Individuals with Disabilities Education Act (IDEA),[1] defines children with disabilities as those "with mental retardation, hearing impairments including deafness, speech or language impairments, visual impairments including blindness, serious emotional disturbance, orthopedic impairments, autism, traumatic brain injury, other health impairments, or specific learning disa-

---

[1]The use of the term *handicapped* has recently been challenged by those of us who are sensitive to its negative connotation and prefer the term *children with disabilities* to define this population. This trend was reflected in the passing of Public Law 101-476, which revised Public Law 94-142, the Education for All Handicapped Children Act, and replaced the term *handicapped* with the term *disability* throughout the law. However, much of the literature, no matter how recent, still uses the earlier terminology.

bilities" and who (because of those impairments) need special education and related services. Kline and Kline (1987) emphasized that the "other health impairments" group includes children with a variety of health problems and cautioned that children with disabilities are not always "developmentally disabled." Furthermore, Tucker and Goldstein (1992) posited that only those children who are "educationally disabled" are covered by Public Law 101-476.

A developmentally disabled child, defined in Public Law 95-602 (the Developmental Disabilities and Bill of Rights Act), is one who is physically or mentally impaired, has manifestation of the disability before age 22, and is likely to be affected indefinitely. In addition, the child must meet at least three of the following seven conditions: inability to demonstrate self-care, self-direction, economic self-sufficiency, or independent living; receptive–expressive language disorders; difficulty in learning or problems with mobility; and a severe, chronic disability that reflects the person's need for services that are of lifelong or extended duration. When applied to infants, the term means "individuals from birth to age 5, inclusive, who have substantial developmental delays or specific congenital or acquired conditions with a high probability of resulting in developmental disabilities if services are not provided."

Incidence of Abuse in Children with Disabilities

Definitional Problems

Definitional issues limit the accurate assessment of the prevalence of "abuse" not only in children with disabilities, but in the general population as well. Public Law 100-294 (the Child Abuse Prevention and Treatment Act), defines child abuse and neglect as "the physical or mental injury, sexual abuse or exploitation, negligent treatment, or maltreatment of a child ... under circumstances which indicate that the child's health or welfare is harmed or threatened." Although nearly all states adhere to this definition, the terms *abuse, maltreatment, and neglect* are legally defined in each state by legislation, as is the term *child*, and they vary from state to state. To complicate the process further, interpretations of these laws with regard to type and severity, what needs to be reported, and so forth, may vary considerably among different agencies (e.g., child protective services [CPS], educational facilities, medical agencies, mental health agencies, child-care centers).

In their attempt to assess the national incidence of child maltreatment (NIS-2), the U.S. Department of Health and Human Services (U.S. DHHS) developed clear and objective operational definitions of maltreatment (U.S. DHHS, 1988). The general categories of "abuse" and "neglect" were more specifically defined as "physical abuse, sexual abuse, emotional abuse, physical neglect, educational neglect, and emotional neglect (p. 2.6). Moreover, within each of these subcategories, specific forms were defined. For example, forms of sexual abuse included intrusion and genital molestation, and emotional abuse included tying or binding, verbal or emotional assault, and so forth (pp. 4.5–4.20). Specific definitions were provided as well (pp. 3.10–3.12) for the general terms used to describe the degree of severity of maltreatment (e.g., fatal, moderate, inferred or probable, endangered). The results of the study indicated an estimated 1,424,400 countable cases of child maltreatment, only half of which were reported to CPS (Sedlak, 1990).

General Population

According to a recent release from the National Committee for Prevention of Child Abuse (1991), "over 2.5 million reports of child abuse and over 1,200 child abuse-related fatalities were documented across the country in 1990. . . . Overall 39 out of every 1,000 children were reported for maltreatment last year while at least three children a day died from maltreatment" (p. 1).

Children With Disabilities

The reauthorization of the Child Abuse Prevention and Treatment Act directed the National Center on Child Abuse and Neglect (NCCAN) to investigate the incidence of abuse of children with disabilities, as well as the incidence of handicapping conditions resulting from abuse. Information was collected from 35 CPS agencies on all cases of substantiated maltreatment over a 4–6 week period in early 1991, with follow-up information obtained during the summer of 1991 (NCCAN, in press).

The results of the study are limited by the reliance on assessments of disabilities by CPS caseworkers, who are not as qualified as health care professionals to diagnose disabilities. Despite this limitation, it was determined that the caseworkers were indeed in the best position to have information on maltreated children and their characteristics, on services provided to these children, and on case outcomes.

Generalizability may be limited because many of the CPS agencies involved served children only within family settings, thus excluding from consideration children in institutional settings. Moreover, the data do not reflect seasonal variation, if any, because data were collected for cases substantiated during late winter and early spring of 1991. Furthermore, only cases of maltreatment that were reported to CPS agencies were included in the study. However, the strengths of the study were in the use of a longitudinal design, which allowed for following up cases for up to 4 months, and prospective data collection, which yielded more complete and reliable information than would have been obtained via retrospective reliance on case records.

The major findings of the study indicate the following:

- The incidence of maltreatment (including physical, sexual, and emotional abuse, and physical, educational, and emotional neglect) of children with disabilities is 1.7 times greater than for children without disabilities.

- In 47% of the cases analyzed, the disability directly led to or contributed to the maltreatment. This figure represents 67% of children with serious emotional disturbance, 75% of children with physical health problems, and 59% of children with hyperactivity problems.
- In 37% of the cases, the maltreatment definitely contributed to or was likely to have led to disabilities. This figure represents 62% of sexually abused children, 48% of emotionally abused children, and 55% of children who experienced neglect.
- Children with disabilities, relative to children without disabilities, are 2.8 times as likely to experience emotional neglect, 2.1 times as likely to experience physical abuse, and 1.8 times as likely to experience sexual abuse.
- Children with disabilities differed from children without disabilities with respect to demographic characteristics in that they were most likely to be male, White, from one-child families, and over the age of 4; primary caretakers were less likely to have been involved in the maltreatment.

Prevalence Research

With regard to research within the academic or clinical domains, interpretation of findings is limited not only by the definitional difficulties cited earlier, but by methodological considerations (i.e., retrospective design, small or nonrepresentative samples, etc.) and by a lack of differentiation between cases of disability that may have been the result of abuse or neglect and those cases of abuse in children with disabilities. In addition, because many of the physical injuries reported in disabled children may have been the result of self-injurious behavior (i.e., head banging), falls (particularly in the orthopedically or visually impaired and in the hyperactive), and the use of physical restraint with severe behavior problems, it is even more difficult to assess the incidence of "inflicted" abuse.

Although children with disabilities appear to be overrepresented in studies that examined the incidence of maltreatment, there are studies that have reported conflicting data (Ammerman, 1991; Ammerman & Hersen, 1990; Ammerman, VanHasselt, & Hersen, 1988). Moreover, some studies have failed to show disproportionate numbers (Ammerman, 1991; Egeland & Vaughn, 1981; Starr, Dietrich, Fischhoff, Ceresnie, & Zweier, 1984).

Recently, some investigators have attempted to assess disability as a result of abuse, particularly in children receiving services provided by United Cerebral Palsy (UCP) centers. Here, again, the range of incidence is fairly wide: 37% (Souther, 1986), 47% (Diamond & Jaudes, 1983), 38% (Jaudes & Diamond, 1985), 9.4%, and 9% (Cohen & Warren, 1987.) Cohen and Warren's study in particular is noteworthy because it exemplifies the difficulty encountered when attempting to interpret the data presented. The authors collected information on more than 2,000 children served in UCP preschool programs. Their results indicate that almost 9.5% of the children had disabilities of "postnatal onset" and that 24% of these were caused by known or suspected abuse. However, if one adds to these cases those attributed to "accidents, no cause reported, or origin unknown," the resulting percentage more than doubles.

Type of Abuse

Of particular relevance to the purpose of the APA Commission on Violence and Youth, is the literature that addresses the relative incidence of particular types of abuse in children with disabilities. It is generally presumed that the incidence of sexual abuse is grossly underreported, particularly in very young children whose limited verbal skills limit their ability to describe their experiences (Dubowitz, Black, & Harrington, 1992). The difficulty of diagnosis is further compounded when the abuse is directed at a disabled child who may be nonverbal and, if cognitively challenged, may be unaware that abuse had even occurred. The situation is complicated even more when a child is partially or totally dependent on the perpetrator for his or her survival. One finding appears to be consistently reported: In an overwhelming majority of cases, disabled victims are abused by someone known and trusted—a family member, caretaker, close friend, and so forth (Seattle Rape Relief, n.d.; Sullivan, Brookhouser, Scanlan, Knutson, & Schulte, 1991). Ammerman, Van-Hasselt, Hersen, McGonigle, and Lubetsky (1989) reported that the most common form of maltreatment found in his multihandicapped population was physical abuse (69%), followed by neglect (45%), and sexual abuse (36%). Moreover, 49% of the sexually abused and 46% of the physically abused children were abused within the first 2 years of life. A close inspection of the data presented by Benedict, White, Wulff, and Hall (1990) reveals a 58% incidence of physical abuse and a 6% incidence of sexual abuse.

By contrast, in a study of 482 communicatively handicapped children and adolescents, Sullivan et al. (1991) reported percentages for types of abuse as follows: 48% sexual abuse, 23% sexual and physical abuse, and 19% physical abuse. Moreover, sexual abuse was the most frequently reported type of abuse across all handicapping condition subgroups (ranging from 32% to 55%). Furthermore, they reported several other important findings: (a) Handicapped males are at greater risk for sexual abuse than are nonhandicapped males; (b) children in residential schools are at greater risk than are those in mainstreamed settings; and (c) in 97% of the sexual abuse cases, the perpetrator was either a relative or "trusted other" such as a houseparent, older child, or peer.

The diagnosis of physical abuse in children with disabilities is no less difficult, as one must distinguish not only between "intentional" and "accidental" injury, but also injury resulting from behaviors associated with the child's syndrome i.e., self-injurious behavior). Frequently, mental health professionals, educators, physicians, law enforcement personnel, and CPS employees may be confronted with the demand to distinguish among these three types of injury.

Vulnerability

Child Factors

What is clear from a review of the relevant literature is that disabled children are particularly at risk for physical abuse and sexual assault. Although there is no direct causal relationship between handicapping condition and abuse, disability apparently can contribute to maltreatment as well as to its perpetuation. Children with disabilities are vulnerable for many reasons, including an inability to defend themselves physically, an inability to articulate or report the abuse, and an inability in many cases to differentiate between inappropriate and appropriate physical or sexual contact (see Grayson, 1992, for an excellent review). Moreover, their dependency on others for assistance or care may result in making them more trusting of their caregivers and more vulnerable to compliance and passivity, which in turn may lead to a reluctance to report instances of abuse (Zantal-Wiener, 1987). Perhaps most disheartening is the fact that disabled children may be considered less credible than their nondisabled counterparts when they report abuse (Brookhouser, Sullivan, Scanlan, & Garbarino, 1986). Finally, many children with disabilities exhibit a variety of difficult-to-manage behavioral problems (i.e., violence, disruptiveness, hyperactivity, etc.) that contribute to the stress experienced by their caretakers and place them at even greater risk (see also Zirpoli, 1986; Zirpoli, Snell, & Lloyd, 1987).

Parental Factors

Hard data have been emerging recently on the explosive problem of substance abuse and its impact on the developing fetus. It is estimated that 1 out of every 10 children born in the United States are born with positive toxicologies. These "prenatally abused" infants are at ongoing risk due to the pernicious environment of drugs and alcohol that subjects children to all kinds of maltreatment. Furthermore, these infants often exhibit characteristics that may interfere with parent–child attachment. For a parent, it is an unpleasant negative experience to care for a difficult, irritable, unrelating baby who frequently emits shrill, penetrating cries. Thus, if such an infant is given to a mother who is anxious about being a parent, experiencing guilt for using drugs while pregnant, and has limited coping and parenting skills (Bays, 1990), multiple scenarios of how vulnerable such a child would be to abuse or maltreatment can easily be created.

Despite their vulnerability, obviously not all children with disabilities are abused. The relatively few attempts to identify parental characteristics that may play a causative role in the maltreatment of children with disabilities involve studies that assessed parental factors in the abuse of nondisabled children (see, e.g., Ammerman, 1990a; Wolfe, 1985). Not surprisingly, maltreatment of children with disabilities has been found to be significantly associated with single-parent status, fewer years of education, chronic unemployment (i.e., Benedict et al., 1990; Benedict, Wulff, & White, 1992), low socioeconomic status (SES; i.e., Garbarino, 1976; Johnson, 1990), parental psychopathology (White, Benedict, Wulff, & Kelley, 1987), poor parenting skills (Fantuzzo, Wray, Hall, Goins, & Azar, 1986; Ammerman, Drudy, Hersen, & Lubetsky, 1989), and poor social interactive skills (Fantuzzo et al., 1986).

Interactional Factors

As with the "child factors" cited earlier, not all parents who fit the aforementioned profiles abuse their children, disabled or not. To assess the contribution of mother–child interactional style in the abuse of nondisabled children, Bousha and Twentyman (1984) observed mothers and children in their homes and were able to identify differential interactional patterns in abusive and nonabusive mothers. Wasserman, Allen, and Solomon (1985) observed mother–child interactions in a laboratory setting and reported differences in "ignoring" and interactional behaviors in mothers of "physically handicapped," premature, and normal toddlers. Although the sample size was small, and the physical "handicaps" of the children were more cosmetic in nature than "disabling," these researchers at least attempted to assess the influence of early mother–child interaction on the subsequent vulnerability of the disabled child for neglect and understimulation. Most recently, Ammerman, Hersen, Van Hasselt, Lubetsky, and Sieck (1994) reported that psychiatrically hospitalized children and adolescents with developmental disabilities were more likely to be maltreated if they were younger, higher functioning, and behaviorally disruptive *and* their mothers were socially isolated and quick tempered.

Theoretical Models

Most professionals have abandoned the "traditional" models used to explain the development and perpetuation of child abuse and neglect. The psychopathology model (i.e., child abuse is attributed to parental psychiatric disturbance or mental illness) and the social–cultural model (i.e., abuse and neglect are attributed to social and cultural forces) have been replaced by the social interaction models that purport that child abuse and neglect are attributed to the relationship between parent and child and the social context in which maltreatment occurs (Ammerman, 1990a; Ammerman, Lubetsky, & Drudy, 1991; Ammerman, Lubetsky, Hersen, & VanHasselt, 1988).

For example, White, Snyder, Bourne, and Newberger (1987) presented a multidimensional model of family violence. According to this model, child abuse or maltreatment can result from the interaction of a number of variables among sociocultural factors and stressors operating at the levels of society, family, parent, and child. Moreover, two factors appear to be critical in determining how vulnerable a parent is to adopting abusive behavior toward a child: (a) the parent's ability to understand and empathize with the child and (b) the parent's own history, including exposure to violence or deprivation in his or her own family of origin. If one considers the contribution of limited communicative and cognitive skills of a disabled child, as well as increased stress due to the child's greater care requirements, special needs that may involve costs in terms of time and money that are beyond their resources, and the child's difficult-to-manage behavior, it is not too difficult to understand why parents of such children are more vulnerable to abusive behavior.

Most recently, Sobsey (1994) presented the integrated ecological model of abuse, which combines elements from countercontrol and social learning theory models with ecological models. This model looks at the physical and psychological aspects of the interacting individuals (i.e., offender and victim) and the inequitable power relationship between them. Moreover, this interaction is considered within the context of environmental (i.e., interacting social units) and cultural (i.e., sources of support, attitudes, beliefs, etc.) factors. Sobsey's model not only provides a framework for understanding abuse, but serves as well as a basis for prevention strategies and efforts to decrease the vulnerability of children with disabilities.

Treatment and Prevention

Treatment and Prevention Programs

A growing number of primary, secondary, and tertiary prevention programs have been generated over the past decade (for reviews, see Baladerian, 1991; Newman & Lutzker, 1990). With regard to children with disabilities, the interactive models just described have provided the basis for both treatment and prevention programs. The Center for Abused Handicapped Children at Boys Town, the John Merck Program for Multiply Disabled Children at Western Psychiatric Institute and Clinic, the Child Assessment and Management Project (Ammerman, Drudy, et al., 1989), and Project Ecosystems (Lutzker, Campbell, Newman, & Harrold, 1989) modeled after Project 12-Ways (Lutzker & Rice, 1984), for example, offer a multidiscipline, competency-based treatment approach that attends to the needs of the child, the parents, and the family unit. Children are offered counseling and skills training in individual or group sessions (or both). Parents are trained in relaxation, coping skills, parenting and behavior management skills, and social interaction skills, and are provided with counseling. Coordination of related social services, medical and psychiatric services, and so on, is facilitated. Prevention programs, such as the Child Abuse and Disabled Children Training/Outreach Program established by the Lexington Center in New York, and the services provided by the PACER organization, have developed methods to increase public awareness and to dispense information about the special needs of children with disabilities to parents, physicians, school personnel, social workers, law enforcement officers, and child-care professionals in institutions. A variety of materials are now available to educate the disabled child about the difference between "good touch–bad touch" (SAFE and OKAY) and how to say "No! Go tell!" A variety of workshops and training programs on topics related to child abuse prevention and intervention for children with disabilities are available (for a price) to schools and agencies. All programs *claim* to be effective.

Cohen and Warren (1990) described a "major tool for prevention" available in England but desperately needed in the United States: the health visitor system. Nurses specially trained in child development and family dynamics work with families from the time of the baby's birth until the child is 5 years old. Because of this no-cost outreach service, identification of serious problems and potential risk is facilitated. The authors recommend an "American" version, at least targeted at "high-risk" families.

In fact, home visitor, or "Healthy Start," programs have been developed and implemented in 24 states (N. Baladerian, personal communication, February 24, 1993). The Community Caring Project of Denver (Kempe National Center), for example, provides supportive home visitor intervention for new families, most of whom are classified as being at moderate to low risk for abusive or neglectful behavior. The Prenatal/Early Infancy Project (PEIP) in New York provided home visits by nurses to expectant mothers in an effort to decrease low birth weight incidence, preterm delivery, and child health and developmental problems, as well as to improve the life course development of the mothers (Olds, Henderson, Chamberlin, & Tatelbaum, 1986; Olds, Henderson, Tatelbaum, & Chamberlin, 1986).

The Healthy Start program in Hawaii, a multidisciplinary program designed to prevent child abuse and neglect, and to enhance parenting skills and child development, offers services to families identified to be at risk. Services include home-based intervention, linkage to medical facilities, and referral and coordination with community agencies. The Hawaii model has been modified by Virginia's Healthy Start project, which specifically targets indigent families and introduces services prenatally (Grayson, 1992).

Program Efficacy

Where are the efficacy studies? Our scrutiny of the databases provided by the Clearinghouse on Child Abuse and Neglect Information and through our own abstract search efforts with respect to children with disabilities produced only one treatment evaluation study, which describes the efficacy of the treatment program used at the Center for Abused Handicapped Children (Sullivan & Scanlan, 1990; Sullivan, Scanlon, Brookhouser, Schulte & Knutson, 1992). Seventy-two sexually abused adolescents at a residential school for the deaf were offered treatment. Ironically, "an untreated comparison group emerged when about half of their parents refused the offer for psychotherapy" (Sullivan et al., 1992, p. 297). The therapy treatment plan included a relevant case history, specific counseling goals and objectives, and treatment methods (see Sullivan & Scanlan, 1990, for specific details regarding treatment goals and methods). The children's behavioral problems and competencies were assessed with the Child Behavior Checklist. The results indicate a "powerful treatment effect for both boys and girls" with "significantly fewer behavior problems on outcome measures" (Sullivan et al., 1992, p. 303) one year after therapy. Although this study raises concern with regard to methodological issues, including the use of an untreated comparison group, unequal sample sizes (i.e., 21 boys and 14 girls in the treatment group and 30 boys and 7 girls in the untreated group), unequal representation with respect to the severity of abuse, failure to provide differential data with respect to age, severity of disability, and so on, it represents at least an attempt to evaluate a treatment program.

With regard to prevention program evaluation, we have been similarly disappointed in our efforts to find much more than anecdotal information. For example, the SAFE and OKAY curriculum evaluation "reported" in the curriculum guide describes a pilot study of 50 first- through fifth-grade students at the Lexington School for the Deaf and 10 elementary-aged emotionally disturbed and mentally retarded students in a public school. The "results" indicate that the students were able to learn the concepts and that the objectives were successfully reached, according to the pre- and posttest "instrument" used.

The development of prevention-through-education programs for children and preschoolers with disabilities is essentially in its infancy. The difficulties presented by the need to assure that the programs be developmentally appropriate, as well as sensitive to the communication difficulties of children with various disabilities, as well as by various methodological considerations, may have inhibited program development and evaluation efforts for this population (Hazzard, 1990).

With respect to the home visitors programs, Holden, Willis, and Corcoran (1992) described the PEIP study as "the most well-designed comprehensive prevention program to date" (p. 32). The methodology included random assignment of subjects to four groups: (a) a control group that was assessed pre–post but did not receive services; (b) a minimal intervention group that received transportation assistance to medical appointments; (c) a group that received extensive nurse home visits prenatally and transportation assistance, and (d) a group that received home visits both prenatally and postnatally in addition to transportation assistance. Mothers who were visited by nurses and control group mothers were grouped according to risk for maltreatment. Analysis of results indicated that, among other positive effects, although referrals for abuse or neglect had occurred in 25% (8 out of 32 cases) of the untreated (control) high-risk group, only one referral was reported in the high-risk treated group. (See also Chapman, Siegel, & Cross, 1990, for a selective review of home visitors programs.)

According to the developers of the Hawaii Healthy Start Program, the goal of the project was the absence of abuse or neglect in 95% of the targeted children. As reported by Grayson (1992), more than 1,200 high-risk families were served between 1987 and 1989. Only 1 case of abuse and 6 cases of neglect were reported for these families.

Focus on the Future: Needs Areas

Definitional Issues

Clearly, reliable data on abused disabled children are needed. This can be achieved only through the establishment of universally used definitions of both *disability* and *abuse* and of standard service criteria and reporting mechanisms among the states and territories. The terms used by professionals (physicians, psychologists, social workers, attorneys, teachers, CPS workers, law enforcement officers, etc.) involved with abused and maltreated children are often different and confusing, (Helfer, 1990). Even when professionals use the same words to describe abused or maltreated children, they do not always mean the same thing (Paradise, 1990). Moreover, there is need to make mandatory the inclusion of "special characteristics" (i.e., disability or disabling conditions) in maltreatment reports (see Brookhouser et al., 1986).

Evidently, American society accepts the use of corporal punishment as a method of discipline. Many people in different communities use or condone the use of physical punishment. Such societal norms make it difficult at times to recognize and to report child abuse and maltreatment. This further increases the need for clear, national definitions of the different types of abuse. Johnson (1990) provided a good example in the definition of physical abuse used by the Child Abuse Program at Children's Hospital, in Columbus, Ohio:

> an injury to a child caused by a caretaker for any reason, including injury resulting from a caretaker's reaction to an unwanted behavior. Injury includes tissue damage beyond erythema or redness from a slap to any area other than the hand or buttocks. Physical discipline should not be used on children who are under 12 months of age. *The child should be normal developmentally, emotionally, and physically* [italics added]. Tissue damage includes bruises, burns, tears, punctures, fractures, ruptures of organs, and disruption of functions. The use of an instrument on any part of the body is abuse. The injury may be caused by impact, penetration, heat, a caustic, a chemical, or a drug. (p. 793)

The recognition that developmentally delayed and disabled children are more vulnerable for abuse is inferred by the caveat "should be normal developmentally, emotionally, and physically."

Research Issues

Despite the difficulties in conducting research in this area, Ammerman, Cassissi, Hersen, and VanHasselt (1986) offered many recommendations for future research: (a) the need for prospective, as opposed to retrospective, studies; (b) the need to distinguish between the categories of maltreatment (physical sexual, neglect) when forming subject samples; (c) the need to differentiate between the topographical features of abuse (e.g., severity, extent of injury, frequency, duration, time of onset, etc.); (d) the need to use appropriate control groups, matched on relevant variables such as sex, IQ, SES, and age, as well as on the aforementioned features; (e) the need to describe more fully the child characteristics and behavioral manifestations of his or her disability; (f) the need to use more sophisticated statistical techniques such as multivariate approaches to permit consideration of several variables at one time; (g) the need to use psychometrically reliable assessment measures, with operationally defined variables; and (h) the need to develop and use multidimensional assessment devices that include a semistructured interview such as the Child Abuse and Neglect Interview Schedule (CANIS; Ammerman, Drudy, et al., 1989) to identify factors associated with child maltreatment and to detect less overt forms of maltreatment.

Treatment and Prevention Program Evaluation

Clearly, there is a need for the evaluation of treatment programs for parents and families who maltreat their disabled children and for the child victims of abuse. We anxiously await the results of longitudinal studies currently in progress (R. Ammerman, personal communication, May 5, 1994; P. Sullivan, personal communication, May 9, 1994). Moreover, the specific characteristics of the child's disability need to be considered when planning a treatment program, with methods and approaches designed to meet their specific needs (Mansell, Sobsey, & Calder, 1993). The use of sign interpreters and extended sessions described by Sullivan and Scanlan (1990) provides a good example of a program that recognizes the needs of communicatively impaired children and adolescents. Tharinger, Horton, and Millea (1990) reported the need for similar sensitivity to the cognitively impaired person's life circumstances and developmental level when developing therapeutic interventions with victims of sexual abuse.

Another important area of research involves the need to test the various "models" of family violence and child abuse, particularly those that address the issues of "process" and propose specific elements or factors that may increase the likelihood of abuse of children with disabilities (Ammerman & Hersen, 1990; Sobsey, 1994).

Finally, with regard to the "family legacy," which describes the intergenerational transmission of maltreatment, it is important to note that certain types of developmental disabilities may be passed on to succeeding generations. Disabled children who have been abused or neglected may therefore have inherited a "double family legacy" (Souther, 1986) and—more important—may be in danger of passing this double legacy along to their offspring. Recent research efforts have focused on the attempt to elucidate factors that may contribute to likelihood of abuse or neglect by mothers with mental retardation (Tymchuk & Andron, 1990), as well as on the effectiveness of parent and social skills training for mothers with mental retardation referred by CPS for neglect (Fantuzzo et al., 1986). There is clearly a need for continued research in this area.

General Concerns and Ethical Considerations

The prevention of maltreatment of children with disabilities requires that all parties involved in their care be educated with regard to their vulnerability. Parents, at the time of initial diagnosis, should be counseled with regard to the familial stress and frustration often involved in raising a disabled child, how to deal with feelings of guilt or disappointment, and how to set realistic expectations. Physicians need to be familiar with the various community and mental health services available to these families and should make suitable referrals with a follow-up check on parental compliance with recommendations to obtain support services. Moreover, pediatricians should schedule "well child" visits on a frequent and regular basis, and need to be more vigilant with regard to detecting the "soft signs" of abuse, using, if necessary, special techniques or assistance (i.e., the use of sign interpreters, language interpreters, structured interviews, etc.). With regard to children in residential settings, and for hearing impaired or communicatively disabled children, Brookhouser (1986; Brookhouser et al., 1987) emphasized an even greater active role on the part of the specialist-physician, the institution's health care personnel, and the child's primary care physician.

Within the venue of private practice, there is a need to recognize the importance of a "treatment team" approach, wherein specialized treatment can be offered by combining the expertise of a clinician experienced in treating abused children, with that of one experienced in treating children with particular disabilities (Grayson, 1992; Mansell et al., 1993).

With specific regard to education of psychologists, information about people with disabilities should be included in training programs for psychology students, as well as in continuing education programs. Moreover, in addition to specialized training for treating abused children with disabilities, training should include, as stated by N. Baladerian (personal communication, February 26, 1993), "information about the culture of disability, and this cultural distinction should be as elevated as the minority and ethnic cultural trainings, in terms of importance to the fully trained psychologist."

Legal Recourse

Because child abuse cases are often processed through the courts, the challenges to the legal system presented by children are even greater when the children are disabled. The legal system must secure and maintain a fine balance between the rights of the children, the parents or caretakers, and the state, in addition to guaranteeing that the treatment and other services critical to the needs of these children are dispensed. Apparently, however, on a national level, there are no particular guidelines for the advocacy of abused children or of abused disabled children.

Who represents the child who cannot communicate his or her desire to "divorce" his or her parents? Personal telephone communication with agencies such as the Support Center for Child Advocates, Juvenile Law Center, Children's Law Center, Disabilities Law Project, Philadelphia Public Defenders Office, National Legal Resource Center for Child Advocacy and Protection of the American Bar Association, Children's Defense Fund, and Youth Law Center and Advocates for Children indicates that there is no uniform national policy providing assurance of adequate representation by a lawyer for children in protective proceedings or for the consideration of the special needs of abused children with disabilities. Clearly, there is a dire need for such policy.

Public Policy Recommendations

1. Legislation on a national level is needed to mandate uniform definitions of abuse, neglect, and maltreatment, as well as specific, uniform guidelines for reporting and evaluating instances. Definitions should be adopted by all social service systems, public and private agencies, and disciplines involved in providing services to children and to children with disabilities in particular.

2. A task force should be commissioned, on a national level, to review, evaluate, and, if appropriate, reorganize the frequently overwhelmed and understaffed CPS system. These efforts must also include a review and evaluation of legal services and law enforcement policy and services to eliminate inconsistencies and to ensure coordination of services. In addition, emphasis should be placed on proposing legislation to guarantee national guidelines for assessment criteria and reporting procedures. Furthermore, the task force should consider the need for both the family and the public systems to be involved from the beginning in the decisions, evaluation process, and subsequent interventions following a report for suspected child abuse (see Wissow & Mainor, 1992).

3. Funding is needed to assist the CPS system, as well as the legal and law enforcement systems, in procuring assistance from the professional and educational communities with respect to the special needs of children with disabilities, particularly with regard to interviewing and assessing abuse, neglect, and maltreatment, and to providing adequate and appropriate services.

4. Legislation is needed to mandate a national home visitor program to provide services prenatally or postnatally to girls and women classified as being at high risk for abuse (i.e., substance abusers, teenagers, single, low SES, cognitively challenged, victims of abuse, etc.).

5. Funding, both private and federal, is needed to support research efforts to identify all risk factors for child abuse, as well as for the investigation of the long- and short-term consequences of abuse and neglect in children with disabilities.

6. Funding is needed to support methodologically sound longitudinal studies to develop and evaluate prevention and treatment programs that are sensitive to the special considerations and needs of children with disabilities.

7. National policy is needed to liberate children from the triple threat of substance abuse, child abuse, and disability and to interrupt the multigenerational pattern of these problems.

8. Legislation is needed to ensure that all mandated child abuse courses include information about children with disabilities. Moreover, the information should include descriptions and universal definitions of institutional abuse and neglect. Finally, in families in which there is a child with a disability, parents should be encouraged to, and foster parents mandated to, receive similar training.

References

Ammerman, R. T. (1990a). Etiological models of child maltreatment: A behavioral perspective. *Behavior Modification, 14*, 230–254.

Ammerman, R. T. (1990b). Predisposing child factors. In R. T. Ammerman & M. Hersen (Eds.), *Children at risk: An evaluation of factors contributing to child abuse and neglect* (pp. 199–221). New York: Plenum.

Ammerman, R. T. (1991). The role of the child in physical abuse: A reappraisal. *Violence and Victims, 6*(2), 87–101.

Ammerman, R. T., Cassisi, J. E., Hersen, M., & VanHasselt, V. B. (1986). Consequences of physical abuse and neglect in children. *Clinical Psychology Review, 6*, 291–310.

Ammerman, R. T., Drudy, K., Hersen, M., & Lubetsky, M.J. (1989, November). *Competency based treatment of neglect in a mother with a developmentally disabled child.* Paper presented at the 23rd Annual Convention of the Association for Advancement of Behavior Therapy, Washington, DC.

Ammerman, R. T., & Hersen, M. (1990). Research in child abuse and neglect: Current status and an agenda for the future. In R. T. Ammerman & M. Hersen (Eds.), *Children at risk: An evaluation of factors contributing to child abuse and neglect* (pp. 3–19). New York: Plenum.

Ammerman, R. T., Hersen, M., VanHasselt, V. B., Lubetsky, M. J., & Sieck, W. S. (1994). Maltreatment in psychiatrically hospitalized children and adolescents with developmental disabilities: Prevalence and correlates. *Journal of the American Academy of Child and Adolescent Psychiatry, 33*, 567–576.

Ammerman, R. T., Lubetsky, M. J., & Drudy, K. F. (1991). Maltreatment of handicapped children. In R. T. Ammerman & M. Hersen (Eds.), *Case studies in family violence* (pp. 209–230). New York: Plenum.

Ammerman, R. T., Lubetsky, M. J., Hersen, M., & VanHasselt, V. B. (1988). Maltreatment of children and adolescents with multiple handicaps: Five case examples. *Journal of the Multihandicapped Person, 1*, 129–139.

Ammerman, R. T., VanHasselt, V. B., & Hersen, M. (1988). Maltreatment of handicapped children: A critical review. *Journal of Family Violence, 3*, 53–71.

Ammerman, R. T., VanHasselt, V. B., Hersen, M., McGonigle, J. J., & Lubetsky, M. J. (1989). Abuse and neglect in psychiatrically hospitalized multihandicapped children. *Child Abuse and Neglect, 13*, 335–343.

Baladerian, N. J. (1991). Sexual abuse of people with developmental disabilities. *Sexuality and Disability, 9*, 323–335.

Bays, J. (1990). Substance abuse and child abuse: Impact of addiction on the child. *Pediatric Clinics of North America, 37*, 881–904.

Benedict, M. I., White, R. B., Wulff, L. M., & Hall, B. J. (1990). Reported maltreatment in children with multiple disabilities. *Child Abuse and Neglect, 14*, 207–217.

Benedict, M. I., Wulff, L. M., & White, R. B. (1992). Current parental stress in maltreating and nonmaltreating families of children with multiple disabilities. *Child Abuse and Neglect, 16*, 155–163.

Bousha, D. M., & Twentyman, C. T. (1984). Mother-child interactional style in abuse, neglect, and control groups: Naturalistic observations in the home. *Journal of Abnormal Psychology, 93*, 106–114.

Brookhouser, P. E. (1987). Ensuring the safety of deaf children in residential schools. *Otolaryngology—Head and Neck Surgery, 97*, 361–368.

Brookhouser, P. E., Sullivan, P., Scanlan, J. M., & Garbarino, J. (1986). Identifying the sexually abused deaf child: The otolaryngologist's role. *Laryngoscope, 96*, 152–158.

Chapman, J., Siegel, E., & Cross, A. (1990). Home visitors and child health: Analysis of selected programs. *Pediatrics, 85*, 1059–1068.

Cohen, S., & Warren, R. D. (1987). Preliminary survey of family abuse of children served by United Cerebral Palsy centers. *Developmental Medicine and Child Neurology, 29*, 12–18.

Cohen, S., & Warren, R. D. (1990). The intersection of disability and child abuse in England and the United States. *Child Welfare, 69*, 253–262.

Diamond, L. J., & Jaudes, P. K. (1983). Child abuse in a cerebral-palsied population. *Developmental Medicine and Child Neurology, 25*, 169–174.

Dubowitz, H., Black, M., & Harrington, D. (1992). The diagnosis of child sexual abuse. *American Journal of Diseases of Children, 146,* 688–693.

Egeland, B., & Vaughn, B. (1981). Failure of "bond formation" as a cause of abuse, neglect and maltreatment. *American Journal of Orthopsychiatry, 51,* 78–84.

Fantuzzo, J. W., Wray, L., Hall, R., Goins, C., & Azar, S. (1986). Parent and social-skills training for mentally retarded mothers identified as child maltreaters. *American Journal of Mental Deficiency, 91,* 135–140.

Ficke, R. C. (1992). *Digest of data on persons with disabilities.* Washington, DC: National Institute on Disability and Rehabilitation Research.

Garbarino, J. (1976). A preliminary study of some ecological correlates of child abuse: The impact of socioeconomic stress on mothers. *Child Development, 47,* 178–185.

Grayson, J. (1992). Child abuse and developmental disabilities. *Virginia Child Protection Newsletter, 37,* 1–16.

Hazzard, A. P. (1990). Prevention of child sexual abuse. In R. T. Ammerman & M. Hersen (Eds.), *Treatment of family violence* (pp. 354–384). New York: Wiley.

Helfer, R. E. (1990). The neglect of our children. *Pediatric Clinics of North America, 37,* 923–942.

Holden, E. W., Willis, D. J., & Corcoran, M. M. (1992). Preventing child maltreatment during the prenatal/perinatal period. In D. J. Willis, E. W. Holden, & M. Rosenberg (Eds.), *Prevention of child maltreatment* (pp. 17–46). New York: Wiley.

Jaudes, P. K., & Diamond, L. J. (1985). The handicapped child and child abuse. *Child Abuse and Neglect, 9,* 341–347.

Johnson, C. F. (1990). Inflicted injury versus accidental injury. *Pediatric Clinics of North America, 37,* 791–814.

Kline, D. F., & Kline, A. C. (1987). *The disabled child and child abuse* (2nd ed.). Chicago, IL: National Committee for Prevention of Child Abuse.

Lutzker, J. R., Campbell, R., Newman, M. R., & Harrold, M. (1989). Ecobehavioral intervention for abusive, neglectful, and high-risk families: Project 12-Ways and Project Ecosystems. In G. H. S. Singer & L. K. Irvin (Eds.), *Family support services: Emerging partnerships between families with severely handicapped individuals and communities* (pp. 313–326). Baltimore: Paul H. Brookes.

Lutzker, J. R., & Rice, J. M. (1984). Project 12-Ways: Measuring outcome of a large in-home service for treatment and prevention of child abuse and neglect. *Child Abuse and Neglect, 8,* 519–524.

Mansell, S., Sobsey, D., & Calder, P. (1993). Sexual abuse treatment for persons with developmental disabilities. *Professional Psychology: Research and Practice, 22,* 404–409.

Newman, M. R., & Lutzker, J. R. (1990). Prevention programs. In R. T. Ammerman & M. Hersen (Eds.), *Children at risk: An evaluation of factors contributing to child abuse and neglect* (pp. 225–248). New York: Plenum.

National Center on Child Abuse and Neglect. (in press). *A report on the maltreatment of children with disabilities.* Washington, DC: U.S. Department of Health and Human Services.

National Committee for Prevention of Child Abuse. (1991, April 16). *Child abuse reports climb; fatalities level off.* Press release.

Olds, D. L., Henderson, C. R., Chamberlain, R., & Tatelbaum, R. (1986). Preventing child abuse and neglect: A randomized trial of nurse home visitation. *Pediatrics, 78,* 65–78.

Olds, D. L., Henderson, C. R., Tatelbaum, R., & Chamberlin, R. (1986). Improving the delivery of prenatal care and outcomes of pregnancy: A randomized trial of nurse home visitation. *Pediatrics, 77,* 16–28.

Paradise, J. A. (1990). The medical evaluation of the sexually abused child. *Pediatric Clinics of North America, 37,* 839–904.

Seattle Rape Relief. (n.d.). *Sexual exploitation: What parents of handicapped persons should know.* Seattle, WA: Seattle Rape Relief Developmental Disabilities Project.

Sedlak, A. J. (1990). *Technical amendment to the study findings—National incidence and prevalence of child abuse and neglect: 1988.* Washington, DC: U.S. Department of Health and Human Services.

Sobsey, D. (1994). *Violence and abuse in the lives of people with disabilities.* Baltimore: Paul H. Brookes.

Souther, M. D. (1986). Developmentally disabled, abused and neglected children: A high risk/ high need population. In *Perspectives on child maltreatment in the mid-80's* (DHHS Publication No. OHDS 84-30338). Washington, DC: Department of Health and Human Services.

Starr, R. H., Dietrich, K. N., Fischhoff, J., Ceresnie, S., & Zweier, D. (1984). The contribution of handicapping conditions to child abuse. *Topics in Early Childhood and Special Education, 4,* 55–69.

Sullivan, P. M., Brookhouser, P. E., Scanlan, J. M., Knutson, J. F., & Schulte, L. E. (1991). Patterns of physical and sexual abuse of communicatively handicapped children. *Annals of Otology, Rhinology and Laryngology, 100,* 188–194.

Sullivan, P. M., & Scanlan, J. M. (1990). Psychotherapy with handicapped sexually abused children. *Developmental Disabilities Bulletin, 18,* 21–34.

Sullivan, P. M., Scanlan, J. M., Brookhouser, P. E., Schulte, L. E., & Knutson, J. F. (1992). The effects of psychotherapy on behavior problems of sexually abused deaf children. *Child Abuse and Neglect, 16,* 297–307.

Tharinger, D., Horton, C. B., & Millea, S. (1990). Sexual abuse and exploitation of children and adults with mental retardation and other handicaps. *Child Abuse and Neglect, 14,* 301–312.

Tucker, B. P., & Goldstein, B. A. (1992). *Legal rights of persons with disabilities: An analysis of federal law.* Horsham, PA: LRP Publications.

Tymchuk, A. J., & Andron, L. (1990). Mothers with mental retardation who do or do not abuse or neglect their children. *Child Abuse and Neglect, 14,* 313–323.

U.S. Department of Health and Human Services. (1988). *Study findings. Study of national incidence and prevalence of child abuse and neglect: 1988.* Washington, DC: Author.

Wasserman, G. A., Allen, R., & Solomon, C. R. (1985). At-risk toddlers and their mothers: The special case of physical handicap. *Child Development, 56,* 73–83.

Wissow, L. S., & Mainor, P. (1992). Advocating for the abused child: Can ethics and the law be in conflict? *Pediatric Annals, 21,* 303–310.

White, R., Benedict, J. I., Wulff, L., & Kelley, M. (1987). Physical disabilities as risk factors for child maltreatment: A selected review. *American Journal of Orthopsychiatry, 57,* 93–101.

White, K. M., Snyder, J., Bourne, R., & Newberger, E. H. (1987). *Treating family violence in a pediatric hospital: A program of training, research, and services.* (DHHS Publication No. ADM 87-1504). Washington, DC: U.S. Department of Health and Human Services.

Wolfe, D. A. (1985). Child abusive parents: An empirical review and analysis. *Psychological Bulletin, 97,* 462–482.

Zantal-Wiener, K. (1987). *Child abuse and the handicapped child.* (ERIC Digest No. 446). Reston, VA: Clearinghouse on Handicapped and Gifted Children.

Zirpoli, T. J. (1986). Child abuse and children with handicaps. *Remedial and Special Education, 7,* 39–48.

Zirpoli, T. J., Snell, M. E., & Lloyd, B. H. (1987). Characteristics of persons with mental retardation who have been abused by caregivers. *Journal of Special Education, 21*(2), 31–41.

Part IV

Societal Influences on Youth Violence

Introduction

Membership in gangs, the ready availability of guns, the formation of mobs, and glamorized violence in the media are among the primary societal factors contributing to the likelihood that a given individual will commit an act of violence at a given time. In this section, these four phenomena are examined as they affect youth violence and as they provide opportunities for prevention and intervention.

In chapter 11 on "The Mass Media and Youth Aggression, Edward Donnerstein, Ronald Slaby, and Leonard Eron stress the one overriding finding in research on the mass media and aggression over the past 20 years: The mass media are significant contributors to aggressive behavior and aggression-related attitudes among youth. Viewing violence in the media can lead to increased violence toward others, increased fearfulness about becoming a victim of violence, increased callousness toward violence among others, and increased self-initiated behavior that exposes one to further risk of violence.

The authors describe a pernicious cycle in which children's viewing of violence leads to identification with aggressors and the cognitive encoding of aggressive solutions to various problems, making aggression more likely in a given context, such as school. Habitual aggressive behaviors lead to academic and social failures, and these failures in turn lead to more regular television viewing. Strategies to help interrupt this cycle include encouraging parents to monitor their children's viewing habits, applying pressure toward modifying the film-rating system currently in place, and teaching children critical viewing skills.

In the context of the raging debate regarding the role of gun control in combatting violence, Leonard Berkowitz, in chapter 12 on guns and youth, examines research to answer crucial questions, such as, Is firearm availability primarily responsible for the high homicide rate in the United States? Do only a relatively few youths make use of the available firearms? Do guns bring safety? Does the presence of a firearm lead to stronger aggressive actions than otherwise would have occurred? Does children's exposure to and play with guns, even toy ones, facilitate the development of an enduring disposition to aggression? Refuting some of the arguments against gun control and concluding that a relatively small number of youth account for a disproportionate share of violent crimes, Berkowitz stresses solutions that offer the possibility of reducing the availability of guns to these high-risk youth and research that better delineates their characteristics and the processes involved in their acts of aggression.

Mob violence, which frequently involves youth, is the topic of chapter 13, by Ervin Staub and Lori Rosenthal. The authors outline instigating events, such as assassinations, killings, arrests, police brutality, and withdrawal of privileges, which they note are often exacerbated by rumors and associated distortions. Background characteristics that make mob violence more likely include social change and disorganization; a cluster of poverty, deprivation, and injustice; cultural and subcultural characteristics; features of cities; and, paradoxically, hope. Once instigating conditions and background characteristics are present, social and psychological processes, such as contagion and modeling, deindividuation, group polarization, and loss of self, make violence more likely to escalate. The authors consider developmental needs of youth in terms of both their involvement in mob violence and the effects of such violence on both participating and nonparticipating youth.

In chapter 14 on juvenile gangs, Arnold Goldstein and Fernando Soriano provide history, definitions, and demographics related to gang membership and summarize theory and programming related to gang intervention from several disciplines. They note a change in public response over the years, from a willingness to provide more work, school, and family opportunities for such youth in the 1960s to the surveillance, deterrence, and incarceration strategies in the 1980s, to the multimodal, multilevel, multidisciplinary models of comprehensive programming that hold the most promise in the 1990s.

The authors explore the role of drugs, turf disputes, codes of honor, and the ready availability of guns in the increase in homicide and aggravated assaults among gang members. They also identify opportunities for clinical, developmental, social, and community psychology to contribute to the sparse contemporary research by psychologists on gangs.

Finally, they provide a model of culturally sensitive programming that not only applies to juvenile gangs but to other groups as well. This model focuses on awareness, knowledge, and skill as needed for working with those of a different ethnic origin, and stresses the need for meaningful, ongoing contact with ethnic minority gang members in developing and implementing interventions.

11

The Mass Media
and Youth Aggression

Edward Donnerstein, Ronald G. Slaby,
and Leonard D. Eron

So far in this book there have been many recurrent themes related to youth violence. Developmental issues and ethnic and cultural factors have been described, and concerns about gangs and weapons are addressed in chapters that follow. Cutting across many of these factors is the involvement of the mass media, particularly television, in the development, maintenance, and facilitation of aggression and violence among children and adolescents. The mere presence of violence in the media, the lack of nonviolent role models, the constant imaging of a society in which "the good life" can and must be attained, and the media portrayal of aggression as a means to solve conflict were influences described by many youth who testified before the APA Task Force on Violence and Youth.

In many ways, as psychologists, we should not be surprised at the relation suggested by these youth between exposure to the mass media and subsequent aggressive behavior. Over the last few decades the academic community, particularly psychology, has produced exhaustive reviews of the best available evidence on the relation between exposure to violence in the media and aggressive behavior. The reports commissioned, for example, by the Surgeon General (1972), the National Institute of Mental Health (1982), and the American Psychological Association (Huston et al., 1992) have all been consistent in their conclusions. And, for the last 20 years there has been one overriding finding: The mass media are significant contributors to the aggressive behavior and aggression related attitudes of many children, adolescents, and adults. There is also a great deal of consensus (save a few psychologists), as to the direction, magnitude, and reasons for an association between the mass media and violence.

Our intent in this chapter is not to "reinvent the wheel," but to suggest ways to mitigate the influences of the mass media by examining and suggesting effective intervention strategies and policy recommendations. However, effective interventions and policy must be guided by an empirical and theoretical understanding of the relation between media violence and aggression. Consequently, we begin this chapter with a review of the existing knowledge in the form of research findings, summarize conclusions from previous reports, and describe the theoretical processes that we believe can account for the conclusions that we reach. After this overview, we explore the gaps in knowledge, consider the potential interventions to reduce the media's influence, and make some policy recommendations regarding the media's role in preventing and reducing violence among youth.

Viewing Habits and Televised Violence

It would be safe to say that American society is preoccupied with television. Recent surveys indicate that about 98% of American households have television and that many of these homes have multiple sets (Huston et al., 1992). Within these homes the television is on about 28 hours per week for children 2 to 11 years of age and 23 hours per week for teens. These are fairly stable patterns that have been found over many years of research. It is now known that television viewing occupies more time than any other nonschool activity and accounts for more than half of leisure activity time, particularly among children. Furthermore, there is more viewing among African American and U.S. Latino children, independent of socioeconomic status (Tangney & Feshbach, 1988), and many of the poorest and potentially most vulnerable groups in society are the heaviest viewers of television, because of the lack of alternative activities (Kuby & Csikszentmihalyi, 1990).

If one asks the question, "How much violence is on television?" one finds that the level of violence on television has remained relatively constant over the last 2 decades. Research shows that there are about 5 to 6 violent acts per hour on prime time and 20 to 25 acts on Saturday morning children's programs (Gerbner & Signorielli, 1990). Within the United States, this accounts for about 188 hours of violent programs per week, or around 15% of program time (Huesmann, 1992). In addition to broadcast television, cable TV adds to the level of violence through new, more violent, programs, and by recycling older violent broadcasts. A recent survey by the Center for Media and Public Affairs (Lichter & Amundson, 1992) identified 1,846 violent scenes broadcast and cablecast between 6 a.m. and midnight on one day in Washington, DC. The most violent periods were between 6 and 9 a.m. with 497 violent scenes and between 2 and 5 p.m. with 609 violent scenes. Most of this violence is presented without context or judgment as to its acceptability, and most of the violence in the morning and early afternoon is viewed by children.

If one considers these data for a moment one might note that if children watch an average of 2 to 4 hours a day of television, then by the time a child leaves elementary school he or she would have seen 8,000 murders and more than 100,000 other acts of violence. As the child nears the end of his or her teenage years he or she has been witness to over 200,000 violent acts within the media (Huston et al., 1992). This figure would actually increase with more exposure to cable premium channels or VCR viewing of R-rated films. Popular films like *Die Hard 2* (264 violent deaths), *Robocop* (81), and *Total Recall* (74) have far more violence than commercial prime time TV, where the above figures are estimated. This is important to note given the changes in technology and program access for children over the last decade. We address this issue shortly.

Minorities in the Media

Although the greatest concerns are with violence in the media, it is also important to be aware of the issue of minority representations on television. Many of the minority youth with whom we spoke expressed a great deal of concern about the representation of various minorities within the media. They talked of lack of models with whom to identify, the message that minorities are violent, and an overall concern for how minorities are portrayed. Research on minority representations supports these concerns. TV images of minority groups are either nonexistent or presented within a negative context. When minority groups such as U.S. Latinos, Asian/Pacific Island Americans, and Native Americans appear, they are usually stereotyped as criminals, dangerous, or victims of violence (Gerbner, Gross, Signorielli, & Morgan, 1986). Although African American representation has shown a change over the last 25 years, the increased representation has not been linear and does not approach their actual representation in society (e.g., Berry, 1988; Greenberg, 1986). Furthermore, when African Americans do appear on television, there is a tendency for them to be segregated from Whites (Liebert & Sprafkin, 1988).

It has been suggested that the effects of this type of minority representation are twofold. First, nonrepresentation and negative portrayals maintain negative stereotyping, facilitating prejudice and racism as well as encouraging the expression of violence against minorities. Second, it leads to negative effects on the self-esteem of the minority group member (Fairchild, 1988). These are indeed important concerns, and we address this issue later in the chapter when we discuss policy.

Issues of New Technologies

Television is much different today than it was a decade or so ago. Today the average viewer has access to numerous program channels including very specialized "pay cable" (e.g., Home Box Office) stations. In addition, the introduction of video cassette recorders (VCRs) has also changed the types of media that are now available in private homes. It is obvious that children and adults are exposed to different types of programs on cable than those available on commercial television. Some of this content would be considered positive (i.e., educational and cultural programs), whereas other programs might be considered to have a negative impact (i.e., more graphic violence). VCR access also presents problems in that material is now available to which children would not otherwise be exposed via commercial television, cinema, and perhaps even cable. Consequently, when such issues as violence on TV are considered, it seems appropriate to take into account the types of media that individuals may be viewing besides normal commercial television.

To date there has not been much research that has directly focused on the effects on behavior of exposure to cable or VCR programs. Most of the available research has concerned itself with the penetration of these new media and their content. This information, however, should provide the psychological community with fertile ground for new research initiatives. For example, in 1970 around 7% of homes had cable TV. It is estimated that today this figure is over 60%, and it is expected to be on a continual climb over the next decade. VCRs, which were almost unheard of in 1970, now have a 42% penetration, with an expectation of double that in the years to come. Of more interest are findings (Greenberg, 1988) indicating increased VCR viewing by children, not only in the United States but in many other countries. Furthermore, VCR use is greater among children and teens than among adults (Sims, 1989).

Recent studies have indicated that children with VCR or cable access have seen more R-rated films than their non-cable, non-VCR counterparts (see Houston et al., 1992). The fact that many of these films would not be shown on commercial TV, or if they were, much of the violence and sex would be cut, suggests that children are being exposed to much different materials today than they were in the past. Graphic violence, sexual content, and mature themes are more readily available for children today. For example, MTV, one of the more popular types of cable program formats, has at least one occurrence of violence in over 50% of its videos. This rate of violence far exceeds that of commercial television. There is no evidence of more restrictive viewing with premium cable or VCR use, in fact there seem to be more liberal rules, particularly regarding PG-13 and R-rated films (Atkin, Heeter, & Baldwin, 1989; Greenberg & Heeter, 1987; Lin & Atkin, 1989). This suggests that the VCR, and to a lesser degree cable, has greatly increased access to content of all types by young viewers (Huston et al., 1992).

Although we are not certain at this time about the specific impact of this new type of viewing on children, it certainly merits future research consideration. Given the findings and theoretical models that we discuss next regarding the relation between media violence and aggression, even more pronounced effects might be anticipated given the nature of cable and VCR content.

A Summary of the Research Evidence

As we noted earlier, psychologists have been involved in numerous investigations into the relation between exposure to mass media violence and aggressive behavior. These investigations have been summarized in major governmental and organizational reports over the last 2 decades. The conclusions of these reports, which are based on exhaustive reviews of the literature (in addition to the initiation of new research), are the prime basis for our own conclusions about the media violence and aggression association. The research on which these reports are based now spans 3 decades, and the researchers have been consistent in their acknowledgement of how televised violence is related to the aggressive behavior of many children, adolescents, and adults. The three major reports from which we draw our conclusions are the 1972 Surgeon General's report on television and social behavior (Surgeon General's

Scientific Advisory Committee on Television and Social Behavior, 1972), the 1982 National Institute of Mental Health (NIMH) report on television and behavior (NIMH, 1982), and the 1992 American Psychological Association Task Force on Television and Society (Huston et al., 1992). It is important to note that these do not reflect the totality of major investigations into the media violence issue, and within this discussion we note the conclusions from other investigative bodies. However, the three major reports involved significant inputs from the psychological community and, therefore, reflect most closely our own evaluation. The conclusions from these investigations are briefly summarized here.

The 1972 Surgeon General's Report

The Surgeon General's report was based not only on a review of existing literature, but on research specifically commissioned for the committee. This research was quite clear in demonstrating that children are exposed to a substantial amount of violence on TV and that they have the capacity to remember and learn from this type of material. These findings naturally make the content of TV programming and how violence is portrayed subjects for concern. There was every indication from the studies reviewed that the consequences of violence were rarely shown, characters children could identify with were just as violent as other characters, and programming directed at children (cartoons) was especially violent. These content observations were especially troublesome given the findings from an examination of the current state of the research. These findings, based on an examination of both correlational and experimental studies were rather conclusive. First, there was strong evidence to indicate that across a number of measures of aggressive behavior there was a significant and consistent correlation between television viewing and aggressive behavior. Second, the report was able to conclude, based on experimental evidence as well as longitudinal field studies, that there was a direct, causal link between exposure to televised violence and subsequent aggressive behavior on the part of the viewer. Although many scientists concluded that the evidence established a causal relationship between televison violence viewing and real-life aggressive behavior, the report's summary was extensively qualified and weakened to appease television industry interests (e.g., Liebert & Sprafkin, 1988). The report's summary put forth the following conclusion:

> At least under some circumstances, exposure to televised aggression can lead children to accept what they have seen as a partial guide for their own actions. As a result, the present entertainment offerings of the television medium may be contributing, in some measure, to the aggressive behavior of many normal children. Such an effect has now been shown in wide variety of situations. (Surgeon General's Scientific Advisory Committee on Television and Social Behavior, p. 5)

National Institute of Mental Health 10-Year Update

Ten years after the release of the Surgeon General's report, the National Institute of Mental Health, at the request of the Surgeon General, issued a report that summarized the state of knowledge on television's effects since the time of the 1972 report. This review and update was entitled *Television and Behavior: Ten Years of Scientific Progress and Implications for the Eighties* (NIMH, 1982). The report concentrated on many areas in which television could influence the behavior of individuals, with only about 10%–15% of its content dealing with televised violence. Its conclusions on violence, however, were quite strong.

> After 10 more years of research, the consensus among most of the research community is that violence on television does lead to aggressive behavior by children and teenagers who watch the programs. This conclusion is based on laboratory experiments and on field studies. Not all children become aggressive, of course, but the correlations between violence and aggression are positive. In magnitude, television violence is as strongly correlated with aggressive behavior as any other behavioral variable that has been measured. The research question has moved from asking whether or not there is an effect to seeking explanations for the effect. (NIMH, 1982, p. 6)

This conclusion, adding significantly to those of the Surgeon General's report, was based on a number of important new findings over the 10-year period. First, the age range of the effects could now be extended to include preschoolers and older adolescents, and were not considered to be gender specific. Research was now demonstrating that both boys and girls were affected by exposure to televised violence. Second, and somewhat disturbing given the findings of a decade before, the amount of violence on television had not decreased since the Surgeon General's report. Finally, and perhaps more importantly, viewers learn more from violence on TV than aggressive behavior. They learn to be victims and to identify with victims. Heavy viewing may lead to aggression, but for some individuals it will lead to fear and apprehension about being aggressed against. It is more than aggressive behavior, the report concluded, that should concern us.

American Psychological Association Task Force on Television and Society

Both the 1972 Surgeon General's report and the 10-year follow up from NIMH concluded that television occupied a significant role in the lives of both children and adults. Both of these reports were unanimous in their position that televised violence can influence aggressive behavior. In 1985, the American Psychological Association (APA) released a position paper that endorsed the findings that televised violence had a causal effect on aggressive behavior. The APA thus joined other professional groups (American Medical Association,

American Academy of Pediatrics, American Academy of Child Psychiatry) in taking the position that violence in the mass media needed to be reduced. In their statement, the APA approved the following resolution:

> WHEREAS, the great majority of research studies have found a relationship between televised violence and behaving aggressively, and WHEREAS, the conclusions drawn on the basis of 25 years of research and a sizeable number of experimental and field investigations is that viewing televised violence may lead to increases in aggressive attitudes, values, and behavior, particularly in children, and
> WHEREAS, many children's programs contain some form of violence,
> BE IT RESOLVED that the American Psychological Association (1) encourages parents to monitor and to control television viewing by children; (2) requests industry representatives to take responsible attitudes in reducing direct imitatable violence in "real life" fictional children's programming or violent incidents on cartoons and in providing more programming for children designed to mitigate possible effects of television violence, consistent with the guarantees of the First Amendment; and (3) urges industry, governmental and private foundations to support relevant research activities aimed at the amelioration of the effects of high levels of televised violence on children's attitudes and behavior. (Abeles, 1985, pp. 648–649)

Following this resolution, in 1986, the APA established a Task Force to review the existing literature on the positive and negative influences of television, particularly on targeted populations such as children, the elderly, women, and minorities. In addition to this charge, the Task Force was instructed to make recommendations about how to mitigate the negative influences and to find ways of working more closely with the media industry in promoting improved mental health aspects of television. The task force made it clear that its concerns were with a large domain of human behavior and that it wanted to move beyond violence and aggression. Nevertheless, its conclusions, which were released in 1992 (Huston et. al., 1992) and were based on an exhaustive review of the literature, were straightforward. Just like the NIMH report of 10 years earlier, the Task Force discussion of media violence occupied only a small portion of the overall review of mass media influences. And like the NIMH conclusions, the American Psychological Association report was firm and conclusive in its beliefs about the relation between televised violence and aggressive behavior.

It was acknowledged that high levels of television viewing are correlated with aggressive behavior and the acceptance of aggressive attitudes. Furthermore, these correlations are fairly stable over time, place, and demographics. An examination of hundreds of experimental and longitudinal studies supported the position that viewing violence in the mass media is causally related to aggressive behavior. More importantly, naturalistic field studies and cross-national studies supported the position that the viewing of televised aggression leads to increases in subsequent aggression and that such behavior can become part of a lasting behavioral pattern (e.g., Huesmann & Eron, 1986). For example, Huesmann and his colleagues (Huesmann, 1986; Huesmann,

Eron, Lefkowitz, & Walder, 1984) found a clear and significant relation between early exposure to televised violence at age 8 and adult aggressive behavior (seriousness of criminal acts) 22 years later. As Huesmann noted,

> Aggressive habits seem to be learned early in life, and once established, are resistant to change and predictive of serious adult antisocial behavior. If a child's observation of media violence promotes the learning of aggressive habits, it can have harmful lifelong consequences. Consistent with this theory, early television habits are in fact correlated with adult criminality. (Huesmann, 1986, pp. 129–130)

In addition then to supporting the NIMH conclusions reached 10 years earlier on the relation between TV violence and aggression, the APA report added the following: "The behavior patterns established in childhood and early adolescence are the foundation for lifelong patterns manifested in adulthood (Huston et al., 1992, p. 57)."

Recent Additional Support

Paralleling the APA report, a number of other recent major reviews have substantially confirmed the media violence and aggression link. After a major conference of media researchers and industry representatives, *Television and Teens: Health Implications*, convened in Los Angeles in 1988, a study group report concluded that media portrayals of violence are of major concern as they are related to adolescent health (Hoberman, 1990). First, media violence can teach adolescents social scripts about violence. Second, it can create and maintain attitudes in society that condone violence. Third, constant exposure can lead to emotional desensitization toward violence. Finally, the social, political, and economic roots of violence are rarely explored, leaving one with the impression that violence is mainly an interpersonal issue. The study group also raised concerns about the portrayal of sexual violence in the media and its relation to sexual aggression, a topic that we will consider later.

In a recent report released by the Centers for Disease Control (CDC, 1991), the concerns about exposure to mass media violence as a factor in the development of aggression in children were once again reinforced. As part of its recommendation to reduce violence, the CDC called on parents to avoid exposing their children to mass media depictions that "aggrandize" violence and to search out alternative programs that educate families in the use of nonviolent alternatives.

All of these reports lend substantial support to the premise that exposure to media violence can influence the perceptions, attitudes, and behaviors of many young children and adolescents. An accurate assessment of this research evidence was best presented by Eron in his recent testimony before the United States Senate Committee on Governmental Affairs (Eron, 1992):

> There can no longer be any doubt that heavy exposure to televised violence is one of the causes of aggressive behavior, crime and violence in society. The evidence comes from both the laboratory and real-life studies. Televi-

sion violence affects youngsters of all ages, of both genders, at all socio-economic levels and all levels of intelligence. The effect is not limited to children who are already disposed to being aggressive and is not restricted to this country. The fact that we get this same finding of a relation between television violence and aggression in children in study after study, in one country after another, cannot be ignored. The causal effect of television violence on aggression, even though it is not very large, exists. It cannot be denied or explained away. We have demonstrated this causal effect outside the laboratory in real-life among many different children. We have come to believe that a vicious cycle exists in which television violence makes children more aggressive and these aggressive children turn to watching more violence to justify their own behavior. (Eron, 1992, p. S8539)

We are well aware, however, that not all forms of televised violence are equally effective in encouraging aggressive behavior. In a major recent review of this literature, Comstock (Comstock & Paik, 1994; Comstock & Strausburger, 1990) considered what types of conditions tend to produce aggressive behavior following exposure.

For Comstock, there are four dimensions that, if heightened, can be seen to contribute to aggressive behavior following exposure to violent media. The first is *efficacy*, which considers whether the aggressive behavior seen on the screen is rewarded or punished. The second is *normativeness*, which examines whether the violence is justified or lacks any consequences. Third is *pertinence* which looks at similarity to the viewer or the viewer's social context. Finally, there is *susceptibility* of the viewer. Does he or she become aroused or frustrated, or is he or she predisposed to aggression? From these dimensions, Comstock has offered the following 15 types of situations whose effects on violent behavior are most supported in the experimental literature (Comstock & Paik, 1994).

1. Those who act aggressively are rewarded or fail to be punished (e.g., Bandura, 1974).
2. The aggressive behavior is seen as justified (e.g., Berkowitz & Rawlings, 1963).
3. There are cues in the portrayed violence that are similar to those in real life (e.g., Berkowitz & Geen, 1967; Donnerstein & Berkowitz, 1981).
4. There is a similarity between the aggressor and the viewer (e.g., Rosekrans, 1967).
5. There is strong identification with the aggressor, such as imagining being in their place (e.g., Turner & Berkowitz, 1972).
6. There is behavior that is motivated to inflict harm or injury (e.g., Geen & Stonner, 1972).
7. There is violence in which the consequences are lowered, such as no pain, sorrow, or remorse (e.g., Berkowitz & Rawlings, 1963).
8. Violence is portrayed more realistically or seen as a real event (e.g., Atkin, 1983; Feshbach, 1972).
9. Violence is not subjected to critical commentary (e.g., Lefcourt, Barnes, Parke, & Schwartz, 1966).

10. There are portrayals that seem to please the viewer (e.g., Slife & Rychiak, 1982).
11. There is violence that includes physical abuse in addition to or compared with verbal aggression (e.g., Liberman Research, 1975).
12. There is violence that leaves the viewer in a state of arousal (e.g., Zillmann, 1971).
13. Viewers are predisposed to act aggressively (e.g., Thomas, 1982).
14. Individuals are in a state of frustration after they view violence, either from an external source or from the viewing itself (e.g., Geen, 1968).
15. There is violence that is unrelieved or is not interrupted (Liberman Research, 1975).

Additional Considerations

The evidence of televised violence effects comes from laboratory experiments, field studies, correlational data, and longitudinal studies of up to 22 years. Although there occasionally are departures from a pattern of findings, or conflicts in findings, the research taken as a whole is rather conclusive. There have been those who disagree (e.g., Freedman, 1984, 1986, 1992) but any examination of these criticisms (Freidrich-Cofer & Huston, 1986; Huesmann, Eron, Berkowitz, & Chaffee, 1991) would certainly reveal the inconsistency in such critical arguments. In fact, scholars in the field of mass media overwhelmingly support the assumption of a strong relation between televised violence and aggressive behavior (Bybee, Robinson, & Turow, 1982). Furthermore, recent methodological techniques such as meta-analysis and effect size estimations have strengthened the conclusions of a media violence and aggression relationship (Comstock & Paik, 1994). There have been two major meta-analyses conducted. One examined 67 studies and over 30,000 subjects (Andison, 1977), and the other looked at 230 studies and close to 100,000 subjects (Hearold, 1986). These analyses support a number of conclusions. First, there is a positive association between televised violence exposure and aggressive behavior over a wide range of ages and measures of aggressive behavior. Second, exposure to violent programming not only increases aggressive behavior but is associated with lower levels of prosocial behavior. As Comstock & Strausberger (1990) pointed out, "the literature gives little comfort to those who assert that the findings are evenly divided, the studies are inferior, or that violence on TV does not influence behavior"(p. 32).

Those studies that have examined effect sizes in the research have found that they range from 5%–15%, according to Comstock (Comstock & Paik, 1994; Comstock & Strausburger, 1990), and for statistical and other reasons, they more than likely underestimate the true size. In fact, there is some evidence to suggest that the effect is higher for more serious antisocial behavior. In considering the issue of effect size, Robert Rosenthal of Harvard, an eminent authority in this area of statistics, notes the following regarding the link between TV violence and viewer aggression:

This paper shows in practical, quantitative, yet intuitive terms just what the social consequences are likely to be [of the effects] typically found in the research on media violence and social behavior. Estimates are provided for how well we can predict . . . current antisocial behavior from current exposure to media violence [and] subsequent antisocial behavior from earlier exposure to media violence, adjusting for earlier levels of antisocial behavior . . . . the practical consequences associated with [both] estimates were found to be substantial. (Rosenthal, 1986, p. 141)

The Special Case of Sexual Violence

In its 1992 report on televised violence, the APA Task Force on Television and Society addressed the concerns about sexual violence in the media. This report and other recent inquiries into media violence (e.g., Comstock & Paik, 1994; Hoberman, 1990) have begun to consider the implications of exposure to sexually violent materials because of the opportunities for exposure to such materials within the confines of cable or VCR viewing. Both R- and X-rated materials are available (with X-rated mainly available through VCR viewing), and images that are restricted from commercial television can be viewed. There are two types of materials that would be of concern, mainly because of their presumed contribution to sexually aggressive behavior. It is important to keep in mind that the research related to this material has been conducted with older youth (17 and above), and we can only begin to speculate about its impact on much younger viewers.

The first type of material of concern is sexualized violence against women. The media depictions in this category are usually R-rated, and although they are less sexually explicit than X-rated materials, they are far more graphic in terms of violence. These films and the violence in them can be either explicit sexual violence (e.g., rape) or images of torture, murder, and mutilation, particularly directed at women. The unique feature of this material is the sexual context in which the violence occurs. Indeed, research indicates that sex and violence are common themes in mass media presentations. Content analyses of the mass media indicate that one out of eight Hollywood films depicts a rape (Wilson, Linz, & Donnerstein, 1992) and analyses of X- and R-rated videotapes revealed approximately as much sexual violence in R-rated materials, widely available to teenagers, as was found in X-rated tapes (Yang & Linz, 1990). Both selected cable channels (e.g., HBO) and VCRs would be the main routes of access to these films for youth.

Research indicates that some males exposed to these materials can become sexually aroused, report calloused attitudes about rape, and increase their laboratory aggression against women (e.g., Donnerstein & Berkowitz, 1984; Donnerstein, Linz, & Penrod, 1987; Linz, 1989; Linz & Donnerstein, 1989; Malamuth & Donnerstein, 1982). In addition, research indicates that these attitude and arousal patterns may have some relation to actual "real world" aggression toward women (Malamuth, 1986). Two issues are important, however. The first is that these effects seem to occur for those who already have certain calloused attitudes about rape. Second, these effects can occur without any sexual content. In other words, it is the violence or message about violence that is important, not the sexual nature of the materials.

A second type of material involves nonexplicit sexual aggression against women. This category includes depictions of sexual violence against women, such as a rape scene, that would be permissible under TV broadcast standards. Although the material is not sexually explicit, the idea that women derive pleasure from sexual abuse is nonetheless a recurring theme. This material can be seen on commercial TV as well as cable and VCR.

Research suggests that exposure to mass media portrayals that depict women as the willing recipients of rape are also problematic. One study, for example (Malamuth & Check, 1981) found that exposure to *The Getaway* (a film shown on nonpay cable television) and another film depicting rape increased men's beliefs in myths that women desire rape and deserve sexual abuse. Other studies have found similar effects in addition to increased laboratory aggression (e.g., Donnerstein, Linz, & Penrod, 1987).

Studies of the effects of sexual violence on older youth (ages 17–22) have found several antisocial effects. The research consistently indicates that exposure to violence against women that is either juxtaposed with mildly erotic scenes (slasher films) or is sexually nonexplicit (but contains rape scenes) results in callousness toward female victims of violence, especially rape. If anything, one might expect even stronger effects of such content on younger viewers who may lack the necessary critical viewing skills and the experience to discount these portrayals. It is not unreasonable to assume that a young adolescent's first exposure to sex will come in the form of a mildly erotic, but violent scene from a rented video or a late-night cable movie. To a young adolescent who is searching for information about relationships, sexual violence in popular films may be a potent source of influence on initial attitudes toward sexuality.

Theoretical Models to Account for Effects

Theorizing and empirical research about the effects of violence in the mass media on aggressive attitudes and behavior have shifted away from an emphasis on "one-sided" conditioning and learning principles toward more "reciprocal" analyses. These more recent theoretical analyses have also benefited from work within the burgeoning field of cognitive psychology. One of the more sophisticated of these reciprocal cognitive models (Huesmann, 1986), for example, attempts to explain how a heavy diet of television violence sets into motion a sequence of cognitive processes that results not only in viewers being more aggressive but also in their developing an increased interest in seeing more television violence.

In this section, we examine the various theoretical models that have been offered by psychologists over the last 30 years to account for the relation between aggressive behavior and exposure to mass media violence and that we have reviewed up to this point. We begin with general theories, including early learning theories and cognitive models; then we describe more recent developmental models. Because of the widespread sexual violence against women by men, including male adolescents, we also discuss current theorizing on exposure to mass media sexual violence.

Learning Theories and Mass Media Violence

Two theoretical approaches dominated early investigations of the impact of mass media violence. Both of these approaches applied basic principles of learning to the notion of learning through observation. These early conceptions of the effects of violent mass media on behavior were often guided by a kind of one-sided determinism: Violent mass media (the environmental factor) was theorized to shape and control behavior through rather automatic processes.

One of the first theoretical accounts of mass media violence effects extended the principles of classical conditioning, whereby certain stimuli come to elicit aggressive behavior impulsively or involuntarily. For example, Berkowitz (1973) reasoned that verbal and other symbolic stimuli could produce aggressive responses because of their conditioned emotional value. Certain stimuli (such as media violence) would elicit impulsive aggressive responses from people who are set to respond in an aggressive manner as a result of the pairing of previously neutral stimuli with aggressive events.

A series of investigations demonstrated that certain aggressive "cues" often elicited aggressive behavior. For example, studies indicated that if a viewer associates cues of violence in a media portrayal that resemble cues encountered later, such as the victim in a portrayal who has the same name or similar characteristics as someone toward whom the viewer holds animosity, this will lead to higher levels of aggression (Berkowitz & Geen, 1967). Later laboratory studies that examined male aggression against a female following media exposure showed that physical aggression against a female by a male was greatest when the media victim was portrayed as similar to a likely real-life target (e.g., Donnerstein, 1980; Donnerstein & Hallam, 1978).

Social learning theory (Bandura, 1971, 1973) held that aggressive modes of response are acquired either through direct experience or indirectly through the observation of aggressive models. Unlike the Berkowitz approach, which emphasized that many violent media effects are not produced voluntarily, social learning theory as advanced by Bandura extended some of the basic principles of instrumental learning to propose that individuals could learn, without practice and without rewards, through observation. Through the observation of aggressive models, the observer comes to learn which behaviors are "appropriate," that is, which behaviors will later be rewarded and which will be punished. Implicit in this approach is the assumption that most human behavior is voluntarily directed toward attaining some anticipated reward. Many laboratory studies have demonstrated that children acquire novel aggressive behaviors on the basis of examples set by models. Studies such as these suggested that viewing a model's aggressive behavior could inhibit or disinhibit aggressive behavior. In the parlance of observational learning embraced by theorists at the time, a model's actions, and the rewards or punishments received by the model, could come to serve as informative cues or *discriminative stimuli.* These cues signaled to the viewers their probable consequences for behaving in similar ways to that of the model, disinhibiting them if they saw the model rewarded and inhibiting them if they saw the model punished. This relatively straightforward approach to mass media effects gained wide acceptance among social psychologists.

One of the first demonstrations outside of the laboratory of the relation between violence viewing and aggressive behavior was a study done in 1960 (Eron, 1963). The author interpreted his findings as fitting Bandura's social learning theory model. Most research in the ensuing years has centered on those variables that facilitate the acquisition of aggressive responses through observational learning. Another factor that is important for predicting when a model will be imitated is the viewer's identification with the actor or actress. Research has supported the notion that children (and adults) are more likely to imitate a model they perceive as having valued characteristics (Singer & Singer, 1981). Although males and females commonly develop a preference for attending to and identifying with models of the same sex as themselves (Luecke & Anderson, 1993; Ruble, Balaban, & Cooper, 1981), females more often identify with male models than vice versa (Bandura, Ross, & Ross, 1963; Huesmann, 1986).

The Original Formulations Revised

In the last decade researchers have taken issue with the idea that simple one-directional learning theory gives a full account of the effects of exposure to violence in the mass media, particularly if the viewer's cognitions are not taken into account (Berkowitz, 1984). Berkowitz and his colleagues (Berkowitz & Rogers, 1986) have proposed that, far from being firmly learned patterns of response, many media effects are immediate, transitory, and relatively short-lived. But, these researchers have rejected classical conditioning as the appropriate model for explaining these effects. Instead, they have offered an explanation influenced by theorizing in cognitive psychology (Neisser, 1967). Basically, the explanation is as follows: When people witness an aggressive event through the mass media, ideas are activated that, for a short period of time, tend to evoke other related thoughts. These thoughts then come to influence subsequent social evaluations or interactions. Berkowitz (1984) suggests that aggressive ideas brought on by viewing violence in the mass media can prime other semantically related thoughts, increasing the probability that they will come to mind. Once these additional thoughts have come to mind they influence aggressive responding in a variety of ways.

The reformulation offered by Berkowitz is appealing because it provides a way of unifying several tangents of mass media violence research by invoking one relatively simple explanation. As we have noted, several authors (e.g., Dorr, 1981; Huesmann, Lagerspetz, & Eron, 1984; Tannenbaum & Gaer, 1965) have suggested that the observer's identification with media characters influences the extent to which the observer will mimic the aggressive behavior. The reformulation by Berkowitz suggests that viewers who identify with the actors they see are vividly imagining themselves as these characters and are thinking of themselves as carrying out the depicted actions. Such identification with the aggressor in a movie should activate high imagery-aggressive thoughts and the subsequent priming of this kind of idea might influence subsequent behavior.

New Questions to Be Addressed

So far the theories of media violence effects that we have discussed all share one common problem: They are primarily one-sided. Media effects are presumed to arise from the environment. There has been no attempt to account for recipient expectations, active audience construal of messages, or the continued interaction of the viewer with the mass media.

This leaves at least two very important questions unaddressed: First, what are the consequences of exposure to mass media violence for future violent media use? Once the individual has been exposed to mass media violence is he or she altered in a way so that future goals and plans incorporate violence viewing? A second and perhaps more narrowly focused question concerns the emotional consequences of repeated viewing of mass media violence. Does repeated exposure to violence cause viewers to become desensitized or less emotionally reactive to the consequences of "real-life" violence? We will attempt to answer the first question by describing a model that emphasizes the reciprocal nature of the viewer and the media event, a developmental theory of mass media violence effects proposed by Huesmann (1986). The second question is addressed in work on the effects of repeated exposure to violence and desensitization.

A Reciprocal Effects Developmental Model

Huesmann (1986) drew on ideas in social cognitive theory to explain the effects of televised violence, especially the notion that learning the appropriate course of action in a situation involves the retention of behavioral rules or "scripts" through active rehearsal. In this model, as in social cognitive modeling, social strategies that are learned through watching violent television are tried in the immediate environment and, if reinforced, are retained and used again. The most important contribution of the social developmental model proposed by Huesmann (1986), however, is the explication of personal and interpersonal factors as intervening variables that link violence viewing and aggression.

Past empirical research has established five variables as particularly important in maintaining the television viewing–aggression relation (Huesmann & Malamuth, 1986). These are the child's (a) intellectual achievement, (b) social popularity, (c) identification with the television characters, (d) belief in the realism of the violence shown on television, and (e) amount of fantasizing about aggression. According to Huesmann, a heavy diet of television violence sets into motion a sequence of processes, based on these personal and interpersonal factors, that results not only in increased aggressiveness on the part of the viewer, but also in his or her development of an increased interest in seeing more television violence.

Research suggests that children who have poorer academic skills behave more aggressively. They also watch television with greater regularity, watch more violent programs, and believe violent programs are accurate portrayals of life (Huesmann & Eron, 1986). Huesmann speculates that aggressiveness interferes with the social interactions between the viewer and his or her teachers and peers that are needed in order to develop academic potential. Slow intellectual achievement may be related to heightened television violence viewing for two reasons. First, heightened television viewing in general may interfere with intellectual achievement (Huesmann & Eron, 1986). It may also be that children who cannot obtain gratification from success in school turn to television shows to obtain vicariously the successes they cannot otherwise obtain. Aggressive children may also be substantially less popular with their peers (Huesmann, Eron, & Yarmell, 1987). Longitudinal analyses suggest, however, that the relation between unpopularity and aggression is bidirectional. Not only do more aggressive children become less popular, but less popular children seem to become more aggressive. In addition, less popular children view more television and therefore see more violence on television.

Identification with television characters may also be important. Children who perceive themselves as like television characters are more likely to be influenced by the aggressive scripts they observe (Huesmann, Lagerspetz, & Eron 1984). This may be particularly true for boys. At the same time, highly aggressive children tend to identify with aggressive characters, and those who identify more with television characters behave more aggressively.

For an aggressive behavior script to be encoded in memory and maintained it must be salient to a child. Huesmann (1986) speculated that realistic depictions are relatively salient depictions. If a violent action is perceived as totally unrealistic, it is unlikely to receive very much attention. Early investigations of televised violence have emphasized this variable as a determinant of imitative effects (e.g., Feshbach, 1972). Later investigations by Huesmann and his colleagues have confirmed that the relation between violence viewing and aggression is heightened for children who believe the violence is representative of real life (Huesmann et al., 1984).

Finally, the maintenance of aggressive scripts might be accomplished through the rehearsal of these scripts in the child's mind. Research has shown that children's self-reports of violent fantasies are positively correlated with both aggression and greater television viewing (Huesmann & Eron, 1986).

Considered together, the interrelations of each of these variables suggest a reciprocal process in which violence viewing and aggressive behavior perpetuate each other. This process is illustrated in Figure 1. It may be described as follows: Children who are heavy viewers of television violence will see characters solving interpersonal problems by behaving aggressively. To the extent that these children identify with the aggressive characters they observe and believe the aggression is realistic, they will fantasize about and encode in memory the aggressive solutions they observe. If aggressive behaviors are emitted in the appropriate situations, the aggressive behaviors will be reinforced with desirable outcomes. But, if aggressive behavior becomes habitual

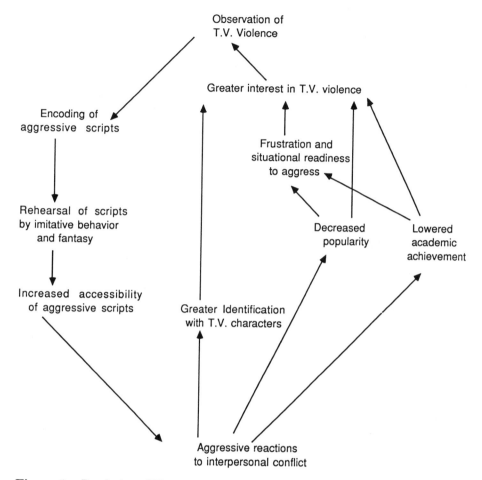

Figure 1.   Rendering of Huesmann's reciprocal model of long-term effects of mass media violence.

it will interfere with social and academic success. The more aggressive child will become less popular at school with peers and especially with teachers. These academic and social failures may lead to aggression, but, just as important, they may also lead to more regular television viewing. It is hypothesized that children might obtain satisfaction that they are denied in their social lives from television and might be better able to justify their own aggressive behavior after seeing more aggression in the media. The self-perpetuating cycle of aggression, academic and social failure, violence viewing, and fantasizing then continues.

An Indirect Effects Model for Exposure to Mass Media Sexual Violence

The developmental model proposed by Huesmann (1986) attempts to account for the effects of mass media violence on interpersonal behavior and how certain interpersonal factors (specifically failures with peers and teachers at school) might then compel the viewer to seek out more violent media. This model is especially interesting as it emphasizes a few of the social interaction variables that may be thought of as both causes and consequences of mass media violence. What other questions might an integrative theory of interpersonal processes and violent mass media effects address? One of particular interest is the effects of mass media sexual violence, especially those depictions that juxtapose violence against women with sexual scenes (e.g., "slasher" films).

Malamuth and Briere (1986) have proposed an "indirect effects" model in which they consider a variety of individual, interpersonal, and societal variables that may be causally related to sexual violence. According to these authors, cultural factors such as the mass media may influence sexually aggressive behavior, but they do so only indirectly through changes in attitudes, perceptions, and beliefs about sexual aggression, sexual arousal to aggression, and other motivations and personality characteristics. In complex combinations, these intermediate variables may lead to antisocial behaviors including aggression. Like Huesmann (1986) and Bandura (1988), Malamuth and Briere devote special attention to potential media influences on thought patterns that are stored in memory as "rules" for guiding behavior. These rules may form part of a larger cognitive structure that includes beliefs about what behaviors are appropriately desirable or acceptable in male–female relations. These belief systems may be thought of as "schemas," or "scripts" for behavior. Regardless of the label, the important assumption, as with Huesmann (1986) and Bandura (1988), is that the information is stored in the form of abstract rules for behavior rather than as a collection of specific experiences.

Experimental laboratory research has linked certain messages about violence against women that are common in the mass media to changes in thought patterns. Several studies (Malamuth & Check, 1980; Malamuth, Haber, & Feshbach, 1980) in which males were exposed to either rape with a "positive" consequence for the victim (e.g., she became sexually aroused), rape with negative consequences, or mutually consenting sex have revealed that those exposed to positive rape portrayals perceived a second rape depiction as less negative than those first exposed to other messages.

Thought patterns supportive of aggression against women, in combination with other variables, may be related to aggression in naturalistic settings. Malamuth (1986) measured 155 men on three sets of variables: motivational factors for sexual aggression (sexual arousal to aggression, hostility toward woman, dominance as a motive for sex), disinhibition factors including attitudes condoning sexual aggression and antisocial personality characteristics, and an "opportunity" variable level of sexual experience. These rape predictors were then correlated with self-reports of sexual aggression. Considered individually, each of the variables was only moderately related to sexual aggression. Interactive combinations of these variables, on the other hand, allowed for far more accurate predictions. Men who had relatively high scores on all of these variables were also highly aggressive in their sexual interactions with women.

Desensitization to Mass Media Violence

The model advanced by Huesmann (1986) deals nearly exclusively with cognitive processes that may operate with long-term exposure to media violence. In this model, heavy emphasis is placed on cognitive scripts and abstract rules for social behavior that may be imparted to the viewer through continued use of violent mass media. Another important factor, however, is the role of emotions. Generally, research on affective reactions to violent messages has been concerned with the possibility that continued exposure to violence in the mass media will undermine feelings of concern, empathy, or sympathy that viewers might have toward victims of actual violence. Most of the previous work on desensitization to media violence has involved exposure to rather mild forms of television violence for relatively short periods of time (e.g., Cline, Croft, & Courrier, 1973; Thomas, 1982; Thomas, Horton, Lippencott, & Drabman, 1977). More recently, Linz, Donnerstein, and Penrod (1984, 1987) measured the reactions of college-age men to films portraying violence against women often in a sexual context that were viewed across a 5-day period. Comparisons of first and last day reactions to the films showed that, with repeated exposure, initial levels of self-reported anxiety decreased substantially. Furthermore, subjects' perceptions of the films also changed from the first day to the last day. Material that was previously judged to be violent and degrading to women was seen as significantly less so by the end of the exposure period. Subjects also indicated that they were less depressed and enjoyed the material more with repeated exposure. Most important, these effects generalized to a victim of sexual assault presented in a videotaped reenactment of a rape trial. Subjects who were exposed to the sexually violent films rated the victim as less severely injured compared with a no-exposure control group. In another study (Linz, Donnerstein, & Penrod, 1988), subjects were also less sympathetic to the rape victim portrayed in the trial and less able to empathize with rape victims in general, compared with no-exposure control subjects and subjects exposed to other types of films. Longer film exposure was necessary to affect the violence-viewing subjects' general empathetic response.

Linz et al. (1984, 1988) suggested that the viewers were becoming comfortable with anxiety-provoking situations much as they would if they were undergoing exposure therapy. Further, it was suggested that self-awareness of reductions in anxiety and emotional arousal may be instrumental in the formation of other perceptions and attitudes about the violence portrayed in the films which are then carried over to other contexts.

A substantial literature now exists on the behavioral treatment of pathological fears which demonstrates that simply exposing a patient to the situations or objects of which he or she is frightened will significantly diminish the anxiety or negative affect that was once evoked by the objects or situations (Foa & Kozak, 1986). It has recently been proposed that exposure therapy is effective because it first evokes a fear memory (Lang, 1977, 1979). Once evoked, this memory is then available for some form of cognitive modification. Certain self-awareness processes have also been suggested as factors contributing to the effectiveness of exposure therapy (Wilkins, 1971). Foa and Kozak

(1986) have speculated that a patient's perception of his or her own habituation in the presence of a feared stimulus plays an important role in helping the patient habituate to that stimulus. Self-awareness of reduced anxiety may provide the patient with information that short-term physiological habituation has occurred and lead to dissociation of response elements from stimulus elements of the fear structure. The new information might also facilitate changes in negative valence associated with the feared stimulus. Patients may also begin to evaluate the "badness" of the feared stimuli in a less exaggerated manner.

Similar processes may operate when subjects are repeatedly exposed to graphic media violence. Once viewers are emotionally "comfortable" with the violent content of the films, they may also evaluate the films more favorably in other domains. Material originally believed to be offensive or degrading to the victims of violence may be evaluated as less so with continued exposure. A reduction in the level of anxiety may also blunt viewers' awareness of the frequency and intensity of violence in the films. Reductions in anxiety may serve to decrease sensitivity to the emotional cues that are associated with each violent episode and thereby reduce viewers' perceptions of the amount of violence in the films. Consequently, by the end of an extensive exposure period, viewers may perceive aggressive films as less violent than they had initially. These altered perceptual and affective reactions may then be carried over into judgments made about victims of violence in other, more realistic, settings.

The Education Gap

A major gap exists between what is known from research evidence on the effects of television and film violence and what is known by the general public, by practitioners in related fields, and even by many professionals. This education gap is characterized by lack of awareness, misperception, and failure to understand and apply the scientific research evidence to the problem of youth violence in America. The large education gap on this particular issue may be due not only to a failure by behavior scientists to articulate the evidence in terms that are most understandable and useful to practitioners, but also to the way this issue has been presented to the American public by the television industry itself (Slaby, 1994). As noted by Murray, Menninger, & Grimes (1993), there has been very little acknowledgment on the part of the television industry that violence still very much exists on television and that there is a relation between exposure to this violence and aggressive behavior in children. Not until July of 1993 did the heads of the major television broadcast companies publicly admit in a national press conference that research evidence indicated that the viewing of television violence contributes to violence in real life.

Although practice and public understanding commonly lags behind the research evidence, the major research findings in most fields are eventually incorporated into practice and public awareness. For example, the latest evidence linking cigarette smoking and various forms of disease will eventually be incorporated into practice by health care practitioners and transmitted to the general public through practitioners and the media. The model that research evidence will eventually be disseminated, incorporated, and applied works well for many areas that affect the health and well-being of the general public, such as in the fields of health, education, and technological development.

In contrast, this model has not worked to influence the television industry's practice and public presentation of the issue of TV violence. Instead, the research evidence on the effects of TV violence has been treated by the industry as a threat to the business of television. Unlike other businesses that might react in a similar self-protective manner while having to face scrutiny by the media and the general public, however, the television industry's self-protective stance also affects the way in which research evidence is presented to the American public. Research evidence on TV violence effects has for decades been actively ignored, denied, attacked, and even misrepresented in presentations to the American public, and popular myths undermining the effects have been perpetuated. As a consequence, a major education gap exists regarding television's contribution to the problem of violence in America.

One index of this education gap is that many popular myths prevail specifically about mass media effects on violence, despite research evidence to the contrary. Such myths include:

1. Television and film violence has no effect on the viewer.
2. Television and film violence has a "catharsis effect" of actually reducing violence by allowing viewers to vicariously "blow off steam" or get violence "out of their system."
3. Television programs and films are no more violent in America than they are in other countries.
4. Violence presented in cartoons is even more innocuous than live action violence.
5. The violence presented in American television programs and films is simply a case of giving the viewers what they want.
6. American television programs and films usually present violence in ways that minimize their harmful effects on the viewer.
7. Any attempts by the public to move the television industry toward responsible action to solve the violence problem constitutes censorship and an infringement of the guarantees of "freedom of speech" provided by the First Amendment of the U.S. Constitution.
8. American citizens are not the rightful owners and ultimate controllers of the airwaves; rather, the licensed station operators are authorized (or even obliged) to deal with television violence in whatever manner they choose and without input from American citizens.

This gap in public knowledge about TV and film effects on violence, and the industry's role in maintaining or widening this gap, is particularly unfortunate in light of the research evidence indicating that television can play an effective educational role in promoting healthful behavior. Evidence indicates that television can and does influence viewers' information, skills, values, and behavior (NIMH, 1982). In addition to regular television programming and outreach activities, coordinated educational campaigns presented on television can also be effective, particularly when programming is supplemented with educational outreach activities that enhance the value of the programming. Thus, television has the potential to play an effective role in educating the American public about the nature of the violence problem and the effective preventative actions that can be taken by children and by adults, by professionals and by ordinary citizens, by individuals and by communities. Television can become an important part of the solution, rather than continuing to primarily contribute to the problem of violence in America. As Murray et al. (1993) noted:

> Forty years of research has removed the excuse for inaction by programmers and policymakers by removing the fiction that TV's harmful effects are merely conjecture. It has been said that every society is only 20 years away from barbarism—20 years is all that is available to help a newborn child learn the ways of society and become a productive adult. There are many sources of influence on young minds and spirits but one of the chief sources of information about our society's values are the stories we tell young viewers in television entertainment. Surely, we can provide more thoughtful stories if we invest our minds and talents in this task. Now is the time and the opportunity for us to face up to our obligations to the next generation. (p. 22)

Research Evidence and Knowledge Gaps

As a result of our review of the research literature we are confident about certain effects of viewing violence in the mass media. Evidence indicates that there are at least four major effects (Parke & Slaby, 1983; Slaby, 1994):

1. an *aggressor effect* of increased meanness, aggression, and even violence toward others;
2. a *victim effect* of increased fearfulness, mistrust or "mean world syndrome," and self-protective behavior (such as carrying a gun, which ironically increases one's risk of becoming a victim of violence);
3. a *bystander effect* of increased desensitization, callousness, and behavioral apathy toward other victims of violence; and
4. an *appetite effect* of increased self-initiated behavior to further expose oneself to violent material.

We are also aware that there are also effects of viewing of prosocial behavior in television programming. Evidence indicates that there are at least two major effects:

1. a *prosocial effect* of increased helpful behavior toward others; and
2. an *antiviolence effect* of decreased violence toward others.

In our review of the existing research on mass media effects, a number of future research agendas have become evident. Although recent research attention has begun to shift away from simple identification and documentation of these media effects and toward more challenging issues, major research gaps exist regarding the interconnection among these effects and their specific application to the issue of how best to prevent violence.

First, research is needed to address those questions that have direct significance for preventing violence among youth. These questions include:

Who is most susceptible or resilient to these media effects?

What are the key factors of susceptibility and resilience?

Which individuals are most susceptible and which are most resilient to each of the different media effects?

Under what circumstances are each of the various media effects most likely to occur?

By what means (mechanisms) do these effects occur?

How do the mechanisms underlying these different effects interrelate and differ?

In what ways can these effects be altered through interventions to prevent violence?

How do effective interventions for these effects interrelate and differ?

Second, we need to investigate the influences on youth violence of depictions of violence in news and recent reality-based programs (e.g., COPS, America's Most Wanted, Eye Witness Video). Specifically:

What mechanisms might account for differences between reactions to media violence presented in a realistic or fantastic context?

What are the effects of TV news broadcasts on violence?

Third, we need to develop a better understanding of why particular youth come to prefer or seek out violent media while others do not. For example, there exists a strong popularity among many youth for graphically violent media, such as "slasher" or horror films.

What are the psychological processes that lead to this selective exposure?

What is the relation, if any, between the popularity of TV programs, TV characters, and violent content?

Finally, little is known about the relation between TV and film effects and other risk factors and social experiences that are related to violence among youth.

In what ways do television and film portrayals of violence connect with the use of firearms and the use of alcohol and other drugs to contribute to violence by youth?

Interventions to Reduce or Prevent Violence Among Youth

A large number of professional organizations that are concerned with the well-being of children and families (e.g., American Academy of Pediatrics, American Medical Association, American Psychological Association, Group for the Advancement of Psychiatry, National Parent Teachers Association) have recommended that professionals take a more active role in reducing the impact of violent media (Huston et al., 1992). Research and intervention programs have indicated that some of the impact of media violence can be reduced by "empowering" parents in their roles as monitors of children's television viewing (e.g., Singer & Singer, 1981). Several investigations have indicated that parents rarely monitor either the content or the extent of children's television viewing (e.g., Bower, 1973). Effective potential strategies for parents to use have been summarized (e.g., Comstock & Paik, 1994).

Another strategy has been to develop social–cognitive resources in the child viewers themselves. An excellent example is provided in a study by Huesmann, Eron, Klein, Brice, and Fischer (1983) who tried to motivate children not to encode and later enact aggressive behaviors observed in certain mass communications. This study was based on ideas from counter-attitudinal advocacy research that were found effective in producing enduring behavioral changes in other domains. The research is predicated on notions contained in both dissonance and attribution theory that people are motivated to achieve some degree of consistency between their attitudes and behaviors. When a person finds himself or herself advocating a point of view that is either unfamiliar or even counter to an original belief, he or she is motivated to shift attitudes into line with what is being advocated.

Children in the experimental group were first credited with the antiviolence attitudes that the experimenters wished them to adopt and then asked to make videotapes for other children who had been "fooled" by television and "got into trouble by imitating it" even though they themselves knew better. The children composed persuasive essays explaining how television is not like real life and why it would be harmful for other children to watch too much television and imitate the violent characters. A videotape of each child reading his or her essay was then played before the entire group. This gave the child an opportunity to see himself or herself advocate an antiviolence position and also made the child's position public. The intervention was successful both in changing children's attitudes about television violence and in modifying aggressive behavior. Four months after the intervention there was a significant increase in the experimental group's belief that television violence is harmful and a decrease in their peer-nominated aggressive behavior.

In addition to the interventions noted above, a number of programs have been designed to build "critical viewing skills" that may ameliorate the impact of televised violence on children (Eron 1986; Singer & Singer, 1991), although the effectiveness of these programs is still under evaluation. It is argued that providing viewers with a set of critical skills to evaluate violence in the mass media may also be important in modifying reactions to these depictions. Curricula are designed to teach students to recognize certain types of negative portrayals of social behavior and to provide them with alternative ways of interpreting these portrayals (Anderson, 1980). Dorr, Graves, and Phelps (1980) have suggested that the effects of exposure to certain mass communications could be modified if a viewer has the ability to devalue the source of information, assess motivations for presenting information and to perceive the degree of reality intended. Specifically, they have identified five critical television evaluation skills: explicit and spontaneous reasoning, readiness to compare television content with outside information sources, readiness to refer to industry knowledge in reasoning about television content, tendency to find television more fabricated or inaccurate, and less positive evaluation of television content.

In this chapter we have also discussed the problems of exposure to mass media sexual violence. Some of the techniques discussed above have also been used successfully to mitigate the impact of exposure to this type of material (Linz, Arluk, & Donnerstein, 1990; Linz & Donnerstein, 1989). In a recent review of this literature, Linz, Wilson, and Donnerstein (1992) suggested a future program of research whose goal is the development of a formal, easily administered educational program, including instructional materials and videotapes, for high school educators to use to educate adolescent populations about the realities of sexual violence and about the inaccuracies in media depictions of such occurrences. This program of research would need to examine (a) what types of information would be most powerful in changing adolescents' attitudes about mass media sexual violence, (b) the optimal format for adolescents to learn and incorporate these messages into their repertoire of values, (c) the most effective communication source for conveying this educational information, and (d) to what extent social psychological factors, such as a critical viewing companion, may facilitate immediate and long-term changes in beliefs and attitudes about sexual violence.

Recommendations regarding regulatory and policy issues in relation to children's television have also been made (e.g., Kunkel & Watkins, 1987; Huston et al., 1992). The potential for the medium of television not only to reduce its role as a source of risk, but also to play a major beneficial role as the most powerful public teacher in reducing violence and other sources of injury deserves thorough consideration in light of television's previous successes in health campaigns (NIMH, 1982; Palmer, 1988). Furthermore, it is important to encourage responsible portrayals of conflict and conflict resolution.

The Film Rating System

Another possible intervention is to rely more extensively on an informational system that is already in place, the film rating system (Linz, Wilson, & Donnerstein, 1992). An excellent discussion of this system has been presented by Wilson, Linz, and Randall (1990). The rating scheme was created by the Motion Picture Association of America (MPAA) over 20 years ago. The system is based on the familiar movie rating codes "G," "PG," "PG-13," "R," "X," and now "NC-17" (no children under 17) that accompany most commercial films and that are publicized on many videocassette copies of these films. The stated purpose of the rating scheme is to inform parents about objectionable movie content (Valenti, 1987). The system is designed to be a heuristic for parents; parents are thought to approve of it and to see it as informative because it corresponds to their implicit notion of which materials are unsuitable for children. Given that this system is already in place, we might recommend that parents be encouraged to use the ratings more often and more systematically. The vast quantity of adult material now available on cable and on videocassettes places many parents in the position of having to make daily decisions about what their children should and should not view. Any information that would help in this decision-making process presumably would be welcome. In order to assist parents, the rating system should be publicized more extensively, along with a guide for how to use it in making movie selections. Additionally, cable television operators and videocassette distributors should be strongly advised to display ratings more prominently when featuring, renting, or selling various films.

There are, however, a number of potential problems with the current rating system that might make it problematic when dealing with concerns about excessive or sexual violence in the media. First, the system attempts to rate films on the basis of what has been traditionally considered offensive rather than what is assumed to be or known to be "harmful" to viewers. The MPAA has asserted that it is concerned with attempting to determine what "most American parents will think about the appropriateness of film content" (Valenti, 1987, p. 5). The assumption that ratings should be based on what is offensive to parents rather than on what is assumed to be or known to be "harmful" to children often leads to peculiar classifications that ignore psychological facts and may ultimately not be all that informative to parents. For example, the system does not explicitly consider graphic horror as part of its criteria for rating films, in spite of the fact that numerous studies show that such content can cause intense emotional reactions in young viewers (see Wilson et al., 1990, for review). Thus, the rating system would be much more useful to parents who need information on violence effects if violent content were rated separately rather than mixing it in unspecified ways with factors of sex, nudity, profanity, and adult themes.

Second, the system assumes that excessive and explicit sex is more offensive and problematic than excessive violence. According to the ratings board's guidelines, any depiction of sexuality will automatically render a film an R rating, and explicit sex will often earn a film an X rating. In contrast, a film can contain violence and still be given a G, PG, or PG-13 rating. The general rule is that the violence must be "rough" or "persistent" before a film will receive an R rating, and "excessive and sadistic" before a film will warrant an X rating. In most cases, however, films that contain graphic and brutal violence are assigned R ratings even when the violence is directed against women in an erotic context (e.g., slasher films). As an illustration of these differential standards regarding sex and violence, the film *The French Lieutenant's Woman* is rated R because of sexual references and a few brief sex scenes, whereas a film such as *Conan the Destroyer* is rated PG despite scenes of "bloodthirsty battlers at every turn" (Martin & Porter, 1987, p. 1049).

Third, the ratings system presumes that films should be rated primarily on the basis of the amount of violence and sex or the explicitness of such content rather than on the context in which these depictions occur. Little attention appears to be given to contextual features of the violence, such as how realistic it is, the rewards and punishments associated with the violent act, and the degree of justification for the violence. The same approach is applied to depictions of sex. The Board appears to pay little attention to motives of the character or other features of the situation in which the sexual contact takes place. Consequently, movies containing depictions of rape and sexual brutality seem to receive the same ratings as movies depicting mutually affectionate lovemaking, so long as they both contain the same amount of sexual activity. Moreover, the ratings board has a policy that two or more uses of a sexually derived word as an expletive in a film will earn it an "R" rating. As a result, a movie like *Rain Man*, which depicts the growing relationship between a man and his autistic brother, receives the same rating (R) as the so-called "slasher" films that gratuitously depict violence against women.

Most recently, the MPAA has attempted to respond to some of its critics by creating the "NC-17" (no children under 17) rating to warn viewers about content that may include "adult" themes that are not necessarily deemed pornographic. Interestingly, this change coincided with strong pressure from influential film producers who objected to the X rating as a label for films that are somewhat sexually explicit but that deal with a serious topic. The addition of another rating category does not, however, address the more deep-seated problems. More fundamental changes in the system are necessary before these issues can be resolved. It has been argued elsewhere that both the age specifications and the actual ratings need to be more informative to parents (Wilson et al., 1990). An alternative scheme could be based on the same two factors used by the MPAA: age level and type of film content. However, the categories of film content need to specify the precise type of content in a film and the most vulnerable age groups. For example, a slasher film such as *Toolbox Murders* might be labeled "SV: 13–17," suggesting that it contains sexual violence or violence in the context of sexual depictions, and that it is particularly unsuitable for 13– to 17–year-olds, but also not appropriate for younger children.

Policy Implications and Recommendations

Based on our review and evaluation of the research literature, we recommend the following:[1]

Recommendation 1: We call upon the Federal Communications Commission to review, as a condition for license renewal, the programming and outreach efforts and accomplishments of television stations in helping to solve the problem of youth violence in America.

Research evidence shows that media violence can and does serve as a contributing cause of youth violence (APA, 1992; NIMH, 1982). Research evidence also indicates that television programming can help to reduce the likelihood of violence by viewers (Hearald, 1986). Whereas the media, and particularly television and film, have for decades contributed to the problem of youth violence in America, the media clearly has the potential and the responsibility to become part of the solution. The Federal Communications Act of 1934 requires broadcasters to "serve the public interest, convenience, and necessity." The Children's Television Act of 1990 (H.R. 1677) requires broadcasters to serve the "educational and informational needs of children" through both programming and nonbroadcast efforts designed to "enhance the educational and information value of such programming."

---

[1]These recommendations were prepared for this chapter and presented earlier in the Commission's summary report, *Violence and Youth: Psychology's Response* (APA Commission on Violence and Youth, 1993).

Recommendation 2: We recommend that an educational campaign involving television programming, supplemented with educational outreach activities for parents, educators, and health care providers be developed and implemented to help solve the problem of youth violence in America.

Recommendation 3: The Film Rating System should be reexamined with an emphasis toward that which is harmful to children rather than that which might be offensive to parents. A stronger consideration needs to be placed upon violent and sexually violent content in the assignment of ratings, as well as providing for the viewer more information of the kind and scope of violence present.

Along these same lines, the video rental market needs to be more in harmony with even the present rating system. Easy access by young adolescents to R-rated graphically violent videos undermines the meaning of the R rating. This rating indicates that children under 17 are restricted from such films unless accompanied by a parent or guardian. Such restrictions are rather uncommon within the video market.

Recommendation 4: The 1985 APA resolution on television violence should be modified so as to include the mass media (television, film, video) in general as a contributor to aggressive behavior and attitudes on the part of children. This modification should be worded as follows:

"WHEREAS, the great majority of research studies have found a relationship between mass media violence and behaving aggressively, and WHEREAS, the conclusions drawn on the basis of over 30 years of research and a sizeable number of experimental and field investigations is that viewing mass media violence may lead to increases in aggressive attitudes, values, and behavior, particularly in children, and WHEREAS, many children's television programs and films contain some form of violence, BE IT RESOLVED that the American Psychological Association (1) encourages parents to monitor and to control television, video, and film viewing by children; (2) requests representatives from the television and film industry to take a responsible attitude in reducing direct imitatable violence in "real life" fictional children's programming or violent incidents on cartoons or other television or film productions and in providing more programming for children designed to mitigate possible effects of television and film violence, consistent with the guarantees of the First Amendment; and (3) urges industry, governmental and private foundations to support relevant research activities aimed at the amelioration of the effects of high levels of mass media violence on children's attitudes and behavior."

References

Abeles, N. (1985). Proceedings of the American Psychological Association for the year 1984. *American Psychologist, 40*, 621–653.

Anderson, J. (1980). The theoretical lineage of critical viewing curricula. *Journal of Communication, 30*, 64–70.

Andison, F. S. (1977). TV violence and viewer aggression: A cumulation of study results. *Public Opinion Quarterly, 41*, 314–331.

APA Commission on Violence and Youth. (1993). *Violence and youth: Psychology's response.* Washington, DC: Public Interest Directorate, American Psychological Association.

Atkin, C. K. (1983). Effects of realistic TV violence vs. fictional violence on aggression. *Journalism Quarterly, 60,* 615–621.

Atkin, D., Heeter, C., & Baldwin, T. (1989). How presence of cable affects parental mediation of television viewing. *Journalism Quarterly, 66,* 557–578.

Bandura, A. (1971). *Social learning theory.* New York: General Learning Press.

Bandura, A. (1973). *Aggression: A social learning analysis.* Englewood Cliffs, NJ: Prentice Hall.

Bandura, A., (1988). Social cognitive theory of mass communication. In J. Groebel & P. Winterhoff (Eds.), *Empirische Medienpsychologie* (pp. 226–249). Munchen: Psychologie Verlags Union.

Bandura, A., Ross, D., & Ross, S. A. (1963). Imitation of film-mediated aggressive models. *Journal of Abnormal and Social Psychology, 66,* 3–11.

Berkowitz, L. (1973). Words and symbols as stimuli to aggressive responses. In J. Knutson (Eds.), *Control of aggression: Implications from basic research* (pp. 171–195). Chicago: Aldine.

Berkowitz, L. (1984). Some effects of thoughts on anti and prosocial influences of media events: A cognitive-neoassociation analysis. *Psychological Bulletin, 95,* 410–427.

Berkowitz, L., & Geen, R. G. (1967). Stimulus qualities of the target of aggression: A further study. *Journal of Personality and Social Psychology, 5,* 364–368.

Berkowitz, L., & Rawlings, E. (1963). Effects of film violence on inhibitions against subsequent aggression. *Journal of Abnormal and Social Psychology, 66,* 405–412.

Berkowitz, L., & Rogers, K. H. (1986). A priming effect analysis of media influences. In J. Bryant & D. Zillmann (Eds.), *Perspectives on media effects* (pp. 57–82). Hillsdale, NJ: Erlbaum.

Berry, G. L. (1988). Multicultural role portrayals on television as a social psychological issue. In S. Oskamp (Ed.), *Applied social psychology annual. Vol. 8: Television as a social issue* (pp. 118–129). Newbury Park, CA: Sage.

Bower, R. T. (1973). *Television and the public.* New York: Holt, Rinehart & Winston.

Bybee, C., Robinson, D., & Turow, J. (1982, April). *Mass media scholars' perceptions of television's effects on children.* Paper presented at the Annual Convention of the American Association for Public Opinion Research, Hunt Valley, MD.

Centers for Disease Control. (1991). *Position papers from the Third National Injury Conference: Setting the national agenda for injury control in the 1990s.* Washington, DC: Department of Health and Human Services.

Cline, V. B., Croft, R. G., & Courrier, S. (1973). Desensitization of children to television violence. *Journal of Personality and Social Psychology, 27,* 360–365.

Comstock, G. A., & Paik, H. (1994). The effects of television violence on antisocial behavior: A meta-analysis. *Communication Research, 21,* 516–546.

Comstock, G., & Strausburger, V. C. (1990). Deceptive appearances: Television violence and aggressive behavior. *Journal of Adolescent Health Care, 11,* 31–44.

Donnerstein, E. (1980). Aggressive-erotica and violence against women. *Journal of Personality and Social Psychology, 39,* 269–277.

Donnerstein, E., & Berkowitz, L. (1981). Victim reactions in aggressive-erotic films as a factor in violence against women. *Journal of Personality and Social Psychology, 41,* 710–724.

Donnerstein, E., & Berkowitz, L. (1984). *Effects of film content and victim association on aggressive behavior and attitudes.* Unpublished manuscript, University of Wisconsin-Madison.

Donnerstein, E., & Hallam, J. (1978). Facilitating effects of erotica on aggression against women. *Journal of Personality and Social Psychology, 36,* 1270–1277.

Donnerstein, E., Linz, D., & Penrod, S. (1987). *The question of pornography: Research findings and policy implications.* New York: Free Press.

Dorr, A. (1981). Television and affective development and functioning: Maybe this decade. *Journal of Broadcasting, 25,* 335–345.

Dorr, A., Graves, S. B., & Phelps, E. (1980). Television literacy for young children. *Journal of Communication, 30,* 71–83.

Eron, L. D. (1963). The relationship of TV viewing habits and aggressive behavior in children. *Journal of Abnormal and Social Psychology, 67,* 193–196.

Eron, L. D. (1986). Interventions to mitigate the psychological effects of media violence on aggressive behavior. *Journal of Social Issues, 42,* 155–169.

Eron, L. D. (1992, June 18). Testimony before the Senate Committee on Governmental Affairs. *Congressional Record, 88,* S8538–S8539.

Fairchild, H. H. (1988). Creating positive television images. In S. Oscamp (Ed.), *Applied social psychology annual. Vol. 8: Television as a social issue* (pp. 118–129). Newbury Park, CA: Sage.

Feshbach, S. (1972). Reality and fantasy in filmed violence. In J. Murray, E. Rubinstein, & G. Comstock (Eds.), *Television and social behavior* (Vol. 2, pp. 318–345). Washington, DC: Dept. of Health, Education, and Welfare.

Foa, E. B., & Kozak, M. J. (1986). Emotional processing of fear: Exposure to corrective information. *Psychological Bulletin, 99,* 20–35.

Freedman, J. L. (1984). Effect of television violence on aggressiveness. *Psychological Bulletin, 96,* 227–246.

Freedman, J. L. (1986). Television violence and aggression: A rejoinder. *Psychological Bulletin, 100,* 372–378.

Freedman, J. L. (1992). Television violence and aggression: What psychologists should tell the public. In P. Suedfeld & P. E. Tetlock (Eds.), *Psychology and public policy* (pp.179–190). New York: Hemisphere.

Freidrich-Cofer, L., & Huston, A. C. (1986). Television violence and aggression: The debate continues. *Psychological Bulletin, 100,* 364–371.

Geen, R. G. (1968). Effects of frustration, attack, and prior training in aggressiveness upon aggressive behavior. *Journal of Personality and Social Psychology, 9,* 316–321.

Geen, R. G., & Stonner, D. (1972). Context effects in observed violence. *Journal of Personality and Social Psychology, 25,* 145–150.

Gerbner, G., Gross, L., Signorielli, N., & Morgan, M. (1986). *Television's mean world: Violence profile no. 14–15.* Unpublished manuscript, Annenberg School of Communication, University of Pennsylvania, Philadelphia.

Gerbner, G., & Signorielli, N. (1990). *Violence profile, 1967 through 1988–89: Enduring patterns.* Unpublished manuscript, Annenberg School of Communication, University of Pennsylvania, Philadelphia.

Greenberg, B. S. (1986). Minorities in the mass media. In J. Bryant & D. Zillmann (Eds.), *Perspectives on media effects* (pp. 165–188). Hillsdale, NJ: Erlbaum.

Greenberg, B. S. (1988). Some uncommon television images and the drench hypothesis. In S. Oskamp (Ed.), *Applied social psychology annual. Vol. 8: Television as a social issue* (pp. 88–102). Newbury Park, CA: Sage.

Greenberg, B. S., & Heeter, C. (1987). VCRs and young people. *American Behavioral Scientist, 30,* 509–521.

Hearold, S. (1986). A synthesis of 1043 effects of television on social behavior. In G. Comstock (Ed.), *Public communication and behavior* (Vol I, pp. 65–113). San Diego, CA: Academic Press.

Hoberman, H. M. (1990). Study group report on the impact of television violence on adolescents. *Journal of Adolescent Health Care, 11,* 45–49.

Huesmann, L. R. (1986). Psychological processes promoting the relation between exposure to media violence and aggressive behavior by the viewer. *Journal of Social Issues, 42*(3), 125–140.

Huesmann, L. R. (1992, March). *Violence in the mass media.* Paper presented at the Third International Conference on Film Regulation, London, England.

Huesmann, L. R., & Eron, L. D. (Eds.). (1986). *Television and the aggressive child: A cross-national comparison.* Hillsdale, NJ: Erlbaum.

Huesmann, L. R., Eron, L. D., Berkowitz, L., & Chaffee, S. (1991). The effects of television violence on aggression: A reply to a skeptic. In P. Suedfeld & P. E. Tetlock (Eds.), *Psychology and public policy* (pp. 191–200). New York: Hemisphere.

Huesmann, L. R., Eron, L. D., Klein, R., Brice, P., & Fischer, P. (1983). Mitigating the imitation of aggressive behaviors by changing children's attitudes about media violence. *Journal of Personality and Social Psychology, 44,* 899–910.

Huesmann, L. R., Eron, L. D., Lefkowitz, M. M., & Walder, L. O. (1984). The stability of aggression over time and generations. *Developmental Psychology, 20,* 1120–1134.

Huesmann, L. R., Eron, L. D., & Yarmel, P. W. (1987). Intellectual functioning and aggression. *Journal of Personality and Social Psychology, 52,* 232–240.

Huesmann, L. R., Lagerspetz, K., & Eron, L. D. (1984). Intervening variables in the TV violence-aggression relation: Evidence from two countries. *Developmental Psychology, 20,* 1120–1134.

Huesmann, L. R., & Malamuth, N. (1986). Media violence and antisocial behavior: An overview. *Journal of Social Issues, 42,* 1–6.

Huston, A. C., Donnerstein, E., Fairchild, H., Feshbach, N. D., Katz, P. A., Murray, J. P., Rubinstein, E. A., Wilcox, B. L., & Zuckerman, D. (1992). *Big world, small screen: The role of television in American society.* Lincoln: University of Nebraska Press.

Kuby, R. W., & Csikszentmihalyi, M. (1990). *Television and the quality of life: How viewing shapes everyday experience.* Hillsdale, NJ: Erlbaum.

Kunkel, D., & Watkins, B. (1987). Evolution of children's television regulatory policy. *Journal of Broadcasting & Electronic Media, 31,* 367–389.

Lang, P. J. (1977). Imagery in therapy: An information processing analysis of fear. *Behavior Therapy, 8,* 862–886.

Lang, P. J. (1979). A bio-informational theory of emotional imagery. *Psychophysiology, 16,* 495–512.

Lefcourt, H. M., Barnes, K., Parke, R., & Schwartz, F. (1966). Anticipated social censure and aggression-conflict as mediators of response to aggression induction. *Journal of Social Psychology, 70,* 251–263.

Liberman Research. (1975). *Children's reactions to violent material on television.* Report to the American Broadcasting Corporation. New York: Author.

Lichter, R. S., & Amundson, D. (1992). *A day of television violence.* Washington, DC: Center for Media and Public Affairs.

Liebert, R. M., & Sprafkin, J. N. (1988). *The early window: Effects of television on children and youth.* Elmsford, NY: Pergamon Press.

Lin, C. A., & Atkin, D. J. (1989). Parental mediation and rulemaking for adolescent use of television and VCRs. *Journal of Broadcasting and Electronic Media, 33,* 53–67.

Linz, D. (1989). Exposure to sexually explicit materials and attitudes toward rape: A comparison of study results. *The Journal of Sex Research, 26,* 50–84.

Linz, D., Arluk, I. H., & Donnerstein, E. (1990). Mitigating the negative effects of sexually violent mass media through pre-exposure briefings. *Communication Research, 17,* 641–674.

Linz, D., & Donnerstein, E. (1989). The effects of counter-information on the acceptance of rape myths. In D. Zillmann and J. Bryant (Eds.), *Pornography: research advances and policy considerations* (pp. 259–287). Hillsdale, NJ: Erlbaum

Linz, D., Donnerstein, E., & Penrod, S. (1984). The effects of multiple exposures to filmed violence against women. *Journal of Communication, 34,* 130–147.

Linz, D., Donnerstein, E., & Penrod, S. (1987). Sexual violence in the mass media: social psychological implications. In P. Shaver & C. Hendrick (Eds.), *Review of Personality and Social Psychology* (Vol. 7, pp. 95–122). Newbury Park, CA: Sage.

Linz, D., Donnerstein, E., & Penrod, S. (1988). The effects of long-term exposure to violent and sexually degrading depictions of women. *Journal of Personality and Social Psychology, 55,* 758–768.

Linz, D., Wilson, B., & Donnerstein, E. (1992). Sexual violence in the mass media: Legal solutions, warnings, and mitigation through education. *Journal of Social Issues, 48,* 145–171.

Luecke, D. M., & Anderson, D. R. (1993, March). Gender constancy and attention to television. Paper presented at the Biennial Meeting of the Society for Research in Child Development, New Orleans, LA.

Malamuth, N. M. (1986). Predictors of naturalistic sexual aggression. *Journal of Personality and Social Psychology, 50,* 953–962.

Malamuth, N. M., & Briere, J. (1986). Sexual violence in the media: Indirect effects on aggression against women. *Journal of Social Issues, 42,* 75–92.

Malamuth, N. M., & Check, J. V. P. (1980). Penile tumescence and perceptual responses to rape as a function of victim's perceived reactions. *Journal of Applied Social Psychology, 10,* 528–547.

Malamuth, N., & Donnerstein, E. (1982). The effects of aggressive-pornographic mass media stimuli. In L. Berkowitz (Ed.), *Advances in experimental social psychology* (Vol. 15, pp. 104–136). San Diego, CA: Academic Press.

Malamuth, N., Haber, S., & Feshbach, S. (1980). Testing hypotheses regarding rape: Exposure to sexual violence, sex differences, and the normality of rape. *Journal of Research in Personality, 14*, 121–137.

Martin, M., & Porter, M. (1987). *Video movie guide, 1988.* New York: Ballantine Books.

Murray, J. P., Menninger, R. W., & Grimes, T. (1993). *Media mayhem and children.* Unpublished manuscript, Kansas State University, Manhattan.

National Institute of Mental Health. (1982). *Television and behavior: Ten years of scientific progress and implications for the eighties, Summary Report* (Vol. 1). Washington, DC: U.S. Government Printing Office.

Neisser, U. (1967). *Cognitive psychology.* New York: Appleton-Century-Crofts.

Palmer, E. L. (1988). *Television and America's children.* New York: Oxford University Press.

Parke, R. D., & Slaby, R. G. (1983). The development of aggression. In P. H. Mussen (Series Ed.), *Handbook of child psychology* (Vol. 4, 4th ed., pp. 547–641). New York: Wiley.

Rosekrans, M. A. (1967). Imitation in children as a function of perceived similarities to a social model of vicarious reinforcement. *Journal of Personality and Social Psychology, 7*, 305–317.

Rosenthal, R. (1986). Media violence, antisocial behavior, and the social consequences of small effects. *Journal of Social Issues, 42*, 141–154.

Ruble, D., Balaban, T., & Cooper, J. (1981). Gender constancy and the effect of televised toy commercials. *Child Development, 52*, 667–673.

Sims, J. B. (1989). VCR viewing patterns: An electronic and passive investigation. *Journal of Advertising Research, 29*, 11–17.

Singer, D. G., & Singer, J. L. (1991). *Creating critical viewers.* Denver, CO: Pacific Mountain Network.

Singer, J. L., & Singer, D. G. (1981). *Television, imagination, and aggression: A study of preschoolers.* Hillsdale, NJ: Erlbaum.

Slaby, R. G. (1994). Combating television violence. *The Chronicle of Higher Education, 15,*(18), pp. B1–B2.

Slife, B. D., & Rychiak, J. F. (1982). Role of affective assessment in modeling behavior. *Journal of Personality and Social Psychology, 43*, 861–868.

Surgeon General's Scientific Advisory Committee on Television and Social Behavior. (1972). *Television and growing up: The impact of televised violence.* Washington, DC: U.S. Government Printing Office.

Tangney, J. P., & Feshbach, S. (1988). Children's television-viewing frequency: Individual differences and demographic correlates. *Personality and Social Psychology Bulletin, 14*, 145–158.

Tannenbaum, P., & Gaer, E. P. (1965). Mood changes as a function of stress of protagonist and degree of identification in film-viewing situation. *Journal of Personality and Social Psychology, 2*, 612–616.

Thomas, M. H. (1982). Physiological arousal, exposure to a relatively lengthy aggressive film, and aggressive behavior. *Journal of Research in Personality, 16*, 72–81.

Thomas, M. H., Horton, R. W., Lippencott, E. C., & Drabman, R. S. (1977). Desensitization to portrayals of real-life aggression as a function of exposure to television violence. *Journal of Personality and Social Psychology, 35*, 450–458.

Turner, C. W., & Berkowitz, L. (1972). Identification with film aggressor (covert role taking) and reactions to film violence. *Journal of Personality and Social Psychology, 21*, 256–264.

Valenti, J. (1987). *The voluntary movie rating system.* New York: Motion Picture Association of America.

Wilkins, W. (1971). Desensitization: Social and cognitive factors underlying the effectiveness of Wolpe's procedure. *Psychological Bulletin, 76*, 311–317.

Wilson, B., Linz, D., & Donnerstein, E. (1992). The impact of social issue television programming on attitudes toward rape. *Human Communication Research, 19*, 179–208.

Wilson, B. J., Linz, D., & Randall, B. (1990). Applying social science research to film ratings: A shift from offensiveness to harmful effects. *Journal of Broadcasting and Electronic Media, 34*, 443–468.

Yang, N., & Linz, D. (1990). Movie ratings and the content of adult videos: The sex-violence ratio. *Journal of Communication, 40*, 28–42.

Zillmann, D. (1971). Excitation transfer in communication-mediated aggressive behavior. *Journal of Experimental Social Psychology, 7*, 419–433.

12

Guns and Youth

Leonard Berkowitz

> Andre, who was 15 years old at the time, remembers the bang of the .32-caliber revolver and the little red spot that blossomed on the cheek of the boy he shot.
>
> "I didn't intend to kill him," Andre said in a visiting room at the Harlem Valley Secure Center, a prison for teenagers in the rolling hills north of New York City. "I just wanted to scare him. I didn't know it would go off so easily."
>
> Tall and fleshy with a loping, insouciant walk, Andre is one of a growing number of American teen-agers who have murdered with guns. (Treaster, 1992, p. 1)

One sees here the kind of tragedy, apparently mounting in frequency, that does not seem to figure much in the debate about gun control. Andre insisted he had not set out to murder his victim and had shot the other boy more or less unintentionally while in a fight with that youngster and his friends. Was this so? Had the killing been an accident, or maybe only an impulsive and not consciously intended squeeze of the trigger, made all too possible by the ready availability of handguns? Firearms evidently are very easy to get in many parts of the United States. Joseph Treaster (1992), the journalist who interviewed Andre, observed that

> "guns are so plentiful in New York these days that teen-agers don't even have to buy them. . . . Andre merely told a friend—a crack dealer—that he was being menaced by boys from another neighborhood, and the dealer handed him the .32-caliber revolver. (Treaster, 1992)

And yet, one should also recognize that Andre apparently was inclined to commit violence. According to the interviewer, not only had the youth sought out the weapon, but he also had a long history of antisocial behavior. The boy admitted to more than 120 muggings by the time he was 14 years old, often (Andre said) because "it was fun." Perhaps Andre's aggressive personality is also revealed by his seeming lack of remorse after the killing. From the story he told, his initial reaction at realizing the other boy was dead had not been sorrow or guilt, only concern as to how he could get out of the trouble he was in.

Treaster (1992) believed Andre's situation was far from unique. He noted that

> a decade ago, when an exchange of punches was a probable outcome of two boys' facing each other down, 10 to 15 percent of the teen-agers who got into serious trouble in New York were carrying guns. Now, state officials estimate, it is 60 to 65 percent. (p. 1)

This case is illustrative of several of the questions that are pursued in this chapter. First, I examine the magnitude of the problem: How prevalent are firearm-produced homicides generally, and has there indeed been the rise in the killing of youngsters by youngsters using guns, as Treaster (1992) indicated? After these statistics are presented, I discuss the availability of firearms and the reasons for handgun ownership. Andre claimed he had gotten his revolver for protection. Do most people who have handguns think these weapons will enhance their safety from violence? This question leads to the main arguments that have been raised against legal restrictions on the ready availability of handguns. It is often believed, for example, that laws preventing citizens from obtaining guns interfere with their right to protect themselves. What is the evidence that gun control will increase honest citizens' likelihood of becoming the victims of lawless criminals? And more pertinent to the purposes of this chapter, I consider whether gun control laws might lessen the chances that youngsters such as Andre would engage in violent crimes. Some behavioral scientists believe that these legal restrictions are futile; people engage in violence, it is said, because they want to do so. So, for these skeptics, if Andre had not had the revolver, he would have used another weapon to assault his victim. Is it not possible, though, that guns have a special quality that makes them different from other objects such as knives or clubs and that increases the likelihood of a fatal outcome? Firearms can kill at a distance, of course, but they might also have other effects. Maybe Andre had not really wanted to shoot the other boy and the homicide had actually been inadvertent. Could the gun in his hand somehow have led him to pull the trigger?

The Magnitude of the Problem

A truly adequate understanding of the effects of firearms on American youths requires an examination of all of the benefits and costs guns bring to young people. Although some attention is given to the possible gains for society arising from the widespread availability of firearms, I leave it to others to spell out these social advantages in detail and instead focus on the possible damage firearms do to the social order. However, even this latter consideration is somewhat restricted. Much of my attention is given to guns and youth. Guns hurt and kill a large number of children in the United States. The U.S. Justice Department (Mason & Proctor, 1992) has reported that in the late 1980s, teenagers were actually more likely than adults to be the victims of violent crimes and that many of these offenses were carried out with guns. As one indication of how many children are affected by these weapons, in 1986 12% of all of the deaths of children under 19 years of age in the United States were caused by gunshot wounds. However, in order to narrow the coverage to reasonable dimensions for this book, I have little to say about child victims generally and disregard youthful suicides with guns altogether even though the suicide rate for children has doubled in the past 30 years, with almost all of this increase being firearm related (Koop & Lundberg, 1992). Instead of taking up these other matters, as important as they are, I concentrate here mostly on the violent actions of armed male youths toward others. It should also be noted in this connection that I do not discuss violence committed by females, generally because relatively few serious violent crimes in this country are carried out by women (Berkowitz, 1993; Kellermann & Mercy, 1992).

Statistics On Youthful Homicides

Partly because there is not good information on how many crimes of all kinds have been committed over the years by youngsters with guns,[1] but primarily in order to highlight the problem of armed children more dramatically, I begin this chapter by examining some of the statistics on youthful homicides. This violence should first be placed in context, however.

National statistics. As noted in chapter 1 of this book, the United States has the highest homicide rate of any western industrialized country, so high that homicide is the 10th leading cause of death in this nation (Novello, 1992). Guns clearly have a major role in these crimes. Firearms were used in about 60% of the murders and nonnegligent manslaughters reported to the police in the United States between 1964 and 1989 (Jamieson & Flanagan, 1989, p. 446; Maguire & Flanagan, 1991, p. 378). Similarly, according to the U.S. National Center for Health Statistics (as cited in the *New York Times*, Apr. 3, 1992, p. A11), between 1983 and 1986 the rate of homicides with guns in this country was 44.6 per million people compared with a rate of 31.3 per million for homicides without guns. This latter survey also indicated that the firearm homicide rate in the United States during this period was approximately twice as high as that in France (21.4 per million), more than 5 times greater than that in Canada (8.4 per million), and more than 10 times higher than the Switzerland rate (4.0 per million). A disproportionate share of the U.S. deaths were produced by handguns. Basing their information on Federal Bureau of Investigation reports, the Coalition to Stop Gun Violence (1992) estimated that handguns were used in about half of all murders committed in the United States in 1991 even though they evidently constitute only about one third of all of the firearms circulating in the country.

---

[1]The Uniform Crime Reports (UCRs) issued by the U.S. Department of Justice (1992) provided an analysis of juvenile crimes (crimes committed by 10–17-year-olds) for the first time in 1992. This latest report indicated that juveniles were arrested for violent offenses in 1990 at a rate of 430 per 100,000, a 27% increase over the 1980 rate. The UCRs noted that there was a rise in violent crimes in all races, social classes, and lifestyles.

Homicides involving young males. More important here are the figures for young men. In the late 1980s, homicide was the second leading cause of death for 15–24-year-old men in the United States, with firearms, mostly handguns, being involved in more than three quarters of the adolescent killings (Fingerhut, Kleinman, Godfrey, & Rosenberg, 1991). According to Fingerhut and Kleinman (1990) of the National Center for Health Statistics, the firearm-produced homicide rate for this age group in the United States during this period was 21.9 per 100,000, 4–73 times higher than the comparable rate in other industrialized nations (e.g., 1.4 per 100,000 in France, 2.9 per 100,000 in Canada, and 1.4 per 100,000 in Switzerland).

Increase in youthful homicide rates. The high homicide rates just reported might rise even more in future years as indicated by extrapolation from past statistics. Making use of the Compressed Mortality File, a county-level database maintained by the National Center for Health Statistics, Fingerhut, Ingram, and Feldman (1992a) recently calculated that there were changes between 1979 and 1989 in the rate at which 15–19-year-old White and African American youths (taken together) fatally shot someone. After a small decline in firearm-related homicide rates from 1979 to 1984, the adolescent gun-produced homicide rate increased through 1987 and then rose even more sharply from 1987 through 1989. Overall, there was a 61% rise in homicides by shootings for these teenagers.[2] Interestingly, this jump was not paralleled by a corresponding increase in non-firearm-involved killings; the rate of homicides produced by objects other than guns actually decreased 29% during this period. As a matter of fact, considering White and African American youths together, the researchers concluded that for older adolescents "firearm homicides. . . . [have] been increasing more rapidly than any other cause of death" (Fingerhut et al., 1992a, p. 3048).

The growth in teenage homicides by guns has been sharper in metropolitan than in nonmetropolitan areas. According to Fingerhut et al. (1992a), the 1989 firearm homicide rate was twice the 1984 rate in the metropolitan strata, whereas the 1989 and 1984 rates were similar in the outlying sections of the counties. However, the researchers put this latter finding in perspective:

> It is important to remember that, even though the firearm homicide rates in the fringe, medium, small, and nonmetropolitan strata are so much lower than in the core stratum, they are still very high compared with firearm homicide rates in other countries. (Fingerhut, 1992a, p. 3053)

Differences between African American and White youths in homicide rates. Research dating at least as far back as Wolfgang's (1958) classic investigation of Philadelphia homicides has consistently shown that African Americans are

---

[2]According to the latest Uniform Crime Reports (UCRs; U.S. Department of Justice, 1992), there was a 79% increase in the number of juveniles (youngsters aged 10–17 years) committing murder with guns over the decade of the 1980s. In 1990, the UCRs reported, approximately 3 out of 4 youthful murderers used a gun. Several authorities have suggested that the sharp rise in firearm homicides in recent years is partly due to the increasing use of automatic and semiautomatic weapons.

greatly overrepresented in homicide cases (for further discussion, see chapter 3 in this book). This overrepresentation has persisted to this day. Thus, out of the approximately 10,000 incidents in 1987 in which a single offender killed one person and the slayer's race was known to the police, about half of the killers were African Americans, even though this racial group constitutes only about 12% of the U.S. population. The victims were also apt to be African American; 88% of the persons slain by African Americans in these one-on-one cases were also African American (Jamieson & Flanagan, 1989, p. 453).

Young African American males are largely responsible for this high killing rate in their group. According to a report from the Centers for Disease Control (1991), the homicide rate for African American males aged 15–24 from 1978 through 1987 was four to five times higher than for same-aged young African American females and five to eight times higher than for young White males of the same age cohort. What is even more troublesome for American society, these gun-related homicide rates have increased in recent years. The U.S. Department of Justice's (1992) latest Uniform Crime Reports showed that the arrest rate for murder jumped 145% over the decade of the 1980s for African American youths between 10 and 17 years old, compared with a 48% increase for Whites of this age and, interestingly, a 45% *decline* for other races.

Here again, it should be noted that guns are heavily involved in these statistics. According to the Centers for Disease Control (1991), firearms accounted for about three fourths of the killings by African American youths. Also of interest, just as all segments of U.S. society have not had the same rise in shooting homicides, teenagers are killed by guns more frequently in some areas of the nation than in others. The Fingerhut et al. (1992a) data indicate that large metropolitan areas are the most dangerous sections of counties for 15–19-year-olds; for this age group in the late 1980s, the firearm homicide rate was four to six times higher in these highly populated sections than in the less populated parts of the counties. And, again, within the large metropolitan areas the rate of killings with guns was almost seven times higher for African American than for White teenage males.[3]

Fingerhut, Ingram, and Feldman (1992b) at the Center for Health Statistics have also reported that there have been some changes in which U.S. counties have the highest firearm homicide rates by African American teenagers. On examining the records for 80 U.S. counties having at least 10,000 African American males between 15 and 19 years of age, they found that in the early 1980s, the 5 counties with the highest rates of African American teenagers killing someone with a gun were (in order) Wayne, Michigan; Los Angeles, California; Baltimore City, Maryland; Fairfield, Connecticut; and Brooklyn, New York. By the late 1980s, however, the firearm homicide rates were highest for African American youths in Washington, DC; Los Angeles, California; Wayne, Michigan; Brooklyn, New York; and Duval, Florida. The increase in the gun killing rate over the decade was truly substantial for these counties.

---

[3]It is worth noting that there are some areas of the nation in which White youths have a very high rate of violent crimes. Greenberg, Carey, and Popper (1987) reported that the overall violent death rate for young White males in the six most dangerous rural counties in western states was 13% higher than the comparable African American rate in six eastern inner cities.

Two other points should also be made. For one, although Fingerhut et al. (1992b) noted that Baltimore and Fairfield did not experience a statistically significant rise in firearm homicide rates for African American youths over this relatively brief period, they advised that these and other comparatively low rate communities not to be complacent. There seem to be "crime waves" in at least some areas, they said. In the early 1980s, the rate of homicides by shooting in Duval County, Florida, was significantly lower than the average for all 80 counties in the study, but by the end of the decade the gun killing rate for African American teenagers in this county was in the upper quartile of the sample. The past is not always a clear guide as to the future. Matters could get worse.

And then, too, it is important to realize that the great majority of the people slain by African Americans are also African Americans of about the same age as the killers. The epidemiologists of the Centers for Disease Control have calculated that homicide has now become the leading cause of death for young African American men between 15 and 24 years of age (Centers for Disease Control [CDC], 1991). Indeed, these killings have become so frequent that one CDC scientist was quoted as saying,

> in some areas of the country it is now more likely for a black male between his 15th and 25th [birthdays] to die from homicide than it was for a United States soldier to be killed on a tour of duty in Vietnam. (*New York Times*, December 7, 1990)

These all too frequent deaths and deaths brought about mostly by shootings are, of course, deplorable, and other chapters in this book consider at length the factors that seem to contribute to the high rates of criminal violence by African American youths (see chapters 3 and 4 in this book). This matter obviously is very important, and it is discussed later. To anticipate the argument, it is suggested that the high homicide rate in this segment of U.S. society is not due primarily to a widespread "subculture of violence," as some writers have proposed (e.g., Wolfgang, 1958), but is more apt to grow out of a number of personal, social, and economic influences that can, and do, affect both Whites and African Americans.

Is Firearm Availability Primarily Responsible for the High U.S. Homicide Rate?

Although the rise in the firearm homicide rate is commonly linked to narcotics (to either the illegal substances' effect on the drug takers or to battles between rival dealers), some authorities contend that many violent crimes actually have little if anything to do with illegal substances. They do not deny that drug use and violence are often intertwined, but in their view these two forms of antisocial conduct are also frequently separate. Findings reported by Block and Block (1993) provide one example of how antisocial violence is often not directly related to drug trafficking. According to the National Institute of Justice-sponsored investigation of gang violence in Chicago from 1987 to 1990, gang fights in that city's high-crime neighborhoods were much more likely to arise from territorial conflicts (in which "disrespect" was shown for another gang's "turf") than from disputes over the sale and use of drugs. Authorities studying criminal violence maintain that the ready availability of guns is a major contributor to the growing number of shooting deaths (cf. Marwick, 1992). In this connection, the Block and Block study also noted that almost all of the homicides stemming from the gang fights were caused by firearms, which increasingly were high-caliber automatic or semiautomatic in nature.

Guns certainly abound in America. The National Rifle Association maintains that private citizens have approximately 200 million firearms (AMA Council on Scientific Affairs, 1992), whereas other estimates range from 100 to 400 million (Cook, 1982). It has also been estimated that 40%–50% of U.S. households have guns, with half of these owning a handgun (Cook, 1982). With the United States being flooded by so many lethal weapons, the advocates of gun control insist that firearms must play some part in the violence plaguing U.S. society.[4]

Relation between firearm availability and homicide rates. Various statistics have been cited in support of this argument, many having to do with the relation between homicide rates in various regions or countries and their population adjusted number of firearms. Only two examples are mentioned here. In the first of these, Sloan et al. (1988) compared the number of gun-related deaths from 1980 through 1986 in Seattle and Vancouver. Although these two cities are relatively comparable in size and at that time had similar unemployment rates, income, general educational levels, and even burglary and robbery rates, they differ markedly in the ease with which their residents can obtain firearms. Whereas Seattle permits pistols to be acquired legally for self-defense and also has little regulation of the recreational use of firearms, its neighboring Canadian city does not regard self-defense as a legal reason for buying a gun and also allows firearms to be discharged only in licensed shooting clubs. As a result of the tighter restrictions on firearm ownership in Vancouver, Sloan et al. concluded, its residents were much less likely to be murdered than the people living in Seattle. More specifically, although the rate of killings involving knives was comparable in the two communities (3.5 and 3.1 per 100,000 in population for Vancouver and Seattle, respectively), a Vancouver resident was much less apt to be shot to death than a person residing in the American city (1.0 per 100,000 population compared with a rate of 4.8 per 100,000 in Seattle).

The other type of evidence often cited has to do with national comparisons. Therefore, in one of the studies along these lines, Lester (1991) reported that his measure of the availability of firearms in each of 16 European nations was significantly associated with the firearm homicide rates in these countries. An

---

[4]Because of space limitations, I cannot adequately summarize the many thoughtful discussions of the pros and cons of gun control and also cannot summarize all of the highly relevant investigations bearing on this controversy. The following section is necessarily highly selective and undoubtedly omits a number of relevant considerations. Readers interested in a fuller discussion would do well to consult, among other sources, Cook (1982), Kates (1984), Nisbet (1990), Wright (1988), Wright, Rossi, and Daly (1983), and Zimring and Hawkins (1987).

informal examination of published statistics that I carried out supports this relationship. When the 10 Western industrialized nations are rank ordered in terms of the percentage of their households having firearms—(in order) the United States, Switzerland, Canada, Finland, France, Australia, Belgium, West Germany, England and Wales, and The Netherlands—(based on data from the National Center for Health Statistics reported in the *New York Times*, April 3, 1992), there is a significant positive correlation between this ordering and the countries' ranking in terms of their rate of homicides with guns ($r = .61, p < .05$).

Some questions about these findings. Results such as these obviously do not show unequivocally that the number of guns in a given area has a causal influence on its rate of violent crimes. As Kleck (1990) observed, "virtually all of [this] evidence . . . could just as easily be interpreted as showing that more gun violence leads to more people acquiring guns for defensive purposes rather than the reverse." (pp. 123–124).

And then too, one does not know how many people in any given population use the readily available firearms in an illegal manner. Skeptics such as Kleck (1990) pointed out that "most people who own guns do not use them for inflicting harm on others. . . . The mere possession of a gun alone does not necessarily make deadly violence more likely." (p. 124). Gun ownership among the law abiding, the skeptics maintain, has no effect on the homicide rate. Society should be concerned only with those violence-prone persons who possess firearms.

Do only a relatively few youths make use of the available firearms? Even if one assumes that the reported correlations between firearm availability and homicide rates stem from the former's causal impact on the latter, one can ask whether the findings, regarding firearm homicides in general and based on community and national comparisons, can truly be generalized to teenage shootings. Moreover, however valid such a generalization might be, it does not necessarily mean (extending Kleck's, 1990, last-mentioned argument) that ever larger numbers of youths will take advantage of the readily available firearms and use them. The greater number of guns may only heighten the chances that these weapons will be used by a *relatively few* violence-prone adolescents.

There are good reasons to believe that this is indeed the case. A mounting body of research (cf. Weiner, 1989) has shown that a fraction of the general population accounts for far more than their share of the violent crimes committed in the United States. Furthermore, whereas the great majority of offenders commit violent crimes at a low rate over time, a small proportion commit these offenses at a high rate. On the basis of this evidence as well as his own youth surveys, Elliott (cited in Marriott, 1992) estimated that "50 to 60 percent of all crime is being committed by 5 to 7 percent of young people from the ages of 10 to 20 years old" (p. E6). These highly antisocial persons typically do not specialize in the ways they break the law. Thus, in one of his studies, Elliott found that seriously violent (three or more designated violent offenses within a year's time) male and female youngsters ... reported involvements in a wide range of infractions. For example, in 1976 the youths averaged per year, among their other offenses, 8.3 serious violent incidents, 65.2 minor assaults, 51.0 public disorders, 6.5 felony thefts, and 49.7 drug sales. (Weiner, 1989, p. 92)

Is it possible somehow, one might ask, to restrict these violence-prone persons' access to firearms?

The problem of assault weapons. Advocates of gun control usually also highlight the increasing deadliness of the firearms in widespread circulation in the United States. As one psychiatrist observed,

> Certainly the "Saturday night specials" were cheap and available, but they were also inaccurate. These newer weapons tend to be easier to use, more accurate, and can deliver more firepower than most weapons in circulation. They are far more lethal and require little or no experience to use effectively. (cited in Marwick, 1992, p. 2993)

Although the U.S. Bureau of Alcohol, Tobacco, and Firearms has estimated that there are 1–3 million assault weapons in private hands in this country, there is no good information as to how many violent crimes are committed with these guns or even how many injuries and deaths they have caused. Nevertheless, authorities are greatly concerned about the spread of these particular firearms. According to the California Attorney General's Office (cited in AMA Council on Scientific Affairs, 1992, p. 3068), semiautomatic firearms are now the weapon of choice for drug gangs, and these guns are increasingly used where crack cocaine is endemic. The American Medical Association has been so troubled by the growing number of traumatic firearm injuries that it has labeled assault weapons a "public health hazard" and has called for restrictions on "the sale and private ownership of large-clip, high-rate-of-fire automatic and semiautomatic firearms" (AMA Council on Scientific Affairs, 1992, p. 3067).

Why Adolescents Own Firearms

Few systematic studies have examined the specific motives propelling violence-prone youths to obtain firearms. Nevertheless, the results obtained in several recent surveys of gun ownership by teenagers suggest that handguns are more apt to be possessed by socially deviant youths than by their more "normally" acting counterparts even in those sections of the country in which firearms and hunting are fairly common.

In the first of these investigations, Sadowski, Cairns, and Earp (1989) surveyed the firearm ownership of a biracial cohort of male and female adolescents in two school districts of a southeastern state. The researchers found, as would be expected in this area, that gun ownership, including the ownership of a handgun, was associated positively with hunting experience, being a male rather than a female, and being White rather than African American. More interestingly, though, the only demographic characteristic having a significant association with the reported ownership of a handgun was school enrollment status; the male teenagers who dropped out of school were more than three times likely to say they owned one or more handguns than were their nondropout counterparts.

The second study, by Callahan and Rivara (1992), was much more detailed. In this survey of 11th-grade students in Seattle high schools, about 6% of the respondents reported owning handguns, and only about 25% of these particular youngsters indicated that they possessed these weapons mainly for hunting or target shooting. Also unlike the previously cited southeastern state study, the ownership rate in this later, more urban, sample was almost twice as high for African American students as for their White schoolmates.[5] However, even with these differences from the Sadowski et al. (1989) survey, other findings seem to be consistent with the earlier investigation's observation that handgun owners tended to be school dropouts: A disproportionately high fraction of the handgun owners (controlling for age, racial or ethnic group membership, and gender) were socially deviant in that they admitted having been expelled or suspended from school, having sold drugs, and having engaged in assault and battery.

The researchers also went beyond ownership to look at the teenagers' general access to handguns. Overall, the lower the students' social status, the more likely they were to say guns were readily available to them, with a larger proportion of the African American youths (49%) than the White youths in the sample (34%) reporting that they could obtain such a weapon easily. Again, those who claimed this easy access, compared with the other adolescents, also were more apt to indicate a tendency to engage in socially problematic behavior such as selling drugs and being assaultive (including having struck a teacher), and were more likely to have been convicted of a crime and expelled or suspended from school.

Also of interest, of course, is what the teenagers did with the handguns. Almost 50% of the handgun owners said they had carried a weapon to school, compared with about 7% of all of the male adolescents in the sample, and one third of the owners even indicated that they had shot at another person.

Guns in school. Although this Seattle survey provides little information as to why teenage urban youths own handguns—except to indicate that recreation is probably not the main reason[6]—it does suggest that a sizable fraction of youthful handgun owners might bring their weapons along with them when they go to school. If this is the case, a report from the CDC (cited in Callahan & Rivara, 1992) provides a rough idea as to the possible magnitude

---

[5]On the basis of the relatively low rate of adolescent firearm homicides in Seattle, Washington, the investigators suggested that firearms are probably less prevalent among this city's youths than among the teenage residents of other urban centers.

[6]Wright, Rossi, and Daly (1983) indicated that firearms are more apt to be owned for crime-oriented reasons in urban than nonurban areas.

of this problem for the United States as a whole. Twenty percent of the 9th–12th-grade students queried in this investigation said they had carried a weapon in the month before the survey, and in about a fifth of these cases, the weapon was a firearm, usually a handgun. Assuming that some of the gun-carrying youths had taken their weapon with them to school on at least some occasions, this would suggest that guns are not at all uncommon in many U.S. schools.[7]

These figures could well be higher in many urban neighborhoods according to a 1991 study carried out by Joseph Sheley and James Wright for the U.S. Department of Justice (Rowley, 1993). In this investigation of youths at 10 inner-city high schools in California, Illinois, Louisiana, and New Jersey, 22% reported owning guns and 12% said they carried weapons routinely. However, many of those who did not personally own a firearm evidently could get one fairly easily; over half of the students indicated that they could borrow a gun from a family member, and more than 33% said that they could get a gun on the streets if they wanted to do so. However, whatever the percentage of students having easy access to weapons, this study, like the others, showed that there was an association between gun possession and participation in antisocial behavior, in this case involvement in drug dealing.

Unfortunately, many of the youths who take guns to their schools do more than just show them off in a more or less innocent display of "show and tell"; they may, at least, use their firearms to intimidate other students. Some quantitative data point to such a possibility. For more than a decade now, investigators at the University of Michigan's Institute for Social Research have asked national samples of high school seniors whether they had been threatened with a weapon during the past year (summarized in Maguire & Flanagan, 1991). Generally speaking, from 1979 to 1990 about 22% of the African American seniors answered they had been so threatened with a weapon without having been hurt and about 6% said they had been injured. These figures averaged about 16% and 4%, respectively, for the White seniors. What all of this means, of course, is that American schools are now increasingly being viewed as possibly dangerous places. A 1991 survey of school crimes reported by the U.S. Department of Justice (cited by Coalition to Stop Gun Violence, 1992) indicated that more than one third of all public high school students and more than 25% of those enrolled in private schools feared being attacked in or on their way to school.

These school altercations obviously can result in serious injuries or even deaths. Combing through published news stories in U.S. papers, the Center to Prevent Handgun Violence (1990) found that 65 students were killed with guns in U.S. schools between 1986 and 1990 and that another 201 people were severely wounded. Also testifying to the magnitude of this problem, in recent years there evidently have been so many gun-related incidents in supposedly peaceful schoolrooms and hallways that it is now distressingly commonplace to have firearm detectors mounted at school entranceways. The Los Angeles

---

[7]Adding to these troubling statistics, a 1990 survey conducted by the National Center for Educational Statistics (cited in Coalition to Stop Gun Violence, 1992) indicated that about 1 out of 5 eighth graders has seen a weapon at school.

school district, for one, has decided to initiate spot checks with portable metal detectors in many of its schools (Hull, 1993).

The Controversy: Cons and Pros of Gun Control

The Arguments Against Gun Control

Academics and other professionals critical of gun control legislation are not necessarily dissuaded by these and other statistics questioning the easy availability of firearms. In the next section I summarize some of the more important points they make, concentrating on matters that are most relevant to the problem of guns in the hands of youth and ignoring the legal issues involved in this controversy.

Three of the major arguments these scholars raise against gun control legislation have to do with (a) the already great numbers of guns circulating in the United States, (b) the protective value of these weapons, and (c) the possibility that other types of weapons will be used if firearms are not available (see, e.g., Wright, 1988; Wright, Rossi, & Daly, 1983). Taking these propositions up briefly in order, I have already referred to the estimates that there are 100–400 million guns in private hands in this country. More than a decade ago, when U.S. citizens probably had many fewer firearms than they now possess, Wright et al. (1983) held that the existing stock of guns was already adequate "to supply all conceivable criminal purposes for at least the entire next century" (p. 320). With this vast pool of weapons now present, the critics say, it is too late to achieve any significant reduction in the availability of firearms and too late to lessen whatever ill effects arise in society from the widespread possession of guns.

The second argument against gun control is voiced frequently by both laypersons and academic scholars: Firearms are perceived to provide protection against criminal intruders. According to some public opinion surveys, the great majority of gun owners say that they have these weapons in their home at least partly for protection, whereas at least 20% of them identify "self-defense" as their most important reason for owning a gun (cf. Kellermann & Reay, 1986).[8]

Adding to their objections, many of the critics contend that restrictions on the availability of firearms would lead only to the substitution of other weapons. Wolfgang (1958) expressed this substitution argument in his classic study of Philadelphia homicides: "Few homicides due to shooting could be avoided," he maintained, "merely if a firearm were not immediately present. . . . The

---

[8]On the basis of a number of studies inquiring into weapon ownership *generally*, Wright, Rossi, and Daly (1983) maintained that there actually is no good evidence that fear of crime promotes gun ownership. However, when Smith and Uchida (1988) more recently examined the factors predictive of the reported purchase of a gun *for self-protection* in three U.S. metropolitan areas, they found that the households claiming to own a gun for self-protection tended to have been victims of a crime in the past, thought there was a risk they would be criminally victimized in the future, or had little confidence that the police would protect them from crime.

offender would select some other weapon to achieve the same destructive goal" (p. 83). Indeed, Kleck (cited in Zimring & Hawkins, 1990a, p. 168) went even further along these lines. He contended that if people could not obtain handguns to protect themselves—or to commit a violent crime—they would seek more lethal weapons such as rifles and shotguns, and this would result in an even higher death rate.

Although these arguments seem persuasive, it is worth looking at some of the available research bearing on them. However, because there are many more studies pertinent to the complex issues than can be adequately examined here (cf. Nisbet, 1990), the review to follow is admittedly highly selective.

"There Are So Many Guns"

Whatever the exact number, it is clear that there are now several hundred million guns in private hands in the United States and that it is impossible, legally and practically, to confiscate these weapons. Opponents of gun control sometimes go beyond these figures to maintain that even if steps could be taken to reduce the vast size of this private arsenal, criminals would still be able to obtain firearms. The great majority of law-abiding citizens might give up their weapons as ordered by some gun control law, but surely, the opponents say, felons would not comply because they repeatedly violate other laws.

More than this, the gun control skeptics add, as long as there are *any* firearms, or *any* handguns, in circulation, criminals would still buy them. Wright (1988) estimated that a handgun could be obtained in any major U.S. city in only a few hours for about $100. Robbers certainly would be willing and able to pay much more than this if fewer handguns were available and the price of these weapons on the street were to increase markedly because they could recoup the purchase price in just a few "transactions."

There is another side to this argument, however. The greater the number of guns that are readily available in society, the lower would be their price, permitting more and more people to obtain deadly weapons from legal or illegal dealers. Even youngsters might be able to buy them cheaply if their price was low enough. Indeed, handguns apparently were so plentiful in Andre's neighborhood that an acquaintance gave him one free. Restricting the number of handguns might at least raise their price above the ability of youths to pay.

Do Guns Bring Safety?

Any consideration of the costs and benefits of the plentiful supply of firearms in the United States obviously must take the protective value of these weapons into account. However, it is difficult to establish a clear and relatively unequivocal estimate of the degree to which private citizens are more secure because of the guns in their possession. The research into this question has yielded often contradictory findings, and plausible arguments have been raised on both sides of the issue (cf. Nisbet, 1990). In this section I delve only briefly into this controversy.

Do firearms deter robberies and assaults? Kleck (1988), one of the leading opponents of gun control legislation, presented evidence indicating that handguns in private hands have a significant value in crime control. As an example, according to a 1981 national public opinion survey of registered voters that he cited, about 6% of the adult respondents said that either they or another member of their household had used a handgun for self-protection or to protect property in the preceding 5 years. Buttressing these results, Kleck also reported his analysis of the criminal incidents between 1979 and 1985 that were recorded in national crime surveys during this period. This analysis indicated, among other things, that victims who used guns or other weapons to resist robbers were less likely to lose their property than were other victims who did nothing or who used other means of resistance. Moreover, Kleck also reported, in the case of both robberies and assaults, those victims who had used a firearm for protection were less likely to have been either attacked physically or injured than were other persons not using a gun, including those who did not resist at all. Considering all this as well as other findings, Kleck (1988) maintained that "civilian ownership and defensive use of guns has a deterrent and social control effect on violent crime and burglary" (p. 289).

Yeager (1990) presented opposing evidence in a report endorsed by the U.S. Conference of Mayors. He agreed with Kleck (1988) that firearms might lead to effective resistance to robberies. However, he also went on to say that a "study of robberies in eight American cities suggests that in only 3.5 percent of the victimizations did the person have the opportunity to use a weapon for self-protection" (Yeager, 1990, p. 215). Furthermore, Yeager (1990) added, "data from Chicago and New York indicate that a victim's weapon (if it is a firearm) is more likely to be stolen than used against the robber" (p. 215). His conclusion from all of the research he examined was that "ownership of handguns by private citizens for self-protection against crime appears to provide more of a psychological belief in safety than actual deterrence to criminal behavior" (Yeager, 1990, p. 234).

A comprehensive examination of more than 1,800 homicides has shown findings consistent with Yeager's (1990) argument. When A. L. Kellermann et al. (1993) looked into the circumstances surrounding the homicides in three counties in Ohio, Tennessee, and Washington (state), they noted that most of the people killed were family members or close acquaintances, not unwelcome intruders, and that there was no evidence that guns in the home had any protective benefits. All in all, they concluded, "rather than confer protection, guns kept in the home are associated with an increase in the risk of homicide by a family member or intimate acquaintance" (Kellerman, 1993, p. 1084). This relationship held for women as well as men and for Whites as well as African Americans. The data also suggested that in many of these instances, the killing had grown out of a fight in the home. Because the households involved in a homicide were more likely than matched nonhomicide homes to have had a firearm kept loaded or unlocked (see Kellerman et al., 1993, p. 1087), someone involved in the conflict might have quickly taken up the readily available weapon and fired it in a fit of temper. I say more about this type of impulsive outburst of violence later.

Unintended costs. Whatever benefits accrue from the use of guns to deter crime, there is another consideration that should also be weighed in the balance: the unintended injuries and deaths that firearms can also bring. Innocent persons are at times shot as well as criminal intruders.

Many of these unwanted shootings occur in the home, as a number of studies attest, sometimes because children have found the guns the homeowners keep for defense against criminal intruders. Wintemute, Feret, Kraus, Wright, and Bradfield (1987) documented some of these tragic instances in an examination of the 88 cases in California between 1977 and 1983 in which one child had unintentionally shot another youngster to death. They found that the shooting had usually occurred at home and that the firearm had been kept loaded, mostly for self-protective reasons, in about half of these residential killings.

Kellermann and Reay (1986) have added to this picture of nondefensive shootings. Their investigation of the 743 firearm-related deaths in King County, Washington, from 1978 through 1983 indicated that more than 50% of them had occurred in the residences where the firearms, usually handguns, were located. The great majority of all of the cases were suicides, and only about 2% of the others could be regarded as legally justified (i.e., to have been the result of an attempt at self-protection). All in all, Kellermann and Reay (1986) calculated that there were about 43 legally unjustified deaths by firearms (suicides, accidents, and criminal homicides) for every incident in which a gun was used to kill someone in self-defense. They then asked "whether keeping firearms in the home increases a family's protection or places it in greater danger" (Kellermann & Reay, 1986, p. 1560). In summary, considering all of the incidents in which people other than criminals have been shot in places of residence, there seems to have been good reason for Yeager (1990) to conclude that "a gun kept in the home for self-protection is far more likely to cause serious injury or death to family and friends than to an intruder. Children and young adults are most vulnerable to firearms misuse" (p. 215).

In recent years there has also been an apparent increase in another kind of unintended consequence: the random wounding or killing of bystanders. According to Sherman, Steele, Laufersweiler, Hoffer, and Julian (1989), there has been a rapid rise in the number of innocent people who are shot, not because they are in conflict with the person wielding the gun, but only because they just happen to be "in the wrong place at the wrong time." Sherman et al. looked at all of the instances between 1977 and 1988 in which residents of Boston, Los Angeles, New York City, and Washington, DC, were hit by bullets not intended for them personally, as recorded in the major newspapers in these communities. Although there were not many of these incidents, in numerical terms,[9] enough took place so that there had been a marked jump over the years in the number of bystanders shot apparently by chance in all

---

[9]To give the reader an idea of how often these shootings occurred, 105 apparently innocent persons were shot in Los Angeles in 1986 through 1988, for an annual rate of 1 shooting per 94,000 persons, whereas 120 bystanders were hit by bullets in New York City during this period, for an annual rate of 1 per 175,000.

four cities. Intriguingly, though, the shootings were not alike in these four areas. A good proportion of the New York and Los Angeles victims evidently had been wounded or killed by bullets fired into crowds, whereas in Boston and Washington the victims were more apt to have been lone bystanders hit by stray bullets.

Sherman et al. (1989) believed that the rise in crowd shootings in New York and Los Angeles was more apt to have been the result of fighting between individuals or gangs motivated by their struggle for pride and vengeance than by battles between drug dealers competing for markets. They also thought that many of the victims in these cities had been shot by automatic or semi-automatic weapons fired more or less indiscriminately.

Will Other Weapons Be Substituted?

Finally, coming to the last-mentioned antigun control proposition, the idea that people will turn to other weapons if handguns (or other firearms) were unavailable, basically assumes that violent actions are largely intentional. Wolfgang (1958) clearly had made this assumption when he held that the offender would select some other weapon to achieve his or her destructive goal.[10]

The difference between instrumental and hostile aggression. However popular this general notion might be, it fails to recognize the important difference between hostile aggression on one hand and instrumental aggression on the other. Together with other experimentally oriented investigators of aggression (e.g., Feshbach, 1964), I have long maintained that these two kinds of aggression arise in different ways and have different primary objectives (e.g., Berkowitz, 1978, 1993). Although all aggression is intended to injure or destroy some target, this injury is in service of some other aim in the case of instrumental aggression. Examples are the drug dealer who kills a competitor trying to sell narcotics in his or her "territory," the youth who assaults a member of a rival gang in order to gain his or her friends' approval, and even the homeowner who shoots a criminal in self-defense. In all of these instances, the action is instrumental to fulfilling some other purpose besides the victim's

---

[10]The findings reported by Sloan et al. (1988) in their previously cited comparison of the gun-related deaths in Seattle and Vancouver are inconsistent with the substitution thesis. Because guns were not readily available in Vancouver, this notion would hold that the persons intent on killing someone would then use knives or other such weapons. However, as I noted earlier, the rate of killings involving knives was comparable in Vancouver and Seattle (both approximately 3 per 100,000).

Other evidence contrary to the substitution thesis has been published by Loftin, McDowall, Wiersema, and Cottey (1991). In 1976, Washington, DC, had adopted one of the most restrictive handgun policies in the nation, one prohibiting the purchase, sale, and possession of handguns by civilians who had not owned a weapon previously. Until 1988, when conflicts over the crack market increased sharply, the result apparently was a reduction of about 25% in the number of homicides by firearms and a decline of about 23% in the number of gun-caused suicides. This decrease was *not* accompanied by a rise in the number of homicides and suicides by other means, as the substitution proposition would have predicted.

injury, such as attaining money or social status, or the elimination of a threat. In the case of hostile aggression, by contrast, the attacker is mainly interested in injuring or killing the victim.

Some highly aggressive individuals have learned to enjoy hurting others for the intrinsic pleasure this brings them, and they may sometimes seek another's injury even when they are relatively calm. However, when most people are assaultive, information that they have hurt their victim is gratifying only if they are angry at that time (cf. Baron, 1977). This behavior has often been referred to as emotional aggression (Berkowitz, 1993). The attackers carrying out this form of aggression may well be reinforced afterward by social approval, the lessening of noxious circumstances, or other extrinsic rewards, but their primary objective is to inflict pain or even destruction. It has been argued repeatedly (e.g., Berkowitz, 1974, 1993) that the assaults made by emotionally aroused people are apt to be somewhat impulsive, carried out with relatively little thought and planning, and governed to some extent by particular kinds of stimuli in the surrounding situation. Therefore, as was indicated earlier, a provoked individual could well attack his or her victim more strongly than he or she had consciously intended after he or she sees a stimulus in the surrounding situation that reminds him or her of the gratifications he or she had previously obtained through aggression (Berkowitz, 1974, 1993). I say more about this kind of phenomenon later.

Instrumental and hostile aggression in crimes of violence. This distinction between instrumental and hostile aggression has also been recognized by several students of criminal violence (e.g., Block, 1977; Weiner, 1989). Block (1977), as a notable example, held that "instrumental" offenses are not the same as "impulsive" ones. In the former case the victim and offender "are both acting to maximize their benefits and minimize their costs," whereas there is little weighing of costs and benefits, "only the desire to injure or kill," in the case of impulsive behavior (Block, 1977, p. 9). Block (1977) proposed that many robberies are best viewed as instrumental actions because "the robber usually does not intend to injure the victim but to take his property. Aggravated assault, on the other hand, is a crime whose goal is the serious injury or death of a participant" (p. 9). Of course, these are the "pure" forms of these two types of crime, and the instrumental–hostile aggression distinction can blur at times. The instrumental feature of robberies is occasionally overriden by emotionally impulsive aggression, Block (1977) pointed out (p. 10), perhaps because of the victim's resistance or maybe because of the weapon in the offender's hand. When this happens, the robber may be so carried away by emotion that he or she fires his or her gun with relatively little thought and injures the victim. From Block's perspective, though, robberies are usually acts of instrumental, not emotional, aggression.

Block (1977) believed his analysis of violent crimes in Chicago supported his interpretation of aggravated assaults as emotional actions. Looking at the murders that occurred in Chicago from the late 1960s to the mid-1970s, he concluded that homicides and other injury-producing violent crimes were more alike than is widely supposed and that the people arrested for killing someone were similar in important respects to those who were arrested for aggravated assaults. They were not very different kinds of personalities, he maintained, with the killers being more violently disposed and more determined to take a life. Instead, for Block, the homicides and aggravated assaults had arisen in somewhat similar ways but had different outcomes only because of the kinds of weapons or objects that were at hand. Zimring and Hawkins (1990b) have made the same argument, largely on the basis of an examination of the deaths from gun and knife attacks in Chicago from 1965 through 1967. According to these writers,

> the circumstances in which most [of these] homicides were committed suggested that they were committed in a moment of rage and were not the result of a single-minded intent to kill . . . also the choice of a gun did not appear to indicate such intent. The similarity of circumstances in which knives and guns were used suggested that the motive for an attack did not determine the weapon used. (Zimring & Hawkins, 1990b, p. 172)

Using the distinction between instrumental and hostile aggression, one would say that Block (1977) and Zimring (1968; also compare Zimring & Hawkins, 1990b) regarded many serious acts of violence as relatively impulsive outbursts carried out under intense emotion rather than planned instrumental behaviors. Thinking only of their desire to hurt (or kill, depending on the intensity of their feelings), and not considering the possible long-term consequences, the offenders made use of whatever was available. In the absence of a gun, the highly aroused persons could only employ whatever other weapon was available—a knife, a club, their fists and/or their feet—but serious injury and death was unlikely with such implements. If a firearm was present, however, they might have used it, and if they happened to shoot accurately, death could have resulted.

Zimring (1968) has long interpreted many domestic homicides as emotionally generated crimes of violence. More than a generation ago, he suggested that most of the persons who killed someone they knew well probably had not planned to murder their victim beforehand. Rather, he proposed, they might have become intensely enraged in an altercation with that individual and then struck at him or her using whatever weapon was close at hand, such as a handgun.

Some of the gun control skeptics have questioned whether emotional aggression of the kind just discussed is as common as Block and Zimring implied. Wright (1988; Wright et al., 1983) acknowledged that "crimes of passion certainly occur," but he argued that many murders are actually more thought out than the idea of impulsive aggression would suggest. Wright et al. (1983) pointed to a study of family homicides in Kansas City to buttress their position. This investigation showed that in 85% of the cases there had been a domestic quarrel in the past 5 years that was so intense the police were called and that the fighting was so frequent in half of the families that the police had been summoned five or more times. This means, Wright et al. (1983) maintained, that the killing was "the culminating event in a pattern of interpersonal abuse, hatred, and violence that stretches well back into the history of the parties involved" (p. 193). Because of this kind of history, it is argued, the wife who shot her abusive husband might have planned to kill him the next time he beat her, and when he then did assault her, used the weapon she had previously intended to use.[11]

Obviously, no one can say with any assurance how many crimes of violence, in or outside of the family, are the planned actions conjectured by Wolfgang, Wright, and others, and how many are the relatively impulsive aggressive reactions that Berkowitz, Block, and Zimring have postulated. Berkowitz (1993) has suggested, answering the Wright group, that an abused woman's prior history of having been battered frequently could increase the chances that a later beating would provoke her into an explosive outburst of rage. In her fury, her usual restraints are overwhelmed, and she might then strike out at her oppressor with little thought, using whatever weapon is available. Consistent with such a possibility, the National Crime Survey sponsored by the U.S. Justice Department indicates that more than half of all the handgun produced murders and nonnegligent manslaughter incidents in the United States between 1979 and 1987 occurred during arguments or fights (Jamieson & Flanagan, 1989).

In my view, this notion of emotionally generated acts of violence is pertinent to Andre's case mentioned at the start of this chapter. One cannot be certain, of course, but it could be that the boy had not consciously intended to shoot the other youngster, as he claimed. His high level of emotion arousal, compounded of anger, fear, and sheer excitement, conceivably could have heightened the likelihood that he would pull his gun's trigger unintentionally.

Instrumental aggression in attacks on strangers. It may be that other violent crimes can also be understood better by recognizing this difference between instrumental and hostile aggression. Consider homicide cases in which the victims are strangers rather than people previously known to the perpetrators. Williams and Flewelling (1988) showed that strangers are more likely to be killed in instrumental than in more emotionally involved "conflict" crimes (cf. Berkowitz, 1993). This finding is consistent with other crime statistics, for example, homicide data from 1987. In the approximately 18,000 murders and nonnegligent manslaughters known to the police in that year, the person slain was unknown to the killer in almost 33% of the clear felony crimes (which are likely to be instrumental in nature), as compared with only 7%–11% of the emotional conflict situations (Jamieson & Flanagan, 1989, p. 448). One of Zimring's observations is relevant here. Commenting on the growing number of homicides involving persons not known to each other, he noted that, "while the majority of all killings are still committed by friends or acquaintances of the victim, a substantial and increasing proportion of the 'new American homicide' is the outcome of robbery—an event [in which] victim and offender are usually strangers" (Zimring, 1979, p. 31). On the basis of all this,

---

[11]In this connection, Wright (1988) commented that, "in denying the wife of an abusive man the right to have a firearm, we may only be guaranteeing her husband the right to beat her at his pleasure. [Because firearms increase the woman's power vis-à-vis the man] one argument against 'stricter gun control' is thus that a woman should have as much right to kill her husband as a man has to kill his wife" (p. 32).

then, it seems reasonable to assume that violent offenses involving strangers, such as robberies, are apt to be largely instrumental rather than more emotional actions, whereas assaults on relatives, friends, or acquaintances are more likely to be fairly emotional in nature.

This possibility, that violent crimes against strangers are apt to be largely acts of instrumental aggression, is pertinent to an interesting article by Kleck and McElrath (1991). Their sophisticated statistical analysis of data from national crime surveys and homicide reports for the period from 1979 to 1985 indicated that the presence of a firearm in a criminal encounter (a) lessened the chance that an open physical attack would be made in the situation and (b) if such an attack were carried out, reduced the probability that an injury would result. The offenders' deadly weapons had apparently enhanced their ability "to terrify, to coerce compliance with [their] demands" (Kleck & McElrath, 1991, p. 673) and thus made it unnecessary for them to attack their victims physically. The researchers did find, as one would expect, that the presence of a firearm increased the likelihood of death *once there was an injury*, but still, they concluded that "the overall net effect of the availability of guns on the probability of the victim's death is very close to zero" (Kleck & McElrath, 1991, p. 669). In support of their findings, Kleck and McElrath (1991) also reported that "at least nine prior studies have found, without exception, that robbers armed with guns are less likely to injure their victims than robbers without guns" (p. 673).

This evidence of a gun-produced reduction in crime injuries is noteworthy, but it may be important to keep in mind the nature of the crimes. Concerned that "violent incidents among persons who knew one another were most likely to go unreported" (Kleck & McElrath, 1991, p. 676), Kleck and McElrath believed they would have a less biased sample of violent offenses if they restricted themselves to incidents involving strangers. As reasonable as this restriction might be, however, the exclusive use of stranger crimes conceivably could have resulted in an overrepresentation of instrumental actions and a comparative slighting of the more impulsive emotionally generated offenses. Most people do often weigh the costs and benefits of the actions they might undertake on a given occasion. If they are relatively calm when they hold a firearm, or when they face a gun pointed at them, they might then become even more cautious so that they carefully consider the advantages and disadvantages of each step they might take. The question is, though, what might happen if they are highly aroused at the time? Would they still be so thoughtful and deliberate?

The "Weapons Effect" and Impulsive Aggression

In basic agreement with the position taken by such writers as Block and Zimring, the analysis offered here holds that many, but certainly not all, acts of aggression are in large part impulsive reactions propelled by intense internal agitation. I have argued elsewhere (e.g., Berkowitz, 1989, 1990, 1993) that this aggression-impelling emotion arousal can be generated by a wide variety of unpleasant occurrences and not only by threats, insults, and frustrations.

It is quite conceivable, then, that any fear and anxiety that Andre had experienced when he faced his antagonist had intensified whatever aggressive inclinations he possessed at that time. More pertinent to this chapter, as I have also proposed (e.g., Berkowitz, 1974, 1993), the aggressive urge can also be heightened by stimuli in the surrounding situation that have either an aggressive or decidedly unpleasant meaning for the person. If an individual is intent on hurting someone, the presence of such a stimulus can cause him or her to strike harder at the victim than was consciously intended.

The "weapons effect" first reported by Berkowitz and LePage (1967) is an excellent, but by no means the only, example of how aggression-related stimuli can strengthen activated aggressive tendencies. Guns (or other objects) having a clear aggressive meaning can give the people holding or seeing them hostile ideas and may even set aggression-related motor reactions into operation, so that they then impulsively lash out at their target, especially if they are ready to attack someone at the time and their restraints against aggression are correspondingly weak.

Although several failures to replicate the original Berkowitz and LePage (1967) findings have been reported, there now have been an impressive number of studies supporting the existence of such a weapons effect (cf. Berkowitz, 1993; Carlson, Marcus-Newhall, & Miller, 1990; Turner, Simons, Berkowitz, & Frodi, 1977). Moreover, these confirming investigations have been conducted in other countries, including Belgium, Croatia, Italy, and Sweden, as well as the United States (cf. Berkowitz, 1993).

I do not offer a detailed review of this research here. Several points are worth mentioning, however. For one, even the sight of photographed guns can produce the weapons effect if people are suitably uninhibited at the time. Experiments in both Belgium (Leyens & Parke, 1975) and Italy (Caprara, Renzi, Amolini, D'Imperio, & Travaglia, 1984) have demonstrated that unrestrained persons can become more punitive than they otherwise would have been after only looking at pictures of firearms. Second, according to several experiments conducted by Turner and his associates (see Berkowitz, 1993), the heightened aggression can be displayed even when the research participants are not aware they are taking part in an experiment. In one of these studies, Turner and his colleagues set up a booth at a college-sponsored carnival and invited students to throw sponges at a target person, allowing them to "assault" the target as often as they wished. More sponges were hurled at the target when a rifle was lying nearby than when no weapon was present.

Other research indicates that "real" as well as playful aggression can be affected by the presence of a weapon and that the effect is influenced by the context within which the firearm is seen. Thus, Zuzul (cited in Berkowitz, 1993) found that Croatian schoolchildren fought with each other more (on a playground but in a nonplayful manner) after being exposed to guns than after not seeing a weapon, but primarily if the situation was relatively permissive for the display of aggression. And then, too, Turner, Layton, and Simons (1975) reported that the sight of a rifle was most likely to draw expressions of impatience and annoyance from frustrated relatively high-status persons when the gun appeared in a hostile rather than friendly context. In this experiment, the weapon effect was revealed only indirectly, not in a direct attack on some target. Yet another study also pointed to a restrained and indirect effect arising from the sight of a gun. According to Boyanowsky and Griffiths (1982), Canadian motorists who were stopped by a police officer for a traffic violation were more likely to exhibit anger in their facial expressions, and also reported stronger felt anger shortly afterward, when the officer carried a pistol at his or her side than when he or she did not have a gun.

Considering all of the research on the weapons effect, it does appear that a firearm's presence can lead to stronger aggressive reactions than otherwise would have occurred. However, it is also clear, as Kleck and McElrath (1991), among others, have properly noted, that this heightened aggressivity is not always manifest. People will restrain their aggressive inclinations, even if these have been intensified by the sight of a gun, if they believe their aggression will be punished in some way or is inappropriate in the given situation. Furthermore, the weapon may not activate any aggressive reactions at all if it is associated with sports and recreation,[12] or provokes strong anxiety and moral repugnance, and thus does not have an aggressive meaning.

Still, the many studies showing the weapons effect demonstrate that guns *are* often regarded as aggressive objects (i.e., as things that can be used to deliberately hurt and kill others), that restraints against aggression are not always operative, even in presumably well-socialized middle-class university students, and that many persons believe it would be appropriate for them to assault someone else under certain circumstances. Given these facilitating factors, the weapon might well increase the probability of an open attack at times, especially if the firearm is held by an individual who has few inhibitions against aggression and is characteristically prone to violence and who also happens to be emotionally aroused on that occasion.

All of this seems to apply to Andre and other youths like him. Judging from the journalist's description, the boy probably had a fairly strong aggressive disposition as well as weak restraints against many different forms of antisocial conduct. He evidently was a tinderbox that could easily explode into violence. This readiness to become aggressive could have been heightened even further by his excitement, anger, and possibly also fear, as he confronted his antagonist. The revolver in his hand might have been the extra spark that then ignited an extra strong aggressive impulse. Consciously, Andre might have only wanted to scare the other youngster by pointing the gun at him, just as he told the journalist. However, the weapon he held was not the truly neutral object that the opponents of gun control often suppose. It had an aggressive meaning for him and thus could have stimulated a relatively involuntary aggressive reaction—the trigger could have pulled his finger.

Some Observations About the Role of Guns in Developing Violence Proneness

Any truly comprehensive account of the relation between weapons and youth obviously should consider why some youngsters are so ready to use

---

[12]Epstein (1979) suggested that people who have had prior experience with guns in hunting and target shooting are less apt to display heightened aggressivity in the presence of a firearm.

firearms when they are in conflict with others and what influence, if any, exposure to guns in childhood has on the development of violent inclinations. Unfortunately, however, there is little good research on these questions, although several studies provide suggestive answers to the second one dealing with the formation of violence proneness. In looking into this latter issue, I first offer a reason why children's play with guns, even toy ones, might, under the right circumstances, facilitate the development of an enduring disposition toward aggression. Then, after this, and adding to the discussion of the high rate of criminal violence by African American youths in other chapters of this book, I suggest that the frequent sight of people being shot might contribute to the violent inclinations apparently possessed by too many African American teenagers.

Children's Play With Toy Guns

As most American parents know all too well, many of their very young sons want to play with toy weapons. The boys insistently ask their mothers and fathers for plastic soldiers, aggressive superheroes, water pistols, make-believe assault guns, and videogames, all of them objects by means of which they can fantasize their destruction of their enemies. Does this seemingly innocent play have an influence on the growing child?

One possible consequence can be ruled out: It is highly unlikely that the make-believe aggression displayed in the play with the toy weapons will bring about a beneficial cathartic reduction of the children's existing aggressive tendencies. Indeed, controlled experiments looking into the short-run effects of play with aggressive toys indicate that the youngsters are far more apt to become aggressively stimulated for a time afterward than to become more peaceful and cooperative (Feshbach, 1956; Turner & Goldsmith, 1976). The violent game evidently primes aggression-related ideas and feelings (Anderson & Ford, 1986) and may even activate aggressive action tendencies (cf. Berkowitz, 1993).

But what about the long-term consequences of frequent play with toy weapons? Although I do not know of any investigations that have sought an answer to this specific question, I can reasonably suppose what might happen under some conditions: Even though the children are engaged only in fantasy aggression, their make-believe play could be an opportunity for them to find that aggression brings rewards. If they do learn this, their existing aggressive inclinations could well be strengthened so that they are then persistently more likely to be assaultive in other, more realistic situations (Bandura, 1973). Suggesting just such a process, Walters and Brown (1963) showed that youngsters who were rewarded intermittently when they hit a toy in a series of learning trials were subsequently more aggressive in their interactions with another child. Huesmann (1988) referred to the process of rehearsing scripts for behavior. As scripts for aggressive behaviors become more firmly entrenched through rehearsal, and as the aggressive behaviors suggested by these scripts are reinforced during play, it becomes more likely that the aggressive scripts will generalize to realistic situations.

However, even though make-believe aggression with toy weapons could possibly have the unfortunate effects I have just identified, this does not necessarily mean that parents should rigidly reject all of their boys' insistent pleas for toy guns and aggressive games. It might be, for one thing, that the youngsters delight in these games at least partly because the play enables them to think of themselves as having some control and mastery over mysterious forces in their lives. Parents might then try to help their offspring think of the fantasy activity as control achieving more than sheer killing and destroying. Above all, they would do well to avoid praising and approving their children's make-believe aggression.

Why Do Black Males Have a High Rate Of Criminal Violence? Possible Effects of Childhood Exposure to Violence

At least some of the relatively high rate of criminal violence by young African American males might be due to their frequent exposure to guns in childhood, an exposure that weakens their faith in traditional social institutions of law and order and that might even teach them that weapons can be useful in their dealings with others. It might be helpful to contrast this possibility with other interpretations.

Are there subcultures of violence? Some sociologists and criminologists (e.g., Wolfgang, 1958) have attributed the high rate of criminal violence by young African Americans to widely shared attitudes and beliefs within the poverty-stricken African American community that presumably are favorable to aggression. According to these writers, working-class African Americans (and people in other poor minority groups as well) often live in a "subculture of violence" that teaches them to interpret challenges, altercations, and other interpersonal difficulties as provocations and then calls on them to respond aggressively to these perceived threats. Young men residing in this kind of subculture thus presumably are easily angered by the threats they frequently see in the world around them and then are quick to react aggressively, in large part because they are expected to behave in this manner; the only way they supposedly can receive the respect and approval they desire when they are provoked is to lash out at the offending party.

However plausible and popular this thesis might be, research has now shown it is deficient as a *general* explanation of the high violence rates in various U.S. minority groups. A relatively few segments of minority communities, such as members of violent teenage gangs and youngsters like Andre, might hold the attitudes and values that are said to make up the violent subculture. The persons in these narrow segments could subscribe to a code of conduct that emphasizes the inviolability of their "manhood" and defines interpersonal difficulties as deliberate challenges to their personal identity. They could also be so alienated from the mainstream society that they repudiate many of its rules and ideals, as Andre apparently had done. Contrary to the original subculture of violence thesis, however, studies have shown that violence-supporting beliefs and attitudes are not as widespread throughout the poorer sections of society, including African American communities, as Wolfgang (1958) and others had supposed (cf. Berkowitz, 1993; Erlanger, 1974).

Effects of growing up in a disorganized, violent environment. If this relatively small, antisocial, and violence-prone segment of economically deprived minority groups is responsible for a good many serious violent crimes in society, as indicated earlier, the question is, How do they acquire the attitudes, beliefs, and personal qualities that are conducive to aggression? A wide variety of influences undoubtedly play a part (cf. Berkowitz, 1993), but I point here only to the possible ill effects of life in a harsh, uncaring, and violent environment.

Few members of the relatively affluent U.S. middle-class realize how many inner-city children continually witness extreme violence in their poverty-stricken and socially disorganized neighborhoods. The statistics here are truly startling, according to a study conducted by Richters and Martinez (1993). On interviewing children and mothers residing in a low-income, "moderately violent" section of Washington, D.C., these investigators found that 72% of the fifth and sixth graders had seen violence done to someone else, with 11% having watched someone be shot, and 6% having been shot at themselves.

This observed killing and shooting must be highly disturbing to children. In Richters and Martinez's (1993) Washington research, there was a significant relation between the amount of violence the children had witnessed and the number of adverse psychological symptoms they had. If one can generalize from studies of children in war-torn Beirut (cf. Berkowitz, 1993), it is reasonable to suggest that this emotional turmoil probably contributes to the development of violent tendencies. In summary, the guns these inner-city youngsters see used on others could help form the personal qualities that lead to a readiness to use firearms themselves.

What all this seems to mean, then, is that urban African Americans and other poor minority youths do not have to be explicitly taught to favor violence in order to become aggressively disposed. Suffering from mistreatment and frustrations in their homes and in their surroundings, and living in a relatively lawless, disorganized, and violent social environment full of disturbances that also provide an abundance of aggressive models, they could easily come to regard their social world as a dangerous, lawless place in which only crime and aggression pay. Ready access to guns could heighten the already too high chances that they will assault and even kill someone else.

Conclusion

Public Policy Implications

My review has summarized some of the disagreements between those favoring and those opposing the imposition of greater restrictions on the availability of firearms. In particular, there is a substantial difference of opinion, and no clear and consistent evidence on one side or the other, as to whether the huge arsenal of weapons in private hands in the United States is a deterrent to crime or a source of considerable danger. However, many of the proponents and opponents actually agree on one point: the desirability of keeping guns away from that small fraction of the population, including violence-prone youths such as Andre, who are particularly apt to use these lethal weapons in an illegal and destructive manner. Thus, in an interview with the *New York Times*, Wright, the critic of gun control said, "the Holy Grail of gun control has been to find some way to keep guns out of the hands of the bad guys, yet leave the legitimate firearms-owning population alone" (*New York Times*, April 3, 1992, p. A11).

Is it possible to achieve this compromise? It is true, of course, as was already noted, that there are now several hundred million firearms in U.S. households, and it is unlikely that this number can be reduced substantially. Many guns will therefore always be available for both legal and illegal use. Yet, according to the U.S. Bureau of Alcohol, Tobacco, and Firearms (as reported in the *New York Times*, April 3, 1992), in New York City at least, most of the guns that have been seized by the police were manufactured in the past 5 years. Restricting the availability of new weapons might therefore help somewhat in reducing the number of firearms that could be used for criminal purposes. Perhaps more important, as was mentioned earlier, any substantial lessening of the handguns in widespread circulation probably would raise their street market price substantially and thus might aid in keeping them away from aggressively disposed youths such as Andre. The U.S. Public Health Service has stated that "children and firearms are a dangerous and impermissible combination" and called for a reduction in "weapon-carrying by adolescents" (Mason & Proctor, 1992). It could be that the only way to achieve this reduction, especially in the number of handguns and semiautomatic weapons to which youths have access is to diminish the supply of new weapons of these types to ordinary citizens.

Questions for Further Research

In this chapter I have singled out a relatively small group of highly antisocial adolescents as being especially troublesome for society. I suggested that these particular youngsters account for a greatly disproportionate share of the violent crimes now occurring in the United States, implying (perhaps overoptimistically) that psychologists can do a great deal to lessen the level of serious violent offenses in America by somehow reducing or controlling their proclivity to antisocial conduct. It obviously is very important to determine how much of the mounting rate of assaults and homicides in the United States is indeed due to this group of persistently violence-prone youths and whether their numbers are growing.

However many crimes they perpetrate, these teenagers are clearly a serious problem, and much more has to be known about them. What are they like, and what forces have shaped their personalities and aggressive disposition? Some questions come readily to mind about their personality qualities.

Interested observers and newspaper stories such as the one about Andre mentioned at the beginning of this chapter repeatedly refer to the violent youngsters' seeming indifference to the suffering of others. Is this apparent callousness truly characteristic of seriously violence-prone youths? Moreover, one might also ask, how do their personal characteristics operate when they assault someone? Does their callousness mean only that they have few inhibitions against aggression so that their attacks are carried out more or less dispassionately and for instrumental reasons? Or, as was suggested in discussing Andre, are they also highly reactive emotionally so that many of their assaults are emotional acts of hostile aggression that they are unable to restrain? Clearly, there is much more to learn about these youths.

References

AMA Council on Scientific Affairs. (1992). Assault weapons as a public health hazard in the United States. *Journal of the American Medical Association, 267,* 3067–3070.

Anderson, C. A., & Ford, C. M. (1986). Affect of the game player: Short-term effects of highly and mildly aggressive video games. *Personality and Social Psychology Bulletin, 12,* 390–402.

Bandura, A. (1973). *Aggression: A social learning analysis.* Englewood Cliffs, NJ: Prentice Hall.

Baron, R. A. (1977). *Human aggression.* New York: Plenum.

Berkowitz, L. (1974). Some determinants of impulsive aggression: Role of mediated associations with reinforcements for aggression. *Psychological Review, 81,* 165–176.

Berkowitz, L. (1978). Is criminal violence normative behavior? Hostile and instrumental aggression in violent incidents. *Journal of Research in Crime and Delinquency, 15,* 148–161.

Berkowitz, L. (1989). The frustration–aggression hypothesis: An examination and reformulation. *Psychological Bulletin, 106,* 59–73.

Berkowitz, L. (1990). On the formation and regulation of anger and aggression: A cognitive–neoassociationistic analysis. *American Psychologist, 45,* 494–503.

Berkowitz, L. (1993). *Aggression: Its causes, consequences, and control.* New York: McGraw-Hill.

Berkowitz, L. & LePage, A. (1967). Weapons as aggression-eliciting stimuli. *Journal of Personality and Social Psychology, 7,* 202–207.

Block, R. (1977). *Violent crime.* Lexington, MA: Heath.

Block, R., & Block, C. R. (1993, November). Street gang crime in Chicago. *National Institute of Justice research in brief.* Washington, DC: U.S. Department of Justice.

Boyanowsky, E. O., & Griffiths, C. T. (1982). Weapons and eye contact as instigators or inhibitors of aggressive arousal in police-citizen interaction. *Journal of Applied Social Psychology, 12,* 398–407.

Callahan, C. M., & Rivara, F. P. (1992). Urban high school youth and handguns. *Journal of the American Medical Association, 267,* 3038–3042.

Caprara, G. V., Renzi, P., Amolini, P., D'Imperio, G., & Travaglia, G. (1984). The eliciting cue value of aggressive slides reconsidered in a personological perspective: The weapons effect and irritability. *European Journal of Social Psychology, 14,* 313–322.

Carlson, M., Marcus-Newhall, A., & Miller, N. (1990). Effects of situational aggression cues: A quantitative review. *Journal of Personality and Social Psychology, 58,* 622–633.

Center to Prevent Handgun Violence. (1990). *Caught in the crossfire: A report on gun violence in our nation's schools.* Washington, DC: Center to Prevent Handgun Violence.

Centers for Disease Control. (1991). Weekly morbidity and mortality report. *Journal of the American Medical Association, 264,* 183–184.

Coalition to Stop Gun Violence. (1992). *Handgun fact sheet.* Washington, DC: Author.

Cook, P. J. (1982). The role of firearms in violent crime: An interpretive review of the literature. In M. E. Wolfgang & N. A. Weiner (Eds.), *Criminal violence* (pp. 236–291). Beverly Hills, CA: Sage.

Epstein, J. F. (1979). *Prior experience with firearms can mitigate the weapons effect.* Unpublished master's thesis, Tulane University, New Orleans, LA.

Erlanger, H. S. (1974). The empirical status of the subculture of violence thesis. *Social Problems, 22,* 280–292.

Feshbach, S. (1956). The catharsis hypothesis and some consequences of interaction with aggressive and neutral play objects. *Journal of Personality, 24,* 449–462.

Feshbach, S. (1964). The function of aggression and the regulation of aggressive drive. *Psychological Review, 71,* 257–272.

Fingerhut, L. A., Ingram, D. D., & Feldman, J. J. (1992a). Firearm and nonfirearm homicide among persons 15 through 19 years of age. *Journal of the American Medical Association, 267,* 3048–3053.

Fingerhut, L. A., Ingram, D. D., & Feldman, J. J. (1992b). Firearm homicide among black teenage males in metropolitan counties. *Journal of the American Medical Association, 267,* 3054–3058.

Fingerhut, L. A., & Kleinman, J. C. (1990). International and interstate comparisons of homicide among young males. *Journal of the American Medical Association, 263,* 3292–3295.

Fingerhut, L. A., Kleinman, J. C., Godfrey, M. S., Rosenberg, H. (1991). Firearm mortality among children, youth, and young adults 1–34 years of age, trends and current status: United States, 1979–1988. *Monthly Vital Statistics Report, 39,* 1–15.

Greenberg, M. R., Carey, G. W., & Popper, F. J. (1987). Violent death, violent states, and American youth. *Public Interest, 87,* 38–48.

Hull, J. D. (1993, February 8). The knife in the book bag. *Time,* p. 37.

Huesmann, L. R. (1988). An information model for the development of aggression. *Aggressive Behavior, 14,* 13–24.

Jamieson, K. M., & Flanagan, T. J. (Eds.). (1989). *Sourcebook of criminal justice statistics: 1988.* Washington, DC: U.S. Government Printing Office.

Kates, D. B., Jr. (Ed.). (1984). *Firearms and violence: Issues of public policy.* San Francisco: Pacific Institute for Public Policy Research.

Kellermann, A. L., & Mercy, J. A. (1992). Men, women, and murder: Gender-specific differences in rates of fatal violence and victimization. *Journal of Trauma, 33,* 1–5.

Kellermann, A. L., & Reay, D. T. (1986). Protection or peril? An analysis of firearm-related deaths in the home. *New England Journal of Medicine, 314,* 1557–1560.

Kellermann, A. L., Rivara, F. P., Rushforth, N. B., Banton, J. G., Reay, D. T., Francisco, J. T., Locci, A. B., Prodzinski, J., Hackman, B. B., & Somes, G. (1993). Gun ownership as a risk factor for homicide in the home. *New England Journal of Medicine, 329,* 1084–1091.

Kleck, G. (1988). Crime control through the private use of armed force. *Social Problems, 35,* 1–19.

Kleck, G. (1990). The relationship between gun ownership levels and rates of violence in the United States. In L. Nisbet (Ed.), *The gun control debate* (pp. 123–129). Buffalo, NY: Prometheus Books.

Kleck, G., & McElrath, K. (1991). The effects of weaponry on human violence. *Social Forces, 69,* 669–692.

Koop, C. E., & Lundberg, G. D. (1992). Violence in America: A public health emergency [Editorial]. *Journal of the American Medical Association, 267,* 3075–3076.

Lester, D. (1991). Crime as opportunity: A test of the hypothesis with European homicide rates. *British Journal of Criminology, 31,* 186–188.

Leyens, J.-P. & Parke, R. (1975). Aggressive slides can induce a weapons effect. *European Journal of Social Psychology, 5,* 229–236.

Loftin, C., McDowall, D., Wiersema, B., & Cottey, T. (1991). Effects of restrictive licensing of handguns on homicide and suicide in the District of Columbia. *New England Journal of Medicine, 325,* 1615–1620.

Maguire, K., & Flanagan, T. J. (Eds.). (1991). *Sourcebook of criminal justice statistics: 1990.* Washington, DC: U.S. Government Printing Office.

Marriott, M. (1992, September 13). On meaner streets, the violent are more so. *New York Times,* p. E6.

Marwick, C. (1992). Medical news and perspectives. *Journal of the American Medical Association, 267,* 2993.

Mason, J., & Proctor, R. (1992). From the assistant secretary for health, US Public Health Service. *Journal of the American Medical Association, 267,* 3003.

Nisbet, L. (Ed.). (1990). *The gun control debate.* Buffalo, NY: Prometheus Books.

Novello, A. C. (1992). From the surgeon general, US Public Health Service. *Journal of the American Medical Association, 267,* 3007.

Richters, J. E., & Martinez, P. (1993). The NIMH Community Violence Project: I. Children as victims of and witnesses to violence. *Psychiatry, 56,* 7–21.

Rowley, J. (1993, December 13). Availability of guns to young. *Capital Times.*

Sadowski, L. S., Cairns, R. B., & Earp, J. A. (1989). Firearm ownership among nonurban adolescents. *American Journal of Diseases of Children, 143,* 1410–1413.

Sherman, L. W., Steele, L., Laufersweiler, D., Hoffer, N., & Julian, S. A. (1989). Stray bullets and "mushrooms": Random shootings of bystanders in four cities, 1977–1988. *Journal of Quantitative Criminology, 5,* 297–316.

Sloan, J. H., Kellermann, A. L., Reay, D. T., Ferris, J. A., Koepsell, T., Rivara, F. P., Rice, C., Gray, L., & LoGerfo, J. (1988). Handgun regulations, crime, assaults, and homicide: A tale of two cities. *New England Journal of Medicine, 319,* 1256–1262.

Smith, D. A., & Uchida, C. D. (1988). The social organization of self-help: A study of defensive weapon ownership. *American Sociological Review, 53,* 94–102.

Treaster, J. B. (1992, May 24). Teen-age murderers: Plentiful guns, easy power. *New York Times,* p. 1.

Turner, C. W., & Goldsmith, D. (1976). Effects of toy guns and airplanes on children's antisocial free play behavior. *Journal of Experimental Child Psychology, 21,* 303–315.

Turner, C. W., Layton, J. F., & Simons, L. S. (1975). Naturalistic studies of aggressive behavior: Aggressive stimuli, victim visibility, and horn honking. *Journal of Personality and Social Psychology, 31,* 1098–1107.

Turner, C. W., Simons, L. S., Berkowitz, L., & Frodi, A. (1977). The stimulating and inhibiting effects of weapons on aggressive behavior. *Aggressive Behavior, 3,* 355–376.

U.S. Department of Justice. (1992). *Uniform crime reports.* Washington, DC: U.S. Government Printing Office.

Walters, R. H., & Brown, M. (1963). Studies of reinforcement of aggression: III. Transfer of responses to an interpersonal situation. *Child Development, 34,* 563–571.

Weiner, N. A. (1989). Violent criminal careers and "violent career criminals": An overview of the research literature. In N. A. Weiner & M. E. Wolfgang (Eds.), *Violent crime, violent criminals* (pp. 35–138). Newbury Park, CA: Sage.

Williams, K. R., & Flewelling, R. L. (1988). The social production of criminal homicide: A comparative study of disaggregated rates in American cities. *American Sociological Review, 53,* 421–431.

Wintemute, G. J., Teret, S. P., Kraus, J. F., Wright, M. A., & Bradfield, G. (1987). When children shoot children. *Journal of the American Medical Association, 257,* 3107–3109.

Wolfgang, M. (1958). *Patterns in criminal homicide.* Philadelphia: University of Pennsylvania Press.

Wright, J. D. (1988). Second thoughts about gun control. *The Public Interest, 91,* 23–39.

Wright, J. D., Rossi, P. H., & Daly, K. (1983). *Under the gun: Weapons, crime, and violence in America.* Chicago: Aldine.

Yeager, M. G. (1990). How well does the handgun protect you and your family? In L. Nisbet (Ed.), *The gun control debate* (pp. 213–238). Buffalo, NY: Prometheus Books.

Zimring, F. E. (1968). Is gun control likely to reduce violent killings? *University of Chicago Law Review, 35,* 721–737.

Zimring, F. E. (1979). Determinants of the death rate from robbery: A Detroit time study. In H. M. Rose (Ed.), *Lethal aspects of urban violence.* Lexington, MA: Heath.

Zimring, F. E., & Hawkins, G. (1987). *The citizen's guide to gun control.* New York: Macmillan.

Zimring, F. E., & Hawkins, G. (1990a). On the needle-in-the-haystack and the deadly long gun. In L. Nisbet (Ed.), *The gun control debate* (pp. 165–169). Buffalo, NY: Prometheus Books.

Zimring, F. E., & Hawkins, G. (1990b). Firearms and assault: "Guns don't kill people, people kill people." In L. Nisbet (Ed.), *The gun control debate* (pp. 170–176). Buffalo, NY: Prometheus Books.

13

Mob Violence: Cultural–Societal Sources, Instigators, Group Processes, and Participants

Ervin Staub and Lori H. Rosenthal

The 1992 Los Angeles riots, which were instigated by mob violence by the police and consisted of mob violence by citizens, have once again drawn attention to this complex phenomenon. In this chapter, we examine the instigating events, background conditions, and social and psychological processes that generate mob violence, as well as the characteristics of individuals who participate in it, with a particular focus on youth. Examples from the urban riots of the 1960s in the United States will be emphasized somewhat, partly because of the relative wealth of information about them and partly because we know that the majority of the participants in them were young people. However, we also consider other examples of mob violence, including the 1992 L.A. riots, soccer violence, prison riots, revolutionary mob violence, lynchings, and "wildings," most of which involve a substantial number of youth. Of special concern, despite limited information, are the reasons for the apparently high frequency of participation by youth in mob violence and the impact of mob violence on both participating and nonparticipating youth. Recommendations for research and for policies aimed at reducing mob violence are also made.

Introduction

Definitions

Before examining mob violence, a number of terms need to be defined and differentiated: crowd, mob, riot, mob violence, group violence, and crowd behavior. According to a dictionary of psychology (Chaplin, 1985), a *crowd* is a collection of people who share a common interest and whose emotions may be easily aroused; a *mob* is a crowd acting under strong emotional conditions that often lead to violence or illegal acts. The primary distinction between a crowd and a mob is the level of shared emotion, as well as some forms of (destructive) expressions of emotion. A riot is an instance of *mob violence*, with the destruction of property or looting, or violence against people. A *riot* has been described as an unplanned or unorganized expression of anger or rage, without a focused goal (Levin & Mehlinger, 1975). However, riots can and often do serve shared motives of the participants.

Milgram and Toch (1969) suggested that mob violence is primarily expressive or serves a need for immediate gratification, whereas social movements are organized efforts to change social conditions (which may be the background activators of mob violence). However, we contend that crowd behavior and mob violence can also be vehicles of social movements.

We use the term *group violence* to refer to organized violence by the state or by a dominant group in society against subgroups that are defined as enemies. Examples of group violence include genocide, mass killing, and the systematic use of torture (Staub, 1989). *Crowd behavior*, in the form of marches, demonstrations, and mob violence can also be part of group violence (e.g., the Kristallnacht in Nazi Germany).

There is little discussion in the literature of the minimum number of people that constitutes a crowd or mob. LeBon (1895) wrote that at certain moments half a dozen men might constitute a psychological crowd. One of the defining criteria for Spilerman (1970) in studying racial disorders was the involvement of 30 or more individuals. In contrast, Morgan and Clark (1973) defined a crowd as "the activities of four or more people acting in concert" (p. 612), although the disorders they actually studied involved 50 or more people.

The level of prior organization of violent groups varies. Truly spontaneous mob action and highly organized group violence represent end points of a continuum. Our consideration of mob violence includes the behavior of groups that have an informal organization, but not of groups, like the SS in Nazi Germany, that have carried out institutional mandates.

Theories and Data Regarding Crowd Behavior

There are a number of theories of crowd behavior: LeBon's early, influential theory (1895), psychoanalytic theory (Freud, 1922), emergent norm theory, and contagion and convergence theories among others. Given space limitation and the fact that good reviews exist (Milgram & Toch, 1969; Perry & Pugh, 1978), these theories are not reviewed comprehensively here, but some of their concepts are used in the analysis of mob violence.

The actual study of crowd behavior and mob violence has been limited, presumably because of the difficulties in conducting such research. Social and psychological processes studied in laboratory research, like deindividuation, have been used in interpreting crowd behavior but not directly studied in crowds. The use of interviews with participants in mob violence requires investigators to deal with questions of credibilitiy, limited or inaccurate awareness, and self-serving reporting. Participant observation, which can be used especially for repeated forms of mob violence like soccer violence (Buford, 1992), has been rare.

Most research on mob violence has been sociological in its focus on the social conditions that create riots and its use of demographic information about participants. As is shown in this chapter, only limited information is available about the psychological characteristics and processes of participants and the actual social influence processes in crowds.

A Conception of Group Violence

A conception of group violence has been developed and applied to the analyses of four instances of group violence—the Holocaust, the genocide of the Armenians in Turkey, the autogenocide in Cambodia, and the disappearances in Argentina (Staub, 1989)—and less formally to the analyses of other manifestations of groups turning against others, like racism or unnecessary violence by the police (Staub, 1991, 1992a, 1992b). Elements of this conception, which may be called a social theory of basic needs, appear useful for understanding mob violence as well.

Briefly, difficult social or life conditions, like intense and prolonged economic problems, intense political conflict in a society, or rapid and substantial social change, create social chaos and disorganization and give rise to intense needs in whole groups of people. These needs include the need for security, a positive identity, usable world views that help people comprehend reality and their place in the world, connection to other people, and hope for a better life.

Certain characteristics of a group's culture make it likely that members deal with the needs that arise by elevating the group relative to other groups, scapegoating these other groups, and adopting ideologies that promise a better future while identifying enemies who stand in the way of the ideology's fulfillment. The cultural characteristics include a history of devaluation of a subgroup of society, a monolithic culture or social organization without access by all groups to the social or political domain, a history of aggression in dealing with conflict, strong respect for authority that makes people seek leaders in difficult times, and certain group self-concepts.

As the perpetrator group turns against the victims, often a subgroup of society, and begins to harm the victim group, an evolution begins. Acts that harm the victims change the perpetrators, and make more harmful acts possible and probable. These "steps along a continuum of destruction" can lead to extreme violence. Bystanders, who could exert influence to inhibit this evolution, frequently remain passive. They change themselves as a result, accepting and justifying the victims' fate. With some variation in specifics, the historical data and analyses supported this general conception in all four instances (Staub, 1989).

Group violence is usually an outcome of either a historically or newly dominant group, or the government that represents it, turning against subgroups of society. Mob violence can be enacted both by majority groups (e.g., lynching) and subgroups of society that have been experiencing discrimination, repression, or relative deprivation.

A distinction between two types of mob and group violence, which will be called *conserving* and *reforming* types, may be useful. The conserving type is a response by a group to threats of identity or status, whether real or experienced, and whether the group's status is high or low. The reforming type is an attempt, usually by a less powerful group, to change the social order.

Organization and Leadership

Destructive actions by mobs can vary from spontaneous emergence to various degrees of leadership and preexisting organization. For example, in the United States around the turn of the century, lynchings frequently occurred relatively spontaneously, but also occurred as the result of the planned activity of a Klu Klux Klan group with an organized leadership. In contrast, Milgram and Toch (1969) note the relative absence of planning and leadership in the civil rights riots in the 1960s.

Violence at soccer games initiated by groups of young English soccer fans (Buford, 1992) has been neither truly spontaneous nor highly organized. The fans share an understanding, a mindset or preparedness for violence. Over time an informal blueprint has developed that guides the actions of the participants, who are united as fans of the same team, with a shared history. New fans are socialized into the ways of the group. An informal leadership also exists. Disruptive and violent confrontation between police and spectators at the Australian Grand Prix motorcycle races also showed an "institutionalization" of the conflict or normative elements (Cuneen & Lynch, 1988).

A similar implicit blueprint or normative pattern is suggested by newspaper accounts of lynchings in the South that occurred around the turn of the century (Ginzburg, 1988; Peretti & Singletary, 1981). Usually, an African American was accused of a crime, like the murder of a White person or the rape of a White woman, and the community responded with outrage. A mob formed, usually of men and boys (who were thereby socialized into mob conduct and lynching). The mob captured the accused, or overran a jail in which he (occasionally she) was held. The victim was carried to a place of execution and frequently underwent horrendous torture. By this time, women and children were often present as spectators. The victim was then hanged or burned. Not infrequently, the "real" perpetrator was later found, who was then also lynched.

An implicit blueprint or normative pattern of behavior also appears to exist for inner city riots, with their focus on looting and destruction of poverty. There has been a long tradition of riots in the United States; between the 1830s and 1850s in just four cities (Baltimore, Philadelphia, New York, and Boston), 35 major riots took place (Perry & Pugh, 1978). In recent times, television images have spread scripts for rioting. (In addition, radio and TV reporting in the 1960s and helicopter surveillance of the 1992 L.A. riot pointed out areas that had no police protection, encouraging people to join rioting in those areas.)

Instigating Events, Background Conditions, and Participant Characteristics

Early Theories

LeBon (1895) wrote that collective outbursts arise in particular historical periods, conditioned by important cultural factors. At the same time he believed that unruly or violent crowds, like those in revolutionary movements, are made up of criminals, social misfits, and other marginal people. This potential inconsistency (if there are understandable social reasons why would only the socially marginal act?) led to approaches emphasizing either social–environmental conditions or the personal frustration and social marginality of participants as explanations of mob violence, the latter sometimes referred to as the riff-raff theory.

Convergence theories (see Milgram & Toch, 1969; Sears & McConahay, 1973) propose that people with similar characteristics join to form crowds and violent mobs. Perpetrators of group violence tend to share certain characteristics, like an "authority orientation," and ideology (Staub, 1989). People who become "soccer hooligans" or participants in a race riot or revolutionary mob violence, are also likely to share certain characteristics.

However, convergence theories tend to be theories of social marginality. They suggest that members of unruly or violent crowds are violence prone, antisocial, criminal persons. But the combination of characteristics that lead individuals to join a crowd and remain part of it when it becomes a violent mob is likely to depend on a combination of specific factors, like the nature of instigating conditions and the population and location involved (e.g., a minority group, neighborhood, or prison).

Contagion theories emphasize immediate environmental conditions that act on individuals who happen to be nearby when some precipitating event occurs (Sears & McConahay, 1973). Contagion, "the spread of affect or behavior from one crowd participant to another" (Milgram & Toch, 1969, p. 550), is an important process that helps in understanding how a collection of individuals join in a shared purpose, but does not explain what instigates the affect and creates the sensitivity of people to it. A few people whose interests and inclinations are at odds with the rest of a crowd are unlikely to be the source of contagion. Neither convergence nor contagion theories emphasize the important role of social conditions, cultural characteristics, and their interaction with instigating events as origins of mob violence.

Instigating Events

Observation and evidence suggest that, frequently, specific events are the starting points for violent collective disturbances. Only 10% of urban riots that occurred between 1964 and 1968 did not have an apparent precipitating incident (Downes, 1968). A high percentage of contemporary civil disorders in the United States, including the Watts riot, were precipitated by the killing, arrest, assault on, or search of African American men and women by the police (Feagin & Hahn, 1973). Innocent verdicts against police officers who were believed to be guilty have been starting points for riots, notably in the Rodney King case. The killing of Martin Luther King also precipitated many riots (Downes, 1968). The lynching of African Americans often followed criminal acts or rumors of such acts against a White person (Ginzburg, 1988).

Downes (1968) made an important distinction among three types of hostile racial "outbursts": early pogroms in which Whites attacked African Americans who offered little resistance; race riots in Northern cities in 1915, 1935, and 1943 in which Whites and African Americans engaged in collective violence against each other; and riots in the 1960s with mostly African American participants, whose actions were directed primarily against local merchants and police "whom they consider responsible for a great deal of racial injustice" (Downes, 1968, p. 505).

Lieberson and Silverman (1965), who examined race riots in the United States between 1913 and 1963, noted that there were only four instances in which they did not have an identifiable precipitating event. The precipitating events of these riots, some of which were started by Whites, tended to be violations of important mores involving violence or interracial relations.

There was a relatively substantial percentage of "spontaneous" outbursts of hostility by African Americans against Whites in 1967, without identifiable precipitating events (Downes, 1968). According to Morgan and Clark (1973) this was the year when "the perceived value of racial disorders as social protest" (p. 613) was greatest in the African American communities. However, the many earlier riots in the 1960s may have made rioting a relatively normative behavior. Moreover, this was a period of general social disorder in the United States, with societal changes arising out of the civil rights movement, feminism, and the escalation of the Vietnam war and antiwar protest. Conditions of social disorganization contribute to the motivation for civic disturbances, like riots, and weaken inhibitions.

Authorities taking away a privilege can be a specific instigator, as in the case of some prison riots (Colvin, 1982). The starting point for the Berkeley Free Speech movement, which included the occupation of university buildings by students, was the University administration's decision to prohibit political activities by students, like the distribution of leaflets and solicitation of funds, on a piece of land where such activity had customarily taken place (Lipset & Wolin, 1965). Especially when a predisposition exists, frustrating events can instigate mob violence. For violence-prone soccer fans, their team's loss or taunts and other provocation by opposing fans can be precipitating events for rioting (Buford, 1992).

Moreover, specific instigation is often a process rather than an event. The investigation of precipitating incidents in the 1960s of 24 riots in 20 cities and 3 universities, showed that a series of incidents preceded each. These occurred over a period of weeks or months, both expressing and creating tension in the community. These incidents, or rumors based on them, involved either police action (40%), African American protest (22%), or White racist acts (17%) (U.S. Riot Commission, 1968).

The incidents were interpreted in light of community grievances. One of them, frequently, has been police brutality. Although the extent of police violence is not clear, there is evidence of strong devaluation and fear of African American people among the White officers of the 1960s and a tendency to favor the use of excessive force (Stark, 1972). In one study, 15 previously safe drivers who put Black Panther stickers on their rear bumper received 33 tickets for traffic violations in 17 days (Heussenstamm, 1971).

Frequently reciprocal changes in the behavior of involved parties are the precursors of mob violence. Rumors and mounting tension affected the behavior of correction officers in Attica preceding the prison riot (Perry & Pugh, 1978). Similarly, rumors and mounting tension in a community are likely to affect police behavior. Inappropriate control attempts and undue force by the police in turn create hostility in the community.

The same types of events only occasionally, not inevitably, instigate mob violence. At least part of the explanation of why they do so at specific times lies in background conditions (which are discussed in the next section). Frequently, in the context of these conditions, the instigator is not the event, but rumors that greatly transform it. Social conditions that give rise to feelings of injustice, anger, or hostility give certain events their instigating power or lead to the creation of rumors.

Social and Cultural Background Conditions

Background conditions can create the underlying motives for mob action. These motives are then activated by instigating events. These background conditions include societal climate, a cluster of poverty, deprivation, injustice and, paradoxically, improving conditions that engender hope; societal change and social disorganization; cultural and subcultural characteristics; the characteristics of riot cities, like unemployment and density; and climatic conditions, such as heat.

Societal climate. There are periods of time that have a dominant societal climate, and maybe even more than one, that influences both the occurrence and the interpretation of instigating events. For example, in the Berkeley Free Speech movement the students reacted to the university administration taking away their rights to political activity in a climate formed by the civil rights movement. In addition, potential leadership existed through the experience of some students in the civil rights movement (Milgram & Toch, 1969).

The urban riots in the 1960s occurred in a societal climate created by the desegregation decisions of the Supreme Court and the civil rights movement. There was an increased awareness of discrimination and injustice, and increased expectation by African Americans of improvement in their social and economic conditions. There was also a less punitive climate for intense expressions of African American frustration.

The disappearance of lynching also had to do with a changing societal climate. Such acts became unacceptable, and violators could expect forceful negative reactions. Changes in societal climate in part express changes in and in part help to transform, over time, culture and societal institutions, such as segregation.

Riots are more frequent during wars (Perry & Pugh, 1978), probably in part because of greater acceptance of violence. Usually, however, a number of background conditions coexist: substantial social changes in wartime create social upheaval, which is another background condition for mob violence.

Poverty, deprivation, injustice, and hope. Deprivation by itself is not viewed as an originator of mob violence (Perry & Pugh, 1978). People can suffer poverty, bad housing, and other aversive conditions without civic disturbance. Moreover, stable differences in the rights or economic conditions of groups can exist without giving rise to mob violence (Staub, 1989).

It is likely, however, that poverty exerts an influence in combination with other background conditions. For example, severe poverty is a substrate for the periodic rioting and violence between Hindus and Moslems in India, that is seemingly the result of religiously and culturally based antagonism. In the United States, it is under conditions that limit hope, usually for subgroups of society, so that education and other avenues are not seen as offering an improved future, that poverty appears to increase violence, for example, youth violence (Prothrow-Stith, 1991).

Losses or worsening conditions, however, are a source of mob violence. Economic decline in the South was associated with lynchings, historically the most common form of group violence in the United States, especially in the southern states. More than 5,000 black people were killed by lynch mobs between 1865 and 1955 (Bureau of Census, 1960). There were many more lynchings during periods when cotton prices were low than when they were high (Hovland & Sears, 1940; Morgan, 1977; Peretti & Singletary, 1981).

Traditional theorizing might suggest that worsening economic conditions created frustration that resulted in displaced hostility and aggression (Allport, 1954). Another view might be based on the combination of basic needs theory (Staub, 1989) and social identity theory (Tajfel, 1982a; Tajfel & Turner, 1979). Economic problems and other difficult life conditions frustrate basic needs, such as the needs for identity, comprehension, and connection, which can be fulfilled by group violence as well as mob violence. Specifically, people may strengthen their group identity—which is essential for a positive individual identity, particularly in difficult times—by elevating, through violence, their group over another. However, some lynchings were apparently motivated by material self-interest as well, a White person initiating a rumor about a provocative or criminal act by an African American business competitor, and that rumor acting as a specific instigator (Brown, 1965).

While the data are not uniform, overall, the perception of relative deprivation and the experience of injustice seem to be important conditions for mob violence. The role of these factors in the urban riots of the 1960s is suggested by the findings that riot participants were better informed politically than nonparticipants and either had experiences with or strong feelings about discrimination and police violence (McPhail, 1971). Moreover, the urban African

American community interpreted the riots as protests against racial discrimination (Caplan & Page, 1968; Sears & Tomlinson, 1978).

As mentioned earlier, prison riots frequently occur after previously granted privileges are withdrawn. The 1980 New Mexico prison riots occurred after employment opportunities and recreational programs that had been introduced were sharply curtailed (Colvin, 1982; Useem, 1985). According to the Official Report of the New York State Special Commission (New York State Special Commission, 1972), very bad conditions preceded the Attica prison riot. Inmates were deprived of phone calls and letters. There were complex rules of which inmates were not informed and which were enforced arbitrarily, with some inmates but not with others. Many rules were petty, used to harass and abuse inmates. There were unclear and unfair parole practices. There was also strong racism with abusive treatment, as White correction officers from rural areas interacted with inner city African American and U.S. Latino inmates. All this occurred when the social climate of the 1960s, including the riots, increased awareness of injustice and strengthened the identity of African Americans, including inmates (New York State Special Commission 1972; Perry & Pugh, 1978; Wicker, 1975). One can also argue that social disorganization characterized Attica preceding the riot (see discussion in next section).

Societal changes sometimes create awareness of injustice without changes in the actual conditions of people. But frequently crowd disturbances and mob violence occur after improved social and economic conditions, as profoundly repressed or downtrodden people seldom are able to rise to action. The French revolution, characterized by mob actions like the storming of the Bastille, followed improved social conditions (Milgram & Toch, 1969). Rioting in prisons has increased in spite of general improvement in prison conditions (Deroches, 1983) or perhaps because of them.

Based mainly on his analysis of the Russian and French revolutions, Davis (1969) proposed a J-curve of rising expectations to explain this. In this view, groups riot and revolutions begin under improved social conditions because expectations outpace the actual improvement in conditions. The New Urban Black theory (Caplan, 1970; Sears & McConahay, 1973), for example, suggests that certain individuals (e.g., young, from the North or West, with at least some high school education) were brought up to expect social and political equality. But in spite of progress, they continued to experience discrimination. A precipitating incident sparks their frustration and leads to a riot.

In addition to rising expectations, there may be another dynamic at work as well. For motives even to arise, and for their expression in action, it is necessary for people to have at least minimal confidence in their ability to fulfill their expectations (Staub, 1980). Under extreme conditions of poverty or repression, people may be preoccupied with survival, afraid of the dangers inherent in public protest or crowd behavior, and lack confidence that their actions can lead to desired outcomes. The easing of conditions may allow anger and the desire for change rooted in social conditions to arise and to be expressed in action.

The inability to exert influence by peaceful means is another background condition for mob violence. Based on an analysis of "racial controversies" involving New York City's African American and Puerto Rican populations, Monti (1979) suggests that violence followed unsuccessful efforts by minority groups to get government and nonminority individuals to act on their grievances. The lack of existing avenues for exerting influence and the experience of empowerment through group action are important elements in mob violence.

Societal change and social disorganization. In many instances, substantial changes in society (in technology, jobs, mores, etc.) or in a particular group's life (e.g., in a prison) precede mob violence. Great social changes often create the experience of chaos and disorganization. They threaten security as well as personal and group identity, make the world and one's future place in it difficult to understand, and loosen community ties and connections among people (Staub, 1989).

Downes (1968), in an analysis of 238 "hostile outbursts" between 1964 and 1968, found that those that reached a high intensity were more likely to occur in larger cities with a larger percentage of non-White population and large influx of non-Whites since 1950. Spilerman (1970) also found that non-White population size was important in the likelihood of community disorders. A certain size of the non-White population appears required to create enough strength and power for crowd actions. Moreover, the influx of a non-White population was likely to change social conditions and affect both minority groups and the White majority.

Frequently, increases in the African American population were not accompanied by similar increases in African American representation in city governments and civic institutions (Perry & Pugh, 1978). Thus, the avenues for dealing with the needs and grievances of the African American population remained restricted as their numbers increased.

The behavior of violent English soccer fans, many of whom had good jobs, according to Buford (1992), may be due to the experience of social disorganization. Tremendous social changes have taken place in many countries in the past few decades, including England, frustrating needs for group identity, connection, and power. Most of these can be satisfied, at least to a degree, by belonging to a group that engages in the shared devaluation of outsiders, like foreigners or fans of other teams, and shared violence against them.

Cultural and Subcultural Characteristics

A preexisting negative orientation toward members of another group is almost always a contributing element in mob violence, making it more likely that other background conditions and instigating events provoke mob violence. This negative orientation can take the form of deep-seated devaluation of and hostility toward certain groups in society, as in the case of lynchings of African Americans. Frustration and hostility can be displaced into a target "preselected" by the history of devaluation; basic needs for identity, comprehension, and connection can be served as members of a group turn together against a scapegoated group. Another form of negative orientation is mutual antagonism between two groups. Relations between police and minority groups in many U.S. cities have been one example of this.

Both in violent confrontations between police and spectators at Australian Grand Prix motorcycle races (Cuneen & Lynch, 1988) and disruptive group behavior at motorcycle races in the United States (Shellow & Roemer, 1966), cultural differences between a working class, motorcycle subculture on the one hand and community and police on the other hand appear to play a role. Overreactions by the police in exercising control and the opportunity for motorcyclists to act out anti-authority feelings appear to contribute to the riots.

In the United States, great social changes, and in earlier times economic problems, have reactivated hostility and violence against devalued minorities, as noted elsewhere in this chapter. In East European countries the collapse of communism has created economic problems, loss of security, and tremendous social change. In East Germany a historically authoritarian culture (Staub, 1989) and a nearly unbroken history of authoritarian rule have made it difficult for people to face the uncertainties of a democratic, capitalistic system. This has combined with a German history of devaluation of non-Germans and led to mob violence against "foreign" residents in Germany. In Yugoslavia, in addition to great social change, deep-seated mutual devaluation by ethnic groups has played a role in both mob violence and organized military actions.

A history of hostility can create an "ideology of antagonism" (Staub, 1989, 1992a), a view of the other as an enemy who is a threat to the self. When such an ideology of antagonism exists, even without threatening action, simply a gain by the other group can lead to negative social comparison (Tajfel & Turner, 1979) that diminishes and threatens the self. The first attacks by Azerbaijanis on Armenians in the dissolving Soviet Union were apparently the result of rumors that the Armenians were getting better housing. This happened, however, in the overall context of profound social change, as the Soviet Union was collapsing.

A history of violence in society, and specifically mob violence, makes such violence more normal and acceptable (Staub, 1989). The United States does have a history of frequent violence of many kinds, including rioting, labor violence, and vigilante actions (Levin & Mehlinger, 1975; Perry & Pugh, 1978). As noted earlier, cultural and subcultural norms that develop for these kinds of activities frequently appear to guide mob violence.

The Characteristics of Riot Cities

Findings about the characteristics of cities in which riots occurred in the 1960s and those in which they occurred earlier in the century may provide further information about background conditions and group relations as sources of riots.

Downes (1968) and Spilerman (1970) found that in the African American riots of the 1960s, the educational level and median family income was lower in cities where riots took place, unemployment higher, and the quality of housing worse. All of these factors usually affect the African American population more than the White population. In addition, as noted earlier, there was an influx of non-White population. Residential mobility, divorce, separation, and illegitimacy rates were all high in the non-White population of riot cities (Lieske, 1978). Lieberson and Silverman (1965) compared cities in which riots did and did not take place between 1913 and 1963. During this period, many riots were started by Whites (Downes, 1968). Riot and nonriot cities did not differ in population change and quality of housing. The economic conditions of African Americans were better in riot cities, with less unemployment, and a lower percentage of African American men holding traditional jobs like laborer or domestic. There was also lower White income and a relatively greater equality between Whites and African Americans in employment and income.

The relative equality may have represented a threat to the identity of Whites, leading to discriminatory behavior and perhaps "conserving" mob attacks on African American people. There was a smaller number of African American policeman as a proportion of the African American population in riot cities, and a smaller proportion of African Americans owning stores. The empowerment of African Americans through improved economic conditions, along with intensified White hostility, discrimination, and unresponsive government, may have created an explosive situation.

Kapsis (1976), in studying 1968 "riot zones" in California, found that in two racially changing neighborhoods with higher pre-riot delinquency rates the incidence of violence during the riots was greater. In a racially stable neighborhood, where the incidence of pre-riot delinquency was low, riots were shorter and their level of violence lower. Social disorganization appeared to characterize the former, friendship and institutional ties the latter neighborhood. Kapsis concluded that riots represent a direct continuity rather than sharp discontinuity with preexisting social conditions.

Other environmental conditions in a particular city or at a particular time, such as heat and crowding, also affect mob behavior. Temperature was positively related to rioting in the hot summers of the 1960s (Baron & Ransberger, 1978; Carlsmith & Anderson, 1979). Crowding in cities was related to riots as well (Downes, 1968), and in an analysis of 65 nations, civil disorders were related to the number of people per room (Welch & Booth, 1974). Experimental research and theory both suggest that heat and crowding are likely to increase aggressive behavior primarily following instigation to aggression, like frustration of goal-directed behavior, threat, or attack (Baron, 1977). These factors may also increase aggressive mob behavior when cultural and societal background conditions are present. Crowding in a society may itself be related to difficult socioeconomic conditions.

When do particular background conditions lead to mob violence and when do they not? It is likely that general background conditions must be present for instigating events to exert an influence, and it may be that particular combinations of conditions and events are most inflammatory. An important task for research is to identify the relative and interactive influence of instigating events and background conditions on mob violence. Their joint presence is rarely identified and almost never carefully assessed. The use of varied data sources is required to assess the degree to which each of the background conditions and instigating events was present during a particular episode or affected the particular population that engaged in mob violence.

The evidence we reviewed suggests that the sources of mob violence that we identified usually gain expression in rioting when there is a context of intergroup hostility (see also Reicher & Potter, 1985), whether it consists of the devaluation or mistreatment of one group by another, or of mutual antagonism. But examining the characteristics of participants in mob violence as well as the role of leaders, bystanders, and control agencies may also help us understand whether and to what extent mob violence occurs.

Characteristics of Mob Participants

Participant characteristics vary. Contrary to LeBon and other early theorists, at least when riots or mob actions are in part motivated by reforming tendencies, participants in them usually have not been marginal individuals.

There has been substantial research on the participants in urban riots in the United States in the 1960s, using a variety of data: interviews of riot area residents, interviews with eyewitnesses, arrest records, and a study of arrestees in Detroit. Rioters tended to be lifelong residents of their cities. The typical rioter was an African American unmarried male between 15 and 24 years of age (61.3% of self-reported rioters, 52.5% of arrestees; for ages 15 to 35, 86.3% and 80.8% are the comparable percentages). Rioters were substantially better informed about social and political issues, somewhat better educated, and more involved in civil rights efforts than uninvolved residents in the same areas. The two groups were equal in income and education, but the rioters were more often unemployed. Riot participants expressed strong racial pride, were hostile to Whites—as well as middle-class African Americans—and felt that they were barred from better jobs, which they deserved, because of discrimination (Caplan & Paige, 1968; Sears & McConahay, 1969; U.S. Riot Commission, 1968, especially pp. 128–129). As in the urban riots, in a riot on an inpatient treatment ward no difference was found between rioters and nonrioters in socioeconomic status, number of prior arrests and incarcerations, or age (Marohn, Dalle-Molle, Offer, & Ostrov, 1973).

The U.S. Riot Commission report (1968) indicated that early property damage in the 1960s riots was targeted against symbols of the White establishment, whereas later destruction was associated with profitable looting. Youth with lower socioeconomic status, according to Mason and Murtagh (1985) got involved in this second phase. However, the looting in the inner city riots appeared to be an expression of community beliefs that because of past persecution and discrimination the people had a right to the goods they were taking. Friends and family groups participated together (Perry & Pugh, 1978). Similarly, in revolutionary France, criminals frequently joined crowds, changing their focus from revolutionary ideals to destruction and thievery (Craik, 1837).

The McCone Commission (McCone, 1966) depicted the Watts rioters as consisting of fringe members of the community, criminals, and the chronically unemployed, who were expressing their personal frustration without community support. Sears and Tomlinson (1978) found, in contrast, that members of the African American community saw the Watts riot as a meaningful protest against injustice and repression by the White society. They saw rioters as people like themselves and were more sympathetic to them than to those who tried to stop them. Rioters were, in fact, connected to their communities, as measured by church attendance and other indexes (Sears & McConahay, 1973).

There were riots and mob actions, however, in which participants compare unfavorably with nonrioters. In the Detroit riots of 1943, 97 African Americans and 8 Whites were imprisoned for their participation. A much larger percentage of African American participants were from the Southern states than people in a nonrioting control group. The rioters were older and less educated, and 74% were unskilled workers with records of prior conflicts with law enforcement agencies (Akers & Fox, 1944).

Many disturbances during the period that includes 1943 were started by Whites, with African Americans defending themselves (Downes, 1968), rather than acting out of discontent with social conditions. In addition, rioting in 1943 may have been a greater deviation from social norms, involving more risk of extreme consequences. Therefore, people who participated were less established in their communities and perhaps more desperate, with less to lose.

In a prison riot (Moss, Hosford, Anderson, & Petracca, 1977), African American inmates involved in the riot had more prior arrests, more prior prison commitments, were younger at the age of first arrest, and had lower grade achievement tests and more deviant scores on the MMPI than those inmates in a control group. In a riot at an impatient treatment center for delinquent adolescents (Marohn et al., 1973), riot participants engaged in more delinquent behavior and showed less impulse control in the days preceding the riot than those who did not participate. The instigators were well-liked by the staff and were not dealt with firmly when they began to act up, supporting the literature that indicates that the use of too much power by control agencies like the police tends to provoke riots, while laxness and undercontrol also makes rioting more likely (Shellow & Roemer, 1966).

In a study of Italian soccer fans, those who participated in serious disturbances were generally young, unemployed, poorly educated, and fanatical in their commitment to their team. Researchers reported that aggressive mob action depended on group norms and on the group's acceptance of violence (Zani & Kirchler, 1991). In contrast, Buford (1992) believed that many of the highly fanatical English soccer fans had decent jobs. Social and family disorganization and the more normative nature of soccer violence in England may have brought a wider range of people to it.

Research on Indiana University basketball fans found that after their team's loss, strongly committed fans experienced more negative moods and lower self-esteem, and predicted that they would perform worse on a task (Hirt, Zillman, Erickson, & Kennedy, 1992). English soccer fans, and perhaps Italians as well, for whom being a fan is a way of life and a form of group membership, may be intensely affected by their team's loss. Through violence and the experience of power over others, they may regain positive group and individual identities.

Research on the psychological characteristics of mob participants is very limited and research in this area is badly needed, even retrospective research. Research on rescuers of Jews in the Holocaust (Oliner & Oliner, 1988) is a good example of how interviews and questionnaires can bring forth meaningful information about the psychological characteristics of participants in even long past events.

The Role of Leaders, Bystanders, and Control Agencies

These are topics about which relatively little firm knowledge exists. In political movements, it is clear that leaders at times incite followers to mob action. However, mob violence or riots that are not tied to political movements seem frequently leaderless, or the process of their instigation by individuals has not been identified. Buford (1992) described an informal leadership among violent soccer fans, the group looking up to certain individuals who at times emerge to initiate and guide violence. He described one case in which such a person guided the group with the help of very young teenage "lieutenants."

We also know relatively little about the role of bystanders, witnesses who do not participate. The potential of bystanders to influence the behavior of other people, by their passivity or action (Latane & Darley, 1970), or by what they say (Staub, 1974), is great. There is also real life evidence that bystanders can influence the behavior of perpetrators of organized group violence (Hallie, 1979; Staub, 1989).

We know that in the urban riots of the 1960s, some members of the community tried to stop violence by rioters (U.S. Riot Commission, 1968), but they had little success (Waskow, 1966). As in the case of organized group violence (Staub, 1989), the earlier bystanders act in the evolution of mob formation the greater their potential influence. Their impact is likely to be greatest during the build-up period, before intense feelings and a shared purpose arise and turn into destructive action.

The role of control agencies, like the police and other authorities, is important. Police behavior has often been a specific instigator of urban riots. However, we do not know how often police behavior was overly forceful and how often it was perceived that way because of the operation of background instigators, longstanding grievances, or repeated incidents before the instigating event. Individuals who interpret, for others, particular police actions as violence, or who create rumors, may have significant influence.

Both overly forceful and provocative behavior by police and relinquishing control and influence appear to have a role in initiating and maintaining mob violence. Police behavior is often shaped by lack of understanding, devaluation, and fear of particular groups of people. With careful planning to shape police perception and action, riots of certain kinds can be avoided, as they were during motorcycle races in Maryland in 1965 (Shellow & Roemer, 1966). When riots begin, a fast police response has been found to limit the extent of violence (Downes, 1968).

The unresponsiveness of societal institutions and agencies to the problems and grievances of groups of people, and their feelings of powerlessness to exert influence through legitimate channels are important sources of rioting. Depending on circumstances, the power to exert a relatively specific influence, like inhibiting police violence or getting a response to prisoner grievances, or political influence to bring about social change, should make mob violence less likely.

But the kinds of changes people seek are not always in the power of governments to provide. In Eastern European countries there have been demonstrations and riots when collapsing communist governments reduced subsidies for basic staples, like bread or milk. In Germany following the loss of World War I, intensely difficult life conditions created both unorganized and organized mob actions. These conditions were the result of longstanding cultural, economic, and historical processes, which involved other nations as well.

Democratic and responsive political institutions, relative economic equality among subgroups of a society, and the absence or weakness of cultural characteristics that promote intergroup conflict (devaluation, authority orientation, etc.) are among the conditions that can be expected to minimize the chances of mob violence in difficult times.

Social and Psychological Processes That Generate Mob Violence

Instigating events, background conditions, and the characteristics of the actors involved, especially when combined with the behavior of control agencies and bystanders, may go a long way to explain the occurrence of mob violence. But such an account would be incomplete without an understanding of the social and psychological processes that occur during and after a group is formed. These include shared definitions; contagion and modeling; deindividuation; group polarization, group mind, and the loss of self; and evolution toward increasing violence. These processes can lead to crowd formation and can change a crowd into a violent mob.

Shared definitions. People "milling around" and spreading information are part of the definitional process in the formation of a mob. As Festinger (1950) suggested, especially when there is situational ambiguity, people turn to information from other people to define the meaning of events. Research on rumor indicates, however, that information is greatly transformed in the course of transmission (Perry & Pugh, 1978). For example, Lieberson and Silverman (1965) wrote

> The Harlem riot during World War II started when a Negro woman was arrested by a white policeman for disorderly conduct. A Negro soldier, on leave, tried to stop him and the ensuing fight ended with both men in the hospital, the policeman with a battered head and the soldier with a pistol wound in the shoulder. Of greatest interest here is the account of the incident that spread through the Negro community: a Negro soldier was said to have been shot in the back and killed by a white policeman in the presence of the Negro's mother. (p. 889)

Contagion and modeling. Starting with LeBon, those concerned with crowds have stressed the speed by which feelings and actions spread. Contagion can contribute to crowd formation, to a shared definition of events, and to the formation of a shared purpose.

Observations indicate that affect can spread fast both among animals and people (Staub, 1987). How affect spreads is unclear. Psychoanalysts view the spread of affect as an inborn, unconscious process that is observable in infants. Empathy can certainly be an automatic response to and at least a partial matching of another's emotion.

It may also be the case that given shared inclinations and specific instigators, people freely express and even exaggerate their emotions in a crowd. This is in contrast to their usual tendency to hide their emotions in public (Latane & Darley, 1970).

There is likely to be a sensitivity to other people that underlies contagion, perhaps because of identification with others who are seen as members of one's group, shared dissatisfactions, concerns, and values, or shared antagonism toward a potential victim group. Without that, affect in some people can arouse the opposite affect in others. Although in interviews after riots people sometimes express shock at their own actions (Freedman, Carlsmith, & Sears, 1974), it is unclear whether people who participate in mob violence ever act contrary to their inclinations.

The role of modeling has been noted in contagion. Circular reaction has been proposed as a mechanism: one person responding to another's affect and that person's reaction feeding back to the first one (Allport, 1924). Affect and actions spread not only within a group, but, as a result of information in the media and images on TV, to other people as well.

Contagion has been used to describe the spread of affect and action among an already assembled group of people, as well as beyond a group to people in other locations. Although riots can spread like contagion in classical epidemics (Burbeck, Raine, & Stark, 1978), there are both contagion and noncontagion periods (Midlarsky & Suda, 1978), and civil disturbances have spread more contagion-like in some Latin American countries than in others (Govea & West, 1981). The reasons for these differences require further exploration.

Deindividuation. LeBon suggested the role of anonymity in crowd behavior. Festinger, Pepitone, and Newcomb (1952) proposed the related concept of deindividuation, further developed and elaborated by others (Diener, 1980; Zimbardo, 1969). In deindividuation, self-awareness and personal identity are lost and replaced with identification with the goals and actions of the group. Over time, the concept has taken on the meaning as well of the loss of the operation of personal moral standards.

Research findings suggest that anything that makes people less identifiable increases deindividuation, as suggested by behavioral outcomes. Wearing hoods and not being called by name led female subjects to give twice as many shocks to others (Zimbardo, 1969). Lack of identifiability also increased the use of obscene language in group discussion (Singer, Brush, & Lublin, 1965). The use of masks by warriors was related to greater aggression (Watson, 1973).

Anonymity and the psychological condition of deindividuation are likely to lead to a diffusion of responsibility for the welfare of others, and a reduction in fear of blame and punitive consequences. This is suggested by decreased helping in emergencies as the number of bystanders increases (Latane & Darley, 1970). When people are alone, social norms focus reponsibility on them for helping a distressed person (Staub, 1978); in groups responsibility is diffused.

As the number of people in a group increases, deindividuation may also increase. For example, when a person contemplates jumping off a building, the larger the number of observers, the more likely they are to encourage jumping (Mann, 1981). Mullen (1983, 1986) proposed, on the basis of an analysis of 60 newspaper accounts, that as the ratio of members of crowds, specifically of lynch mobs, to the number of potential victims increases, lynchers become less self-attentive and their level of atrocity increases.

But being in a group does not by itself increase aggression. Individuals alone with a victim are sometimes more aggressive than a group of people (Diener & Wallbom, 1976). Being with others can decrease anonymity. In actuality, people often join crowds with friends and know at least some other people present (Reicher & Potter, 1985). Perhaps anonymity is not a necessary condition for the loss of a separate identity and loss of the operation of customary moral standards when a group becomes cohesive and emotions rise. And members of a mob are usually anonymous to outsiders.

Reicher and Potter (1985) suggest that the focus on anonymity, deindividuation, and contagion show a continued adherence by social psychologists to early and conservative notions about the mindlessness of groups and the social marginality of participants. They argue, and the review and analysis in this chapter supports their argument, that mob violence frequently arises out of social conditions that give rise to a collective perception by members of a group of themselves and their social world. The members of a crowd act in terms of common social identification.

At the same time, mob violence is extreme behavior that is often at odds with the prior behavior of participants. These social–psychological processes appear to be involved in their facilitation. With repetition, as particular mob actions become normative, these processes are less likely to be required in order for violence to occur.

Group polarization, group mind and the loss of self. LeBon has stressed that in a crowd a group mind takes over, which he believed was irrational. Marx (1848), in contrast, believed that crowds are purposeful and serve an important role in creating social change. The earlier discussion suggests that the behavior of mobs is guided by understandable motives. But a group is more than a collection of separate individuals.

Research in social psychology has shown that members of a group arrive at positions that are more extreme than the average position of those who make up the group (Moscovici & Zavalloni, 1969; Myers & Bishop, 1970; Stoner, 1962). Such "group polarization" happens even in the course of orderly discussions of issues. In crowds, mutual influence is likely to be greater because of contagion, deindividuation, and conformity pressures that increase as a group identity develops.

There can be a loss of individual self and a giving of oneself over to the group, which may be experienced as a falling away of the limitations inherent in the self and of the boundaries restricting connections to other people. The resulting sense of abandon and feelings of connection and oneness can be intensely satisfying, whether they happen in mobs, or in self-development groups that are fashionable in the United States. Mob action can also create or enhance feelings of excitement and power.

Buford (1992) gives a sense of this groupness as he describes how English soccer fans in Italy respond to a policeman firing a gun into the air. They begin with the destruction of property; then they turn against the police:

> I had never seen trouble escalate so quickly. The firing of the handgun now seemed ludicrous; it had served only to inflame. The crowd that was now running back down the street was a different crowd from the one that had fled in panic from the tear gas. It had become different the moment it started destroying property—the familiar border. It was liberated now, and dangerous, and had evolved to that giddy point where it was perfectly happy to run amok with a comprehensive sense of abandon and an uninhibited disregard for the law. It was running hard, the people in it angry and wild. They were screaming something, I couldn't make it out—it was some kind of aggressive howl—but its object was clear enough: It was the police. (Buford, 1992, p. 292)

Buford (1992) also described the experience of English soccer fans in the course of violent action as a form of peak exerience, seemingly addictive in nature.

Evolution toward increasing violence. Psychological and behavioral evolution takes place in groups and in individual members of groups. People change as a result of their own actions. Children who are led to help others become more helpful (Staub, 1975, 1979). "Teachers" who shock "learners" tend to increase the level of shock they use over time (Buss, 1966; Goldstein, Rosnow, Raday, Silverman, & Gaskell, 1975). In the course of organized group violence, whole groups enter into a process of change along a "continuum of destruction" that may end in extreme violence, like mass killing or genocide (Staub, 1989). Such evolution can take place even in the course of a single incidence of mob violence and even more so over repeated instances (e.g., of lynching, soccer violence, or mob action that is part of a social movement). Even vicarious participation, through TV or other media, can be a source of such change (Staub, 1989).

Buford (1992) described what he regarded as "threshold acts" that may be performed by a single person but that move violence from one level to another. Redl (1943) wrote about initiatory acts among violent youths. Threshold acts may exert influence through modeling, disinhibition, and contagion, and may be one means by which change or evolution in a group is furthered. Turner and Killian's (1972) emergent norm theory proposes the emergence of group norms as an explanation of crowd behavior. Groups norms are an outcome of an evolution.

Buford (1992) describes a pattern of behavior in which a group of fans surrounds and kicks a person lying on the ground. This action had become part of the script for the group's behavior. Once a group develops such violent scripts and norms, it is extremely difficult for individuals to deviate from them.

As in the case of organized group violence (Staub, 1989), the psychological changes in individuals may include increased devaluation of victims and changes in the self that make violence more acceptable. People may turn to beliefs and "ideals" that justify destructive actions as just or moral. Individual standards are lost as people give themselves over to the group and adopt group standards. As a shared perspective and identification with the group evolve or enlarge, deviation by individuals becomes less likely. The social controls that people normally exert on each other to inhibit violence now serve violence.

The Participation of Youth in Mob Violence

Although adequate information about the percentage of participants by age is not available, both in urban riots (Sears & McConahay, 1973; U.S. Riot Commission, 1968) and in groups of violent soccer fans (Buford, 1992), male adolescents and young adults seem to be the most frequent participants. As discussed earlier, participants, especially in postwar African American urban riots, have not usually been criminals or delinquents: 56% of juveniles between the ages of 10 and 19 who were arrested or referred to the L.A. probation department during the Watts riot had one or no previous contact with the police, 48% attended church regularly, and 53% were doing average or better in school (Sears & McConahay, 1973).

The motives of young participants may include frustration, hostility, the desire to create social change, and personal gain. But part of the reason for their greater participation may be that the motives fulfilled through participation in a crowd or mob activity are especially satisfying for young, developing persons.

Developmental Issues

In cultures where young people are led to distance themselves from their families, they need to create their own, separate identity. This attracts them to groups, including cults and gangs (see chapter 14). But even semi-organized groups like violent soccer fans or a crowd that becomes a mob can provide them with connection, belonging, and self-definition. The positive social identity they gain from group membership (Tajfel & Turner, 1979) depends partly on the group's perceived status and rank, which in certain subcultures will depend on toughness and violence (Gaskell & Smith, 1986). As needs increase under difficult life conditions, the satisfaction gained from connection to a group would also increase.

As they seek self-definition and identity, young people may be more open to the lure of "higher ideals," both legitimate ones like fighting injustice and illegitimate ones proclaimed by leaders and advocated by destructive ideologies. Because they seek separateness from their families, but still need guidance and support, the potential influence of leaders on young people is greater.

In addition, to the extent that young people are less socialized, have fewer internalized societal norms and prohibitions, and have developed less impulse control, they are likely to be more vulnerable to contagion and deindividuation. They may change more easily, adopt emerging group norms, and lose their identity in a group.

Other factors intrinsic to youth may be attraction to the excitement of mob action and less fear of legal consequences or harm to themselves. This may be partly due to feelings of invulnerability; it is due to their courage as well as their malleability that armies and revolutionary groups induct them or work to attract them, or that youth are attracted to them (Etcheson, 1984; Staub, 1989). For example, the Khmer Rouge soldiers were extremely young (Etcheson, 1984) and the Greek torturers were young people inducted into the military police (Haritos-Fatouros, 1988). Young people may also feel they have less to lose, because they have few possessions and limited obligations and commitments.

There are other factors contributing to young people's participation that are not intrinsically tied to age, but are more likely to be present among young people, especially young black males in the United States at this time. These are unemployment and limited opportunity.

Individual and Family Characteristics

There has been very little research on the personal characteristics and family experiences of youthful participants in crowd action and mob violence. Particularly when mob violence does not arise as a relatively direct protest against social conditions and is not the result of intense devaluation and hate shared by a society or subculture, it is important to investigate these characteristics and experiences. Even if participants have no criminal record, they may possess personal characteristics that create an inclination for aggressive behavior, such as a negative view of human beings, weak or undeveloped moral values (Staub, 1971, 1989), lack of aggression anxiety (Baron, 1977) or a perception of aggression as acceptable and normal (Huesmann & Eron, 1984), and low self-esteem. Experiences in the home, like rejection or hostility (Bandura & Walters, 1959; Dodge, 1993; Huesmann, Eron, Lefkowitz, & Walder, 1984; Staub, 1993b), can contribute to the development of such predisposing characteristics. To the extent that this occurs, interpersonal aggressiveness and participation in some types of mob violence would be related.

Youth Groups as Mobs

Violence committed by loosely knit groups of adolescents appears to be an emerging form of youth violence in the United States. The information about these groups is, as yet, extremely limited and speculative.

The word "wilding" was made familiar by the group of adolescents who, after they attacked several victims in Central Park in New York, severely beat and raped a female jogger. Only one of the youths involved had prior police contact. Other instances of violence by small groups of youth have also been recently reported (Gibbs, 1989).

Scheidlinger (1992) suggests the emergence of "loosely structured 'packs' (small crowds) of teenagers who engage in senseless violence" (p. 1). He suggests that these groups have shifting membership and lack affectionate ties and a sense of shared identity among members. He contrasts them with the organized gangs of the 1960s, which were characterized by group loyalty, cohesion, and stable leadership. Whereas gangs in the 1960s usually fought with each other, violence by packs is more random, with little empathy for the victims. In Scheidlinger's view, moblike processes such as deindividuation, contagion, and "group psychological intoxication" (Redl, 1943) characterize these groups. Scheidlinger's (1992) hypotheses about the existence and nature of such groups come from limited observations and discussions with adolescent participants in group counseling.

Crimes by teenagers have often been committed in small groups. For example, one extensive study found that 43% of rapes in Philadelphia were committed by pairs or groups of youth mainly between 15 and 19 years old. Among the Kikuyu, which Sanday (1981) identifies as a rape-prone society, it is normative for boys to roam the countryside looking for women to rape as an initiation into sexual behavior.

Research is needed to determine how common "packs" are, the characteristics of participants in them, the social and psychological processes by which they operate, and the similarities and differences between them and violent groups of teenagers in the past. Deindividuation and contagion probably always characterized groups of teenagers engaged in violence. However, in stable groups norms develop that guide behavior, which may make violence less random, if not less extreme.

Many authors, including Scheidlinger (1984), have noted the crucial role of the peer group in social and moral maturation. He suggests that when deviant behavior among adolescents becomes frequent, causes are likely to reside in social patterns of families and communities.

Tremendous societal changes have taken place in the United States in the past 25 years. The civil rights movement, feminism, changes in sexual mores, divorce, increase in single parent families, and drug use are among the examples and consequences of social change (Staub, 1989, 1992b, in press). The impact on families and children has been profound. The children who are most severely affected, a kind of "new youth" who experienced lack of affection as well as disorganization and lack of structure in their early lives, may find it difficult to establish and to function within structures in their peer groups.

Experiences of neglect and of abuse would intensify the problem, limiting affective ties to others, trust, and caring.

In the absence of persistent affective ties and stable sources of identity, even temporary connections, such as packs, can be of substantial emotional value. The violence by such groups may be intensified by the excitement that results from the experience of connection to some and power over others. The absence of affective ties and mistrust of people would limit empathy and concern about the welfare of others. In their home, through films and TV, and in their peer group such teenagers may even have learned to value violence and see it as a source of manhood (Toch, 1969).

The Impact of Mob Violence on Young People

As suggested in the discussion of evolution in groups, mob violence will shape participants and may particularly shape the younger ones. The nature of actions (destruction of property, looting, physically harming others, killing people), their frequency, and the combination of motives they serve—political, ideological, psychological need-fulfillment, excitement, or material gain—should all influence how participants change. Among the likely effects are a changed perception (devaluation) of victim groups and human beings in general, an increase in the acceptability of aggression, changes in self-perception and feelings of empowerment, and in many cases stronger group ties, especially if the mob has an identifiable composition (Staub, 1989, 1990, 1993b). Laboratory research on the psychological and behavioral effects of engaging in aggressive behavior, alone and with others, is greatly needed.

The effect of violence on nonparticipating young people depends on many factors. There is substantial evidence that a wide range of conditions traumatize children and create posttraumatic stress (McCann & Pearlman, 1990). For example, following a fatal schoolyard sniping incident, being physically closer to the shooting and knowing the deceased child both contributed to a greater posttraumatic syndrome. This included intrusive imagery, emotional constriction and avoidance, loss of interest in significant activities, fears of recurrence, anxiety, sleep difficulties, and difficulties in paying attention in school (Pynoos et al., 1987).

Children and youth who are part of a victim group, especially in the case of recurrent violence, like lynchings in the United States or pogroms against Jews in Eastern Europe, can be expected to show not only intense posttraumatic stress, but fear of and hostility toward the perpetrators and, based on just world thinking (Lerner, 1980; Staub, 1989), in-group devaluation (Tajfel, 1982a, 1982b). Those who are not members of a victim group are also likely to show posttraumatic stress, probably based on physical proximity, age and discriminatory ability, empathy, degree of identification with the victims, and general security and anxiety level.

Other research, for example, with Cambodian children who were relocated to the United States following concentration camp experiences (Kinzie, Sack, Angell, Manson, & Rath, 1986; Sack, Angell, Kinzie, & Rath, 1986), suggests that the characteristics of children's families and family relationships will moderate both the short-term and long-term impact of witnessing violence. Close in-group ties lessen the extent to which devaluation and discrimination by out-groups become in-group devaluation (Tajfel, 1982b).

Summary and Conclusions

When it comes to mob violence, difficult life conditions can affect a whole society, or a specific group of people. These conditions can involve economic problems or decline, political upheaval, or great social changes that create the experience of disorganization and chaos with loss of guiding values and sense of community. Relative deprivation, the perception of unfair treatment and injustice, and powerlessness in improving one's fate or affecting change also function as instigators of mob violence. The easing of repression, discrimination or economic problems can also give rise to mob violence by decreasing fear, empowering people, and increasing hopes for change that may remain essentially unfulfilled. In addition, the changes involved in creating such improvements can themselves contribute to social disorganization. Under these conditions, devaluation of or antagonism between groups can create a persistent cultural potential for mob violence.

Evidence suggests that specific instigating events are often the starting points for mob violence. The assassination of political leaders, police brutality, and withdrawal of privileges are among the kinds of precipitants often found. Frequently, the interpretation of the event rather than simply the event's occurrence seems to be the potent precipitant.

Particular group processes are also implicated in mob violence. Rumors about an event, contagion, modeling, deindividuation, group polarization, group mind, loss of self, and evolution toward increasing violence are among the processes that may change a crowd into a violent mob. Leaders and bystanders can also function to provoke or inhibit violence.

An individual's reasons and motivations for participation in mob violence can include frustration, hostility, exploding anger, and the desire to hurt; the desire for institutional and social change motivated partly by self-interest and partly by response to perceived injustice; feelings of connection to and unity with others; a sense of identity the person gains; feelings of control, power, and even intense excitement and peak experience that arise from group processes; or the desire for personal gain.

When a mob turns against a particular victim group, as in the case of lynching, perhaps the most prejudiced will participate. But given shared prejudice, or a shared cultural devaluation of and hostility toward the group to which potential victims belong, it may be other characteristics that lead participants to join. The people who joined the SS shared the general German and Nazi anti-Semitism, but only a percentage (mostly in leading positions) were extremely anti-Semitic (Merkl, 1980).

Under some conditions, demographic characteristics like employment status, race, class, and other group memberships may be powerful selectors.

Under other conditions, the types of needs that arise in response to difficult circumstances, and the extent to which individuals possess these needs (for positive identity, connection to others, a comprehension of reality), may determine participation. Clearly, self-selection for participation in mob violence needs to be further explored.

To gain a better understanding of mob violence, fine grained analyses are needed that identify background conditions, the groups that are most affected, relevant aspects of culture and current societal norms and climate, and not only demographic but personality characteristics of participants. In the discussion that follows, specific research and policy recommendations related to some of the determinants of mob violence that we identified are briefly outlined.

Research Recommendations

Background conditions. Identifying the relative and interactive influence of background conditions would be of great value. Already existing information could be used, and assessment techniques could be developed to determine the degree to which the varied background conditions have been present at different times when riots did or did not occur. Regression analyses can determine their separate and interactive influence. The psychological effects of background conditions are the direct, proximal influences on mob violence. When it is possible to assess these, using already existing information or in future instances, more accurate specification of the origins of mob violence could result because some background conditions probably have greater psychological impact than others.

Certain background conditions are likely to have an especially strong impact on youth. For example, difficult life conditions and societal change, chaos, and disorganization make identity formation more difficult. When these factors create family disorganization, as they currently do in the United States, they also interfere with the fulfillment of the needs for security and connection, and with the receiving of guidance needed for a "usable" comprehension of reality and the development of meaning and purpose in life. Economic problems that create unemployment may have an especially strong impact on youth, making it more difficult to form a working, adult identity. A perception of injustice may provoke stronger anger in youth searching for ideals than in older people. The relative impact of such cultural–societal conditions on youth could be assessed even in the absence of youth violence. Differences between youth and adults in responding to specific instigating conditions could also be assessed.

Participant characteristics. Research on the psychological characteristics of participants in mob violence has been very limited. Such research could use retrospective interviews, as in previous studies, to compare participants and control subjects. Instead of focusing on demographic information, however, the research would assess personal characteristics like self-concept related variables (self-esteem and self-efficacy) and positive and negative orientations toward other people and groups (empathy, prosocial and antisocial orientation, devaluation of particular groups, and prejudice).

A potential problem in such research is that participation would be expected to change participants on certain dimensions. The nature and length of participation would have to be considered. The impact of participation on youth, given their greater malleability, should be greater than on adults. To address the effects of participation, laboratory analogue research offers the best avenue (see below).

Child rearing. Although it depends on background circumstances, the resulting motivations, and types of mob violence, some participants in mob violence may be inclined to varied types of violence by their childhood experience and parental socialization. What is the relationship between participation in mob violence and other kinds of violence? Can childhood antecedents be identified for at least certain types of participants?

Evolution in persons and groups. We have offered the evolution of persons and groups as an important concept in explaining mob (and group) violence. Although supporting research is noted in the chapter, a great deal of important research could be and should be conducted in this area. What are the changes in individuals as they participate (or resist engagement) in mob violence or laboratory analogues of it? How do their self-concept, beliefs about the acceptability of violence, and orientation toward other people change?

Changes in group norms over time could be assessed in laboratory analogue research (which might be constrained, however, by ethical considerations) or through participant observations, a technique that would be important to further develop and use, especially in repetitious mob behavior like soccer violence. As group norms and individuals' identification with groups evolve, even when temporary, the increasing embeddedness of individuals in the group would make deviation by them increasingly difficult. This would also be important to study.

Participation in mob violence may affect self-esteem and mood, and at least temporarily make participants feel empowered. As already noted, given their less well-developed identity, youth should be more affected. Research could be conducted to explore these effects both in laboratory analogues and in real life. Moreover, what happens when self-esteem, a feeling of efficacy, and positive mood are enhanced by other means? Would that increase resistance to entering into mob violence? Or would it increase openness to joining with other people, especially when this joining is not initially violent, but then evolves into violence?

Packs and wilding. We have little knowledge of how common are packs of adolescents and wilding type behaviors, or what are the characteristics of participants and the processes by which they operate. These are questions of great importance in light of the recent increase in such violence by young people. Finding young informants who are part of the relevant youth culture, identifying participants through them, and interviewing and in other ways studying participants, may be the best initial approach.

Policy Recommendations

Police training. The relation between citizens and control agencies, particularly the police, can be a background condition, while specific instances of interaction can be instigators of riots. The devaluation of minorities and excessive use of force by police remain continuing problems in the 1990s. They have been evident in community–police relations in Los Angeles and elsewhere, and specifically in the beating of Rodney King, which qualifies as an instance of mob violence by the police. Police violence may itself have increased from the 1960s on, because of the impact of great social changes in the United States, including changes in the roles of minorities and changed definitions of maleness (Staub, 1991).

To reduce police violence, intensive police training in cultural awareness should be required. This should include training to enhance the understanding of young people and their needs, including face saving in front of peers and conduct that may seem disorderly and even threatening but is, developmentally, relatively normal peer group interaction and can remain harmless with the appropriate response.

Close ties ought to be developed between police and the communities they serve through joint projects that involve significant interaction or "cross-cutting relations" (Deutsch, 1973; Staub, 1988, 1989). This would help to overcome both the tendency of the police, like other uniformed groups, toward an "us–them" differentiation and devaluation of outsiders and minorities, as well as helping to overcome the distrust of the police by their communities. Changes in the police culture and special training are required to make police officers active bystanders who intervene when their fellow officers use unnecessary force (Staub, 1991, 1992a, 1992c,1992d). National selection and training standards for officers, rather than state and local standards, would be highly desirable.

Using the schools to overcome antagonism between groups. Certain classroom experiences and to a lesser degree instruction can be used to overcome devaluation and create positive connections across groups lines.

For example, cooperative learning practices, like the jigsaw technique (Aronson, Blaney, Stephan, Sikes, & Snapp, 1978), can bring children from different groups to work intensively together. Among their beneficial effects are more subsequent interaction of children from different groups and more prosocial behavior toward peers (Johnson, Maruyama, Johnson, Nelson, & Skon, 1981). Educating children about cultures from a functional perspective and focusing on how different characteristics of cultures evolved as groups dealt with their life circumstances can promote both understanding and acceptance (Staub, 1986, 1988). Intensive teacher training is required to create these and other relevant school practices (Staub, 1993a, in press).

Service on behalf of others. People learn by their own actions both to help and to harm others (Staub, 1979, 1989). An extensive and well-constructed version of President Clinton's plans for national youth service would be of great value. It could fulfill the psychological functions that gangs, violent mobs, or packs serve for young people, while developing a positive orientation toward and caring about other people, and an identity that is positively connected to others. Such a youth service could also be an avenue for some for increased opportunities, partly by improving participants' capacity for effective functioning. It is of special importance to make such a service attractive for a wide range of young people. A service requirement that high schools are beginning to introduce, although the object of controversy, could also well serve these aims. Moreover, schools can provide children with opportunities and guidance to help others and learn by doing (Staub, 1993a, in press).

Parent training. Families require strengthening in many realms. Training in positive parenting may be of special value, however. The great social changes in the United States left many parents uncertain about whether and how parents should guide and discipline children. Parents need to learn that affection, reasoning with children, having expectations of them, and guiding them to fulfill these expectations contribute to healthy development, to a positive self-esteem and caring about other people. Learning and practicing these skills of "positive socialization" (Staub, 1992a) can create feelings of effectiveness in parents and help generate affection for children.

Community and authority. Creating responsive communities may be an extremely important way to reduce the potential for youth violence while improving the quality of people's lives.

Human beings need connections with others; positive connection is a basic human need (Staub, 1989). Such connections are especially important when difficult life conditions exist, as they now do in the United States as a result of great societal changes and within certain subgroups because of economic problems as well. The support that a community provides contributes to better parenting and helps develop positive identities and social responsibility in young people. Responsiveness to people by authorities and control agencies is an aspect of a functioning community. Community development should be one central direction of efforts aimed at reducing both youth violence and the likelihood of mob violence. Creating alliances between schools and parents (Staub, 1993a, 1993b) is one method; this and many other approaches should converge in creating communities.

References

Akers, E. R., & Fox, V. (1944). The Detroit rioters and looters committed to prison. *J. Crim. Law Criminol.*, *35*, 105–110.

Allport, F. H. (1924). *Social psychology*, Boston: Houghton Mifflin.

Allport, G. (1954). *The nature of prejudice*. Reading, MA: Addison-Wesley.

Aronson, E., Blaney, N., Stephan, C., Sikes, J., & Snapp, M. (1978). *The jigsaw classroom*. Beverly Hills, CA: Sage.

Bandura, A., & Walters, R. H. (1959). *Adolescent aggression*. New York: Ronald Press.

Baron, R. A. (1977). *Human aggression*. New York: Plenum.

Baron, R. A., & Ransberger, V. M. (1978). Ambient temperature and the occurrence of collective violence: The "long, hot summer" revisited. *Journal of Personality and Social Psychology, 36*, 351–360.

Brown, R. W. (1965). *Social Psychology*. New York: Free Press.

Buford, B. (1992). *Among the thugs: The experience, and the seduction, of crowd violence*. New York: Norton.

Burbeck, S. L., Raine, W. J., & Stark, M. J. (1978). The dynamics of riot growth: An epidemiological approach. *Journal of Mathematical Sociology, 6*, 1–22.

Bureau of Census. (1960). *Historical statistics of the United States, colonial times to 1957*. Washington, DC: U.S. Government Printing Office.

Buss, A. (1966). Instrumentality of aggression, feedback, and frustration as determinants of physical aggression. *Journal of Personality and Social Psychology, 3*, 153–162.

Caplan, N. S. (1970). The new ghetto man: A review of recent empirical studies. *Journal of Social Issues, 26*, 59–73.

Caplan, N. S., & Paige, J. M. (1968). A study of ghetto rioters. *Scientific American, 219*, 15–21.

Carlsmith, J. M., & Anderson, C. A. (1979). Ambient temperature and the occurrence of collective violence: A new analysis. *Journal of Personality and Social Psychology, 37*, 337–344.

Chaplin, J. P. (1985) *Dictionary of psychology* (2nd ed.). New York: Doubleday.

Colvin, M. (1982). The 1980 New Mexico prison riot. *Social Problems, 29*, 119–153.

Craik, G. L. (1837). *Sketches of popular tumults*. London: Knight.

Cuneen, C., & Lynch, R. (1988). The social meanings of conflict in riots at the Australian Grand Prix motorcycle races. *Leisure Studies, 7*, 1–19.

Davis, J. L. (1969). The J-curve of rising and declining satisfactions as a cause of some great revolutions and a contained rebellion. In H. D. Graham & T. R. Gurr (Eds.), *Violence in America*. New York: Bantam Books.

Deroches, F. J. (1983). Anomie: Two theories of prison riots. *Canadian Journal of Criminology, 25*, 173–190.

Deutsch, M. (1973). *The resolution of conflict: Constructive and destructive processes*. New Haven, CT: Yale University Press.

Diener, E. (1980). Deindividuation: The absence of self-awareness and self-regulation in group members. P. P. Paulus (Ed.), *Psychology of group influence*. Hillsdale, NJ: Erlbaum.

Diener, R., & Wallbom, M. (1976). Effects of self-awareness on anti-normative behavior. *Journal of Research in Personality, 10*, 107–111.

Dodge, K. A. (1993). Social cognitive mechanisms in the development of conduct disorder and depression. *Annual Review of Psychology, 44*, 559–584.

Downes, B. T. (1968). Social and political characteristics of riot cities: A comparative study. *Social Science Quarterly, 49*, 504–520.

Etcheson, C. (1984). *The rise and demise of democratic Kampuchea*. Colorado: Westview Press.

Feagin, J. F., & Hahn, M. (1973). *Ghetto revolts*. New York: Macmillan.

Festinger, L. (1950). Informal social communication. *Psychological Review, 57*, 271–292.

Festinger, L., Pepitone, A., & Newcomb, T. (1952). Some consequences of deindividuation in a group. *Journal of Abnormal and Social Psychology, 47*, 382–389.

Freedman, J. L., Carlsmith, J. M., & Sears, D. O. (1974). *Social psychology* (2nd ed.). Englewood Cliffs, NJ: Prentice Hall.

Freud, S. (1922). *Group psychology and the analysis of the ego*. London: Hogarth Press.

Gaskell, G., & Smith, P. (1986). Group membership and social attitudes of youth: An investigation of some implications of social identity theory. *Social Behaviour, 1*, 67–77.

Gibbs, N. C. (1989, May 8). Wilding in the night. *Time*, pp. 20–21.

Ginzburg, R. (1988). *100 years of lynchings*. Baltimore, MD: Black Classic Press.

Goldstein, J. H., Rosnow, R. L., Raday, T., Silverman, I., & Gaskell, D. (1975). Punitiveness in response to films varying in content: A cross-national field study of aggression. *European Journal of Social Psychology, 5*, 149–165.

Govea, R. M., & West, G. T. (1981). Riot contagion in Latin America. *Journal of Conflict Resolution, 25*, 319–358.

Hallie, P. P. (1979). *Lest innocent blood be shed. The story of the village of Le Chambon, and how goodness happened there.* New York: Harper & Row.

Haritos-Fatouros, M. (1988). The official torturer: A learning model for obedience to the authority of violence. *Journal of Applied Social Psychology, 18,* 1107–1120.

Heussenstamm, F. K. (1971). Bumper stickers and the cops. *Trans-action, 8,* 32–33.

Hirt, E. R., Zillman, D., Erickson, G. A., & Kennedy, C. (1992). Costs and benefits of allegiance: Changes in fans' and self-ascribed competencies after team victory versus defeat. *Journal of Personality and Social Psychology, 63,* 724–734.

Hovland, C. I., & Sears, R. (1940). Minor studies of aggression: Correlation of lynchings with economic indices. *Journal of Psychology, 9,* 301–310.

Huesmann, L. R., & Eron, L. D. (1984). Cognitive processes and the persistence of aggressive behavior. *Aggressive behavior, 10,* 243–251.

Huesmann, L. R., Eron, L. D., Lefkowitz, M. M., & Walder, L. O. (1984). Stability of aggression over time and generations. *Developmental Psychology, 20,* 1120–1134.

Johnson, D. W., Maruyama, G., Johnson, R., Nelson, D., & Skon, L. (1981). The effects of cooperative, competitive and individualistic goal structures on achievement: A meta-analysis. *Psychological Bulletin, 89,* 47–62.

Kapsis, R. E. (1976). Continuities in delinquency and riot patterns in Black residential areas. *Social Problems, 23,* 567–580.

Kinzie, J. D., Sack, W. H., Angell, R. H., Manson, S., & Rath, B. (1986). The psychiatric effects of massive trauma on Cambodian children: I. The children. *Journal of the American Academy of Child Psychiatry, 25,* 370–376.

Latane, B., & Darley, J. M. (1970). *The unresponsive bystander: Why doesn't he help?* New York: Appleton-Century-Crofts.

LeBon, G. (1895). *The crowd.* London: Unwin.

Lerner, M. J. (1980). *The belief in a just world: A fundamental delusion.* New York: Plenum.

Levin, M. A., & Mehlinger, H. D. (1975). *Violence and society.* Boston: Houghton Mifflin.

Lieberson, S., & Silverman, A. R. (1965). The precipitants and underlying conditions of race riots. *The American Journal of Sociology, 62,* 14–20.

Lieske, J. A. (1978). The conditions of racial violence in American cities: A developmental synthesis. *The American Political Science Review, 72,* 1324–1340.

Lipset, S. M., & Wolin, S. S. (1965). *The Berkeley student revolt.* New York: Anchor Books.

Mann, L. (1981). The baiting crowd in episodes of threatened suicide. *Journal of Personality and Social Psychology, 41,* 703–709.

Marohn, R. C., Dalle-Molle, D. Offer, D., & Ostrov, E. (1973). A hospital riot: Its determinants and implications for treatment. *American Journal of Psychiatry, 130,* 631–636.

Marx, K. (1888). *Manifesto of the communist party.* Chicago: Charles H. Kerr. (Original work published 1848)

Mason, D. T., & Murtagh, J. A. (1985). Who riots? An empirical examination of the "new urban Black" versus the social marginality hypotheses. *Political Behavior, 7,* 352–373.

McCann, L., & Pearlman, L. A. (1990). *Psychological trauma and the adult survivor.* New York: Brunner/Mazel.

McCone, J. A. (Ed.). (1966). *Violence in the city: An end or a beginning?* Los Angeles: Governor's Commission on the Los Angeles Riots.

McPhail, C. (1971). Civil disorder participators: A critical examination of recent research. *American Sociological Review, 36,* 1058–1073.

Merkl, P. H. (1980). *The making of a storm trooper.* Princeton, NJ: Princeton University Press.

Midlarsky, E., & Suda, W. (1978). Some antecedents of altruism in children: Theoretical and empirical perspectives. Psychological Reports, *13,* 187–208.

Milgram, S., & Toch, H. (1969). Collective behavior: Crowds and social movements. In G. Lindzey & E. Aronson (Eds.), *The handbook of social psychology* (2nd ed., Vol. IV). Reading, MA: Addison-Wesley.

Monti, D. J. (1979). Patterns of conflict preceding the 1964 riots: Harlem and Bedford-Stuyvesant. *Journal of Conflict Resolution, 23,* 41–69.

Morgan, C. T. (1977). *Introduction to Psychology* (2nd ed.). New York: McGraw Hill.

Morgan, W. R., & Clark, T. N. (1973). The causes of racial disorders: A grievance-level explanation. *American Sociological Review, 38,* 611–624.

Moscovici, S., & Zavalloni, M. (1969). The group as a polarizer of attitudes. *Journal of Personality and Social Psychology, 12,* 124–135.

Moss, C. S., Hosford, R. E., Anderson, W. R., & Petracca, M. (1977). Personality variables of Blacks participating in a prison riot. *Journal of Consulting and Clinical Psychology, 45,* 505–512.

Mullen, B. (1983). Operationalizing the effect of the group on the individual: A self-attention perspective. *Journal of Experimental Social Psychology, 19,* 295–322.

Mullen, B. (1986). Atrocity as a function of lynch mob composition: A self-attention perspective. *Personality and Social Psychology Bulletin, 12,* 187–197.

Myers, D. G., & Bishop, G. D. (1970). Discussion effects on racial attitudes. *Science, 169,* 778–789.

New York State Special Commission on Attica. (1972). *Official report.* New York: Praeger.

Oliner, S. B., & Oliner, P. (1988). *The altruistic personality: Rescuers of Jews in Nazi Europe.* New York: Free Press.

Peretti, P. O., & Singletary, D. (1981). A theoretical–historical approach to black lynching. *Social Behavior and Personality, 9,* 227–230.

Perry, J. B., & Pugh, M. D. (1978). *Collective behavior: Response to social stress.* New York: West.

Prothrow-Stith, D. (1991). *Deadly consequences: How violence is destroying our teenage population and a plan to begin solving the problem.* New York: HarperCollins.

Pynoos, R. S., Frederick, C., Nader, K., Arroup, W., Steinberg, A., Eth, S., Nunez, F., & Fairbanks, L. (1987). Life threat and posttraumatic stress in school-age children. *Archives of General Psychiatry, 44,* 1057–1063.

Redl, R. (1943). Group psychological elements in discipline problems. *American Journal of Orthopsychiatry, 13,* 77–81.

Reicher, S., & Potter, J. (1985). Psychological theory on intergroup perspective: A comparative analysis of "scientific" and "lay" amounts of crowd events. *Human Relations, 38,* 167–189.

Sack, W. H., Angell, R. H., Kinzie, J. D., & Rath, B. (1986). The psychiatric effects of massive trauma on Cambodian children: II. The family, the home and the school. *Journal of the American Academy of Child Psychiatry, 25.*

Sanday, P. R. (1981). The sociocultural context of rape: A cross-cultural study. *Journal of Social Issues, 37,* 5–27.

Scheidlinger, S. (1984). The adolescent peer group revisited. Turbulence or adaptation? *Small Group Behavior, 15*(3), 387–397.

Scheidlinger, S. (1992). *On adolescent violence: Some preliminary group process observations.* Unpublished manuscript, Albert Einstein College of Medicine, Bronx, NY.

Sears, D. O., & McConahay, J. B. (1969). Participation in the Los Angeles riot. *Social Problems, 17,* 3–20.

Sears, D. O., & McConahay, J. B. (1973). *The Politics of Violence: The New Urban Blacks and the Watts Riot.* Boston: Houghton Mifflin.

Sears, D. O., & Tomlinson, T. M. (1978). Riot ideology in Los Angeles: A study of Negro attitudes. *Social Science Quarterly, 49,* 485–503.

Shellow, R., & Roemer, D. V. (1966). The riot that didn't happen. *Social Problems, 14,* 221–233.

Singer, J. E., Brush, C. A., & Lublin, S. C. (1965). Some aspects of deindividuation: Identification and conformity. *Journal of Experimental Social Psychology, 1,* 356–378.

Spilerman, S. (1970). The causes of racial disturbances: A comparison of alternative explanations. *American Sociological Review, 20,* 408–414.

Stark, R. (1972). *Police riots, collective violence and law enforcement.* Belmont, CA: Wadsworth.

Staub, E. (1971). The learning and unlearning of aggression: The role of anxiety, empathy, efficacy and prosocial values. In J. Singer (Ed.), *The control of aggression, violence: Cognitive and physiological factors* (pp. 93–125). San Diego, CA: Academic Press.

Staub, E. (1974). Helping a distressed person: Social, personality and stimulus determinants. In L. Berkowitz (Ed.), *Advances in experimental social psychology* (Vol. 7, pp. 293–344). San Diego, CA: Academic Press.

Staub, E. (1975). To rear a prosocial child: Reasoning, learning by doing and learning by teaching others. In D. DePalma & J. Folley (Eds.), *Moral development: Current theory and research.* Hillsdale, NJ: Erlbaum.

Staub, E. (1978). *Positive social behavior and morality: 1. Personal and social influences.* San Diego, CA: Academic Press.

Staub, E. (1979). *Positive social behavior and morality: 2. Socialization and development*. San Diego, CA: Academic Press.

Staub, E. (1980). Social and prosocial behavior: Personal and situational influences and their interactions. In E. Staub (Ed.), *Personality: Basic aspects and current research* (pp. 236–295). Englewood Cliffs, NJ: Prentice Hall.

Staub, E. (1986). A conception of the determinants and development of altruism and aggression: Motives, the self, the environment. In C. Zahn-Waxler (Ed.), *Altruism and aggression: Social and biological origins* (pp. 135–165). Cambridge, England: Cambridge University Press.

Staub, E. (1987). The meanings, clarification and functions of empathy: A commentary. In N. Eisenberg & J. Strayer (Eds.), *Empathy and its development*. Cambridge, England: Cambridge University Press.

Staub, E. (1988). The evolution of caring and nonaggressive persons and societies. In Wagner, R., De Rivera, J., & Watkins, M. (Eds.), Psychology and the promotion of peace. *Journal of Social Issues, 44*(2), 81–100.

Staub, E. (1989). *The roots of evil: The origins of genocide and other group violence*. Cambridge, England: Cambridge University Press.

Staub, E. (1990). The psychology and culture of torture and torturers. In P. Suedfeld (Ed.), *Psychology and torture* pp. 49–77). New York: Hemisphere.

Staub, E. (1991, September 26). *Understanding and overcoming police violence*. Lecture at the POST (Peace Officers Standards and Training) Symposium on Law Enforcement Training Issues, San Diego, CA.

Staub, E. (1992a). *Bystandership with focus on the use of force*. Manual for proposed course, developed for the Commission of Peace Officers' Standards and Training, Department of Justice, State of California. Amherst: University of Massachusetts.

Staub, E. (1992b). The origins of caring, helping and nonaggression: Parental socialization, the family system, schools, and cultural influence. In S. Oliner, P. Oliner, L. Baron, L. Blum, D. L. Krebs, & M. Z. Smolenska (Eds.), *Embracing the other: Philosophical, psychological, and historical perspectives on altruism* (pp. 390–413). New York: New York University Press.

Staub, E. (1992c). Turning against others: The origins of antagonism and group violence. *The Bulletin of Peace Psychology, 1*, 11–14.

Staub, E. (1992d). Understanding and preventing police violence. *Center Review*. Cambridge, MA: Center for Psychology and Social Change, Affiliate of the Harvard Medical School of Cambridge Hospital.

Staub, E. (1993a). *A proposal for a program to develop caring and prosocial behavior, nonaggression, positive relations across group lives, and positive self-esteem in children: The prosocial schools projects*. Unpublished manuscript, University of Massachusetts at Amherst.

Staub, E. (1993b, August). *Societal–cultural, familial and psychological origins of youth violence*. Paper presented at the 101st Annual Convention of the American Psychological Association, Toronto, Canada.

Staub, E. (in press). The cultural–societal roots of violence: The examples of genocide and of contemporary youth violence in the U.S. In R. Feldman (Ed.), *The psychology of adversity*. Amherst: University of Massachusetts Press.

Stoner, J. A. F. (1962). *A comparison of individual and group decisions involving risk*. Unpublished master's thesis, Massachusetts Institute of Technology, Cambridge.

Tajfel, H. (1982a). *Human groups and social categories*. Cambridge, England: Cambridge University Press.

Tajfel, H. (1982b). Social psychology of intergroup relations. *Annual Review of Psychology, 33*, 1–39.

Tajfel, H., & Turner, J. C. (1979). An integrative theory of intergroup conflict. In W. G. Austin & S. Worchel (Eds.), *The social psychology of intergroup relations*. Pacific Grove, CA: Brooks-Cole.

Toch, H. (1969). *Violent men*. Chicago, IL: Aldine.

Turner, R., & Killian, L. M. (Eds.). (1972). *Collective Behavior* (2nd ed.). Englewood Cliffs, NJ: Prentice Hall.

U. S. Riot Commission. (1968). *Report*. New York: Bantam Books.

Useem, B. (1985). Disorganization and the New Mexico prison riot of 1980. *American Sociological Review, 50*, 677–688.

Waskow, A. I. (1966). *From race-riot to sit-in: 1919 and the 1960's*. New York: Doubleday.

Watson, R. I., Jr. (1973). Investigation into deindividuation using a cross-cultural survey technique. *Journal of Personality and Social Psychology, 5*, 4–15.

Welch, S., & Booth, A. (1974). Crowding as a factor in political aggression: Theoretical aspects and an analysis of some cross-national data. *Social Science Information, 13*, 151–162.

Wicker, T. (1975). *A time to die*. New York: Quadrangle/The New York Times Book Co.

Zani, B., & Kirchler, E. (1991). When violence overshadows the spirit of sporting competition: Italian football fans and their clubs. *Journal of Community and Applied Social Psychology, 1*, 5–21.

Zimbardo, P. G. (1969). The human choice: Individuation, reason and order versus deindividuated impulse and chaos. In W. I. Arnold & D. Levine (Eds.), *Nebraska Symposium on Motivation*. Lincoln: University of Nebraska Press.

14

Juvenile Gangs

Arnold P. Goldstein and Fernando I. Soriano

As America enters the 1990s, there are more juvenile gangs, more gang member drug involvement, more violence among such youth, and increasing levels of community concern in response than ever before. In this chapter we examine this social phenomenon, with particular emphasis on the forms and sources of aggression perpetrated by gang members. Two notes of caution must be entered first. With regard to gang demographics, which are considered early in the chapter, accurate data are difficult to acquire. No national-level agency in the United States has assumed responsibility for the systematic collection and dissemination of gang-relevant information. To learn of the number, nature, structure, and functioning of gangs, one must rely primarily on local police or other criminal justice agencies. Such agency information, along with that gleaned from school and mass media sources as well as from gang youth themselves, frequently suffers from exaggeration, minimization, or other distortions because of political, financial, or other "impression-management" factors.

It must also be noted that exceedingly little gang-focused literature exists—theoretical, investigative, or applied—that is of a psychological nature. A substantial literature bearing directly on gangs does exist and will be summarized here, however, its contributors have been sociologists, criminologists, legal scholars, political scientists, and, only very rarely, psychologists. Psychologists have studied a considerable array of domains that appear to be potentially gang relevant, and thus, following our discussion of gang demographics and gang aggression, we sketch some of the productive directions that psychological study of gang formation, behavior, and modification might take. Psychological interventions that are directed individually and collectively toward gang members are among these potential psychological contributions. In light of the racial and ethnic diversity of gang membership, the final section of this chapter examines the means for promoting the cultural sensitivity of such psychological interventions.

The Nature of Contemporary Gangs

How Are Gangs Defined?

Numerous definitions of *gang* have been suggested. Their substance has varied by location, economic and political climate, community conservatism and tolerance for deviancy, the intensity of concern by police and other criminal justice agencies, and with the level and sensationalism of mass media attention. Thus, over time, the answer to "What is a gang?" has varied from a sometimes predatory play group formed out of unconscious pressures and instinctual need (Puffer, 1912), to an interstitial group evolving from conflict with others (Thrasher, 1927/1963), to an aggregation demarcated as "a gang" through community and then self-labeling processes (Klein, 1971), to singular definitional emphasis on territoriality and delinquent behavior (Gardner, 1983), and most recently, to special focus on violence and drug involvement (Spergel, Curry, Ross & Chance, 1989). Until the mid 1970s, gang formation and membership evolved from neighborhood association and protection, as is now the case for a decreasing majority of gangs in America. This led Miller (1974) to create a definition of *gang* that listed the following as defining attributes: (a) structured organization, (b) identifiable leadership, (c) territorial identification, (d) continuous association, (e) specific purpose, and (f) illegal behavior. In the mid-1970s, as a companion to the rapid growth of the illegal drug trade in the United States, a major shift in gang activity occurred, a shift from cultural (Miller's definition) to instrumental gangs (Padilla, 1993). Currently, a large minority of American juvenile gangs are entrepreneurially oriented, illegal youth groups, aggressively protecting not their "hood" but, instead, their piece of the drug marketplace. This continuing shift in focus has engendered a number of attendant shifts in gang demographics.

Current Gang Demographics

Based on an extensive national survey, Spergel et al. (1989) reported that juvenile gangs are located in almost all 50 states. The 35 major cities that they surveyed reported 1,439 gangs. Based on a number of sources, we estimate the current figure to be close to 2,000 and growing (Cummings & Monti, 1993; Goldstein, Glick, Carthan, & Blancero, 1994). California (especially) and both Illinois and Florida appear to contain the largest gang concentrations. Spergel et al. (1989) reported a total of 120,636 gang members; we estimate a current combined population of 200,000.

Juvenile gangs are an urban, suburban, and rural phenomenon. Though the popular mythology indicates that most non-big city gangs are branches that are intentionally exported to less gang-infested locations by particular big city gangs or mega-gangs (especially Los Angeles' Crips and Bloods), the reality appears to be a bit more complex. Although a modest amount of such "franchising," "branching," or "hiving off" may occur, most midsized and smaller-city gangs either originate in these locations or are started by non-resident gang members as a result of kinship, alliance, the expansion of turf boundaries, or the movement of gang members' families into new areas (Moore, Vigil, & Garcia, 1983).

Several categories of actual and potential gang membership have been outlined (Padilla, 1992). Hard core and regular members are the most fully committed to gang involvement and activities. Peripheral or so-called "wanabees" are more on the fringe of membership, whereas *potentials* are neighborhood youth who are not yet involved but who may be ripe for recruitment. In contrast, the *neutrons* are youths who are living in the gang's hood, but who are not interested in membership. *Veterans* or *veteranos* are past members who have aged-out of the gang.

For decades, male gang members outnumbered females approximately 20 to 1 (Goldstein, 1991), although Taylor's (1993) recent work suggests a narrowing to 15 to 1. In the past, girl gangs functioned in a manner largely auxiliary to their associated boy gangs, as weapons carriers, lookouts, social or sexual targets, and so on. Today, there are increasing numbers of independent or unaffiliated girl gangs. Females join gangs later than do males, and they leave earlier (Goldstein, 1991).

Gang surveys have consistently found that, collectively, a large proportion of gangs and gang members are ethnic minorities (Miller, 1974; Needle & Stapleton, 1982; Spergel et al., 1989). According to Spergel et al. (1989), over half or approximately 55% of gang members are African American and another third or 33% are U.S. Latino. Although these figures may in fact reflect law enforcement's disproportional focus on and adjudication of ethnic minority youth (Mirande, 1987) and an undercount of White non-Latino youth, they nevertheless point to incontrovertible gang problems facing ethnic communities throughout the United States.

Until the mid-1970s, juveniles age 12 to 21 constituted the membership of juvenile gangs. Along with the growing shift from cultural to instrumental gangs, the age range of membership expanded at both ends, with members now as young as 9 and members over age 30 (Goldstein, 1991). Why are there both much younger and much older gang members than in the past? Younger members are used as runners, lookouts, and in similar capacities because if they are caught, the criminal justice system is likely to respond with considerable leniency (Goldstein, 1991). Older members frequently remain in the gang because employment opportunities for disadvantaged populations remain low in the legitimate economy, and the profitability of continuing to engage in activities within the illegitimate economy remains high (Goldstein, 1991).

Gang size is the result of several interacting factors, including the size of the youth population in a given area (i.e., the pool to draw on), the presence or absence of police and community pressure, the nature and visibility of the gang's activities, recruitment efforts, time and season of the year, agency activity, and the availability within the youths' community of alternative means of successfully attaining the goals that gang membership provides. Membership tends to continue, and often to solidify further, when and if a gang youth is incarcerated (Camp & Camp, 1985; Lane, 1989). Gott (1989), for example, reports that in 1989 approximately 5,000 of the 9,000 youth incarcerated in California Youth Authority facilities were gang members and that, as others have observed, gang cohesiveness and activity level appeared to accelerate substantially during and as a result of incarceration (Goldstein, 1991).

Moore (1991), long an observer and investigator of gang behavior notes that over the last few decades juvenile gangs in the United States have become more entrenched in their communities, more influential in the lives of their members, more deviant in their behavior, and more socially isolated from other adolescent groups.

Why do youth join gangs? Largely to obtain what all adolescents appropriately seek: peer friendship, pride, identity development, self-esteem enhancement, excitement, the acquisition of resources, and family and community tradition. Such goals may not be achievable through legitimate means in the disorganized and low income environments from which most gang youth are drawn. How are they recruited? According to Jankowski (1991) either in a manner akin to a fraternity or sorority "rush," through a sense of community obligation to gangs that have existed for several generations, or coercively, by means of threats and intimidation. How do they leave gangs? Members may "marry-out," "age-out," or find employment in the legitimate economy. They may shift to individual or organized crime. Many go to prison; some die.

Such are the findings of the professional community (Jankowski, 1991; Padilla, 1992; Sanders, 1994) regarding bases for initiating and terminating gang membership. What are the views of past gang members themselves on these subjects? According to Spergel et al. (1989), ex-gang members list as reasons for joining: gang availability, fun, friendship, protection, lack of home supervision, an older brother in the gang, not knowing that one instantly inherits all of the gang's enemies, status, and power. Reasons for leaving, in their view, include growing up, getting smarter, fear of injury, prison experiences, a girlfriend, marriage, obtaining a job, concern for the community, religious experiences, and assistance from others.

What do gangs do? Mostly they just "hang out," engaging in the diverse interpersonal behaviors characteristic of almost all adolescents. Much of this behavior reflects a dual purpose effort to increase "we-ness" or solidarity within the gang and difference or distinctiveness from all others. To do so, gangs may claim and topographically define their territory; make sometimes extensive use of graffiti to define their turf, challenge rivals, or proclaim their gang's existence; incorporate distinctive colors or color combinations within their dress; tattoo their bodies; and make use of special hand signs as a means of communicating membership and challenging rival gang members. They often commit delinquent acts and engage in various forms and levels of aggressive behavior. Although the total amount of such behavior is small, its effect on the chain of media response, public perception of gang youth behavior, and police and public agency counter-measures is quite substantial.

Gang Violence

Throughout the 1970s and 1980s, the levels and types of gang violence in the United States substantially increased, alongside the levels and types of violence that occur elsewhere on the American scene (Maxson & Klein, 1991).

Whereas the Roxbury Project (Miller, 1980), Group Guidance Project (Klein, 1968), and Ladino Hills Project (Klein, 1968), gang intervention programs of the 1950s and 1960s, collectively revealed few homicides and only small numbers of other types of gang violence, there were 81 gang-related homicides in Chicago in 1981, 351 such deaths in Los Angeles in 1980, and over 1,500 in Los Angeles during the 1985–1989 period (Gott, 1989).

Not only the levels and lethality, but also the types of gang violence have changed in recent years. The individual fair fight (which ended when one participant "gave up") and the group rumble, along with their sticks, bricks, fists, and pipes weaponry, have increasingly given way to new styles of intimidation. The armed drive-through or the drive-by shooting in a rival gang neighborhood; the mission, which is largely a series of drive by's; wilding, in which a loosely structured gang vandalizes and attacks passersby; and swarming or home intrusion, in which a large number of gang members enter an occupied home to commit robbery, assault, or worse, are all characteristic of today's gang violence.

What Do Youth Gang Members Fight Over?

There are certain contextual factors, such as territory, drugs, and guns, that influence whether gang members initiate violence and how serious the effects of the violence become. There are also factors, which we group under the category of "honor" that play a predominant role in instigating violence. Finally, there are immediate provocations, both internal and external, that should be examined in any particular act of youth gang violence.[1]

Territory. The traditional major source of gang violence—territoriality—continues to be a relevant concern. Although enhanced mobility through use of automobiles, dispersal of many school-age youth to schools outside of their neighborhoods because of desegregation efforts, and enhanced focus on economic rather than physical territory are all relevant factors, many gangs continue to mark, define, claim, protect, and fight over their turf. Vigil (1988) quotes one gang youth who makes this point powerfully:

> The only thing we can do is build our own little nation. We know that we have complete control in our community. Its like we're making our stand. . . . We're all brothers and nobody fucks with us. . . . We take pride in our little nation and if any intruders enter, we get panicked because we feel our community is being threatened. The only way is with violence. (p. 131)

Drugs. Increasingly, gang members' fighting is over drug sales and economic territory and less about turf ownership and physical territory, though the latter still fuel their share of violent incidents (Cervantes, 1992). Competition for drug markets, at least in some regions of the United States, appears to be an especially important motivation for gangs to become aggressors.

---

[1]The following discussion of these factors and provocations is based on work that previously appeared in Goldstein (1991).

This tendency is more prevalent in American West Coast cities, where gangs may have control of drug business (Spergel et al., 1989). In East Coast cities, the drug trade is more likely to be controlled by organized adult crime, and gang youth are assigned more ancillary roles, such as runner or lookout (New York State Task Force on Juvenile Gangs, 1990).

Guns. Guns have played a particularly important role in gang violence in recent years. There are 200 million privately owned guns in the United States, and it has been estimated that 270,000 of them are carried to school every day (Center to Prevent Handgun Violence, 1990) (see also chapter 12). Since 1900, over 750,000 American civilians have been killed by privately owned guns. Each year, there are 200,000 gun related injuries and approximately 20,000 gun related deaths: 3,000 by accident, 7,000 by homicide, 9,000 by suicide. Guns are involved in two out of every three murders in America, one third of all robberies, and one fifth of all aggravated assaults. This remarkable amount and use of weaponry has major implications for both the incidence and lethality of American gang violence. Klein and Maxson (1989) put it well:

> Does the ready access to guns explain much of the increase in violence? The notion here is that more weapons yield more shootings; these, in turn, lead to more 'hits'; and these, in turn, lead to more retaliations in a series of reciprocal actions defending honor and territory. . . . The theory is that firearms have been the teeth that transform bark into bite. (p. 219)

Honor. Honor, and its several related qualities (e.g., machismo, self-esteem, status, power, heart, reputation) have long been gang youth characteristics that were purported to contribute to overt aggression, and perhaps do so even more today (Padilla, 1992; Vigil, 1990). Miller (1980) wonders if honor has become less of a factor in the etiology of gang member aggression. As aggression has changed in form and frequency from intergang rumbles defending local turf to individual or small group acts of mugging, robbery, or other "gain" or "control" behaviors, perhaps, he asserts, the protection and enhancement of "rep" becomes less focal. We suggest that the opposite may be true. Gardner (1983) has noted that, in this context, "With few resources available to poor urban young people, a reputation for being tough and a good fighter is one of the only ways to attain status" (p. 27). It is a sad commentary on America's priorities, but we believe that as resources have become even scarcer in the years since Gardner's observation, the potential status-enhancing avenues available to low income youth are even fewer, and, as a result, the need to seek such enhancement by means designated by the larger society as illegal or inappropriate—including overt aggression—is even greater.

Immediate provocations. Contextual features (such as territory, drugs, guns, and honor) and youth gang and member characteristics (such as more gangs in the area and older members) may function collectively as the distal explanations of heightened gang violence in contemporary America. What of its proximal or immediate causes? What are the common internal and external provocations, or triggers that spark the fuse, of gang violence?

There is no doubt that the triggers change with culture, time, and place, but the following (a 1960 list from the New York City Youth Board) appears remarkably current. Exterior provocations include bad looks, rumors, territorial boundary disputes, disputes over girls, out-of-neighborhood parties, drinking or using illegal drugs, and ethnic tensions. Internal provocations include needs to obtain leadership power, to compensate for low self-esteem, to act out in ways that are meant to convince oneself of one's own potency, to obtain group affection, and to retaliate against fantasized aggression.

These are only a sampling of possible provocations to aggression. In addition, there are features of cognitive processing that also lead to violence. For example, Moore, Garcia, Garcia, Cerda, & Valencia (1978) have demonstrated that gang youth are often hypervigilant in their attention to possible slights. Dodge and Murphy (1984) have shown that such attention often leads to misperceptions of hostile intent and related misinterpretations of neutral events. Although the following observation was made long ago (New York City Youth Board, 1960), it too seems pertinent:

> The possibilities [for provocation] are almost limitless since the act itself in many cases is relatively unimportant, but rather is seen in a total context of the past, the present, and the future. Further, the act is seen in a total context of its stated, implied, and imagined meanings, all of which are subject to distortion by the groups, individuals, and the gangs. (p. 69)

Prevention and Intervention

As noted earlier, disciplines other than psychology have mounted the primary efforts to understand and alter gang behavior. Beginning in the 1950s, sociology provided the predominant explanatory theories of gang formation and behavior on which prevention and intervention efforts were based. These include strain theory (Cloward & Ohlin, 1960; Cohen, 1955), subcultural theory (Clarke, 1977; Sutherland & Cressey, 1974), control theory (Hirschi, 1969), labeling theory (Lemert, 1967; Schur, 1971), and radical theory (Abadinsky, 1979; Meier, 1976). Gang intervention programming first took major substantive form in the 1950–1965 period through detached worker and youth outreach agencies across the nation, an approach that was developed and staffed primarily by social workers (Bremmer, 1976; Spergel, 1965). From 1965 to 1980, political science combined with sociology to initiate widespread social and economic opportunities programming in the form of vocational, social, recreational, and academic offerings (Klein, 1968; Quicker, 1983). Then, as the drug scene came to dominate American ganging, and as the violence levels grew, social infusion yielded to social control, and opportunity provision gave way to opportunity withdrawal. From 1980 to the present, the gang intervention era of gangbusting and "just desserts" has predominated, with its criminal justice emphasis on suppression, deterrence, prosecution, and incarceration (Hagedorn & Macon, 1988; Spergel et al., 1989). Throughout this evolution of underlying theories of causation, and the accompanying parade of applied strategies for prevention and intervention, psychology has been largely silent. One recent exception is our own effort in this regard (Goldstein, 1991; Goldstein & Huff, 1993) in which we call for a new era in gang intervention, one based on comprehensive programming. This strategy envisions an array of available interventions: psychological (e.g., Gibbs, 1993; Goldstein, 1993; Hollin, 1993); contextual, involving family (Horne, 1993), school (Stephens, 1993), employment (Corsica, 1993), recreation (Lovell & Pope, 1993), and the larger community (Ribisl & Davidson, 1993); and criminal justice (e.g., Duxbury, 1993; Genelin, 1993; Huff & McBride, 1993). These interventions would be employed in appropriate combinations with gang youth as a function of both individual member and gang demographic, behavioral, group, and criminal history characteristics.

We feel strongly that psychology may well have a great deal to offer in clarification of a host of gang-relevant concerns, and that its collective silence need not and ought not continue. To be sure, the ultimate contributions of a discipline to a social phenomenon is an empirical question, to be answered by theory development, investigative scrutiny, and applied benefit. How might such theorizing, research, and application profitably proceed? We believe there are four subfields of contemporary psychology that may be of particular value in these areas (Goldstein, 1991).

Clinical Psychology

Especially in recent years, clinical psychology has begun to put forth theoretical formulations regarding the development and maintenance of individual and, occasionally, collective aggression and criminal behavior. These perspectives include diverse personality theories (Arbuthnot & Gordon, 1987; Eysenck, 1977), biogenetic and neurohormonal theories (Ellis, 1987; Trasler, 1987), social learning theory (Bandura, 1986), and sophisticated multicomponent theories (Feldman, 1977; Wilson & Hernstein, 1985). Although none of these approaches are explicitly gang-oriented, it is not a far leap—although it is a leap largely not yet taken—to seek to better understand and moderate gang violence and crime through these same theoretical positions. Our own successful gang intervention effort is a start in this extrapolatory direction. In this project, which we termed "The Prosocial Gang," a training program resting securely on social learning principles had a significant impact on such gang youth behaviors as interpersonal skills, community functioning, and criminal recidivism (Goldstein, Glick, Carthan, & Blancero, 1994).

Developmental Psychology

The psychological study of adolescent development has examined and elucidated characteristics of typical adolescents that appear to exist in exaggerated form in many gang youth, namely status seeking behavior, marginality, independence striving, search for identity, heightened need for self-esteem enhancement, challenge of authority, and, perhaps most pointedly, focus on peer relationship. The apparent degree of exaggeration of these qualities in many gang youth has led us to suggest that they might be better described as "hyper-adolescents" (Goldstein, 1991). The familial and peer-group antecedents and concomitants of such hyper-qualities seem central to both gang prevention and intervention efforts, and as a result appear to be especially worthy domains for further investigative inquiry. The possibly greater role of status seeking, versus crime for profit, in the commission of delinquent acts by gang members has been suggested by Cartwright, Schwartz, and Tomson (1975). Miller (1980) is among the several researchers who have underscored gang member susceptibility to peer pressure. Cartwright et al. (1975) have written of a heightened need for approval in this context, and we have stressed the search by gang members for the appearance of adult status (Goldstein, 1991). These notions are developmental psychological characteristics that deserve additional scrutiny by themselves. Collectively, these factors combine to enhance the potential value of developmental psychological scrutiny of gang-relevant variables.

Social Psychology

Of all the domains of psychological inquiry, it is social psychology that may hold the greatest relevance to a fuller understanding of gang formation, maintenance and intervention. Potentially, social psychology offers the gang researcher theories and data concerning group development, the nature of group leadership, facilitators and inhibitors of group cohesiveness, intermember communication, intergroup conflict and conflict resolution, norm and role development, interpersonal influence processes, power, deindividuation, and "groupthink." Social psychological knowledge is just beginning to be used for these purposes. Cartwright, Howard, and Reuterman (1970) have examined the impact on within-gang cohesiveness of selective recruitment, shared neighborhood residence, and diverse, within-group conformity pressures. Cartwright (1975) has also reported that although gang-wide cohesiveness is often considerably lower than is popularly believed, there often exists highly cohesive within-gang cliques, especially among core members. Gang leadership has often been found to be something less than the popular image of considerable centralized power. Instead, it has been described as often hesitant (Klein, 1971), cautious (Quicker, 1983), and tenuous (Tognacci, 1975), and, according to this last source, frequently resting "on the leader's ability to [continually] provide interesting activities, and his ability to [continually] demonstrate his superiority in the gang's status hierarchy" (p. 108). In addition to gang applications of cohesiveness and leadership research, Fox (1971) conducted a creative attempt to reduce the level of conflict between gang youths and their "most hated" police officers by means derived from social psychological study of the use of interpersonal contact as a facilitator of conflict reduction. The positive results of his gang youth–police weekend retreat program further encourages the use in this context of psychological perspectives.

Community Psychology

Yet another domain of contemporary psychology, community psychology contributes in important ways to the pool of theory and data from which gang-relevant hypotheses may be drawn. In particular, we refer to the focus in this arena on natural communities, neighborhoods, social networks, and social support. In a manner that seems especially relevant to gang formation and maintenance, McMillan and Chavis (1986) have examined the notion of a psychological sense of community, defined as "a feeling that members have of belonging and being important to each other, and a shared faith that members' needs will be met by their commitment to be together" (p. 7). Membership, influence, reinforcement, and emotional connection are the processes they posit as constituting this sense of community. The essence of "community," in the sense that we are using it, aids understanding of gang formation and functioning and is further clarified by community psychology's focus on social networks and social support. The former is usefully defined by Boissevain and Mitchel (1973) as "the chains of persons with whom a given person is in actual contact and their interconnection" (p. 24). Social support, an especially active target of psychological inquiry in recent decades, has been defined by Cobb (1976) as "information leading the subject to believe that he/she is cared for . . . esteemed and valued, that he/she belongs to a network of communication and mutual obligation" (p. 300). In what appears to be the single psychological study of how such constructs function in a gang context, Gillis and Hagan (1990) were able to demonstrate the degree to which such youth, in apparent contrast to nongang adolescents, offered more intense social support to a more limited (friends and family only) social network.

The diverse bodies of psychological knowledge that we have touched on—clinical, developmental, social, and community—are each rich sources of gang-relevant theory, research hypotheses, and, perhaps, eventual means for prevention and intervention applications. Their use for such purposes has barely begun.

The Need for Culturally Relevant Gang Interventions

Culturally relevant interventions are important to the success of many prevention and treatment interventions in the area of youth and violence. For gangs, whose membership is often based on ethnicity in addition to geographical proximity, cultural relevance must play a central role in devising interventions.

Gang Membership and Ethnicity

In our view, because of the importance of the ethnic composition of gangs and also because of the paucity of ethnic minority psychologists and others who are likely to plan interventions and perform research (Hagedorn & Macon, 1988), programs targeted toward gang members are likely to fail unless strategic planning and tactical implementation of such programs involve major, sustained, and serious involvement of gang members, as difficult as this may be to orchestrate. An accurate understanding of gang structure, motivation, perception, aspiration, and both routine and dramatic behavior, which may often be related to ethnicity, cannot be gained from the outside in.

African American, U.S. Latino, Asian, and other minority youth do indeed constitute a large portion of America's contemporary gang membership. They bring to their gang participation diverse and often culture-specific membership motivations, perceptions, behaviors, and beliefs (see chapters 2, and 4–7 in this book). The meaning of aggression; the perception of gang as family; the gang as a status, honor, or "rep" acquisition arena; the gang's duration, cohesiveness, typical and atypical legal and illegal pursuits; its place in the community; and many more aspects of gangs are substantially shaped by cultural traditions and mores.

A rich literature, including the following, exists that describes in-depth the cultural patterns and perspectives of America's ethnic and racial subgroups: African American (Beverly & Stanback, 1986; Brown, 1978; Glasgow, 1980; Helmreich, 1973; Keiser, 1979; Kochman, 1981; Meltzer, 1984; Silverstein & Krate, 1975; White, 1984), U.S. Latino (Horowitz, 1983; Mirande, 1987; Moore et al., 1978; Quicker, 1983; Ramirez, 1983; Vigil, 1983, Vigil & Long, 1990), Asian/Pacific Island American (Bloodworth, 1966; Bresler, 1980; Kaplan & Dubro, 1986; Meltzer, 1980; President's Commission on Organized Crime, 1985; Wilson, 1970), and others (Hagedorn & Macon, 1988; Howard & Scott, 1981; Schwartz & Disch, 1970).

The opportunity this culture clarifying provides to view the structure, dynamics, and purposes of delinquent gangs through the cultural lenses of their members, and the support it implies for the crucial necessity of gang member input for effective gang member programming are particularly useful. However, collectively, the extant literature is found wanting in discussing the means of taking the cultural context into consideration in research, particularly when developing gang prevention or intervention programs.

What Is Culturally Sensitive Programming

If asked, most psychologists and other social scientists would agree that in order to be successful, prevention and intervention programs need to be culturally sensitive (Soriano & De La Rosa, 1990), but few would understand what cultural sensitivity really means or how to incorporate it into gang programming. Understanding culturally sensitive programming begins with understanding the repertoire of available gang programming. Spergel (1990) has divided gang programmatic strategies into four types: (a) local community organization or neighborhood mobilization, (b) youth outreach or street gang work, (c) social and economic opportunities provision, and (d) gang suppression and incarceration.

Community organization or neighborhood mobilization efforts attempt to bring together various community groups and agencies to push for coordinated efforts to address concerns related to gangs. Youth outreach and street gang work focus on the use of street workers to assist gang members and at-risk youth in mediating gang conflict and help meet the social, recreational, and educational needs of youth through one-to-one contact. Social and economic opportunities refers to efforts to increase social, employment, and economic opportunities within deprived communities. Gang suppression and incarceration efforts focus on removing or incarcerating criminal gang members.

The type of gang programming determines the level of interpersonal contact and rapport that is needed with community residents and individuals. The development of trust and rapport is particularly important for community organization or street outreach programming. By contrast, economic opportunity provision and suppression efforts require less interpersonal contact. It is the extent, nature, and importance of interpersonal and intercultural contact that determine the level of importance of cultural sensitivity. Yet, the question still remains: What is cultural sensitivity, and how do we achieve it in gang programming?

Does cultural sensitivity mean having ethnic minority members incorporated into the staffing of gang prevention and intervention programs? Others may argue that cultural sensitivity means that those working in a particular gang project should be able to communicate linguistically with targeted ethnic groups, such as U.S. Latino or Asian/Pacific Island American youth. Still others may suggest that cultural sensitivity means that project staff need to acquire a level of knowledge and familiarity with a particular cultural group or groups that are represented by gang members.

Most personnel running gang programs will readily admit that cultural sensitivity is important, if not critical, to their success. However, all too often this recognition does not result in implementation. As a result, far too many gang programs fail to specifically plan and ensure that their programs are culturally sensitive and relevant to various groups in their catchment area. Usually the problem does not arise from lack of interest or cultural regard, but in a lack of understanding of what sensitivity means and how it is incorporated within gang programming. Soriano (1993) recently reviewed the literature on cultural sensitivity and suggested both a definition of cultural sensitivity and ways that gang prevention and intervention programs can be made more culturally sensitive and relevant. According to Soriano (1993), cultural sensitivity refers to a person's or a program's objective understanding, appraisal, appreciation, and knowledge of a particular cultural group that are used equitably in behavioral dispositions toward members of the cultural group. Cultural sensitivity is developed through self-awareness, the elimination of stereotypes and unfounded views, and through gaining objective knowledge and actual interaction with members of a particular cultural group.

This definition has various implications for gang programming. First, it encompasses many of the characteristics that are commonly used as indicators of cultural sensitivity, such as language capability, ethnic background, social science training, cultural training, and background experience of program staff members. Gang prevention and intervention programs have commonly relied on any one of these characteristics singly or in combination in order to engender cultural sensitivity. This definition emphasizes the importance of objectivity and knowledge in developing fair evaluative judgments and behavioral responses that are related to gang members and cultural groups they represent. But it also suggests that objective evaluations and positive or appropriate behavioral patterns toward cultural groups are developed through a candid and dispassionate introspective assessment of one's current attitudes and views toward them. Finally, this definition also points to the importance of having contact with gang members and the cultural group they represent in order to develop cultural sensitivity.

In essence, this definition emphasizes the multiple conditions necessary for developing cultural sensitivity. It encompasses the various commonly used indicators of cultural sensitivity and points to three main components of cultural sensitivity: Awareness, knowledge, and skill (Pedersen, 1988). These three components are encompassed by what is called the tridimensional view of cultural sensitivity (Soriano, 1993).

Awareness. According to Pedersen (1988), awareness refers to an initial assessment of a person's current attitudes, opinions, and assumptions regarding a particular culture. It reveals assumptions about cultural differences and similarities in behavior, attitudes, and values compared with one's own. According to Sue and Sue (1982), awareness training involves acquiring several competencies. The first competency consists of an understanding of one's own cultural values and biases. A second competency involves awareness of how one's cultural values and biases affect ethnic minority subjects and clients. The third competency involves comfort with cultural differences between one's own values and norms and those of culturally different individuals. The fourth competency is sensitivity and understanding in situations in which working with a culturally different person is not advisable for various reasons (e.g., personal biases, preferences because of ethnic identity).

As mentioned earlier, current gang surveys suggest that the majority of gang members and gangs are ethnic minorities (G. D. Curry, personal communication, April 18, 1994). Moreover, among U.S. Latinos, the largest proportion of gang members are second or third generation gang members (Moore, 1991; Vigil, 1988). This suggests that at least among U.S. Latinos gang members tend to adopt a hybrid of cultural values borrowed from mainstream culture and traditional Latino culture. To some researchers, gangs and gang members compose part of a subculture with its own values and beliefs (Cohen, 1966; Miller, 1958). In achieving cultural sensitivity, engendering awareness requires an understanding of the unique patterns of attitudes, values, and beliefs held by gang members that are separate from those held by nongang members living in the same community. For example, U.S. Latino gang members, like African American members, may adopt strong values of toughness, smartness, excitement, fate, and autonomy (Goldstein, 1991; Miller, 1958), which would need to be considered and acknowledged by those who want to develop rapport with them. Developing cultural sensitivity may require gang program workers to understand how their own values differ from such values.

Knowledge. Knowledge is considered the beginning of true cultural understanding. It consists of facts about a culture's history, social position, cultural values, norms, and beliefs. According to Sue and Sue (1982), cultural knowledge training for counselors should offer several competencies that are geared specifically toward working with multicultural persons. First, cultural knowledge training should offer a good understanding of the sociopolitical system in the United States and of its past and present treatment of ethnic minorities. For example, Asian/Pacific Island American gang members, as members of a broader Asian community, have a distinctively different sociopolitical experience from that of African Americans. Moreover, they are different in different parts of the country and in different time periods (e.g., Asian immigrant railroad workers of the 1800s vs. Asian immigrants in the U.S. workforce more recently).

Second, knowledge training should include specific information about the culture itself, about its salient cultural values, beliefs, practices, and norms. This information should also describe the heterogeneity that is found in cultural groups, including the role of assimilation and acculturation in altering cultural characteristics. Third, knowledge training should develop an acute understanding of those intervention strategies that are being considered for implementation and their appropriateness in light of knowledge of the culture, including the role of language. Fourth, cultural knowledge training should include information about institutional barriers to access to services and intervention efforts. Common institutional barriers include language, geographic access, a perceived lack of confidentiality, and mistrust resulting from cultural ignorance.

Moore (1991) and Hagedorn and Macon (1988) point to the industrial and other economic changes that affect the marginalization of U.S. Latino and African American populations, leading to increases in delinquency and gang membership. Similarly, Rodriguez and Zayas (1990) point to the adverse role of discrimination and institutional disrespect of minority cultures and how this increases the functional role of gangs for minority youth. Developing cultural knowledge includes understanding these historical and systemic developments.

Skill. Skill refers to the stage at which one is able to use what is learned through awareness and knowledge about oneself and about a particular cultural group, and when one is able to apply this knowledge in order to have effective interpersonal contact with members of the ethnic group. Once again, Sue and Sue (1982) provide guidance in developing relevant skill competencies. First, cultural knowledge gained previously needs to be used to develop a broad range of verbal and nonverbal responses that are acceptable, appropriate, and sensitive to the values and norms of ethnic minorities. Second, cultural skill requires the ability to receive both verbal and nonverbal communications from culturally different groups and to interpret them accurately. Third, skill development requires implementation of gang intervention and prevention efforts in a respectful manner that is mindful of the cultural context.

As mentioned earlier, an additional requirement for intercultural skill development is having actual interaction and meaningful contact with minority group members and in this case gang members. It is the actual contact with culturally different groups that refines and puts the cultural awareness and knowledge to the test. This knowledge allows for the emergence of behavioral and verbal repertoires that are mindful and respectful of cultural beliefs, values, and norms of gang members.

Taken together, the tridimensional components of cultural awareness, knowledge, and skill are comprehensive and dynamic. However, according to Pedersen (1988), many cultural sensitivity training programs traditionally emphasize one component over another, to the detriment of their effectiveness. For example, by itself, knowledge about a cultural group or gang does not mean a counselor or community worker knows how to apply this knowledge in a programmatic setting. Similarly, over-emphasis on awareness can lead to guilt and self-consciousness because of false assumptions and stereotypes regarding a cultural group. At the same time, a premature emphasis on skill development, without the necessary awareness or knowledge of a particular cultural group, can lead to immediate misunderstandings, mistrust, and the blind or inappropriate development of verbal and nonverbal communication and behavioral patterns.

Within the tridimensional perspective, knowledge—whether gained through self-awareness, through attending training programs, or through interpersonal interaction with members of the culture—is a central part of developing cultural sensitivity. In working with ethnic gang members this knowledge needs to include the universal, but also the unique, social and cultural experiences of gang members. They are members of larger minority groups, but hold their own unique youth values as gang members.

Developing culturally sensitive gang prevention and intervention programs requires, first, a programmatic commitment and, second, an individual commitment to gaining cultural understanding and intercultural skills on the part of those implementing gang programs. Sufficient time and resources need to be committed to programs and their staff in order both to acknowledge the need for developing cultural sensitivity toward minority youth and to be effective at developing it.

The preceding discussion has obvious public policy implications. First, it suggests that gang programs need to consider the social, historical, economic, and political context of communities that are plagued with gang problems (e.g., gang violence). This view counters prevailing views that are held by many who see all gang members—whether Asian/Pacific Island American, African American or U.S. Latino—as the same (a view commonly held among those in law enforcement). There may be similarities (particularly in marginalization), but there are certainly cultural and social differences. This view also poses a challenge to psychologists who would rather believe that social deviance can be examined by simply focusing on the psychological maladjustment of youth. Psychologists who work with gang members, regardless of theoretical persuasion, need to be trained to understand the social and cultural context of youth. Finally, acknowledging the importance of cultural sensitivity requires that public policymakers press for providing gang programs with adequate resources to train their staff to work with culturally different youth.

Conclusion

Gangs in the United States are growing rapidly in number, breadth of location, drug involvement, amount and lethality of aggression, and, more generally, their impact on citizen awareness and concern. We have examined the nature and characteristics of contemporary gangs and the extent of the violence that occurs among them. We have looked at the role gangs play in the lives of youth, psychologically, interpersonally, and economically.

Within this framework, gangs cannot be seen as the problem that is responsible for the increased violence and delinquency in communities. A broader, but deeper understanding of the unmet, but basic, physical, social, and psychological needs of particular communities is needed, in order to point to the etiological factors that are truly responsible for the increase in gang participation and violence throughout the United States.

In this chapter, we have also examined psychology's preliminary contribution and substantial potential contribution to the study of youth gangs, and have explored the necessity and benefits of gang intervention programming that is culturally sensitive. Most promising, in our view, is the period of gang intervention work that we may now be entering. Comprehensive programming draws selectively and prescriptively on the full range of available interventions—psychological, contextual, and criminal justice—in a broad effort to meet the diverse needs and aspirations of both gang youth and the larger society of which they are a part. Psychology, with its wealth of theory, research, and practice still largely untapped when it comes to youth gangs, can have a major role in this endeavor. It is our hope that this chapter serves as an invitation to psychologists to play such a role.

References

Abadinsky, H. (1979). *Social service in criminal justice.* Englewood Cliffs, NJ: Prentice Hall.

Arbuthnot, J., & Gordon, D. A. (1987). Personality. In H. C. Quay (Eds.), *Handbook of juvenile delinquency* (pp. 139–183). New York: Wiley.

Bandura, A. (1986). *Social foundations of thought and action.* Englewood Cliffs, NJ: Prentice Hall.

Beverly, C. C., & Stanback, H. J. (1986). The Black underclass: Theory and reality. *The Black Scholar, 17,* 24–31.

Bloodworth, D. (1966). *The Chinese looking glass.* New York: Dell.

Boissevain, J., & Mitchel, J. C. (1973). *Network analysis: Studies in human interaction.* The Hague, Netherlands: Mouton.

Bremmer, R. H. (1976). Other people's children. *Journal of Social History, 16,* 83–103.

Bresler, F. (1980). *The Chinese mafia.* New York: Stein & Day.

Brown, W. K. (1978). Black gangs as family extensions. *International Journal of Offender Therapy and Comparative Criminology, 12,* 39–48.

Camp, G. M., & Camp, C. G. (1985). *Prison gangs: Their extent, nature and impact on prisons.* South Salem, NY: Criminal Justice Institute.

Cartwright, D. S. (1975). The nature of gangs. In D. S. Cartwright, B. Tomson, & H. Schwartz (Eds.), *Gang delinquency* (pp. 1–22). Monterey, CA: Brooks/Cole.

Cartwright, D. S., Howard, K., & Reuterman, N. A. (1970). Multivariate analysis of gang delinquency: II. Structural and dynamic properties of groups. *Multivariate Behavioral Research*, 5, 303–324.

Cartwright, D. S., Schwartz, H., & Tomson, B. (1975). *Gang delinquency*. Monterey, CA: Brooks/Cole.

Center to Prevent Handgun Violence. (1990). *Caught in the crossfire: A report on gun violence in our nation's schools*. Washington, DC: Center to Prevent Handgun Violence.

Cervantes, R. E. (Ed.). (1992). *Substance abuse and gang violence*. Newbury Park, CA: Sage.

Clarke, R. V. G. (1977). Psychology and crime. *Bulletin of the British Psychological Society*, 30, 280–283.

Cloward, R. A., & Ohlin, L. E. (1960). *Delinquency and opportunity: A theory of delinquent gangs*. New York: Free Press.

Cobb, S. (1976). Social support as a moderator of life stress. *Psychosomatic Medicine*, 38, 300–314.

Cohen, A. K. (1955). *Delinquent boys: The culture of the gang*. New York: Free Press.

Cohen, A. K. (1966). The delinquency subculture. In R. Giallombardo (Ed.), *Juvenile delinquency* (pp. 103–118). New York: Wiley.

Corsica, J. Y. (1993). Employment training interventions. In A. P. Goldstein & C. R. Huff (Eds.), *The gang intervention handbook* (pp. 301–318). Champaign, IL: Research Press.

Cummings, S., & Monti, D. J. (Eds.). (1993). *Gangs*. Albany, NY: State University of New York Press.

Dodge, K. A., & Murphy, R. R. (1984). The assessment of social competence in adolescents. In P. Karoly & J. J. Steffen (Eds.), *Advances in child behavior analysis and therapy* (Vol. 4, pp. 169–187). New York: Plenum.

Duxbury, E. B. (1993). Correctional interventions. In A. P. Goldstein & C. R. Huff (Eds.), *The gang intervention handbook* (pp. 427–440). Champaign, IL: Research Press.

Ellis, L. (1987). Neurohormonal bases of varying tendencies to learn delinquent and criminal behavior. In E. K. Morris & C. J. Braukmann (Eds.), *Behavioral approaches to crime and delinquency* (pp. 499–520). New York: Plenum.

Eysenck, H. J. (1977). *Crime and delinquency*. London: Routledge & Kegan Paul.

Feldman, M. P. (1977). *Criminal behavior: A psychological analysis*. New York: Wiley.

Fox, H. G. (1971). Gang youth and police: Live in. *The Police Chief*, 37, 233–235.

Gardner, S. (1983). *Street gangs*. New York: Franklin Watts.

Genelin, M. (1993). Gang prosecutions: The hardest game in town. In A. P. Goldstein & C. R. Huff (Eds.), *The gang intervention handbook* (pp. 417–426). Champaign, IL: Research Press.

Gibbs, J. C. (1993). Moral–cognitive interventions. In A. P. Goldstein & C. R. Huff (Eds.), *The gang intervention handbook* (pp. 159–188). Champaign, IL: Research Press.

Gillis, A. R., & Hagan, J. (1990). Delinquent samaritans: Networks, structures, social conflict and the willingness to intervene. *Journal of Research in Crime and Delinquency*, 27, 30–51.

Glasgow, D. G. (1980). *The Black underclass: Poverty, unemployment, and entrapment of ghetto youth*. San Francisco: Jossey-Bass.

Goldstein, A. P. (1991). *Delinquent gangs: A psychological perspective*. Champaign, IL: Research Press.

Goldstein, A. P. (1993). Interpersonal skills training interventions. In A. P. Goldstein & C. R. Huff (Eds.), *The gang intervention handbook* (pp. 87–158). Champaign, IL: Research Press.

Goldstein, A. P., Glick, B., Carthan, W., & Blancero, D. (1994). *The prosocial gang*. Newbury Park, CA: Sage.

Goldstein, A. P., & Huff, C. R. (Eds.). (1993). *The gang intervention handbook*. Champaign, IL: Research Press.

Gott, R. (1989, May). *Juvenile gangs*. Paper presented at Conference on Juvenile Crime, Eastern Kentucky University, Richmond.

Hagedorn, J., & Macon, P. (1988). *People and folks*. Chicago: Lake View Press.

Helmreich, W. B. (1973). Race, sex and gangs. *Society*, 11, 44–50.

Hirschi, T. (1969). *Causes of delinquency*. Berkeley: University of California Press.

Hollin, C. R. (1993). Cognitive–behavioral interventions. In A. P. Goldstein & C. R. Huff (Eds.), *The gang intervention handbook* (pp. 55–86). Champaign, IL: Research Press.

Horne, A. M. (1993). Family-based interventions. In A. P. Goldstein & C. R. Huff (Eds.), *The gang intervention handbook* (pp. 189–218). Champaign, IL: Research Press.

Horowitz, R. (1983). *Honor and the American dream*. New Brunswick, NJ: Rutgers University Press.

Howard, A., & Scott, R. A. (1981). The study of minority groups in complex societies. In R. H. Monroe, R. L. Monroe, & B. B. Whitings (Eds.), *Handbook of Cross-Cultural Human Development* (pp. 74–104). New York: Garland STPM Press.

Huff, C. R., & McBride, W. (1993). Gangs and the police. In A. P. Goldstein & C. R. Huff (Eds.), *The gang intervention handbook* (pp. 401–416). Champaign, IL: Research Press.

Jankowski, M. S. (1991). *Islands in the street*. Berkeley: University of California Press.

Kaplan, D. E., & Dubro, A. (1986). *Yakuza: The explosive account of Japan's criminal underworld*. Reading, MA: Addison-Wesley.

Keiser, R. L. (1969). *The Vice Lords: Warriors of the streets*. New York: Holt, Rinehart & Winston.

Klein, M. W. (1968). *The Ladino Hills Project (Final report)*. Washington, DC: Office of Juvenile Delinquency and Youth Development.

Klein, M. W. (1971). *Street gangs and street workers*. Englewood Cliffs, NJ: Prentice Hall.

Klein, M. W., & Maxson, C. L. (1989). Street gang violence. In N. A. Weiner & M. W. Wolfgang (Eds.), *Violent crime, violent criminals* (pp. 40–53). Newbury Park, CA: Sage.

Kochman, T. (1981). *Black and White styles in conflict*. Chicago: University of Chicago Press.

Lane, M. P. (1989, July). Inmate gangs. *Corrections Today*, pp. 98–99, 126–128.

Lemert, E. M. (1967). *Human deviance, social problems, and social control*. Englewood Cliffs, NJ: Prentice Hall.

Lovell, R., & Pope, C. E. (1993). Recreational interventions. In A. P. Goldstein & C. R. Huff (Eds.), *The gang intervention handbook* (pp. 319–332). Champaign, IL: Research Press.

Maxson, C. L., & Klein, M. W. (1991). Street gang violence: Twice as great, or half as great. In C. R. Huff (Ed.), *Gangs in America* (pp. 71–100). Newbury Park, CA: Sage.

McMillan, D. W., & Chavis, D. M. (1986). Sense of community: A definition and theory. *Journal of Community Psychology, 14*, 6–23.

Meier, R. (1976). The new criminology: Continuity in criminological theory. *Journal of Criminal Law and Criminology, 67*, 461–469.

Meltzer, M. (1980). *The Chinese Americans*. New York: Crowell.

Meltzer, M. (1984). *The Chinese Americans*. New York: Crowell.

Miller, W. B. (1958). Lower class culture as a generating milieu of gang delinquency. *Journal of Social Issues, 14*, 5–19.

Miller, W. B. (1974). American youth gangs: Past and present. In A. Blumberg (Ed.), *Current perspectives on criminal behavior* (pp. 291–320). New York: Knopf.

Miller, W. B. (1975). *Violence by youth gangs and youth groups as a crime problem in major American cities*. Washington, DC: National Institute for Juvenile Justice and Delinquency Prevention.

Miller, W. B. (1980). Gangs, groups, and serious youth crime. In D. Shicker & D. H. Kelly (Eds.), *Critical issues in juvenile delinquency* (pp. 186–197). Lexington, MA: Lexington Books.

Mirande, A. (1987). *Gringo justice*. Notre Dame, IN: University of Notre Dame.

Moore, J. W., Garcia, R., Garcia, C., Cerda, L., & Valencia, F. (1978). *Homeboys, gangs, drugs, and prison in the barrios of Los Angeles*. Philadelphia: Temple University Press.

Moore, J., Vigil, D., & Garcia, R. (1983). Residence and territoriality in Chicano gangs. *Social Problems, 31*, 182–194.

Moore, J. W. (1991). *Going down to the barrio*. Philadelphia: Temple University Press.

Needle, J. A., & Stapleton, W. V. (1982). *Police handling of youth gangs*. Washington, DC: National Juvenile Justice Assessment Center.

New York City Youth Board. (1960). *Reaching the fighting gang*. New York: Author.

New York State Task Force on Juvenile Gangs. (1990). *Reaffirming prevention*. Albany: Division for Youth.

Padilla, F. (1992). *The gang as an American enterprise*. New Brunswick, NJ: Rutgers University Press.

Padilla, F. (1993). The working gang. In S. Cummings & D. J. Monti (Eds.), *Gangs* (pp. 173–192). Albany, NY: State University of New York Press.

Pedersen, P. (1988). *A handbook for developing multicultural awareness*. Alexandria, VA: American Association for Counseling and Development.

President's Commission on Organized Crime. (1985). *Organized crime of Asian origin*. Washington, DC: U.S. Government Printing Office.

Puffer, J. A. (1912). *The boy and his gang*. Boston: Houghton Mifflin.

Quicker, J. S. (1983). *Seven decades of gangs*. Sacramento, CA: State of California Commission on Crime Control and Violence Prevention.

Ramirez, M. (1983). *Psychology of the Americas*. Elmsford, NY: Pergamon Press.

Ribisl, K. M., & Davidson, W. S. (1993). Community change interventions. In A. P. Goldstein & C. R. Huff (Eds.), *The gang intervention handbook* (pp. 333–358). Champaign, IL: Research Press.

Rodriguez, O., & Zayas, L. H. (1990). Hispanic adolescents and antisocial behavior: Sociocultural factors and treatment implications. In A. R. Stiffman & L. E. Davis (Eds.), *Ethnic issues in adolescent mental health* (pp. 137–171). Newbury Park, CA: Sage.

Sanders, W. B. (1994). *Gangbangs and drive-bys*. New York: Aldine de Gruyter.

Schur, E. (1971). *Labeling deviant behavior: Its sociological implications*. New York: Random House.

Schwartz, B. N., & Disch, R. (1970). *White racism*. New York: Dell.

Silverstein, B., & Krate, R. (1975). *Children of the dark ghetto*. New York: Praeger.

Soriano, F. I. (1993). Cultural sensitivity and gang intervention. In A. P. Goldstein & C. R. Huff (Eds.), *The gang intervention handbook* (pp. 441–462). Champaign, IL: Research Press.

Soriano, F. I., & De La Rosa, M. R. (1990). Cocaine use and criminal activities among Hispanic juvenile delinquents in Florida. In R. Glick & J. Moore (Eds.), *Drugs in Hispanic communities* (pp. 55–73). New Brunswick, NJ: Rutgers University Press.

Spergel, I. A. (1965). *Street gang work: Theory and practice*. Reading, MA: Addison-Wesley.

Spergel, I. A. (1990). Youth gangs: Continuity and change. *Crime and justice: A review of research, 12,* 171–275.

Spergel, I. A., Ross, R. E., Curry, G. D., & Chance, R. (1989). *Youth gangs: Problem and response*. Washington, DC: Office of Juvenile Justice and Delinquency Prevention.

Stephens, R. D. (1993). School-based interventions: Safety and security. In A. P. Goldstein & C. R. Huff (Eds.), *The gang intervention handbook* (pp. 219–256). Champaign, IL: Research Press.

Sue, D. W., & Sue, S. (1982). Cross-cultural counseling competencies. *The Counseling Psychologist, 19*(2), 45–52.

Sutherland, E. H., & Cressey, D. R. (1974). *Criminology*. Philadelphia: Lippincott.

Taylor, C. S. (1993). *Girls, gangs, women and drugs*. East Lansing: Michigan State University Press.

Thrasher, F. M. (1927/1963). *The gang*. Chicago: University of Chicago Press.

Tognacci, L. (1975). Pressures toward uniformity in delinquent gangs. In D. W. Cartwright, B. Tomson, & H. Schwartz (Eds.), *Gang delinquency* (pp. 102–110). Monterey, CA: Brooks/Cole.

Trasler, G. (1987). Biogenetic factors. In H. C. Quay (Ed.), *Handbook of juvenile delinquency* (pp. 184–215). New York: Wiley.

Vigil, J. D. (1983). Chicano gangs: One response to Mexican urban adaptation in the Los Angeles area. *Urban Anthropology, 12,* 45–75.

Vigil, J. D. (1988). *Barrio gangs: Street life and identity in southern California*. Austin: University of Texas Press.

Vigil, J. D. (1990). Cholos and gangs: Cultural change and street youth in Los Angeles. In C. R. Huff (Ed.), *Gangs in America* (pp. 116–198). Newbury Park, CA: Sage.

Vigil, J. D., & Long, J. M. (1990). Emic and etic perspectives on gang culture: The Chicano case. In C. R. Huff (Ed.), *Gangs in America* (pp. 55–70). Newbury Park, CA: Sage.

White, J. L. (1984). *The psychology of Blacks*. Englewood Cliffs, NJ: Prentice Hall.

Wilson, J. Q., & Hernnstein, R. J. (1985). *Crime and human nature*. New York: Simon & Schuster.

Wilson, R. W. (1970). *Learning to be Chinese*. Cambridge, MA: MIT Press.

Part V

Preventive and Treatment Interventions

Introduction

Previous sections of this book dealt with developmental and sociocultural factors in youth violence, risk and resilience factors related to ethnicity, vulnerability of selected groups to violence, and societal influences on violence. In this section, many of these elements are viewed through the prism of prevention and intervention in youth violence. Previous chapters detailed much of what is known about how violence is learned; this section examines how to arrange the conditions of learning so that violence as a response to interpersonal difficulties is not learned in the first place. If violent responses have already been learned, how they can be unlearned and replaced by prosocial behavior is a crucial concern. Therefore, the chapters in this section take a developmental perspective consistent with the thrust of the previous chapters.

In chapter 15, Alan Kazdin reviews in detail interventions with children that attempt to prevent the development of violent behaviors and, where these have already begun to develop, to correct the behaviors and induce youngsters to develop more prosocial ways of interacting with others.

Kazdin emphasizes that aggressive and violent behavior patterns in children are often seen in combination with other dysfunctions, such as academic deficiencies, poor interpersonal relations, and deficits in cognitive and attributional processes. In addition, parent and family characteristics, such as disciplinary practices, criminal behavior and alcoholism, and defensive communications are also associated with aggressive child behavior. Prevention programs that target these areas do so at different points in time and in different settings. For example, early preventive interventions may begin during a mother's pregnancy and involve home visitation. Some school-based prevention programs begin in preschool, whereas others target the elementary school years.

In examining treatment programs for children who have already evidenced problems with aggression, violence, and other comorbid conditions, Kazdin argues for treatment in the context of children's everyday lives and highlights four promising approaches: problem-solving skills training; parent management training; family therapy; and school and community-based treatment, which may include components of the three earlier approaches.

Kazdin points out that to be effective, preventive and treatment interventions must be based on the interplay of basic and applied research in many of the areas already covered in this book. Indeed, he notes, the findings from basic research, such as in developmental psychology, provide the underpinnings for informed interventions; and applied research, such as on the efficacy of intervention programs, provides direct tests of models that are derived from basic research.

In chapter 16, Nancy Guerra, Patrick Tolan, and W. Rodney Hammond focus on preventive and treatment interventions for aggression and violence among a slightly older group—adolescents—using a public health model of primary, secondary, and tertiary (treatment) programs. The programs they describe vary on a number of dimensions, including the targeted population and guiding theoretical framework, as well as in whether efforts are directed toward changing individuals or toward changing the systems that influence individual behavior (e.g., family, peers, school, and community).

Guerra and her colleagues note that at the individual level, programs that promote social–cognitive skills (e.g., perspective taking, alternative solution generation, self-esteem enhancement, peer negotiation skills) are likely to have the most impact on adolescent violence at the primary and secondary prevention levels. At the systems level, programs that attempt to influence environmental factors related to the learning of aggression (e.g., the presence of aggressive models or reinforcement for aggressive behavior), as well as those that attempt to affect situational variables (e.g., the presence of police or the availability of guns in a community) appear promising. They also note that with regard to treatment of already violent adolescents who come from impoverished environments, single dimension, short-term interventions are unlikely to be successful. Integration of individual, family, peer group, and community interventions over a long period of time seem necessary to make any real difference.

In the last chapter in this section, chapter 17, Eva Fiendler and Judith Becker focus on children and adolescents as victims of family violence, both physical and sexual, because children so victimized may develop delinquent and criminal careers, may victimize their own children, or may be prime targets for victimization outside of the family. (Although it should be emphasized that most victims of family violence do not go on to physically and sexually victimize others; for a discussion of cycle-of-violence theory and research, see Emery, 1989.)

The authors describe prevention and intervention programs for both victims and perpetrators of such abuse. Traditionally, parents have been the focus of prevention and treatment programs, but more recently, child characteristics that may influence violent family patterns have been identified, and the interaction of these characteristics with environmental stressors has been emphasized.

Like other authors in this book, Feindler and Becker emphasize that programs that view family violence as interactive and influenced by all three factors are likely to be most effective in preventing family violence, in treating violent parents, and in dealing with the sequelae of child and adolescent abuse, which may include both the transmission of intergenerational violence and the spread of violence beyond the confines of the family to the community at large.

In this spirit, Fiendler and Becker also review programs targeting juvenile sex offenders, because a high percentage of such offenders may have been victims of childhood violence themselves. Various treatment programs exist for juvenile sex offenders, but outcome studies in this area are sorely lacking. The majority of such programs have as their aim enhancing social and assertiveness skills, developing victim empathy and nondeviant sexual interests, teaching sex education, and decreasing deviant arousal.

Attention to interventions in the prevention of violence and the treatment of youthful perpetrators and victims of violence has been a traditional way in which psychologists have contributed to the reduction of violence in society. Although this book advocates expanding the role of psychologists in other pursuits (e.g., policy making and research), the role of practicing psychologists working directly with youth will continue to be a major and integral part of psychology's contribution to preventing and reducing violence among America's youth.

Reference

Emery, R. (1989). Family violence. *American Psychologist, 44,* 321–328.

15

Interventions for Aggressive and Antisocial Children

Alan E. Kazdin

Aggressive behavior includes a variety of acts such as fighting, cruelty, vandalism, fire-setting, and threatening others, to mention a few. Such behaviors in children often are associated with other antisocial and conduct problem behaviors including stealing, using and abusing harmful substances, lying, truancy, and running away. Aggressive and antisocial behaviors can vary markedly in severity, chronicity, and frequency; they can also come in various combinations. The development and identification of effective interventions for aggressive and antisocial behavior are critically important for several reasons. First, antisocial behavior represents a prevalent and significant clinical and social problem. Epidemiological studies indicate that between 2% and 6% of youth evince clinically severe forms of antisocial behavior (Institute of Medicine [IOM], 1989). In the United States alone this translates into approximately 1.3 to 3.8 million cases. Although less than half of these youth are likely to continue the pattern of aggressive and antisocial behavior, the majority suffer significant impairment in adulthood (Robins, 1978). The problem of antisocial behavior is not "only" life long but often continues across generations (e.g., Huesmann, Eron, Lefkowitz, & Walder, 1984; Robins, West, & Herjanic, 1975). Obviously, identifying effective interventions or making any effort to interrupt the pattern and course are high priorities.

Second and related, aggressive and antisocial behavior often has severe consequences for others. Siblings, peers, parents, and teachers of aggressive children, as well as strangers, are victims of aggressive acts perpetrated by children. As aggressive and antisocial behaviors continue over the course of development, there are more victims of acts of murder, rape, robbery, arson, drunk driving, and spouse and child abuse that are carried out to a greater extent by adults with a history of aggressive behavior in childhood than by other persons (Kazdin, 1987a). Consequently, effective intervention for ag-

Completion of this chapter was greatly facilitated by the support of a Research Scientist Award (MH00353) and a grant (MH35408) from the National Institute of Mental Health. The support of these projects is gratefully acknowledged. Correspondence concerning this paper should be directed to: Alan E. Kazdin, Department of Psychology, Yale University, P.O. Box 20805, New Haven, CT 06520–8205.

gressive behavior in children can have significant consequences for others in society.

Third, the monetary costs of aggressive and antisocial behavior make identification of effective interventions critically important. The precise costs are difficult to estimate because youth with aggressive and antisocial behavior often traverse several systems including mental health, juvenile justice, special education, and social services. The expense is more concretely conveyed by identifying specific examples of aggressive acts among juveniles. In the mid-1970s, separate estimates of the costs of vandalism and firesetting among juveniles in the United States were approximately $600 and $700 million, respectively, in a single year ("Fire in the U.S.," 1978; U.S. Senate Judiciary Committee, 1976). The costs for psychological treatment, family social work, juvenile adjudication and incarceration, special programs in education, and those incurred by social agencies are difficult to estimate. Because a large proportion of antisocial youth remain in contact with mental health and criminal justice systems well into adulthood, antisocial behavior has been identified as possibly the most expensive mental health problem (Robins, 1981).

This chapter focuses on interventions designed to prevent and to treat aggressive and antisocial behavior in children. It begins with an elaboration of the scope and nature of aggressive and antisocial behavior. Characteristics of children who engage in antisocial behavior convey the special challenges that this domain of functioning places on developing effective interventions. Prevention and treatment programs are illustrated to convey promising interventions. Several issues and research priorities are also discussed including the importance of basic and applied research, the need for expanded models of intervention, and the integration of a developmental perspective in identifying opportunities for intervention.

Characteristics of Aggressive and Antisocial Behavior

Scope and Focus

Aggressive behavior serves as the primary focus of this chapter. However, there are a number of complexities that affect the scope of the topic. To begin, aggression has been defined and measured in many different ways. Different types of aggression are included, such as physical aggression (e.g., assaults against others or destruction of objects), verbal aggression (e.g., verbal threats), nonverbal (e.g., facial) expressions, and gestures. Second, aggression is sometimes defined by a particular act as well as the accompanying purpose or intent. The APA Commission on Youth and Violence, for example, stressed the interpersonal and intentional nature of the behaviors they considered violent, thus helping to clarify what is meant by aggression in ambiguous situations. For example, juvenile firesetting is often a purposeful and aggressive act, as attested to by the motive and intent of the child. Yet, sometimes the motive and intent are quite different (e.g., curiosity), and therefore the act would not be considered aggressive in these terms. Third, the characteristics of aggression vary over the course of development. What is aggressive at one age may change in form, scope, severity, and consequences over time. Finally, and to be discussed in greater length, aggressive behavior is often associated with other problem behaviors such as vandalism, theft, truancy, and substance use. A constellation of antisocial behaviors that includes aggression is likely to be present in the repertoires of individual children. Consequently, discussion of research, particularly intervention research, focuses on both aggression and antisocial behavior.

There are a large number of youth who engage in aggressive and antisocial behavior in everyday life. When community samples of youth are surveyed about the aggressive and antisocial behaviors in which they engage, the prevalence rates are extraordinarily high. For example, among youth (ages 13–18) more than 50% admit to theft, 35% admit to assault, 45% admit to property destruction, and 60% admit to engaging in more than one type of antisocial behavior (e.g., aggressive acts, drug abuse, arson, vandalism) (Feldman, Caplinger, & Wodarski, 1983; Williams & Gold, 1972). Although most of the data are available for adolescents rather than children, the scope of the problem in adolescents has important and immediate implications for childhood. Preventive efforts in childhood are obviously one line of attack to avert the onset of antisocial behavior in adolescence.

Most children who engage in aggressive and antisocial behavior are not brought to the attention of mental health or juvenile justice systems because their behavior is not systematically detected or viewed as a problem among those with whom they are in contact. Such youth may become involved in occasional fights with peers, use and abuse drugs, drop out of school, engage in sexual activity early for one's age, run away from home, not attend school, and become pregnant early in adolescence. Youth who engage in such behaviors often are referred to as youth at risk because their behaviors place them at risk for more serious antisocial behavior and untoward long-term outcomes (Dryfoos, 1990; Hechinger, 1992; U.S. Congress, 1986, 1991).

Aggressive and antisocial behavior often is identified as problematic in youth and leads to contact by the child and his or her family with mental health and juvenile justice systems. It is important to comment on antisocial behavior as designated in psychiatric and legal spheres because much of the research designed to understand aggression and violence has relied on these designations. In contemporary psychiatric diagnosis, persistent aggressive and antisocial behavior in children and adolescents is designated as conduct disorder. For example, in the *Diagnostic and Statistical Manual of Mental Disorders,* 4th edition (*DSM–IV*; American Psychiatric Association, 1994), to meet criteria for the disorder the child or adolescent must show (for at least 12 months) any three of the following behavioral characteristics: bullying, threatening, or intimidating others; initiating physical fights; using a weapon to harm others; being physically cruel to people or animals; stealing from someone; forcing someone into sexual activity; setting fires with the intention of causing damage; destroying property of others; breaking into someone else's house, building, or car; lying to obtain goods or favors or to avoid obligations;

staying out late at night despite parental prohibitions; running away from home overnight; and being truant from school.

Merely listing the behaviors does not adequately convey those features that distinguish clinically referred youth. First, among youths whose behavior meets diagnostic criteria for conduct disorder many of the behaviors such as fighting, temper tantrums, stealing, and others are relatively frequent. In some cases, the behaviors may be of a low frequency (e.g., firesetting), in which case intensity or severity is the central characteristic. Second, repetitiveness and chronicity of the behaviors are critical features. The behaviors are not likely to be isolated events or to be restricted to a brief period during which other influences or stressors (e.g., change in residence, divorce) are operative. Third, the breadth of the deviant behaviors is central as well. There are usually several behaviors that occur together and form a constellation. Fourth, included with the diagnosis is the criterion that the individual suffers impairment in everyday life. This is usually reflected in significant problems in interpersonal relations (e.g., parents, teachers, siblings, peers) and deficiencies in meeting role expectations (e.g., academic impairment, deportment problems at school).

Antisocial behavior also is recognized as a legal designation referred to as *delinquency*, based on official contact with the courts. There are several specific acts that can be referred to as delinquent. These include index offenses that are criminal if committed by anyone (e.g., homicide, robbery), as well as status offenses that include a variety of behaviors that are illegal because of the age of the youth (e.g., use of alcohol, driving a car, not attending school).

Delinquency, as a legal designation, and conduct disorder, as a psychiatric designation, overlap but are not the same. Youth whose behaviors meet criteria for conduct disorder may or may not engage in behaviors that are defined as delinquent or have any contact with the police and courts. Official contact with police is unlikely to take place or to be recorded for young children. Delinquent acts in early and middle childhood usually are dealt with informally rather than officially. On the other hand, conduct disorder may be identified and brought to attention early, as the child's behavior comes into conflict on a daily basis with parent and teacher expectations. Youth who are identified as meeting criteria for conduct disorder are not necessarily defined as delinquent. Similarly, delinquent youth, adjudicated by the courts, would not necessarily be considered as having conduct disorder. The youth may have committed crimes (homicide, selling of narcotics, prostitution) on one or more occasions but not be regarded as impaired, emotionally disturbed, or functioning poorly in the context of everyday life. Although the distinction can be drawn, many of the behaviors that make up conduct disorder and delinquency overlap and fall under the general rubric of antisocial behavior.

Special Features

Antisocial behaviors often come in "packages." Several studies have shown that aggressive, conduct problem, and antisocial behaviors go together (e.g.,

Elliott, Huizinga, & Menard, 1988; Farrell, Danish, & Howard, 1992; New-comb, & Bentler, 1988). For example, drug abuse, delinquent acts, and aca-demic dysfunction are likely to go together. These behaviors do not invariably co-occur, yet, a sample of youth identified with one of the behaviors (e.g., early sexual activity) is more likely to have higher rates of other behaviors (sub-stance use and abuse, delinquent acts) than a comparison sample similar in age and sex.

A dominant theoretical view that captures these findings is referred to as *problem behavior theory*, which emerged from the study of adolescents (Jessor & Jessor, 1977). The theory is based on the view that multiple problem be-haviors are similar in the functions they serve for the individual. Several problem behaviors may bring similar rewards (e.g., peer acceptance) or serve common purposes (e.g., obtaining autonomy from parents). The finding that at-risk behaviors come in packages has implications for prevention and treat-ment, as is addressed later.

"Packages" of more serious dysfunction are also evident among youth. Ep-idemiological studies of community (nonclinic) samples suggest that youth who meet criteria for a psychiatric disorder often meet criteria for at least one other disorder as well (Caron & Rutter, 1991). The presence of two or more disorders, referred to as comorbidity, is more prevalent in clinically referred youth. For example, in our own outpatient service where youth (ages 7–13) are referred for aggressive and antisocial behavior, approximately 70% meet criteria for more than one diagnosis (DSM–III–R) (Kazdin, Siegel, & Bass, 1992). As is well known, hyperactivity (attention-deficit/hyperactivity disor-der [ADHD]) co-exists with conduct disorder in a large percentage (e.g., 45–70%) of cases. Other comorbid conditions (e.g., depression, substance abuse) may be present as well. The findings that antisocial behavior in community and clinic samples come in "packages" and co-occur with other conditions is important to note because of the implications for designing interventions as well as for evaluating their impact.

Associated features. Children with aggressive and antisocial behavior are likely to show a number of other characteristics in their repertoires that are potentially relevant for intervention (Henggeler, 1989; Kazdin, 1987a; U.S. Congress, 1991). Youth with antisocial behavior are likely to show academic deficiencies, as reflected in achievement level, grades, being left back, early termination from school, and deficiencies in specific skill areas, especially reading. Such youth are also likely to evince poor interpersonal relations, as reflected in diminished social skills in relation to peers and adults and higher levels of peer rejection. Youth who engage in antisocial behavior also may show a variety of cognitive and attributional processes. Deficits and distor-tions in cognitive problem-solving skills, predisposition to attribute hostile intent to others, and resentment and suspiciousness are a few cognitive fea-tures associated with aggressive and antisocial behavior.

Parent and family characteristics. Parent and family characteristics are associated with aggressive and antisocial child behavior (Kazdin, 1987a; Robins, 1991; Rutter & Giller, 1983; U.S. Congress, 1991). Criminal behavior and alcoholism, particularly in the father, are two of the stronger and more consistently demonstrated characteristics of parents of aggressive and antisocial youth. Parent disciplinary practices and attitudes that are harsh, lax, erratic, or inconsistent often characterize the parents of aggressive and antisocial youth. Dysfunctional relations are also evident in parents as reflected in less acceptance of their children; less warmth, affection, and emotional support; and less attachment, compared with parents of nonreferred youth. At the level of family relations, less supportive and more defensive communications among family members, less participation in activities as a family, and more clear dominance of one family member are also evident. In addition, unhappy marital relations, interpersonal conflict, and aggression often characterize the parental relations of antisocial children.

Contextual conditions. The conditions in which youth live often serve as risk factors for antisocial behavior. Examples include large family size, overcrowding, poor housing, poor parental supervision, disadvantaged school settings, and others (Kazdin, 1987a). These conditions are relevant to prevention and treatment both on conceptual and applied grounds. Many of the untoward conditions in which families live place stress on the parent or diminish the threshold for coping with everyday stressors. The net effect can be evident in parent–child interaction in which parents inadvertently engage in patterns that sustain or accelerate aggressive interactions (e.g., Patterson, Capaldi, & Bank, 1991). Stress and socioeconomic disadvantage relate to remaining in and profiting from treatment (e.g., Dumas & Wahler, 1983; Kazdin, 1990) and hence cannot be neglected in intervention research.

General Comments

Although the present focus emphasizes aggression, much of the literature has focused on the broader pattern of antisocial behavior of which aggression is often a part. Thus, many interventions are designed to address a broad range of antisocial behaviors including aggression because of the repertoires of the children who serve as the target focus. This chapter emphasizes interventions and outcomes related to aggression and violence, although the broader domain may be the usual focus of intervention research.

Aggression and antisocial behavior reflect more than a pattern of behavior within youth themselves. There is a child–parent–family context that includes multiple and reciprocal influences that affect each participant (child and parent) and the systems in which they operate (family, school). The interactive context poses challenges for developing models of aggressive and antisocial behavior as well as for identifying effective interventions. The challenge is to identify how the interventions can, in theory, alter the constellation of antisocial behaviors and the relevant contexts in which these behaviors are embedded and then, of course, to implement the interventions in practice.

Underpinnings of Intervention Research

The development of effective interventions depends on the accumulation of controlled trials in which well-defined and described interventions are contrasted against each other and the various control conditions. Examples of such research are readily available in both prevention and treatment and will be highlighted later. In a fundamental way, advances in the development of effective interventions stem from understanding the emergence of aggressive behavior, the risk factors and mechanisms that contribute to its emergence, and paths that might be influenced by interventions. Advances in understanding as well as in methods of research are highlighted here because they provide the underpinnings of progress in intervention research.

Understanding Aggressive and Antisocial Child Behavior

Several areas relating to the nature of aggressive and antisocial child behavior illustrate the important advances that underlie intervention research. First, the study of processes that may underlie aggressive behavior represents a foundation on which treatments can draw. For example, Dodge and his colleagues have identified a significant *attributional bias* among aggressive children and adolescents (e.g., Dodge, Price, Bachorowski, & Newman, 1990; Dodge & Somberg, 1987). Aggressive youth tend to view ambiguous situations (in which the intention of others is unclear) as hostile. The attribution of hostility to others precipitates aggressive acts that are merely retaliatory from the standpoint of the aggressive child. These acts, however, do not seem justified in the views of the child's peers. Peer rejection appears to follow aggressive behavior. The reactions of the peers and their dislike of and isolation of the aggressive child provide additional cues to the aggressive child that the environment is hostile. Thus, a vicious circle of aggressive behavior and untoward peer reactions can be sustained. Research such as the work on attributional bias serves to identify potential points of intervention to interrupt aggressive behavior. Further research that would elaborate the development of attributional biases and related maladaptive cognitions might have potential implications for developing interventions to prevent aggression.

As another area of research, different types and patterns of antisocial behavior have been hypothesized among clinically referred youth. Different subtypes of youth who engage in aggressive and antisocial behavior have been proposed including those whose antisocial behavior emerges in childhood versus adolescence (Hinshaw, Lahey, & Hart, 1993), those who engage in aggression rather than theft (e.g., Patterson, 1982), those whose aggression seems to be reactive (in response to others) rather than proactive (as an initial way of goal attainment) (Dodge, 1991), and those whose antisocial behavior is primarily overt (fighting) rather than covert (lying, truancy) (Loeber & Schmalling, 1985). Additional ways of subtyping antisocial behavior among children depend on other characteristics with which antisocial behavior is associated. Aggressive youth who vary in social withdrawal (Serbin, Moskowitz, Schwartzman, & Ledingham, 1991) or in positive prosocial behavior (Eron & Huesmann, 1984; Tremblay, 1991) have different prognoses for long-term adjustment. Generally, children with social deficits in addition to their antisocial behavior have a poorer long-term outcome.

The many different ways of dissecting aggressive and antisocial behavior are highly promising for research. Different subtypes are designed to draw attention to possible developmental paths that lead to antisocial behavior. It is likely that identification of varied paths will have implications for early identification, prevention, and treatment. For example, for some time, it has been known that coercive parent–child interactions are likely in the homes of aggressive children (Patterson, 1982). The implication is that parent training that restructures these interactions is likely to be more appropriate in dealing with aggressive children. To date, few studies have attempted to match youth who vary in patterns or type of antisocial behavior and various treatments or to test predictions of type of aggressive and antisocial behavior by treatment interactions. However, the underpinnings for more specific types of predictions about the impact of treatment for varied subtypes continue to develop.

Longitudinal studies of youth and identification of factors that place youth at risk for aggressive behavior also have critical implications for intervention. Factors that predispose children to aggressive behavior, as highlighted previously, have been studied extensively in the context of community samples, clinical referrals, and adjudicated delinquents (Pepler & Rubin, 1991; Robins & Rutter, 1990). Diverse factors have been identified related to the child (e.g., temperament, early onset of unmanageable behavior), parents (e.g., criminal behavior, harsh child-rearing practices), family (e.g., large family size, marital discord), school (e.g., poor work ethos, physical disarray), and other domains (Kazdin, 1987b). Obviously, not all individuals at risk will show later dysfunction. This can be attributed to imperfections of assessment of risk (the predictors) and subsequent antisocial behavior (the criterion) as well as changes in risk status on a particular factor over time. A conceptually interesting and potentially critical set of influences that may affect onset are referred to as *protective factors*. These factors refer to influences that may cancel or attenuate the influence of known risk factors. Researchers have identified protective factors by studying groups of individuals known to be at risk because of the presence of several risk factors, and by identifying a subgroup that does not later evince antisocial behavior.

For example, in a longitudinal study from birth through young adulthood, youth were identified as at risk for delinquency based on a number of risk factors (Werner & Smith, 1992). Those at-risk youth who did not evince delinquency by adolescence were more likely to be first born, to be perceived by their mothers as affectionate, to show higher self-esteem and locus of control, and to have alternative caretakers in the family (other than the parents), and a supportive same-sex model who provided structure. Such factors are important in helping to suggest why many individuals who are at risk do not develop antisocial behavior. In general, the study of risk and protective factors is important not only to describe the characteristics associated with aggressive and antisocial behavior, but also to provide the building blocks for theories about mechanisms of dysfunction and for the design of prevention efforts.

Research has focused on how factors might interrelate and lead to dysfunction. For example, Elliott, Huizinga, and Ageton (1985) examined delinquency and drug use in a sample of youth (ages 11–17) who were evaluated annually. A variety of constructs was measured (e.g., the youths' family and school aspirations and involvement; exposure to delinquent peers; personal characteristics such as isolation, educational goals, attitudes toward deviance) and used to predict self-reported delinquency and drug use 3 years later. Bonding (or attachment) to deviant peers was directly related to delinquency and later drug use for both males and females and across multiple measures of delinquency and drug use. Moreover, weak conventional bonding (i.e., poor connections with family and school) was a factor that led to increases in deviant bonding. Thus, early in the path toward delinquency there is a breakdown in connections to home, school, and family. The model suggests that interventions would be advised to focus on these connections to effect change or to prevent delinquency.

In general, the previous example represents only a small portion of the research on which current interventions rely. Research that examines aggressive and violent behavior and its developmental course not only tests theory about the nature of aggressive and antisocial behavior, but also has implications for intervention research. The specific predictions about what interventions to apply, for whom, and when during their development should be guided by basic research.

Improved Methods of Evaluation

Along with improved understanding of aggressive and antisocial behavior, advances have been made in research practices, procedures, and methods of evaluation. Methodological developments that have contributed directly to progress in child intervention research can be illustrated with several examples. First, development of measures of child functioning has accelerated greatly (e.g., Rutter, Tuma, & Lann, 1988). The assessment of child problem behaviors with standardized measures has permitted diverse lines of research including the study of prevalence and incidence of dysfunction and developmental course. In general, development of standardized measures has broad implications for better description and identification of aggressive and antisocial youth, evaluation of a broad range of theoretical constructs to evaluate youth, and finer-grained evaluation of intervention outcomes.

A second and related methodological development has been the assessment of community samples of youth of different ages (e.g., Achenbach & Edelbrock, 1981). The assessment of normative levels of functioning at different age levels charts the patterns of individual behaviors as well as constellations of behavior that wax and wane over the course of development. Description of normative levels of functioning serves as a basis to help understand the course of development and provides baseline information for evaluating the functioning of clinically referred youth before and after treatment.

A third methodological advance in research has been improved operationalization of intervention procedures, particularly in the area of treatment. A large number of manuals have appeared for a variety of treatments for children and adolescents including psychoanalytically and psychodynamically oriented treatments (e.g., Kernberg & Chazan, 1991), diverse cognitively based treatments (e.g., Horne & Sayger, 1990), parent training (e.g., Forehand & McMahon, 1981), behavioral social skills training (e.g., King & Kirschenbaum, 1992), experiential psychotherapy (e.g., Wright, Everett, & Roisman, 1986), and community-based treatment (e.g., Steen & Monnette, 1989). The manuals specify critical events and practices and serve to guide the therapist. By providing concrete guidelines for carrying out particular techniques, one can better assess treatment integrity, that is, the extent to which those persons delivering the treatment have actually adhered to the treatment prescriptions. Specification of treatment in manual form can also facilitate replication studies among researchers and dissemination of empirically developed treatments to clinical practice (Kazdin, 1992).

A final illustration of methodological advances that have enhanced intervention research includes expansion of the range of statistical models and data analytic methods. As one example, the description and evaluation of models of dysfunction, already mentioned, have profited from such methods as structural equation modeling (e.g., Newcomb & Bentler, 1988). The ability to evaluate multiple measures of a given construct (latent variable), to examine relations among variables at a given point in time and over time, and to identify possible paths of influence and direct and indirect influences on a particular outcome can clarify possible points of intervention. Meta-analysis is another analytic method that has contributed to treatment research. Although meta-analyses are driven by substantive questions (e.g., the effectiveness of treatment), their use has helped identify weaknesses and areas of neglect in both the focus and reporting of treatment research with children (e.g., Kazdin, Bass, Ayers, & Rodgers, 1990; Weiss & Weisz, 1990).

General Comments

The substantive and methodological examples highlighted here do not exhaust the range of developments that contribute to identifying effective interventions. The full scope of research on "normal" development is relevant. For example, theory and research on prenatal development, child temperament, attachment, and parent child-rearing practices relate to affective, cognitive, and behavioral development and to patterns of adjustment. The important point to make is the critical role that basic research and improved research methods plays in providing the underpinnings of intervention research. The quality of intervention research and the likelihood of identifying effective and replicable interventions very much depend on the extent to which substantive and methodological advances are made.

Promoting Prosocial Competence and Preventing Aggressive and Antisocial Behavior

Overview and Current Status

Logically, prevention of antisocial behavior should be practiced prior to considerations of treatment. Prevention programs, if successful, can avert and minimize antisocial behavior in childhood. Treatment could be reserved for those cases for whom preventive efforts have failed. Although prevention might be logically practiced before treatment in the effort to intervene, treatment of aggressive and antisocial behavior has received greater attention.

The scope of interventions designed to improve social competence and to prevent dysfunction among children is vast in light of the many distinguishing characteristics of the programs and their objectives (Rickel & Allen, 1987; U.S. Congress, 1991). First, different goals of preventive efforts can be distinguished. Primary prevention is directed toward reducing the rate of onset of dysfunction (incidence); secondary prevention is directed toward reducing the severity, duration, and manifestation among cases with early signs of dysfunction.[1] Second, programs differ in their central focus. Some programs are aimed at developing prosocial competence or adaptive functioning; others focus on reducing onset of dysfunction or preventing a specific problem (e.g., substance abuse, delinquency). Third, programs often vary in whether they are applied universally (e.g., all students in a school, district, or city) or whether they are aimed at a special subgroup of youth who are selected and screened because of their high-risk status. Fourth, programs rely on different settings and hence on the resources and interventions deployed to achieve their goals. For example, programs in the schools, at home, and at special daycare or activity centers, alone and in various combinations, have all served as the basis for prevention. These characteristics lead to a broad range of interventions and provide multiple options to improve adjustment and to prevent maladjustment.

Prevention programs generally are designed to reduce factors that place youth at risk for antisocial behavior. At-risk factors refer to conditions that increase the likelihood, above base rates in the population, that individuals will show the condition or dysfunction. A great deal of research is available on factors that increase risk for aggressive and antisocial behavior (see Farrington, 1985; Kazdin, 1987a; Loeber, 1990; Patterson, Reid, & Dishion, 1992; Rutter & Giller, 1983). Child, parent, and family factors are salient domains that have been studied. For example, among the child factors, pre- and perinatal complications (e.g., maternal infections during pregnancy, low birth weight), "difficult" temperament, early signs of aggressive behavior, and academic delays or dysfunction can place youth at risk later for aggressive and antisocial behavior. Among parent and family factors, parent psychopathology

---

[1] Tertiary prevention is occasionally defined as the effort to reduce disability or dysfunction and its complications among individuals who already experience the dysfunction.

or criminality, harsh and inconsistent discipline practices, poor supervision and monitoring of the child, parent conflict and marital discord, and large family size are salient influences. Several risk factors have been identified that relate to onset and course of aggressive and antisocial behavior. Even so, there remain several complexities that have direct implications for how the risk factors might be used to identify children for preventive interventions. First, risk factors come in packages; at a given point in time several factors may be present, such as low income, large family size, overcrowding, poor housing, poor parental supervision, parent criminality, and marital discord, to mention a few. The co-occurrence makes identifying the unique contribution of individual factors somewhat difficult. Second, over time several risk factors become interrelated because the presence of one factor can augment the accumulation of other risk factors. For example, early academic dysfunction can lead to truancy and dropping out of school, which further increase risk for antisocial behavior. The accumulation of risk factors means that the specific role of a given factor in the sequence leading to antisocial behavior is difficult to discern. Third, factors combine and vary in their effects as a function of other variables such as the child's sex and age. For example, boys may be more vulnerable to discontinuous mothering and adverse home conditions than girls as risk factors for antisocial behavior (Kazdin, 1987a). In some cases, both sexes may be influenced by a given factor but the strength of association may vary. In other cases, the influence may be a risk factor for one sex but not the other. The central point is that multiple risk factors related to the onset of antisocial behavior have been identified. The accumulation of risk factors, rather than any single factor, appears to be important. Prevention programs often use risk factors to identify target populations for intervention. In addition, programs also focus on altering risk factors (e.g., child-rearing practices) as illustrated later, and developing competencies (e.g., problem-solving skills) to protect children against the influence of such factors.

Several reviews and monographs on prevention attest to the burgeoning literature and the positive outcomes that can be achieved (Goldston, Yager, Heinicke, & Pynoos, 1990; Price, Cowen, Lorion, & Ramos-McKay, 1988; Rickel & Allen, 1987). From many demonstration projects, several conclusions seem warranted:

- Prevention programs directed early in life (e.g., pre- and post-natal counseling, continued contact with family and child in first few years of life) can reduce factors that increase risk for antisocial behavior (e.g., school dropout) and clinical dysfunction in childhood and adolescence (McCord & Tremblay, 1992; Zigler, Taussig, & Black, 1992);
- School-based programs for children and adolescents have improved prosocial competence and reduced at-risk behavior (Schinke, Botvin, & Orlandi, 1991; Weissberg, Caplan, & Harwood, 1991);
- Programs vary in the breadth of impact. Sometimes, programs alter multiple domains of functioning including, for example, several at-risk behaviors (e.g., school dropout, teen pregnancy, substance use) (e.g., Allen, Philliber, & Hoggson, 1990). Broad impact is critically important to document in light of evidence that was highlighted previously

noting that multiple problem behaviors often co-occur. On other occasions, however, programs are more specific in their effects (e.g., altering use of one substance but not others, improving social competence but not altering at-risk behaviors) (e.g., Caplan & Weissberg, 1989; Johnson et al., 1990); and

■ Occasionally, programs have not been effective or have exacerbated the problem domain (e.g., antisocial behavior, drug use) they were trying to redress (e.g., Bangert-Drowns, 1988; Shaffer et al., 1990), a point commented on later.

Illustrations of Promising Interventions

Efforts to prevent aggressive and antisocial behavior, particularly delinquency, are vast. A number of efforts have shown little or no effect (Lundman, 1984). Within the last decade there has been considerable promise; a number of programs have shown that antisocial behavior can be reduced with preventive interventions (McCord & Tremblay, 1992; Zigler et al., 1992). Improved results appear to have arisen from better understanding of the emergence of antisocial behavior, implementation of comprehensive and protracted intervention programs, and more careful evaluation of long-term intervention effects. Three types of prevention programs are illustrated below to convey the scope of interventions and the types of results that are evident over the course of follow-up. No effort is made to comprehensively review results from the full range of available programs (McCord & Tremblay, 1992; U.S. Congress, 1991; Zigler et al., 1992).

Early parent / family intervention. Several studies have focused on the reduction of risk factors that portend child aggressive and antisocial behavior. In many studies, the purpose was not to prevent antisocial behavior of the children nor were measures of antisocial behavior even included to evaluate outcome. Nevertheless, the connection between risk reduction and later aggressive and antisocial behavior is evident in a few studies and conveys the relevance of this focus.

Provence and Naylor (1983) completed a project designed to aid disadvantaged young parents to support the development of their children and to improve family life. The rationale was that impairment and stress of the parents impede family functioning and increase risk of dysfunction for the child. Mothers at the poverty level were recruited for the project. After the project was completed, a sample matched on several variables (e.g., income level, parents in the home, ethnicity) was recruited and served as a nonintervention control group. The intervention consisted of services to the mothers for a period of 2 1/2 years after delivery. These included home visits by a social worker to address various needs (e.g., safety, obtaining adequate financial and housing aid), child visits for day care at the program center, and developmental and pediatric exams of the child. Within the structure of the program and contacts with program staff, services were tailored to the needs of individual families.

For present purposes, the 10–year follow-up data are particularly interesting (Seitz, Rosenbaum, & Apfel, 1985). Mothers who had received the intervention, when compared with control mothers, were more likely to be self-employed, to have had fewer children, and to have spaced the births of their children more widely. Birth rate and spacing of children (density of the family or family size) address risk factors for antisocial behavior. Children of intervention parents showed higher rates of school attendance, required fewer special services, and were rated more positively by their teachers. Teacher ratings reflected less aggression, acting out behaviors (required for special classroom placement), and school suspensions. Mothers of control children reported more antisocial behavior of their children such as staying out all night without the mother's knowledge, cruelty to animals, and aggressive behavior toward parents and siblings. This study is significant in demonstrating direct changes in risk factors, reductions in aggressive and antisocial behavior, and long-term consequences of early intervention.

Lally, Mangione, and Honig (1988) also provided a program for economically disadvantaged families. Mothers who were low on a socioeconomic scale were recruited and in the last trimester of pregnancy. The intervention consisted of contact with paraprofessionals who provided diverse services related to mother and child care (e.g., nutrition, child development, parent–child interactions, assistance with community services, and other features). Home visits were provided weekly to assist families with such issues as child-rearing, family relations, employment, and community functioning. Although parent contact was viewed as the primary intervention, a central part of the program was day-care which was provided to children for approximately 5 years. Intervention families were compared with a nonrandomly composed control group selected in the same way as the intervention group and matched on several subject and demographic variables.

Follow-up evaluation was completed 10 years after the program had ended at which point the children were between 13 and 16 years of age. Among the changes, those related to aggressive and antisocial behavior are particularly noteworthy. Intervention youth, compared with controls, showed fewer instances of probation, less severity of recorded offenses (including aggressive behavior and physical assult), and lower degree of chronicity. Costs of antisocial behavior (e.g., court costs, probation, placement, detention and related costs) also were lower for youth who received the intervention. Thus, the early intervention had a direct impact on antisocial behavior.

School-based interventions. Several interventions have been based primarily in the schools. Prominent among the examples, Schweinhart and Weikart (1988; Schweinhart, Weikart, & Larner, 1986; Weikart & Schweinhart, 1992) reported a program that was designed to help children who were at risk for school failure. Risk of school failure was based on parental lack of education, low income, and living in a stressful environment. The study began with 3 to 4 year old children who were randomly assigned to intervention or no-intervention groups. The intervention included a classroom program for a 2–year period. The program for the children was 5 mornings per week for 7 months each year. Weekly teacher home visits were also included during this period. Curricula and teacher–child activities were designed to address diverse needs (e.g. intellectual, social, physical) guided by Piagetian views of development for decision making and cognitive processes.

The program ended when the children were 5 to 6 years old. Follow-up assessments continued over several years. The follow-up at age 19 conveyed several noteworthy findings. At age 19, youth who had participated in the preschool program showed lower levels of mental retardation, school drop-out rates, and reliance on welfare assistance compared with youth in the nonintervention group. They also showed greater literacy, higher levels of employment, and greater attendance at college or vocational school. At age 19, women who as youth received the preschool program reported fewer pregnancies and births than women who had not received the program. Thus, the program altered risk factors for aggressive and antisocial behavior in the index youth for their own offspring (e.g., family size, education, presumably social class as a result of employment status). In addition, on self-report measures and arrest records, youth who participated in the program showed lower antisocial behavior. Fewer youth who received the intervention had come to the attention of juvenile authorities or had been arrested. This program, conducted early in life, provides strong evidence for the prevention of aggressive and antisocial behaviors and of factors that place offspring of the target youth at risk for aggressive and antisocial behavior.

Hawkins and his colleagues (Hawkins, Catalano, & Morrison, 1989; Hawkins, Doueck, & Lishner, 1988) developed a program specifically intended to curb antisocial behavior. The program focused on increasing opportunities, skills, and rewards of children in an effort to develop prosocial bonding to conventional social institutions (family, school, peer relations) and values. The intervention included multiple components. The classroom and school components focused on classroom management to address deportment, interactive teaching, and cooperative (peer involved) learning techniques. Each of these was directed toward increasing child involvement in class and attachment to teachers and nondeviant peers. The classroom programs altered the environment to support appropriate behavior, academic skills, and interpersonal attachments to others. A family-based component was designed to improve family management skills (parent management training) and to assist in conflict resolution in relation to misconduct at home and at school. Other components included peer-focused social skills training and community-focused interventions in which career education and counseling are introduced. Data available at the end of one year of the program indicated that intervention youth showed fewer suspensions and expulsions from school than no-intervention youth. Subsequent evaluations have shown reduced rates of self-reported delinquency (e.g., aggressive acts, truancy, and theft) and alcohol use among 5th-grade youth exposed to a program from grades 1 through 4 (Hawkins et al., 1989).

The previous illustrations reflect interventions for children who have not yet evinced significant aggressive and antisocial behavior or related problems. Preventive efforts have also focused on populations in which dysfunction has been evident and where the effort is to limit further development of antisocial behavior. For example, Bry and George (1979, 1980) provided an intervention for 7th-grade youth at risk for school failure. Intervention programs were evaluated that included frequent meetings with students at which specific behaviors were rewarded (e.g., attending school, punctuality, no disciplinary action). Contacts were also made by program staff with teachers and parents. Youth were assigned to intervention or no-intervention groups and evaluated during and after the program. After 2 years of the program, significantly better grades and attendance were found for the intervention group. No differences were evident in disciplinary actions at school. Follow-up evaluations were conducted 1 and 5 years after the program was completed (Bry, 1982). At the 1-year follow-up, intervention youth showed significantly less self-reported criminal behavior than the control group. At the 5–year follow-up evaluation, at which point the youths averaged 19.5 years of age, intervention youth showed fewer court contacts than nonintervention youth.

Olweus (1991) also conducted a novel program that was primarily school-based. The program was a nationwide intervention for schools (grades 1–9) in Norway. The purpose of the program was to reduce and to prevent "bullying" in the schools, that is, repeated victimization (e.g., verbal or physical aggression) by one's peers where there was a power differential (e.g., in strength, age, status). The intervention encompassed teachers, parents, and students. Written materials and other sources of information (e.g., a video cassette) were provided to teachers and parents. Efforts with teachers, parents, and children were made to increase knowledge about the problem of bullying. Within the school, rules were provided and enforced regarding bullying, and efforts were made to support and protect victims. The large-scale effort and the mobilization of multiple influences across settings at a micro and macro level are unique strengths of this program. The impact was evaluated in a quasi-experimental design involving several cohorts of students. After 2 years of the program, bullying was reduced by 50% or more across all grades. Effects were evident for boys and girls. In addition, several antisocial behaviors such as theft, vandalism, and truancy, which were not focused on directly, decreased as well. The program is worth highlighting as an intervention because it conveys an effort to institutionalize an intervention and to deploy teachers, parents, and students in a consistent and concentrated fashion. However, it must be pointed out that there was no control group in the research design.

Community-based interventions. Community-based interventions use existing facilities in the community (e.g., recreational centers, parks) or bring the intervention to youth in the contexts of their everyday lives. For example, Fo and O'Donnell (1975; O'Donnell, Lydgate, & Fo, 1979) conducted programs for children and adolescents (ages 11 to 17) who were referred from a number of agencies (public schools, courts, social welfare agencies) for their behavioral and academic problems. Some of the youth who participated had prior arrest records; others did not. Hence, the project at once addressed treatment (remediation of adjudicated youth) and prevention (for those at risk for delinquency). Adults were recruited from the community to work as therapists and to conduct behavior modification programs individually with the youths. They met with the youths, engaged in a variety of activities (e.g., arts and crafts, fishing, camping) and implemented and evaluated a behavior modification program. Individualized reward programs focused on such behaviors as truancy, fighting, completing chores at home, and homework.

The results indicated changes in fighting, truancy, staying out late, and other problem behaviors in relation to control youth who did not receive treatment. Also, over a 2–year follow-up period, arrest records reflected treatment gains relative to no-treatment controls. However, the effects of the program varied as a function of whether the children had a prior record of offenses. Youth who completed the program and who had no prior arrest record became worse with the intervention, as reflected by an increase in rates of major offenses. This finding might be due to the increased contact these youth had with more deviant peers during the project. The program was effective, however, in decreasing antisocial behavior among those youth who had begun with more severe arrest records.

Among community-based interventions, those devoted to curbing recidivism with individuals early in their careers are particularly noteworthy. Davidson and his colleagues (Davidson & Redner, 1988; Davidson, Redner, Blakely, Mitchell, & Emshoff, 1987) developed a program for youth (12–16 years old) who have been apprehended and referred to juvenile court but have not been formally adjudicated. The intervention consisted of close contact of individual youths with a college student volunteer. The volunteer was trained and supervised by graduate students who were in turn supervised by university faculty. The student and youth were in close contact (6–8 hrs per week) for 18 weeks. The intervention included behavioral contracting, child advocacy, help for youth to obtain access to community resources, and involvement in the community. The contacts between the student volunteer and the youth took place in the youth's home, recreational settings, or other convenient locales. Carefully controlled and large-scale evaluations of the diversion program have shown that the intervention reduced recidivism among those who participated. Recidivism rates reflect police contacts up to 2 years after the point of intake (Davidson et al., 1987). In general, there are several notable features of this program including the replication of intervention effects in several studies, the comparison of the intervention and diverse control (attention placebo) and alternative intervention (e.g., traditional court processing) conditions, and others. The results suggest a viable and well-replicated intervention for reducing severity of dysfunction in youths who are apprehended for offenses.

Current Issues and Limitations

The above illustrations sample several programs with promising leads. A number of points are worth underscoring. To begin, many of the programs are multifaceted and protracted. Interventions often attempt to attenuate and to controvert the influence of multiple risk factors associated with onset and poor prognosis of antisocial behavior. The multiple components (e.g., parent training, academic training of youth) for a period of years reflects the view that strong interventions are needed to produce enduring effects (Kazdin, 1987b;

Zigler et al., 1992). The examples highlighted previously, along with other programs, support the utility of multiple component and protracted programs (McCord & Tremblay, 1992). Available evidence indicates that aggressive and antisocial behavior can be reduced with prevention programs early in childhood, as reflected on a variety of measures (e.g., misconduct records at school, self-report, other report, arrest and court records).

Although many programs have demonstrated a positive impact, several humbling exceptions are available in prevention research in general in which programs have not worked or have demonstrated deleterious effects (e.g., Bangert-Drowns, 1988; Shaffer et al., 1990). Programs may be ineffective for a variety of reasons such as poor staff training, the use of weak interventions (e.g., dissemination of information and education materials only), departures from the intended procedures while the interventions are in effect, lack of administrative support, and others (see Allen et al., 1990; Johnson et al., 1990; Schinke et al., 1991). On the more constructive side, there is general agreement that effective programs draw on the understanding of causes and risk factors leading to antisocial behavior and use intervention methods or techniques that are known to change behavior (e.g., reinforcement, problem-solving skills training).

The multiple goals of prevention programs raise important issues. Many programs focus on developing prosocial competence; others on reducing risk factors and conditions that lead to risk. These foci and goals may overlap in their impact on improving adjustment and adaptive functioning, and reducing impairment. However, the interrelations need to be better understood. For example, developing personal and social competencies may be important in their own right given the stressors and influences that impinge on children. The impact of developing prosocial competence on the prevention of aggressive and antisocial behavior is less clear. Prosocial competence and adaptive functioning are not the inverse of antisocial behavior, and increases in prosocial behavior are not invariably associated with decreases in antisocial behavior (Kazdin, 1993). The importance of understanding how aggressive behavior and prosocial functioning unfold and the relevance of this information for sequencing interventions that promote prosocial behavior apply to both prevention and treatment and hence are addressed later.

As a related issue, prevention programs may have immediate (proximal) and long-term (distal) goals. The long-term goals often are of major concern and serve as the impetus for intervention. For example, one would want to know if an intervention in early childhood improved resilience or decreased the incidence of aggressive and antisocial behavior in childhood and adolescence or if a certain intervention during adolescence had an impact on functioning in adulthood. The impact may be examined years (e.g., 5–20) after the program is completed (e.g., Lally et al., 1988; Seitz et al., 1985). Not all prevention programs require long-term follow-up to be of value. Short-term outcomes (e.g., not beginning to smoke cigarettes or to use alcohol in adolescence) are important in their own right. In many cases, the immediate effects of a program may help youth pass through a sensitive or vulnerable period of development in which they might be susceptible to deleterious influences.

Treatment of Aggressive and Antisocial Behavior

Overview and Current Status

Aggressive, antisocial, and conduct problem behaviors represent the domain most frequently focused on in clinical practice (Kazdin, Siegel, & Bass, 1990) and in therapy research with children and adolescents (Kazdin, Bass, Ayers, & Rodgers, 1990). Many forms of therapy, medication, home, school, and community-based programs, residential and hospital treatment, and social services have been evaluated (for reviews see Brandt & Zlotnick, 1988; Dumas, 1989; Kazdin, 1985, 1987b; Pepler & Rubin, 1991; U.S. Congress, 1991). Psychotherapy, one of many interventions to address emotional and behavioral problems of children, is of special interest for at least two reasons. First, outpatient psychotherapy can preempt the use of more restrictive, costly, and disruptive interventions such as hospitalization and residential care. Maintaining children in the context of their everyday lives, if possible, is much more desirable from the standpoint of adjustment and family preservation. Second, models of psychotherapy and the specific treatment techniques themselves are used in diverse settings including schools, day-treatment and residential inpatient hospital services, and juvenile justice programs. Thus, even when restrictive treatment programs are used, psychotherapy in some form often bears the burden of producing the desired change.

Psychotherapy includes a wide range of interventions designed to decrease or eliminate problem behaviors and maladjustment and to improve adaptive and prosocial functioning. The interventions rely on interpersonal interaction, counseling, or activities following a specific treatment plan. The focus is on how persons feel (affect), think (cognition), and act (behavior). A broad range of conceptual views is in use as reflected in psychoanalytic, psychodynamic, client-centered, behavioral, cognitive, and family approaches. Within and among approaches, techniques vary greatly based on who is seen in treatment (youth, parents, family), the medium of treatment (talk, play), the central therapeutic focus (e.g., the individual, family), and the setting where the intervention is carried out (e.g., clinic, home, school). Over 230 different treatment techniques have been identified that are currently in use for children and adolescents (Kazdin, 1988). The vast majority of these techniques have not been studied empirically.

Several reviews of the effectiveness of psychotherapy for children and adolescents have appeared within the last decade. The evaluation of treatment has been aided by the development of meta-analysis, a set of quantitative procedures that permit the combination of data from several different studies. The most common way of evaluating the literature through meta-analysis is to compute *effect size*, which provides a common metric across investigations.[2]

---

[2]Effect size is calculated as the difference between means of a treatment and a no-treatment or an alternative treatment group, divided by the standard deviation of the control group (or of the pooled sample of both groups). Effect size constitutes the dependent variable for the meta-analysis and is used as a summary statistic to examine the impact of other variables (e.g., types of treatment and clinical problem).

From meta-analyses of child/adolescent therapy (e.g., Casey & Berman, 1985; Hazelrigg, Cooper, &, Borduin, 1987; Kazdin, Bass, Ayers, & Rodgers, 1990; Weisz, Weiss, Alicke, & Klotz, 1987), several conclusions can be drawn:

- The effectiveness of psychotherapy appears to be better than no treatment. This finding has been consistent across reviews that have sampled over 300 studies.
- The magnitude of these effects closely parallels those obtained from outcome research with adults (Brown, 1987). Effect sizes for treatment versus no treatment tend to hover within the range of .7–.8, although reviews of some treatments (e.g., cognitive therapies, family therapies) have shown different effect size estimates (higher and lower, respectively).
- Classes of treatment (e.g., behavioral vs. nonbehavioral) and individual treatment techniques within a given class of treatments do not consistently vary in effectiveness. The paucity of studies of a given technique and their variation with respect to clinical problems and populations may render such comparisons difficult to interpret.
- The effects of treatment are not clearly different for internalizing (e.g., anxiety, depression, withdrawal) and externalizing problems (e.g., hyperactivity, aggression). The absence of consistent methods of delineating problems and the mixture of multiple ages in the reviews make firm conclusions difficult to reach (Kazdin, 1994).

Illustrations of Promising Treatments

Diverse treatments have been applied to youth referred clinically for aggressive and antisocial behavior. Yet, advances have been evident for a number of different treatments (Kazdin, 1987b). Four promising approaches are illustrated below.

Problem-solving skills training. Cognitive processes (perceptions, self-statements, attributions, and problem-solving skills) frequently are accorded a major role in aggressive behavior. As a case in point, aggression is not merely triggered by environmental events, but rather through the way in which these events are perceived and processed. The processing refers to the child's appraisals of the situation, anticipated reactions of others, and self-statements in response to particular events. As mentioned earlier, aggressive youth show a predisposition to attribute hostile intent to others when the cues of actual intent are ambiguous (Dodge et al., 1990; Dodge & Somberg, 1987). Understandably, when situations are initially perceived as hostile, youth are more likely to react aggressively. Other cognitive processes and predispositions have been identified in relation to aggressive children and behavioral adjustment. For example, Spivack and Shure (1982; Spivack, Platt, & Shure, 1976) have identified several interpersonal cognitive problem-solving processes (e.g., generating alternative solutions, means-end thinking, consequential thinking) related to social behavior. Deficits and distortion among these processes of aggressive children relate to teacher ratings of disruptive behavior, peer evaluations, and overt behavior (Rubin, Bream, & Rose-Krasnor, 1991).

Problem-solving skills training consists of developing interpersonal problem-solving skills. Although many variations have been applied to children with conduct problems (Camp & Bash, 1985; Kendall & Braswell, in press; Spivack et al., 1976), several characteristics are shared. First, the emphasis is on how children approach situations. Although it is obviously important that children ultimately select appropriate means of behaving in everyday life, the primary focus is on the thought processes rather than the outcome or specific behavioral acts that result. Second, children are taught to engage in a step-by-step approach to solve interpersonal problems. They make statements to themselves that direct attention to certain aspects of the problem or tasks that lead to effective solutions. Third, treatment uses structured tasks involving games, academic activities, and stories. Over the course of treatment, the cognitive problem-solving skills are increasingly applied to real-life situations. Fourth, therapists usually play an active role in treatment. They model the cognitive processes by making verbal self-statements, apply the sequence of statements to particular problems, provide cues to prompt use of the skills, and deliver feedback and praise to develop correct use of the skills. Finally, treatment usually combines several different procedures including modeling and practice, role-playing, and reinforcement and mild punishment (loss of points or tokens). In an example from my own research, my colleagues and I examined the effectiveness of problem-solving skills training, nondirective relationship therapy, and minimal treatment contact with hospitalized children (ages 7–13) referred for aggressive and antisocial behavior (Kazdin, Esveldt-Dawson, French, & Unis, 1987). In the problem-solving skills training condition, youth were seen individually and trained to apply the skills to interpersonal interactions in which the children had engaged in aggressive and antisocial behavior. Relationship therapy consisted of sessions that focused on developing a close therapeutic relationship, providing empathy, positive regard, and warmth, and helping the child to express feelings. Minimal-contact children met briefly in sessions with a therapist and played games or engaged in other activities that provided contact but no specific treatment regimen to alter antisocial behavior. The results showed significant improvements in antisocial behavior and other problem areas for children who received problem-solving skills training, as reflected on parent and teacher checklists of child functioning at home and at school immediately after treatment (after discharge from the hospital) and up to 1 year later. Children who received problem-solving skills training were more improved than relationship therapy and minimal contact children, who did not reliably improve.

Several other studies have attested to the effectiveness of cognitively based treatment in changing aggressive and antisocial behavior (see Durlak, Fuhrman, & Lampman, 1991; Kazdin, 1987b; Kendall, 1991; Pepler & Rubin, 1991). Gains have been evident in measures of child functioning at home, at school, and in the community. Benefits of treatment often are evident up to 1 year later, although improvements are not invariably maintained (e.g., Kendall, Ronan, & Epps, 1991).

There are limitations to outcome research in this area. To begin with, the magnitude of therapeutic changes must be bolstered. Typically, treatments lead to improvements but do not place children within the levels of functioning of nonreferred peers. Second, few studies have elaborated the factors that contribute to treatment outcome. For example, it is not clear that changes in cognitive processes, the presumed focus of treatment, are related to therapeutic change. Also, level of cognitive development has been proposed as a moderator of outcome but has not been specifically tested (Durlak et al., 1991). In general, the bases of treatment effects are not well understood. Nevertheless, gains have been achieved with cognitively based treatment in relation to aggressive and antisocial behavior.

Parent management training. Parent management training refers to procedures in which parents are trained to alter their child's behavior in the home. The parents meet with a therapist or trainer who teaches them to use specific procedures to alter interactions with their child, to promote prosocial behavior, and to decrease deviant behavior. Training is based on the view that aggressive behavior is developed and sustained in the home by maladaptive parent–child interactions. Indeed, inept discipline practices, coercive interaction sequences between parent and child, and increasingly aggressive child behavior over time as a result of these interactions have been well-documented (Patterson, 1982, 1986; Patterson et al., 1992). Parent management training alters interaction patterns to promote prosocial behavior.

Although many variations exist, several common characteristics can be identified. First, treatment is conducted primarily with the parent or parents who directly implement several procedures in the home. Usually there is no direct intervention by the therapist with the child. Second, parents are trained to identify, define, and observe problem behavior in new ways. The careful specification of the behavior of interest is essential for the delivery of reinforcing or punishing consequences and for evaluating whether the program is achieving the desired goals. Third, the treatment sessions cover social learning principles and the procedures that follow from them, including positive reinforcement (e.g., the use of social praise and tokens or points for prosocial behavior), mild punishment (e.g., use of time out from reinforcement, loss of privileges), negotiation, and contingency contracting. Fourth, the sessions provide opportunities for parents to see how the techniques are implemented, to practice using the techniques, and to review the behavior change programs in the home. The immediate goal of the program is to develop specific skills in the parents, so they can implement procedures effectively in the home.

As an illustration, Webster-Stratton, Kolpacoff, and Hollinsworth (1988) evaluated parent training with parents of children (ages 3–8) who were referred for conduct problems including noncompliance, aggression, and oppositional behavior. Families were randomly assigned to one of four conditions that examined variations of the presentation and delivery of parent training. Three treatment conditions included parenting materials, group discussion, and videotaped presentation of the parent training content; individually administered videotaped presentation without group discussion; and group discussion of parenting but without the videotapes. Each of these groups received parent training over a period of 10–12 weeks, in weekly 2–hour sessions. A waiting-list control group did not receive treatment during this period.

At posttreatment, all three treatment groups showed significant improvement in child functioning on rating scales and home observations. Among the three intervention groups, the outcomes were similar. However, the group discussion and videotaped presentation group tended to show greater improvements on outcome measures and significantly lower dropout rates, higher rates of attendance to the sessions, and greater satisfaction with treatment. Assessment of a 1–year follow-up indicated that the effects were maintained (Webster-Stratton, Hollinsworth, & Kolpacoff, 1989). At follow-up, the three treatments were significantly improved on several outcome measures relative to pretreatment. Overall, 67% and 78% of treated cases across the three groups achieved clinically significant change, as defined by returning to the normative range of functioning on mother- and father-completed standardized rating scales.

Several other studies of parent training have shown improvements in child behavior at home, at school, and in the community (see Kazdin, 1987a; Miller & Prinz, 1990). Parent training has brought the problematic behaviors of treated children within normative levels of their peers who are functioning adequately. Treatment effects are maintained for up to a year; few studies have assessed treatment beyond that point. Parent training usually is used with young children (under 10 years of age). Extensions to delinquent adolescents have shown treatment to have significant impact on offense rates, days of incarceration, and nonstatus offenses (e.g., felonies, misdemeanors) (Bank, Marlowe, Reid, Patterson, & Weinrott, 1991).

Family therapy. Family therapy refers to a broad class of interventions in which clinical dysfunction is viewed from the standpoint of the family as a system. The child or adolescent referred for treatment is considered to be the "identified patient," that is, the person whom the family identifies as problematic but who actually is considered to reflect dysfunction, conflict, and maladaptive processes within the family. There are multiple approaches to and techniques of family therapy based on different views about the structure, functions, roles, and sources of conflict that lead to dysfunction.

Family therapy approaches are mentioned only in passing because of two features of existing studies. First, interventions tend to focus on adolescents and hence extend beyond the focus of this chapter. Second, interventions have shown reductions in delinquency. Typically, aggressive behavior is included in the outcome assessment but not separated from broader outcome measures (e.g., arrests, recidivism). Interventions are mentioned in passing because of the promise they have shown and the importance of considering their use in extensions to children.

Among alternative approaches, functional family therapy (Alexander & Parsons, 1982) has been especially promising with delinquent youth. With this treatment, clinical problems are conceptualized from the standpoint of the functions (e.g., intimacy, distancing, support) that they serve in the family as a system, as well as for individual family members. Treatment focuses on directly altering interaction and communication patterns in such a way as to foster more adaptive functioning. Behavioral (e.g., altering contingencies at home) and cognitively based interventions (e.g., identifying attributions, expectations) are integrated into a family focus of treatment. The main goals of treatment are to increase reciprocity and positive reinforcement among family members, to establish clear communication, to help specify behaviors that family members desire from each other, to negotiate constructively, and to help identify solutions to interpersonal problems.

The few available outcome studies of functional family therapy have produced relatively clear effects. The initial study included male and female delinquent adolescents who were referred to juvenile court for such behaviors as running away, truancy, theft, and unmanageability (Alexander & Parsons, 1973). For example, in comparison with other treatments (e.g., client-centered or psychodynamically oriented family treatment) and control conditions (e.g., attention-placebo, no treatment), family therapy has led to greater improvement on family interaction measures and lower recidivism rates from juvenile court records up to 18 months after treatment. Follow-up data obtained 2 1/2 years later indicated that the siblings of those who received family therapy showed significantly lower rates of referral to juvenile courts (Klein, Alexander, & Parsons, 1977). The available studies also provide information regarding factors that influence outcome. The effectiveness of treatment is influenced by the relationship (e.g., warmth, integration of affect and behavior) and structuring (e.g., directiveness) skills of the therapist (Alexander, Barton, Schiavo, & Parsons, 1976). Also, process measures of family interactions at posttreatment are related to subsequent recidivism (Alexander & Parsons, 1973). This finding lends credence to the model from which treatment was derived.

Other family approaches such as multisystemic family therapy also have shown promise in treating delinquent youth (see Henggeler & Borduin, 1990). The approach provides multiple components to address problems of individual family members, extrafamilial systems (e.g., peers, school performance), and developmental issues of the identified youth. Outcome studies with juvenile offenders have shown reductions in rates of arrest as well as self-reported delinquent behavior and improvements in family and peer relations and school performance (e.g., Henggeler et al., 1986).

School- and community-based treatments. Occasionally, treatment is conducted in school and community settings. In each case, treatment attempts to take advantage of the resources in the everyday environment that can support prosocial behavior and help to integrate individuals into the network and influences of their prosocial peers. For example, Kolvin et al. (1981) conducted a large-scale outcome study in England between 1972 and 1979 to evaluate different interventions for maladjusted children in the schools. Two different types of child dysfunction were investigated, namely, neurotic problems (e.g., overcontrolled problems such as depression, anxiety) and conduct problems (e.g., undercontrolled problems such as disruptive behavior, bullying, delinquency) with children at two different age levels (ages 7–8 and 11–12).

Children were assigned randomly to one of four conditions. The conditions varied slightly for younger and older children; for each age group there was a no-treatment condition that provided the basis for comparison over the course of treatment and follow-up. Parent counseling plus teacher consultation consisted of social work consultation with parents and teachers in an effort to coordinate school and home activities, casework with the family, and support for the teacher. Nurture work consisted of providing enrichment activities for the children, close interaction with the child, and behavioral shaping for individual child goals. Group therapy was based on client-centered principles and practices and consisted of play group therapy (for younger children) or discussion (more traditional) group therapy for older children. In each case, the focus was on the expression of feelings, acceptance of the child, warmth, and the therapeutic relationship. Behavior modification (for older children) consisted of classroom reinforcement systems relying on social and token reinforcement to improve deportment and classroom performance.

Among the major findings, for the younger children, play group therapy and nurture work led to significantly greater changes than the parent–teacher and no-treatment conditions. However, these effects were evident primarily for neurotic rather than conduct problem behavior. For the older children, group therapy and behavior modification led to greater changes than the parent–teacher condition or no treatment. Among the different treatments, children with neurotic problems, as defined earlier, responded better than children with conduct problems. Also, girls responded better to treatments than did boys. There were no consistent interactions between the type of treatment and type of child problem nor between treatment and sex of child.

Treatments for youth have been evaluated outside of the school setting. As an example, Feldman et al. (1983) conducted a community-based treatment project for youth who engaged in a variety of behaviors that hurt, disrupted, or annoyed others (e.g., hitting, slapping, and threatening others, destroying objects). Treatment was integrated with activities of the Jewish Community Centers Association in St. Louis, Missouri. The study included youth (ages 8–17) who were referred for antisocial behavior (referred youth) or who normally attended the regular activities programs and were not identified as showing problem behavior (nonreferred youths).

The study evaluated the effects of three types of treatment, two levels of therapist experience, and three different ways to compose the groups. The three treatments were traditional group social work (focus on group processes, social organization, and norms within the group), behavior modification (use of reinforcement contingencies, focus on prosocial behavior), and minimal treatment (no explicit application of a structured treatment plan; spontaneous interactions of group members). Activity groups within the center were formed and assigned to one of these three interventions. The groups were led by trainers, some of whom were experienced (graduate students of social work with previous experience) and others who were inexperienced (undergraduate students). Finally, the groups were composed in three ways: all members were youth referred for antisocial behavior, all members were nonreferred ("normal") youth, and a mixture of referred and nonreferred youth. Treatment was conducted over a period of a year (mean = 22.2 sessions, each lasting about 2–3 hours) in which the participants attended sessions and engaged in a broad range of activities (e.g., sports, arts and crafts, fundraising) as part of the usual structure of the facility.

The results indicated that youth with experienced, rather than inexperienced, leaders showed greater reductions in antisocial behavior. Referred (antisocial) youth in mixed groups (that included nonreferred children) showed greater improvements than those in groups made of only antisocial youth. Very modest outcome differences were noted as a function of technique. Behavior modification tended to lead to greater reductions in antisocial behavior than did traditional group treatment. Traditional treatment led to some decrements in antisocial behavior relative to the minimal contact group. Evaluation of treatment integrity indicated that each of the active treatments was not executed as intended and that the activity (no-treatment) condition received some therapy. Thus, lack of clear differences in outcome among treatment conditions could be explained on methodological grounds. Overall, antisocial youth benefited from the program, especially those who received the most favorable intervention condition (i.e., behavior modification with an experienced leader and in a mixed group of referred and nonreferred peers). Several features of the study are noteworthy including evaluation of therapist characteristics and group composition in relation to outcome, the assessment of treatment integrity, and others.

As evident by these examples, school- and community-based treatments do not necessarily involve different conceptual approaches to treatment than those highlighted previously. Yet, the settings provide special opportunities to intervene and reach larger numbers of youth than those seen in or referred for treatment. Also, such settings can draw on resources and sources of influences (e.g., peers) that would be difficult to mobilize in more traditional mental health and private practice treatment settings.

Current Issues and Limitations

Treatment research has made considerable progress in developing interventions for aggressive behavior. Even so, several limitations are easily identified. First, treatment research for children has focused on a relatively narrow range of techniques. For example, behavior modification and cognitive–behavioral techniques account for approximately one half of the treatment research (Kazdin, Bass, Ayers, & Rodgers, 1990). Other "more traditional" techniques such as psychodynamic therapy, psychoanalysis, and client-centered therapy, and combinations as part of eclectic approaches are infrequently studied, although they are commonly used in clinical practice (e.g., Kazdin, Siegel, & Bass, 1990; Koocher & Pedulla, 1977; Silver & Silver, 1983). A critical research priority is to investigate a wider range of treatment approaches. Second, the range of questions that guide treatment research is somewhat limited. The majority of studies of child and adolescent therapies focus on the impact of treatment techniques (Kazdin, Bass, Ayers, & Rodgers, 1990). Treatment technique is one source of influence and is likely to operate in conjunction with a host of other factors (e.g., child and parent characteristics) that also contribute to change. Expansion of research beyond the focus on techniques is an important research priority.

Third, the long-term effects of treatment are infrequently studied. In most studies of child therapy, no follow-up assessment is conducted; in the studies that do evaluate follow-up, assessment typically takes place 5 to 6 months after treatment ends (Kazdin, Bass, Ayers, & Rodgers, 1990; Weisz et al., 1987). The effects of treatment and the relative effectiveness of different treatments often vary at posttreatment and follow-up (Kazdin, 1988). Thus, treatments that appear more effective at posttreatment may not be those that are most effective at follow-up. A longitudinal perspective of therapy is especially important in relation to children. Marked changes in deviant and prosocial behavior are a matter of course during childhood, independent of intervention effects. Treatments that appear to be effective or differentially effective in the short run may not surpass the impact of developmental change.

Issues, Challenges, and Research Directions

Several issues and challenges are raised by intervention research and more generally address the larger research agenda of achieving a significant impact on aggressive and antisocial behavior.

Scope of Intervention Effort

A critical issue in prevention and treatment research pertains to the scope of the intervention effort, which refers to the degree and intensity of intervention that is required and the range of influences brought to bear to achieve a particular outcome (Newman & Howard, 1986). A relatively small intervention effort, for example, might consist of fairly circumscribed and focused interventions (e.g., 10–week school-based program) to achieve a particular preventive outcome (e.g., reduced incidence of vandalism). At the other extreme, a more extended intervention might involve the schools, parents and families, and community (out of school) activities over a period of several years. Obviously, for the range of antisocial behaviors and diverse youth who are involved, there is no single intensity or dosage of intervention effort that can be advocated.

In the case of many preventive efforts, multicomponent programs may be needed that involve home and school, parents, teachers, peers, and the community. The use of multicomponent programs is reasonable because many high-risk behaviors and conditions co-occur; narrowly focused or brief programs would not be expected to have significant and enduring impact. Moreover, multiple components may be required to address the many influences (family, peers, media) that may unwittingly promote or contribute to at-risk behavior. Multiple counterinfluences may need to be brought to bear to achieve significant impact.

In the case of treatment research, a similar issue emerges. The vast majority of treatment studies focus on single treatment modalities for a very abbreviated period (e.g., 8–10 sessions). The scope of such intervention efforts may be quite limited as far as the outcomes that are likely to result. By the time youth with antisocial behavior are referred clinically, their dysfunction is often severe and pervasive. Several domains of functioning (e.g., academic performance, peer relations) are likely to be impaired. Aggressive and antisocial behavior also is likely to be embedded in a child–parent–family-context configuration mentioned earlier. A single or simplistic approach to treatment, on a priori grounds, may be unlikely to have the necessary impact. A range of interventions and their protracted delivery may be needed to achieve change. This is not a call for a haphazard combination of all interventions. We still wish to use as a guide conceptual models and evidence that the intervention will address critical facets of aggressive and antisocial behavior. Several interventions hold promise. For example, parent training in various forms has occupied a central role in both preventive and intervention efforts. In light of the evidence, this particular component would be one likely to be considered further. Other interventions might be evaluated in a similar fashion. As efficacy is demonstrated, the interventions may be added to develop a broader intervention package to address a range of domains. Treatment combinations may be needed to effect broader changes than those achieved with individual components (e.g., Kazdin et al., 1992) and to achieve durable changes (Satterfield, Satterfield, & Schell, 1987).

More intervention (prevention or treatment) is not invariably better (more effective). There is no substitute for understanding the onset, basis, and course of aggressive and antisocial behavior. Improved understanding can help refine the focus of interventions. However, at present, evidence has suggested that the scope of intervention efforts for many youth may need to be broad. It may be that multiple component programs for extended periods are required, depending on the goals of the program and stages at which youth are identified for intervention. Alternatively, more focused and circumscribed interventions may be possible with early identification of small changes in the beginning of a developmental trajectory toward maladjustment.

Interplay of Basic and Applied Research

The development of effective preventive and treatment interventions requires the interplay of basic and applied research. In this context, basic research refers to investigations that are designed to understand development and paths leading to adaptive and maladaptive functioning. Basic research encompasses broad areas of study (e.g., child and adolescent development) and multiple disciplines (e.g., psychology, biology, psychiatry, epidemiology, pediatrics). The findings from basic research provide the underpinnings for informed interventions. Applied research in this context represents an effort to achieve a therapeutic goal for those youth who are involved in the program. Efforts to promote prosocial functioning, to avert aggressive behavior, and to ameliorate dysfunction have applied goals.

Basic research has as its higher priority the understanding of critical processes. In the context of child aggressive and antisocial behavior, multiple areas of research are relevant because of the many influences, determinants, and processes that shape functioning. Advances in research on brain development, genetics, patterns of dysfunction, and psychosocial adversity, to mention a few, are all critical to understanding development (IOM, 1989). Basic research on development encompasses many areas that affect biological, psychological, and social spheres and their interface (see, e.g., Petersen, 1988; Powers, Hauser, & Kilner, 1989).

As an example, developmental research has shown that the onset of puberty and timing of pubertal change (relative to one's peers) relate to important psychological changes (Richards & Peterson, 1987). Biological maturation occurs in a social context, that is, in relation to the timing of maturation of one's peers, the meeting, as it were, of biological and social clocks. Being early (in relation to one's peers), "on time," or late has implications. Early entry into puberty for girls is often associated with low self-esteem, poor body image, and concern with being overweight. Maturing early or late in relation to one's peers exacerbates these reactions. Girls early or late are more likely to show high levels of depression and a propensity toward self-harm. Entry into puberty for boys, on the other hand, is associated with increases in self-esteem and feelings of attractiveness. Early maturation is not associated with negative views but merely brings on an earlier onset of positive reactions. Similarly, transitions to new schools (elementary to junior high; junior to senior high) are associated with decreases in self-esteem for girls but not for boys. Basic research on gender, age, and development is designed to describe differences, to place these into theoretical contexts, and then to identify processes and mechanisms that account for the differences. Improved understanding from such research can then be translated into intervention programs in which the critical processes serve as the central focus.

Research on the mechanisms underlying at-risk behavior concretely convey the role of basic research in guiding interventions. For example, much of prevention research is based on identifying factors that place youth at risk. The goal is often to reduce those risk factors that can be altered. At-risk behaviors and conditions often come in packages. It would be helpful if basic research could increase understanding of the interrelations among risk factors and whether some conditions or factors can be identified as more central influences than others.

Statistical modeling techniques (e.g., path analyses, structural equation modeling) have helped to evaluate the relations among risk factors and to determine whether these factors operate directly on the onset of problem behaviors, indirectly through the influence of other variables, or are moderated by other variables (e.g., Newcomb & Bentler, 1988; Patterson et al., 1991; Swaim, Oetting, Edwards, & Beauvais, 1989). For example, previously mentioned was the finding that bonding to deviant peers is directly related to delinquency and subsequent drug use and that weak bonding to family and school was a precursor to deviant bonding (Elliott et al., 1985). Thus, early in the path toward delinquency there is a breakdown in connections to home, school, and family. Prevention programs draw on such findings in an effort to develop bonding to conventional home and school activities and values (e.g., Hawkins, Von Cleve, & Catalano, 1991).

Applied research provides direct tests of models devised from basic research. Prevention and treatment trials are obviously designed to have impact. At the same time, such studies can raise and address issues that augment the understanding of aggressive and violent behavior. Thus, applied investigations often encompass theoretical issues and mechanisms of change in a way that complements basic research (West, Sandler, Pillow, Baca, & Gersten, 1991). Consider the interplay and complementary role of basic and applied studies in prevention. In basic research, alternative conceptual models of dysfunction are developed to suggest possible risk factors and paths in development that lead to maladaptive behavior (e.g., violence). Research provides a test of alternative models. As part of this research, measures of critical processes (e.g., peer relations, nonconforming beliefs, deviance) and outcomes (e.g., delinquency, clinical dysfunction) are developed. The plausible paths of factors that influence outcome are identified. The paths suggest a theory that can subsequently guide interventions. Applied research draws directly on the theory by altering those processes or factors whose importance is suggested by basic studies. For example, a prevention study is not only designed to benefit participants (e.g., at-risk youth) but also to test the model. If processes identified in the original model are altered and the desired outcome is achieved, support for the theory is increased. Quite possibly, and equally important, many exceptions may emerge from the prevention study. For example, outcome differences may occur as a function of gender or race. The pattern of results may call into question the original theory, suggest other factors that need to be considered, or show the boundary conditions of its applicability.

Priorities for Research and Policy

Finer-grained analyses of samples and populations. Progress in developing interventions for aggressive and antisocial behavior has resulted from longitudinal studies of youth that track the development of aggressive behavior. Also, intervention trials that directly test viable approaches and their impact have contributed in an obvious way to current advances. The performance of basic and applied research to understand and to apply this understanding to youth who may be aggressive continues to be a high research priority. In addition, a high priority for research is the integration of a developmental perspective in the design and evaluation of interventions.

A developmental perspective considers changes over time in child functioning and the interface of these changes with the interpersonal environment. Many lines of work might be advocated under the guise of a developmental perspective. Two broad lines are recommended in light of current findings. First, research ought to consider the emergence, course, and amelioration of aggressive behavior in light of salient subject characteristics. For example, chronological age, sex differences, and cultural, ethnic, and racial differences can influence patterns of aggressive and antisocial behavior and their correlates.

Sex differences can be highlighted to illustrate the point. Boys and girls, whether in community or clinic samples, vary in aggressive and antisocial behavior in many ways including the extent to which they are perpetrators and victims of aggression and in the constellation of factors in early development that predict the onset and long-term course of aggressive and antisocial behavior (e.g., Eron, Huesmann, & Zelli, 1991; Kazdin, 1987a; Olweus, 1991). The implications of such differences can be important in relation to interventions. For example, Tremblay et al. (1992) evaluated childhood predictors of delinquent acts in adolescents to isolate the contribution of early disruptive behavior and poor school accomplishment. For boys, early signs of disruptive behavior (at age 7) predicted later delinquency (at age 14); poor school accomplishment did not predict delinquent acts once disruptive behavior was taken into account. For girls, neither early disruptive behavior nor poor school achievement were especially useful in predicting delinquent acts. If the factors that influence onset of antisocial behavior vary for male and female youth, effective preventive and treatment interventions may vary as well. In general, the task is to identify developmentally meaningful ways to delineate youth so that interventions can be optimally applied. Differences in normal development of boys and girls at different ages and stages point to domains that will need to be integrated into intervention research. Similarly, the differential effects of interventions that are occasionally reported for youth of different ages (e.g., Kolvin et al., 1981) or racial composition (e.g., Hawkins et al., 1991) further suggest the importance of subject characteristics.

One research priority is to attend to subject characteristics in relation to the development and reduction of aggressive and antisocial behavior. No doubt there remain influences that affect aggressive behavior fairly broadly across samples and population characteristics; however, there are important age, sex, and cultural, ethnic, and racial differences in relation to aggressive and antisocial behavior. Developmentally and culturally sensitive methods of intervention are needed. Integration of subject characteristics in the conceptualization, design, and evaluation of intervention trials is a critical research priority.

Identifying opportunities for intervention. Another research priority is the identification of developmental opportunities for intervention. Opportunities for intervention are periods of development in which specific age-appropriate influences can be harnessed. As an example, research on antisocial behavior in adolescence has pointed to the strong role of peer relations and bonding (e.g., Elliott et al., 1985; Newcomb & Bentler, 1988; Swaim et al., 1989). Drawing on the influence of peers may provide special opportunities for treatment. As a case in point, Feldman et al. (1983) found that the types of peers included in group therapies affected outcome among aggressive and antisocial youth. Youth in treatment groups with nonantisocial peers improved more than youth in groups composed of all antisocial youth. Moreover, within different groups, the single best predictor of change was prior behavior change of peers in the group (Feldman, 1992). The more active use of nonantisocial peers in the treatment process (e.g., as therapeutic agents or adjunctive roles to assist in treatment) would follow from current research.

Peer influences and their changing role in development is only one type of influence that is prompted by developmentally based research. Also, children and youth undergo a variety of transition periods in which change and varying influences operate. The transition that occurs in periods of progression from one level of school to the next represents potential stress for youth but at the same time opportunities for intervention (e.g., Felner & Adan, 1988). Changes in cognitive development, peer influences, and transition periods (e.g., in schools) in childhood and adolescence may provide special intervention opportunities. The challenge for theory, research, and practice is to identify intervention windows of opportunity in which processes that are critically related to antisocial behavior can be interrupted and redirected. The range and degree of opportunity are not necessarily an inverse linear function of age. Different ages, stages, and developmental periods may provide different opportunities for intervention.

Policy commitment to prevention and treatment. This chapter highlights preventive and treatment interventions that are aimed at averting and ameliorating aggressive and antisocial behavior among children. From a policy as well as a research perspective, prevention and treatment are often juxtaposed in a competitive fashion in which one is proposed as the better way to address aggressive and antisocial behavior. Arguments are advanced that prevention is particularly important given the obstacles to effective intervention once aggressive and antisocial behavior become severe and stable in children. The costs of treatment, the greater difficulty of treating more severe impairment, and limited professional resources to deliver treatment are advanced as central reasons to emphasize early preventive interventions.

From the standpoint of reducing aggressive and antisocial behavior, there is little point in justifying one focus (e.g., treatment or prevention) at the expense of the other. The limited funding resources contribute to the polarization of prevention and treatment. The resource constraints themselves need to be reconsidered. Also, neither prevention nor treatment, nor one type of approach or intervention within these domains (e.g., primary prevention, social competence promotion) can be expected to single-handedly resolve aggression and antisocial behavior among children. For example, it is unlikely that primary prevention will be unequivocally successful across the full range of at-risk behaviors and conditions that contribute to aggression so as to obviate treatment. Few proponents of prevention would suggest this is a reasonable expectation. Within even very high quality programs, considerable variability is often evident in how the intervention is implemented and the degree of impact (e.g., Allen et al., 1990; Botvin, Baker, Filazzola, & Botvin, 1990). In principle as well as in practice there may be limits on the impact of prevention. Identification of all individuals who might evince antisocial behavior, for example, is constrained by the imperfect relation of risk factors (e.g., biological, psychological, social) to particular outcomes and the inherent limits of assessment methods.

Diverse intervention efforts and a broad portfolio of approaches are central to reducing aggressive and antisocial behavior in children. As a beginning, large-scale programs for maternal care and child intervention that are directed toward early risk factors for poor adjustment involving maternal nutrition, baby care, child-rearing and early education can have broad effects on mothers and their offspring for an extended period (Zigler et al., 1992). The focus of such programs is on packages of risk factors that are known to have adverse effects. Large-scale universal programs for children and adolescents in the schools are also important for promoting positive social competence and resistance to internal and peer pressures that might lead to aggressive and antisocial behavior. Universal programs do not necessarily replace more focused or targeted interventions for youth who do not show antisocial behavior but are at high risk (primary prevention), for those who show early signs of antisocial behavior (secondary prevention), or for those who are referred because they already show a pattern of antisocial behavior that interferes with their functioning and causes them to interact violently with peers and others (treatment). The task is to identify a range of interventions, settings in which they can be deployed, ages at which they are maximally effective, and so on. In this process, prevention and treatment are complementary, interdependent, and united in their contribution to developing prosocial behavior. The cost savings are not necessarily from prevention that obviates the need for treatment but from a broad range of intervention opportunities that achieve a significant impact on the costly, burdensome, social problem that aggressive and antisocial behavior represents.

Beyond prevention and treatment to social intervention. Research and policy professionals should consider the full range of interventions that might be used to reduce aggression and violence. Prevention and treatment are important segments of this effort but are incomplete. There are broader social issues regarding aggression and violence. The use of corporal punishment in child-rearing and school discipline; violence in the media, especially television and films; and social practices that permit violence and aggression (e.g., availability of weapons), to mention salient issues, are some of the practices that are relevant to the issue of aggression and antisocial behavior in society. As a matter of social policy, one should take as a given a backdrop of factors and practices that may contribute in significant ways to aggression and antisocial behavior in society. The factors need to be scrutinized in relation to policy regarding child management and care. For example, the use of corporal punishment (i.e., physical aggression against children) is already implicated as a contributor to child aggression. The extensive use of corporal punishment is one of the givens in society that might be challenged if there is broad interest in delimiting aggression and antisocial behavior. In this regard, it is instructive to note that corporal punishment in child discipline at home and at school has been banned in a number of countries (e.g., Austria, Denmark, Finland, Norway, and Sweden; Greven, 1992).

Prevention and treatment, as discussed in this chapter, focus primarily on youth at risk for more severe aggression and antisocial behavior or who evince these behaviors already. However, this leaves unaddressed the social matrix in which aggression and violence are accepted in several domains that warrant attention. Social efforts to reduce aggression and violence on a large scale are no less important than interventions developed, implemented, and evaluated in the context of small scale prevention and treatment trials.

Influences that might affect violence (e.g., gun control, limits of permissible violence on television, categorization of films based on violence) often are discussed in the media as well as in policy deliberations. Efforts to limit aggression and violence in everyday life are particularly difficult to implement because they clash with specific constitutional rights or the perception and interpretation of these rights. A more difficult obstacle in setting policy may come from oversimplistic interpretations of individual influences. For example, one might argue for strong gun control as a means to influence aggression and violence. The standard counterargument for such control is that the presence of guns and their misuse account for relatively little violence or are not the cause or main influence on aggression in society. From a policy standpoint, such logic warrants more critical analysis (see chapters 12 and 14). No one influence accounts for or causes aggression and antisocial behavior. It might be useful to conceptualize the full range of influences in terms of a risk-factor model in which there are multiple influences that contribute to some outcome. In this case, the outcome is the overall level and type of aggression in society. The search is not for single, simple causes, but rather to identify a range of influences. Even influences that are arguably small in their impact on the outcome (e.g., small beta weight in a regression equation) can be exceedingly important. In a risk-factor model, multiple influences add and combine to increase the likelihood of the outcome (e.g., aggression). Small influences can combine and add appreciably, even though their individual contribution would be nugatory. Also, individual influences can interact (synergistically combine) with other influences and very much affect the outcome.

As a matter of policy, it would be worthwhile to make a legislative and social commitment to the reduction of aggression and violence in society. Prevention and treatment programs of the type that are reviewed in this chapter are important but in this larger context quite limited. In a different social setting and context, the program by Olweus (1991) that was designed to reduce bullying in Norway represents an effort along the lines suggested. The specifics of that program or the applicability of the details to different countries are not the issues. Rather, the intervention represented a multiple-component effort at the level of public policy to ameliorate the problem. A commitment at the policy level and at the level that can mobilize social forces that influence, express, or model aggression are recommended in order to have an impact on the problem. Social influences involving the matrix of societal displays, encouragement, and implicit endorsement of aggression, including the media at all levels, ought to be mobilized more systematically for a broad effort to ameliorate aggression and antisocial behavior.

Conclusions

Aggressive behavior can vary widely in type, severity, and chronicity. Moreover, aggressive behavior often is present with other antisocial behaviors (e.g., stealing, lying, truancy, substance abuse) and other sources of impaired functioning (e.g., academic dysfunction and delays, poor peer relations, and cognitive deficits and distortions). Beyond the repertoires of the children themselves, parent and family dysfunction (e.g., marital discord, spouse abuse), socioeconomic disadvantage, high stress, and parental social isolation may be present as well. The multiple response domains of the child and the broad influences in which these are often embedded must be considered in the development of effective interventions.

The task of prevention is to avert the onset of aggressive and antisocial behavior (primary prevention) and to delimit dysfunction among youth with early signs of the behaviors (secondary prevention). Promising prevention approaches have been illustrated by highlighting early parent and family programs, and school-based and community-based interventions. The illustrations provide evidence that early intervention can reduce aggressive and antisocial behavior, as reflected in arrests, court appearances, school misconduct, and self-reported delinquency, and in risk factors associated with aggressive and antisocial behavior such as low educational achievement and large family size. A few studies provide long-term follow-up (10–20 years) and convey the impression that enduring effects can be achieved. The evidence suggests that the interventions in controlled trials have had an impact on aggressive and antisocial behavior among children and adolescents. Nevertheless, the paucity of long-term follow-up evaluations and the limited assessment of aggressive and antisocial behavior constrains the strength of the conclusions that can be reached.

Promising treatments have also been discussed. Illustrations were drawn from cognitive problem-solving skills training, parent management training, family therapy, and school- and community-based treatment. In each area, research has shown that children with aggressive, antisocial, or delinquent behavior improve with treatment and that the effects are maintained at least up to 1 year. Notwithstanding demonstrated advances, there remain unresolved basic questions about the durability of treatment effects, the mechanisms through which effects are achieved, and the factors with which treatments interact to produce a given outcome.

Progress has resulted from an increase in controlled trials of various prevention and treatment programs. In addition, basic research on the characteristics of antisocial youth, information regarding risk and protective factors, and paths leading to antisocial behavior have played a central role in contemporary progress. The design of effective interventions has depended on advances in such research. In addition, several methodological advances in assessment, operationalization of treatment, and evaluation of treatment integrity have improved the quality of intervention trials and their yield.

Basic and applied research remain critically important in developing effective interventions. The development of aggressive and antisocial behavior and paths and influences that contribute to that behavior have only begun to be charted. Even so, critical influences (e.g., child-rearing practices, peer bonding) suggest points of intervention to alter the course of development of aggressive and antisocial behavior. Further research on development and the impact of contextual influences is important as a means of identifying optimal points of intervention.

Advances in understanding aggressive and antisocial behavior and translation of these into effective interventions are likely to continue. At the same time, effective interventions may be limited in their potential accomplishments if they are restricted to the prevention and treatment models that are currently in place. There are broad social influences and, therefore, opportunities to address the societal backdrop in which violence and aggression are accepted or viewed as reasonable expressions. The policy implications that should be derived from this review are to encourage the examination of all influences on aggression and antisocial behavior and to consider broad social programs, on an experimental basis, in which multiple influences are harnessed in an effort to decrease aggression in everyday life. Advances in prevention and treatment are obviously important; but it would be an unfortunate consequence of such progress if promising interventions inadvertently diverted attention from other factors in society that might be altered on a larger scale in an effort to reduce aggression and antisocial behavior. Among the tasks for researchers is the identification of factors that contribute to aggression and antisocial behavior. Once identified, integration of these into interventions and then policy are further steps. Significant impact on the reduction of aggression, violence, and antisocial behavior is likely when intervention research is conceived of as a continuity of commitment at multiple levels (e.g., individual, families, classroom, and society at large) with multiple influences that are mobilized toward the goal.

References

Achenbach, T. M., & Edelbrock, C. S. (1981). Behavioral problems and competencies reported by parents of normal and disturbed children aged four through sixteen. *Monographs of the Society for Research in Child Development, 46*, 188.

Alexander, J. F., Barton, C., Schiavo, R. S., & Parsons, B. V. (1976). Systems-behavioral intervention with families of delinquents: Therapist characteristics, family behavior, and outcome. *Journal of Consulting and Clinical Psychology, 44*, 656–664.

Alexander, J. F., & Parsons, B. V. (1973). Short-term behavioral intervention with delinquent families: Impact on family process and recidivism. *Journal of Abnormal Psychology, 81*, 219–225.

Alexander, J. F., & Parsons, B. V. (1982). *Functional family therapy*. Monterey, CA: Brooks/Cole.

Allen, J. P., Philliber, S., & Hoggson, N. (1990). School-based prevention of teenage pregnancy and school dropout: Process evaluation of the national replication of the Teen Outreach Program. *American Journal of Community Psychology, 18*, 505–524.

American Psychiatric Association. (1994). *Diagnostic and statistical manual of mental disorders* (4th ed.). Washington, DC: Author.

Bangert-Drowns, R. L. (1988). The effects of school-based substance abuse education: A meta-analysis. *Journal of Drug Education, 18*, 243–264.

Bank, L., Marlowe, J. H., Reid, J. B., Patterson, G. R., & Weinrott, M. R. (1991). A comparative evaluation of parent-training interventions for families of chronic delinquents. *Journal of Abnormal Child Psychology, 19*, 15–33.

Botvin, G. J., Baker, E., Filazzola, A. D., & Botvin, E. M. (1990). A cognitive–behavioral approach to substance abuse prevention: One-year follow-up. *Addictive Behaviors, 15*, 47–63.

Brandt, D. E., & Zlotnick, S. J. (1988). *The psychology and treatment of the youthful offender*. Springfield, IL: Charles C Thomas.

Brown, J. (1987). A review of meta-analyses conducted on psychotherapy outcome research. *Clinical Psychology Review, 7*, 1–23.

Bry, B. H. (1982). Reducing the incidence of adolescent problems through preventive intervention: One- and five-year follow-up. *American Journal of Community Psychology, 10*, 265–276.

Bry, B. H., & George, F. E. (1979). Evaluating and improving prevention programs: A strategy from drug abuse. *Evaluation and Program Planning, 2*, 127–136.

Bry, B. H., & George, F. E. (1980). The preventive effects of early intervention on the attendance and grades of urban adolescents. *Professional Psychology, 11*, 252–260.

Camp, B. W., & Bash, M. A. S. (1985). *Think aloud: Increasing social and cognitive skills—A problem solving program for children.* Champaign, IL: Research Press.

Caplan, M. Z., & Weissberg, R. P. (1989). Promoting social competence in early adolescence: Developmental considerations. In B. H. Schneider, G. Attili, J. Nadel, & R. P. Weissberg (Eds.), *Social competence in developmental perspective* (pp. 371–385). Boston: Kluwer.

Caron, C., & Rutter, M. (1991). Comorbidity in child psychopathology: Concepts, issues, and research strategies. *Journal of Child Psychology and Psychiatry, 32*, 1063–1080.

Casey, R. J., & Berman, J. S. (1985). The outcome of psychotherapy with children. *Psychological Bulletin, 98*, 388–400.

Davidson, W. S. II, & Redner, R. (1988). The prevention of juvenile delinquency: Diversion from the juvenile justice system. In R. H. Price, E. L. Cowen, R. P. Lorion, & J. Ramos-McKay (Eds.), *14 ounces of prevention: A casebook for practitioners* (pp. 123–137). Washington, DC: American Psychological Association.

Davidson, W. S. II, Redner, R., Blakely, C. H., Mitchell, C. M., & Emshoff, J. G. (1987). Diversion of juvenile offenders: An experimental comparison. *Journal of Consulting and Clinical Psychology, 55*, 68–75.

Dodge, K. A. (1991). The structure and function of reactive and proactive aggression. In D. J. Pepler & K. H. Rubin (Eds.), *The development and treatment of childhood aggression* (pp. 201–218). Hillsdale, NJ: Erlbaum.

Dodge, K. A., Price, J. M., Bachorowski, J., & Newman, J. P. (1990). Hostile attributional biases in severely aggressive adolescents. *Journal of Abnormal Psychology, 99*, 385–392.

Dodge, K. A., & Somberg, D. R. (1987). Hostile attributional biases among aggressive boys are exacerbated under conditions of threats to the self. *Child Development, 58*, 213–224.

Dryfoos, J. G. (1990). Adolescents at risk: Prevalence and prevention. New York: Oxford University Press.

Dumas, J. E. (1989). Treating antisocial behavior in children: Child and family approaches. *Clinical Psychology Review, 9*, 197–222.

Dumas, J. E., & Wahler, R. G. (1983). Predictors of treatment outcome in parent training: Mother insularity and socioeconomic disadvantage. *Behavioral Assessment, 5*, 301–313.

Durlak, J. A., Fuhrman, T., & Lampman, C. (1991). Effectiveness of cognitive–behavioral therapy for maladapting children: A meta-analysis. *Psychological Bulletin, 110*, 204–214.

Elliott, D. S., Huizinga, D., & Ageton, S. S. (1985). *Explaining delinquency and drug use.* Beverly Hills, CA: Sage.

Elliott, D. S., Huizinga, D., & Menard, S. (1988). *Multiple problem youth: Delinquency, substance abuse, and mental health problems.* New York: Springer-Verlag.

Eron, L. D., & Huesmann, L. R. (1984). The relation of prosocial behavior to the development of aggression and psychopathology. *Aggressive Behavior, 10*, 243–251.

Eron, L. D., Huesmann, L. R., & Zelli, A. (1991). The role of parental variables in the learning of aggression. In D. J. Pepler & K. H. Rubin (Eds.), *The development and treatment of childhood aggression* (pp. 169–188). Hillsdale, NJ: Erlbaum.

Farrell, A. D., Danish, S. J., & Howard, C. W. (1992). Relationship between drug use and other problem behaviors in urban adolescents. *Journal of Consulting and Clinical Psychology, 60*, 705–712.

Farrington, D. P. (1985). Predicting self-reported and official delinquency. In D. P. Farrington & R. Tarling (Eds.), *Prediction in criminology* (pp. 150–173). Albany, NY: State University of New York Press.

Feldman, R. A. (1992). The St. Louis Experiment: Effective treatment of antisocial youths in prosocial peer groups. In J. McCord & R. E. Tremblay (Eds.), *Preventing antisocial behavior* (pp. 233–252). New York: Guilford Press.

Feldman, R. A., Caplinger, T. E., & Wodarski, J. S. (1983). *The St. Louis conundrum: The effective treatment of antisocial youths.* Englewood Cliffs, NJ: Prentice Hall.

Felner, R. D., & Adan, A. M. (1988). The school transitional environment project: An ecological intervention and evaluation. In R. H. Price, E. L. Cowen, R. P. Lorion, & J. Ramos-McKay (Eds.), *14 ounces of prevention: A casebook for practitioners* (pp. 111–122). Washington, DC: American Psychological Association.

Fire in the United States. (1978). Washington, DC: United States Fire Administration, U.S. Department of Commerce.

Fo, W. S. O., & O'Donnell, C. R. (1975). The buddy system: Effect of community intervention on delinquent offenses. *Behavior Therapy, 6,* 522–524.

Forehand, R., & McMahon, R. J., (1981). *Helping the noncompliant child: A clinician's guide to parent training.* New York: Guilford Press.

Goldston, S. E., Yager, J., Heinicke, C. M., & Pynoos, R. S. (Eds.). (1990). *Preventing mental health disturbances in childhood.* Washington, DC: American Psychiatric Press.

Greven, P. (1992). Exploring the effects of corporal punishment. *Child, Youth, and Family Services Quarterly, 15*(4), 4–5.

Hawkins, J. D., Catalano, R. F., & Morrison, D. M. (1989, April). *Seattle social development project: Cumulative effects of intervention in grades 1–4.* Paper presented at the meeting of the Society for Research on Child Development, Kansas City, MO.

Hawkins, J. D., Doueck, H. J., & Lishner, D. M. (1988). Changing teaching practices in mainstream classrooms to improve bonding and behavior of low achievers. *American Educational Research Journal, 25,* 31–50.

Hawkins, J. D., Von Cleve, E., & Catalano, R. F. (1991). Reducing early childhood aggression: Results of a primary prevention program. *Journal of the American Academy of Child and Adolescent Psychiatry, 30,* 208–217.

Hazelrigg, M. D., Cooper, H. M., & Borduin, C. M. (1987). Evaluating the effectiveness of family therapies: An integrative review and analysis. *Psychological Bulletin, 101,* 428–442.

Hechinger, F. (1992). *Fateful choices: Healthy youth for the 21st century.* New York: Carnegie Corporation of New York.

Henggeler, S. W. (1989). *Delinquency in adolescence.* Newbury Park, CA: Sage.

Henggeler, S. W., & Borduin, C. M. (1990). *Family therapy and beyond: A multisystemic approach to treating the behavior problems of children and adolescents.* Pacific Grove, CA: Brooks/Cole.

Henggeler, S. W., Rodick, J. D., Borduin, C. M., Hanson, C. L., Watson, S. M., & Urey, J. R. (1986). Multisystemic treatment of juvenile offenders: Effects on adolescent behavior and family interaction. *Developmental Psychology, 22,* 132–141.

Hinshaw, S. P., Lahey, B. B., & Hart, E. L. (1993). Issues of taxonomy and comorbidity in the development of conduct disorder. *Development and Psychopathology, 5,* 31–49.

Horne, A. M., & Sayger, T. V. (1990). *Treating conduct and oppositional disorders in children.* Elmsford, NY: Pergamon Press.

Huesmann, L. R., Eron, L. D., Lefkowitz, M. M., & Walder, L. O. (1984). Stability of aggression over time and generations. *Developmental Psychology, 20,* 1120–1134.

Institute of Medicine (1989). *Research on children and adolescents with mental, behavioral, and developmental disorders.* Washington, DC: National Academy Press.

Jessor, R., & Jessor, S. L. (1977). *Problem behavior and psychological development: A longitudinal study of youth.* San Diego, CA: Academic Press.

Johnson, C. A., Pentz, M. A., Weber, M. D., Dwyer, J. H., Baer, N., MacKinnon, D. P., Hansen, W. B., & Flay, B. R. (1990). Relative effectiveness of comprehensive community programming for drug abuse prevention with high-risk and low-risk adolescents. *Journal of Consulting and Clinical Psychology, 58,* 447–456.

Kazdin, A. E. (1985). *Treatment of antisocial behavior in children and adolescents.* Homewood, IL: Dorsey Press.

Kazdin, A. E. (1987a). *Conduct disorder in childhood and adolescence.* Newbury Park, CA: Sage.

Kazdin, A. E. (1987b). Treatment of antisocial behavior in children: Current status and future directions. *Psychological Bulletin, 102,* 187–203.

Kazdin, A. E. (1988). *Child psychotherapy: Developing and identifying effective treatments.* Elmsford, NY: Pergamon Press.

Kazdin, A. E. (1990). Premature termination from treatment among children referred for anti-social behavior. *Journal of Child Psychology and Psychiatry, 31,* 415–425.

Kazdin, A. E. (1992). *Research design in clinical psychology* (2nd ed.). Needham Heights, MA: Allyn & Bacon.

Kazdin, A. E. (1993). Changes in behavioral problems and prosocial functioning in child treatment. *Journal of Child and Family Studies, 2,* 5–22.

Kazdin, A. E. (1994). Psychotherapy for children and adolescents. In A. E. Bergin & S. L. Garfield (Eds.), *Handbook of psychotherapy and behavior change* (4th ed., pp. 543–594). New York: Wiley.

Kazdin, A. E., Bass, D., Ayers, W. A., & Rodgers, A. (1990). Empirical and clinical focus of child and adolescent psychotherapy research. *Journal of Consulting and Clinical Psychology, 58,* 729–740.

Kazdin, A. E., Esveldt-Dawson, K., French, N. H., & Unis, A. S. (1987). Problem-solving skills training and relationship therapy in the treatment of antisocial child behavior. *Journal of Consulting and Clinical Psychology, 55,* 76–85.

Kazdin, A. E., Siegel, T. C., & Bass, D. (1990). Drawing upon clinical practice to inform research on child and adolescent psychotherapy: A survey of practitioners. *Professional Psychology: Research and Practice, 21,* 189–198.

Kazdin, A. E., Siegel, T., & Bass, D. (1992). Cognitive problem-solving skills training and parent management training in the treatment of antisocial behavior in children. *Journal of Consulting and Clinical Psychology, 60,* 733–747.

Kendall, P.C. (Ed.). (1991). *Child and adolescent therapy: Cognitive–behavioral procedures.* New York: Guilford Press.

Kendall, P. C., & Braswell, L. (in press). *Cognitive–behavioral therapy for impulsive children* (2nd ed). New York: Guilford Press.

Kendall, P. C., & Ronan, K. R., Epps, J. (1991). Aggression in children/adolescents: Cognitive–behavioral treatment perspectives. In D. J. Pepler & K. H. Rubin (Eds.), *The development and treatment of childhood aggression* (pp. 341–360). Hillsdale, NJ: Erlbaum.

Kernberg, P. F., & Chazan, S. E. (1991). *Children with conduct disorders: A psychotherapy manual.* New York: Basic Books.

King, C. A., & Kirschenbaum, D. S. (1992). *Helping young children develop social skills.* Pacific Grove, CA: Brooks/Cole.

Klein, N. C., Alexander, J. F., & Parsons, B. V. (1977). Impact of family systems intervention on recidivism and sibling delinquency: A model of primary prevention and program evaluation. *Journal of Consulting and Clinical Psychology, 45,* 469–474.

Kolvin, I., Garside, R. F., Nicol, A. R., MacMillan, A., Wolstenholme, F., & Leitch, I. M. (1981). *Help starts here: The maladjusted child in the ordinary school.* London: Tavistock.

Koocher, G. P., & Pedulla, B. M. (1977). Current practices in child psychotherapy. *Professional Psychology, 8,* 275–287.

Lally, R., Mangione, P. L., & Honig, A. S. (1988). The Syracuse University Family Development Research Program: Long-range impact on an early intervention with low-income children and their families. In D. Powell (Ed.), *Parent education as early childhood intervention: Emerging directions in theory, research, and practice* (pp. 79–104). Norwood, NJ: Ablex.

Loeber, R. (1990). Development and risk factors of juvenile antisocial behavior and delinquency. *Clinical Psychology Review, 10,* 1–41.

Loeber, R., & Schmalling, K. B. (1985). Empirical evidence for overt and covert patterns of anti-social conduct problems: A meta-analysis. *Journal of Abnormal Child Psychology, 13,* 337–352.

Lundman, R. J. (1984). *Prevention and control of juvenile delinquency.* New York: Oxford University Press.

McCord, J., & Tremblay, R. E. (Eds.). (1992). *Preventing antisocial behavior.* New York: Guilford Press.

Miller, G. E., & Prinz, R. J. (1990). Enhancement of social learning family interventions for child conduct disorder. *Psychological Bulletin, 108,* 291–307.

Newcomb, M. D., & Bentler, P. M. (1988). *Consequences of adolescent drug use: Impact on the lives of young adults.* Newbury Park, CA: Sage.

Newman, F. L., & Howard, K. I. (1986). Therapeutic effort, treatment outcome, and national health policy. *American Psychologist, 41*, 181–187.

O'Donnell, C. R., Lydgate, T., & Fo, W. S. O. (1979). The buddy system: Review and follow-up. *Child Behavior Therapy, 1*, 161–169.

Olweus, D. (1991). Bully/victim problems among school children: Basic facts and effects of a school based intervention program. In D. J. Pepler & K. H. Rubin (Eds.), *The development and treatment of childhood aggression* (pp. 411–448). Hillsdale, NJ: Erlbaum.

Patterson, G. R. (1982). *Coercive family process*. Eugene, OR: Castalia.

Patterson, G. R. (1986). Performance models for antisocial boys. *American Psychologist, 41*, 432–444.

Patterson, G. R., Capaldi, D., & Bank, L. (1991). An early starter model for predicting delinquency. In D. J. Pepler & K. H. Rubin (Eds.), *The development and treatment of childhood aggression* (pp. 139–168). Hillsdale, NJ: Erlbaum.

Patterson, G. R., Reid, J. B., & Dishion, T. J. (1992). *Antisocial boys*. Eugene, OR: Castalia.

Pepler, D. J., & Rubin, K. H. (Eds.). (1991). *The development and treatment of childhood aggression*. Hillsdale, NJ: Erlbaum.

Petersen, A. C. (1988). Adolescent development. *Annual Review of Psychology, 39*, 583–607.

Powers, S. I., Hauser, S. T., & Kilner, L. A. (1989). Adolescent mental health. *American Psychologist, 44*, 200–208.

Price, R. H., Cowen, E. L., Lorion, R. P., & Ramos-McKay, J. (Eds.). (1988). *14 ounces of prevention: A casebook for practitioners*. Washington, DC: American Psychological Association.

Provence, S., & Naylor, A. (1983). *Working with disadvantaged parents and children: Scientific issues and practice*. New Haven, CT: Yale University Press.

Richards, M., & Petersen, A. C. (1987). Biological theoretical models of adolescent development. In V. B. Van Hasselt & M. Hersen (Eds.), *Handbook of adolescent psychology* (pp. 34–52). Elmsford, NY: Pergamon Press.

Rickel, A. R., & Allen, L. (1987). *Preventing maladjustment from infancy through adolescence*. Newbury Park, CA: Sage.

Robins, L. N. (1978). Sturdy childhood predictors of adult antisocial behavior: Replications from longitudinal studies. *Psychological Medicine, 8*, 611–622.

Robins, L. N. (1981). Epidemiological approaches to natural history research: Antisocial disorders in children. *Journal of the American Academy of Child Psychiatry, 20*, 566–680.

Robins, L. N. (1991). Conduct disorder. *Journal of Child Psychology and Psychiatry, 32*, 193–212.

Robins, L. N., & Rutter, M. (Ed.). (1990). *Straight and devious pathways from childhood to adulthood*. Cambridge, England: Cambridge University Press.

Robins, L. N., West, P. A., & Herjanic, B. (1975). Arrests and delinquency in two generations: A study of black urban families and their children. *Journal of Child Psychology and Psychiatry, 16*, 125–140.

Rubin, K. H., Bream, L. A., Rose-Krasnor, L. (1991). Social problem solving and aggression in childhood. In D. J. Pepler & K. H. Rubin (Eds.), *The development and treatment of childhood aggression* (pp. 219–248). Hillsdale, NJ: Erlbaum.

Rutter, M., & Giller, H. (1983). *Juvenile delinquency: Trends and perspectives*. New York: Penguin Books.

Rutter, M., Tuma, A. H., & Lann, I. S. (Eds.). (1988). *Assessment and diagnosis of child psychopathology*. New York: Guilford Press.

Satterfield, J. H., Satterfield, B. T., & Schell, A. M. (1987). Therapeutic interventions to prevent delinquency in hyperactive boys. *Journal of the American Academy of Child and Adolescent Psychiatry, 26*, 56–64.

Schinke, S. P., Botvin, G. J., & Orlandi, M. A. (1991). *Substance abuse in children and adolescents: Evaluation and intervention*. Newbury Park, CA: Sage.

Schweinhart, L. J., & Weikart, D. P. (1988). The High/Scope Perry preschool program. In R. H. Price, E. L. Cowen, R. P. Lorion, & J. Ramos-McKay (Eds.), *14 ounces of prevention: A casebook for practitioners* (pp. 53–66). Washington, DC: American Psychological Association.

Schweinhart, L. J., Weikart, D. P., & Larner, M. B. (1986). Consequences of three preschool curriculum models through age 15. *Early Childhood Research Quarterly, 1*, 15–35.

Seitz, V., Rosenbaum, L. K., & Apfel, N. H. (1985). Effects of family support intervention: A 10–year follow-up. *Child Development, 56*, 376–391.

Serbin, L. A., Moskowitz, D. S., Schwartzman, A. E., & Ledingham, J. E. (1991). Aggressive, withdrawn, and aggressive/withdrawn children in adolescence: Into the next generation. In D. J. Pepler & K. H. Rubin (Eds.), *The development and treatment of childhood aggression* (pp. 55–70). Hillsdale, NJ: Erlbaum.

Shaffer, D., Vieland, V., Garland, A., Rojas, M., Underwood, M., & Busner, C. (1990). Adolescent suicide attempters: Response to suicide prevention programs. *Journal of the American Medical Association, 264*, 3151–3155.

Silver, L. B., & Silver, B. J. (1983). Clinical practice of child psychiatry: A survey. *Journal of the American Academy of Child Psychiatry, 22*, 573–579.

Spivack, G., Platt, J. J., & Shure, M. B. (1976). *The problem-solving approach to adjustment*. San Francisco, CA: Jossey-Bass.

Spivack, G., & Shure, M. B. (1982). The cognition of social adjustment: Interpersonal cognitive problem solving thinking. In B. B. Lahey & A. E. Kazdin (Eds.), *Advances in clinical child psychology* (Vol. 5, pp. 323–372). New York: Plenum.

Steen, C., & Monnette, B. (1989). *Treating adolescent sex offenders in the community*. Springfield, IL: Charles C Thomas.

Swaim, R. C., Oetting, E. R., Edwards, R. W., & Beauvais, F. (1989). Links from emotional distress to adolescent drug use: A path model. *Journal of Consulting and Clinical Psychology, 57*, 227–231.

Tremblay, R. E. (1991). Aggression, prosocial behavior, and gender: Three magic words, but no magic wand. In D. J. Pepler & K. H. Rubin (Eds.), *The development and treatment of childhood aggression* (pp. 71–78). Hillsdale, NJ: Erlbaum.

Tremblay, R. E., Masse, B., Perron, D., Leblanc, M., Schwartzman, E., & Ledingham, J. E. (1992). Early disruptive behavior, poor school achievement, delinquent behavior, and delinquent personality: Longitudinal analyses. *Journal of Consulting and Clinical Psychology, 60*, 64–72.

United States Congress, Office of Technology Assessment. (1986). *Children's mental health: Problems and services—A background paper* (Publication No. OTA-BP-H-33). Washington, DC: U.S. Government Printing Office.

United States Congress, Office of Technology Assessment. (1991). *Adolescent health* (Publication No. OTA-H-468). Washington, DC: U.S. Government Printing Office.

United States Senate Judiciary Committee, Subcommittee to Investigate Juvenile Delinquency. (1976). *School violence and vandalism: The nature, extent and cost of violence and vandalism in the nation's schools*. Washington, DC: U.S. Government Printing Office.

Webster-Stratton, C., Hollinsworth, T., & Kolpacoff, M. (1989). The long-term effectiveness of treatment and clinical significance of three cost-effective training programs for families with conduct problem children. *Journal of Consulting and Clinical Psychology, 57*, 550–553.

Webster-Stratton, C., Kolpacoff, M., & Hollinsworth, T. (1988). Self-administered videotape therapy for families with conduct problem children: Comparison with two cost-effective treatments and a control group. *Journal of Consulting and Clinical Psychology, 56*, 558–566.

Weikhart, D. P., & Schweinhart, L. J. (1992). High/Scope Preschool Program outcomes. In J. McCord & R. E. Tremblay (Eds.), *Preventing antisocial behavior* (pp. 67–86). New York: Guilford Press.

Weiss, B., & Weisz, J. R. (1990). The impact of methodological factors on child psychotherapy outcome research: A meta-analysis for researchers. *Journal of Abnormal Child Psychology, 22*(18), 639–670.

Weissberg, R. P., Caplan, M., & Harwood, R. L. (1991). Promoting competent young people in competence-enhancing environments: A systems-based perspective on primary prevention. *Journal of Consulting and Clinical Psychology, 59*, 830–841.

Weisz, J. R., Weiss, B., Alicke, M. D., & Klotz, M. L. (1987). Effectiveness of psychotherapy with children and adolescents: Meta-analytic findings for clinicians. *Journal of Consulting and Clinical Psychology, 55*, 542–549.

Werner, E. E., & Smith, R. S. (1992). *Overcoming the odds: High risk children from birth to adulthood*. Ithaca, NY: Cornell University Press.

West, S. G., Sandler, I., Pillow, D. R., Baca, L., & Gersten, J. C. (1991). The use of structural equation modeling in generative research: Toward the design of a preventive intervention for bereaved children. *American Journal of Community Psychology, 19*, 459–480.

Williams, J. R., & Gold, M. (1972). From delinquent behavior to official delinquency. *Social Problems, 20*, 209–229.

Wright, L., Everett, F., & Roisman, L. (1986). *Experiential psychotherapy with children.* Baltimore, MD: The Johns Hopkins University Press.

Zigler, E., Taussig, C., & Black, K. (1992). Early childhood intervention: A promising preventative for juvenile delinquency. *American Psychologist, 47*, 997–1006.

16

Prevention and Treatment of Adolescent Violence

Nancy G. Guerra, Patrick H. Tolan,
and W. Rodney Hammond

The dramatic rise in violent behavior in the United States over the last four decades has been accompanied by a decrease in the modal age for violent offenses (Blumstein, Farrington, & Moitra, 1985). Both self-report and arrest data reveal that the majority of antisocial and criminal acts of violence are committed by teenagers and young adults (Elliott, Ageton, Huizinga, Knowles, & Canter, 1983; Hirschi & Gottfredson, 1983). Indeed, if violence in this country is to be prevented or ameliorated, considerable attention must be devoted to the development of effective interventions for adolescents.

The purpose of this chapter is to review a variety of programs that are focused on the prevention and treatment of adolescent aggression and violence. Using a public health model of primary, secondary, and tertiary (treatment) prevention, one can identify a diverse portfolio of intervention programs at each level. These programs vary on a number of dimensions including the targeted population and guiding theoretical framework, as well as whether efforts are directed toward changing individuals, or the systems and settings that influence behavior (e.g., family, peers, school, community). Programs that target individual development tend to cluster around several identified areas of risk including physical development and health, academic performance, social and behavioral skills, affect awareness and regulation, and social–cognitive processes. Systems-based interventions either attempt to influence factors related to the learning of aggression (e.g., decrease observation of aggressive models and reinforcement for aggressive behavior), promote supports for behaviors other than aggression, or lessen situational opportunities that may provoke a violent act (e.g., increase police patrols, reduce availability of guns in a community).

A discussion of intervention programs for adolescents first requires at least brief consideration of the nature of aggression and violence during this developmental period. Although adolescence has often been neglected in developmental studies because of its status as a transitional stage between childhood and adulthood, more recent models of adolescent development emphasize the unique features of this period (e.g., Petersen, 1988). With regard to the etiology of adolescent aggression and violence, two important observations can be made.

First, most aggressive teenagers do not limit their antisocial behavior to aggression, but rather display a broad repertoire of antisocial behavior. Although we are concerned here primarily with violent behavior and how it can be prevented or reduced, empirical studies suggest that rates of co-occurrence of aggression with other types of disruptive behaviors are quite high (Achenbach & Edelbrock, 1981; Elliott, Huizinga, & Menard, 1989; Osgood, O'Malley, Bachman, & Johnston, 1989). In a corresponding manner, intervention programs rarely distinguish aggressive and violent behavior from other antisocial and delinquent behavior, but instead seek to remediate a broad class of antisocial outcomes including aggression. Therefore, any discussion of adolescent interventions that is focused on violence prevention must include programs targeting a range of maladaptive behavioral outcomes including conduct disorder, delinquency, or general problem behaviors. However, because violence seems to be an extreme version of general patterns of antisocial behavior, one can expect that broad-based programs would reduce violence (Tolan & Loeber, 1993), although when there seems to be no demonstrated effects of these programs on violent behavior it will be pointed out in our description of them.

Second, intervention programs must address the sharp peak in rates of antisocial and violent behavior during the teenage years. One possibility is that the incidence of antisocial behavior increases during adolescence, so that already aggressive children simply become more aggressive and violent during this particular time. Alternately, it may be that the stressors of adolescence cause more individuals to flirt with antisocial and violent behavior from time to time, causing an increase in prevalence rates.

Recent studies suggest that this adolescent peak is due primarily to an increase in prevalence (Farrington, 1983; Wolfgang, Thornberry, & Figlio, 1987). This means that many adolescents engage in some antisocial behavior, including violent acts. For example, in a national survey of 17–year-olds, 35% of males and 20% of females reported committing an aggressive offense in the preceding year (Osgood et al., 1989). For most teenagers such behavior is relatively infrequent and is part of the typical course of adolescent development (Moffitt & Silva, 1988). In fact, most adolescents simply do "grow out of" a number of age-specific behavioral problems. This suggests that certain phenomena related to adolescence, per se, produce a temporary surge in antisocial behavior for a large number of individuals.

However, the normative status of aggressive and antisocial behavior during adolescence should not overshadow the more serious and habitual acts of violence committed by a select few. For some adolescents, violent behavior does not taper off, but continues to escalate. There is considerable evidence that most individuals who display habitual aggressive behavior during adolescence develop this behavior during childhood (Farrington, 1986; Huesmann, Eron, Lefkowitz, & Walder, 1984; Robins, 1978). Although these adolescents represent a small portion (5%–10%) of the population, they are responsible for as many as half of the serious violent acts committed (Wolfgang, Figlio, & Sellin, 1972).

Bringing this back into the public health approach to prevention, the data on patterns of adolescent antisocial behavior suggest several issues that intervention programs must consider. The acceleration in prevalence rates implies that population-based primary prevention programs are warranted. To the extent that this upswing is due to the nuances of adolescence, such programs may be well-advised to concentrate on preparing children to navigate effectively the transitions of adolescence. To the extent that aggression and violence co-occur with other types of antisocial behavior and represent a general risk pattern, programs may also do well to target children who are at-risk to effect multiple problem behaviors rather than focusing exclusively on reducing their aggression. However, even the best primary and secondary prevention programs may be unable to counteract the developmental histories of more chronic and seriously aggressive youth. These behaviors, if left uncorrected until adolescence, may require more substantial targeted intervention efforts.

In reviewing intervention programs for adolescents, we attempt to evaluate programs not only in terms of measured outcomes, but in terms of how various programs may or may not fit into an overall model for understanding and treating adolescent violence. We discuss the benefits and limitations of programs at each level of prevention, and consider how programs for adolescents might best form part of a comprehensive violence prevention strategy.

Population-Based Primary Prevention Programs

Primary prevention focuses on preventing aggression and violence before any signs of such behavior are noted. Although such programs cover a broad span of approaches and address an array of risk factors for aggression, most frequently they try to promote prosocial behavior through psycho-educational programming directed at children and their teachers, schools, peers, or families. It is believed that bolstering prosocial competencies should relate to reductions in antisocial and aggressive behavior. These programs are often a mainstay of intervention programming during the elementary school years, with fewer programs available for adolescents.

Individual-level programs typically try to build children's skills in one or more areas including school achievement, social skills, social problem solving, social perspective taking, and impulse control. Programs that address systems or setting characteristics usually focus on altering environmental contingencies for aggressive and prosocial behavior, although some programs attempt to reduce opportunities to behave aggressively either by enhancing surveillance or by providing opportunities for involvement in prosocial activities (e.g., after school recreation). Regardless of program orientation, a major advantage of primary prevention programs is that individuals do not have to be identified as "high-risk," although preventive efforts may rely on community-level risk factors to identify target populations for intervention (e.g., adolescents living in economically disadvantaged urban communities).

However, a significant disadvantage of primary prevention programs is that they typically consist of a uniform intervention provided to all members of a given population. In many cases, the specific foci (e.g., social skills training) are clearly connected to a general class of risk factors for aggression (e.g., peer rejection, poor social skills). Yet, because these programs are offered to all individuals, they cannot be sensitive to differences in need for or receptivity to a particular type of program. It is naive to expect that all teenagers will respond equally to the same intervention and need the same type and level of services. In particular, it is unlikely that youth who have progressed from childhood aggression to more serious and habitual adolescent violence will respond to broad-based educational or social development programs, although there is some evidence to suggest that primary prevention conducted during the preschool years may generate reductions in aggression that last into adolescence (for a review, see Zigler, Taussig, & Black, 1992). Still, it is likely that such programs are most beneficial for adolescents who display milder forms of age-typical aggressive and antisocial behavior and whose status affords ready access to such programs (e.g., being a full-time student rather than a high school dropout).

At the primary prevention level, the majority of these programs have been conducted in school settings. Schools are an especially appropriate locale for violence prevention initiatives. Epidemiological data indicate that the school campus itself has increasingly become a site for violent behavior, including assaults and even homicide (Center to Prevent Handgun Violence, 1990). Increases in reported incidents of violence at school and in violence-provoking behavior (e.g., carrying weapons to school) have been particularly evident in inner-city schools and among ethnic minority adolescents (Centers for Disease Control, 1991; Goldstein, 1992; Menacker, Weldon, & Hurwitz, 1990). For example, in a survey of 1,653 urban high school students, Sheley, McGee, and Wright (1992) found that 46% of the students said they knew someone who had carried a gun to school within the past year.

In addition to the fact that aggressive and violent behavior often takes place at school, schools are perhaps the most feasible settings for implementing intervention programs. In recent years, school-based violence prevention programming has been a prominent recommendation of task forces, conferences, and individuals studying youth violence (Centers for Disease Control, 1991; Prothrow-Stith, 1991; Wilson-Brewer & Jacklin, 1990). Reasons cited include the elimination of barriers to service accessibility such as cost and need for transportation, and the "captive audience" phenomenon, that is, the ability to reach a broad youth population base whose attendance is mandated (Hammond & Yung, 1991).

For example, Sarason and Sarason (1981) developed a 13-session social problem-solving training program for urban high school students that was delivered during the students' regular health course. The intervention focused on modeling and role-playing effective, nonaggressive solutions to common social problems. Compared with no-treatment control students, students who participated in the intervention displayed improvements in social problem-solving skills, fewer absences, and decreases in office referrals for problem behaviors. However, the impact of the intervention on serious violent behavior was not measured, and no long-term follow-up was conducted, making it difficult to determine if even the modest short-term effects were maintained.

In another study conducted in both an urban and a suburban setting, Caplan et al. (1992) provided a 20-session curriculum, the Positive Youth Development Program, to 6th and 7th grade children in their regular school classrooms. Six areas of social competence were emphasized: stress management, self esteem, social problem solving, health information, assertiveness, and social networks. Classrooms were randomly assigned to intervention and attention control conditions (i.e., classrooms where children received extra attention but did not receive social competency training). When compared with children in attention control classrooms, intervention children were rated by their teachers as less impulsive and more constructive in prosocial conflict resolution. Still, we are unable to ascertain whether this program had any impact on serious aggressive and violent behavior.

In recent years, other curricula specifically designed as population-based violence prevention programs have begun to appear. Reporting on the results of a national survey of such programs, Cohen and Wilson-Brewer (1991) provided case studies of several of the newly developed curricula. Included among these are two potentially promising interventions, the Second Step Program of the Committee for Children in Seattle and the Violence Prevention Curriculum of Prothrow-Stith (1991). The Second Step program focuses specifically on self-esteem development and anger control training for students through adolescence. Initial results indicate short-term knowledge and skill gains in anger management, impulse control, empathy, social problem-solving, and conflict resolution, but the researchers do not report any data indicating a reduction in aggressive and violent behavior. However, a larger-scale outcome study is still in progress. The Prothrow-Stith intervention targets high school students and includes didactic and informational components as well as skill development practice in conflict resolution. Initial evaluations have shown that participating youth demonstrate marginally significant decreases in self-reports of fighting and arrests. Again, the effectiveness of these programs in reducing serious aggressive and violent behavior remains undetermined. For example, there have been no well-controlled comparisons between treatment, no treatment control groups, and no long-term follow-ups.

In contrast to programs that attempt to directly influence individual attitudes, skills, and behavior, systems-based interventions focus on restructuring settings and environments that bear on the learning and performance of aggression. For example, Goldstein (1992) enumerates a panoply of intervention techniques that rely on changing school operations and services, including teacher self-defense training, enhanced school administrator–police coordination, changes in the physical environment such as installation of better lighting or metal detectors, increases in security personnel, and community-oriented media campaigns about school violence and vandalism. Unfortunately, because these techniques are rarely implemented as part of controlled experimental studies but more commonly as stop-gap measures in response to particular incidents, it is virtually impossible to evaluate their effectiveness as violence prevention techniques. Furthermore, although it is possible that they may reduce the occurrence of violent acts in schools, it is less likely that their effects will generalize to other settings or, more broadly, to an individual's propensity to engage in violent acts. These programs can be seen as "opportunity-reduction" strategies, rather than behavior change approaches.

The most enduring behavior changes should result from interventions that influence the psychological underpinnings of aggression and violence. To the extent that the upswing in antisocial behavior during the teenage years is related to the particular developmental tasks of adolescence, programs that ease this transition should engender corresponding reductions in problem behaviors. To date, only a limited number of experimental studies have focused on changing school environments in order to facilitate the transition into adolescence.

For example, Felner and Adan (1988) report on the evaluation of a program designed to ease students' transition into high school. The School Transitional Environmental Program (STEP) involves only a minimal reorganization focused on keeping students together in common groups and in close proximity and expanding the role of the homeroom teacher to include a variety of counseling and administrative functions. In one study, low-income 9th grade minority students entering a large urban high school participated during their first (transitional) year. When compared with matched control students, intervention students showed fewer decreases in academic performance, fewer absences, and lower dropout rates. However, these differences did appear to diminish over time, and few differences were evident two to three years following the intervention. Replication studies are consistent (Felner & Adan, 1988). Short-term gains on a number of outcome measures (including substance abuse and delinquency) have been shown by intervention subjects, although assessments of long-term maintenance effects are still underway. In addition, it is unclear how the effects were distributed across the sample in regard to risk. Thus, it is uncertain if such a program would effect population violence and the most violence-prone portion of the population.

In summary, a number of population-based preventive interventions have reported short-term reductions in problem behaviors, although only a few have focused specifically on violence and aggression. In several studies, long-term maintenance of such effects has not been demonstrated, although many studies have not included follow-up beyond the intervention period. The general orientation and short duration of most programs suggests that they may have only limited impact on changing the behavior of more serious and chronically violent youth. Instead, broad-based approaches may be most useful in promoting nonviolent norms, lessening the opportunity for and elicitations of violent acts, and in preventing the sporadic violence that emerges temporarily during adolescence.

Secondary Prevention Programs for High-Risk Youth

Secondary prevention consists of mitigating the further development of aggression and violence in children who already display earlier forms of aggressive behavior or other risk factors associated with such behavior. Efforts are directed toward preventing either the risk factors or the further development of the behavior. An advantage of secondary prevention programs is that they target those individuals who should benefit most from the services. Not only are overall costs reduced, but programs can be tailored more specifically to the needs of the targeted group. Also, the risk of harm to those not in need is reduced (McCord, 1978), a topic that is further discussed later in this chapter.

Identification may occur through a number of methods (e.g., multiple gating or identification by teachers, parents, law enforcement), and intervention may take place in a variety of settings. Although individuals may be referred for services, they are not always interested in being assigned to intervention, and participation is often a problem. To counteract this difficulty, the most frequent venue for such programs is the school, although children who are not in school (and therefore, probably most in need of services) cannot be included. Another popular approach to secondary prevention (that differs somewhat from targeted interventions) consists of diverting identified juvenile offenders into specialized services. Diversion is meant to stem the development of more serious behaviors by shielding the adolescent from harmful, violence-encouraging exposure to the legal and correctional system. A practical advantage of this method is that individuals should be motivated to participate, especially when failure to do so can result in more serious court action. In both targeted and diversion programs there are marked differences in both length of intervention and types of services provided. Some programs target specific individual affective, cognitive, or behavioral skills. Other programs focus on changing social contextual influences including school, peers, and family.

Interventions that have focused on individual skills range from narrowly focused programs to more broad-based approaches. It appears that even when interventions are limited to a narrow range of skills, behavior change is possible. For example, Arbuthnot and Gordon (1986) randomly assigned 7th through 10th grade students identified by teachers as "behavior disordered" (based on histories of aggressive and disruptive behavior) to intervention and control groups. Intervention students met weekly in small groups for a period of 16–20 weeks to discuss a variety of moral dilemma situations. The dilemma discussions focused primarily on the rights, perspectives, and moral obligations of the dilemma characters, embedded in a more general context of human rights and responsibilities. Presumably, exposure to reasoning (of other students and group leaders) that is slightly more advanced should promote disequilibrium and generate moral growth ("+1 stage method"). Post-intervention assessments indicated that students in the intervention, but not those in the control condition, improved on moral reasoning abilities and displayed reductions in behavior referrals for official disciplinary action as well as reductions in contacts with police or juvenile authorities. One-year follow-up data on approximately one half of the students showed that intervention and control students continued to diverge on outcome measures, although no students in either group had experienced recorded police or court contacts. Apparently, a strength of this type of program is that it teaches students to consider more carefully the moral consequences of their actions and, hence, increases their motivation to refrain from behavior that harms others.

Some programs have attempted to teach individuals a specific set of self-regulatory or social interaction skills, without considering the motivational underpinnings of prosocial behavior or particular moral worldviews. For example, a number of interventions teach aggressive youth how to control and manage their anger. Conceptualizations of anger management or aggression control explicate the cognitive bases of anger, deficit coping responses, and the chain of related events that lead in some cases to acts of physical hostility and aggression (Feindler & Ecton, 1986; Novaco, 1975). Intervention strategies include behavioral modeling with feedback and cognitive self-regulating methods that train youth to recognize triggers and arousal cues in order to apply self-instruction, self-evaluation, and other behavioral means to control their responses to anger. Anger control programs with teenagers have reported successful outcomes, as evidenced by increases in self-reports of anger management skills and reductions in aggressive behavior (Feindler & Ecton, 1986; Feindler, Marriott, & Iwata, 1984). Such interventions also have been extended to residential treatment settings (Dangel, Deschner, & Rapp, 1989).

Although self-regulation is clearly vital if teenagers are to manage relationships effectively, it is also important for them to develop behavioral repertoires for dealing with conflict. Addressing this need, some individual change programs are more broad-based, linking anger management with the development of social and behavioral skills to use in situations of interpersonal conflict that typically engender anger and hostility. The Positive Adolescents Choices Training (PACT) program developed by Hammond and his colleagues (Hammond, 1991; Hammond & Yung, 1991) represents a unique, broad-based, violence-prevention approach developed specifically for African American youth to reduce their disproportionate risk for becoming victims or perpetrators of violence. Addressing the problem of expressive violence or primary homicide that involves loss of control between family, friends, or acquaintances, the PACT program uses a cognitive–behavioral group training program for identified high-risk youth. A key feature of the intervention is the use of a project-developed culturally sensitive series of videotapes, *Dealing With Anger: Givin' It. Takin' It. Workin' It Out.* The target skills addressed in the program include giving negative feedback (expressing criticism or displeasure calmly), receiving negative feedback (reacting to criticism and anger of others appropriately), and negotiation (identifying problems and potential solutions and learning to compromise) (Hammond, 1991; Hammond & Yung, 1991).

In a preliminary outcome study, Hammond and Yung (1993) randomly assigned 169 middle school students to treatment or control groups. Treatment youth received 20 1-hour weekly sessions in PACT training over the course of one semester. During the 3-year period following training, 17.6% of students who had received the training were referred to juvenile court, compared with 48.7% of control youth. Furthermore, of these referrals, control youth were more likely to have been charged with violent offenses.

In contrast to interventions that emphasize individual skills, systems-based secondary prevention programs are organized around modifying contextual influences on adolescent behavior. Some of these programs focus on improving services that are provided in the school setting. Interventions that are directed at modifying the characteristics of peer group interactions are also a mainstay of intervention programming in schools. However, because schools infrequently provide services for families, family-focused interventions are usually part of a community-based service delivery network.

In one example of a general secondary prevention program for 7th grade urban students, Bry and George (1980) randomly assigned identified problem children to treatment or control conditions. In the treatment condition, children were provided with a battery of school support services designed to increase monitoring of behavior and provide reinforcements for desired behaviors. Specifically, target children received daily monitoring and feedback about school behavior, structured reinforcement for appropriate behaviors (e.g., attending school, punctuality, no disciplinary action), biweekly teacher consultations, and periodic parent meetings. At postassessment, intervention youths showed increases in grades and decreases in disruptive behavior and fewer delinquent and criminal offenses a full 5 years after the intervention.

Given the prominent influence of peers during adolescence, it is not surprising that a number of intervention programs have focused on redirecting the norms and behaviors of antisocial peer groups and encouraging affiliations with prosocial peers. Several peer group programs have been derived from the Guided-Group Interaction (GGI) approach (Bixby & McCorkle, 1951), including Positive Peer Culture (Vorrath & Brendtro, 1974), Peer Group Counseling (Howlett & Boehm, 1975), and Peer Culture Development (National School Resource Network, 1980). Through structured discussions with peers, these groups are designed to enhance the leadership skills and positive involvement of selected peers. In turn, it is also expected that these leaders will influence their own peer groups to behave in a more conventional and positive manner.

Although these programs have enjoyed popular support in schools, few controlled studies have been conducted. One exception is a multiple-cohort evaluation, the School Action Effectiveness Study (Gottfredson, Gottfredson, & Cook, 1983) of a Peer Culture Development (PCD) program. The program was implemented in several urban elementary and high schools. The overall goals of the program were to alter peer interaction patterns in order to reduce negative peer influences, increase students' sense of responsibility, increase their support of conventional rules, promote attachment to school, reduce alienation, and increase self-esteem. Identified students were randomly assigned to intervention and control groups. Students in the intervention groups attended daily group meetings for a period of at least one semester. In order to mix "problem" students with "successful" students, the groups included a mix of referred students and students who were expected to be positive role models.

Following the intervention, multiple behavioral outcomes were assessed for students in both intervention and control conditions. These outcomes included self-reports and teacher reports of problem behavior, school referrals for disciplinary action, tardiness, and absences. For the elementary school students, no significant differences between groups were found on any of the outcome measures. In a more disturbing finding, the high school intervention appeared to have an adverse effect on participants. Compared with control students, intervention youth showed significantly more tardiness, less attachment to parents, more "waywardness," and more self-reported delinquent behavior. These differences were due primarily to the poorer performance of the identified problem youth, although on some outcome measures the students selected as role models were most adversely affected by the intervention. This vividly illustrates the potentially iatrogenic effects of interventions (see also McCord, 1978; Lorion, Tolan, & Wahler, 1987). These findings also suggest that intervention effectiveness declines as programs adopt a more general group discussion or group therapy format.

The limits of general therapeutic interventions are also evident in reviewing the literature on juvenile diversion. Juvenile diversion programs can be considered secondary prevention efforts because they involve early identification of delinquent youth, presumably before such behavior has become more serious and habitual. Contact with the justice system is used to identify at-risk youth, and services are intended to prevent further delinquent behavior. Although the types of services that are offered vary considerably, the underlying impetus behind diversion is to avoid formal processing and "labeling" of individuals as delinquents. Unfortunately, most diversion efforts consist of vaguely-formulated counseling programs, and the overall effectiveness of diversion programming has not been demonstrated.

Dunford, Osgood, and Weichselbaum (1981) reported the results of a national evaluation of diversion projects. They assessed 4 out of 11 federally funded programs in which delinquent youth had been randomly assigned to either diversion or regular court processing. The most prevalent type of diversion programming involved some type of individual or group counseling, although two of the projects functioned as service brokers, wherein a variety of services were contracted for. Their findings revealed that across all four sites, diversion was no more successful in improving social behavior or reducing delinquency than either court processing or release.

Gensheimer, Mayer, Gottschalk, and Davidson (1986) conducted a meta-analysis of 44 outcome studies of interventions with officially delinquent youth who were diverted from the formal juvenile justice system, which were reported from 1967 to 1983. These programs covered an array of intervention techniques, including group psychotherapy (25%), casework (14%), behavior therapy (14%), individual psychotherapy (5%), educational/vocational guidance (5%), and "nonspecific" treatment (37%). In general, their analysis cast serious doubt on the utility of diversion programs for effecting positive changes in attitudes and behavior and for reducing future delinquency. They conclude that, "Overall, the results drawn from both the qualitative ratings of effectiveness and those obtained from quantitative methods lead to the conclusion that diversion interventions produce no effects with youths diverted from the justice system" (Gensheimer et al., 1986).

Why have diversion programs fared so poorly? Perhaps the most critical feature of any intervention, the guiding rationale, has been virtually overlooked. It is unfortunate that most programs have provided some type of vaguely formulated, nonspecific services, rather than theoretically driven and solidly developed interventions. In essence, diversion programs have developed around a specific level of intervention, without much regard for identifying the characteristics of effective interventions. Furthermore, delivery of services without controlled evaluation has almost always been the norm.

One exception can be found in a recent study by Davidson, Redner, Blakely, Mitchell, and Emshoff (1987). In this study, identified delinquent youth were randomly assigned to one of six experimental conditions. One of the conditions was an attention placebo group, and one was a return to court control group. Of the remaining four experimental conditions, three of these represented distinct types of intervention approaches: behavioral contracting/child advocacy, family-focused behavioral treatment, and interpersonal relationship therapy. The fourth condition involved a relatively nonspecific intervention equal in intensity to the other treatments but administered within the court system rather than as a diversion program.

Although there were no significant differences reported between groups on the outcome measure of self-reported delinquency, significant differences were found on recidivism, with all three diversion treatment conditions resulting in significantly lower recidivism rates than the court intervention, attention placebo, and court control (regular court processing) groups. In addition, no significant differences were reported between the court intervention and court control groups. Interestingly, there were no significant differences between the three treatment conditions on recidivism rates, suggesting that each of the three types of treatment represented an effective intervention technique. Thus, some support is offered for the utility of theoretically well-grounded interventions in diversion programming.

The benefits of theory-driven interventions are perhaps most evident in studies of family interventions. Family-focused interventions have been used as secondary prevention programs with "predelinquent" youth and as tertiary programs for serious offenders and their families. A wide variety of family therapy techniques have been used, including behavioral contracting (Beal & Duckro, 1977), communication skills training (Parsons & Alexander, 1973), providing information and education about family processes (Kifer, Lewis, Green, & Philips, 1974), modifying family interaction patterns (Minuchin, 1974), and behavior management training (Wade, Morton, Lind, & Newton, 1977). These diverse intervention modalities are woven together by the assumption that children's behavior is a reflection of the family as an organized system. Therefore, changing system organization should prevent further development of aggressive and violent behavior (Tolan & Mitchell, 1989). Such a perspective is supported by an accumulating literature that suggests that family variables are important in the development and treatment of antisocial and violent behavior (for a review, see Tolan, Cromwell, & Brasswell, 1986).

Several studies with predelinquent youth have yielded encouraging results. For example, in a study with adolescents who were referred to juvenile court for minor infractions (e.g., running away, unruliness), Alexander and Parsons (1973) used a functional family therapy model. This approach uses a family systems framework to identify maladaptive family interaction patterns, followed by direct instruction in remedial family management skills. The main goals of the intervention were to improve communication, negotiation, and problem-solving skills. When compared with other treatments (client-centered individual therapy and combined individual–family therapy) and no treatment, functional family therapy resulted in improved family interactions and lower recidivism rates for identified youth up to 18 months after treatment. In addition, sibling delinquency rates were also lowered. However, there was no direct evidence of a lower incidence of violent behavior.

In another illustrative study with predelinquent youth, Stratton (1975) devised a family problem-solving intervention that focused on defining family problems, expressing feelings about problems, discussing how family members respond to such problems, and generating new coping methods. The overall goal was to reduce family tension and disorganization through the introduction of more effective coping strategies. When compared with no-treatment controls, intervention participants were less likely to be arrested for a delinquent offense.

In summary, secondary prevention programs that are based on vague theory and unspecific techniques have not proven useful. In general, unstructured programs for high-risk or predelinquent youth have not been successful. Still, the prognosis for secondary prevention is bright. In particular, programs that focus on improving individual affective, cognitive, and behavioral skills and modifying the learning conditions for aggression appear most promising. Although several successful programs have been narrow in scope and focused on single skill areas (e.g., moral reasoning development), programs that combine multiple components (e.g., anger management and behavioral skills training) should be more effective. Furthermore, to the extent that development is an ongoing process, programs that target learning contexts such as the family should produce the most enduring effects over time. Nevertheless, a caveat is warranted. Given the relatively brief duration and psycho-educational emphasis of most interventions, such programs still may fall short of achieving the magnitude of change that is needed to have an impact on the behavior of the most chronic and seriously aggressive youth.

Tertiary Prevention (Treatment) Programs

The distinction between secondary and tertiary prevention is often blurred, because both approaches involve the identification of at-risk children for intervention services, and the type of services provided may be quite similar. Furthermore, because behavior is often used to identify risk, what is tertiary intervention for the target behavior functions is secondary prevention for any later, more serious behavior. Presumably, treatment programs should target the most seriously troubled youth who are either referred for psychiatric care or committed to day treatment or residential correctional facilities. However, referral for more extensive services is not always related to severity of problems (Tolan, Jaffe, & Ryan, 1988). Clearly, the differentiation of secondary prevention from treatment is less important than being able to understand fully the comparative effectiveness of different programs for adolescents whose antisocial behavior ranges in severity from infrequent fighting to chronic and malicious violent acts. Therefore, our review of treatment programs is predicated on the assumption that such programs inform us about the effectiveness of different approaches with the most seriously disturbed youth, although we recognize that the referral process is influenced by variables other than severity. (See chapter 17 by Feindler & Becker, for a description of tertiary interventions for adolescent sexual offenders.)

Individual psychotherapy has traditionally been a cornerstone of rehabilitative efforts with delinquent youth. This counseling may be provided by various individuals and agencies. For example, although individual counseling by probation officers generally serves a more supervisory function, more intensive treatment services have been used. For example, one concept that has gained popularity over the last few decades as a means of providing higher quality probation and correctional services and that has received some empirical support is based on the differential treatment of juvenile offenders. Derived from the Community Treatment Project (CTP) of the California Youth Authority (Palmer, 1971), these programs rely on the Interpersonal Maturity Level Classification System (I-Level) to match juvenile offenders with appropriate treatment methods, treatment workers, and treatment environments. When applied in community-based settings, the use of the I-Level system has been shown to result in enhanced performance on school work, improved attendance, and reductions in recidivism (Barkwell, 1980). But again there is no direct evidence of the effect on frequency of violent behavior.

Probation departments have also relied on volunteers and nonprofessionals to provide individual counseling services for delinquent youth. These programs do, however, appear to be more effective when a structured treatment approach is applied. For example, O'Donnell, Lydgate, and Fo (1979) reported on the effectiveness of a structured treatment model, "The Buddy System," for 11–17–year-old at-risk youth and juvenile offenders. Using a community-based approach, participating youth were matched with adult volunteers who participated in various recreational activities with the youth and implemented individualized behavior modification programs. Compared with control youth, participants showed reductions in fighting, truancy, and other problem behaviors. However, these effects were only found for the most seriously antisocial youth who had been arrested for at least one major offense in the preceding year. In fact, iatrogenic effects were noted for youth with no prior arrest records; their rates of offending actually increased after the treatment (see also chapter 15 by Kazdin). Individual psychotherapy has also been offered as part of more comprehensive treatment programs. For example, in a series of studies conducted in the 1960s and 1970s by Shore and Massimo (Massimo & Shore, 1963; Shore & Massimo, 1966, 1969, 1973), individual psychotherapy was embedded in a vocationally oriented community-based treatment program. Following the original 10–month intervention program, results indicated changes on a variety of attitudinal and behavioral measures, including a reduction in delinquent behavior for those youth in the treatment but not in the control group. In subsequent follow-up studies, these differences were maintained for up to 15 years following the original intervention (Shore & Massimo, 1979).

The eclectic nature of many treatment programs involving individual psychotherapy makes it difficult to pinpoint the precise mechanisms of change. Many of these programs combine elements of diverse strategies including specialized treatment plans (Barkwell, 1980), vocational training (Shore & Massimo, 1979), and behavior modification (e.g., O'Donnell et al., 1979). However, programs that have isolated some of these components can provide information about their independent contributions to behavior change.

An illustrative example of a community-based behavior modification program can be found in the work of Schwitzgebel and colleagues (Schwitzgebel, 1964; Schwitzgebel & Kolb, 1964). Using a rather unique approach as part of a street corner project, male delinquent multiple offenders were recruited and paid to participate in interviews. Interview attendance and content was then shaped using a variable reinforcement schedule. After 1 year, treatment subjects improved in both attendance and interview content, compared with matched controls. They also had significantly fewer arrests for up to 3 years following the intervention.

More recently, behavior modification programs have been displaced by treatments that emphasize training in cognitive and behavioral skills. Similar to many primary and secondary prevention programs, a number of treatment programs have been developed that emphasize skill building and behavioral rehearsal. The more extremely aggressive and delinquent youth is seen as a person who is weak or deficient in certain skills that are necessary for effective interpersonal functioning (Slaby & Guerra, 1988). Presumably, individuals can be taught these skills, and such skills should generalize to a range of interpersonal situations (Goldstein & Pentz, 1984). These programs have been implemented in a variety of settings, including day treatment centers, psychiatric hospitals, and correctional facilities.

Such treatment programs vary in terms of their relative emphasis on cognitive skills or behavioral skills. Some programs focus on one specific skill, whereas other programs target a range of skills. For example, in a community-based intervention for seriously delinquent youth, Chandler (1973) focused on developing social perspective-taking skills. This was accomplished by having youth in the treatment condition develop, act out, videotape, and critique several skits related to real-life situations experienced by themselves and their peers. Participants met weekly in small groups for approximately 3 hours per day over the course of 10 weeks. Compared with youth in an attention control and no contact control group, youth in the treatment condition improved on social perspective-taking skills and showed significant reductions in recidivism for up to 18 months following treatment. The effect on reducing violent behavior, again, is not clear.

Still, it is often suggested that social perspective taking is a necessary but not sufficient condition for socially competent behavior (Gordon & Arbuthnot, 1987). In fact, the success of programs focused on a single process may be partially due to the fact that participants are also inadvertently practicing a range of other skills including problem solving, communication, decision making, and so on. Although it is important to specify the particular skills that are implicated in the etiology of adolescent aggression, and hence, indicated as viable intervention foci, it may be more realistic to develop interventions that combine training in a broad range of cognitive and behavioral skills.

A more elaborate social skills program is found in the structured learning approach of Goldstein and his colleagues (Goldstein, 1986; Goldstein, Sprafkin, Gershaw, & Klein, 1980) that has been used with aggressive adolescents. Of particular importance in this training is the grouping together of youth with shared skill deficits as well as the application of specific procedures to maximize transfer and maintenance of skills (e.g., stimulus variability, programmed reinforcement). In general, this training has proven effective with various populations, including assaultive incarcerated youth.

Other recent work focused on a highly aggressive population is the Viewpoints Training Program, a treatment program directed toward changing the beliefs and attitudes of violent youth about the legitimacy of violence as a response to conflict and also emphasizing specific social problem-solving skills (Guerra & Panizzon, 1986). In a controlled evaluation study with juvenile offenders who were incarcerated for violent crimes, Guerra and Slaby (1990) randomly assigned aggression offenders to the cognitive–behavioral treatment group, an attention control group, or a no-treatment control group. The 12-session, small group treatment program resulted in decreases in posttest aggression for the treatment participants only, and these decreases were related to changes in the targeted social–cognitive variables. In another treatment program for hospitalized antisocial children and preadolescents, youth were randomly assigned to either problem-solving skills training, nondirective relationship therapy, or minimal contact conditions (Kazdin, Esveldt-Dawson, French, & Unis, 1987). This program did not involve small group treatment, but consisted of individual sessions for participating youth. In the social problem-solving training, children were taught to apply problem-solving skills to interpersonal interactions that most commonly provoked them to respond aggressively. The focus of the relationship therapy treatment was on developing a close therapeutic relationship and learning to express feelings. The minimal contact condition involved brief interaction with a therapist but no specific treatment plan. Results indicated that the problem-solving training had significantly greater effects on aggression reduction than did the relationship therapy treatment, and the minimal therapy children showed no significant improvements.

In addition, there has been a recent burgeoning of literature on psychopharmacological treatment for extremely violent adolescents. However, much of this literature focuses on managing violent outbursts (Kreusi & Johnson, in press). Less is known about pharmacological efficacy as a primary intervention method or as one component of an articulated multimodal program. Although drugs may be an effective component of a treatment package for the most violent youth, it is unlikely that drug treatment alone will be sufficient.

Instead, a common element related to treatment effectiveness appears to be a focus on a battery of social interaction skills. These skills can be trained directly and strengthened through structured reinforcement contingencies. Recall the elaborate skills training program of Goldstein and his colleagues (Goldstein et al., 1980), and the emphasis on vocational skills within the psychotherapeutic interventions of Shore and Massimo (1966, 1969, 1973, 1979). Improved social skills not only help individuals resolve conflict-producing situations with their peers, but enable them to get along in multiple social contexts.

Given the influence of these multiple social contexts, some treatment programs begin by intervening at the systems level, with the assumption that system changes will translate into decreases in individual aggressive behavior.

In the treatment literature, the most common type of intervention involves family therapy. The theoretical basis of such programs does not differ significantly from secondary prevention efforts with high-risk children and their families, and programs appear to be quite effective with seriously antisocial youth. For example, Barton, Alexander, Waldron, Turner, and Warburton (1985) applied a functional family therapy model to 30 adolescents (who each averaged 20 past adjudicated offenses) and their families. Fifteen months after the end of the intervention, youth in the treatment group were compared with a matched sample of 44 youth who were part of a general intervention program. Whereas 60% of the treatment youth had a subsequent criminal charge, a striking 93% of control subjects reoffended.

New models of family therapy for serious offenders are also being tested. For example, Henggeler and his colleagues have used a multisystemic family therapy approach (MST) in the treatment of serious juvenile offenders and their families (Henggeler & Borduin, 1990; Henggeler et al., 1986). This home-based treatment involves individualized treatment plans based on assessments of the strengths and weaknesses of the teenager and his or her family, peer system, and school. The treatment is designed to help alleviate family organization problems that impede family functioning and to aid the family in addressing and overcoming social impediments that are constraining them. In a recent outcome report, Henggeler, Melton, and Smith (1992) reported that, in comparison with the typical intensive probation services, families participating in their treatment had much lower recidivism rates. This report suggests that an integrative approach (targeting the family to improve family relations and aiding the family in addressing the external demands of their social world) has the most promise for reducing violence and other antisocial behavior among those most involved in such acts.

Summarizing the treatment literature, there are isolated examples of effective interventions that are based on a diversity of theoretical approaches. Interpersonal relations oriented psychotherapy, behavior modification, social skills development, cognitive–behavioral, and family interventions all have had some effect in some instances. However, it appears that effectiveness is most consistent and extensive when the intervention is multimodal, and consists of carefully designed and coordinated components. For that reason, it may be that treatment programs for the adolescents who are most seriously involved and most likely to be violent should work through the family and coordinate interventions around family implementation.

Conclusions and Recommendations

The available literature includes demonstrations of a variety of programs that target violence-related problems at the primary, secondary, and tertiary levels of prevention. There are programs that recognize the social basis of such violence and that violent acts are most prevalent during adolescence. There are programs that target at-risk populations to "inoculate" children in order to limit the harmful impacts of environmental impediments. There are programs that target individuals based on their exhibition of at-risk behavior. There are also programs that attempt to help those already exhibiting serious chronic behavior.

The promising components of such programs can be identified. At the individual level, it seems that those programs that promote social–cognitive skills including perspective taking, alternative solution generation, self-esteem enhancement, and peer negotiation skills, and that aid students in learning violence avoiding behavior, are likely to have the most impact. In addition, their impact seems likely to be greatest at the primary and secondary prevention levels. At the primary level, prevention programs can modify group norms and increase group skills to help children develop fully (and nonviolently). At the secondary level, when delivered with greater intensity, such skills can reduce the risk in children who are living in the most impeding environments or exhibiting early signs of reliance on aggressive behavior. At the family level, programs that help parents establish clear and consistent discipline and family responsibilities, clarify communication and increase positive affect, and that aid the family in navigating normal and unusual transitions and stresses seem most promising. At the school level, organization of transitions, inclusion of social problem-solving and nonviolence-promoting curricula are likely to have a significant impact, particularly at the primary prevention level. Social group and community level interventions are also likely to have a significant impact on the overall prevalence rates and provide social supports for development of nonaggressive behavior among the already involved youth.

Thus, one can see a diverse portfolio of interventions, which suggests that psychologists can and should invest their energy and skills into prevention of violence and related behaviors. Although there is a promising base, there also is a need for more extensive empirical evaluation of many of these promising approaches, and for the articulation of a comprehensive strategy that defines the intervention approaches of choice at the primary, secondary, and tertiary levels.

Furthermore, the available studies suggest that there is a concurrent need for development of evaluation methods that adequately reflect the diversity of approaches and the specific issues in applying prevention. In particular, there is a need to move to a next step of evaluation and make comparisons between competing interventions with specific populations, with the aim of identifying the relative merits of each approach. This is a very complex activity that demands high fidelity of intervention application and cooperative investigations. However, if the rising tide of adolescent violence and its enormous costs are to be stemmed, such work is sorely needed.

In addition to these comparisons, there is a concurrent need to develop multimodal interventions that consider individual as well as contextual factors. Given the trends indicating that inner-city and minority children are disproportionately at-risk, single-dimension, short-term interventions are unlikely to be sufficient to enable them to overcome or be insulated from the difficult social conditions and environments in which they are developing.

Psychologists must be cognizant of the limitations that are placed on the predictability of their procedures by the social and economic conditions under which their target populations live. When parents are unavailable to respond to requests for cooperation and information (e.g., if they have no telephone or permanent address), or when children are not attending school or are living in extreme poverty with no adult supervision, it is overly optimistic to expect that the psychological intervention procedures described here can be of help before there are significant changes in the social and economic conditions under which these young people live.

Integration of individual, family, social group, and community interventions seems necessary to make any real difference. In some cases, it may be necessary to address the need to bring teenagers and their families up to a level at which they demonstrate sufficient "readiness" for preventive intervention services. For instance, school-based programs are ineffective for children not in school, just as family therapy is ineffective if families cannot keep scheduled appointments. Although such developments may seem daunting in complexity and intimidating in cost, the cost of not doing so and the problems of complexity of uncoordinated services should serve as an impetus toward these goals.

References

Achenbach, T. M., & Edelbrock, C. S., (1981). Behavioral problems and competencies reported by parents of normal and disturbed children aged four through sixteen. *Monographs of the Society for Research in Child Development, 46*, 188.

Alexander, J. F., & Parsons, B. V. (1973). Short-term behavioral intervention with delinquent families: Impact on family process and recidivism. *Journal of Abnormal Psychology, 81*, 219–225.

Arbuthnot, J., & Gordon, D. A. (1986). Behavioral and cognitive effects of a moral reasoning development intervention for high-risk behavior-disordered adolescents. *Journal of Consulting and Clinical Psychology, 54*, 208–216.

Barkwell, L. (1980). Differential treatment of juveniles on probation. In R. R. Ross & P. Gendreau (Eds.), *Effective correctional treatment* (pp. 363–378). Toronto, Canada: Butterworths.

Barton, C., Alexander, J. F., Waldron, H., Turner, C. W., & Warburton, J. (1985). Generalizing treatment effects of functional family therapy. *American Journal of Family Therapy, 13*, 16–26.

Beal, D., & Duckro, P. (1977). Family counseling as an alternative to legal action for the juvenile status offender. *Journal of Marriage and Family Counseling, 3*, 77–88.

Bixby, F. L., & McCorkle, L. W. (1951). Guided group interaction and correctional work. *American Sociological Review, 16*, 455–459.

Blumstein, A., Farrington, D. P., & Moitra, S. (1985). Delinquent careers: Innocents, desisters, and persisters. In M. Tonry & N. Morris (Eds.), *Crime and justice: An annual review of research* (Vol. 6, pp. 187–219). Chicago: University of Chicago Press.

Bry, B. H., & George, F. E. (1980). The preventative effects of early intervention on the attendance and grades of urban adolescents. *Professional Psychology, 11*, 252–260.

Caplan, M., Weissberg, R. P., Grober, J. S., Sivo, P. J., Grady, K., & Jacoby, C. (1992). Social competence promotion with inner-city and surburban young adolescents: Effects on social adjustment and alcohol use. *Journal of Consulting and Clinical Psychology, 60*, 56–63.

Centers for Disease Control. (1991). Weapon-carrying among high school students. *Journal of the American Medical Association, 266*, 2342.

Center to Prevent Handgun Violence. (1990). *Caught in the crossfire: A report on gun violence in our nation's schools*. Washington, DC: Author.

Chandler, M. (1973). Egocentrism and antisocial behavior: The assessment and training of social perspective taking skills. *Developmental Psychology, 9*, 326–332.

Cohen, S., & Wilson-Brewer, R. (1991) *Violence prevention for young adolescents: The state of the art of program evaluation.* Newton, MA: Educational Development Center.

Dangel, R., Deschner, J., & Rapp, R. (1989). Anger control training for adolescents in residential treatment. *Behavior Modification, 13,* 447–458.

Davidson, W. S., Redner, R., Blakely, C. H., Mitchell, C. M., & Emshoff, J. G. (1987). Diversion of juvenile offenders: An experimental comparison. *Journal of Consulting and Clinical Psychology, 55,* 68–75.

Dunford, G. W., Osgood, D. W., & Weichselbaum, H. F. (1981). *National evaluation of diversion projects: Final report.* Washington, DC: National Institute of Juvenile Justice and Delinquency Prevention.

Elliott, D. S., Ageton, S. S., Huizinga, D., Knowles, B. A., & Canter, R. J. (1983). *The prevalence and incidence of delinquent behavior: 1976–1980* (National Youth Survey Report No. 26). Boulder, CO: Behavioral Research Institute.

Elliott, D. S., Huizinga, D., & Menard, S. (1989). *Multiple problem youth: Delinquency, substance use, and mental health problems.* New York: Springer-Verlag.

Farrington, D. P. (1983). Offending from 10 to 25 years of age. In K. Van Dusen & S. A. Mednick (Eds.), *Prospective studies of crime and delinquency* (pp. 17–38). Norwell, MA: Kluwer Academic.

Farrington, D. P. (1986). Age and crime. In M. Tonry & N. Morris (Eds.), *Crime and Justice: An Annual Review of Research* (Vol. 7, pp. 189–250). Chicago: University of Chicago Press.

Feindler, E., & Ecton, R. (1986). *Adolescent anger control.* Elmsford, NY: Pergamon Press.

Feindler, E., Marriott, S. A., & Iwata, M. (1984). Group anger control training for junior high school delinquents. *Cognitive Therapy and Research, 8,* 299–311.

Felner, R. D., & Adan, A. M. (1988). The school transitional environment project: An ecological intervention and evaluation. In R. H. Price, E. L. Cowen, R. P. Lorion, & J. Ramos-McKay (Eds.), *14 ounces of prevention: A casebook for practitioners* (pp. 111–122). Washington, DC: American Psychological Association.

Gensheimer, L. K., Mayer, J. P., Gottschalk, R., & Davidson, W. S. (1986). Diverting youth from the juvenile justice system: A meta-analysis of intervention efficacy. In S. P. Apter & A. P. Goldstein (Eds.), *Youth violence: Programs and prospects* (pp. 39–57). Elmsford, NY: Pergamon Press

Goldstein, A. P. (1986). Psychological skill training and the aggressive adolescent. In S. P. Apter & A. P. Goldstein (Eds.), *Youth violence: Programs and Prospects* (pp. 89–119). Elmsford, NY: Pergamon Press.

Goldstein, A. P. (1992, May 4). *School violence: Its community context and potential solutions.* Testimony presented to the Subcommittee on Elementary, Secondary, and Vocational Education Committee on Education and Labor, U.S. House of Representatives.

Goldstein, A. P., & Pentz, M. A. (1984). Psychological skill training and the aggressive adolescent. *School Psychology Review, 13,* 311–323.

Goldstein, A. P., Sprafkin, R. P., Gershaw, N. J., & Klein, P. (1980). *Skillstreaming the adolescent.* Champaign, IL: Research Press.

Gottfredson, G. D., Gottfredson, D. C., & Cook. M. S. (1983). *The school action effectiveness study: Second interim report* (Report No. 342). Center for Social Organization of Schools. Baltimore, MD: Johns Hopkins University.

Guerra, N. G., & Panizzon, A. (1986). *Viewpoints training program.* Santa Barbara, CA: Center for Law-Related Education.

Guerra, N. G., & Slaby, R. G. (1990). Cognitive mediators of aggression in adolescent offenders: 2. Intervention. *Developmental Psychology, 26,* 269–277.

Hammond, R. (1991). *Dealing with anger: Givin' it. Takin' it. Workin' it out.* Champaign, IL: Research Press.

Hammond, R., & Yung, B. (1991). *Dealing with anger: Given' it. Takin' it. Workin' it out: Leader's guide.* Champaign, IL: Research Press.

Hammond, R., & Yung, B. (1993). *Evaluation and activity report: Positive adolescent choices training.* Unpublished grant report, U.S. Maternal and Child Health Bureau, Washington, DC.

Henggeler, S. W., & Borduin, C. M. (1990). *Family therapy and beyond: A multisystemic approach to treating the behavior problems of children and adolescents.* Pacific Grove, CA: Brooks/Cole.

Henggeler, S. W., Melton, G. B., & Smith, L. A. (1992). Family preservation using multisystemic therapy—An effective alternative to incarcerating serious juvenile offenders. *Journal of Consulting and Clinical Psychology, 60,* 953–961.

Henggeler, S. W., Rodick, J. D., Borduin, C. M., Hanson, C. L., Watson, S. M., & Urey, J. R. (1986). Multisystemic treatment of juvenile offenders: Effects on adolescent behavior and family interaction. *Developmental Psychology, 22,* 132–141.

Hirschi, T., & Gottfredson, M. (1983). Age and the explanation of crime. *American Journal of Sociology, 89,* 552–584.

Howlett, F. W., & Boehm, R. G. (1975). *School-based delinquency prevention: The Rock Island experience.* Austin, TX: Justice Systems.

Huesmann, L. R., Eron, L. D., Lefkowitz, M. M., & Walder, L. O. (1984). Stability of aggression over time and generations. *Developmental Psychology, 20,* 1120–1134.

Kazdin, A. E., Esveldt-Dawson, K., French, N. H., & Unis, A. S. (1987). Problem-solving skills training and relationship therapy in the treatment of antisocial child behavior. *Journal of Consulting and Clinical Psychology, 55,* 76–85.

Kifer, B. E., Lewis, M. A., Green, D. R., & Philips, F. L. (1974). Training predelinquent youths and their parents to negotiate conflict situations. *Journal of Applied and Behavioral Analysis, 3,* 357–364.

Kreusi, M. J. P., & Johnson, A. (in press). Pharmacologic treatment of problematic aggression in children and adolescents. *School Psychology Review.*

Massimo, J. L., & Shore, M. F. (1963). The effectiveness of a comprehensive vocationally oriented psychotherapy program for adolescent delinquent boys. *American Journal of Orthopsychiatry, 33,* 634–643.

McCord, J. (1978). A thirty-year follow-up of treatment effects. *American Psychologist, 33,* 284–289

Menacker, J., Weldon, W., & Hurwitz, E. (1990). Community influences on school crime and violence. *Urban Education, 25,* 68–80.

Minuchin, S. (1974). *Families and family therapy.* Cambridge, MA: Harvard University Press.

Moffitt, T. E., & Silva, P. A. (1988). Self-reported delinquency: Results from an instrument for New Zealand. *Australian and New Zealand Journal of Criminology, 21,* 227–240.

National School Resource Network. (1980). *Peer culture development* (Technical Assistance Bulletin 28). Washington, DC: National School Resource Network.

Novaco, R. (1975). *Anger control: The development and evaluation of an experimental treatment.* Lexington, MA: DC Heath.

O'Donnell, C. R., Lydgate, T., & Fo, W. S. O. (1979). The buddy system: Review and follow up. *Child Behavior Therapy, 1,* 161–169.

Osgood, D. W., O'Malley, P. M., Bachman, J. G., & Johnston, L. D. (1989). Time trends and age trends in arrests and self-reported illegal behavior. *Criminology, 27,* 389–417.

Palmer, T. B. (1971). California's treatment program for delinquent adolescents. *Journal of Research in Crime and Delinquency, 8,* 74–92.

Parsons, B. V., & Alexander, J. F. (1973). Short-term family intervention: A therapy outcome study. *Journal of Consulting and Clinical Psychology, 41,* 195–201.

Petersen, A. C. (1988). Adolescent development. *Annual Review of Psychology, 39,* 583–607.

Prothrow-Stith, D. (1991). *Deadly consequences: How violence is destroying our teenage population and a plan to begin solving the problem.* New York: HarperCollins.

Robins, L. N. (1978). Sturdy childhood predictors of adult antisocial behaviour: Replications from longitudinal studies. *Psychological Medicine, 8,* 611–622.

Sarason, I. G., & Sarason, B. R. (1981). Teaching cognitive and social skills to high school students. *Journal of Consulting and Clinical Psychology, 49,* 908–918.

Schwitzgebel, R. L. (1964). *Streetcorner research.* Cambridge, MA: Harvard University Press.

Schwitzgebel, R. L., & Kolb, D. (1964). Inducing behavior change in adolescent delinquents. *Behavior Research and Therapy, 1,* 297–304.

Sheley, J., McGee, Z., & Wright, J. (1992). Gun-related violence in and around inner-city schools. *American Journal of Diseases of Childhood, 146,* 677–682.

Shore, M. F., & Massimo, J. L. (1966). Comprehensive vocationally oriented psychotherapy for adolescent delinquent boys: A follow-up study. *American Journal of Orthopsychiatry, 36,* 609–616.

Shore, M. F., & Massimo, J. L. (1969). Five years later: A follow-up study of comprehensive vocationally oriented psychotherapy. *American Journal of Orthopsychiatry*, *39*, 769–774.

Shore, M. F., & Massimo, J. L. (1973). After ten years: A follow-up study of comprehensive vocationally oriented psychotherapy. *American Journal of Orthopsychiatry*, *43*, 128–132.

Shore, M. F., & Massimo, J. L. (1979). Fifteen years after treatment: A follow-up study of comprehensive vocationally oriented psychotherapy. *American Journal of Orthopsychiatry*, *49*, 240–245.

Slaby, R. G., & Guerra, N. G. (1988). Cognitive mediators of aggression in adolescent offenders: 1. Assessement. *Developmental Psychology*, *24*, 580–588.

Stratton, J. G. (1975). Effects of crisis intervention counseling on predelinquent and misdemeanor juvenile offenders. *Juvenile Justice*, *26*, 7–18.

Tolan, P. H., Cromwell, R. E., & Brasswell, M. (1986). Family therapy with delinquents: A critical review of the literature. *Family Process*, *25*, 619–649.

Tolan, P. H., Jaffe, C., & Ryan, K. (1988). Adolescents' mental health service use and provider, process, and recipient characteristics. *Journal of Clinical Child Psychology*, *17*, 228–235.

Tolan, P. H., & Loeber, R. L. (1993). Antisocial behavior. In P. H. Tolan and B. J. Cohler (Eds.), *Handbook of clinical research and practice with adolescents* (307–331). New York: Wiley.

Tolan, P. H., & Mitchell, M. E. (1989). Families and the therapy of antisocial and delinquent behavior. *Journal of Psychotherapy and the Family*, *6*, 29–48.

Vorrath, H. H., & Brendtro, L. K. (1974). *Positive peer culture*. Chicago: Aldine.

Wade, T. C., Morton, T. L., Lind, J. E., & Newton, R. F. (1977). A family crisis intervention approach to diversion from the juvenile justice system. *Juvenile Justice*, *28*, 51–53.

Wilson-Brewer, R., & Jacklin, B. (1990). *Violence prevention strategies targeted at the general population of minority youth*. Background paper prepared for the Forum on Youth Violence in Minority Communities: Setting the Agenda for Prevention. Newton, MA: Educational Development Center

Wolfgang, M. E., Figlio, R. M., & Sellin, T. (1972). *Delinquency in a birth cohort*. Chicago: University of Chicago Press.

Wolfgang, M. E., Thornberry, T. P., & Figlio, R. M. (1987). *From boy to man, from delinquency to crime*. Chicago: University of Chicago Press.

Zigler, E., Taussig, C., & Black, K. (1992). Early childhood intervention: A promising preventative for juvenile delinquency. *American Psychologist*, *47*, 997–1006.

17

Interventions in Family Violence Involving Children and Adolescents

Eva L. Feindler and Judith V. Becker

Child and adolescent physical and sexual abuse within the family are two of the most prevalent forms of violence against youth. Almost 1.5 million children and adolescents are targets of domestic abuse and neglect every year and a significant proportion of these victims die as a result of this maltreatment (Ammerman & Hersen, 1990). Other victims suffer severe negative sequelae in terms of physical, cognitive, and socioemotional functioning, and the long-term effects on their development can be overwhelming.

In a recent synthesis of data concerning the victimization of children, Finkelhor and Dziuba-Leatherman (1994) not only underscored the high frequency of victimization of children but revealed that children suffer from certain types of violence that have largely been excluded from traditional criminologic concern. In particular, assaults against young children by other children including siblings may be as traumatic as assaults by adults. These authors suggested the following three-level categorization that might be used to direct research and intervention efforts: a) pandemic victimizations that occur to a majority of children in the course of growing up (assault by siblings, physical punishment by parents, peer assault, etc.), b) acute victimizations (physical abuse, neglect, and family abduction), and c) extraordinary victimizations (homicide, child abuse homicide, and nonfamily abduction). Because the obvious child risk factors such as small physical stature, dependency status, and little choice as to whom they associate with are an inherent part of childhood status, childhood victimization represents the most serious clinical problem (Finkelhor & Dziuba-Leatherman, 1994).

The impact of child abuse does not stop with the victim, however. Widom's (1992) data suggest that the incidence of childhood abuse increased the odds of future delinquency and adult criminality by 40%. And, clearly, the oft cited "cycle of violence" hypothesis suggests that a childhood history of abuse may predispose the survivor to become a victim or perpetrator of violence later in life (Widom, 1992).

For both perpetrators and victims, there are enormous needs for effective clinical prevention programs and intervention programs designed to rectify the often devastating psychological consequences that are associated with violence against children and adolescents within the family. The primary purpose of this chapter is to provide an overview of empirically evaluated intervention and prevention programs that are targeted at youth victims and perpetrators of physical violence and sexual violence, primarily within the context of the family. The chapter begins with an overview of incidence and prevalence data regarding both the physical and sexual abuse of children and adolescents. Then, in each of these areas respectively, we describe empirically tested prevention and intervention programs. Because new avenues of clinical application have been suggested by reviewing some programs that target aggressive adolescents or juvenile sex offenders—those who may be both victims and perpetrators—the chapter also includes a discussion of adolescent sexual offenders and relevant programs for them.

Unfortunately, there are precious few reports of well-described, rigorously evaluated, and clinically effective prevention and treatment programs in these areas. Definitional issues as well as difficulties experienced in securing reliable and valid assessment instruments certainly have hindered the progress of clinical research. However, it is our intent, through this integration of available literature, to emphasize the urgent need for further psychological research on prevention and intervention with individuals and families to help reduce the startling prevalence of physical and sexual abuse of children and adolescents.

The Extent of the Problem

Because of their inherent dependency, children and adolescents represent one of the populations that is most vulnerable to physical and sexual abuse, particularly within the context of the family. Clearly, just being a child in an American family increases vulnerability to violent victimization, and being a female increases one's chances of sexual abuse within the family. Although there are wide variations in estimates of the incidence and prevalence of child maltreatment, between 12 and 16 children per 1,000 suffer from maltreatment each year (Ammerman & Hersen, 1990). According to the American Humane Association, in 1986 about 2.1 children were reported as suspected victims of child abuse or neglect, and their curcumstances were suggestive of parental maltreatment (Rivera & Widom, 1990). Younger children are more susceptible to physical abuse and fatalities and older children are more likely to be sexually abused. In general, there is a tendency for boys to be more maltreated except for sexual abuse of which girls are more frequently victims (Ammerman & Hersen, 1990). (Chapter 2 of this book provides further data on the incidence and prevalence of child abuse for both girls and boys.)

The sexual abuse of children continues to be a major societal problem, although awareness of the problem has increased in recent years. Research initially focused on the incidence and prevalence of sexual abuse and the impact that abuse has on victimized youth.

Estimates of the national incidence rate of reported child sexual abuse in the United States range from 0.7 (National Center on Child Abuse and Neglect [NCCAN], 1981) to 1.4 (American Humane Association, 1984) victims per 1000 children in the population; however, only 2% to 5% of child victims ever report the abuse to a responsible adult (Finkelhor, 1979; Russell, 1984). A random survey of college students and the general population revealed that 27% of women and 16% of men reported being molested as children and adolescents, and 39% of these people reported the occurrence of abuse (Timnick, 1985). In terms of the relationship between victim and perpetrator, Conte and Berlinger (1981) found that the offender was a family member among 47% of the 383 children seen in their study for evaluation and treatment. Finally, Russell (1983) reported that 77% of perpetrators of intrafamial abuse were uncles, brothers, or grandfathers, and 23% were natural fathers or stepfathers. Interestingly, of that sample only 15% of extrafamilial sexual abuse perpetrators were strangers.

A review of the available psychological literature reveals that even though adolescents are least likely to be reported by public service providers and are usually labeled as having other correlated behavior problems, adolescent abuse accounts for some 42% of all cases of maltreatment (Schellenbach & Guerney, 1987). Nationwide data indicate that parents were the perpetrators in 81% of the more than 500,000 cases of adolescent physical abuse, sexual abuse, or neglect that were officially reported in 1986 (Williamson, Bordwin, & Howe, 1991). These findings certainly refute the assumption that young children are the primary victims of abuse and neglect and that the risk of maltreatment declines as children grow older (Powers & Echenrode, 1988).

Traditionally, the discussion of risk factors in child maltreatment has emphasized inadequate parenting skills such as low frustration tolerance, inappropriate expression of anger, social isolation, unrealistic expectations of children and impaired parenting skills (Wolfe, 1987).

In terms of vulnerability to child sexual abuse, a survey of 795 college students helped to identify several risk factors that might help guide the development of effective interventions. Presence of a stepfather, separation of a child from the natural mother, the mother's failure to finish high school, the mother's punishment of the child's sexual curiosity, the father's lack of physical affection toward the child, family income of under $10,000 per year, and child's limited friendships (Finkelhor, 1979) are factors that may place a child at greater risk.

Parents have been the primary focus of clinical intervention and prevention efforts related to child and adolescent abuse. More recently, child characteristics and family interaction patterns that may contribute to violent family interactions have been identified. Empirically tested prevention and intervention efforts involving each of these are described in the sections that follow.

Physical Abuse of Children and Adolescents

Although some child characteristics (e.g., prematurity and low birth weight) are not appropriate targets for direct child interventions, other characteristics of the child that may influence the occurrence of physical abuse (e.g., aggressive and oppositional behavior patterns) may be targeted. Parent–child relationships, such as disrupted mother–infant/child attachments) and dysfunctional family coping mechanisms, may also serve as relevant treatment targets. (Social stressors, such as unemployment, that may influence violence in various forms are described in chapter 3.) However, conceptualizations that view family violence as interactive and influenced by parent, child, family, and stress factors are most helpful in directing multimodal treatment efforts.

Perpetrator-Focused Interventions

Necessarily, prevention and intervention efforts with families who are involved in child maltreatment must focus on the perpetrators of physical child abuse, and almost all efforts have focused on mothers and fathers. Cognitive–behavioral models have emphasized parent–child coercive interactions (Wolfe & Wekerle, 1993), faulty parental cognitions, expectations, and attributions (Milner, 1993), and poor parental impulse control (Azar & Siegel, 1990) as factors in child abuse. Comprehensive parent training programs that provide instruction, modeling, and rehearsal procedures to increase parents' positive reinforcement, to reward compliance, to teach parents to give clear, concise demands, and to implement time-out procedures as alternatives to punishment have proven an effective approach to prevention with parents at risk for abuse and neglect (Wolfe, Edwards, Manion, & Koverola, 1988). Additional skill deficiencies that characterize abusive parents include problem-solving skills for child-related problems, which may result in the use of punishment as the predominant strategy in response to child noncompliance. Problem-solving skills and social skills that are necessary for healthy parent–child interactions have all been effectively taught to abusive parents in comprehensive and methodologically sound parent intervention programs (Azar & Siegel, 1990).

An extremely comprehensive program for the treatment and prevention of child maltreatment is Project 12-Ways, operative since 1979. This ecobehavioral approach focuses on parent skills and deficits and has included skills training in stress management, self-control, problem solving, child management, pre- and post-natal care and home safety and cleanliness. Admirably, these component interventions have been repeatedly empirically evaluated through sample-subject and group designs and indicate clear acquisition of necessary skills. Lutzker and Rice (1987) presented program evaluation data that examine recidivism over 5 years across more than 700 families. Although early differences between treatment and comparison groups decreased across the years, those families who participated in Project 12-Ways training were less likely to be involved in recidivistic child abuse and neglect than the comparison families. The authors suggest booster services or additional monitoring of high risk families to ensure maintenance of behavior change (Lutzker & Rice, 1987).

The most recent focus on the development of interventions for abusive parents has been on the social information processing model reviewed by Milner (1993). Clinical strategies must target dysfunctions and distortions at the three cognitive processing stages (perceptions of social behavior; interpretations, evaluations and expectations that give meaning to social behavior; and information integration and response selection stage). Because cognitive activities are believed to mediate a parent's selection and implementation of responses to their children, the treatment of child abusive parents must incorporate cognitive restructuring approaches in addition to skills training in child management. This approach clearly dovetails with effective intervention when negative affect accompanies aggressive attributional styles of those with anger management difficulties (Feindler, 1990), with stress management interventions for abusive parents (Schinke, Schilling, Barth, & Gilchrist, 1986), and with cognitive problem-solving skills in areas related to child care in neglectful families (Dawson, de Armas, McGrath, & Kelly, 1986). Interventions with abusive parents have proven quite effective, and the recent emphasis on social information processing only promises to enhance further treatment efforts and the maintenance and generalization of gains. (Social information processing models of the development of violence among youth are reviewed in chapter 2.)

In keeping with approaches to parent training, it is important to hear the message in Straus' (1992) National Family Violence Survey, which indicated that over 90% of American parents use physical punishment to correct misbehavior. Data indicate that parents who believe in physical punishment hit more often, more often go beyond ordinary punishment strategies, and have a child abuse rate that is four times the rate of parents who do not approve of physical punishment (Straus, 1992). Clearly, further research is needed on the relation of physical punishment to child maltreatment and to the intergenerational transmission of the abuse cycle. Moreover, it has been demonstrated (Eron & Huesmann, 1990) that physical punishment of children by parents is related to the children's aggressive behavior, and when these children in turn confront their own children's behavior, the punishment patterns continue in a cycle that extends across three generations. It is imperative that the clinical community continue to develop and implement parent treatment and prevention programs that specifically train parents in alternative child management techniques.

Child-Focused Interventions

Psychological treatment of violent families must also target the young abused victim of child abuse. Not only do physically abused children suffer physical and neurological damage, but they suffer severe emotional and social consequences. Many young victims experience chronic anxiety, depression, and even posttraumatic distress disorder, which may lead to a dissociative disorder. Youngblade and Belsky (1990), in their excellent review of consequences of child maltreatment, describe additional psychological difficulties such as dysfunctional parent–child relations, coercive interpersonal exchanges, dysfunctional and aggressive peer relations, lower self-esteem, and significantly higher rates of externalizing and internalizing behavior problems compared with nonmaltreated children. Given these conclusions, it is critical for treatment efforts to focus not just on the abusive adult but on the youthful victims of family violence.

Although children who have been victims of physical abuse have been described as having a number of cognitive, emotional, and social difficulties (e.g., anxiety, impulse control, poor social and academic adjustment; Friedrich & Einbender, 1983; Hoffman-Plotkin & Twentyman, 1984; Perry, Doran, & Wells, 1983; Wolfe & Mosk, 1983), there are precious few studies of psychological treatment interventions for abused children. This serious omission in the field of clinical psychology may be due to the emphasis on the role of the parent in the abuse and on ensuring the safety of the child by removal and placement in foster care. However, family focused interventions have recently begun to be described and evaluated as more successful because they target the entire dysfunctional family system, not just the parents, and seek to modify the typically coercive parent–child interactions (Daro, 1988).

Daro's (1988) review of demonstration projects for treatment of violent families indicated that therapeutic dayschool services for preschoolers and a combination of group counseling, temporary shelter, and personal skill development for adolescents were the most effective interventions for victims of abuse. But as Gaudin (1993) pointed out, the lack of control groups and reliance on clinicians' judgments of treatment outcome restrict the reliability and generalizability of these conclusions. Heide and Richardson (1987) reported significant gains for neglected but not necessarily abused preschoolers in day treatment for approximately 8 months in a well-evaluated project. Compared with waiting list controls, treated children improved in perceptual–motor skills, cognition, social and emotional adjustment, and language, but, unfortunately, the exact treatment interventions were not well-described.

For very young children, intensive child care programs that enhance skills development in cognitive, social, and emotional areas seem promising. Documented deficits in peer interaction skills have been effectively treated with a behavioral social skills training approach with young children (Davis & Fantuzzo, 1989) and could well be extended to older children. Others are beginning to develop comprehensive social skills training programs for maltreated children that it is hoped will prove as effective as other social skills interventions (Howing, Wodarski, Kurtz & Gaudin, 1990), but comprehensive clinical evaluations with valid and reliable assessments will need to be completed. Classroom behavior problems and deficits in academic functioning that may lead to school failure and dropping out could easily be targeted for behavioral interventions in the school setting. Difficulties in managing emotional sequelae of domestic violence, namely the anxiety patterns exhibited by some youngsters and the anger and aggression exhibited by others, could also be significant targets for the cognitive–behavioral interventions that have proven so effective with children and adolescents. (See chapter 15 for a comprehensive summary of the treatment of aggressive children.) Mannarino and Cohen (1990) review several other treatment approaches, such as group counseling for middle school victims to improve problem-solving skills and self-esteem and a more psychodynamic emphasis on "reattachment therapy" for young abuse victims to ameliorate deficits in adult–child relationships. However, these authors again point to the paucity of well-described and rigorously evaluated psychological intervention outcomes for child victims of family violence. The urgent mandate for the psychology community is clear.

Family-Focused Interventions

Family intervention models emphasize active involvement in enhancing communication, decision making, effective child management, and mobilization of family strengths (Gaudin, 1993). These models may provide in-home intensive skills training, behavioral interventions, and contracting. This would seem to be a promising approach in that family focused treatment may prevent out-of-home placement of child victims of violence. However, recent program evaluations of such family preservation programs have shown only minimal results and require much more comprehensive data-based evaluations (Gaudin, 1993). In order for methodologically sound program evaluations to be completed, the treatment interventions themselves and steps toward implementation need to be fully described. But, clearly, this family retraining approach seems most promising.

Recent research has made it clear that violence affects all family members, not just the victims and perpetrators (Emery, 1989). In a model that emphasizes family systems theory, emotional regulation, and expression in children who witness or experience family violence, Emery conceptualized a three component process wherein a) parental conflict serves as an aversive event that creates distress in the child, b) the child reacts emotionally or instrumentally in an attempt to alleviate the distress, and c) the child's actions that reduce the conflict are likely to be maintained because of the function they serve for the child and for the family as a whole. Family systems analyses that identify scapegoating (wherein only one child in the family is singled out for abuse) or collusion (wherein children are sexually abused repeatedly because mothers collude in the process of making the child the substitute object of the father's desires) may help to guide structured family interventions that shake up this homeostatic dysfunction (Emery, 1989). Indeed, Polansky and colleagues (Polansky, Chalmers, Williams, & Buttenweiser, 1981) have suggested that assertive, intrusive intervention is often needed with abusive and neglecting families in order to disturb the dysfunctional family balance. Those family interventions might include re-allocation of family roles and tasks, establishing clear intergenerational boundaries, clarifying mixed communications, reframing dysfunctional perceptions of parents, and empowering parents to assume leadership and appropriate control roles (Polansky et al., 1981). Unfortunately, although these suggestions for strategic family interventions make good clinical sense, the lack of empirical data to support family focused interventions in cases of child physical or sexual abuse may indicate caution.

Some theorists have identified stages in family violence that are important to consider. For example, Wolfe's (1987) transitional model of escalating conflict between family members highlights the following dynamic stages: a) reduced tolerance of stress and disinhibition of aggression, b) poor management of acute crises and provocation, and c) habitual patterns of arousal and aggression. We believe that remedial programs for abusing parents, recovery programs for abused children, and prevention programs for high risk children and parents should incorporate intervention strategies to address each of these stages and that only comprehensive treatment of both parents and children can halt the cycle of family violence. (See chapter 2 for an overview of some of the interactive theories and models of the development of violence and aggression.)

Treatment Interventions for Adolescent Physical Abuse

According to Schellenbach and Guerney (1987), the age-appropriate behaviors of the normal adolescent (self-assertion, increased peer interaction, higher levels of cognitive and verbal ability) place tremendous strain on the family system, its rules, parenting techniques, and parental expectations. Clearly, significant differences exist between adolescent maltreatment and child maltreatment in terms of identification, etiology, and treatment (Powers & Echenrode, 1988). Abuse and neglect in the adolescent age group are frequently unrecognized and under-reported because of behavioral manifestations such as drug abuse, running away, suicide attempts, and antisocial responses that only mask the precipitating maltreatment. In their review of samples of Child Protective Services (CPS) reports from New York State, Powers and Echenrode (1988) indicated that substantiated reports of maltreatment of adolescents peak around age 15 and that adolescent victims are predominantly female across all types of maltreatment.

From an etiological perspective, Pelcovitz, Kaplan, Samit, Krieger, and Cornelius (1984) proposed that adolescent abuse is primarily a symptom of family dysfunction and less a product of environmental stress. In support of this, results from the study by Williamson et al. (1991), which examined individual characteristics, family relations, and stress and social support of 50 maltreated adolescents and their mothers, indicated the following: Adolescent physical abuse is associated with rigidity in family relations, poorer maternal understanding of adolescent development, and adolescent externalizing behavior problems, whereas adolescent sexual abuse is related to maternal emotional problems in that the marital relationship is dysfunctional or the mother is not able to provide safety for her adolescent. Because the quality of parent–child relationships is linked to a realistic match between parental expectations, discipline techniques, and adolescent behavior (Schellenbach & Guerney, 1987), the focus on family interactions as causative and maintaining seems logical.

Pelcovitz et al. (1984) suggest a typology of adolescent abuse indicative of three different familial situations: a) a continuing abuse case in which abuse has existed prior to the child's adolescence, b) families in which a qualitative change in parenting occurs from strict authoritarian discipline and harsh punishments during childhood to physical abuse during adolescence, and c) families in which the onset is related to an inability to accommodate to behavioral and developmental changes that occur in puberty.

Considering this typology, there may be several key etiological factors to consider in the development of intervention and prevention strategies for this population. First of all, adolescence is a period marked by a number of developmental tasks that not only place strain on the family system, but that may lead to impulsive behavior patterns on the part of the adolescent. Separation from family, greater autonomy, shifting allegiance toward peers, emerging sexuality, and the temptation of high-risk activities create challenges to parents' abilities to shift their expectations and give up some control (Azar & Siegel, 1990). In response to this, physically abusive parents seem to be less flexible in their choice of disciplinary strategies (Williamson et al., 1991) and tend to communicate with either excessive authority or excessive permissiveness enforced by abusive punishment (Schellenbach & Guerney, 1987). Moreover, these parents appear to use maladaptive interpretive processes, including unrealistic expectations of their children, a negative attribution bias in their interpretation of the causes of children's misbehavior, poor problem-solving skills, and an expectation that children will provide them with continued comfort and support (Azar & Siegel, 1990). Although these deficits in parenting may seem overwhelming to the treatment planner, the hypothesis that adolescent abuse is a symptom of family dysfunction may make it less intractable (Pelcovitz et al., 1984) and a ready target for clinical intervention.

Given the severity of the problems that are associated with adolescent maltreatment, it is astounding that there are so few reports of psychological intervention programs for either adolescents or their parents who are experiencing physical violence in the family.

Parent-Focused Interventions

Azar & Siegel (1990) hypothesize that there should be four main areas of clinical focus in the treatment of parents who abuse their adolescents. These are: a) improving communication and negotiation strategies, b) cognitive restructuring to decrease unrealistic expectations regarding adolescent behavior and misinterpretations of developmentally normal responses, c) anger and impulse control training, and d) appropriate contingency management techniques. Furthermore, because the emergence of adolescence tests the flexibility of the family organization and may upset the homeostasis of the family dynamics, family therapy may be indicated to assist in altering dysfunctional family structures (Pelcovitz et al., 1984).

Schellenbach and Guerney (1987) detail their seven-session parent education group, titled the Family Interaction Project. In addition to information on parenting challenges to expect during adolescence, parents receive training in skills for enhancing communication, discipline alternatives to physical punishment that are appropriate to the developmental level of adolescence, developing empathy and genuine understanding of the changing needs of adolescents, and conflict resolution to address control issues between parents and their adolescents. Although this is a promising treatment program, no data have yet been provided as to the efficacy of this approach to intervention. Such a program is clinically useful; however, an empirical evaluation of short-term and long-term treatment effects is needed before generalizations can be made.

Family-Focused Interventions

Pelcovitz et al. (1984) reported their clinical impressions of 22 families with adolescents who were referred to their child abuse treatment program. Their family-focused interventions varied according to the family structure and the time of abuse, but emphasized alternative approaches to exercising authority and control, developing appropriate child management skills, and developing defined parental boundaries and realistic expectations. Although neither pre-post assessments nor comparisons to control groups were obtained, the short-term goal of cessation of physical abuse was met relatively effectively with most families. Again, this appears to be a promising intervention approach; however, the results are anecdotal and must be interpreted with caution.

Other interventions described in the psychological literature, which have been evaluated in a controlled fashion, primarily target parents of young children. Although these published reports (see Isaacs, 1982; Lutzker & Rice, 1987; Wolfe et al., 1988) provide evidence for the efficacy of parent training efforts, the behavioral and developmental challenges of adolescence are so different that only limited extension of those results is possible (see Wolfe & Wekerle, 1993, for extensive review).

Because of this paucity of available treatment literature on intervention in adolescent maltreatment, to focus briefly on effective treatment of parent–adolescent conflict may be useful. Early work in the area of family problem solving (Alexander, Barton, Schiavo, & Parsons, 1977) suggested that families with delinquent adolescents were characterized by defensive communications, dominance by one family member, and a lack of communication focus. Using a behavioral–communications focus in which family members were directly targeted for changes in verbal behaviors, Alexander et al. (1977) obtained improvements in family interactions. Another early study reported by Kifer, Lewis, Green, and Phillips (1974) focused on behavioral family therapy with adolescents using instruction, behavioral rehearsal, and feedback strategies to improve the negotiation skills of three predelinquents and their parents. Each family identified three specific problem situations in which to practice the newly acquired communication and problem-solving skills. Results from the multiple-baseline across problem situations design indicated acquisition and use of negotiation skills and reduced family conflicts, and presumably, although this is not stated, instance of abuse.

A very comprehensive communications skills training program for adolescents and their families has been developed by Robin and his colleagues (Foster, Prinz, & O'Leary, 1983; Robin & Foster, 1984; Robin, Koepke, & Nayar, 1986), which includes skills training in appropriate interpersonal communication and in discrete problem-solving strategies. During sessions, parent–

adolescent dyads practice newly acquired skills while discussing a "hot topic" selected from a previously determined list. Although not yet evaluated with severely disordered adolescents, research assessing this communication skills training approach has shown improvements in verbal skills, problem solving, family cohesiveness, and in beliefs and attitudes about family relationships. Furthermore, the concomitant reduction in parent–adolescent conflict may be instrumental in the reduction of adolescent maltreatment. Certainly, the comprehensiveness of the program and the rigorous development of assessment methodology (Foster & Robin, 1988) make this package an extremely promising one. Again, however, there are no data to indicate that this program specifically results in lessening the instance of abuse.

Another interesting study was reported in which reciprocal parent–adolescent social skills training was used in the treatment of court adjudicated adolescents (Serna, Schumaker, Hazel, & Sheldon, 1986). After the training of discrete social skills (giving positive and negative feedback, accepting negative feedback, negotiation, resisting peer pressure, following instructions, and problem-solving), the parents and adolescents in the experimental group practiced their newly acquired skills while engaging in parent–adolescent interactions. Results from the multiple-baseline evaluation across skills indicated that social skills improved for youth and their parents after training and were maintained at a 10-month follow-up. Furthermore, these families were rated by outside judges as being more pleasant and as having more positive parent–youth interactions than comparison families. In essence, it seems that the focus on the parent–adolescent dyadic interaction is an important one. Changes in family communication and problem-solving behaviors can affect changes in a variety of adolescent behavior problems and may be crucial in the treatment of families with abuse history. The underpinnings and correlates of abuse, such as poor communication, poor problem-solving and coercive and aggressive interaction styles must be targeted, as well as the cessation of abuse.

An extensive social-interactional parent training program for adolescent offenders was compared with a family systems therapy program (Bank, Marlowe, Reid, Patterson, & Weinrott, 1991). Parents were trained to monitor both prosocial and antisocial behaviors, to develop behavior contracts incorporating both positive and negative consequences, and to implement effective punishment strategies designed to reduce delinquent behaviors. Results indicated large and significant reductions in both rates and prevalence of juvenile arrests across the three follow-up years were obtained for both treatment conditions. However, the more behavioral parenting intervention produced quicker results that were at least as strong and durable as those produced by the more labor intensive family therapy approach and obtained these results with one third less reliance on incarceration (Bank et al., 1991). The authors suggested that the effectiveness of the intervention may be due to changes in parent behavior, as compared with child behavior focused interventions, and recommend that intervention efforts need to begin much earlier in the delinquency process in order to have the greatest impact. Although these were not families evidencing violence in the home, this approach represents a comprehensive approach to parent training of aggressive adolescents and might be worthy of evaluation with aggressive parents to see if it lowers the incidence of child and adolescent abuse. As in the other programs discussed thus far, this has not yet been documented. In order to address other parenting difficulties, programs targeting anger control (Nomellini & Katz, 1983) and stress management (Schinke et al., 1986) for abusive parents may serve to reduce impulsive and aggressive responses toward children and to restructure cognitive distortions, such as unrealistic expectations and negative attributions that precede poor problem-solving and faulty discipline strategies. But, again, these approaches have been subject to little empirical investigation and have not been applied to parents of adolescents.

Adolescent-Focused Interventions

Another aspect of treatment of adolescent abuse involves effective interventions for adolescent victims. As mentioned above, behavioral manifestations of abuse and its consequences are difficult to identify and assess, and recovery from victimization seems equally individualized and may, therefore, obscure treatment and clinical research efforts. However, if there is a higher likelihood of abuse by parents if they themselves were abused as children (Widom, 1989), and if the rate of intergenerational transmission of abuse is approximately 30% (Kaufman & Zigler, 1987), then treatment of the abused adolescent is imperative to help break the cycle of family violence.

Research has indicated that abused children manifest more aggressive and problematic behaviors early on and that this aggressiveness is a fairly stable personality trait predictive of later antisocial behavior (Widom, 1989). However, because the psychological literature on the treatment of adolescents who are victims of family violence is sparse, we must again turn to empirically evaluated interventions for conduct-disordered and aggressive youth (see also chapters 15 and 16) to obtain potentially effective treatment strategies for youth victims.

Feindler (1990) provided a comprehensive review of the assessment and cognitive–behavioral treatment of adolescent anger and aggression and concluded that outcome research has provided equivocal results. Anger control interventions have resulted in reductions in self-reported anger, decreases in distorted cognitions and misattributions about provocations, increased problem-solving abilities, and decreased fines for aggressive and disruptive behaviors in existing institutional contingency management programs. There is, however, little evidence for direct inhibition of aggressive impulses and overt aggressive responding. Although none of the studies reviewed had targeted interventions for abused adolescents and their families, Feindler (1990) suggested that the adolescent's aggressive behavior patterns become part of a coercive family interaction process and are not only reinforced but are functional as well. It is possible that adolescent aggression serves to maintain a dysfunctional interaction pattern in abusive families and aggressive responses, whether verbal or physical, may precipitate episodes of abuse by adults (Williamson et al., 1991). It seems then that aggressive adolescents require much clinical focus, not only because their aggressiveness may be a consequence of early maltreatment, but also because parents of aggressive adolescents display the same aggressive response to provocation and hostile and defensive attributions (Feindler, 1990), and together both parties continue to maintain the level of family violence. Researchers and clinicians are urged to extend the already existing treatment technology for aggressive youth to violent families.

Clinicians need to consider two other overlooked aspects of adolescent family violence, namely, witnessing spousal abuse and teenage violence toward parents. Clinical investigations have indicated that exposure to marital violence is related to a greater frequency of behavior problems such as peer aggressiveness, destructiveness, mood changes, and noncompliance, and to less social competence in children (Carlson, 1990; Jaffe, Wolfe, Wilson, & Zak, 1986). Kalmuss (1984) used survey data from adults to explore the relationship between two types of family aggression (parent to teen and parent to parent) and severe marital aggression in the next generation. Although results rely solely on retrospective self-report data, these data indicate that observing parents hitting each other was more strongly related to involvement in severe marital aggression than was actually being hit during adolescence.

Witnessing family violence has a profound effect on socioemotional development and behavioral responses, but a clear understanding of the effects on youth and goals for clinical intervention have received little attention. Jaffe et al. (1986) described a pilot investigation of group counseling for 8- to 13-year-old witnesses to family violence. Therapy sessions focused on identifying feelings, dealing with one's own anger, prevention of child abuse and acquiring basic safety skills, identifying and using social support, enhancing social competence and self-concept, and dealing with feelings of responsibility for violence. Post-treatment structured interviews indicate numerous gains in positive self-perception and reductions in attitudes condoning violence in the family, but controlled comparisons to nontreated children have yet to be completed. Finally, the effects on the adolescent and the relevance and effectiveness of such an approach need to be evaluated for adolescent witnesses (Carlson, 1990).

Adolescent violence toward parents has rarely been mentioned in either theoretical or therapeutic aspects of family violence. In reporting their results from a survey of 1,545 White male high school youth, Peek, Fischer, and Kidwell (1985) indicated that the incidence of violence toward parents is relatively low (from 2% of seniors reportedly hitting their mothers to 11% of sophomores having hit either parent), but fathers were more likely than mothers to be targets. Furthermore, several family structural variables were associated with the incidence of violence directed toward parents. Although greater family cohesion is linked with lower levels, a punitive or nonstrict parental style of exerting power and the display of parental violence toward youth are clearly related to higher levels of youth violence against parents (Peek et al., 1985). Again, although this critical aspect of family violence has been identified, adolescent violence toward parents has yet to be adequately assessed, understood in terms of etiological and maintaining factors, and treated effectively.

Prevention of Violence in Families With Children and Adolescents

According to Donnelly (1991), prevention efforts in the area of child physical abuse have multiplied rapidly during the last decade. Common prevention services such as educational and support programs for parents have been developed by community groups with teams of volunteers. Programs that offer support and information on child development or that offer training in parenting skills seem promising but appear to focus primarily on pre- and postnatal parenting education and support for parents of young children. Prevention programs for adults and teens who have not actually committed acts of abuse or neglect are founded primarily on the premise that promoting a positive and responsive parent–child relationship is both a desirable intervention target as well as a viable child maltreatment prevention strategy (Wekerle & Wolfe, 1993).

Grotberg, Feindler, White, and Stutman (1991) reported the development of a comprehensive anger management program for the prevention of child abuse. Parents who are at risk for abusing children and adolescents are trained in specific skills a) to express and manage anger, b) to understand developmental challenges and conflicts from birth through adolescence, and c) to improve behavior management and learn discipline strategies that are appropriate for every age. Through role-play and discussion, parents of adolescents are taught to reinterpret typical adolescent behavior, to manage their own anger reactions, to communicate solutions to conflict and to model anger control for their adolescents (Grotberg et al., 1991). Although this is a promising prevention program, data have not been obtained to evaluate the effectiveness and long-term effects of this effort.

Another approach might be an even earlier prevention effort to teach parents appropriate responses to their children. Because a large proportion of teenagers eventually become parents, and because there are many teenage parents, preventive parent education for high school students seems to be a reasonable goal. Zoline and Jason (1985), citing the importance of the parental role and the problems associated with inadequate parenting skills, developed a prevention program involving behavioral skills training, parent training, child development information, and an effort to modify cognitions about parenting. Forty male and female seniors from an urban parochial school were randomly assigned to either a five-session treatment group or a control group. Material on parent–infant interaction, parental influences on development, parent–child communication, time limitations, lifestyle changes, and child abuse was presented and discussed. A number of infant care skills were modeled and then role-played by students as well. Data from a parenting knowledge quiz, a self-efficacy inventory, and a pre-post behavioral role-play of various childcare tasks indicate that such a prevention program results in significant changes in parenting knowledge, especially in males, and in parenting expectations. The insignificant, slight improvements in behavioral skills were attributed to the already achieved competencies by seniors. The authors suggested that future projects use more advanced child care and parenting skills such as behavior management techniques, communication skills, and infant stimulation techniques. We might also suggest that the evaluations of interventions focus on aggressive behaviors of parents toward their children.

A further extension of prevention approaches would be to target adolescents who are at risk for becoming abusive parents. Margolin and Craft (1990) investigated the frequency and severity of child abuse committed by adolescents in nonparental caregiving roles (i.e., babysitters). Earlier surveys had indicated that adolescents engaged in much caregiving but that some felt poorly prepared for the task, felt afraid of losing control and not knowing what to do, and admitted spanking young children (Kourany, Gurnin, & Martin, 1980). In their larger survey of approximately 8,300 cases of physical and sexual abuse substantiated in Iowa during 1985 and 1986, Margolin and Craft (1990) found that although caregivers who were 19 and younger accounted for a substantial volume of physical abuse (25% of cases), the abuse was neither more nor less severe than abuse by others. However, their results indicate that adolescents did account for 44% of cases of sexual abuse, and this abuse was likely to involve threats, physical injury, and intercourse. Despite potential biases in official reporting policies, these data represent an astounding concern, and call for immediate and effective intervention and prevention efforts for this high-frequency contact between adolescents and young children. Unfortunately, no treatment or prevention programs for adolescent caregivers have been reported as yet in the psychological literature.

Adolescent mothers and their infants represent another group at high risk for child maltreatment and are therefore most likely to benefit from early prevention efforts. Given the fact that not all adolescent parents succumb to the obvious stresses and become maltreating parents, Bolton, Charlton, Gai, Laner, and Shrumway (1985), examined the characteristics of maltreating and nonmaltreating adolescent mothers during the perinatal period and up to 27 months following this assessment. Screening adolescent deliveries at a public hospital, Bolton et al. (1985) assessed the pregnancy and birth experience, maternal and infant health status, previous experiences with violence, maternal caretaking behaviors, and attitude toward the child, as well as demographic, environmental, and social conditions. Results indicate that adolescent mothers who subsequently maltreated their infants were more likely to a) have delayed confirmation of pregnancy and not to have wanted it, b) have held a poor health record, c) have been victims of maltreatment, d) be inadequate in infant interaction behaviors such as touching, eye-contact, and early stimulation, and e) be isolated from family and friends and to have reduced financial resources. The implications for a massive prevention effort are obvious and necessary to prepare adolescents for parenthood and to arrest the cycle of child maltreatment.

A final focus in the development of prevention programs would be to identify factors that protect adolescents from maltreatment and promote their resilience and resistance to violence. According to Masten, Best, and Garmezy (1990), many maltreated children become effective parents, despite the considerable risk for intergenerational transmission of abuse. These authors indicated that children who experience chronic adversity recover more successfully when a) they have a positive relationship with some adult, b) they are good learners and problem-solvers, c) they are socially engaging with others, and d) they have an area of competence or perceived efficacy. Not only could these characteristics be targeted for intervention with maltreated adolescents, but they could also be incorporated into prevention programs for children and adolescents who may eventually become parents.

Kruttschnitt, Ward, and Sheble (1987) examined the influence of caregiving environments on subsequent criminal behavior. Factors influencing later antisocial behavior focused on unresolved parental conflict, criminality among other family members, and inconsistent discipline. Factors identified as protective, and therefore as promoting resilience, focused on support systems, close relationships with other caregivers, and involvement with team sports. Theoretically, identification of these factors could help in the development of both intervention and prevention efforts as the psychological community dedicates itself to the problem of youth and violence. It is hoped that these efforts will be carefully delineated and evaluated with reliable and valid assessment tools so that the application and generalizability of results will readily be completed.

Sexual Abuse of Children and Adolescents

Prevention of Sexual Abuse in the Family

In terms of prevention approaches, the major clinical effort has been aimed at protecting children against stranger perpetrators of sexual abuse even though the incidence of intrafamilial sexual abuse is much greater. A number of studies have focused on teaching children "personal safety skills" and on educating youth in order to promote awareness and prevention of child sexual abuse. One such program compared the effectiveness of three interventions: a film, a behavioral skills training program (which included modeling, behavioral rehearsal, and social reinforcement), and a combination of the two. A no-treatment control presentation was also used (Wurtele, Saslawsky, Miller, Marrs, & Britcher, 1986).

The participants were 71 youths in public schools in the following grades: kindergarten, first, fifth, and sixth. Dependent measures included a personal safety questionnaire and the "What if" situations test. Follow-up testing was conducted at 3 months. Compared with the control presentation, the behavioral skills program alone or in combination with the film was more effective than the film alone in enhancing knowledge of sex abuse. Intervention effectiveness was maintained at 3-month follow-up. Older youth performed better on the dependent measures than younger youth. These authors noted that their study cannot, however, address how children would react in actual encounters with a sexual abuser.

Binder and McNeil (1987) evaluated a public school based sexual-abuse prevention program that consisted of 2-hour workshops for children, parents, and their teachers. The children were between 5 and 12 years of age. The teachers' in-service and parents' workshops were conducted before the children experienced the workshop. The workshops were 2 hours long.

The youth portion of the program was also 2 hours long and consisted of a role-play and guided-group discussions providing information about sexual abuse. Children and parents completed a questionnaire 1 week before the participation in the program and 2 to 4 weeks after the program. Two weeks after the program, teachers also completed a questionnaire. Both parents and teachers were asked to rate the children's level of emotional distress and anxiety postintervention. For the youth, pre- and post-testing revealed significant increases in knowledge about strategies for coping with potential abuse situations. Parents reported that they talked more with their children about sex abuse after the workshop. Neither teachers nor parents noticed any increased emotional distress in the children who participated. Children also reported that they felt safer and better able to protect themselves after the workshop. As with the previous study, these authors noted that their studies could not address how much the observed increase in knowledge would lead to actual use of self-protection techniques.

In an attempt to assess whether kindergarten-age children would benefit from sexual abuse prevention, 71 kindergarten children were randomly assigned to either a prevention program or a placebo-control group (Harvey, Forehand, Brown, & Holmes, 1988). The sexual-abuse prevention program, which was entitled "Good Touch/Bad Touch," involved 3 half-hour sessions occurring across 3 consecutive days with approximately 20 children in each session. Instructions, modeling, rehearsal, and social reinforcement were used as teaching procedures. For the placebo-control group, none of the material presented was related to sexual abuse. Measures included a direct test and a generalization test of knowledge obtained. Compared with the control group, the children receiving the behavioral interventions at both the 3-week and 7-week follow-up demonstrated more knowledge about preventing abuse and performed better on simulated scenes involving sexual abuse. These authors noted that further research needs to focus on demonstration of maintenance of skills at much longer follow-up intervals and that research should also focus on a wider range of dependent measures; specifically, ones that would demonstrate that children can use the skills in actual or potentially sexually abusive situations.

The use of teachers versus the use of expert consultants has been evaluated in teaching prevention programs (Hazzard, Kleemeier, & Webb, 1990). The design included three treatment conditions. In Condition One, 15 regular classroom teachers presented the prevention program to their own students. In Condition Two, 8 teachers conducted the program in classrooms within schools but not with their own students. In Condition Three, 3 expert consultants conducted the intervention program. Measures consisted of a knowledge scale administered pre- and post-testing, a video vignettes measure, and a subjective rating measure administered at post-testing only. Results indicate that there were no significant differences in the impact of prevention programs as presented by teachers versus those presented by child abuse expert consultants. Children demonstrated equivalent knowledge gains and equivalent scores on the video vignettes measure of preventive skills.

Harbeck, Peterson, and Starr (1992) rigorously evaluated the effects of the prevention program "The Touch Continuum" with 4- to 16-year-old male and female children with a history of sexual abuse. Because sexually abused children are at high risk for victimization (Browne & Finkelhor, 1986), this study represents a most important extension of the prevention approach. Unfortunately, pre-post treatment effects were largely absent and the authors suggested that such a didactic program does not specifically allow the children opportunities to practice new behavioral skills that are required for protection against re-abuse. Generally, outcome measures indicated that this at-risk population could adequately identify preventive information but had great difficulty in using that information. Therefore, the prevention of revictimization may require additional therapeutic interventions that are implemented in a more intense fashion.

These studies offer hope in that they demonstrate that teachers are effective in implementing sex abuse prevention programs and that children as young as kindergarten age benefit from such programs, at least according to the outcome measures used. It is important to state, however, that the burden should never be placed on children to deter their own abuse. Although it is important that they be made aware of their vulnerability and taught to assert themselves and also to disclose abuse, the responsibility always lies with family and the community. Further, it seems that the perhaps sensitive issue of prevention of intrafamilial abuse needs to be considered, and strategies for children need to be developed.

Treatment of Child and Adolescent Victims of Sexual Abuse

The awareness of the severe sequelae of sexual victimization of children and adolescents has spurred the development and dissemination of individual, group, family, and systems interventions. However, as Kolko (1987) concludes, the absence of empirical, controlled design, objective assessment data, and follow-up data have made it difficult to determine the effectiveness of interventions. The psychology community needs to overcome obstacles to further clinical research such as misperceptions about the extent, nature, and causes of abuse; lack of coordination and integration in multimodal clinical services; need to protect children through placement or termination of parental rights; and disagreements as to whether the focus of treatment should be directed toward the acquisition of skills that are likely to improve the child's cognitive and behavioral repertoire and subsequent psychological adjustment (Kolko, 1987). Only with intensive efforts at the design and evaluation of both prevention and intervention programs will the sexual abuse and victimization of vulnerable children and adolescents and the subsequent serious impact be reduced.

Child- and family-focused interventions. There is a considerable body of literature on the incidence of childhood sexual abuse and the impact that sexual abuse has on children (Alter-Reid, Gibbs, Lachenmeyer, Siegel, & Massoth, 1986). There is, however, a paucity of literature, other than clinical anecdotes and case studies, on the treatment of sexually abused children. Deblinger, McLeer, and Henry (1990) presented the first empirical evaluation of a therapy approach to 19 children suffering from PTSD from contact-sexual abuse. The female children ranged in age from 3 to 15 years with a mean age of 7 to 8 years. Among the children 68.4% had suffered from genital–oral contact or penile penetration, and 5% experienced inappropriate sexual touching or kissing. The majority of the perpetrators (52.5%) were fathers or stepfathers, 21% were other male relatives, 21% were nonrelative trusted males, and one child was abused by a male stranger.

Both the child and the nonoffending primary caretaker participated in the treatment. The child intervention consisted of gradual exposure, modeling, education, and prevention skills training. The nonoffending parents received three modules consisting of education and coping, communication modeling and gradual exposure, and behavior management skills. Dependent measures included the Child Behavior Checklist, the Child Depression Inventory, and the Spielberger State–Trait Anxiety Inventory. There were two baseline data collection periods: at initial evaluation and 2 to 3 weeks before the initiation of treatment. The dependent measures were again administered following 12 treatment sessions. Results indicated that PTSD symptoms for all 19 subjects revealed significant improvement across the PTSD subcategories. Although the treatment did not eliminate all PTSD symptoms, no subjects continued to meet full diagnostic criteria for PTSD. The authors concluded that this open clinical trial holds considerable promise.

Group therapy. Verleur, Hughes, and Dobkin de Rios (1986) report on a controlled comparison study of female adolescent incest victims who received group therapy. The adolescents ranged in age from 13 to 17. Unfortunately, little detail is given on what occurred over the 6 months of homogenous group therapy. Results indicate that the experimental group, pre- and post-test comparisons were significant in the two areas of focus (self-esteem and sexual awareness). The control group's pre-tests and post-tests indicate change in self-esteem but the change in their sexual awareness scores was not significant. Because all of these children were in residential treatment, it is possible that the increase in self-esteem was perhaps related to other therapy that they might have been receiving. Although the authors noted that the control group was a matched comparison group, we are not informed as to whether there was a random assignment to groups.

Others (Berman, 1990; Kitchur & Bell, 1989) have described psychodynamic group therapy for sexually abused girls. Group goals included education about abuse, personal self-control, increased problem solving, family trust, and anger, and insight into emotional consequences of abuse. Unfortunately, only cursory pre-post assessments of self-esteem were included (Kitchur & Bell, 1989). Furniss, Bingly-Miller, & Van Elberg (1988) described ongoing group therapy for sexually abused teens that was coordinated with family therapy. Through discussion, members worked to boost self-esteem, regain a sense of power, decrease personal responsibility for abuse and desexualize other interpersonal relationships. Follow-up questionnaire data obtained 2 years after treatment indicated for 7 of 9 girls improved self-esteem, peer relationships, family communication, and social adjustment. However, without data from comparison groups it is hard to interpret these self-report data. Future research on sexual abuse victims should include larger sample sizes,

random assignments of subjects to different conditions, longer term follow-
ups, and more comprehensive and multimodal assessments of functioning.

Intervention With Adolescent Sex Offenders

A very high proportion of juvenile sexual offenders were victims of abuse
themselves (Pierce & Pierce, 1987), and they may be at risk for perpetrating
abuse in their own families in the next generation. Therefore, another means
by which to prevent future child and adolescent abuse is to provide treatment
to those youth who engage in sexually abusive behavior (see also chapter 16).

The literature to date on treatment and recidivism of this population focuses for the most part on program descriptions and uncontrolled program
evaluations. Davis and Leitenberg (1987) report low recidivism rates in their
review of follow-up studies of juvenile sex offenders treated in the 1940s and
1950s (10% and 3%, respectively).

It is surprising that few treatment outcome studies have been conducted,
given that there are over 600 treatment programs in the United States for
adolescent sex offenders, with 80% of them being community-based. Although
there are diverse approaches to treatment, the majority of the programs center
around the following treatment goals: (a) developing social and assertiveness
skills, (b) developing victim empathy and nondeviant sexual interests, (c)
teaching sex education, and (d) decreasing deviant arousal. Programs also
focus on cognitive restructuring and identifing the precursors to deviant behavior for proper self-monitoring. Becker, Kaplan, and Kavoussi (1988) described a seven-component treatment plan based on a cognitive–behavioral
model. The components include verbal satiation, cognitive restructuring, covert sensitization, social skills training, anger control, sex education and values
clarification, and relapse prevention. More recently, Becker (1990) presented
1-year follow-up data on a sample of adolescents who were treated on an
outpatient basis. Of the 52 adolescents on whom follow-up data had been
completed, five adolescents had recommitted sexual crimes.

Borduin, Henggeler, Blaske, and Stein (1990) provided a controlled evaluation of the efficacy of specific treatment approaches to adolescent sexual
offenders. Sixteen adolescent sexual offenders were randomly assigned to either multisystemic therapy or individual therapy conditions. The multisystemic treatment attempted to ameliorate deficits in the adolescent's cognitive
processes, family relationships, peer relationships, and school performance.
The individual therapy focused on personal, family, and academic issues. The
therapist offered support, feedback, and encouragement for behavioral change.

Those adolescents receiving individual therapy received an average of 45
hours of therapy compared with an average of 37 for those who received the
multisystemic therapy. The length of follow-up ranged from 21 months to 49
months. Those youths who received the multisystemic therapy had recidivism
rates of 12.5% for sexual offenses and 25% for nonsexual offenses, compared
with those receiving individual therapy, whose recidivism rates were 75% for
sexual offenses and 50% for nonsexual offenses. These authors demonstrated

significant treatment effects for those who received the multisystemic therapy related to the commission of sexual offenses.

Kahn and Chambers (1991) provided a summary of a 2-year program for juvenile sex offenders in the state of Washington who were treated in either community-based or institution-based treatment programs. Youths were followed for a mean of 20 months. This study was not a controlled-outcome study in that the 221 juvenile sex offenders were enrolled in 10 treatment programs. A total of 44.8% of the juveniles were convicted of one or more subsequent criminal offenses; however, new convictions for sexual offenses were only 7.5%. A few variables were found to be related to sexual reoffending. Juveniles who participated in outpatient programs were less likely to offend than those in residential settings. Juveniles who victimized a nonrelated child who was known to them were most likely to be convicted for a new sexual offense. Youths whose therapists had identified them as having deviant arousal patterns were more likely to reoffend. Youths who used verbal threats in the commission of their offense were more likely to reoffend sexually. Youths who blamed their victims for their crimes were more likely to reoffend sexually. Of interest is that eight youths who completely denied their offenses did not reoffend sexually.

Although clinicians have realized the importance of providing treatment to youthful offenders, research on assessment, treatment outcome, and recidivism has lagged seriously behind. Future research should focus on the development of forensic assessment instruments for adolescent sexual offenders as well as on therapy outcome studies with significant follow-up periods of at least 5 years.

A related area of investigation concerns the increased prevalence of courtship violence among adolescents. White and Koss (in press), in their review of risk factors for juvenile sexual aggression, indicated that familial and peer group attitudes and behaviors that condone violence as an interpersonal strategy and that degrade women appear to be important. Furthermore, acceptance of the stereotyped male sex role and of certain assumptions concerning dating behaviors may encourage the misrepresentation of women's behaviors "justifying" the use of force in sexual interactions (White & Koss, 1993). As the understanding of the prevalence, the characteristics, and probable causes of dating violence becomes clear, it is imperative for the psychological community to develop multilevel intervention strategies for young males in terms of their attitudes and behaviors while dating. A large scale primary prevention program on violence in intimate relationships was designed, implemented, and evaluated in four high schools in Ontario, Canada (Jaffe, Sudermann, Reitzel, & Killip, 1992). The target audience, 737 male and female students in grades 9 through 12, received a brief intervention: a large group presentation on wife assault and dating violence, followed by a classroom discussion facilitated by community professionals from domestic violence agencies. The either half day (2 high schools) or full day (2 high schools) intervention was evaluated by an assessment of adolescents' attitudes, knowledge, and behavioral intentions concerning violence in dating relationships. Results from pre-post and follow-up assessments indicated changes in all of these areas; awareness of abuse in relationships, sensitivity toward child victims of family violence, and ideas concerning intervention strategies to obtain help were desired changes. There was, however, a small sample of male students who reported more negative attitudes concerning power and control in relationships and excuses for condoning date rape after intervention. This "backlash" effect may indicate an increase in defensiveness following the program's focus on abuse of women or may reflect attitudes of males already engaged in abusive behavior in intimate relationships (Jaffe et al., 1992). Although based only on self-report data, this effort to implement and evaluate such a wide scale prevention program is to be commended. The authors suggested that the negative results indicate a need for even earlier prevention efforts regarding boys' attitudes about girls and dating. Certainly, future research on school-based primary prevention programs is in order.

Summary

This chapter has primarily focused on prevention and intervention efforts that have been empirically evaluated and are targeted toward children and adolescent victims and survivors of physical and sexual abuse and their families.

Further research on both the causes and consequences of family violence is clearly needed. With regard to child and adolescent physical and sexual abuse, it is time for researchers to shift their focus from the consequences of victimization to the identification of effective and efficient psychological treatments. The pros and cons of family versus individual intervention, the additive effects of corollary group treatment, and the most effective therapeutic orientations all require experimental inquiry. Additional research efforts could be focused on the identification of protective factors in children and adolescents and the incorporation of these skills and abilities into prevention efforts as attempts are made to enhance resiliency. The long-term consequences of early abuse on later intimate relationships, such as dating relationships, needs much exploration, and both prevention and intervention programs need to be designed and evaluated. Finally, the role of bystanders or witnesses, who may be other family members not being victimized, needs to be clarified and results channeled into broader scope family interventions.

It is imperative for the psychological community to develop even more effective prevention and early intervention strategies for child and adolescent victims of family violence, to continue to identify at-risk children and families for massive prevention efforts, and to evaluate all intervention strategies rigorously to determine the most effective and efficient ones. In this way, not only will the overwhelming negative sequelae of child victimization be addressed, but the intergenerational transmission of patterns of violence can begin to be eliminated.

References

Alexander, J. F., Barton, C., Schiavo, R. S., & Parsons, B. V. (1977). Systems–behavioral intervention with families of delinquents: Therapist characteristics, family behavior, and outcome. *Journal of Consulting and Clinical Psychology, 44,* 656–664.

Alter-Reid, K., Gibbs, M. A., Lachenmeyer, J. R., Siegel, J., & Massoth, N. A. (1986). Sexual abuse of children: A review of the empirical findings. *Clinical Psychology Review, 6*(2) 49–266.

American Humane Association. (1984). Highlights of official child neglect and abuse reporting. Denver, CO: Author.

Ammerman, R. T., & Hersen, M. (1990). *Children at risk: An evaluation of factors contributing to child abuse and neglect.* New York: Plenum.

Azar, S. T., & Siegel, B. R. (1990). Behavioral treatment of child abuse: A developmental perspective. Child abuse and neglect [Special issue]. *Behavior Modification, 14*(3), 279–300.

Bank, L., Marlowe, J. H., Reid, J. B., Patterson, G. R., & Weinrott, M. R. (1991). A comparative evaluation of parent-training interventions for families of chronic delinquents. *Journal of Abnormal Child Psychology, 19*(1), 15–34.

Becker, J. V. (1990). Treating adolescent sexual offenders. *Professional Psychology: Research and Practice, 21*(5), 362–365.

Becker, J. V., Kaplan, M., & Kavoussi, R. (1988). Measuring the effectiveness of treatment for the aggressive adolescent sexual offender. *Annals of New York Academy of Science, 528,* 236–247.

Berman, P. (1990). Group therapy techniques for sexually abused pre-teen girls. *Child Welfare, 69*(30), 239–252.

Binder, R., & McNeil, D. (1987). Evaluation of a school based sexual abuse prevention program: Cognitive and emotional effects. *Child Abuse and Neglect, 11,* 497–506.

Bolton, F. G., Charlton, J. K., Gai, D. S., Laner, R. H., & Shrumway, S. M. (1985). Preventive screening of adolescent mothers and infants: Critical variables in assessing risk for maltreatment. *Journal of Primary Prevention, 5,* 169–187.

Borduin, C. M., Henggeler, S. W., Blaske, D. M., & Stein, R. J. (1990). Multisystemic treatment of adolescent sexual offenders. *International Journal of Offender Therapy and Comparative Criminology, 34,* 105–114.

Browne, A., & Finkelhor, D. (1986). The impact of child sexual abuse: A review of the research. *Psychological Bulletin, 99,* 66–77.

Carlson, B. E. (1990). Adolescent observers of marital violence. *Journal of Family Violence, 5*(4), 285–299.

Conte, J. R., & Berlinger, L. (1981). Sexual abuse of children: Implications for practice. *Social Casework, 62,* 601–606.

Daro, D. (1988). *Confronting child abuse.* New York: Free Press.

Davis, G., & Leitenberg, H. (1987). Adolescent sex offenders. *Psychological Bulletin, 101,* 417–427.

Davis, S., & Fantuzzo, J. W. (1989). The effects of adult and peer social initiations on social behavior of withdrawn and aggressive maltreated preschool children. *Journal of Family Violence, 4,* 227–248.

Dawson, B., de Armas, A., McGrath, M. L., & Kelly, J. A. (1986). Cognitive problem solving training to improve the child-care judgement of child neglectful parents. *Journal of Family Violence, 1,* 209–221.

Deblinger, E., McLeer, S., & Henry, D. (1990) Cognitive–behavioral treatment for sexually abused children suffering posttraumatic stress: Preliminary findings. *Journal of the American Academy of Child and Adolescent Psychiatry, 29,* 747–752.

Donnelly, A. (1991). What we have learned about prevention: What we should do about it. *Child Abuse and Neglect, 15* (Supplement 1), 99–106.

Emery, R. E. (1989). Family violence. *American Psychologist, 44*(2), 321–328.

Eron, L. D., & Huesmann, L. R. (1990). The stability of aggressive behavior—even into third generation. In M. Miller & S. Miller, (Eds.), *Handbook of developmental psychotherapy* (pp. 147–156). New York: Plenum.

Feindler, E. (1990). Adolescent anger control: Review and critique. In M. Hersen, R. M. Eisler, and P. M. Miller (Eds.), *Progress in behavior modification* (Vol. 26, pp. 11–59). Newbury Park, CA: Sage.

Finkelhor, D. (1979). *Sexually victimized children.* New York: Free Press.

Finkelhor, D. & Dziuba-Leatherman, J. (1994). Victimization of children. *American Psychologist,* *49*(3), 173–183.

Foster, S. L., Prinz, R. J., & O'Leary, K. D. (1983). Impact of problem solving communication training and generalization procedures on family conflict. *Child and Family Behavior Therapy, 5,* 1–23.

Foster, S. L., & Rabin, A. (1988). Family conflict and communication in adolescence. In E. J. Mash & L. G. Terdal (Eds.), *Behavioral assessment of childhood disorders* (2nd ed., pp. 717–775). New York: Guilford Press.

Friedrich, W. N., & Einbender, A. J. (1983). The abused child: A psychological review. *Journal of Clinical Psychology, 12,* 244–245.

Furniss, T., Bingly-Miller, L., & Van Elberg, A. (1988). Goal oriented group treatment for sexually abused adolescent girls. *British Journal of Psychiatry, 152,* 97–106.

Gaudin, J. M. (1993). Effective intervention with neglectful families. *Criminal Justice and Behavior, 20,* 1, 66–89.

Grotberg, E. H., Feindler, E. L., White, C. B., & Stutman, S. S. (1991). Using anger management for prevention of child abuse. In L. Vandercreek (Ed.), *Innovations in clinical practice: A source book* (Vol. 10). Sarasota, FL: Professional Research Exchange.

Harbeck, C., Peterson, L., & Starr, L. (1992). Previously abused child victims' response to a sexual abuse prevention program: A matter of measures. *Behavior Therapy, 23,* 375–387.

Harvey, P., Forehand, R., Brown, C., & Holmes, T. (1988). The prevention of sexual abuse: Examination of the effectiveness of a program with kindergarten-age children. *Behavior Therapy, 19,* 429–435.

Hazzard, A. P., Kleemeier, C. T., & Webb, C. (1990). Teacher versus expert presentations of sexual abuse prevention programs. *Journal of Interpersonal Violence, 5*(1), 23–36.

Heide, J., & Richardson, M. T. (1987). Maltreated children's developmental scores: Treatment versus nontreatment. *Child Abuse and Neglect, 11,* 29–35.

Hoffman-Plotkin, D., & Twentyman, C. T. (1984). A multimodal assessment of behavioral and cognitive deficits in abused neglected preschoolers. *Child Development, 55,* 794–802.

Howing, P. T., Wodarski, J. S., Kurtz, P. D., & Gaudin, J. M. (1990). The empirical base for the implementation of social skills training with maltreated children. *Social Work, 34,* 330–338.

Isaacs, C. D. (1982). Treatment of child abuse: A review of behavioral interventions. *Journal of Applied Behavior Analysis, 15,* 273–294.

Jaffe, P. G., Sudermann, M., Reitzel, D., & Killip, S. M. (1992). An evaluation of a secondary school primary prevention program on violence in intimate relationships. *Violence and Victims, 7,* 129–146.

Jaffe, P. G., Wolfe, D. A., Wilson, S., & Zak, L. (1986). Similarities in behavioral and social maladjustment among child victims and witnesses to family violence. *American Journal of Orthopsychiatry, 56,* 142–146.

Kahn, T., & Chambers, H. J. (1991). Assessing reoffense risk with juvenile sexual offenders. *Child Welfare, 19,* 333–345.

Kalmuss, D. (1984). The intergenerational transmission of marital aggression. *Journal of Marriage and the Family, 46,* 11–19.

Kaufman, J., & Zigler, E. (1987). Do abused children become abusive parents? *American Journal of Orthopsychiatry, 57,* 186–192.

Kifer, R., Lewis, M., Green, D., & Phillips, E. (1974). Training predelinquent youths and their parents to negotiate conflict situations. *Journal of Applied Behavior Analysis, 7,* 357–364.

Kitchur, M., & Bell, R. (1989). Group psychotherapy with preadolescent sexual abuse victims: Literature review and description of an inner-city group. *International Journal of Group Psychotherapy, 39*(3), 285–319.

Kolko, D. (1987). Treatment of child sexual abuse: Programs, progress and treatment. *Journal of Family Violence, 2*(4), 303–318.

Kourany, R. F., Gurnin, M., & Martin, J. E. (1980). Adolescent babysitting: A thirty year phenomenon. *Adolescence, 15,* 939–945.

Kruttschnitt, C., Ward, D., & Sheble, M. (1987). Abuse resistant youth: Some factors that may inhibit violent criminal behavior. *Social Forces, 66*(2), 501–519.

Lutzker, J. R., & Rice, J. M. (1987). Using recidivism data to evaluate Project 12-Ways: An eco-behavioral approach to the treatment and prevention of child abuse and neglect. *Journal of Family Violence, 2,* 283–290.

Mannarino, A. P., & Cohen, J. A. (1990). Treating the abused child. In R. T. Ammerman & M. Hersen (Eds.), *Children at risk: An evaluation of factors contributing to child abuse and neglect* (pp. 249–268). New York: Plenum.

Margolin, L., & Craft, J. L. (1990). Child abuse by adolescent caregivers. *Child Abuse and Neglect, 14*(3), 365–373.

Masten, A. A., Best, K. M., & Garmezy, N. (1990). Resilience and development: Contributions from the study of children who overcome adversity. *Development and Psychopathology, 2,* 425–444.

Milner, J. S. (1993). Social information processing and physical child abuse. *Clinical Psychology Review, 13,* 275–294.

National Center on Child Abuse and Neglect. (1981). *Study findings: National study of the incidence and severity of child abuse and neglect.* Washington, DC: U.S. Government Printing Office.

Nomellini, S., & Katz, R. (1983). Effects of anger control training on abusive parents. *Cognitive Therapy and Research, 7,* 57–68.

Peek, C. W., Fischer, J. L., & Kidwell, J. S. (1985, November). Teenage violence toward parents: A neglected dimension of family violence. *Journal of Marriage and the Family,* 1051–1058.

Pelcovitz, D., Kaplan, S., Samit, C., Krieger, R., & Cornelius, D. (1984). Adolescent abuse: Family structure and implication for treatment. *Journal of the American Academy of Child Psychiatry, 23,* 85–90.

Perry, M. A., Doran, L. D., & Wells, E. A. (1983). Development and behavioral characteristics of the physically abused child. *Journal of Clinical Child Psychology, 12,* 320–324.

Pierce, L. H., & Pierce, R. L. (1987). Incestuous victimization by juvenile sex offenders. *Journal of Family Violence, 2,* 351–364.

Polansky, N. A., Chalmers, M. A., Williams, D. P., & Buttenweiser, E. W. (1981). *Damaged parents: An anatomy of child neglect.* Chicago: University of Chicago Press.

Powers, J. L., & Echenrode, J. (1988). The maltreatment of adolescents. *Child Abuse and Neglect, 12*(2), 189–199.

Rivera, B., & Widom, C. S. (1990). Childhood victimization and violent offending. *Violence and Victims, 5*(1), 19–35.

Robin, A. L., & Foster, S. L. (1984). Problem-solving communication training: A behavioral-family systems approach to parent-adolescent conflict. In P. Karoly & J. J. Steffen (Eds.), *Adolescent behavior disorders: Foundations and contemporary concerns* (pp. 195–240). Lexington, MA: Lexington Books.

Robin, A. L., Koepke, T., & Nayar, M. (1986). Conceptualizing, assessing, and treating parent–adolescent conflict. In B. B. Lahey & A. E. Kazdin (Eds.), *Advances in clinical child psychology* (pp. 87–124). New York: Plenum.

Russell, D. E. H. (1983). The incidence and prevalence of intrafamilial and extrafamilial sexual abuse of female children. *Child Abuse and Neglect, 7,* 133–146.

Russell, D. E. H. (1984). The prevalence and seriousness of incestuous abuse: Stepfathers vs. biological fathers. *Child Abuse and Neglect, 8,* 15–22.

Schellenbach, C., & Guerney, L. F. (1987). Identification of adolescent abuse and future intervention prospects. *Journal of Adolescence, 10,* 1–12.

Schinke, S. P., Schilling, R., Barth, R., Gilchrist, L. (1986). Stress management intervention to prevent family violence. *Journal of Family Violence, 1*(1), 13–26.

Serna, L., Schumaker, J. B., Hazel, J. S., & Sheldon, J. B. (1986). Teaching reciprocal social skills to parents and their delinquent adolescents. *Journal of Clinical Child Psychology, 15,* 64–77.

Straus, M. A. (1992, April). *Corporal punishment of children and depression and suicide in adulthood.* Paper presented at the Society for Life History Research, Philadelphia, PA.

Timnick, L. (1985, August 25.) 22% in survey were child abuse victims. *Los Angeles Times,* p. 1.

Verleur, D., Hughes, R. E., & Dobkin de Rios, M. (1986). Enhancement of self-esteem among female adolescent incest victims: A controlled comparison. *Adolescence, 21,* 843–854.

Wekerle, C., & Wolfe, D. A. (1993). Prevention of child physical abuse and neglect: Promising new directions. *Clinical Psychology Review, 13,* 501–540.

White, J. W., & Koss, M. P. (in press). Adolescent sexual agression within heterosexual relationships: Prevalence, characteristics and causes. In H. G. Barbanee, W. L. Marshall, & D. R. Laws (Eds.), *The juvenile sexual offender*. New York: Guilford Press.

Widom, C. S. (1989). Does violence beget violence? A critical examination of the literature. *Psychological Bulletin, 106*(1), 3–28.

Widom, C. S. (1992, October). The cycle of violence. *National Institute of Justice: Research in Brief*, pp. 1–4.

Williamson, J. M., Bordwin, C. M., & Howe, B. A. (1991). The ecology of adolescent maltreatment: A multilevel examination of adolescent physical abuse, sexual abuse and neglect. *Journal of Consulting and Clinical Psychology, 59*(3), 449–457.

Wolfe, D. A. (1987). *Child abuse: Implications for child development*. Newbury Park, CA: Sage.

Wolfe, D. A., Edwards, B., Manion, I., & Koverola, C. (1988). Early intervention for parents at risk of child abuse and neglect: A preliminary investigation. *Journal of Consulting and Clinical Psychology, 56*, 40–47.

Wolfe, D. A., & Mosk, M. D. (1983). Behavioral comparisons of children from abused and distressed families. *Journal of Consulting and Clinical Psychology, 51*, 702–708.

Wolfe, D. A., & Wekerle, C. (1993). Treatment strategies for child physical abuse & neglect: A critical progress report. *Clinical Psychology Review, 13*, 473–500.

Wurtele, S. K., Saslawsky, D. A., Miller, C. L., Marrs, S. R., & Britcher, J. C. (1986). Teaching personal safety skills for potential prevention of sexual abuse: A comparison of treatments. *Journal of Consulting and Clinical Psychology, 54*(5), 688–692.

Youngblade, L. M., & Belsky, J. (1990). Social and emotional consequences of child maltreatment. In R. T. Ammerman & M. Hersen (Eds.), *Children at risk: An evaluation of factors contributing to child abuse and neglect* (pp. 109–146). New York: Plenum.

Zoline, S. S., & Jason, L. (1985). Preventive parent education for high school students. *Journal of Clinical Child Psychology, 14*, 119–123.

Part VI

Research and Policy Recommendations

Introduction

In many of the preceding chapters, authors have outlined research and policy recommendations germane to their areas of focus. They have identified gaps in current knowledge about the causes of violence and the prevention of violence, and they have described some of the intervention strategies that hold the most promise to date and are thus pertinent for researchers and for those who develop policy.

In addition, the APA Commission on Violence and Youth has developed a set of recommendations for research and policy that are presented in the two chapters in this section. The 12 commissioners conducted a careful review of psychological research,[1] heard testimony from experts and from young people living in the midst of violence, commissioned the chapters in this book, and publicly presented and received critical feedback from the public and from colleagues. Then, with this information in hand, the commissioners developed a set of research and policy recommendations that were first published in *Violence and Youth: Psychology's Response* (APA Commission on Violence and Youth, 1993). Authors of the two chapters in this section discuss research and policy needs and then present the specific recommendations of the commission.

Recommendations for research and policy should inform each other. Policymakers who are considering legislation or the deployment of funds for basic and applied research need to be aware of the most promising findings and of the consistent gaps in the empirical literature. Researchers who are designing studies and are evaluating interventions must, of course, be guided by their own convictions supported by research. Within this context, however, they would also do well to consider the information needs of policymakers at the federal, state, and local levels.

Psychologists, regardless of their role, bear a responsibility to "give psychology away," as George Miller, past-president of the American Psychological Association, so eloquently said. This is particularly important in areas of behavior such as youth violence, where the stakes are perhaps the highest and

---

[1]The commissioners limited their review to psychological aspects of interpersonal violence among children and youth between the ages of 3 and 22.

the mistakes the costliest. Whether they do basic research on violence and aggression, apply that research to prevention and intervention, or evaluate efforts toward those ends, psychologists have an opportunity to imbue the nation's efforts toward preventing and reducing violence with the best psychology has to offer.

In the first chapter of this section, Judith Becker, Joyce Barham, Leonard Eron, and S. Andrew Chen describe the present status and future directions for psychological research on youth violence. They comment on the absence of an overarching theory to guide research and on the limitations of past studies in terms of methodology. They also highlight a number of important issues to consider in future research: culturally diverse perspectives, universal definitions of violent behaviors, common variables and measurement instruments, full descriptions of intervention and treatment strategies, inclusion of evaluation and outcome measures, early development of program evaluations, broader scope of interventions, long-term follow-up, inclusion of girls and women, and attention to ethical issues in conducting violence research. They then present the APA Commission's specific recommendations for future psychological research in six major areas.

In the second chapter, Ronald Slaby, Joyce Barham, Leonard Eron, and Brian Wilcox stress important considerations for policy formation: the vulnerability of some groups of youths to becoming involved in violence; the need for increased attention to early childhood experiences that foster or inhibit the development of violence; the influence of media, firearm availability, alcohol, and other drugs that help perpetuate violence; and the variety of ways to implement programs to prevent and treat violence, particularly within the schools. Moreover, they each echo a theme supported throughout this book: Violence among youth is not inevitable. In this spirit, they present the APA Commission's specific recommendations for policy in 10 major areas.

Although knowledge about violence and youth is not complete, enough is known to assist researchers, practitioners, and policymakers as they search for solutions to the distressing increase of violence perpetrated and experienced by young persons in the United States. It is hoped that future initiatives to address the problem of violence and youth will be built on the solid foundation of accumulating knowledge in psychology as well as other important disciplines.

Reference

American Psychological Association Commission on Violence and Youth. (1993). *Violence and youth: Psychology's response*. Washington, DC: APA Public Interest Directorate.

18

The Present Status and Future Directions for Psychological Research on Youth Violence

*Judith V. Becker, Joyce Barham, Leonard D. Eron,
and S. Andrew Chen*

Psychologists have made major strides over the past 50 years in understanding the multiple etiologies of youth violence. As noted in many of the chapters in this book, violent and aggressive behavior in children and youth is an outgrowth of an array of historic, ecological, cultural, demographic, biological and psychological risk factors, many of which have been studied by psychologists as well as other scientists.

In this regard, many of the chapters in this book have noted that violence is not randomly distributed throughout the population. For example, now, as in times past, both perpetrators and victims of violence are concentrated in low-income areas. However, the fact that only a small percentage of the children living in these environments engage in aggressive and violent behaviors emphasizes that there is still much to be learned about why some youth become violent and others do not.

A synthesis of the research reviewed in this book demonstrates the multiple and varied processes that can thrust individual children on a developmental pathway or trajectory leading to violence. Although by no means inevitable, too often the trajectory suggested involves the following sequences.

Economic and social disorganization in communities promotes family disequilibrium. Weak bonding to caretakers in infancy and ineffective parenting techniques including a lack of supervision, inconsistent discipline, and failure to reinforce positive, prosocial behavior in young children all have been shown to lead to subsequent poor peer relations and high levels of aggressiveness. Extremely aggressive young children tend to be rejected by many of their more conforming peers and perform poorly in school. Later, many of these highly aggressive youngsters have poor school attendance and numerous suspensions. Such peer-rejected children tend to establish relationships with others similar to themselves and enter into deviant peer groups. The more such children are exposed to violence in their homes, communities, and the media, the greater the risk for aggressive and violent behaviors. Although psychologists cannot yet predict precisely which children will become violent and which will not, what has been called "a violence-prone trajectory" has been identified.

Present Status of Research on Youth Violence

Over the years, numerous small-scale psychological studies have demonstrated that early interventions at points in this violence-prone trajectory can, at least in the short run, modify or redirect the developmental pathways of some of these high-risk children. Small-scale, experimental prevention, early intervention, and treatment studies have demonstrated that parent–child bonding can be strengthened; parents can be taught more effective ways of supervising, disciplining, and teaching their children; and children can be taught to improve their social skills, develop their cognitive skills in solving problems nonviolently, change their cognitions about the appropriateness of violence, and improve their sense of self-efficacy. Furthermore, they can learn techniques for anger management, impulse control, and conflict resolution. However, researchers do not yet know whether the changes achieved by these procedures are long-lasting, if such changes actually serve to reduce the frequency of violent behavior, or if similar efforts can be replicated on a wider basis.

Also, even though this book has presented much data, theory, and application with regard to youth and violence, in many chapters authors directly or indirectly have noted the absence of an overarching theoretical approach that could help guide research and interpret data about violence among youth. For example, Goldstein and Soriano (chapter 14) cite the absence of viable contemporary theory to understand youth gang behavior amid rapid social changes. Donnerstein, Slaby, and Eron (chapter 11) report theories of media violence have been inadequate and "one-sided." Hill, Soriano, Chen, and LaFromboise, in the chapter on social and cultural influences (chapter 3), expressed the need to develop realistic and culturally appropriate models which could guide the generation of research questions, procedures, interpretation, and application of findings. Kazdin (chapter 15) emphasizes the need for greater integration of a developmental approach in the conceptualization and design of research. In virtually every area of research reviewed in this book, there is a call for a more applied and ecologically valid approach to the understanding of youth violence.

Therefore, despite a half century of research progress in generating formulations, methods, measures, and findings that substantially contribute to the understanding of violence, there still is a wide gap between understanding of the problem of violence and the knowledge needed to prevent it completely or lower the frequency of its occurrence. Because of the complex pathways to the expression of violence by youth, a comprehensive theory that encompasses the complex interactions of factors on societal, community, family, and individual levels while allowing that psychological variables have explanatory power at each of these levels, would further the field immensely.

Psychological knowledge about youth violence and what to do about it is limited by other factors as well. Forces in the larger society, gaps in existing research on violence, and limitations in the state of the science limit the understanding of its etiology and of remedial possibilities.

Many of the existing studies on violence and youth, for example, have methodological problems. Future studies must have sound methodologies including clearly stated hypotheses and study designs as well as clearly defined descriptions of the study populations. They must use state-of-the art assessment instruments and include process–outcome measures and control or comparison groups. As mentioned earlier, future studies on violence should also be theory driven.

Future Directions in Psychological Research

Those doing research in the area of violence and youth should also pay careful attention to the following issues:

1. *Integration of culturally diverse perspectives.* Much of the current research fails to attend sufficiently to the issue of cultural diversity and the overwhelming implications of cultural differences in understanding all aspects of child and family behavior and its relation to youth violence.

2. *Need for universal definitions.* There is little agreement across studies as to what constitutes aggressive behavior, maltreatment, child abuse, sexual abuse, disability, and so on. There is a need for federal, state, and local data-gathering agencies, funding agencies, and psychologists and others conducting research in these areas to develop standardized definitions.

3. *Establishment of common variables and measurement instruments.* Many researchers develop their own measurement instruments (which may or may not have been validated). Research efforts would be enhanced if researchers use existing instruments when appropriate or collaborate to develop and share new, more rigorous ones. The acceptance of a basic minimal set of variables to be included in all studies would allow for aggregation of data across studies.

4. *Full descriptions of intervention and treatment strategies.* Intervention research needs clear descriptions of the strategy for change, as well as safeguards to ensure consistency and integrity of the intervention and research procedures; if changes to procedures are made they should be documented.

5. *Inclusion of evaluation and outcome measures.* Although innumerable intervention programs have been launched by agencies of the federal government, communities, and schools, few have included outcome measures of program efficacy or any indication of cost effectiveness. Millions and even billions of dollars have been spent on the prevention of violence, child abuse, and sexual assault, as well as on drug and alcohol abuse prevention programs, but most of these programs have not included outcome measures of efficacy in reducing violence. As one example, programs such as good touch–bad touch have been implemented widely in schools with minimal evaluation and no documentation of generalization to out of school situations.

If psychologists are to move beyond their present understanding in the prevention and treatment of violence, variables such as self-esteem, anger control, problem solving, social skills, and conflict resolution can be considered only as mediating variables, not as outcome measures. It now remains to be demonstrated that an improvement in these variables does in fact lead to a reduction of violent behavior.

6. *Early development of implementation program evaluations.* Whether an intervention or treatment program is conducted on an individual, group, school, or community level, the evaluation design should be part of the original study design. Many intervention programs are well into the implementation stage before the issue of evaluation arises, and therefore the ability to obtain crucial baseline measures have been lost. Process evaluation should be conducted throughout all stages of the program.

7. *Broader scope of the interventions.* Given the multiple pathways to the expression of violence, existing interventions may be too narrowly focused. The need for comprehensive, broad-based efforts should be stressed.

8. *Need for long-term follow-up.* Those existing prevention or treatment studies that have outcome measures generally follow study participants only for brief periods: 3 months, 6 months, or at most 1 year. The need to follow the participants for longer periods is stressed.

9. *Inclusion of girls and women in studies of aggression research.* Virtually all research on violent behavior has been done with males, and thus little is known about the extent to which the etiology and development of violence among girls similar or different from boys. Until such differences are understood, appropriate prevention and treatment models cannot adequately be developed.

10. *Ethical issues in conducting violence research.* There are a number of ethical issues that are not always well addressed in current research. As in medicine, the first concern is that the research should do no harm.

The selection of the population to be studied raises ethical as well as theoretical and methodological issues. For example, the question of whether all children in a classroom should be targeted for intervention or only those at high risk has many implications for ethics and for the design of the study. The issue of whether labeling children as "at risk" may in fact stigmatize them and thus further increase their risk is one that needs consideration.

Once the study population has been identified, the ethical issue of random assignment to a no-intervention group becomes pertinent. Research designs that provide comparison groups assigned to alternate interventions are one viable option.

It is particularly relevant that informed consent or assent be obtained and that research participants are free from any degree of coercion to participate. Confidentiality of data when studying violence becomes critical, and consequently researchers may wish to apply for a certificate of confidentiality from the National Institutes of Health. It is particularly important that research participants be informed, prior to any history taking or assessment, what the limits of confidentiality are. This is particularly relevant when participants are being questioned relevant to child abuse or neglect or intent to harm others.

These are not all of the potential ethical issues in conducting research on violence, but they are meant to urge due consideration of ethical issues in the design and execution of research.

The American Psychological Association (1982) has published guidelines for research with human participants and these guidelines should be followed.

11. *Beyond research: Public policy considerations.* There is a wide gap between what psychologists know how to do and what they do. A broad range of social policies can be informed by research, but ultimately must be shaped by the personal preferences of the American public and their representatives in legal and social institutions. Psychologists are urged to take steps to make their research findings widely available to inform such action (see chapter 19 in this book). Individual psychologists and psychological organizations should disseminate their research findings widely within and beyond the scientific community.

Recommendations for Future Psychological Research on Youth Violence

To improve the scope and quality of research on violence involving youth, the APA Commission on Violence and Youth developed the following recommendations for planning and implementation of future research efforts.[1]

1. Research to identify effective intervention programs that address the continuum of prevention, early intervention, treatment, and rehabilitation.

1.1 *Community Interventions:* We recommend that culturally appropriate, comprehensive interventions for youth in the context of their ecological environments be developed and implemented. To facilitate this end, we urge psychologists to:
- Participate in studies on how to mobilize and empower communities to take responsibility for addressing violence within their own communities; and
- Become involved in preventive interventions launched by city governments, police departments, schools, social agencies, and civic or church groups in their own communities by providing consultation on the design and conduct of evaluation efforts.

1.2 *Interventions With Children:* We recommend that interventions begin as early as possible to interrupt and redirect processes related to the development of violent behavior. Among the research activities needed to support this end are:
- Meta-analyses of the numerous small-scale studies that have demonstrated the ability to interrupt a child's trajectory toward violence;
- Identification of developmental opportunities for intervention, including a consideration of critical periods in development at which age-appropriate interventions can be introduced;

[1]These recommendations were prepared for this chapter and presented earlier in the commission's summary report, *Violence and Youth: Psychology's Response* (APA Commission on Violence and Youth, 1993, pp. 63–66).

- Integration of a developmental perspective into the design and evaluation of interventions, including consideration of changes over time in child functioning and the interface of these changes with the interpersonal environment; and
- Investigation of a wider range of treatment approaches for both short-term and long-term effects, including psychodynamic and client-centered treatments commonly used with aggressive and violent children as well as cognitive–behavioral interventions.

1.3 *Interventions With Parents:* We recommend that interventions involving parents or prospective parents be a key part of a continuum model of violence prevention and intervention. Among the research activities needed to facilitate such interventions are:

- Research on home visiting programs, which have demonstrated effectiveness in improving parental care, supervision, and discipline techniques among extremely young parents and single parents. Research is needed on: (a) how to adapt such interventions to various cultural groups; (b) how to integrate such services into existing health and social services; (c) how to minimize the cost of such interventions; and (d) most importantly, to determine how effective such interventions are in reducing violence;
- Research to test and refine training programs to improve parenting skills with various racial and ethnic groups and in different geographic areas and to find ways of implementing the programs on a larger scale with parents of children at high risk; and
- Research on parents' beliefs and practices in disciplining children and adolescents, including the use of corporal punishment, and their effect on concurrent and future aggression and violent behavior.

1.4 *Interventions in the Schools:* We recommend that schools play a critical part in any comprehensive plan for preventive intervention to reduce youth violence. Among the most important research priorities for school-based interventions are:

- Research on the effects of altering factors in the school environment that have been shown to be conducive to aggression. These factors include a high number of students in a limited amount of space, heavy-handed and inflexible use of rules in the classroom, teacher hostility and lack of rapport, and inconsistencies in the limits of tolerance for students' misbehavior;
- Development and evaluation of school-based curricula and teaching strategies to help build children's resistance to violence as perpetrators and victims. Ongoing school programs should be evaluated for efficacy in reducing violent behavior both inside and outside the school setting; and
- Development and evaluation of school-based programs to teach children and their parents "critical media viewing skills." The effect of these programs on current and subsequent aggressive behavior should be evaluated.

2. Expansion of basic research efforts.

2.1   We recommend that psychologists expand efforts to develop collaborative, multidisciplinary research and to include such fields as anthropology, criminology, education, neurology, physiology, psychiatry, public health, sociology, and urban geography, recognizing the multiplicity of factors involved in the etiology of violent behavior.

2.2   We recommend that basic developmental research using a biopsychosocial approach be undertaken to shed new light on the interaction between nature and nurture in the development of aggressive and violent behavior.

2.3   We urge that studies of the role of culture in fostering and preventing violence be conducted for each ethnic minority group, including studies that examine the impact of strengthening cultural identity as a preventive strategy and studies that test the theoretical concepts of conflicting cultural demands as influences on violence.

2.4   We recommend that, although the concept that "violence breeds violence" is widely accepted, further research be conducted to confirm the extent to which victims of violence in one sphere of life may later become perpetrators of violence in another.

2.5   We recommend that there be more careful examination of the developmental pathways to violence and victimization among ethnic minority youth, with particular attention to contextual factors such as living conditions and life stressors.

2.6   We recommend that research be conducted to identify factors that serve to protect children who share in those risk factors but do not exhibit violent behavior, given that only some children who grow up in high-risk situations become violent.

2.7   We urge that research be conducted to identify the mediating factors that may act to buffer or protect children who have experienced harsh and continual physical punishment in the home, school, or community from developing aggressive interpersonal behavior as adolescents and adults, because many children who receive physical punishment at home do not become violent.

2.8   We encourage further research on the demographic characteristics of perpetrators of hate crimes and on their beliefs and attitudes. Research sites should include the community, schools, the workplace, and the military.

2.9   We recommend that research be conducted on the incidence of "random violence"—homicide and assault that appears unconnected with any ostensible motive—and on the characteristics of the perpetrators and the circumstances under which such violence occurs.

2.10   We urge the development of research efforts to determine whether the huge arsenal of weapons in private hands is a deterrent to crime or a source of danger. This research effort should inform the development of public policy in this area.

2.11   We recommend that research be conducted to study how the documented effects of watching violence in the mass media are engendered in the individual viewer of media violence. Among the questions to be answered are: Who is most susceptible to these media effects? Which media effects are most likely for particular individuals? Under what circumstances are these media effects most likely? Which effects are most likely under particular circumstances? By what mechanisms do these media effects occur? How do the mechanisms underlying these effects interrelate and differ? In what ways can these media effects be altered to prevent violence? and How do effective interventions for these effects interrelate and differ?

3. Recognition of the complex influence of racial, ethnic, and cultural differences in all research.

3.1   We recommend that all research be conceptualized, designed, and conducted with unfailing attention to the traditions, beliefs, attitudes, and behaviors of the groups being studied as well as the circumstances under which they are living.

3.2   We urge investigators to examine their own racial and cultural assumptions for bias in conceptualization, design, methodology, and selection of participants.

3.3   We recommend that representatives of the study population participate at every stage of the research, from planning through execution and publication.

4. Improved data collection and analysis.

4.1   We ask that collection of data on youth violence by the U.S. Department of Justice, the U.S. Public Health Service, and other state and local governmental agencies be expanded and improved.

4.2   We urge the U.S. Department of Justice to make further attempts to reconcile and explain the differences between its two major data sets, the Uniform Crime Reporting Program and the National Crime Victimization Survey.

4.3   We recommend that data be collected, analyzed, and reported on the risk and prevalence of violence by and toward the various racial and ethnic groups and subgroups of Asian and Pacific Island Americans, Hispanics, and Native Americans in addition to African Americans and Whites. We further recommend that whenever possible, fine-grained distinctions should be made; for example, data should be collected not just on "Asian Americans", but specifically on Chinese, Koreans, Japanese, Vietnamese, Thai, Cambodians, Pacific Islanders, and other subgroups.

4.4   We recommend collection of basic data on the prevalence of gay and lesbian sexual orientation among youth and on the problems these youth experience, including discrimination, sexual and other physical assaults, health practices and disease, suicide and suicide attempts, and substance abuse.

4.5 We recommend that more data be collected on the risk of violence among youth with disabilities, using standardized definitions of key terms such as "disability" and "handicapped." Wherever possible, studies should differentiate between disability caused by violence and disability that precedes the violence.

4.6 We urge the collection of current data on the prevalence of gangs, their breadth of location, their activities, their involvement with drug distribution and use, and their use of violence, and on the psychological attributes and functioning of boys and of girls who participate in gangs.

4.7 We recommend that data be collected on participants and matched groups of nonparticipants in mob violence, and on the psychological aftermath of mob violence on both the participants and the victims. Such data gathering should go beyond basic demographic characteristics and include information on personal psychological characteristics, family experience, affectional ties, and group affiliations.

4.8 We recommend that data be collected on the prevalence of violence perpetrated by women and girls. Because women and girls are less frequently the perpetrators of sexual and other physical violence than are boys and men, samples must be of sufficient size to analyze for the characteristics of perpetrators and victims.

4.9 We urge that data be collected on the prevalence of domestic violence and on characteristics of perpetrators and victims.

5. New and improved measurement and instrumentation.

5.1 We recommend the development of new and improved gender-sensitive and culturally sensitive measures, psychological tests, and assessment instruments. These instruments should be normed on different ethnic and racial groups and the subcultures that comprise [sic] each group.

5.2 We recommend the development of new measures to assess the characteristics of communities and the institutions with which children and youth interact.

5.3 We recommend that, whenever possible, multiple psychological assessment measures be used, including self-report, reports of others (i.e., teachers, parents, and peers), observations of behavior in standard controlled situations, and archival data. Multilevel assessments should be used (i.e., community, family, and individual).

5.4 We urge that new instruments be developed and validated that use behavioral assessment strategies appropriate to various groups of children, in addition to self-reports, teacher and parent reports, and archival data. Ideally, measures should be both quantitative and qualitative.

5.5 We recommend development of new measures of the cost-effectiveness of intervention programs.

6. Consideration of key issues in the review, funding, and dissemination of research.

6.1   We recommend that funding agencies assess, as part of the review of scientific merit, the extent to which research applications (a) include subjects of varied racial and ethnic groups, genders, and sexual orientations, or justify the case when special groups have been selected; and (b) are culturally sensitive in all aspects of the planning and execution of the research projects. Scientists who are members of the study populations should have the opportunity to provide opinions in the review of applications for support. Review committees should include scientists who are members of the study populations. Furthermore, experts with community ties should have the opportunity to provide input to review committee deliberations.

6.2   We encourage the support of studies for understudied groups and problems, recognizing that research resources may need to be allocated to populations most at risk and to problems of widespread concern.

6.3   We ask that federal agencies and foundations recognize the vital interplay between basic and applied research, and reduce the dichotomy in funding categories. Basic research provides the underpinnings for informed interventions. Applied research provides direct tests of models derived from theory and basic research and represents an effort to achieve the goal of reducing or eliminating violent behavior; at the same time it generally provides new understandings of basic processes. Therefore, it is important that funding agencies issue requests for applications that permit investigation of basic and applied research within the same study.

6.4   We recommend that federal agencies and private foundations seek to develop greater coordination of research and funding plans and longer funding periods that would allow meaningful follow-up.

6.5   We urge funding agencies to increase support for follow-up of previously completed studies in which short-term reductions of either mediators of violent behavior or violent behavior itself have been demonstrated. Such follow-up studies could provide important information on the duration of effects now so often lacking in the body of prevention and treatment research.

6.6   We urge that new longitudinal studies be initiated utilizing multicomponent interventions in home, school, and community, with sufficient sample size and of sufficient duration to test long-term effects.

6.7   We support an increase in federal funding commitments to comprehensive, accelerated, longitudinal designs with multiple cohorts to trace the developmental trajectory of aggression and violence across transitional stages from early childhood into late adolescence and young adulthood. The planning for such studies should take into account and complement existing longitudinal studies.

6.8   We urge every investigator involved in psychological research related to youth violence to be aware of their professional and scientific responsibilities to the community and to the society in which they work and live. These responsibilities include promoting collegial exchange of knowledge with members of other disciplines engaged in research related to youth violence; disseminating the results of studies to the scientific community and to the general public; sharing data with other investigators seeking to verify the results of the research, within the limits of any legal barrier or confidentiality restrictions applying to the data; seeking to assure that their research efforts contribute to the welfare of their subjects and the community; and encouraging the development of law and social policy that serve the interests of the study population and the general public.

References

American Psychological Association. (1982). *Ethical principles in the conduct of research with human participants*. Washington, DC: Author.

APA Commission on Violence and Youth. (1993). *Violence and youth: Psychology's response*. Washington, DC: Public Interest Directorate, American Psychological Association.

19

Policy Recommendations: Prevention and Treatment of Youth Violence

Ronald G. Slaby, Joyce E. Barham,
Leonard D. Eron, and Brian L. Wilcox

Violence, like all behavior, is fostered, developed, and enacted within a broad environmental, social, and individual context, as demonstrated in the chapters in this book. Because many factors in these contexts interact in complex ways to influence violent behavior, there is no simple or single effort that can solve the problem of violence among our youth in the United States. Therefore, policymakers need to consider a broad and coordinated set of policies if they hope to reduce violence. It is with such policies that this chapter is concerned.

The APA Commission on Violence and Youth conducted a careful review of psychological research, heard testimony from experts in the field, and listened carefully to the young people who are actually living in the midst of violence. They reached a number of conclusions, many of which have important policy implications that are summarized here (specific policy recommendations issuing from these conclusions are detailed later in this chapter).

First, although violence is a potential threat to all youth, some groups are more vulnerable than others to becoming involved in violence as perpetrators, victims, or bystanders (who may provide social support for violence). For example, those youth who are at highest risk because of their life circumstances are the socioeconomically disadvantaged ethnic and racial minority group members. However, too often the public has associated violent behavior with race or ethnicity rather than with the social and economic conditions that create the difficult life circumstances in which violence thrives. There are also groups who are particularly vulnerable to violence because of gender, sexual preference, religious beliefs, or physical condition. Prejudice and hostility toward individuals on the basis of such group membership can foster hate crimes and associated violence.

Second, early childhood experiences play a pivotal role in the learning of violent behavior or effective nonviolent alternative behaviors. Physically aggressive young children who receive no systematic support for learning alternatives to violence may grow up to become violent teenagers and adults. Children are more apt to become aggressive and grow up to become involved in violence when they experience or witness violence and abuse in the home and community, when they lack consistent supervision and emotional support from caring adults, or when they receive encouragement or pressure from peers to engage in violence. Individuals who do not receive adequate opportunities to learn adaptive patterns of response in early childhood are likely to continue to show low levels of social competence and high vulnerability to violence.

Third, the exposure to media that glorify violence, the fairly easy access to firearms that increases the lethality of aggressive encounters, and the availability of alcohol and other drugs that contribute to the frequency of aggressive behaviors may separately and in combination help to perpetuate youth violence.

Fourth, effective interventions to prevent and treat violence can also be implemented in a variety of ways, including parent training and support, Head Start and school-based programs, peer mentoring and support programs, individual counseling and therapy, community-based programs, and media presentations with related outreach activities. Opportunities for children to learn, adopt, and use their inner resources are most effective when they are introduced early, presented in a coordinated way across many social domains, tailored to the community and cultural priorities, and repeated and expanded systematically over the long term. Because of their access to the nation's youth, schools can have a powerful effect on the prevention and amelioration of youth violence.

Finally, psychological research has shown that although increasingly prevalent and lethal, violence is not inevitable: Most children who grow up under the most adverse circumstances do not become violent. Researchers need to know more about the mechanisms that protect such children from environmental hazards and what causes other children to proceed on an accelerated pace along the pathways to violence.

The remainder of this chapter distills these conclusions into more detailed policy recommendations in 10 specific areas.[1] Although socioeconomic issues are not specifically addressed, members of the APA Commission on Violence and Youth often noted the broad and pervasive influence on violence of the living conditions associated with poverty, social inequality, and lack of opportunity. They stressed the need for expansion and systematic implementation of governmental and private efforts to reduce poverty and socioeconomic inequality, improve general living conditions, and increase educational and employment opportunities.

Public Policy Recommendations

1. Early childhood interventions can help children learn to deal with social conflict effectively and nonviolently. In their early years, children learn fundamental ways of dealing with social conflict. Parents, guardians, child-care providers, and health care providers play an important role in help-

---

[1] These recommendations were prepared for this chapter and presented earlier in the commission's summary report, *Violence and Youth: Psychology's Response* (APA Commission on Violence and Youth, 1993, pp. 73–84).

ing young children learn basic aspects of effective nonviolent social behavior. These primary agents of child socialization need effective intervention strategies, materials, training, technical assistance, and support services designed to help them lay the critical foundations on which children can learn to reduce aggressive behavior and prevent future violence.

1.1   We recommend that Congress ask all relevant federal agencies to identify successful and promising interventions, programs, and resources for preventing and treating youth violence and develop and disseminate a report that is based on these programs. (Such agencies would include the U.S. Department of Education, the U.S. Department of Health and Human Services, the U.S. Department of Housing and Urban Development, and the U.S. Department of Justice.)

1.2   We recommend that funding and technical assistance for implementing local violence prevention programs be distributed through such mechanisms as state block grant programs. Special attention should be directed to continuous comprehensive intervention and follow-up in health and educational programs for families at risk for violence. Such families would include very young mothers, single parent families, those with parental mental health or substance abuse problems, those with parental histories of violent offenses or domestic violence, and those at high risk for child neglect and abuse. We also ask Congress to expand funding for Head Start and other school readiness programs both to improve the overall quality of such programs and to include all eligible children.

1.3   We encourage parent–teacher associations, community health centers, child care centers, and other organizations at which parents gather, to provide parent–child management training programs to foster the development of a repertoire of parental disciplining techniques to replace coercive ones. These programs should include behavior management and social skills training curricula, which have been shown to be effective in improving family communication and reducing child behavior problems.

2. Schools can become a leading force in providing the safety and the effective educational programs by which children can learn to reduce and prevent violence. On the one hand, schools often provide multiple opportunities for bullying, harassment, intimidation, fights, and other forms of violence to occur. Students who feel that their personal safety is threatened may bring weapons to school with them. Students who show poor school achievement and poor peer relations show an increased risk of becoming involved in violence. On the other hand, schools also can provide children with repeated and developmentally appropriate opportunities to follow sound principles of personal safety, strengthen academic and social skills, develop sound peer relationships, and learn effective nonviolent solutions to social conflict. A number of promising programs in classroom management, problem solving skills training, and violence prevention for school children have been developed, but not all of them have been adequately evaluated.

2.1 We ask Congress to encourage federally supported efforts to develop, implement, and evaluate violence prevention and aggression reduction curricula for use in the schools from early childhood through the teen years. Such efforts would involve teacher training, training for other school personnel, curricular activities, coordinated parental support activities, and technical assistance in implementing programs that apply techniques known to be effective in reducing aggression and preventing violence.

2.2 We recommend that school systems take a long view of children's education regarding violence and make every effort to develop and implement a coordinated, systematic, and developmentally and culturally appropriate program for violence prevention beginning in the early years and continuing throughout adolescence.

2.3 We ask state educational agencies to support the development, implementation, and evaluation of programmatic comprehensive school-based violence prevention programs designed to provide a safe learning environment and to teach students sound and effective principles of violence prevention. Furthermore, we underscore the need to provide a safe school environment for all children.

2.4 We recommend that professional organizations involved with school-based programs prepare and disseminate effective and promising program materials, assessment tools, and evaluation findings germane to violence prevention for broad and flexible use by schools, even while ongoing research attempts to improve their effectiveness and adapt them for particular circumstances and local cultural groups. Such organizations would include the American Psychological Association, the National Association of School Psychologists, the National Education Association, and the National Association for the Education of Young Children, among others.

2.5 We encourage schools to engage in the early identification of children who show emotional and behavioral problems related to violence and to provide to them or refer them for appropriate educational experiences and psychological interventions.

2.6 We ask Congress, state governments, and local governments to support the funding and development of after-school programs and recreational activities in schools with high proportions of at-risk children and youth. Initiation into gangs and delinquency is commonly linked to unsupervised time after school.

2.7 We recommend that those state governments and school boards that have not already done so adopt policies and provide training to prohibit the use of corporal punishment in schools and to encourage positive behavior management techniques to maintain school discipline and safety. We also encourage early childhood educators and health practitioners to teach parents alternative methods of discipline in the home.

2.8 We recommend that violence reduction training be made a part of preservice and inservice training for teachers, administrators, school staff, and health professionals likely to serve children of school age.

3. All programmatic efforts to reduce and prevent violence will benefit from heightened awareness of cultural diversity. Throughout every aspect of the review, the increasing cultural diversity of the United States was stressed. An understanding, appreciation, and integration of the benefits of culturally diverse perspectives is an important component not only of the content of the program but also of the process by which it is developed, implemented, and evaluated. It was noted that well-intentioned people and programs often have lacked sensitivity to cultural differences and have failed to develop violence prevention programs that are responsive to those differences. The effectiveness of programmatic efforts to reduce and prevent violence is likely to be increased by involving the members of the communities as partners in the development, implementation, and evaluation of these efforts.

3.1　We call for a variety of efforts aimed at increasing sensitivity to cultural differences and reducing discrimination and prejudice that create a climate conducive to violence. Such efforts should begin in the earliest school years with specialized curricula for children and be continued throughout the school years. To foster more widespread acceptance of cultural diversity, human relations education should be provided for adults in a variety of settings, including public and private employment, the armed services, churches, and schools.

3.2　We recommend that all public programs designed to reduce or prevent youth violence be developed, implemented, and evaluated with a sensitivity to cultural differences and with the continued involvement of the groups and the communities they are designed to serve. Current programs designed to prevent violence should also be reviewed for their appreciation and integration of diverse cultural perspectives.

4. Television and other media can contribute to the solutions rather than to the problems of youth violence. For more than 4 decades, psychologists and other researchers have investigated and reviewed the best available evidence on the relation between violence in the media and aggressive behavior. Findings have been consistent: Television and other media contribute to children's and youths' involvement with violence as aggressors, victims, and bystanders who support violence. Research investigation of television and other media has also provided some techniques by which the effects of violence in the media may be mitigated through the teaching of critical viewing skills. Finally, evidence indicates that television is an effective and pervasive teacher of children and youth that has the potential, consistent with its new legal obligation to educate and inform children, to make a major contribution to solving the violence problem, rather than contributing to it. Our recommendations on this subject appear in two sections: Recommendations 4.1, 4.2, and 4.3 address public policymakers, and Recommendations 10.1 and 10.2 address the policy-making bodies of the American Psychological Association.

4.1   We call upon the Federal Communications Commission (FCC) to review, as a condition for license renewal, the programming and outreach efforts and accomplishments of television stations in helping to solve the problem of youth violence. This recommendation is consistent with the research evidence indicating television's potential to educate young children and with the legal obligation of broadcast stations to "serve the educational and informational needs of children," both in programming and in outreach activities designed to enhance the educational value of programming. We also call on the FCC to institute rules that would require broadcasters, cable operators and other telecasters to avoid programs containing an excessive amount of dramatized violence during "child viewing hours" between 6 am and 10 pm.

4.2   We ask Congress to support a national educational violence prevention campaign involving television programming and related educational outreach activities to address the dire need for public education to help prevent youth violence in America. This campaign would be based on our best available scientific evidence about which changes will be most effective in helping to prevent violence, and our best educational and media strategies for fostering such change.

4.3   We recommend that the Film Rating System be revised to take into account the violence content that is harmful to children and youth. We also recommend that producers and distributors of television and video programming be required to provide clear and easy to use warning labels for violent material to permit viewers to make informed choices.

5. Major reductions in the most damaging forms of youth violence can be achieved by limiting youth access to firearms and by teaching children and youth how to prevent firearm violence. Youth and guns often are a fatal combination. Although interpersonal violence can occur through a variety of means, the use of firearms has dramatically increased the prevalence of violent death and the severity of violent injury to America's youth. For example, in 1987 firearms accounted for 60% of all homicides in the United States and for 71% of homicides of youth 15 to 19 years of age. For every firearms fatality there were an estimated 7.5 nonfatal injuries. Although national debates about adult access to guns continue, few would advocate that children and youth should have easy access to guns. Nevertheless, children and youth in America generally have widespread, easy, and unsupervised access to firearms, exposure to media portrayals that glorify the use of firearms, and little opportunity to learn how to prevent firearm violence. Without society-wide restrictions it will not be possible to effectively restrict youth access to firearms. Our recommendations on this subject appear in two sections: Recommendations 5.1 and 5.2 address public policymakers, and Recommendation 10.3 addresses the policy-making bodies of the American Psychological Association.

5.1 We support the initiative of the U.S. Public Health Service to reduce weapon-carrying by adolescents.

5.2 We recommend that Congress provide funding for the development, implementation, and evaluation of school-based programs to educate children regarding the prevention of firearm violence and the reduction of both unintentional and intentional death and injury caused by firearms.

6. Reduction of youth involvement with alcohol and other drugs can reduce violent behavior. Violent behavior associated with the use of alcohol commonly accounts for about 65% of all homicides, 40% of all assaults, and 55% of all fights and assaults in the home. In addition, an estimated 10% of homicides occur in the business of trafficking illegal drugs. Alcohol and other drugs are involved in youth violence in several ways. Abuse of alcohol and other drugs by parents has often been associated with violent behavior toward children. Alcohol and use of some other drugs by youth themselves also is associated with increased rates of violence. Youth involvement in the illegal business of drug trafficking is associated with violence. Although our Commission report does not provide a thorough review of this issue, the following recommendations were nevertheless clear.

6.1 We encourage community, school, family, and media involvement in prevention and treatment programs that focus on the links between substance abuse and the prevalence of violence.

6.2 We encourage federal, state, and local agencies to provide funding for such education, prevention, and treatment programs.

7. Psychological health services for young perpetrators, victims, and witnesses of violence can ameliorate the damaging effects of violence and reduce further violence. Research has shown that a history of previous violence is the best predictor of future violence. Actually, a relatively small proportion of the population accounts for much of the serious criminal violence. More than one-half of all crime is committed by 5% to 7% of young people between the ages of 10 and 20. Therefore, it is important to target young violent offenders for a variety of interventions, including cognitive, behavioral, and social skills training, counseling, and therapy. A number of effective and promising programs have been identified for treatment of children and youth who have committed violent offenses or been referred for problems of antisocial, aggressive, and violent behavior. However, too few publicly funded mental health services have been made available for child and family treatment that can help prevent violence.

7.1 We recommend that public mental health services be reallocated so that more services are available for prevention and for early treatment of children and families with problems of aggression and violence.

7.2 We recommend that more treatment programs be developed and increased counselling services for victims be made available to the large numbers of young children and youth who witness high levels of violence in their homes, streets, and schools.

8. Education programs can reduce the prejudice and hostility that lead to hate crimes and violence against social groups. Hate crimes can be committed by individuals or groups, sometimes loosely organized, sometimes more formally organized. Hate crimes can be directed against individuals or groups. Children and youth who appear "different" in any way are more apt to be harassed and victimized by others. Children and youth often victimized include African Americans, Hispanics, Asian and Pacific Island Americans, Native Americans, girls and young women, gays and lesbians, Jews, and those with physical disabilities. There are many competing explanations about the origins of this type of violence, but it is always associated with learned prejudice, group polarization, and hostility.

8.1   We encourage schools, colleges, and universities to adopt human relations education to dispel stereotypes, encourage broader intercultural understanding and appreciation, and reduce the incidence of hate violence. Training in mediation techniques should be provided to community leaders.

8.2   We recommend that effective interventions be developed to help victims of hate violence to recover from attacks.

8.3   We recommend that, in conjunction with these efforts, the U.S. Civil Rights Commission undertake a review of federal antidiscrimination laws, statutes, and regulations regarding race, ethnicity, religion, gender, sexual orientation, and physical disability.

8.4   We recommend that federal, state, and local governments pursue strict enforcement of antidiscrimination laws regarding race, ethnicity, religion, gender, sexual orientation, and physical disability.

9. When groups become mobs, violence feeds on itself. Mob violence may occur under a variety of conditions, including when rising expectations are unfulfilled, when social and economic conditions appear to be worsening, or when injustice is perceived. Often a specific event precipitates the violence. Mob violence may be directed against individuals or groups or may appear to be undirected. In the course of group violence, the members enter into a process of change along a "continuum of destruction." Many of the recommendations previously made are relevant here to address the underlying conditions that encourage mob behavior, including relief from conditions of socioeconomic disadvantage, access to increased opportunities and resources, increased cultural awareness, and reduced discrimination. Whatever the underlying roots of the disturbance, the police are called on to restore control. They are often caught in a dilemma between responding too early and too late, too much and too little. Experience has shown that the participation of community leaders in restoring early control is important.

9.1   We recommend that human relations training for community leaders and police be conducted jointly.

9.2   We recommend that police departments implement or expand their training and community policing efforts, that these efforts include social and cultural sensitivity training, and that increased participation by members of the community be included in these efforts.

10. Psychologists can act individually and in our professional organizations to reduce violence among youth. The Commissioners noted that there were many activities in which psychologists can contribute to the reduction of youth violence, in addition to those already being conducted. Such activities can be carried out through national, state, and local associations and divisions, as well as through individual actions.

10.1   We propose that the American Psychological Association resolution on television violence and children's aggression be modified to cover all the mass media, including film and video as well as television.

10.2   We recommend that the American Psychological Association develop video and other educational materials designed to enhance the critical viewing skills of teachers, parents, and children regarding media violence and how to prevent its negative effects.

10.3   We recommend that the American Psychological Association revise and expand its current policy on handgun control to incorporate the following as APA policy:

Support for nationwide restrictive licensing of firearm ownership based on attainment of legal voting age; clearance following a criminal record background check; and demonstrated skill in firearm knowledge, use, and safety.

Support for federal, state, and local governments to increase specific legal, regulatory, and enforcement efforts to reduce widespread, easy, and unsupervised access to firearms by children and youth.

10.4   We propose that the American Psychological Association hold a series of training programs for its members on youth violence with special sessions for clinicians and for researchers.

10.5   We recommend that the American Psychological Association take an active role in identifying model interventions that have been demonstrated to be effective in preventing or reducing youth violence. These should be disseminated to professional audiences and to the general public.

10.6   We recommend that psychologists review the research findings presented in this and other reports and provide consultation to community groups interested in implementing programs to prevent youth violence.

10.7   We suggest that psychologists make a coordinated presentation of models of successful violence prevention programs at such workshops as the Vermont Conference on Primary Prevention.

10.8   We recommend that the American Psychological Association sponsor further reviews of influencing factors in violence—for example, gender, ethnicity, psychophysiology, and substance abuse.

10.9   We recommend that the report and recommendations of this Commission on Violence and Youth be presented to Congress, to the U.S. Department of Health and Human Services, to the U.S. Commission on Civil Rights, to the U.S. Department of Justice, and to other relevant agencies.

10.10   We recommend that education and training on youth violence be incorporated into the graduate preparation of psychologists. We also recommend that psychological training programs institute cultural sensitivity courses and training to increase cultural awareness and sensitivity to underrepresented groups that are affected by violence.

Afterword

Ronald G. Slaby and Leonard D. Eron

The authors in this volume have reviewed the efforts over the last 50 years of organized psychology as well as the work of selected individual psychologists in the area of violence and youth. We believe that psychology has accomplished much over this period in advancing knowledge of the origins and development of violence among youth. We have also begun to understand what is involved and what is needed to intervene effectively to reduce and prevent this behavior. Proceeding from the conviction that aggression is ultimately a learned behavior, we have demonstrated, we believe, how it is learned and how it endures.

Our message of hope is that because aggression and violence are learned, they can also be unlearned, or, even better, we can create and maintain the kinds of conditions in which violence is not learned in the first place. In this volume, we have largely limited our consideration of what psychology has to offer in this regard to certain areas of the discipline. We have dealt extensively with developmental, social psychological, and cognitive–behavioral contributions and somewhat less with the contributions of clinical and educational psychology. We have not focused on biological psychology, behavior genetics, psychopharmacology, neuropsychology, or psychophysiology (see discussion in the introduction to this volume), all of which contribute to a comprehensive understanding of violence, its origins, and ways to prevent it. We have not included interdisciplinary work by such researchers as criminologists and educators, although that is one of the goals we have set for the future (see next section). Excluding these areas of psychology and other disciplines by no means devalues their important contributions to the understanding and amelioration of youth involvement in violence. It only signifies the need to limit the scope of this book in order to permit adequate depth of coverage for the topics we do address. Future directions for psychology indicate a need to expand this scope considerably.

Future Directions for Psychology

Although psychology has a great deal to offer in addressing the problem of youth violence in America, it also faces many new challenges in attempting to develop effective solutions. To play a central role in helping to solve the problem of violence in America, the field of psychology needs to develop: (a) new definitions of the problem, (b) new partnerships with other disciplines, (c) new perspectives on the problem, (d) new applications of current knowledge, and (e) new roles by which to address the problem.

New Definitions

The psychological study of aggression has faced several definitional problems (Eron, Walder, & Lefkowitz, 1971; Parke & Slaby, 1983). *Aggression* has been defined conceptually and operationally in a wide variety of ways, many of which are overlapping, artificially limited, or ambiguous. Furthermore, the definition of aggression that is used by psychologists for research has consistently produced major communication problems with other disciplines and with the general public. Although psychologists generally attempt to exclude from their definition the generally positive attributes of "assertiveness," "forcefulness," or "initiative," these meanings nevertheless remain an integral part of the widely held popular concept of aggressiveness. Thus, there is currently no single definition of aggression that simultaneously satisfies both the diversity of popular meanings and the variety of psychological research strategies that are applied to the concept.

In contrast, the term *violence,* despite its variations in usage, is generally more clearly and uniformly understood by researchers within and across disciplines, as well as by the general public. In this volume, the words have often been used interchangeably, and "violence" is sometimes used when referring to the acts of younger children for which the term *aggression* has normally been used. Always, however, the intention to cause harm was understood as part of the meaning of this term.

The popular concept of violence is closely connected with the common psychological definition of *aggressive behavior* as an interpersonal act of intentional harm-doing, but it excludes the more positive attributes that are associated with aggressiveness. The term violence also draws attention to its more extreme consequences of injury and death. It also challenges one to examine distinctions and commonalities between interpersonal acts of violence (e.g., homicide, assault, rape, and abuse of children, intimate partners, elders) and self-directed acts of violence (e.g., suicide, attempted suicide) (see Earls et al., 1992).

New Partnerships

Although psychology has approached research on the development of aggression largely as a single discipline, the problem of violence in the United States is multidimensional, and its solution requires an interdisciplinary approach. Because the perspectives of the various disciplines that are involved in the issue of violence overlap to some degree, common ground exists on which to build an interdisciplinary approach to violence prevention that incorporates, unites, and transcends each individual discipline. But important differences among disciplines in their concepts, theoretical formulations, practical strategies, and research findings must be appreciated in order for an interdisciplinary approach to become valuable, generative, and greater than the sum of its parts. Indeed, within psychology itself efforts must be made for collaboration, cooperation, and mutual understanding among the various subdisciplines (e.g., biological, clinical, developmental, social psychological, and community organizational) in order for a comprehensive picture to emerge of how violent behavior originates and develops within the individual.

New Perspectives

The understanding of violence and how to prevent it could be greatly enhanced by integrating the varying perspectives on violence that are held by the major disciplines that address the issue:

- Public health has addressed violence as a potentially preventable societal problem that often results in physical injury and death.
- Criminal justice has viewed violence as a criminal act that violates the law, requires deliberation of facts and circumstances by a jury of peers to determine an individual's legal guilt and level of responsibility, and requires punishment and/or correctional treatment.
- Education has dealt with violence as a maladaptive interpersonal behavior that can be corrected through the building of knowledge, skills, and strategies that are needed to resolve interpersonal conflict effectively and nonviolently.
- Psychotherapy has often dealt with violence as a symptom of underlying emotional or mental health disorder marked by the "acting out" of aggressive urges that are assumed to reside within all individuals.
- Psychiatry has considered violence as a manifestation of mental disorder, often treatable with psychotropic medications.
- Psychology and other behavioral sciences have commonly investigated violence as a learned, developing, and alterable form of physically aggressive behavior that harms individuals, families, communities, and societies.

New Applications

When viewing psychological research from alternative perspectives, it is clear that the psychological field needs to expand and develop new applications for its findings, formulations, methods, and intervention strategies. For example, public health has addressed the violence problem as one of the prevention of intentional injury in society. From this perspective, the limits of psychology's traditional focus on the individual aggressor can be seen. This focus has largely ignored the role of the victim, who is often carefully chosen by the aggressor, and the role of the bystander, who may either support or help to prevent violence. Psychology has also largely overlooked the need to develop strategies to prevent injuries and death and the need to understand an individual's behavior in the broader context of the community, society, and culture.

From the criminal justice perspective, it can be seen that psychology needs to examine the problem of violence in relation to the use of firearms as well as the trafficking and use of alcohol and other drugs. Psychology also needs to help develop and evaluate effective and enduring correctional treatment of violent offenders.

From the education perspective, it is apparent that psychologists need to help in the planning, development, formative evaluation, refinement, and outcome evaluation of effective school-based curricula and teaching strategies to help build children's resistance to violence. Psychology also needs to contribute to the education of professionals and the general public about violence, by replacing "common sense" notions with the research facts and by identifying effective intervention techniques.

From the counseling and mental health perspective, it can be seen that psychologists need to develop effective diagnostic and evaluation methods as well as effective intervention techniques for individuals and groups at risk for involvement in violence as perpetrators, victims, or bystanders.

New Roles

To address the broad and multidimensional problem of violence, psychologists need to change, refocus, or extend their traditional roles in research, teaching, counseling, and clinical treatment. After decades of carrying out research designed primarily to help us understand the causes and development of aggression and violence, psychologists now need to develop new applied roles to meet the challenge of helping solve the practical problem of violence in America. Psychologists also need to develop new outreach roles to help shape national agendas, formulate public policy, and guide programmatic efforts to reduce and prevent violence. It is indeed time for us to "give away" psychology in the service of preventing and reducing violence.

Conclusion

For too long, Americans have been trying to solve the problems of youth violence by intervening when it is already too late, after violent acts have been committed. Although prisons and detention facilities continue to be built and to be filled with young violent offenders, little has been done to use the present understanding of violence to develop and present early prevention and treatment programs to those youth who are on a developmental pathway toward violence.

Interpersonal violence, as a way of solving interpersonal problems, relieving frustration, coercively controlling others, restoring one's loss of "respect," and gaining material rewards and social approval, is learned early in life and learned very well. The rewards can be substantial, and so, despite frequent attempts to discourage or control violence, the behavior may persist. Characteristic ways of interacting aggressively with others are often established early in childhood and become increasingly resistant to change. Thus, in the absence of effective intervention, the physically aggressive young child is likely to become the violent adolescent and then the violent adult.

Because of the consistency and continuity of this behavior once it has been learned and rewarded, intervention programs that start in late adolescence and young adulthood have had limited success. Rather than waiting until violence has been learned and practiced and then devoting increased resources to hiring policemen, building more prisons, and sentencing three-time offenders to life imprisonment, it would be more effective to redirect the resources to early violence prevention programs, particularly for young children and preadolescents. Certainly, ensuring adequate health care for infants, guiding and training young parents in noncoercive management skills, and providing enrichment programs to prepare toddlers and preschoolers with the interpersonal skills and strategies they need for successful school experiences should be of great help in directing children away from developmental pathways that lead to violent behavior.

The early prevention programs described in this volume that have been scientifically evaluated offer considerable hope for teaching children prosocial ways of solving interpersonal problems and achieving success without resorting to violence. However, the success of these programs can be compromised by the overwhelming macrosocial and macroeconomic conditions under which a substantial proportion of youth and their parents live. Until this country's problems of socioeconomic inequality, joblessness, lack of opportunity, overcrowding, and inadequate health care can be mitigated, the psychosocial and educational intervention programs advocated in this book cannot achieve their full promise. When the citizens of this nation address these larger societal problems, while implementing the violence prevention strategies presented in this volume, the hope for a future free of fear and violence may then be realized.

References

Earls, F. J., Slaby, R. G., Spirito, A., Saltzman, L. E., Thornton, T. N., Berman, A., Davidson, L., Fagan, J., Goodman, A., Hawkins, D., Kraus, J. F., Loftin, D., Moscicki, E., Muehrer, P., O'Carroll, P., Sudak, H., Visher, C., Widom, C. S., Wintemute, G., & Baer, K. (1992). Prevention of violence and injuries due to violence. In *Injury control: Position papers from the third national injury control conference: Setting the national agenda for injury control in the 1990s* (pp. 159–254). Atlanta, GA: Centers for Disease Control.

Eron, L. D., Walder, L. O., & Lefkowitz, M. M. (1971). *The learning of aggression in children.* Boston, MA: Little, Brown.

Parke, R. D., & Slaby, R. G. (1983). The development of aggression. In P. H. Mussen (Series Ed.), *Handbook of child psychology* (Vol. 4, 4th Ed., pp. 547–641). New York: Wiley.

Author Index

Numbers in italics refer to listings in reference sections.

Abadinsky, H., 321, *330*
Abbott, K. A., 151, *160*
Abbott, E. L., 151, *160*
Abeles, N., 225, *246*
Abelson, R. P., 32, *57*
Aboud, F., 12, *18*
Achenbach, T. M., 349, *376*, 384, *400*
Acuna, R., 72, *91*
Adams, D., 44, *52*
Adan, A. M., 372, *378*, 388, *401*
Adorno, T., 12, *18*
Ageton, S. S., 349, 369, 371, *377*, 383, *401*
Ageton, S., 167, 171, 172, *174*
Akers, E. R., 294, *308*
Alexander, G. R., 15, *18*
Alexander, J. F., 17, *18*, 363, 364, *376, 379*, 393, 398 *400, 402*, 414, *427*
Alicke, M. D., 360, 367, *381*
Allen, J. P., 352, 358, 372, *376*
Allen, L., 351, 352, *380*
Allen, N., 106, 110, *116*, 146, *161*
Allen, R., 203, *213*
Allport, F. H., 297, *308*
Allport, G., 12, *18*, 288, *308*
Alter-Reid, K., 422, *427*
Alterkruse, J., 15, *18*
AMA Council on Scientific Affairs, 257, 259, *277*
American Psychological Association Commission on Violence and Youth, 245, *247*, 433, *434*, 439, *445*, 447, 448
American Psychological Association, 343, *376*, 439, *445*
American Humane Association, 407, *427*
Ammerman, R. T., 200, 201, 202, 203, 204, 207, 208, *211*, 405, 406, *427*
Amolini, P., 271, *277*
Amundson, D., 220, *249*
Andereck, N. D., 168, *174*
Anderson, C. A., 273, *277*, 292, *309*
Anderson, D. A., 180, *192*
Anderson, D. R., 232, *249*
Anderson, J., 242, *246*
Anderson, M., 108, *116*, 136, 138, *143*
Anderson, W. R., 294, *311*
Andison, F. S., 228, *246*
Andron, L., 208, *213*
Angell, R. H., 152, 153, *160*, 303, *310, 311*
Annest, J., 134, *144*

Anthony, A., 49, *56*
Anti-Defamation League of B'nai Brith, 178, *192*
Apfel, N. H., 354, 358, *380*
Arbit, J., 123, *130, 131*
Arbutnot, J., 322, *330*, 389, 396, *400*
Arce, C. H., 63, *95*
Arezzo, D., 17, *21*
Arluk, I. H., 243, *249*
Aronson, E., 307 *308*
Arroup, W., 303, *311*
Artichoker, K., 135, 140, *143*
Asbury, J., 107, 108, 109, *115*
Ascione, F. R., 36, *52*
Asher, S. R., 43, *57*
Asian and Pacific Islander Center for Census Information and Services, 145, 151, *160*
Asnis, G. M., 182, *193*
Atkin, C. K., 227, *247*
Atkin, D., 222, *247*
Atkin, D. J., 222, *249*
Attneave, C., 68, 78, 79, *91*
Aurand, S. K., 178, 179, 188, *193*
Axtell, J., 83, *91*
Ayers, W. A., 350, 359, 360, 366, 367, *379*
Azar, S., 203, 208, *212*
Azar, S. T., 408, 413, *427*

Baca, L., 370, *381*
Bachman, J. G., 384, *402*
Bachorowski, J., 347, 360, *377*
Baer, K., 15, *18*, 458, *461*
Baer, N., 353, 358, *378*
Baker, E., 372, *376*
Balaban, T., 232, *250*
Baladerian, N., 204, 205, *211*
Baldwin, O., 84, *91*
Baldwin, T., 222, *247*
Bandura, A., 13, 16, 30, 31, *52*, 85, 86, 87, 88, *91*, 227, 231, 232, 236, *247*, 273, *277*, 301, *309*, 322, *330*
Bangert-Drowns, R. L., 353, 358, *376*
Bank, L., 16, *21*, 346, 363, 369, *376, 380*, 415, *427*
Banton, J. G., *278*
Barkwell, L., 395, *400*
Barnes, K., 227, *249*
Baron, R. A., 267, *277*, 292, 300, *309*

463

Subject Index

About the Editors

Leonard D. Eron, PhD, is an emeritus research professor at the University of Illinois at Chicago, and is currently a professor of psychology and a research scientist at the Research Center for Group Dynamics of the Institute for Social Research, University of Michigan, Ann Arbor. He received his PhD in 1949 from the University of Wisconsin and served on the faculties of Yale University and the University of Iowa. In 1969, he joined the UIC faculty as director of training in Clinical Psychology, then became chair of the department, and later became a research professor of the social sciences in psychology. Eron is a diplomate of the American Board of Professional Psychology. He served as editor of the *Journal of Abnormal Psychology* and associate editor of the *American Psychologist,* and as president of the Midwestern Psychological Association and the International Society for Research on Aggression. In 1980, he received the APA award for Distinguished Professional Contribution to Knowledge.

For the past 40 years he has been doing research on the learning of aggression in children, including two large-scale longitudinal studies, one of which followed 875 subjects from age 8 to age 30. He is the author of seven books, numerous articles in edited journals, and many chapters in edited books. Eron has testified several times before the U.S. Senate and the U.S. House of Representatives on the effects of violence in the media.

Jacquelyn H. Gentry, PhD, is Director of the Public Interest Initiatives Office of the American Psychological Association. She received her PhD from the University of Maryland in 1973, and for many years she directed the development of educational materials for the National Institute of Mental Health. She has a wealth of experience in scientific communications related to mental health and public policy, having produced monographs, books, public education materials, films, and an interactive video disk. Since she joined the APA staff in 1989, she has directed a number of violence-related activities, including the Commission on Violence and Youth, the Presidential Task Force on Violence and the Family, and the development of a violence research agenda for the behavioral and social sciences.

Peggy Schlegel, LCSW, received her masters degree in social work from Virginia Commonwealth University in 1984. She began her career working in a violence prevention program for at-risk families with adolescents. After several years in general practice, Schlegel came to the American Psychological Association in 1991. Currently, she works in the Office of Communications and Publications.